I WANT
MY MTV

THE UNCENSORED STORY OF
THE MUSIC VIDEO REVOLUTION

Craig Marks and
Rob Tannenbaum

DUTTON

DUTTON
Published by Penguin Group (USA) Inc.
375 Hudson Street, New York, New York 10014, U.S.A.
Penguin Group (Canada), 90 Eglinton Avenue East, Suite 700, Toronto, Ontario M4P 2Y3, Canada (a division of Pearson Penguin Canada Inc.); Penguin Books Ltd, 80 Strand, London WC2R 0RL, England; Penguin Ireland, 25 St Stephen's Green, Dublin 2, Ireland (a division of Penguin Books Ltd); Penguin Group (Australia), 250 Camberwell Road, Camberwell, Victoria 3124, Australia (a division of Pearson Australia Group Pty Ltd); Penguin Books India Pvt Ltd, 11 Community Centre, Panchsheel Park, New Delhi—110 017, India; Penguin Group (NZ), 67 Apollo Drive, Rosedale, Auckland 0632, New Zealand (a division of Pearson New Zealand Ltd); Penguin Books (South Africa) (Pty) Ltd, 24 Sturdee Avenue, Rosebank, Johannesburg 2196, South Africa

Penguin Books Ltd, Registered Offices: 80 Strand, London WC2R 0RL, England

Published by Dutton, a member of Penguin Group (USA) Inc.

First printing, October 2011
10 9 8 7 6 5 4 3 2 1

 REGISTERED TRADEMARK—MARCA REGISTRADA

LIBRARY OF CONGRESS CATALOGING-IN-PUBLICATION DATA

Marks, Craig.
I want my MTV : the uncensored story of the music video revolution / by Craig Marks and Rob Tannenbaum.
p.   cm.
Includes index.
ISBN 978-0-525-95230-5
1. MTV Networks—History.   2. Rock videos—United States.   I. Tannenbaum, Rob.
II. Title.
PN1992.8.M87M33   2011
791.45′611—dc23   2011032517

Printed in the United States of America
Designed by Daniel Lagin

To my mom and dad, who loved me unconditionally and always had cable.

And to Porter, for whom I promise to do the same. (C.M.)

*To Gabriela, who links the family that's recently gone
to the family that's soon to arrive. (R.T.)*

Contents

Introduction: "Ridicule Is Nothing to Be Scared Of"   15

PART 1: PICTURES CAME AND BROKE YOUR HEART
"VIDEO KILLED THE RADIO STAR" TO "THRILLER"
1981–1983

1. "It's the Greatest Thing in the World"   25
   FIRST GLIMPSES OF MTV

2. "I Didn't Know How to Plug in a Light"   30
   MUSIC VIDEOS (ONLY THEY WEREN'T CALLED THAT) IN THE 1970s

3. "We Were Just Idiots in Hotel Rooms"   38
   JOHN LACK, BOB PITTMAN, AND THE CREATION OF MTV

4. "What's a VJ?"   55
   HOW MTV HIRED ITS HOSTS (INCLUDING A CASE OF MISTAKEN IDENTITY)

5. "A Total, Unmitigated Disaster"   64
   MTV LAUNCHES WITH THE BUGGLES, BLOTTO, AND THIRTY
   ROD STEWART VIDEOS

6. "Girls Sliding on Poles"   70
   THE FIRST DIRTY MUSIC VIDEO

7. "A Hail Mary Pass"   73
   HOW $1 SAVED MTV FROM BANKRUPTCY

8. "Midgets, Models, and Trannies"   85
   THE FIRST VISIONARIES AND VICTIMS OF THE MUSIC-VIDEO ERA

9. "Pouting and Shoulder Pads"   113
   EFFEMINATE BRITISH BANDS SPREAD WEIRD HAIRCUTS ACROSS THE U.S.

10. "Shut That Door!"   131
    OFFICE SEX AND POWER STRUGGLES AT MTV

11. "They Figured Out a Whole New Persona"   144
    HOW THREE GNARLY OLD DUDES BECAME UNLIKELY VIDEO STARS

12. "Girls Belong in Cages"   149
    METAL TAKES OVER THE AIRWAVES

13. "That Racism Bullshit"   165
    MTV'S AOR FORMAT COMES UNDER FIRE

14. "I'm Not Like Other Boys"   173
    MICHAEL JACKSON SAVES A STRUGGLING NETWORK FROM ITSELF

PART 2: I PLAY MY PART AND YOU PLAY YOUR GAME
"BURNING UP" TO "HERE I GO AGAIN"
1983–1987

15. "The Two M's"   189
    MADONNA TOUCHES MTV FOR THE VERY FIRST TIME

16. "You Got Char-as-ma"   197
    PRINCE, BRUCE, BILLY IDOL, AND THE GODS OF 1984

17. "He's Got a Metal Plate in His Head"   221
    MTV AND VAN HALEN TEAM UP TO NEARLY KILL A SUPER-FAN

18. "Wannabe Cecil B. DeMilles"   225
    EVERYTHING—BUDGETS, IDEAS, HAIR—GETS BIGGER

19. "Why Don't I Just Take $50,000 and Light It on Fire?"   240
    THE BACKLASH AGAINST MTV

20. "Don't Be a Wanker All Your Life"   245
    "DO THEY KNOW IT'S CHRISTMAS?," "WE ARE THE WORLD," AND LIVE AID

21. "A Whopping, Steaming Turd"   250
    THE WORST VIDEO EVER MADE

22. "A Wedding Dress with Nothing Underneath It" 256
MADONNA TAKES—AND POPS OUT OF—THE CAKE
AT THE FIRST VIDEO MUSIC AWARDS

23. "No Cable Network Is Worth $500 Million" 260
MTV GETS NEW OWNERS; THE FOUNDING TEAM TRASHES A HOTEL,
THEN HEADS FOR THE EXIT

24. "Gacked to the Tits" 269
TWENTY-FOUR STORIES ABOUT DRUGS

25. "They Diss the Beatles" 273
RUN-DMC AND THE BEASTIE BOYS SMUGGLE RAP ONTO MTV

26. "We Put Fincher on the Map" 285
RICK SPRINGFIELD, CHRISTOPHER CROSS, AND THE HUMBLE
BEGINNINGS OF A GENIUS

27. "There I Am, with My Rack" 301
THE RISE OF THE SUPERDIVAS, MALE AND FEMALE

28. "The Legion of Decency" 313
CENSORING VIDEOS, FOR FUN AND PROFIT

29. "Hickory Dickory Dock, This Bitch Was . . ." 320
BACKSTAGE AT THE VIDEO MUSIC AWARDS

30. "I'd Like to Thank My Cheekbones" 331
JON BON JOVI AND TAWNY KITAEN TAKE HAIR METAL TO THE TOP

PART 3: WHERE DO WE GO NOW
"WITH OR WITHOUT YOU" TO "U CAN'T TOUCH THIS"
1987–1990

31. "The Island of Misfit Toys" 353
120 MINUTES AND THE RISING UP/SELLING OUT OF ALTERNATIVE ROCK

32. "Martha Was Heartbroken" 367
MTV FINDS A NEW, MOUTHIER SQUAD OF VJs

33. "A True Television Network" 382
THE NEW BOSS ORDERS UP A RIOTOUS SHOW THAT
FOREVER CHANGES THE NETWORK

34. "That's What Hype Can Do to You" 396
CLUB MTV LAUNCHES THE "UPSKIRT SHOT" AND A POP SCANDAL

35. "The First Time I Smelled Freebase" — 404
MTV PARTIES DOWN AT SPRING BREAK

36. "I Brought Snowballs to the Desert" — 411
SUCKING UP TO MTV'S LADDISH NEW POWER BROKER

37. "People in the Hood Rushed to Get Cable" — 418
HOW TED DEMME DID, DIDN'T, MAYBE DID, AND ABSOLUTELY
DID CREATE *YO! MTV RAPS*

38. "We've *Always* Loved Guns N' Roses" — 436
CHICKS AND A SNAKE, *HEADBANGERS BALL*, AND THE RETURN OF HARD ROCK

39. "Those Harem Pants Came Out of Nowhere" — 451
RAP BUSTS A MOVE INTO THE MTV MAINSTREAM

40. "Ego-Fucking-Maniacs" — 464
MICHAEL BAY, CHER, AND ALL 9:08 OF "NOVEMBER RAIN"

41. "I Want to Have a Nickname" — 478
HOW MTV HELPED MICHAEL JACKSON ELECT HIMSELF "THE KING OF POP"

PART 4: NOTHING LASTS FOREVER,
AND WE BOTH KNOW HEARTS CAN CHANGE
"JUSTIFY MY LOVE" TO "JEREMY"
1990–1992

42. "Rhythm Nation" — 483
SUPERSTARS AND ONE-HIT WONDERS STAGE A DANCE-OFF IN YOUR LIVING ROOM

43. "Your Manager's an Asshole" — 498
FISTFIGHTS AND PYRO FARTS: WAR BREAKS OUT
AT THE MOSCOW PEACE FESTIVAL

44. "Kermit Unplugged" — 502
AN ACOUSTIC MUSIC SHOW MORPHS INTO A WORLDWIDE MEGABRAND

45. "Silly, Superficial, and Wonderful" — 509
CINDY CRAWFORD AND JON STEWART BRING BEAUTY AND LAUGHS TO MTV

46. "Tired of Cheap Sex Songs" — 514
R.E.M., U2, AND VAN HALEN (!) ELEVATE THE ART FORM IN THE NINETIES

47. "A Monkey Could Do It" — 520
PAULY SHORE AND THE THIRD GENERATION OF VJs

48. "A Pep Rally Gone Wrong"   526

"SMELLS LIKE TEEN SPIRIT," GRUNGE, AND THE HAIR METAL APOCALYPSE

49. "You're No Better Than a Rabbit!"   543

FEARLESS TWENTYSOMETHINGS SHAPE A PRESIDENTIAL ELECTION

50. "Getting Out of the Music Business"   550

THIS IS THE TRUE STORY . . . OF WHAT HAPPENED WHEN *THE REAL WORLD* . . .
TOOK OVER MTV . . . AND MADE MUSIC VIDEOS . . . OBSOLETE

51. "Let's Get Crazy Tonight"   555

TEARS, TEQUILA, AND BROKEN GLASS: MTV VIPs CELEBRATE THE FIRST DECADE

52. "Fat City"   557

THE BUBBLE BURSTS ON MUSIC VIDEOS' GOLDEN ERA

53. "You Have No Idea How I Miss It"   564

FANS, STARS, STAFF, AND DETRACTORS REFLECT ON THE VIDEO AGE

Acknowledgments   573

Cast of Characters   575

Index   595

So the book covers the years 1981 to 1992 . . .

WALTER YETNIKOFF, record executive: Okay. I don't remember any of that.

Introduction

————

"RIDICULE IS NOTHING TO BE SCARED OF"

ARDLY ANYONE THOUGHT IT WOULD SUCCEED. Upon hearing of the plan to launch a TV channel that would show music videos around the clock, businessmen of wealth and experience—worldly men who ran record companies and partied with rock stars, and visionary men who made fortunes by anticipating the explosion of cable TV—scoffed and snickered. Who would watch this channel? Even if it proved popular, who would advertise there? Why would GM or Anheuser-Busch want to reach this channel's audience, consisting mostly of fourteen- to twenty-four-year-olds? Where's the money in that?

Prior to the launch of this channel on August 1, 1981, only a few dozen people believed it would succeed, and all of them worked at the channel. The start-up staff was a coterie of misfits, inexperienced and determined, and included two one-eyed executives who were later hailed as visionaries. Which is not to say that *everyone* who worked at the channel believed it would succeed. "It sounded like an asinine idea," Bob Pittman (one of the one-eyed executives) admitted five years after the launch, when the channel was the centerpiece of a $525 million bidding war. It's easy to imagine this as the theme of one of the network's early advertising campaigns, which were usually brash and self-mocking: "MTV: It sounds like an asinine idea."

There are two kinds of successful consumer products: some fill an existing need by making people's lives easier (toilet paper, or the dishwasher), and others create a need that didn't previously exist (sanitary wipes, or coffee). It's easy to predict success for the first type of product, but harder for the second. In 1981, there was no need for music videos. MTV was an outlet for something that barely existed; the network had about a hundred of them in inventory, mostly by marginal or unpopular British and Australian bands. Not only that, MTV planned to get more videos by asking someone else, record labels, to make and pay for them, then hand them over for free. That's not a business model, that's chutzpah.

But from asinine beginnings, MTV became the sun around which popular culture rotated. The MTV aesthetic during its Golden Age of 1981 to 1992—quick cuts, celebrations of youth, shock value, impermanence, beauty—influenced not only music, but network and cable TV, radio, advertising, film, art, fashion, race, teen sexuality, even politics. The channel was plotted to captivate an audience whose interests had been ignored: John Lack, who started MTV, called teenagers "the demographic group least interested in TV," because TV wasn't interested in teens. Children had cartoons; adults had the evening news and most of the shows that followed it. Teens were an untapped audience, an invisible power. MTV gave them what they wanted, and got them not only interested in, but obsessed by MTV, making it their clubhouse.

Like MGM in the 1930s, or CBS from the mid-'50s to the mid-'70s, MTV became the preeminent arbiter of celebrity. Constant airplay of Michael Jackson videos helped make *Thriller* the best-selling album of all time. When MTV Europe launched in 1987 as the start of a global expansion that now reaches from Brazil to Pakistan, the network's influence expanded beyond the U.S. *Yo! MTV Raps*, which debuted a year later, gave hip-hop its first international forum and accelerated the music's popularity around the world. The channel's first foray into long-form programming, the faux-game show *Remote Control*, introduced dorm-dwelling smart-alecks to novice comedian Adam Sandler. When *House of Style* arrived the next year, it transformed Cindy Crawford from a model to a mogul. Cannily, MTV never tied success to the fate of any one or two stars. ("MTV works in dog years," Downtown Julie Brown wisecracked, after her VJ tenure ended.) Unlike traditional networks, which spend millions to retain popular shows and actors whose popularity is bound to dwindle, MTV sees talent as disposable and replaceable; the network is the star, not the performer. Martha Quinn got five years. Tawny Kitaen got a year and a half. A-ha got three months.

MTV gave work to young directors, producers, and executives who became power brokers in film and TV, most notably David Fincher, who received Academy Award nominations for *The Curious Case of Benjamin Button* and *The Social Network*, and Michael Bay, who received no Academy Award nominations, but who made shit blow up real good in *Armageddon* and the *Transformers* series. Videos created ample work for *Playboy* playmates and for choreographers, dancers, mimes, animal trainers, pyrotechnicians, hairdressers, aestheticians, dry-ice vendors, coke dealers, and midgets. (Midgets were a staple of music videos. Midget freelance work surely peaked in the '80s.) MTV did a lot for record labels, helping to revive a slumping industry, but it was the bands who benefitted most. The channel gave a platform to new acts, asking only that they be beautiful or outrageous. MTV could make stars out of Brits in eyeliner, rappers in genie pants, permed Jersey boys, even choreographers with weak singing voices. Within weeks, acts went from journeymen or unknowns to stars whose faces were familiar across the country. Their lives were transformed, sometimes ruined. The story of music videos is also the story of overnight celebrity and the experiences created by celebrity: the indulgence and decadence, the backstage sexual exploits, the drugs that were as ever-present as makeup kits and hair weaves. This is true not only for the artists but for the network executives themselves, most spirited among them former radio program director Les Garland, who partied on yachts with Rod Stewart, cameoed in videos with Eddie Murphy, and charmed centerfolds, actresses, stewardesses, and starlets, often on the same night. A history of MTV is also a history of excess that has since vanished from the music business due to dwindling sales. As Simon Le Bon, the Marlon Brando of music videos, mutters darkly, "Nobody's got any money to make videos now." From today's frugal perspective, the stories of the video industry's invention, expansion, and domination read like the last days of the Roman Empire, if Nero had been really into dry ice and pyro.

Not all MTV content was fleeting. If an artist's peak coincided with the Golden Age of music videos, there's a good chance that artist is among the few remaining acts who can still sell out sheds, arenas, even stadiums, testament to MTV's pop-cultural dominance in its first decade. Before Xbox and Facebook, the Disney Channel and text-messaging, kids did one thing, separately but simultaneously: They watched MTV. Now those kids are parents, and when they want to relive their youth, they plunk down $250 for a ticket to see Madonna, the Police, U2, Guns N' Roses, Bon Jovi, Van Halen, Bruce Springsteen, Motley Crue, George Michael, Michael Jackson (until his death), or Janet Jackson. All were synonymous with MTV's first decade, and all continued to pack enormodomes twenty and thirty years later. Oldsters, purists, clergymen, and boomers carped that MTV's corrupt value system promoted style over substance, impermanence over immortality. MTV and its viewers knew this was a false choice. Videos made songs better, not worse. They enhanced the joy of being a music fan, rather than diminishing it. Unless you were Billy Squier. Then, you were fucked. (See Chapter 21: "A Whopping, Steaming Turd.")

As the subject of an oral history, MTV is uniquely compelling; the network identity morphs but never peters out. There's no dreary third act where the star gets old, Learns an Important Lesson, and ceases being relevant. Like Charlie Brown or Beavis and Butt-head, the passing of time does not age MTV. It is perpetually fourteen years old, about to start high school, excited, but not too smart. With vampiric persistence, the network perpetually finds new, young blood.

But for us, 1992 marks the end of MTV's Golden Era, which was brought to a close by a series of unrelated factors. Video budgets rose steeply, leading to wasteful displays; digital editing arrived, making it a snap for directors to flit between shots and angles; all the good ideas had been done; record labels increasingly interfered in video decisions; many of the best directors moved on to film; Madonna made *Body of Evidence*. It's also the year MTV debuted *The Real World*, a franchise show that sped a move away from videos, the network's founding mission, and into reality shows about kids in crisis, whether an unplanned pregnancy or how to un-marry Spencer Pratt. *The Real World* was the culmination of the network's initiative to create its own shows and was also the last time MTV could claim to be revolutionary. MTV created the video music industry, then abandoned it, leaving behind a trail of tears—disgruntled music-video fans have stamped the phrase "MTV sucks" and "Bring back music videos" all over the comments pages of YouTube.

MTV WAS CREATED BY WARNER AMEX SATELLITE ENTER-tainment Company (WASEC), a joint venture between two companies with little in common: Warner Communications, a fast-growing media company committed to "identifying new markets and new technologies," and American Express, the credit-card giant, founded in 1850 as a shipping company. Warner executives believed in a future when all homes would be wired, and they invested heavily in cable TV and Atari home computers. ("The computer's emergence as a commonplace object in the home," Warner's 1981 annual report predicted, "will, in fact, change life all over again for the American consumer." They were right, but they were also too early to profit from their foresight.) Warner Communications envisioned cable TV as a sales tool, to deliver goods and services directly into the home, and American Express rode along in the hope that soon customers would buy the company's traveler's checks and investment services via two-way, interactive cable TV.

MTV first appeared in suburban and rural areas, where the cost per mile of digging and installing cable was far cheaper than in cities. As a result, it was seen first by teens who probably needed it the most—videos brought big-city ideas to the sticks, and terrified parents who had terrified *their* parents by listening to the Beatles. In small towns or big cities, MTV was like an early social network—when Stray Cats videos aired, showing the trio in rockabilly outfits, fans in the Midwest began coming to shows in cowboy shirts and pompadours. And Mike Score of A Flock of Seagulls, owner of early MTV's most unprecedented hair, says video exposure brought like-minded fans together at clubs where outcasts discovered they were part of a tribe.

Even if it accomplished nothing else, MTV pissed off baby boomers, in part because it signified a transition from an era when the biggest rock stars were bands that transformed public consciousness, to one where technology filled that role. Today, that transformation is complete: Apple sold 275 million iPods in the first nine years they were on the market, which is higher than the number of records sold by Elton John, Aerosmith, AC/DC, Pink Floyd, or U2 in their careers. But MTV was the first time technology became a rock star, because—unlike calculators, CD players, or home gaming systems—it was sold at a reasonable price.

Every new technology contains a philosophy. The Walkman told consumers they should never stray far from music, nor were they required to interact with strangers. The iPhone preached permanent access to all media, while also miniaturizing the idea of status. What was the philosophy of MTV? It was best expressed in an Adam Ant song that was an early favorite on MTV: "Ridicule is nothing to be scared of."

MTV was an invention, as many principals in the story emphasized to us.

Music video was "the Wild, Wild West," a lawless place where nerve and cunning hands were rewarded. "All the rules go away," Bob Pittman told a reporter in 1981, and other people recall it as a time when "There were no rules." One cinematographer proudly said, "We had a policy not just to break the rules, but to blow up the fucking rules."

The people behind MTV had almost no TV experience, so they had no habits or allegiances to limit them—except when it came to picking videos. MTV's programmers came from radio, where the trend was "narrowcasting," a way of targeting a specific demographic and selling your popularity within that audience to advertisers, rather than aiming for the broadest possible audience. Broadcasting was Ed Sullivan creating a show that mixed the Beatles with Topo Gigio. Narrowcasting was embodied by MTV's initial commitment to playing rock videos, which meant videos by white musicians.

MTV's narrowcasting mission was challenged by Michael Jackson, whose *Thriller* videos transformed the network from a curiosity into a fulcrum. A similar event repeated five years later with rap, a style of music MTV feared, hesitantly embraced, and then built its brand around. Once that occurred, MTV became The Singularity, the last media force that represented an encompassing view of pop culture.

HISTORY HAS NOT RECORDED THE DATE, LOCATION, OR name of the first musician who was filmed playing or singing, but it's likely to have happened soon after the movie camera was invented. Musicians are not modest, and the first one who saw a camera in operation probably suggested, "Hey, why don't you point that thing at me while I play?"

Each decade had its own variation on music videos. In 1930, Warner Bros. Pictures began making "Spooney Melodies," short performance films of popular songs, including "Just a Gigolo," later revived by David Lee Roth. In the 1940s, thousands of black-and-white "soundies" were made with Duke Ellington, Cab Calloway, Fats Waller, and other suave, camera-ready jazz artists, dancers, and comedians.

Scopitones edged closer to the modern music video—the Scopitone was a coin-operated video jukebox, created in France and bigger than a refrigerator. In the 1960s, they could be found at diners and truck stops across the U.S. An article in *Variety* praised "the jet-paced editing, exceptionally vivid color and generally top-drawer production values" of Scopitone videos, many of which are catalogued on YouTube, where the editing seems, to modern eyes, more tugboat-paced. However, Scopitones were shamelessly lewd and provocative, full of cleavage, bikinis, and enough butt-shaking to match any gratuitous display seen in a Sir Mix-a-Lot or Poison video.

So MTV was the culmination of a fitful relationship that went back twenty-five years. "Since the beginning of time—1956—rock n' roll and TV have never really hit it off," said Keith Richards of the Rolling Stones, shortly after MTV appeared. "But suddenly it's like they've gotten married and can't leave each other alone." Richards picked 1956 because it was the year of Elvis Presley's debut on *The Ed Sullivan Show*, which delivered a giant audience of 60 million. *American Bandstand*, the first regular music show on TV, arrived the next year. After the Beatles topped Elvis by luring 73 million people to their first Ed Sullivan broadcast, the short-lived musical-variety series *Shindig* and *Hullabaloo* appeared in the U.S., as well as the long-lived *Top of the Pops* in the UK. *The Monkees* was a daffy mid-'60s show about a rock band who acted out their songs in a series of comic, almost slapstick vignettes.

Music shows of the '70s centered on live performances: *The Old Grey Whistle Test* in England, and ABC's excellent *In Concert*, quickly followed by *Don Kirshner's Rock Concert* (hosted by Kirshner, who, years later, claimed credit for MTV and music videos), NBC's *The Midnight Special* (often hosted by the bland soft-pop star Helen Reddy), and PBS's more homespun *Austin City Limits* in 1976. There were even music-video programs prior to MTV: Australia had *Countdown* and *Sounds*, neighboring New Zealand had *Radio with Pictures*, the unhosted show *Video Concert Hall* began on the USA Network in 1978, and WNBC-TV in New York had *Album Tracks*, hosted by future MTV execs Bob Pittman and Lee Masters.

There were plenty of precedents for what began on August 1, 1981. And many pieces of film have been cited as "the first music video": The Beatles made short films for "Strawberry Fields Forever" and "Penny Lane"; the Rolling Stones, the Who, the Doors, and Bob Dylan made similar films, as did TV heartthrob Rick Nelson and country star Buck Owens. Queen's 1975 clip for "Bohemian Rhapsody" dazzled forward-thinking Britons and helped the song filibuster at number one across the UK. But the term "music video" (which barely existed before MTV) now connotes a specific set of qualities—aggressive directorship, contemporary editing and FX, sexuality, vivid colors, urgent movement, nonsensical juxtapositions, provocation, frolic, all combined for maximum impact on a small screen—that were not formalized until MTV provided a delivery system. There is no such thing as "the first music video."

What aired on MTV was so strange and unfamiliar that explaining it proved difficult. The channel's first mention in *Time* magazine contained language you might use to explain a laptop computer to a caveman: "The main ingredients in MTV's programming are 'video records' or 'videos': current recordings illustrated by 3- or 4-minute videotapes." A year later, *Time* writer Jay Cocks was still struggling to familiarize the magazine's audience with MTV, referring to videos as "illustrated songs, little three- or four-minute clips" and "production numbers soaked in blotter acid."

Even as MTV struggled financially, and employees worried the network could be shut down any day, its influence rippled across the culture, most quickly in film. In a review of the smash 1983 film *Flashdance*, Pauline Kael of the *New Yorker* wrote, "Basically, the movie is a series of rock videos." She did not intend this as a compliment. The next year, *Flashdance* producer Jerry Bruckheimer got even more MTV-ish with *Beverly Hills Cop*, which spawned videos for the soundtrack songs "Axel F," "Neutron Dance," and "The Heat Is On." "It was free promotion," says Bruckheimer, "another platform to reach a young audience, and it helped enormously."

Network television followed; the hit series *Miami Vice* launched in 1984, according to legend, after NBC's Brandon Tartikoff wrote the phrase "MTV cops" on a piece of paper. Michael Mann, *Vice*'s executive producer, dismisses this as "a nice anecdote without much basis in history, as far as I know." But Mann imbued the show with a video sensibility: "I watched MTV a lot in those days. And *Miami Vice* was a radical departure from everything else on the air. The conventional way of using music in Hollywood was to apply the music to picture, more or less. But MTV influenced editing—now, we were cutting picture to music. And the content of videos on MTV was often what you would today call 'fractals.' They didn't have the beginning, middle, and end of a story. MTV forced feature filmmaking to evolve: you didn't need to bring an audience through so much clunky, conventional exposition of the story. That kind of stuff was obsolete."

Also, John Sayles says, "MTV had a huge influence on independent films."

Sayles, who had been directing independent films since 1980, explains that music videos gave novice technicians access to state-of-the-art equipment; previously, someone would "start as a camera loader and fifteen years later might touch a Panavision. Twenty-three-year-old technicians had horror stories about working on videos, and then they'd say, 'But you should have seen the camera they gave me!'"

THIS BOOK INCORPORATES INTERVIEWS WITH MORE THAN four hundred people who were significant, even if only briefly, in MTV's Golden Era. It's been thirty years since the network signed on with a few videos and a flurry of technical mishaps. Memories change over the years and agendas can conflict, so two people might recall an incident in different ways—when this occurs, we've let each side have his or her say. MTV lent assistance to us; however, this is not an MTV book. No one from the network had any say in its content or read the book prior to publication. We thank them, collectively, for their faith that we'd tell the story with candor, affection, and, where appropriate, criticism.

Throughout our research, the people we interviewed almost unanimously looked back at this period with joy and happiness, even if they now regret some of the clothes they wore, and we hope their enthusiasm—and ours—is obvious on the page. This is the story of how an asinine idea changed the culture of America, and then the world, for better or worse.

—Rob Tannenbaum

Chapter 1

"IT'S THE GREATEST THING
IN THE WORLD"

FIRST GLIMPSES OF MTV

BILLY GIBBONS, ZZ Top: One night I got a phone call from Frank Beard, our drummer. He said, "Hey, there's a good concert on TV. Check it out." So a couple of hours went by while I watched TV, and I called him back and said, "How long does this concert last?" He said, "I don't know." Twelve hours later, we were still glued to the TV. Finally somebody said, "No, it's this twenty-four-hour music channel." I said, "*Whaaaat?*" MTV appeared suddenly—unheralded, un-announced, un-anything.

STEVIE NICKS, Fleetwood Mac: I was living in the Pacific Palisades and I would sit on the end of my bed, watching video after video, just stupefied.

DAVE NAVARRO, Jane's Addiction: I was fourteen when MTV came on the air. My record collection at the time consisted mainly of Black Sabbath and Led Zeppelin, and here I was being exposed to a cross section of hard rock, new wave, and pop music. I still listen to Musical Youth every day. Okay, maybe not.

DAVE GROHL, Nirvana; Foo Fighters: It seemed like a transmission from some magical place. Me and all my friends were dirty little rocker kids in suburban Virginia, so we spent a lot of our time at the record store or staring at album covers. With music videos, there was a deeper dimension to everything. On Friday nights, you'd go to a friend's house to get fucked up before going out to a party, and you'd have MTV on.

"WEIRD AL" YANKOVIC, artist: I was living in a $300-a-month apartment in Hollywood with a Murphy bed and a tiny TV, but man, I wanted my MTV. It was a luxury for me to get cable TV. I would watch all day long. At the time, MTV felt like a local, low-budget station. The VJs would make glaring errors, or forget to turn off their mics. I mean, it was horribly produced and great. I felt like, *This is television for me.*

JANET JACKSON, artist: I loved watching it. How exciting back then, being a teenager and having something so creative, so fresh, so new. It was about waiting for your favorite video, and not really knowing what hour it would hit, so you'd have to watch all day long.

CONAN O'BRIEN, TV host: I was a freshman in college and a friend of mine was staying at her grandfather's apartment in New York. She said, "Come over and hang out." When I got there, she said, "I'm watching this new channel, MTV." What a weird thing. What do you mean, they're showing music videos? What's a music video? Why would you show that? I can't stop watching! We watched for six hours. It's one of those things you can't describe to anyone who's younger than you, like the first year of *Saturday Night Live.* It was like a comet streaking across the sky.

DAVE MUSTAINE, Megadeth: My mom moved out when I was fifteen, so I'd been living alone in my apartment for a few years. People would ditch school, come over, buy pot from me, and watch MTV. I'm telling you, man, I had the coolest house in the town.

LARS ULRICH, Metallica: I lived with my parents, and we didn't have cable TV. We had three channels, and PBS. Dave Mustaine was a couple years older, and he had cable. And as I'm sitting here now, I can clearly see his apartment. In the right-hand corner, under the window, there was a wood-cabinet television and it was tuned to MTV 24/7.

LENNY KRAVITZ, artist: The first time I saw MTV, I was on vacation with my parents in the Bahamas. They had MTV in the hotel we were staying at. It was beautiful outside, eighty degrees and sunny, and I spent the whole week in my hotel room, watching MTV, 24/7. My parents were like, "My god, what is wrong with you?" I did not want to come out. I just wanted to watch videos all day. Duran Duran, Prince, Hall & Oates, Bowie's "Ashes to Ashes," Talking Heads, Bow Wow Wow, Haircut 100, Adam & the Ants. That's when MTV was MTV.

LADY GAGA, artist: The '80s was such a magical time. We'd just come off Bowie's '70s glam rock, and disco was spiraling into this incredible synthetic music. Everything was so theatrical. Once the video was born, all these visuals found a new medium.

PATTY SMYTH, Scandal: I remember watching MTV at my boyfriend's house in Gladwyne, Pennsylvania, in the summer of '81. A year later, I was on it.

PAT BENATAR, artist: I was in a hotel in Oklahoma, just this little roadside motel, and it was one of only about eight places in the United States that actually had MTV on the day that it aired. We were all sitting on my bed—the whole band, my manager, everybody—with our mouths open. I'm telling you, within a week, we couldn't go anywhere without being recognized. It changed everything, in one week.

AL TELLER, record executive: The timing of MTV was perfect. The music industry was in the doldrums and trying desperately to reinvent itself.

CHRIS ISAAK, artist: I had a TV that was from, like, 1959, a portable with rabbit ears and tinfoil. I got two and a half channels, and MTV was not one. My buddy was a photographer for the San Francisco 49ers, and it was a big treat when I went to babysit his kid, because I could watch MTV. At first, it was almost underground or counterculture. I don't think people had gotten to the payola yet.

BRET MICHAELS, Poison: I was eighteen or nineteen, working as a fry cook and maintenance man, and singing in a covers band. We got cable just so we could watch MTV. I'd go to parties, and girls would ask me, "Why are you watching the TV?" I'd say, "I'm waiting for Van Halen." I'd sit there with a little smokage and wait for their video to come on.

MICHAEL IAN BLACK, comedian: We did not have cable. Cable was for millionaires. I grew up in Hillsborough, New Jersey, a terrible place, but there was a local

UHF station, U68, that hopped on the MTV bandwagon. If the weather was clear and the antenna was pointed just so, we could watch videos on U68. It was a ghetto MTV.

CHYNNA PHILLIPS, Wilson Phillips: I saw MTV the first day it aired. I was in New Jersey, visiting my dad, and our friend had MTV. We all crowded around the TV, and "Video Killed the Radio Star" played. I was hooked.

DAVE HOLMES, MTV VJ: I grew up in St. Louis, and when I was ten, somebody told me there was gonna be a thing called MTV and it was just gonna show music videos. First of all, I didn't believe them. And second, I thought, *If that's true, it's the greatest thing in the world.*

B-REAL, Cypress Hill: I think it was the greatest invention ever.

RICHARD MARX, artist: I spent a ton of time watching MTV. I'd set my VHS machine to extended-play mode, to get six hours on a cassette. I videotaped midnight to 6 A.M., because they'd play videos overnight that they wouldn't play during the day. I was studying it.

SEBASTIAN BACH, Skid Row: I'm from Canada, where there was no MTV. Every summer, my dad would send me and my sister to California to be with my grandma. I went to my cousin's basement, put on the TV, and saw the Scorpions on fuckin' television. I was a huge heavy metal fan, and I couldn't believe my cousin had the Scorpions on his TV set! I didn't leave the basement all summer. His parents said, "Are you okay? Do you do this at home?" I'm like, "I've never seen music videos, so you've got to leave me alone."

CHUCK D, Public Enemy: These days, everybody has a hi-def camcorder in their pocket. It's accepted with shrugging shoulders. "Okay, so what? A video." But back then, it was a main event.

RUDOLF SCHENKER, Scorpions: We came on an American tour in 1982 and I exactly remember every night coming from the concert into the hotel. I went in the room, switched immediately MTV on. It was so fantastic.

NANCY WILSON, Heart: Everybody wanted their MTV so bad. I remember *craving* it like crazy.

ANN WILSON, Heart: It was like the difference between silent films and talkies. All of a sudden, records could be seen. You could just put it on and party around the TV.

JANE WIEDLIN, Go-Go's: It was the go-to place to find new music, and you could find out right away what you need to know about a band, like if you liked their style or if they were cute.

STEVIE NICKS: When "Video Killed the Radio Star" came out, we took it with a grain of salt. We thought, *Well, video's not gonna kill the radio star.* It did. The song was prophetic.

Chapter 2

"I DIDN'T KNOW HOW TO PLUG IN A LIGHT"

MUSIC VIDEOS (ONLY THEY WEREN'T CALLED THAT) IN THE 1970s

THE ALLIANCE BETWEEN MUSIC AND PICTURE, WHICH went a long way back, took a different perspective in the '70s. Low-budget video novices were influenced by experimental filmmakers: Andy Warhol, Kenneth Anger, the Kuchar Brothers, and Bruce Conner, who spliced together existing film footage like a cinema DJ, and was hired by Devo, pre-MTV, to create a video for their song "Mongoloid." The *New York Times* film critic Manohla Dargis, writing an obituary for Conner in 2008, noted the wide influence of his "shocking juxtapositions and propulsive, rhythmically sophisticated montage," and concluded, "MTV should have paid him royalties." Later on, music videos would reflect the influences of *Raiders of the Lost Ark, The Shining, West Side Story,* film noir, Russ Meyer's breast-laden film farces, and Saturday-morning cartoons. But here at the beginning, they were bold and wild.

DAVID MALLET, director: Music video was a medium that was not regarded at all. It was like lavatory paper. In England, they were referred to as "fillers." That was an insult.

JERRY CASALE, Devo: Videos were a curiosity at best. The record company thought we were stupid for using promotion money to do low-budget videos. "What's *that* for?"

DAVID MALLET: The first time anybody put film to music satisfactorily, in my opinion, was David Lean in *Brief Encounter* [1945]. The second time I noticed it was *Death in Venice* [1971], which was Luchino Vicsconti. The third and most effective time was "Born to Be Wild" by Steppenwolf, which is at the beginning of *Easy Rider* [1969]. That was the first time images and music went together to illustrate the music, rather than to illustrate the mood.

MICHAEL MANN, film director: The different ways music can collide with dramatic action, complement it, or prepare or surprise us is not new. You can go back to *Alexander Nevsky*—Sergei Eisenstein was writing storyboards on the same long roll of paper Sergei Prokofiev was using to write the score. They were doing this in 1938, and "talkies" were only nine years old. Watch the battle-on-the-ice scene; the planning, the synchronization of music and picture, the premeditated architecture of their collision is as specific as in the best MTV videos.

JERRY BRUCKHEIMER, movie producer: *The Graduate* was the first time I saw contemporary music integrated into a story. The Simon & Garfunkel songs gave you an emotional lift. It told the audience how to feel about those scenes and those characters.

MICK JONES, the Clash: When the Rolling Stones got busted for drugs, they did a promo film for "We Love You," where Keith Richards is the judge and Mick Jagger is Oscar Wilde, and on trial. Really fantastic.

JO BERGMAN, record executive: My first experience with music videos was when I was working for the Rolling Stones in London in 1968, and we shot "Jumpin' Jack Flash" and "Child of the Moon" in the freezing English countryside, with the band dressed as itinerants. They're funny little films.

NIGEL DICK, director: I was at Bath University in 1975, and every Thursday night at 6:30 we'd gather in a common area to watch *Top of the Pops*. The program after it was *Monty Python's Flying Circus*, so it was a big event. There'd be five hundred people watching one television. *Top of the Pops* came on, and number one on the countdown was "Bohemian Rhapsody" by Queen. This video comes on and we're all like, *What the fuck is that?* It was astonishing.

BRUCE GOWERS, director: When I was a cameraman, I worked on at least three Beatles videos—I can't remember the songs, but "Paperback Writer" was one. In 1975, two crooked wheeler-dealer brothers from Queen's management company asked me to do a film for "Bohemian Rhapsody." We started at 7 P.M. and were in the pub before it closed at 11 P.M. That famous multiplying effect during the "thunderbolts and lightning" part, where you see many Freddie Mercurys and Brian Mays? That was corny. I stuck a prism onto the camera lens. It was held on with gaffer's tape.

JOHN TAYLOR, Duran Duran: "Bohemian Rhapsody" could not have held the number one spot for as many weeks as it did if *Top of the Pops* hadn't kept running their film. But nobody called it a "video." Later, there was one for the Boomtown Rats' "I Don't Like Mondays" and for Ultravox's "Vienna" as well—most of the long-running number one songs in the late '70s had some form of filmic presentation, because bands didn't want to keep showing up to play the song on *Top of the Pops*. That was the motivation within the UK market.

ROBERT SMITH, the Cure: "Bohemian Rhapsody" was number one every fucking week. I fucking hated it.

BRIAN GRANT, director: Nobody had seen anything like "Bohemian Rhapsody." I was working on *The Muppet Show* as a cameraman, and at that point I determined I wanted to direct videos.

JULIEN TEMPLE, director: The first video I directed was the Sex Pistols's "God Save the Queen." The Sex Pistols were banned from television in England, so we used to take a projector around and show the video before other bands played, so kids could actually see them.

DEBBIE HARRY, Blondie: We started making music videos in 1976, maybe a little earlier. A lot of times we couldn't go to England to promote a single, and they used a lot of video on TV there. We had a big following in Australia as well, and traveling to Australia every time you released a song was out of the question. Our videos were stunning, and so ahead of their time. They have an innocent flavor to them. My nipples are showing in "Heart of Glass." Maybe that's why people liked the video so much.

MEAT LOAF, artist: For *Bat Out of Hell* [in 1977], I talked the label into giving me $30,000 to shoot three live performance clips, and I got them played as trailers before midnight showings of *The Rocky Horror Picture Show*. That is still the number one selling album in the history of Holland, and I never played there. It's all because of the "Paradise by the Dashboard Light" video.

KEVIN GODLEY, director: Lol Creme and I made our first video in 1979 for the Godley & Creme song "An Englishman in New York." It was post–"Bohemian Rhapsody," which was a watermark. The record label agreed to let us make a little film on the condition that we work with a guy who had done it before. This may sound boastful, but it became obvious to us that we could do better on our own. We used video cameras and hired TV people to do the lighting. It was very low rent.

PERRI LISTER, choreographer: In 1978, in London, I joined a dance group called Hot Gossip. We were like a punk rock dance group. We did a TV pilot for a comedian named Kenny Everett, and when it was shown, Mary Whitehouse, who was the Tipper Gore of England, stood up in the House of Parliament and said we were lewd and should be banned immediately. Which, of course, meant instant fame. Everybody tuned in the next week. *The Kenny Everett Video Show* was a bit like *In Living Color*, and we were like the Fly Girls. We danced to Blondie, Devo, the hits of the day. David Mallet was the director, and he started directing music videos. He did a bunch of early David Bowie videos: "Ashes to Ashes," "DJ," "Fashion." When he began directing music videos full-time, he often used me as his choreographer. And then I started to appear in them as well.

DAVID MALLET: Bowie was at the forefront of anything new and exciting. He was a fan of surrealist cinema and he wanted to mix it into rock n' roll. The video for "Fashion" has a lot of Buñuel in it, a lot of surrealism, which David brought to the party.

ALAN HUNTER, MTV VJ: I'd been in New York for less than a year, attending drama school, and I was one of the six dancers in the "Fashion" video. I wore a mime striped shirt with suspenders, and I got paid $50 a day for three days.

DAVID MALLET: The "Boys Keep Swinging" video is an incredibly straight and normal performance by David Bowie right up to about fifty seconds, when it goes insane with him in drag. He smears lipstick across his face; that's traditional Berlin drag-club stuff. The BBC watched the first twenty seconds and said, "Jolly good, nice to see him doing proper for once." They put it on the air at teatime on a Saturday. And there was a hell of a row. They called it obscene and perverse.

BRIAN GRANT: A guy from MCA Records gave me £2,000 to make a video for M's song "Pop Muzik." It got shown on *The Kenny Everett Video Show*, which was directed by David Mallet, who later became my partner. "Pop Muzik" went to number one, and the phone didn't stop ringing.

ROBIN SLOANE, record executive: In 1978, I got a job as a secretary in the publicity department at Epic Records. I was bored doing administrative work, so I said to my boss, "Can I try and do something with the promotional videos we're getting from England?" No one paid attention to that stuff. I'd get them placed in local news programs if artists were touring, or on HBO between movies, or on late-night video shows popping up in different cities. The higher-ups left me alone.

WAYNE ISHAM, director: When I got out of the army after the Vietnam War, I used my GI bill to go to college, and I saw the David Bowie "Ashes to Ashes" video on a midnight show called *Night Flight* [USA Network, 1981–1996]. I said, "That's exactly what I want to do." I got a Hollywood phone book and ripped out the pages that listed production companies. I went from one to the other, saying, "I'll do whatever it takes to get into the production business," and eventually I got a job as stage manager at the A&M soundstage. I'd literally clean the stage by hand. I didn't know how to plug in a light. But that was the best education I could've had. When Russell Mulcahy showed up, I was the only guy who knew who he was, because I'd seen his video for XTC's "Making Plans for Nigel" on *Night Flight*. All these crazy English directors filmed there—Russell, Godley & Creme, Steve Barron.

STEVE BARRON, director: My mother, Zelda, was a continuity girl in film—they call it "script supervisor" in America—and my father was a sound mixer. They worked on films like *Blow-Up* and *Performance*. I was never much good at school and I left when I was fifteen. This was 1976, and music in London was getting really interesting. I worked as a camera assistant on movies, and eventually that led to the first video I directed, the Jam's "Strange Town."

SIMON FIELDS, producer: Steve Barron and I had our first meeting at Warren Beatty's house; Steve's mother, who worked for Beatty, had just finished work on *Reds*, and she was staying at his place. I had more meetings with Steve and his sister, Siobhan, who was very smart, very wild. She ended up as my fiancée later on. She and Steve started a production company in London called Limelight, and we decided to join forces.

SIOBHAN BARRON, producer: When we started Limelight, we were working out of Steve's house. We were living on Scotch eggs to try and make ends meet. When the phone rang, which was once in a blue moon, Steve would always make me type on the typewriter, so we sounded busy.

BETH BRODAY, producer: I was a producer on a syndicated video-clip show in LA called *Deja View*. Ricci Martin, Dean Martin's son, was the on-camera talent. Response to the rudimentary clips we played was *unbelievable*. Station managers would get calls from viewers saying, "This is fantastic. We've never seen anything like this." This was before MTV, but I knew it was going to explode.

MARK MOTHERSBAUGH, Devo: Groups made videos in the 1940s. The Beatles made "Hello Goodbye" after they weren't willing to tour anymore, and the Monkees movie *Head* was like a music video. Music videos weren't invented in the early 1980s.

STEWART COPELAND, the Police: The first videos were for bands like the Monkees, where somebody with a video camera shot them walking through a park, doing stupid shit. "Hey, one of you guys climb a tree." The band jerks around and someone hoses them down with a camera and cuts it in time with the music.

MICHAEL NESMITH, the Monkees: I recorded a song called "Rio" in 1977, and Chris Blackwell, the head of Island Records, asked me to make a promo for the song—I think he called it a "clip." I wrote a series of cinematic shots: me on a horse in a suit of light, me in a tux in front of a 1920s microphone, me in a Palm Beach suit dancing with a woman in a red dress, women with fruit on their head flying through the air with me. As we edited these images, an unusual thing started to emerge: The grammar of film, where images drove the narrative, shifted over to where the song drove the narrative, and it didn't make any difference that the images were discontinuous. It was hyper-real. Even people who didn't understand film, including me, could see this was a profound conceptual shift.

That wasn't what Island Records had in mind, at all. They wanted me to stand in front of a microphone and sing. These lavish images were more than the medium could really stand. But "Rio" became a mild hit in Europe. I decided to try three or four more of these. And I started to see other music videos popping up.

MARK MOTHERSBAUGH: By the time MTV showed up, it was something Devo had been anticipating for half a decade. In 1974, Jerry Casale, his brother Bob, and I were writing songs for Devo when our friend Chuck Statler came over with a copy of *Popular Science* magazine. On the cover, it had a picture of a young couple holding what looked like a vinyl record, except it was silver and reflective. And it said, "Laser discs. Everyone will have them by Christmas." Chuck had taken filmmaking classes, and then directed commercials. We wanted to make films that used our songs, so they could eventually be on laser discs. We were art students from Kent State who were influenced by Robert Rauschenberg and Andy Warhol. Laser discs looked like the obvious bridge between the conceptual world of art museums and the real world of record stores.

JERRY CASALE: It was a burgeoning, do-it-yourself thing. The Devo videos I directed were hideous and funny. We saw the world as grotesque, and put ourselves right in with it. I grew up loving the New York underground films of the Kuchar Brothers and Kenneth Anger. I hired friends and we'd get extras for $25 a day. The video for "Satisfaction" cost a whopping $5,000. By the time we spent $16,000 on "Whip It," it was like, *Uh-oh, these video budgets are getting out of hand.*

MARK MOTHERSBAUGH: "Whip It" was shot in our rehearsal room. The faux log cabin was made out of the cheapest paneling we could find at Home Depot. We cast a band member's girlfriend, and when I was at the mall, I saw a girl who was really pretty and really cross-eyed, so I asked if she'd be in a video. It was very casual. My dad's in about a half dozen Devo videos. Our management and our agents didn't understand us, and our record company certainly didn't.

STEVE LUKATHER, Toto: We did some lip-synced videos for our first album, in 1978, including "Hold the Line." I had *Mork and Mindy* fucking suspenders on. For our second album, *Hydra*, we decided to try concept videos. This was before MTV. Bruce Gowers shot four videos for us in one day. They're so bad, they're hilarious. The sets looked like the inside of a sewer. Even when we were doing it, we were laughing. We figured, "No one's ever gonna show this."

TOM PETTY, artist: We made a video for "Refugee" because we didn't want to appear on *The Merv Griffin Show*. We thought if we sent a film clip, they'd play it—which they did. We showed up with our guitars, the director said, "Stand here," and that was it. It was meant to be shown once.

Then in 1981, for *Hard Promises*, we did four videos in two days, directed by my high-school buddy Jim Lenahan, who did our lighting and staging on tour. "A Woman in Love" was really good. The Police completely stole that. They stole the cinematographer, Daniel Pearl, the location, everything, for "Every Breath You Take." In those days we were actually cutting film by hand in the editing booth, and I was there right through the cut, through everything. So when MTV came along, I was an old hand at it. But I never dreamed those things would be seen repeatedly.

DAVID MALLET: I directed "Emotional Rescue" and "She's So Cold" for the Rolling Stones. Afterwards, I got an interesting fax from Keith Richards, and it happens to be in front of me because it's framed and hangs on my office wall. Part of it reads, "TV and rock n' roll have always had a weird marriage." He's right. One of the most difficult things to film is rock n' roll. People get bored and want to go home. By the time you've filmed the bloody thing, all the rock n' roll has gone out of it.

Chapter 3

————

"WE WERE JUST IDIOTS
IN HOTEL ROOMS"

JOHN LACK, BOB PITTMAN,
AND THE CREATION OF MTV

I F MTV HAD PLACED A HELP-WANTED AD, IT MIGHT HAVE read: "Novice TV station seeks employees. Ideal candidates must love music, be willing to work long hours and drink a lot, and have no prior TV experience."

It might seem odd that most of the network's original staff had little or no TV background. If you were charged with murder or needed brain surgery, you wouldn't hire a trial lawyer or a doctor who just months ago was selling aluminum siding. But MTV wasn't brain surgery. Many of its most important founders came from radio backgrounds, which freed them from abiding by the existing rules of the TV industry. (On the other hand, it also meant they were bound to the existing rules of the radio industry, which soon proved to be an impediment.)

A successful start-up requires dedication and imagination, but not necessarily expertise. Steve Wozniak, the tech wizard who cofounded Apple Computer with Steve Jobs, has recalled that in the early days of the company, when he didn't know how to design a floppy disk or a printer interface, he'd make something up, "without knowing how other people do it." He added, "All the best things that I did at Apple came from (a) not having money and (b) not having done it before, ever." Similarly, MTV had little money and less experience. If there was a corporate culture, it was based on confidence and pugnaciousness, traits that began at the top of the company's masthead.

In November 1979, *Billboard* magazine's first Video Music Conference, a four-day event at the Sheraton-Universal Hotel in LA, brought together most of the nascent industry's pioneers. Todd Rundgren and Michael Nesmith showed their videos, Jon Roseman presented "Bohemian Rhapsody" and Blondie's *Eat to the Beat* videodisk, with videos for every song from the band's album of the same name, and record labels showed off clips by David Bowie, Meat Loaf, Bruce Springsteen, and Rod Stewart, among others.

During a panel titled "Video Music—Tomorrow Is Here Today," John Lack declared his intention to start a twenty-four-hour video music network. "I got up and gave the presentation, which was pretty classy and elegant," Lack recalls. After he finished, Sidney Sheinberg spoke—Sheinberg was president of MCA and probably the most powerful executive at the conference. "Sheinberg gets up and goes, 'We ain't giving you our fucking music,'" says Lack, still sounding indignant about the slight.

So Lack phoned his boss, Jack Schneider, and quoted Sheinberg's snub. "And Schneider says, 'We'll kick his ass, don't worry about him.'" MTV didn't even have a name yet, and the fight had already begun.

JOHN LACK, MTV executive: A video radio station—that was my dream. I said "video radio" a thousand times.

JAMES D. ROBINSON III, CEO, American Express: American Express was interested in selling financial services into the home, and that led to my buying half of the Warner Cable Corporation in 1979 for $175 million. I did the deal with [Warner Communications chairman] Steve Ross, who was a fascinating guy. A simple deal bored him; a complex, tax-advantaged, convoluted structure really got his focus. Warner Cable had founded QUBE, a state-of-the-art interactive TV programming system, and the technology was desirable for us. So Amex and Warner jointly formed Warner Amex Cable Communications. That eventually split into two divisions: Warner Amex Cable Company, which built local cable systems; and Warner Amex Satellite Entertainment Company, or WASEC, which created and supplied programming, and was run by Jack Schneider.

JACK SCHNEIDER, MTV executive: I came to Warner Amex when it was created in 1979. I was president and chief executive officer of WASEC. I inherited The Movie Channel and Nickelodeon. I said, "What can we do next?"

BOB PITTMAN, MTV executive: John Lack hired me in 1979, when I was a young, hot programmer at NBC Radio. John and Jack Schneider, the CEO of WASEC, decided that the world of cable TV was going to be all about specialized net-works. Radio was a good model for that, so they wanted a radio programmer to work on The Movie Channel, which was the first twenty-four-hour movie service.

JOHN LACK: Bob Pittman had long hair, one eye, and was out of his mind. But he was brilliant. Jack Schneider said, "I'm not hiring some kid from radio to pro-gram movies. What are you, crazy?" Jack and I fought and fought and fought about it. One day, he said, "Look, if we hire him, do I have to listen to your shit anymore?"

BOB PITTMAN: I grew up in Brookhaven, Mississippi, the son of a Methodist preacher. Not only did I have one eye, but I was a small, skinny kid, plus I moved towns—we'd live in a town two years, four years, in towns where people had lived there for centuries, so it made me a bit of an outsider. I think it made me a pretty good observer of people, because you do that to keep from getting beat up.

I started in radio at fifteen, because I needed a job to pay for flying lessons, which was my hobby. I went to a couple of other stations in Mississippi, then Milwaukee, then Detroit, where I called myself "The Mississippi Hippie." I talked someone into letting me program my first station in Pittsburgh at nine-teen and had a big success. I went to Chicago, and they said, "We're gonna change the station to country." I didn't know anything about country. And they go, "That's okay, you know all about research." I was one of the first program-mers to use consumer research to figure out what music to play. In college, I'd been majoring in sociology with an emphasis on social methods research, and I used a lot of that.

CHARLIE WARNER, radio executive: Bob had long hair down his back and a full beard. He looked like he stepped out of a commune. His coiffure got shorter and more conservative as he moved up the corporate ladder.

BOB PITTMAN: I programmed The Movie Channel like a radio station. I figured, Okay, these are the five most popular movies, I'm gonna show them twice a day. These are not so popular, I'm only gonna show them every four days.

JOHN LACK: HBO went off the air at 2 A.M. Research showed that people wanted uncut, unedited movies twenty-four hours a day. So the Movie Channel went from 300,000 customers to 2 million in less than a year. The second channel we did was Nickelodeon—it wasn't called that in those days, but we began developing children's programming. The third channel I had on the drawing board was music. I'd traveled around Europe, and in every country you would see music shows with video clips. I thought we could show them twenty-four hours a day, if we had permission.

JACK SCHNEIDER: We needed cheap programming, which meant we needed somebody to *give* us the programming. And the record companies had videos. The world did not know that the record companies had videos. *I* knew. Why did I know? I knew because Columbia Records once reported to me when I was executive vice president at CBS. They were very cheap videos, maybe one camera shooting at Rod Stewart while he's singing "Da Ya Think I'm Sexy?" No productions values. But it was something.

MICHAEL NESMITH: I haven't talked about my role in the development of MTV, but this would be a good time to do that. I was driving in my car, it was an early evening, and I thought, *What you could do is, you could put together a television show or a television channel that played videos all the time.* And the name *PopClips* came into my mind. I talked to Jerry Perenchio, who was my first agent and has since made a big name for himself as a media tycoon. Jerry was in business with Norman Lear and they had *All in the Family.* We made a pilot, with half a dozen of these clips—"You Light Up My Life" and Paul McCartney's "Mull of Kintyre"—introduced by comedians like Howie Mandel and Charles Fleischer. And we were unable to sell it. The pushback from television was profound. I went to a meeting with one guy who said, "Look, let me tell you, music doesn't work on television. It never has, and it never will."

GARY LIEBERTHAL, TV executive: I was working with Norman Lear and Jerry Perenchio, running their syndication business. We had *All in the Family, Sanford and Son, Maude, The Jeffersons, Facts of Life, Diff'rent Strokes.* We were a significant presence in the TV business.

We financed a pilot, and I went to try to sell it. I sat down with the head of programming at Metromedia—they owned stations in New York, LA, Chicago, Dallas, Houston, Washington—and after he watched the pilot, he said, "But nobody's dancing." He was thinking of *American Bandstand.* He said, "Gary, I've been a programmer for a long time. You'll never have a music show on TV without kids dancing." I was known as a pretty good salesman in the syndica-tion business. But I tell people, "I'm the guy who couldn't sell MTV."

JOHN LACK: Michael Nesmith came to see me. Michael had been in the Monkees and he had funding to do a show he called *PopClips*.

MICHAEL NESMITH: I said, "John, this is a music video. Have you ever seen any-thing like this?" He said, "No, I never have." I said, "Artists are starting to make these things, you could play them all day long." And he said, "Like a music channel? Like music television?" I think John was the first guy I ever heard use the words "music television." He called a few days later and said, "I want to test the pilot on our children's channel." And once they did, from what I under-stand, the needle went off the meter. They called and said, "Can you make more of these?"

SUE STEINBERG, MTV executive: *PopClips* was a half-hour show with music vid-eos, hosted by comedians. The content wasn't great—it had to be repackaged—so Bob and I flew to LA to meet with Michael Nesmith. And he was not in a good mood. He didn't like the changes we suggested.

MICHAEL NESMITH: John said, "You've got to make these shows better for us. If you want to come to New York and maybe head this thing up, that might be interesting." My plan had always been to build it and sell it. They paid me a nice number. That was my exit.

TODD RUNDGREN, artist: I developed an interest in video before MTV. In the early 1970s, I saw a program called *Video Tape Review*, which was on Channel 13 in New York, WNET. They showcased the work of Nam June Paik and some other video experimentalists. I bought a lot of video equipment and set up a studio in the Bearsville, New York, area, mostly to experiment with leading-edge techniques. Since there were a lot of videos around and I had built a studio, my manager got the idea of having a twenty-four-hour music-video channel with a video DJ. To that end, for about $10,000, we bought a transponder on a video satellite, SatCom2. They sent it up and it didn't find its orbit, and it essen-tially turned into junk.

We took the idea to Bob Pittman, who feigned no interest. Eight months or a year later, they announced MTV. It's just an idea that was too damn obvious at that point. Things were reaching a critical mass in terms of video, so I think somebody eventually was going to do it.

JOHN LACK: Every time *PopClips* aired, the phones rang off the hook. I walked into Pittman's office one day in early 1980 and said, "It's time to do music. Let's start the research. I want to go to the board of directors in ninety days."

JORDAN ROST, MTV executive: John loved the idea of putting rock n' roll on television. That interested him much more than The Movie Channel or Nickelodeon. He was the first guy there who owned a Sony Walkman.

We had to do some research, to prove there was a market for the channel, and to get the Warner Amex board to approve it. I was the head of research. The first study had basic questions about the hosts and the sets. And then we asked, What kind of music should we play?

BOB PITTMAN: John Lack was the biggest supporter I could have and a great pal. I hung around with John a lot. In fact, all of us hung around a lot. You went to dinner with your MTV friends, you went on vacation with your MTV friends.

SUE STEINBERG: John knew I loved music, so he plucked me from Nickelodeon and told me and Bob to work on a music channel. I became the founding executive producer.

BOB PITTMAN: I'd worked with Steve Casey in radio, and he knew the science of music programming. He had call-out research down pat.

STEVE CASEY, MTV executive: Bob asked me to fly to New York and see what they were doing. The experience would have turned most people off; there was nothing at the time, only one other employee—Sue Steinberg—and the offices were like an insurance company.

FRED SEIBERT, MTV executive: When I was six weeks into being a chemistry major in college, I was learning how to kill a rat so I could dissect it. I looked at my lab mate and said, "The Beatles are more important to me than this," and I walked out. That was it for being a chemistry major. I marched uptown to the college radio station at Columbia University, because I heard I could get free records if I worked there.

After college, I took a job at a huge country music radio station in New

York, WHN. I found a mentor, Dale Pon. He was the head of promotion, and I was his assistant. And one day Dale quits and goes to work at WNBC radio, where Bob Pittman is running the station. I made commercials at night for Bob and Dale while working for WHN in the day. I saw Bob on TV all the time, because there was an ad campaign he ran for WNBC, with him on camera going, "Hi, I'm Bob Pittman, program director of WNBC, and we're gonna make you rich." During that period he also wrangled a gig where he and Lee Masters did a fifteen-minute show called *Album Tracks*. It was the MTV format in fifteen minutes.

From my standpoint, radio guys were idiots. Bob was much smarter than my boss. He offered me a job at The Movie Channel and I took it the next morning.

LEE MASTERS, MTV executive: Bob and I met in 1972, when we were both teenage disc jockeys, working in the South. A few years later, Bob hired me to work for him at WNBC as on-air talent, and we did *Album Tracks* together, which was a precursor to MTV in many ways. There weren't many outlets for music videos, so Bob had an idea for a show that would run after *Saturday Night Live* on NBC stations in New York, Chicago, Washington, and LA. We wrote the show and we were the on-camera talent, so to speak. We showed "Paradise by the Dashboard Light" and some Styx clips from *The Grand Illusion*. It was always album rock.

ANDY SETOS, MTV executive: I got a call from John Lack, because I was a cool engineer, and I'd had experience doing stereo television at WNET, the public TV station in New York. I think I was the tenth employee at WASEC. All the professional television equipment, all the TV sets, and all the video clips were monaural. I said, "Look, music *is* stereo, just like television is color. If this network is about music, it's gotta be in stereo." Jack Schneider said, "But it's gonna be hard." I said, "The hard part's my problem. Don't worry about that." So we were off on designing a television network in stereo—the first one anywhere, ever.

ROBERT MORTON, MTV executive: I was working at NBC, on *Tomorrow* with Tom Snyder. I got fired by none other than Roger Ailes, who came in as producer. I instantly disliked him, and he disliked me, I guess. Sue Steinberg offered me a job at this new music channel as creative director. I hardly had any experience, but I was the only person there with *any* TV experience.

BOB PITTMAN: My assistant said, "You've got to see this guy named John Sykes. He's calling you all the time." I didn't want to see him. We were done hiring. Finally he came in, and John is one of the more persuasive guys in the world.

JOHN SYKES, MTV executive: This is all I ever wanted to do: music on television. I'd worked for CBS Records as the regional promotion rep. It was my job to deliver radio airplay for our bands: Cheap Trick, Charlie Daniels, REO Speed-wagon, James Taylor.

The international department sent promotional videotapes to our branch from England and Australia. VCRs had just been introduced, so the tapes would be played at a band's in-store appearance. And I loved these tapes. I wanted to pitch CBS Television on a late-night video show. In those days, they were airing a test pattern with an Indian on it at night. CBS Records gave me $5,000 to edit together these videos and present them to a guy at CBS Television. He was sixty-five years old, I had no jacket or tie, and he had no interest whatsoever.

JOHN LACK: See, the whole pitch to the board of directors at WASEC had nothing to do with music videos. It had to do with demographics. At that point, there was no television aimed at the twelve- to thirty-four-year-old demographic. Half of the *Saturday Night Live* audience was over thirty-five. If you were an advertiser buying time on *Saturday Night Live* to reach young adults, half your money was wasted on thirty-five-plus. We said, *If this music channel reaches twelve to thirty-four year olds, we can deliver an audience for advertisers they can't get through broadcast television.* Cable providers would sign up new subscribers, because this would be available only on cable. We would sell second-set hookups because mothers and fathers would not allow this shit to be played in the living room: "Here's a TV, go play it in your own bedroom!"

We needed to get the videos for free, the same way radio got singles. I went to Allen Grubman, a hotshot lawyer. I said, "I want to meet the presidents of the eight large record companies, as quickly as we can." Some agreed because Steve Ross and Warner Communications were involved. PolyGram said no. Clive Davis at Arista laughed at me. He said, "Give us a year or two, let's see how it goes."

ALLEN GRUBMAN, attorney: John Lack invited me to lunch at the Four Seasons Restaurant. He explained that he was launching MTV and needed my help to get videos from the record companies. As a music lawyer, I was wired into all the labels. He said he'd like to retain me as a consultant, to introduce him to the head of a different record company every week, and he would pay me $50,000 a year. I said, "That sounds fair," but inside I was jumping up and down. Fifty-thousand dollars in 1980 was like somebody giving me $10 million today. And from that lunch until this very day, I've been a consultant to MTV.

The meetings were every Monday night, if I remember correctly. We would meet in the Pool Room at the Four Seasons, and John would present what MTV was about. For CBS, it was Walter Yetnikoff; for RCA, it was Bob Summer. *Boom, boom, boom.* Lack was a brilliant salesman. Smooth, well spoken, looked good. He was a great face for MTV. I believe Lack has never been given the appropriate credit that he deserved for MTV, because he left very early on.

JOHN LACK: There was the Walter Yetnikoff meeting. We go to the Four Seasons, Yetnikoff is with his little blond girlfriend, some bimbo with huge tits. Every fifteen minutes, one of them goes to the restroom. They come back sniffing, wiping their noses. By the end of the dinner, Walter is so high that whatever he said, the next day he doesn't remember.

ALLEN GRUBMAN: Walter was—how do I say this politely?—he was *meshuggah.* I'd call him extraordinarily eccentric.

GALE SPARROW, MTV executive: We went on the road to sell the labels on MTV. Bob Pittman would explain the channel, how many videos would be played, and how we'd chyron the artist's name and the song title at the beginning and end of the videos, which was a big deal to the labels, because half the time you'd hear a song on the radio and the DJ would never say who it was. That was a big selling point for us. Still, we hit a lot of brick walls.

JEFF AYEROFF, record executive: Pittman told me he was going to take all A&M Records' international films—that's what we called music videos—and put them on a cable channel. I was like, *What the fuck are you talking about?*

BOB PITTMAN: My mission was to get the labels to give us their videos. We had Warner Bros. locked up. RCA was supportive. Then there were the other labels. There was an ex-lawyer, David Braun, running PolyGram. He said, "I'm not gonna give you those things for free. You've gotta pay." Sid Sheinberg was running MCA Records. He said, "You gotta pay. Nothing's free from MCA." And at CBS, Walter Yetnikoff, obviously he's gonna make a tough deal. So rather than go to him, I went to Dick Asher, his deputy, and got Dick interested. Went to Bruce Lundvall, who was a president at CBS Records. Then we went to a lot of Walter's bands and got them interested. Sykes had worked at CBS, he knew REO Speedwagon. I was gonna flank Walter.

WALTER YETNIKOFF, record executive: When MTV came to me, I was perfectly happy to license our videos to them. My problem was, I wanted CBS to get paid. Their argument was, they were just like radio, and radio didn't pay royalties to labels. But it didn't cost me anything extra to send a record to radio. With videos I'd have to spend money.

JACK SCHNEIDER: Walter Yetnikoff was the toughest nut to crack. I chose not to involve myself personally with Walter. I knew it was going to get theatrical and vulgar and coarse, and he was deep into his chemical period at the time.

DEBBIE NEWMAN, record executive: CBS was the last company to get involved with MTV. They'd started a foray into home video, and they were petrified that giving videos to MTV would devalue the potential for sales. And they were afraid that MTV, which was co-owned by Warner Communications, would give preference to videos from Warner Bros. Records, which was CBS's main rival.

AL TELLER: I wanted MTV to pay CBS for playing music videos in the same way traditional TV networks pay for the programming they put on the air. I was a lone voice in that wilderness, though. My counterparts said, "Just give them the videos. Get the exposure." It was stupid. I fought hard to hold out, but ultimately I had to respond to the competitive realities. I wasn't going to go down in flames on this principle. But the industry sold itself for a pittance. It was like the Indians selling Manhattan for $24 worth of beads.

LEN EPAND, record executive: I felt MTV should pay some sort of licensing fee. This was Warner Communications and American Express, after all. This wasn't some impoverished start-up. PolyGram's president, David Braun, wouldn't budge. So MTV launched without any PolyGram videos. Meanwhile, our competitors' acts were getting all this exposure. Eventually we acceded to their demands.

MILES COPELAND, manager: Almost everybody in the business was skeptical of MTV. I remember the manager of ZZ Top saying, "If you want ZZ Top on TV, you pay ZZ Top." Later on, they gave *everything* to MTV.

TOMMY MOTTOLA, record executive: I represented the hottest duo in pop music at that time: Hall & Oates. Pittman, Sykes, and Lack came to us hat-in-hand, because it was not an easy sell in the beginning.

BOB PITTMAN: I started at MTV when I was twenty-six. We were all very young. And we were worried no one would take us seriously, so we wore suits. We wore suits to everything.

JOHN SYKES: Bob thought if we looked like drug addicts, no one would give us any money.

SIMON LE BON, Duran Duran: You thought, *Who are these guys? They're not very rock n' roll.*

JOHN SYKES: Bob and I would sit in record company offices and wait and wait and wait for them to see us. I'd go to California and sit outside offices and a secretary would say, "He's not ready." I'd go to lunch, use the bathroom five times, and come back the next day. At the end of day two she'd say, "Sorry, he had to leave." I'd come back the next day and do it all over again.

GALE SPARROW: A lot of managers gave us their clients' videos and said, "You have our permission to play them." It was probably illegal. But not only did we play that manager's big acts, we also played the baby acts they were trying to break. So they got double exposure.

LES GARLAND, MTV executive: Pittman and I were friends—we were programming different radio stations in Milwaukee at the same time. I was discovered in my twenties by the legendary radio programmer Bill Drake, and I was given a shot to go to Los Angeles, the biggest market in the country. And that led me to Boston, Detroit, Milwaukee . . . I received a lot of Program Director of the Year awards. I'd always get great ratings and I never got beat.

Doug Morris, who was running Atlantic Records, said, "Garland, you'd be great in the music business. You're friendly with the artists, you understand that language, you're a unique guy." That led to a job in 1979 as West Coast vice president and general manager of Atlantic, the biggest record company in the world: Led Zeppelin, the Rolling Stones, Aretha Franklin.

Pittman invited me to dinner sometime in '80. He said, "Does Atlantic make music videos?" I said, "A few." He said, "How do you determine who you're gonna make one for?" A lot of it had to with touring: if a band wasn't going to Europe, we might shoot a video to send there instead. If we got some traction, *then* we could send the act over. He said, "Garland, do you think music videos twenty-four hours a day, kind of like a radio station, would work on TV?" Immediately, I said, "Yes, I do. I think we're headed into a new age with cable television."

TOM FRESTON, MTV executive: I'd spent the 1970s living in Afghanistan and India. I'd made and lost a lot of money. I decided I wanted to work in the music business; my brother was working for Columbia Records, and I used to say, "Wow, this isn't hard." My brother turned me on to Bob McGroarty, who had started working in sales for a new venture. McGroarty said, "It's a new form of television, and we're looking for people who have no experience in TV." I said, "I'm your man." I started at MTV in October 1980, as head of marketing.

JOHN LACK: McGroarty knocks on my door. He tells me there's a guy in his office he really likes, but has no experience. I meet this guy and ask him what he does. He says, "I'm kind of in the import/export business in India." That was Tom Freston. I assumed "import/export" meant he was selling drugs.

TOM FRESTON: We were like an Internet start-up. We were lean and mean and didn't know what the hell we were doing. At the beginning, we were working out of a couple of rooms at the Sheraton Hotel in midtown New York. We had no office equipment. My first office was a soda storeroom. People thought I was delivering soda to the building.

ROBERT MORTON: It was a dump. The Carnegie Deli was downstairs, so our hotel room stunk like pastrami. We'd explain that we were starting a music channel and we're gonna play videos, and people didn't even know what videos were. It was a crazy pitch. We had, like, three videos we could show to people and say, "Here's what a video is." We were just idiots in hotel rooms.

CAROLYN BAKER, MTV executive: We worked out of a hotel room with puke yellow walls. We were all tense and nuts, because we'd given up jobs, and what if Bob didn't get the money?

JOHN SYKES: I went to work in a conference room with no windows and four phones. It was Carolyn Baker, Sue Steinberg, Steve Casey, and me. I asked Bob, "When do we start?" And he said, "Well, we don't have money to start yet."

BOB PITTMAN: The Warner Amex board of directors said *no* to the idea. They thought it was too crazy, too risky. Then Jack Schneider got us a meeting with Steve Ross and Jim Robinson and Lou Gerstner, the president of American Express. And we loaded it with some friends: Doug Morris from Atlantic Records, whom I'd known since I was a teenager in Detroit, when he had Big Tree Records, and Stan Cornyn from Warner Bros. Records. We played a videotape of what the channel would look like. We tried to make it *very* tame for them, and Jim or Lou said, "Oh that's such noise. Terrible stuff." And we're thinking, *Boy, you should see the stuff we're* really *gonna play.*

JOHN LACK: We were asking for $25 million, half from Warners and half from American Express. Ross turns to Schneider, the gray-haired guy, and says, "Jack, do you believe in this?" I fucking kicked Schneider hard under the table. He said, "Yes, Steve, I believe in it."

JACK SCHNEIDER: The programming concept for MTV was very simple. It was radio with pictures. I spent my whole life working in radio and television at CBS. I knew what a radio station was: It was a microphone, a transmitter, and a stack of records. We were simply adding the video aspect to it.

STEVE CASEY: My first meeting was with Jack Schneider, the guy in charge of the company. He spent the entire meeting telling us it was not going to work. His exact words were that music and television were "an unnatural marriage." I thought, *What a hell of a pep talk.*

LES GARLAND: Jack Schneider was great, he was the big papa, but he didn't really get it. Putting people on TV with purple hair, he just thought it was silly.

JACK SCHNEIDER: I was never comfortable in my role at MTV. I was the only adult there. I was fifty-four. They treated me like the old man, which I was. I always wore a coat and pants that matched. I thought that was an appropriate uniform, and it always served me well. Those kids didn't scare me. I was tougher, smarter, and more successful than any of them could ever dream of being. I had credibility. I had a presence, a maturity. When I met with Jim Robinson and Steve Ross, it was as equals. No, I wasn't chief executive of Warner, but I knew people like Steve Ross and dealt with them all my life. I didn't meet with Steve or Jim as a supplicant. I met with them as a peer.

JAMES D. ROBINSON III: We gathered in a conference room off of Steve Ross's office. Jack Schneider opened up the meeting and turned it over to Bob Pittman. For twenty minutes, Pittman laid out the concept of how to build a music-video channel. Bob was articulate and clearly knew what he was doing. After his presentation, I said, "Where in the devil do you get your raw material?" And he said, "That's not a problem. Every time a recording group creates a new album, they make these promotional films and give them away." I said, "You mean you don't have any cost of goods sold?" He said, "No." I said, "Steve, you've got our $10 million." It was literally as fast as that.

JOHN SYKES: They were in the conference room for three hours, and we waited outside. It was like waiting for a verdict from the jury.

SUE STEINBERG: We were all pretending to work. Some of us were playing a board game to occupy ourselves.

TOM FRESTON: If they'd said *no*, we would have all been fired.

JOHN LACK: We got the okay in January 1981. I said, "We will be on the air in seven months." Once I got approval, I said to Michael Nesmith, "Come be my creative consultant, I'll give you a piece." He said, "I don't want to do it the way you're doing it, and I don't like Bob Pittman." He didn't need the money.

JOHN SYKES: Pittman said, "We have to get it on air by August 1." We hardly knew where to begin. My business card said, "Music Program Development, Warner Amex Satellite Entertainment Company." There was no MTV yet.

JACK SCHNEIDER: People wonder why we picked August 1 for the launch. It was my knowledge that most fads start in the summer. I wanted the kids who saw it to go back to college or their high-school cafeteria and say, "Did you see this new channel?" I told everyone, "We're gonna make it by August 1 or there'll be hell to pay."

FRED SEIBERT: Once they got the green light, right away I said to Pittman, "Hey, I know more about music than anyone here." And he said, "You're right. Start working on the music channel." I said, "Great! Should I find somebody to replace me at The Movie Channel?" He said, "Oh no, no. You have to do that job, too."

One of the first things we needed to do was come up with a name for the new network. At first, Bob wanted to call it The Music Channel. Like The Movie Channel. Then he decided it should be called TV1. We all rebelled. We were adamant about it, so we walked into his office one day and told him we didn't like the name. He said, "Well, come up with a better one." There were six or seven of us, and no one could agree.

STEVE CASEY: I was scribbling down different names, and I liked the way MTV looked when I doodled it. I said, "Let's call it Music Television."

FRED SEIBERT: Music Television became the final compromise. Nobody liked it. We all hated the name MTV.

RICHARD SCHENKMAN, MTV staff: Fred ran the program services department. I'd never heard the phrase "program services" in my life. Fred explained to me that his department was going to make all the stuff that came in between the videos. And even though what he was making would occupy only two minutes an hour, it was the most important stuff on the air, because it explained to the viewers who we were.

FRED SEIBERT: I called my oldest friend, Frank Olinsky, who had started Manhattan Design with two partners. I asked them to design a logo. All I told them was, it's radio on television, and I don't want any musical instruments or notes. At this point it's April or May, and we're down to the wire. Bob is tapping his foot, saying "Where the hell is the logo?"

So one day Frank comes to my office. I'm flipping through one after another. I'm depressed. This one's not gonna work, that one's not gonna work. On the bottom of the pile is a piece of tracing paper that looks like it had been crumpled up and then flattened out. And on it was the *M* that we now know. I'm like,

"*That's* great." Frank spray paints *TV* onto the *M,* leaves the drips on, and comes back. We go, "That's it!" Graffiti. *Done.*

Then I said, "Okay, what colors will it be?" They do a couple dozen treatments, and each one looks good to me. So I put them up on my wall in my cubicle, and for weeks I looked at them, every hour, every day. Finally I said, "What if we use *all* of these in a single piece of animation? What if the logo was constantly changing? Isn't that kind of a rock n' roll thing to do?" You'd see twenty logos in one ten-second piece.

ANDY SETOS: It was changing like every eighth of a second. We had a discussion about that, so it wouldn't go too fast and give people epilepsy.

TOM FRESTON: John Lack hired Ogilvy & Mather to be our ad agency. It was a bad fit. We showed the logo to their creative director, Jerry McGee. He said, "This is the single worst thing I have ever seen. It violates every rule of logo-making. If you do this, you'll ruin your business." Fred said, "Well, too bad, we're gonna do this." Jerry McGee was appalled.

Twenty years later, when I was running MTV, I was at the car park at the Four Seasons Hotel in LA and I saw Jerry McGee getting into his car. He looked at me and said, "I know, I know." It's hard to remember now, but MTV was revolutionary in its day.

MARCY BRAFMAN, MTV staff: We had a sign above the monitor where we viewed the day's work, and it said, THIS IS NOT TRUE. We wanted people to question the voice-of-God aspect of television.

RICHARD SCHENKMAN: Fred Seibert is brilliant. When he walks in the room, he's the smartest guy there.

JACK SCHNEIDER: I have great respect for Fred. He gave MTV a look. The variations he did on the logo were simply brilliant. He did one with French fries and ketchup that was the best of its kind I ever saw. I remember it to this day.

JUDY McGRATH, MTV executive: Fred asked me what bands I liked, and no matter what I answered, he said, "You're wrong, and I'll tell you why."

PETER DOUGHERTY, MTV producer: As someone said to me, Fred thinks he invented television. I like Fred, but he's not humble.

FRED SEIBERT: We were the most conceited, arrogant people. We actually thought what we were doing was important. We thought, *We're gonna change the face of television!* And we needed a station ID that reflected how arrogant we were. So we thought, "What's the most famous moment in television history?" We were gonna steal it. The Kennedy assassination? No, that's not gonna work. And I said, "I think the most famous moment is the moon walk. Why don't we take that footage, and put the MTV logo in the American flag?"

TOM FRESTON: Pittman never gave us any money to do anything. This was a fucking shoestring operation if there ever was.

BOB PITTMAN: We hit upon the NASA moon-landing footage, because it was public domain—it was cheap—and it seemed big. Our original concept was to have Neil Armstrong saying, "One small step for man, one giant leap for mankind." We sent a letter to his lawyer: "If we don't hear back from you, we're going to run this." And like a day before we launched, we got a letter back saying, "No, you do not have our permission." *Shit.*

FRED SEIBERT: At first I wanted Joe Jackson to do all the music for our promos. But I was too scared to call him. So I hired a company called Elias-Peterson. I told them I need ten-second pieces of music, and we picked a dozen of them.

JONATHAN ELIAS, musician: They showed me the moon-landing picture and said, "Because people are so used to seeing that image as holy, let's rip it apart with some rock music." Who knew the MTV theme would turn into a generation's standard-bearer? They still use it every now and then, in various parts of the world. About seven years later, I went on to produce Duran Duran. Simon Le Bon and Nick Rhodes said to me, "You're the only person who's on MTV more than we are." That's how they introduced me to people; not "He's our producer," but "This is the guy who wrote the MTV theme."

Chapter 4

—————

"WHAT'S A VJ?"

HOW MTV HIRED ITS HOSTS (INCLUDING A CASE OF MISTAKEN IDENTITY)

WHEN MTV: MUSIC TELEVISION ANNOUNCED THE hiring of five on-air hosts in a July 1981 press release, the word VJ appeared in quotation marks—it was a new term, bound to cause confusion.

So maybe it was inevitable that the original five grew confused about the duties of their jobs and that MTV executives were also confused about whom to hire. Of the five announced in July, two had not been the network's first choices.

BOB PITTMAN: I decided we needed VJs. Nobody falls in love with a jukebox; you have to bond with a human being.

JOHN LACK: Bob said, "We need a black person. We need a girl next door. We need a little sexy siren. We need a boy next door. And we need some hunky Italian-looking guy with curly hair." They all had roles to play.

KEVIN CRONIN, REO Speedwagon: I was the first person approached to be an MTV VJ, and I turned it down. My publicist, Howard Bloom, said, "I want you to meet some guys who are putting together a twenty-four-hour TV station that plays rock videos." So we went to dinner and these guys who looked like lawyers and accountants offered me a job. I said, "I play in a rock band! We tour eight months of the year and make records the rest of the time!" And their jaws dropped, like this had never occurred to them. I thought, *These guys are clueless.*

SUE STEINBERG: We placed ads in *Variety* and *Hollywood Reporter* and got on the phone with agents. We had serious actors, DJs, record company executives.

A broad variety of people. Richard Belzer auditioned. He was doing stand-up then. Carol Leifer auditioned. She might have been the funniest and most irreverent.

ROBERT MORTON: We auditioned local newscasters. We saw a lot of radio people, who had faces for radio, unfortunately. We held auditions in a hotel room. There were beds in the room. I mean, it just reeked of sleaze.

SUE STEINBERG: For the audition, we wrote up a little script for them to read. But the best part was when we had them do mock interviews. Robert Morton would pretend he was Billy Joel. They would ask, "What did you have in mind when you wrote 'New York State of Mind'?" And he'd say something like "My mother's cooking," and they'd have to banter off that.

ROBERT MORTON: I'd be surly, I'd be falling asleep, I'd be physically touching them—whatever somebody would do who was a little drugged up. I was acting like a big asshole; rock musicians do things that are unexpected, and we were testing potential VJs to see if they could handle situations like that.

SUE STEINBERG: Nina came in through an ad in the paper. She was playing the harp at some hotel near LAX.

NINA BLACKWOOD, MTV VJ: I played rock n' roll–style harp: "Stairway to Heaven," even Bruce Springsteen. I studied acting at the Lee Strasberg Institute. And I was working on three different local prototypes for music-video programs, where I'd do interviews or introduce video clips. I sent in my résumé and an eight-by-ten photo which I drew on with watercolor pens to make it look punky.

SUE STEINBERG: She looked edgy, with that crazy hair, but she wasn't sure she wanted to come to New York, so we flew her in from LA.

NINA BLACKWOOD: Sue told me to come to New York and meet the head guy, Bob Pittman. He reminded me of Sherman, from the *Rocky & Bullwinkle* cartoon. Sherman was the boy genius.

ROBERT MORTON: Sue and I took her to Tavern on the Green, and not three minutes after we sat down, she put a piece of bread in her mouth and started choking on it. She's turning red. I said, "Need a little Heimlich, Nina?" And she nodded her head *yes*. From working in morning television, I knew Dr. Heimlich; I'd had him on shows, demonstrating the Heimlich maneuver. I got behind her and gave her a big squeeze, and this piece of bread popped out. She said, "Now I have to take the job, you saved my life."

NINA BLACKWOOD: Morty, who I love to this day, said, "Now you have to take the job. You owe me!" I moved to New York on July 5. I was the first VJ hired.

SUE STEINBERG: We decided we needed a teen idol, and that was Mark Goodman.

MARK GOODMAN, MTV VJ: I was working at WPLJ radio in New York when I got a call from a friend about this twenty-four-hour video music thing. I knew of Pittman, so I arranged a meeting with an executive producer at Warner Amex. I said, "Where's your office?" He said, "We're at the Sheraton on Seventh Avenue." I'm like, "Okay, this is a gonna be a rape." I was kind of creeped out. The first audition was March '81.

KEVIN CRONIN: If you were to pull up photos from the early '80s of me and Mark Goodman, you'd notice an undeniable similarity in style. Check out those mullet-Afros, or as we call them now: mulfros. It's my contention that Mr. Goodman coattailed into his gig on my hairdo.

MEG GRIFFIN, radio DJ: I really liked my job at WNEW in New York. I was content. I went in kind of begrudgingly one day to audition for MTV, and it felt good that they wanted to hire me. I was in an office next to Bob Pittman, and I overheard him say, "I have my black, my Jew, my WASP, my sex-bomb, and now my tomboy." I was like, *What did he just say?* It rubbed me the wrong way. And to be honest, I was flabbergasted by the $50,000 a year salary for national television; I thought they were shortchanging their talent.

SUE STEINBERG: Just a few weeks before we went on air, Meg didn't show up for work. We started madly dialing her house—we thought maybe she'd been in a car accident. We got her husband on the phone and he said, "Well"—long pause—"Meg has decided this is not for her."

MEG GRIFFIN: Maybe they thought I was being unprofessional. You know what? I didn't give a shit.

MARTHA QUINN, MTV VJ: I had graduated from NYU, where I'd worked at the radio station, WNYU. My radio name was Tiffany and I played urban music, like Shalamar and the Whispers.

MEG GRIFFIN: It was clearly typecast, because look who they hired when I turned it down! Martha Quinn was a duplicate of me. People used to call her "Little Meg," which irked her.

RONALD "BUZZ" BRINDLE, MTV executive: I was talking to Pittman, and he said, "We're looking for a VJ." Martha was an intern at WNBC radio, where I worked, and she was standing in my office. She had a charismatic personality. Bob said, "Have her here in thirty minutes for an audition."

MARTHA QUINN: I said, "What's a VJ?" Buzz said, "It's like being a DJ, but on TV." And I said, "What do I do while the records are playing?" Because I was thinking it was like *WKRP in Cincinnati*.

ROBERT MORTON: She grew into a great personality, but we never thought much of her. It was like, "Oh, she's [*Newsweek* columnist] Jane Bryant Quinn's daughter, we have to give her a shot."

MARTHA QUINN: I walked in to audition and they looked at me like, "Who are you? A messenger?" A couple of days later, Sue Steinberg called me to the studio and said, "We would like you to work for us." That was two weeks before launch.

SUE STEINBERG: Martha was so young, her father had to sign her contract for her.

MARTHA QUINN: I was still involved with my high school boyfriend when I started at MTV. That's how young I was.

KEN R. CLARK, MTV staff: I was hired as production assistant to the VJs. I was the sixth VJ—if they were there, I was there. And they were easy to work with. There was no ego, they loved each other like siblings. There wasn't that animosity or jealousy that came to plague the later years.

JOHN SYKES: The J.J. Jackson we hired wasn't the J.J. we meant to hire.

ROBERT MORTON: That's true. Pittman's one direction to us was "Find a black VJ." He told us about a guy named J.J. Johnson, and said, "He's really good.

Track him down." So I looked all over for J.J. Johnson. Subsequently, I found out who he was; a very good-looking black guy who had a great voice. But I couldn't find him. I called every radio station in the country. Finally I called KMEL in San Francisco and said, "Do you have a guy named J.J. Johnson working for you?" They said, "No, but we have J.J. *Jackson*." I said, "Well, let me talk to him." We auditioned him and I said to Pittman, "Here's your J.J."

MARTHA QUINN: J.J. was the elder statesmen of the VJs. He had Rod Stewart's home phone number. And he was the partier. He knew every doorman at every club.

KEN R. CLARK: J.J. was the most rock star of the VJs. He would be out at the clubs, surrounded by gorgeous, exotic models, and imbibing all the '80s had to offer. He kept a tube of Preparation H in his dressing room to shrink his swollen eyes after a hard night of partying. Apparently it's something models had known and used for years. I recall him saying, "It reduces the swelling brought on by a night of intense partying with the lovely Katrina and Nadia."

ADAM CURRY, MTV VJ: Our car service, Communi-Car, called J.J. "the franchise." He lived it, man. He'd be out all night and leave the car sitting outside for hours. He was larger than life.

KEN R. CLARK: J.J. always came flowing into the studio in his floor-length, black, pimp-daddy mink coat just moments before he was due on set.

MARK GOODMAN: I used to call J.J. "Club Man," because he was always out all night, and he would roll straight from a club to the MTV studio. J.J. had a never-ending stream of women, and they were all pretty and exotic. He was a very unusual guy. He was erudite, a great storyteller. You couldn't help but love him. He was a hugger and a kisser, too; within weeks of knowing him, he was hugging me. He was that kind of guy.

PAM LEWIS, MTV staff: The first major celebrity interview we did was with Robert Plant, who went way back with J.J. Plant walked in, with all his sex appeal and swagger, hugged J.J., and said, "You're wearing fuckin' makeup." Our budget was pretty bare bones and we had no makeup artist. J.J. would apply his own makeup and sometimes he'd overdo it, and get a kind of ocher color. He looked like a brick with eyes.

ALAN HUNTER: I have no idea why they hired me. I think they were desperate. They opened the auditions to every critter on the face of the earth who could speak. Even after I was hired, I kept my bartending job. About half a year into it, J.J. said, "If you're not making at least $40,000, then you got screwed." I was like, "Oh, I'm doing fine!" I couldn't admit to him that Mark and I were making less than that. They picked me out of nowhere, and I was fine with it.

SUE STEINBERG: Martha Quinn was the girl next door. Alan Hunter was Martha's counterpoint, the boy next door.

MARTHA QUINN: Al was the funny one. He was our in-house Mork, complete with rainbow suspenders. He was always doing cartwheels, being goofy.

ALAN HUNTER: For the first six months, they thought they'd made a horrible mistake by hiring me. I don't think I was very good on the air. I was only a year out of college, I was scared and uneasy, and speaking extemporaneously about a Styx concert was hard for me. I'd come home every night and say to my wife, "They're gonna fire me tomorrow." One day I actually did a cartwheel into the teleprompter at the studio, broke the glass all over the place, and popped back out again. Bob Pittman sent me a note that said, "Beautiful." They loved that.

The goal that first year was to break every television mold, by being funny and clowning on camera. Pittman wanted the VJs to be as irreverent as the videos.

JOHN LACK: I took the VJs to dinner at Odeon before the launch, the hot new restaurant in New York. Keith McNally had just opened it, cocaine was everywhere, it was the rock n' roll cafeteria. I stood up and said, "Next week you're going to be famous."

TODD RUNDGREN: I was put off by the slickness of the VJs. They were no different from radio DJs.

THOMAS DOLBY, artist: They'd roll the camera, and J.J. Jackson would go, "So Thomas, you're over here on your first American tour." And I'd say, "No, I'm over here to make a record." It was literally that stupid. It was like a joke; they had to keep stopping and starting.

ALAN HUNTER: They asked me to not wear my wedding ring on the air, so I took it off for a week. One producer told me that if Martha and I were to become more than just friends, it wouldn't hurt ratings.

I was alive and I was a male; who wouldn't have lustful thoughts about Martha and Nina? Martha's kinda flirty anyway. And we all shared the same low-rent dressing room, so I caught a glimpse of Nina naked. I didn't mean to, but I also didn't mind it.

NINA BLACKWOOD: In 1978, when I was living in Cleveland, I posed for *Playboy*. When *Playboy* got wind of my MTV job, they decided to reprint the photos. I got called into the MTV offices over this. I remember feeling like a scolded little girl, having to go to the principal's office. They weren't real thrilled, which I find pretty ludicrous considering what MTV turned into.

ALAN HUNTER: I was doing a personal appearance in a record store, signing autographs and shaking hands, and a guy came up and popped this *Playboy* open to the page where Nina was. I couldn't take a mental snapshot quick enough. There were a thousand people in the store, and all I could think about was Nina naked.

JACK SCHNEIDER: Nina Blackwood was every teenager's wet dream. That's why she was hired. We knew what we were doing. This thing was designed to appeal to young men.

DAVE NAVARRO: I liked Nina Blackwood—she was a little more heavy metal. I always fall for the woman with the smoke and mirrors.

CONAN O'BRIEN: I remember thinking, *Martha Quinn's cute*. She seemed attainable to me. She was the only one whose name I could remember early on. Of course, now they're all in prison.

"WEIRD AL" YANKOVIC: I think everybody in North America had a small crush on Martha Quinn.

ALAN HUNTER: Nina was the vamp, and Martha was the girl next door. Guys always said to me, "What's Nina like? I want to sleep with her." And "What's Martha like? I want to date her."

KEN R. CLARK: Martha looked like the little girl next door, and Nina was thought to be the "video vamp." In reality, Nina was timid. She loved animals. Nina blushed if she even said *damn*. And Martha—I love Martha, we're still close— but she was scrappy. She could be in your face. Martha was the one dating the rock star, [Dead Boys singer] Stiv Bators. Nina was going home to her apartment full of cats.

MARK GOODMAN: Everybody was hot for Nina at some point. There were those who were hot for Martha, too. But by 1983, Martha was already dating rock stars.

JULIAN GOLDBERG, MTV executive: I shared a cab once with a major executive in the business world. I won't tell his name. We were coming back from a party, and he was making friendly small talk about MTV. All of a sudden he said, "How can I fuck Martha Quinn?" A lot of guys I ran across had that same thought.

JOHN KALODNER, record executive: From the second I saw Martha on MTV, I wanted her to be my girlfriend. I met her a few times, and when she moved to LA in 1989, she was my girlfriend for about a year. She was one of my true loves. She was like having a girlfriend and a child in the same person. She was the messiest, dirtiest person. She would throw her clothes everywhere. You'd have to throw her in a bathtub to clean her up.

STEVE SCHNUR, MTV staff; record executive: I was a college intern in the programming department of MTV, and I had a major thing for Martha Quinn. I tried so hard, and I got nowhere. It was pathetic. I went to her house a couple of times, but I failed miserably. Every artist I became friendly with would ask if I could hook him up with Martha, because we all had the same idea, that this girl next door was secretly wild.

MARTHA QUINN: I can't believe more guys didn't ask for my phone number. I was a young girl, cute. I remember going *after* Michael J. Fox. I *begged* his publicist, Bobby Zarem, to give Michael J. Fox my phone number.

STEVE LUKATHER: Steve Porcaro, Toto's keyboardist, dated Martha Quinn on and off for a while. I remember being up all night with her and Steve in a bar. When I walked out, it was eleven in the morning.

KEN R. CLARK: Martha attracted the weirdos. Of the five original VJs, she was the one with the disturbed fans. A couple got so obsessed that Martha had to have security with her all the time. Police got involved.

MARK GOODMAN: When you look at the five of us, we had the benign black guy, the girl next door, the high-school jock, the hot video vamp, and me. I once asked Sue Steinberg and she said, "You were the stud." I was like, "Fuck me, really? The stud? Wow!" I thought I was the guy with the Jewfro.

KEN R. CLARK: I still have a piece of fan mail that was sent to Mark. It said, "Would you like to come meet a girl who can suck the chrome off a trailer hitch? If not, please send Alan. Thanks."

Chapter 5

————

"A TOTAL, UNMITIGATED DISASTER"

MTV LAUNCHES WITH THE BUGGLES, BLOTTO, AND THIRTY ROD STEWART VIDEOS

AFTER MONTHS OF LATE HOURS AND SHORT PAY, MTV employees deserved a great party when the channel debuted on the air. They didn't get one. Because no Manhattan cable operator had yet agreed to carry MTV, the staff schlepped to the Loft, a restaurant and bar in Fort Lee, New Jersey, the nearest town where the signal was available.

To their credit, the surroundings didn't diminish the celebration. "When MTV came on the air at midnight, the Loft's downstairs banquet room resembled a winning candidate's headquarters on election night," wrote the *Los Angeles Times'* Robert Hilburn, the only reporter who covered the event. "Gathered around a half-dozen TV sets, they cheered wildly when anything came on the screen: the music, the commercials, the station logos."

No volume of cheering could drown the technical mistakes that plagued the launch. At the network operations center in Smithtown, Long Island, carefully planned segments aired in the wrong order, which made the broadcast seem like a grade school talent pageant. It's fortunate that so few people could tune in; advertisers, cable operators, and the home audience would have been baffled by what they saw.

BOB PITTMAN: We launched on August 1, 1981. Our first video was the Buggles' "Video Killed the Radio Star." It was too obvious not to do it. When you see the video today, you go, "Don't tell me that's cutting edge." But at the time, it was.

STEVE CASEY: Nobody wanted to launch with "Video Killed the Radio Star." They thought we had to play a hit. I said, "Nobody's going to be watching. It's symbolic." In fact, the second video we played was symbolic, too: Pat Benatar's "You Better Run" was a message to the record labels.

TREVOR HORN, the Buggles: We wrote "Video Killed the Radio Star" in 1979. It came from this idea that technology was on the verge of changing everything. Video recorders had just come along, which changed people's lives. We'd seen people starting to make videos as well, and we were excited by that. It felt like radio was the past and video was the future. There was a shift coming.

RUSSELL MULCAHY, director: "Video Killed the Radio Star" was a one-day shoot in south London. I had a good friend who was trying to break into acting. I told her I needed a girl to dress in a silver costume and be lowered via wires into a test tube. What she didn't know was that we would need about thirty takes. What you see in that scene is actually the wrong take; the tube falls over, which wasn't supposed to be in the final cut. I think it's still in the video to this day. No one really knew what they were doing, including me.

TOM FRESTON: We had a party in Fort Lee, New Jersey, just for staff, so we could watch the network launch at midnight on August 1, 1981. The party couldn't be for advertisers, because we didn't have any. The only cable operator who came was this great guy in New Jersey, who was the first guy to carry us. He was our only customer.

JOHN LACK: The night before we went on the air, Fred Seibert says to me, "We can't just sign on, we have to say something. John, it's like a time capsule. What would you say?" I told him, "I'd say, 'Ladies and gentleman, rock n' roll.'" He goes, "That's it! And you're going to say it!" That's how we started: I say, "Ladies and gentlemen, rock n' roll," the rocket ship goes up, the man lands on the moon, and that's it.

CAROLYN BAKER: When that Buggles video played, we started screaming like maniacs. We were all drunker than skunks.

PAM LEWIS: That night might have been the first time I was ever in a limo. I told John Lack that he looked like he'd given birth—which in essence, he had. It was jubilation.

BOB PITTMAN: The first hour of MTV was a total, unmitigated disaster. The VJs would announce, "That was Styx," right after we'd played REO Speedwagon.

They'd say "This is the Who," and a .38 Special video would begin. We'd gotten everything mixed up. And we'd also done stereo TV for the first time. So if you're listening in stereo, it sounds fine. If you're listening in mono, like 99.9 percent of people, either the audio wasn't there or it was totally muffled. Everything that could have gone wrong did go wrong. It was probably one of the worst nights in my life. While everybody else was celebrating, I was on a telephone with the network operations center, going ballistic.

ANDY SETOS: The first hour was both comical and embarrassing. It was complete chaos. Someone handed me the phone at the network operations center, and it's Pittman. Bob goes, "Andy, that was the wrong clip." He sounded very nervous. I said, "Bob, are we on the air?" And he said nothing, so I hung the phone up.

We were doing things that had never been done before. I'd had broadcast equipment specially modified for stereo, a cartridge system designed by Ampex, which played the video clips. There was some video feedback a couple of times, because we had circuits that were crossed in the wiring. We weren't even finished wiring the place! It was crazy, like any other startup. Two or three weeks before the launch, Bob had contracted with the record companies to include the artist, the name of the song, and the record label in the lower third of the screen, at the beginning and end of the clip, for a certain amount of time. Not being a TV person, Bob hadn't realized how complex it would be to add the overlays. It was a last-minute scramble, and it meant there was no time for any real rehearsal before the launch.

STEVE CASEY: The night we launched is still the proudest moment in my life. I've never experienced that level of energy at any other time. When I got up the next morning, the first thing I did was call my mother in Wichita, Kansas, and tell her. She goes, "Oh yeah, I'm watching." I'm like, *What?* Wichita had a brand-new fifty-channel cable system and so MTV was on from day one. We couldn't watch it in Manhattan, but my mom could in Kansas.

DAVE HOLMES: I've seen the first hour of MTV. I watched it at the Museum of Television and Radio in New York. And it's, like, three Rod Stewart videos and two Pat Benatars. It was like a haphazardly formatted radio station. A British metal band. Then an American female pop singer. But no black people. *No* black people.

PAT BENATAR: I got really angry when we shot "You Better Run." I kept thinking, *What do they think I am, a runway model? Fuck you!* It seemed like we were making a commercial. As a musician, it was your whole life to be edgy and underground. And here come these film people, who weren't like us—they had little shirts with collars that buttoned down. The bad attitude I had was exactly what we needed for that song—I come across as extremely sassy and aggressive, which was perfect for the lyric and for the image I was trying to project.

NEIL "SPYDER" GIRALDO, artist: My wife, Patricia, is very photogenic. MTV was made for her—it was perfect.

DON BARNES, .38 Special: MTV had sent their own film crew from New York to tape our show, and "Hold On Loosely" was one of the first videos they played. We weren't the prettiest guys around: We were Southern dudes with hair down to our chests. And we certainly weren't actors. You see some of our early videos, we're standing there like zombies. *Stoned* zombies.

LEE RITENOUR, artist: I was the only jazz-oriented artist they showed on the first day—they played not one, but two of my videos. I mean, they were looking for content, they were trying to fill twenty-four hours a day. "My God, how are we doing to do this?" I have to laugh, because when people think of Lee Ritenour, they don't think of MTV, and when they think of MTV, they don't think of Lee Ritenour.

JIM DIAMOND, Ph.D.: We were the fifth song they played, "Little Suzi's on the Up." In the video, I'm supposed to be working as a butcher, and there was ballroom dancing—nothing to do with the song. When MTV played it, we said, "Oh shit, what have we done? Not only do *we* know it's the worst video ever made, now the whole *world* knows it's the worst video ever made!" It didn't do anything for our career; the record was never even released in America.

KEVIN CRONIN: When MTV came on the air, our record *Hi Infidelity* had been number one for months, so it was pretty good timing for us. 1978 was the first time we made a video; they'd set up a couple cameras at sound check and we'd run through the song. That was a music video. For *Hi Infidelity*, we'd made four videos in one day with Bruce Gowers. They were horrible. "Keep On Loving You" made us look like even bigger dorks than we were. It starts with me sitting in a psychiatrist's office—a female psychiatrist, because someone figured out that you had to have a hot chick in the video. The psychiatrist was this gorgeous model with librarian glasses. She was out of our league, big-time.

DENNIS DeYOUNG, Styx: "Best of Times" and "Rockin' the Paradise" were among the first videos played on MTV. This is how Styx made videos in the early days: If we were playing several nights in some city, we'd go onstage in the afternoon on the second day and lip-sync three songs. Had we been aware that MTV would emerge, perhaps we would have put a little more thought into our videos.

GREG HAYMES, Blotto: We were a small indie band in Albany, New York, when MTV ran our video on day one, sandwiched between Iron Maiden and Rod Stewart. Not to be overly humble, but they needed content. I think we were the thirty-fourth or thirty-sixth video they played.

JERRY CASALE: In the beginning, they played "Whip It" all the time.

"WEIRD AL" YANKOVIC: Devo was in heavy rotation, not because MTV loved Devo, but because it was a twenty-four-hour network and they needed product.

BOB PITTMAN: I think there were 250 videos in existence.

RICHARD SCHENKMAN: When new videos came in, it was like when you're living in a small port town and the ship comes in with supplies.

ANDY SETOS: After two days, it was getting *really* boring. We had very few clips— and there were no commercials.

MARK GOODMAN: We must have played "Lonely Boy" by Andrew Gold every twenty minutes. He was one of the few American artists with more than one video. We also played Rod Stewart up the wazoo.

TOM FRESTON: When we went on the air, we had something like 165 videos. And thirty of them were Rod Stewart.

RICK KRIM, MTV executive: Damn, there was a lot of Rod Stewart and REO Speed-wagon. But I also remember random videos like Classix Nouveau's "Guilty," and Tenpole Tudor's wacky "Wunderbar."

DAVE HOLMES: There were bands I got into because I thought they were cool, and I thought they were cool because they were on MTV, and they were on MTV because the network had played Rod Stewart too many times. Blotto, or Joe King Carrasco and the Crowns—I thought they were legendary artists. And I wanted to live in a world where Blotto was huge.

GREG HAYMES: I think they appreciated us because we were not afraid to be silly. Alan Hunter wore a Blotto sweatshirt on the air.

GALE SPARROW: We had eight Rod Stewart videos. We played him, like, every five minutes. Rod was lucky we didn't ruin his career. To be honest, we'd play pretty much anyone with a video.

Chapter 6

"GIRLS SLIDING ON POLES"

THE FIRST DIRTY MUSIC VIDEO

FROM THE BEGINNING, MUSIC VIDEOS WERE OFTEN silly, undignified, funny (intentionally? unintentionally? It was hard to know), crass, and artificial. However, they were never dirty—until the arrival of a British band who counted on shock value to make their mark in the U.S. In this narrow sense, "Girls on Film" is the most influential music video ever made, setting in motion three decades of titillation.

JOHN TAYLOR: "Girls on Film" is pretty fucking insane. I mean, it's like *Penthouse* or *Hustler*. It's *cheesy*. But it worked.

LOL CREME, director: Duran Duran's managers, Paul and Michael Berrow, told us they were going to break the band in America by making a video, but not an ordinary video. They wanted an outrageous video. They said we could do whatever we wanted, but they suggested the concept be something sexual.

KEVIN GODLEY: The Berrows discovered there were clubs in the United States that played music videos. They wanted a video that would be controversial. I went to the south of France with a fashion crowd for a few weeks and my partner Lol went to LA. When we came back together, he'd seen some mud wrestling and I'd seen fashion shows. We thought, *What if we did a sort of catwalk show, but with sumo wrestling and sex?*

JOHN TAYLOR: There's no plot to "Girls on Film." The only plot was to set up some sexy scenes with girls. You don't need a plot to make a cool video. You just need something that catches the eye, that's sexy or amusing. Sometimes it's enough just to have style.

KEVIN GODLEY: It had glamour, it had polish, it had sex, it had good-looking boys, it had girls sliding on poles. It was a dirty film. In hindsight, it had the ingredients that became MTV-able. If it was influential, I'm sorry. I can only apologize.

NICK RHODES, Duran Duran: It's the kind of video people now call "politically incorrect."

SIMON LE BON: We were five randy twenty year olds, and management didn't want us around the girls when they took their clothes off. We did sneak in. It was *very sexy* for us at the time.

KEVIN GODLEY: Management kept the band well away from the girls. There were other shoots going on in nearby studios. Word got around, and people began flocking to our shoot.

LOL CREME: We had a closed set, because there were naked ladies about. At one point, I turned around and saw Japanese tourists with their cameras, like a cliché, photographing what we were doing.

SIMON LE BON: My favorite moment is definitely the ice cube on the nipple.

KEVIN GODLEY: Someone mentioned that at porno shoots, in order to get an erect nipple, you put some ice on it. So we said, "Why not?"

SIMON LE BON: I don't know who held the ice cube. I wish it'd been me, but unfortunately it wasn't.

NICK RHODES: It was funny and tongue-in-cheek.

JOHN TAYLOR: It definitely got the juices flowing. It brought out the alpha dog thing, where we were all unconsciously scrambling over each other to get the attention of the brunette.

SIMON LE BON: Those two models in the video completely polarized the band. I liked the dark one. John liked the blond one.

KEVIN GODLEY: Subsequently it was edited for MTV, which made it a little less raunchy than the original.

SIMON LE BON: It was really on the edge. I mean, it was *banned*. That was the best thing that could ever have happened to it, really.

JOHN TAYLOR: It was very clear that we were a band served well by the video medium.

Chapter 7

"A HAIL MARY PASS"

HOW $1 SAVED MTV FROM BANKRUPTCY

WHEN RECORD LABELS GAVE THEIR EXISTING music videos to MTV, they were often reluctant, even though it didn't cost a cent—the videos were already paid for and were, for the most part, sitting around unused. But if MTV was going to succeed, they needed new videos, and better ones, too. This required record labels to spend money, in the midst of a sales slump, and that prospect changed their mood from reluctant to cranky. So MTV needed to present proof that exposure on the network led directly to more albums sales, or the labels would not increase their meager commitments to video.

And MTV had a second reluctant business partner: cable operators. "Remember, cable was in rural communities," John Lack says. The federal government had been moving toward deregulation of cable, but cable operators were still subject to regulation on the municipal and state levels, and they feared that rock videos would incite controversy, viewer objections, protests, and maybe even cause them to lose the virtual monopolies they'd worked hard to win.

The cable operators were MTV's mightiest obstacle, and the network needed a quick solution. If MTV was going to survive past its first year, it had to outsmart the cable operators. The strategy devised inside the network involved a memorable four-word phrase, mixed with the power of celebrity.

BOB PITTMAN: We needed to be very scientific about the impact MTV was having on the record industry. So I sent John Sykes and Tom Freston to Tulsa, Oklahoma. And one night, Sykes and Freston called me *very* excited. They'd been to a record store, and the store had suddenly sold out of the Tubes, and we were the only people playing the Tubes, so it had to be because of us. We had our first evidence that MTV was selling records.

TOM FRESTON: Tulsa was one of the markets where we had the highest concentration of subscribers. We had dinner with guys from the local radio station, and they told us MTV had made them change their format, because people would see all this music they had never been exposed to, like the Stray Cats and Duran Duran, and call to request their songs. Then we met with the record-store guys and they said, "My god, we're selling out of Buggles records." That was the one-two effect of MTV: Exposure on MTV would lead to radio airplay, and together that would lead to sales.

BOB PITTMAN: Before MTV, if you were a big act, no one knew what you looked like. Artists loved MTV, because suddenly people were stopping them on the street and saying, "I saw you on MTV."

AL TELLER: The big challenge for record companies was to build a roster of long-term artists. To do that, you not only had to get your artist on the radio, you had to develop an image for the artist, through live appearances and national and local press. Videos accelerated the artist-imaging process dramatically.

GARY GERSH, record executive: It could take years and several albums for an audience to understand who the artist is or what they mean, but even what they look like. All of a sudden, what you look like is instantaneous. You make a video, and the next day, you're recognized in Peoria.

MICK KLEBER, record executive: Once Duran Duran records started selling in record stores in Oklahoma, it opened up the eyes of everyone who was initially resistant to music video. There was a hiring and spending freeze in the music business in 1981. But not for the video departments. We got our own new offices, we got new equipment, we got our own editing bays. We got everything we needed to move forward.

CLIFF BURNSTEIN, manager: Def Leppard's *High and Dry* came out in '81, and it didn't do well. They came to the U.S. and opened for Blackfoot; that was as good as we could do. Then in early '82, I looked in a trade magazine and saw *High and Dry* listed as a top seller by a record store in Lowell, Massachusetts. A couple of weeks later I saw it listed by a store in Tulsa. I thought it was peculiar, because there was nothing I knew of to link Lowell and Tulsa. I started piecing things together, and here's what I found: MTV had come to Lowell and to Tulsa. MTV had been playing "Bringin' On the Heartbreak" in substantial rotation. MTV wasn't available in New York, so I had no idea.

LES GARLAND: In my travels, I had gone through Tulsa, and I had a buddy there. I called him and said, "There's a new channel on your cable lineup that plays music. Do me favor, hit your VHS machine for me, give me a twenty-four-hour tape." I started getting a tape once a week. And I'd put together constructive feedback for Pittman. I sent notes to him, like "Maybe you ought to try this . . ." He comes out in October to Los Angeles. We go to dinner and he hits me with it: "I want you to come to New York." I go, "To do what?" "Take over MTV." I go, "Done." He goes, "*What?*" No deal, no nothing. He goes, "Garland, between the two of us we'll make this thing huge. One day we'll have jets."

BOB PITTMAN: Les came in to see me at MTV and gave me the big pitch of why he should join. And Les came aboard. Les was a character. Still is.

TOM FRESTON: Les Garland was like a bolt of lightning. He was a pure rock n' roll animal. Constantly vibrating. He loved to have a good time, had a very infectious personality, had a big ego. He brought MTV's profile to a whole other level within the music industry.

JUDY McGRATH: When I saw Justin Timberlake in *The Social Network*, I had a flash of Les Garland. He called everyone "Bud." "How are ya, Bud?!" It was a perfect greeting if he couldn't remember your name. And Pittman was like Marc Zuckerberg. He had the true sense of what this thing was going to be, and nothing was going to get in his way.

JOHN SYKES: Les was the most interesting character of us all. He could say anything to anybody, wild things, and people would just accept it. He had a high-energy, show-business personality. He loved living the rock-star life.

RANDY PHILLIPS, manager: Les Garland and I went to school together at Stanford. We were best friends in San Francisco, and we moved to LA around the same time. One day, I was sitting in his office on Sunset Blvd., and he said, "Bob Pittman has gone to New York to start a thing called music television. They're going to play videos." Now, I was one of the few managers who knew what a video *was*, because I managed Rod Stewart, and he'd made so many. I said to Les, "That's a *terrible* idea. Who the hell is gonna watch back-to-back videos?" He said, "Well, I think I'm going to take the job." I said, "Les, are you crazy? You have a perfectly good job, you're living in LA, the weather's beautiful, you play golf every fucking day. You're gonna move to New York and work for a start-up? That thing is never going to work."

LES GARLAND: There were moments after I got to MTV that I thought we weren't gonna make it. I thought the plug would be pulled. We weren't getting distribution, advertisers weren't coming along, we weren't on the air in LA or New York. We burned through $25 million and had to go back and get $15 million more.

TOM FRESTON: Our success was so ephemeral. We were selling records in some store in Des Moines? Who gives a shit? Where's the fucking money?

BOB PITTMAN: We expected to lose about $10 million on MTV before we turned it around, but we probably lost closer to $50 million.

TOM FRESTON: The advertisers didn't want to buy time on a cable network. They figured, the best we would get was a 1.0 rating. And a 1.0 rating didn't matter. The three networks were bringing in 20–30 rating points on shows. Nowadays, you have 150 networks that do less than a point, and they're all making a fortune.

JORDAN ROST: It wasn't as profitable for ad agencies to buy small ratings on cable channels, when they could buy a 25 rating on NBC. Buying ads on cable TV was actually more work and less money for the media buyers, so it wasn't in their self-interest to help us.

JOHN LACK: Advertisers weren't buying into the idea. Bob McGroarty, who was head of distribution, said, "Procter & Gamble and Coke won't sign on to this." I'd heard that CNN wanted to launch another news network, but they needed to buy a satellite transponder. Luckily, we had an extra one. I thought we could trade them a transponder for the rights to sell CNN ad time. If we sold CNN and MTV in combination, advertisers would have to buy from us.

Ted Turner, who owned CNN, said, "I want to meet Lack face-to-face before

I do this deal." Bob McGroarty and I met him at the Ritz-Carlton in Boston. Ted said, "Johnny, let's go upstairs. I want to smoke a peace pipe with you. I want to look in your eyes." He's out of his mind, Ted Turner.

We went upstairs to a vacant ballroom. He said, "I want a transponder from you. I know you guys are good salespeople. You can sell our ad time for a year. If it works, you can keep selling it for us."

He said, "Do you get high?" Turner always had good weed. He pulled a corncob pipe out of his pocket, lit the thing, took a puff, and put it in my mouth. He said, "Let me see the whites of your eyes, big boy." I smoked. He said, "We're in business." We walked out and I said to McGroarty, "We've got to tell Jack Schneider how the meeting went. You call him. I think I'm a little too high."

RONALD "BUZZ" BRINDLE: At that point, cable wasn't set up like it is now. I mean, you would go to your hardware store and sign up for cable.

JUDY McGRATH: I was writing for *Glamour* magazine when I took a job writing on-air promotions at MTV. My boss said, "You're out of your mind. This cable thing will never last." Saying you were going to work in cable television was like saying you were going to work for your uncle's carpet business.

TOM FRESTON: We thought MTV was irresistible. We thought we were so fucking smart. But our optimism was chipped away by this cascade of rejection from cable operators. Back then, the cable operator was a monopolist: there was no direct home satellite, there was no Internet, so they controlled the geographic area.

JOHN LACK: The biggest cable operator was TCI in Denver. I can't even get their CEO, John Malone, on the telephone. I finally go to his boss, Bob Magness, who was the founder and chairman. Magness is a nice guy and he deigns to see me. I fly to Denver. I said, "Bob, will you please convince John to let me talk to him?" He goes, "Come on, he's in the next office." We go in to see Malone, who is kind of pissed I went over his head. Malone says, "I told you we're not interested." Bob says, "Will you just listen to his presentation?"

I show him the clips, I tell him what's in it for TCI. He says, "This is sex, drugs, and rock n' roll. We're in little markets all over America. We can't put this stuff on the air." I tell him, "Look, you're gonna get new cable subscribers.

These kids are gonna demand it. This is gonna be a sea change for you in basic cable. HBO is the only place you're making money." He literally leads me to the door and throws me out.

JACK SCHNEIDER: John Malone would only consider carrying MTV when I went to see him. I had to humble myself, which was really difficult for me. I'd had a much more influential career in broadcasting than he could ever dream of, so it was very annoying to me to have to go and explain to various cable operators what we were doing. The goddamn pole-climbers didn't get it. They didn't understand that I was offering them a demographic that was going to sell cable connections for them. But we all did what we had to do to get this off the ground. Not just MTV, but the whole segment of advertiser-supported cable. Because without distribution there was no business.

JORDAN ROST: The guy who ran Manhattan Cable, said, "Who the hell cares about you? Who's gonna watch?" He had the most important cable TV system in the country. John and Bob McGroarty and Jack Schneider had been involved in sales at CBS, and they were tough negotiators. But it was a different environment with cable operators. The last thing other networks wanted to do was alienate a cable operator they were pitching. But Warner Amex was getting a little arrogant with them.

BOB PITTMAN: We needed to find a way to get the cable operators to carry us. They were reluctant, because MTV was sex, drugs, and rock n' roll. Ad sales wasn't working, affiliate sales wasn't working. In the first year, we sold only $500,000 of advertising. Coca-Cola didn't think it was a "family environment." The only thing we had going was the consumer liked the product, when they could see it.

I hired Dale Pon, who had worked as the promotion director with me at WNBC radio. Dale had formed an ad agency with George Lois.

FRED SEIBERT: Dale had a reputation as an out-of-control maniac. He was a hothead. And George was also known as a raving lunatic, but he was a famous raving lunatic.

DALE PON, advertising executive: I wanted the MTV account. I thought the idea was huge.

TOM FRESTON: Fred Seibert is a genius. Dale Pon was a genius, too, but he was difficult. He had no interpersonal skills. If you disagreed with him, he thought you were a fucking asshole.

DALE PON: If you're an ad man, you have two jobs: You make 'em rich, and you make 'em famous. No one knew what MTV was. The idea was to acquaint the world with MTV in thirty seconds or less. In any ad campaign, what's central is to convey the essential nature of the product immediately. What was the nature of MTV? For me it was insatiable desire, the Rolling Stones lyric, "I can't get no satisfaction." That's the very nature of Americans: We want what we don't have. One of the characteristics of American consumers in the early '80s was *Shop till you drop.* "I want it. I don't know what it is, but I want it."

FRED SEIBERT: Dale hired a woman who'd been his girlfriend for many years, an unbelievable copywriter named Nancy Podbielniak. They wrote a tagline, "Cable Brats," and a sub-tag: "Rock n' roll wasn't enough for them, now they want their MTV. The exploding twenty-four-hour video music cable network in stereo." George Lois would tell you it was his phrase, but George claims credit for everything, including the MTV logo. I love George, but he's an absolute liar.

DALE PON: We ran that ad in trade magazines for a few months, but MTV didn't like the campaign. Whenever they walked in to see a cable operator, he would say, "Here come the cable brats." So we gave it a twist, and it became "I Want My MTV." That was our slogan.

FRED SEIBERT: In 1956, an animator named John Hubley had come up with an ad campaign for a cereal, in which his four-year-old son, as the voice of a cartoon cowboy, says, "I want my Maypo!" About ten years later, Maypo comes to George Lois's agency and gives him the account. And George, who, like a lot of great creative people, only had a few really good ideas in his pocket, takes the sports stars he'd used in other campaigns and has them sit in front of a bowl of Maypo with a spoon, crying like a kid: "I want my Maypo!"

So we go to a presentation and George shows us pictures of Mick Jagger with a tear coming down his face, going, "I want my MTV." I was so pissed. I said to Dale, "This is what I get? The third version of an ad from thirty years ago? We're gonna have rock stars crying?" And Dale says, "I'm not gonna ask Mick Jagger to cry. That's stupid. But it's a really good idea. Trust me on this."

LES GARLAND: I love George Lois. He *is Mad Men*, a real renegade. George starts off with a little Q&A: "Pittman, who owns MTV?" *Uh, WASEC.* "Wrong. Garland, who owns MTV?" He has everybody engaged now. He says, "They do, the kids do, it's *theirs.* They have a sense of ownership. It belongs to them. A young guy has MTV, all the kids on the block come over to watch it." And it was true, I'd seen it happen.

George says, "Garland, can you get Mick Jagger"—the biggest star in the world—"Can you get Mick Jagger to say, 'I want my MTV'?" Mick had been a friend of mine when I worked at Atlantic Records, and lived across the street from me on the Upper West Side. My assistant Joan Myers had worked for the Rolling Stones, and I buzzed her and said, "Find out where the Stones are." And that happened to be Paris.

DALE PON: If you're asking who said we needed to get rock stars in this campaign, that was me. The "I" in "I want my MTV" was always someone who nobody could doubt loved rock n' roll. So when you see a rock star say, "I want my MTV," they are giving you an example of how to express yourself.

JOAN MYERS, MTV staff: I was Les's secretary. I was serving Bob and Les coffee in Garland's office, and one of them said, "How do we get to the Stones?" I'd worked with them, so I made a phone call, and they agreed. Garland and I flew to Paris. While he was out having fun, I sat in a hotel room waiting for Mick to call and tell us he was ready.

BOB PITTMAN: Les Garland talked Mick Jagger into doing the "I Want My MTV" campaign. He went and sat in Paris for days, waiting for Mick.

LES GARLAND: Joan and I flew to France, along with Dale Pon. I had two days to spare when we got there. I'd been working hard, and I went out rocking. And got lost for a day and a half. I met some women, and I had a pretty good time. Joan was freaked out. She had the police looking for me. I finally come rolling in, and she says, "Where the fuck have you been?"

I get my meeting with Mick. "Okay, Garland, tell me what you want." I go, "I'd like to convince you to go on camera to help us with a new ad campaign, and all I need you to say is, 'I want my MTV.'" And he goes, "You want me to do a commercial?" I go, "It's really more of an endorsement. It's an endorsement for a new phenomenon called music videos." He says, "Yeah, that's a commercial. The Rolling Stones don't do commercials."

I go, "Well, that's not really true. I was at Atlantic when Jovan sponsored your tour." "Well, we got paid a lot of money for that." I said, "So what you're saying is, you do commercials for money." And that got a little laugh. I said, "Mick, we don't have any money. But if this is about money, I'll give you a dollar." And I threw a dollar on the table. He looked up and he said, "I like you, Garland. I'll do it." We shot it the next day. And it blew everybody's mind. From there we called Pat Benatar: "Mick Jagger's in." David Bowie: "Mick Jagger's in." We used Mick to get the cooperation of everyone else.

JACK SCHNEIDER: Jagger saying "I want my MTV"—I don't think we ever thanked him enough. It legitimized us. People called their cable companies and said to the poor operators, in these lousy imitations of Mick Jagger, "I want my MTV."

JOHN SYKES: I had a very thin connection to Pete Townshend's manager, Bill Curtis, through a friend, so I took the red-eye to London. I went straight to see Bill, and they said, "He's not here." So I waited and waited, and all of a sudden, Pete walks in. I said, "Hi, Pete, uh, I'm John Sykes with MTV, it's a new channel that plays videos. Would you do, um, would you do a, a, a commercial for us like you do when you visit a radio station?" He goes, "Okay, I'll do that. When do you want to do it?" I go, "Now? We rented a garage across the street." Six months later, the Who came to our studio to do an interview. Pete saw me and said, "I know you. You're the guy who stuck a carrot up my ass."

ADAM ANT, artist: I didn't know anything about the network, because video didn't exist, really. I turned up at a studio somewhere and did it. They said Pete Townshend had done it, and Jagger had done it, so I thought, *If it's good enough for them . . .*

BILLY IDOL, artist: It made sense for me to help promote MTV because, in a sense, I was promoting myself.

PAT BENATAR: Back then, it was completely taboo to promote any kind of product, so I had a little bit of hesitation. But MTV always had promotional campaigns, and whatever they asked, people did. It was good for you and it was good for them.

JOHN SYKES: I went somewhere to do the Police, and Les did Bowie in Gstaad, Switzerland, where Bowie skied right up to the camera. I think Gale got Cyndi Lauper, and somebody got Pat Benatar. The campaign exploded. The cable phones rang like crazy, and we began to get added to different systems.

DALE PON: Gstaad is one of these places for rich people that you don't imagine you'll ever get to. We shot Bowie in the early morning, and he hired a truck with rental ski equipment of every size, and outfitted everyone in my crew. He opened the back door of a truck and said to one of my producers, "Susan, what shoe size are you?" And he's pulling boots off the truck for her. They skied off with David to a big lunch, which he'd arranged. I'm afraid of speed, afraid of height, afraid of death, so I walked down the mountain.

RANDY PHILLIPS: To the record companies, the managers, and the artists, Les was the face of MTV. He sold MTV to a very skeptical industry. Most of the artists who participated in the early "I Want My MTV" campaign? Les got them to do it. Most of them didn't even know what they were talking about when they did those spots. That should give you a sense of Les's ability to bullshit.

FRED SEIBERT: We fought with Jack Schneider to get $10 or $15 million for advertising. Schneider had made his fortune through advertising, but ironically, he didn't believe it worked. He said we could have $2 million. Dale Pon researched which markets presented the greatest opportunities for us. And he said we had to flood each market with the ad. He figured we'd create a fucking jihad. It meant we'd run through our budget in four to six weeks. Given what our finances were in May of '82, we probably *were* in a go-for-broke strategy.

The spots had stars like Pete Townshend saying, "America, demand your MTV," and "Call your cable operator and say, 'I want my MTV.'" John and Jack thought this was the greatest thing in the world. They hated these cable operators.

JOHN LACK: We were in the Warners boardroom at 75 Rockefeller Plaza: me, Jack Schneider, Bob Pittman, Bob McGroarty, the lawyers. And Pittman says, "I suggest we go right to the consumer." McGroarty stands up. "What are you, out of your mind? We're gonna go around the cable operators? We can't do that!"

DALE PON: I think I'm quoting Bob Pittman: He said it was "a Hail Mary pass." He said, "Whatever we think of this campaign, it's our last chance."

GEORGE LOIS, advertising executive: The plan was, we were going to shove the idea down the throats of cable operators.

TOM FRESTON: We knew our audience had a lot of time on their hands and actually would call their cable company.

TOMMY MOTTOLA: "I Want My MTV" was the best promotion in the history of the music business. They were able to get every single act to stand in a stupid commercial and say that line. The campaign gave MTV integrity and credibility with the audience; their favorite band or icon was endorsing this brand and telling them *this* was the thing they should watch.

DALE PON: The "I Want My MTV" campaign is an immature, rude, impudent campaign.

FRED SEIBERT: "I Want My MTV" was one of the most iconic campaigns of all time.

NICK RHODES: Their corporate identity—the logo, the "I Want My MTV" campaign—was genius.

MARTHA QUINN: Friends would ask what I was doing. I'd say, "Oh, I'm working at this MTV thing." *What?* "Well, I'm a VJ." *What?* It wasn't until the "I Want My MTV" commercials that I could say, "You know where Pete Townshend says, 'I want my MTV'? *That's* where I work."

JOHN LACK: So we launch a campaign in Denver where TCI is headquartered, and where they own the cable system. Within an hour of the first ad, the phone is ringing. Within the first day, they're getting more phone calls than they get in a month. By the second day, they've gotten five thousand phone calls. Newspapers pick up on the story. Within a week, Malone is on the phone with Steve Ross: "I give, call off the dogs." That's how we got TCI.

DALE PON: The cable operators said, "Stop hurting us. Stop. Please stop. I'll sign if you stop."

BOB PITTMAN: We'd go into a city and run the campaign, and people would flood the cable company with phone calls. They'd cave and put us on. Then we'd go to another city and say, "We're gonna run that campaign. Look at what happened in the last city." By the time we'd done it three or four times, we didn't have to run the campaign much, because the threat of running the ad was enough.

FRED SEIBERT: The cable operators all got mad, and they all signed up MTV. The cascade began. And once the cascade began, it never stopped.

Chapter 8

"MIDGETS, MODELS, AND TRANNIES"

THE FIRST VISIONARIES AND VICTIMS OF THE MUSIC-VIDEO ERA

RECORD LABELS ARE ABUNDANTLY STAFFED WITH people who oversee every stage of an album, from recording through publicity, marketing, and promotion. Like nervous parents, labels rarely let musicians out of their sight. But when it came to video, artists were mostly unsupervised. There were no record-label departments to oversee videos, and no one in the executive ranks who had any expertise in filmmaking. Budgets were low, and videos were not yet recognized as important. The job was often delegated to female staffers, who rarely saw opportunities in other departments, and many of them became heavyweights in the music-video industry.

The lack of oversight meant creativity could run rampant, within the limits of a budget. Video directors had a level of freedom film directors could only envy, and video sets were unregulated havens for misbehavior. Unlike films and network TV, where every production carefully hewed to union or guild regulations about pay, schedules, and work conditions, music videos fell into more of a sweatshop model. Hours were cruel and pay was meager, but directors, producers, and technicians could quickly get opportunities that would have taken years of apprenticeship in film or TV. Director Jeff Stein summarized the trial-and-error nature of video with a joke he says was often told on his sets: "How do they make music videos in Poland? The same way we do."

Music videos drew a specific type of characters, brave and hardy men and women bent on exploration and merriment, people whose personalities—and appetites, especially for drugs—often rivaled those of the bands whose videos they made. In short, pirates, lunatics, outcasts, misfits, iconoclasts, and barbarians.

ROBERT LOMBARD, producer: At first, Van Halen were very anti-MTV. They were getting pressure from the network to produce clips, but they didn't want to. They felt they were better than that. Van Halen's record label commissioned Bruce Gowers to shoot a concert, but the band wouldn't cooperate, so there was no augmented lighting onstage. I had my own independent production company, and they dumped the footage on me. It was hard to cut things together, but I worked with an editor to make a video for "Unchained," and the band loved it.

Their next single was the Roy Orbison tune "Pretty Woman," and they asked me to oversee the video. "And you'd better not steal money from us"—they were always saying that. The band chose characters they were going to play: David Lee Roth played Napoleon, Eddie Van Halen played a cowboy, Alex Van Halen played Tarzan, Michael Anthony played a samurai warrior. We had two midgets in the video and a transvestite. At the audition, we put eighty trannies on tape. The band wanted to see some pussy, and I'd have to bring in models so they could look at girls in bikinis. The casting session was midgets, models, and trannies. And we'd drink Jack Daniel's all day—Drambuie for Eddie—and have a little toot here and there. There are line items in a video budget for catering and craft services—that's where you hid the money you used to buy drugs. I would always be able to bury at least a quarter ounce of cocaine in there and then dummy up a catering receipt.

SAMUEL BAYER, director: I grew up in Columbus, Ohio, and I loved MTV. In "Pretty Woman," David Lee Roth dressed up as Napoleon and Eddie Van Halen was a cowboy. It looked like they'd shot it in two hours, in someone's backyard in Pasadena. It was brilliant.

ROBERT LOMBARD: The location was near Valencia, a long drive from LA, so to make sure they were on time, we had a limo pick each one of them up. They had a big trailer, like for a major film star, where we hung out and got high. The shoot took twenty-four hours and everybody was laughing their asses off, especially when the midgets tied the tranny to a stake.

At the end of the video, the girl whips off her wig and she's a man. And the midgets are running their hands up her legs and under her dress. You've got midgets violating a tranny. I thought it was hysterical, but MTV didn't. The video was banned and I thought, *My music-video career is totally over.*

PETE ANGELUS, director: Some bizarre things happened during that video. Two cameramen quit. Why? Maybe because it seemed like we were disorganized. But they might have quit because they were severely hallucinating from the mushrooms that the little people brought to the set and handed out.

MICHAEL ANTHONY, Van Halen: MTV played "Pretty Woman" once or twice and that was it, because of the ending with the transvestite and the midgets and the hunchback. We were going, *Let's be outrageous as we can.* I was wearing about 120 pounds of armor, and walking around in that was not fun. But you know, a couple of beers and everything was okay.

The two midgets—or little people—one is named Jimmy Briscoe. He used to come to Arizona and stay with me and my wife. He went on the road with the band, as "head of security," and he's been in quite a few movies. As it got later in the day and into the evening, everybody'd had a few beers, and the other little guy was copping a bit of a buzz and hitting on the female star. When he found out it was a guy, he didn't care; he was still hitting on him.

PETE ANGELUS: I stood on the set, going, "Seriously, can anybody find the little people? Where are they?" After twenty minutes of searching for them, I thought, *I'll walk around and see if I can turn up anything.* I got to the transvestite's dressing room and I opened the door. This is what I saw; I don't want to be held accountable, it's just what I *saw.* The little guy was wearing a black cape. He was holding the transvestite's penis, which seemed kind of erect, and he was pretending it was a microphone. And he was singing "Satisfaction" by the Rolling Stones while doing a Mick Jagger impersonation. I thought, *This is not going well.* Then I closed the door and let him finish whatever the hell they were doing.

KEVIN GODLEY: From the beginning, the lunatics were running the asylum. It was a new industry; there were no boundaries. It was like the Wild, Wild West.

JEFF STEIN, director: I'm sure you've heard this from many people; it was like the Wild West. And I'm sure you've heard this even more: it was like the inmates were running the asylum.

MICK KLEBER: In the early days, one week you'd be a food stylist, the next you were a producer of music videos. It was the Wild West. Everyone was inventing it as they went along.

MIKE RENO, Loverboy: Nobody knew what the hell was going on, to be honest.

TIM NEWMAN, director: It was completely freewheeling. Nobody knew anything. There wasn't much in the way of rules.

STEVE BARRON: Nobody knew what music videos were going to become, or even what they were. There wasn't any history to go by. There was no one saying, "This is what a music video looks like."

LOL CREME: There were no authorities at the record companies, no authority anywhere, that could say you were doing it wrong. Video directors were the new rock stars. Everyone was crazy, no one was in charge.

JULIEN TEMPLE: The record companies had no real control over the videos. They were very film ignorant, so as long as you could agree on an idea with the band, you were free to do what you wanted. It was very exciting to have an idea as you fell asleep and then two weeks later see it all around the world on TV.

JOHN DIAZ, producer: None of the labels wanted to have anything to do with videos. And since they had a lot of women in less glamorous, lower-paying jobs, they put these women in charge of videos. Debbie Newman and Debbie Samuelson at CBS, Liz Heller at MCA . . . We called them all "The Debbies," as an homage to Debbie Newman, since she was the first. Debbie was hard-driving; we always said she was a woman with balls.

DEBBIE NEWMAN: In 1979, the head of marketing for international at CBS Records needed footage of Journey to send overseas, because it was cheaper than sending the band. I was booking bands to appear on shows like *Midnight Special* and *Don Kirshner's Rock Concert,* and she asked if I could find somebody to shoot a video. There weren't any established music-video production companies in America yet, but I found two Englishmen, Paul Flattery and Bruce Gowers, to shoot some live clips. That was the beginning of my music-video career.

JEANNE MATTIUSSI, record executive: Debbie Newman hired me at Columbia Records, and that's when I got thrown into video production. I was the West Coast girl and Debbie Samuelson was the East Coast girl. A lot of us who did video promotion back then were fairly attractive, so we used to work that angle.

PAUL FLATTERY, producer: At the genesis of the industry, almost everybody at the labels who was commissioning videos was female. The male executives palmed the job off onto the women—the assistants, the secretaries. And for us young Englishmen, that was not a bad thing. At all. We took them to dinner, we wined and dined them. It was part and parcel of the deal.

SUSAN SILVERMAN, record executive: The record business was a man's world. But there was an open door for women who had chutzpah. Video was the one area we could take over. We went in and we fucking kicked ass.

JEFF AYEROFF: Most of the girls in the video business were beautiful, especially Siobhan Barron.

SIOBHAN BARRON: I didn't get along with most of the men in the record industry. They were macho and leather-jacketed, and they didn't accept me. They were of the opinion that women in the industry should shut up and lie down. I was very beautiful—I used to be a model—and bands would tell their labels they wanted to work with Limelight. I used my beauty when I had to.

RANDY SKINNER, record executive: The '80s were amazing for video departments, because the labels didn't have a clue what to do. They didn't really care. The last label I worked for was Virgin in 2006, and twenty people had to approve your treatments.

JEFF AYEROFF: Music videos were like the Internet ten years ago: Nobody at the labels understood them. CBS was so focused on radio promotion, they didn't care about videos—they assigned video production to product managers, who knew nothing about film or art direction. That was how videos got done there. Somebody said, "Here, you deal with this shit."

AL TELLER: Originally, we thought we could budget each video at $15,000 to $20,000. That lasted about twelve seconds.

MICK KLEBER: Some of the early music videos were terrible. There wasn't a blueprint for how to make a cool one.

DARYL HALL, Hall & Oates: I'm not a big fan of any video, especially my own. Visuals are distracting. When the eye and the ear compete, the eye always wins. It has something to do with the way the brain works. In a word, I hated the Hall & Oates videos. But we were realists. If you were popular—which we were, obviously—you couldn't not do videos. But I went kicking and screaming. In the early days, no one knew what to do. For the "Private Eyes" video, somebody said, "Why don't you wear '50s hats and trench coats, like private eyes?" That's what we did. It was so low-budget it was almost laughable.

PAT BENATAR: The "Shadows of the Night" video is about the Nazis during the Holocaust. A woman who's working in a factory, making parachutes for the war, is daydreaming that she's flying a plane and fighting the Nazis. It's so kitschy, we just die laughing when we look at it now. The Nazis were played by my drummer, Myron Grombacher, and my bass player, Roger Capps, a total Aryan from Tennessee. Myron was like, "Why do *I* have to play the Nazi?" *Because your name is Grombacher. Figure it out!*

TIM FARRISS, INXS: In the early '80s, we made a crazy video at home in Australia for "The One Thing." We fed Valium to a few cats and had them running around a table while we had a feast with sexy models and *Playboy* centerfolds, ripping apart a turkey. Next thing we knew, we had a Top 40 hit in America and were opening for Adam Ant, who we called Adam Pissant. We played Long Beach Arena and the crowd mobbed us and we were ushered offstage—which goes to show the power MTV had.

JOE ELLIOTT, Def Leppard: We did our first three videos—"Bringin' on the Heartbreak," "High 'n' Dry," and "Let It Go"—with the same speed you'd go out for a meal. I wouldn't even really call them videos. They were filmed during a sound check. We put the kids from our fan club right in front and angled the camera so it looked like a full house. We wanted to get something on film, so we could get it onto *The Old Grey Whistle Test*, a British music program. We'd grown up watching that show and we thought it would be cool if we gave them a promo film and they played it—which they never did.

MIKE RENO: We were going, "Videos? What are videos?" I remember saying, "Huh? We finally have a day off and we're going to be dancing around the streets in makeup?" I also remember seeing the budget and being like, "We're spending $25,000 to do *this*?" If you look at the beginning of "Turn Me Loose," I'm holding a cigarette and the camera pans over my shoulder. The director said, "Your hand is trembling." It was nerve-wracking for me. For some people it came very easily, and for some it didn't come at all.

JONATHAN CAIN, Journey: Steve Perry was very anti-video. He'd always say, "We're performers, we're entertainers, but we're not actors." And we were *not* a very photogenic band. So we stayed on the sidelines at first. When *Frontiers* came out in 1983, our manager, Herbie Herbert, was tight with the NFL Films guys, so he hired their crew, and they put together the footage you see in the "Faithfully" video. The live stuff looks great. But the shot of Steve shaving off his mustache was a bit much. I mean, did people even have to know he had a mustache? I didn't get that.

JOHN DIAZ: In the late '70s, I became a producer and assistant director on TV commercials. Videos turned my life around. My idea was to bring in young commercial directors I'd been working with. One was Tom Buckholtz, who did the infamous Journey video "Separate Ways," shot on a wharf in New Orleans. That was the first air-guitar video. In fact, it had air guitar, air keyboards, and air drums. It had air everything. Our concepts were so inane. At the end, you see a girl in bed wearing headphones who "dreamed" the whole video while listening to the song.

JONATHAN CAIN: I'm at a loss to explain that video. Good Lord, I will never live down those air keyboards. No matter what else I've done in my career, sooner or later people find a way to ask me about the "Separate Ways" video. And Perry, I don't know what he was thinking, but he cut his hair right before the video. Bad idea. His hair was rocking before the shoot.

RUDOLF SCHENKER: When I saw Journey videos, something was wrong.

DEBBIE NEWMAN: The deal was, none of the band members could bring girlfriends or wives to the shoot in New Orleans. But Steve Perry had started dating

Sherrie Swafford, and he brought her. There was a ton of tension. The band hated Sherrie.

JONATHAN CAIN: Sherrie was jealous and possessive. And when she found out there was gonna be a *girl* in the video—oh my god. There was a big kicking and screaming session. Sherrie was giving Steve a very bad time about that girl: "She's a whore, she's a bitch, I don't want her in the video."

DEBBIE NEWMAN: The video was terrible. I mean, truly terrible. MTV played it constantly.

ADAM DUBIN, director: Here's a band at their commercial peak, and some idiot decided to film them on a wharf, and—here's the worst part—instead of giving them instruments, let them mime playing imaginary instruments. The director should be shot. And the manager should be shot for allowing his band to be put in this position. But this is my point, there really wasn't a music-video aesthetic yet.

JONATHAN CAIN: Beavis and Butt-head made total fun of "Separate Ways." Which was an outrage to me because, you know, we helped *make* MTV. I called our manager and said, "Isn't there anything we can do to stop this?"

KEVIN CRONIN: You were either on MTV and hip, or you weren't on MTV and you didn't even fucking exist. When you were their darling, it was great. When you weren't their darling, you were fucked. We developed a love/hate relationship with them.

BRYAN ADAMS, artist: I didn't really think videos mattered. MTV was a cable channel with minor viewership. Shooting videos? I didn't care. I should have.

FRED SCHNEIDER, the B-52s: We wanted to do videos. Our manager, Gary Kurfirst, said, "What do you want to do videos for? You don't make any money from them. Look at David Byrne, he puts out videos, he doesn't make any money from them." Gary didn't get the point. I guess you wouldn't say he was a visionary in that respect.

JANE WIEDLIN: When Miles Copeland, the president of our record label, said we were gonna shoot a music video for "Our Lips Are Sealed," we were like, "Music video? That's stupid. You suck." We were totally bratty about it. The money he used for the video was, like, left over from the Police's video budget. It was pennies. They got a guy to follow us around Hollywood. We wanted an old-school convertible, so we rented it from Rent-A-Wreck for $10 or $15.

This was the plot: "Get in a car and drive around. Belinda, you sing. Everyone else look cute." When we needed a grand finale, our big idea was to jump in the fountain at the intersection of Santa Monica and Wilshire in Beverly Hills. I remember thinking, *The cops are gonna come any minute, this is gonna be so cool.*

MICHAEL STIPE, R.E.M.: Miles Copeland said, "I want you to make music videos, and I want you to lip-sync." And I said, "No, I'm not going to do it." He said "Okay," and that was the end of the meeting. I was this twenty-three-year-old little shit with acne and a bad haircut, and he allowed us the latitude. But it was a reaction against what other people were doing. It felt like a sellout to lip-sync. Jim Herbert, who was my art professor, drove with us to a place in Georgia where a guy named Mr. Miller made whirligigs and had thousands of them on a hill And Jim filmed us. The first videos we did really were, for lack of a better term, anti-video.

SHARON ORECK, producer: Prince's "1999" and "Little Red Corvette" videos were just smoke, then Prince's face, then smoke, then Prince's butt, and then smoke. Prince was interesting, and I liked the songs, but the videos were profoundly bad. They were, like, porn bad. His videos were so filled with smoke that everyone on the set would get diarrhea, because mineral oil was so thick in the air.

DON LETTS, director: The Gap Band were a handful. They turned up on the set of "Party Train" in a white limo. They stumbled out of the limo, then one of the dudes bit the makeup woman on the ass. I got them to walk fifteen feet twice, did a tracking shot, and then got them the hell out of there.

SIMON FIELDS: The Gap Band wanted to be wheeled onto the sand by white guys. Not in the video, but on the set.

PHIL COLLINS, artist: For "In the Air Tonight," I had a distinct idea of what I wanted the video to be. The best bit is where the album cover sings. But the part where I'm walking down the corridor? That was meant to look scary, like something from *The Blair Witch Project*, where you can only see what's directly in front of you, as though you were wearing a miner's helmet. And it didn't turn out that way at all. Unless you're lucky, you end up looking back on these things with a bit of dread.

STEVE LUKATHER: We hated the "Hydra" video so bad. This was the image the world saw on TV? I might as well have hung myself in a closet with an orange ball gag in my mouth and a dildo up my ass. We were going, "How will we live this down?" So our fuck-you answer for our third album was to film ourselves playing live at A&M Studios. And then MTV didn't want to play that. I'd like to underline how much I hated making videos.

DAVE HOLMES: I loved how acts who were huge before MTV tried to adapt and couldn't. Like "Abracadabra" by Steve Miller, which was a huge song. *Oh, stop it. You're making a fool of yourself.* He just seemed too old. He was probably in his late thirties.

ADAM DUBIN: "Start Me Up" is a great song, but it's like somebody locked down a video camera and said to the Rolling Stones, "Okay, get out there. We've got an hour." That's a ridiculous video. It's almost like they couldn't be bothered.

BILLY JOEL, artist: The Rolling Stones may be the best band that ever was, but their videos were absolutely horrendous. It's as if Mick said, "I refuse to spend money on this."

MICK KLEBER: Bonnie Raitt was one of the artists from the '70s who was nervous about making music videos. Bob Seger wasn't a huge fan of the idea of a music video. They were self-conscious about their *still* photos. You can imagine how uncomfortable they were with a video.

MEAT LOAF: MTV was never very kind to me. They never played any of my videos.

PAUL FLATTERY: The truth is, video did kill the radio star. It was like when the talkies happened and actors lost their careers if they didn't have a good voice. Bob Seger was a great singer, but he felt he was overweight, so he always had to be shot in black-and-white, and at certain angles. There were a lot of people trying to cover up.

MARTHA DAVIS, the Motels: It's a lot harder for a woman to not think about her appearance, because we've been programmed that way for so long. Women didn't have the confidence to be dorks in their videos. It's easier for a guy to be a goofball, because that's what guys do. Especially if you're Huey Lewis.

HUEY LEWIS, artist: On "Do You Believe in Love," we did whatever the record label told us. They hired a stylist, and we were made up to the max, and I sang to a girl who was asleep in a bed with my band. When I saw it, I thought it was the worst thing I'd ever seen. And everybody loved it! We were producing our own records, so I said, "Let's do our own videos, too. We can think of far sillier shit than this."

PATTY SMYTH: We had a hard time getting radio to add "Goodbye to You." At that point, if a station was playing one chick record, like Pat Benatar or the Pretenders, they wouldn't play another. But MTV liked our video, and the song became a huge hit because of MTV. The first time I saw it on MTV I was really surprised, because the label had added cheesy, swirly psychedelic special effects to it. That's so classic record company. "Oh, let's put some schmutz on it to make it look professional." My videos got more and more ridiculous, because the record company got more and more involved.

JOHNNY BARBIS, manager: Elton John felt that he didn't photograph well. He didn't like the way he looked. So getting him to make videos was not easy.

DON LETTS: Chrissie Hynde was not pro-video. She's old-school. She had a few moments when people were staring at her in the street. I said, "Darling if you don't want to be stared at, you shouldn't be making a video."

TOM PETTY: I didn't much like making videos—the hours were insane—but I liked the outcome. My band hated making videos. They didn't want to go anywhere near them. I didn't blame them. But I didn't have a choice. I had to be in them.

ROBERT SMITH: My overriding impression of making videos is that they're incredibly tedious and incredibly hard work.

CHUCK D: I hated doing videos. Anything over four hours, to me, is like, *I want to get the fuck out of here.* I don't like to be photographed and I don't like to be in front of a camera. So my biggest recollection is doing the same thing over and over and over again, which I've never gotten used to.

MARTIN FRY, ABC: Every video was a one-day shoot. And that one day would last forty-eight hours.

ANN CARLI, record executive: We had a fire on the set one time. The lights ignited a bunch of trash, but we didn't want the fire department there, because they would have shut us down. We probably had too many people in the building, we probably shouldn't have been working so late. But at the time, it was unregulated. We'd do an eighteen-hour day with seventy-two setups.

ANN WILSON: It would be ten hours of waiting around in makeup and hair, then ten minutes in front of the camera and five more hours of waiting around. At the end of the two days, when the sun was coming up in the morning, they'd say, "Time for your close-ups!"

MARTIN FRY: The food on set was good. And you got air miles.

TERRI NUNN, Berlin: We shot videos for "The Metro" and "Sex" in a two-day period, back to back, forty-eight hours straight. What I remember from the shoot is crying. There's a sequence in "The Metro" where I'm walking on subway tracks—it was a stage set—and I'm kind of stumbling through it. I was exhausted and pissed off, like, "When are we gonna fucking finish this video? I wanna go to bed and die." I was sobbing, and the director was like "Great! Yeah! Okay, film her now!" It was good for the video.

MICK KLEBER: If you were a music-video executive, you'd want to show up on set around midnight, an hour or two before the thing's supposed to be over, because that's when the shit is really hitting the fan. You're coming face-to-face with the reality that you're not going to be able to get all your shots in the time you've allotted, and you're either gonna have to spend more money or make some creative adjustments.

DAVID ROBINSON, the Cars: I just tried to get through them with my dignity intact.

BRYAN ADAMS: I tried to whinge my way though it.

BILLY JOEL: I hated making videos. See, I became a musician because I knew I wasn't cut out to be a movie star. I'm a piano player, not an actor. I'm not photogenic. Back in the '70s, people who knew my music didn't even know what I looked like until they'd see an album cover. Then they'd meet me and say, "Oh, you're short." Everybody I talked to hated doing videos. Elton hated them. Springsteen didn't like making them. He held out for a while, but the music business became completely geared toward them.

JON LANDAU, manager: When Bruce Springsteen put out *Nebraska* in '82, he wasn't interested in making videos. He hadn't yet decided what MTV had to do with him creatively. Then and now, Bruce is interested in three things: writing songs, making records, and doing concerts. Everything else is secondary. The idea that you had to make a video every time you put out a record wasn't very appealing. So Arnold Levine, the director of creative services at Columbia Records, assembled a video for "Atlantic City" that Bruce doesn't appear in. Bruce loved what Arnold had done. Les Garland and John Sykes were big Bruce fans, and MTV played "Atlantic City." But Bruce had no ambition to become a video artist.

RUSSELL MULCAHY: Rod Stewart didn't like making videos. We shot "Tonight I'm Yours" at the pool at the Sunset Marquis Hotel in LA. We booked twenty rooms that overlooked the pool, and we had lovely girls in bikinis having pillow fights on the balconies. There's some fairly obvious '80s imagery: a nun in a rowboat, that sort of thing. Well, Rod partied the night before, and he didn't want to come out of his trailer. I went to have a chat with him, and he had sunglasses on. I said, "Rod, come on. I'm gonna film the video anyway. Do you want to be in it?" And he went, "Oh fuck, all right."

BRIAN GRANT: I was in LA, and Russell asked if I would operate one of the cameras. It was probably the most debauched evening I've experienced in my life. There were forty or fifty very beautiful women there, some in bikinis, and a helicopter overhead. There was plenty of substance abuse going on all around. In every room, I believe. The police shut down the filming, but they didn't shut down the rest of the night's activities.

RANDY SKINNER: Rod used to act out his lyrics in his videos. For instance, he would do a choo-choo train move when he'd sing a lyric about a train. He was very literal. I'd always howl when I saw that.

CAROL ROSENSTEIN, producer: I became Bruce Gowers's line producer, and Warner Bros. hired us to do four Rod Stewart videos. We were meeting Rod and his manager, Billy Gaff, at the finest restaurant in LA, Le St. Germain. After a while, the maître d' says, "Mr. Gaff called, and he and Mr. Stewart are running a bit late. But he said to have a drink and order an appetizer." A while later, the maître d' comes around again and says, "Mr. Gaff says Mr. Stewart's going to be a little while longer, go ahead and have your dinner." We finish dinner, no Rod.

Next day, the meeting is rescheduled at another super-expensive restaurant. Again, same thing happens. We eat, no Rod. We wait another couple of days. Finally we get the call: "Come to Rod's house at 10 A.M. on Saturday."

We were in the kitchen, waiting for him. Amazing kitchen, by the way. Rod comes in wearing nothing but a loosely tied silk robe. Bruce says, "Rod, we have some ideas for the locations of the videos." Rod says, "Eh, let's just do the whole thing here. It's a nice house." And we did. When we were setting up, we had to store some lights in the master bathroom. There was a large apothecary jar of talcum powder. That's what I thought it was, until I saw somebody reach into it who hadn't taken a bath. Rod was fun to work with, though. And we always ate very well.

PAUL FLATTERY: Jon Roseman Productions was the biggest music-video company in America. I was a producer; Russell Mulcahy, David Mallet, and Bruce Gowers were our directors. And then Roseman fucked it all up. He shared an apartment with a coke dealer who was sent to prison. And he gave interviews where he slammed the record companies and the artists. "I ripped off the Rolling Stones!" "The Atlanta Rhythm Section are a bunch of big, fat Southerners!" "Rod Stewart was doing coke." And the labels said, "Look, we like you guys, but we can't use your company anymore." Roseman completely screwed me. So in 1982 Bruce Gowers, Simon Fields, and I formed our company.

We had John Cougar as a client and we shot a concert with him at the Marquis from which came two live videos, one for "Factory" and one for "I Need a Lover." John was swearing like crazy onstage—"I need a fucking lover, that won't drive me fucking crazy"—and this was in the days of painstaking two-inch editing, so our entire budget was blown editing out the curses. John was a pain to deal with. Always has been. We did all of his videos and he was always a pain in the ass.

Then we got hired to do two videos from his album *American Fool*: "Hurts So Good" and "Hand to Hold On To." We shot them back to back. He said, "Look, there's a song on the album the label doesn't believe in. But I do. Can you do me a favor and save one roll of film, shoot me singing the song, I'll give you some old photos and stuff and then you cobble it together for me?" The song was "Jack and Diane." So we stole some editing time in LA. We projected slides on the edit room wall, and we had the tape op wear white gloves to do the clapping. We didn't charge John a cent. It was his only number one song, and he never, ever called us again.

JULIEN TEMPLE: I wrote the treatment for the Rolling Stones's "Undercover of the Night" as a way of *not* doing the video. I was a punk rocker, and the Stones were regarded as jet-set traitors to the cause. The song was about the death squads then operating in Central America, and I wrote an extreme treatment about being in the middle of an urban revolution, and dramatized the notion of Keith and Mick really not liking each other by having Keith kill Mick in the video. I never thought they would do it. Of course they loved it.

I went to Paris to meet with the band. We were having dinner at Le Cinq, and Keith was looking particularly unhappy. He was glowering with menace from the other side of the table and eventually said, "Come downstairs with me." My producer and I went down to the men's room. Keith had a walking stick, and suddenly he pulled it apart. The next thing I know he's holding a swordstick to my throat. He said, "I want to be in this video more than I am." So we wrote up his part a bit more. That was Keith's idea of collaboration.

STEVE BARRON: Fleetwood Mac were, um, not easy to work with. They'd been through many relationship dynamics, shall we say, and those dynamics were strained at the time of "Hold Me." Four of them—I can't recall which four—couldn't be together in the same room for long. They didn't want to be there. I think Christine McVie was about ten hours getting out of the makeup trailer. By which time it was dark. That wasn't a good video, that one.

SIMON FIELDS: "Hold Me" was a fucking nightmare, a horrendous day in the desert. John McVie was drunk and tried to punch me. Stevie Nicks didn't want to walk on the sand with her platforms. Christine McVie was fed up with all of them. Mick thought she was being a bitch, he wouldn't talk to her. They were a fractious bunch.

STEVIE NICKS: First of all, it was 110 degrees there in the desert, and I'm in flowing chiffon and platform boots with five inch heels, in a chaise lounge on a white sand dune, and I couldn't leave until they got that shot. It was so hot, and we weren't getting along. Lindsey Buckingham wasn't happy with me because I'd broken up with him six years before. I'd had an affair with Mick Fleetwood, which was a secret until Mick told Lindsey, and Lindsey was *horrified.* Then Mick fell in love with my best friend, who left her husband for Mick, so I lost Mick and my best friend in one fell swoop. And everybody hated Mick because of what he had done to me. So it was a bad situation. My advice is, don't ever go out with a rock star.

RUSSELL MULCAHY: I was coupling up the members of Fleetwood Mac in "Gypsy," and people were pulling me aside saying, "No, no. Those two were fucking and then they split up and now he's sleeping with her." I got very confused, who was sleeping with whom.

STEVIE NICKS: There's a scene in "Gypsy" where Lindsey and I are dancing. And we weren't getting along very well then. I didn't want to be anywhere near Lindsey; I certainly didn't want to be in his arms. If you watch the video, you'll see I wasn't happy. And he wasn't a very good dancer.

I wanted to stop doing coke at that point, so I'd been in Corona del Mar, California, in self-imposed rehab, for two weeks. But the "Gypsy" video was scheduled and there was no getting out of it. That video was three days, and by the time we got to the end of the first day of filming, I was exhausted. I said, "I need a little bit of coke." Somebody got it for me, and I wrapped up the little bottle in a Kleenex and hid it behind the makeup mirror. Then I got called to the set, and when I came back, somebody had cleaned up the dressing room and thrown away the bottle. I said to the person who had gotten it for me, "You have to get in the garbage Dumpster and find that little bottle." But the person refused.

I think we probably would have gone on to make many more great videos like "Gypsy," had we not been so into drugs.

JANE WIEDLIN: We'd already had a number one album and we were seasoned rock stars by the time our second album came out. There was a big budget to make "Vacation"—$50,000 or something. We still saw videos as an annoying waste of time. After seven or eight hours we sent somebody out to sneak in booze.

KATHY VALENTINE, Go-Go's: We drank champagne. Lots of champagne. Lots.

JANE WIEDLIN: When I look at that video now and see the parts we filmed at the end of the day—we're smiling and waving our hands, but if you look at our eyes, we're all *so* drunk. We didn't try to make it look like we were really water-skiing.

JOHN KALODNER: The first act I worked with who were dramatically impacted by MTV, both positively and negatively, was Asia. We did MTV's first live concert broadcast from Japan, called "Asia from Asia." But the guys in Asia were older than other acts who were breaking on MTV, and that showed in their videos. They had the biggest-selling record of 1983, but they quickly became unhip.

AL TELLER: The first artist I saw positively affected by MTV was Men at Work. It was because of "Who Can It Be Now?" which was godawful. But it got a good response from the audience, and MTV started pounding it.

COLIN HAY, Men at Work: I think "Who Can It Be Now?" cost $5,000. Greg Ham, our sax player, had a theatrical background, and I loved to perform. We first came to the States towards the end of 1982, and toured for about four months. MTV was already playing "Who Can It Be Now?" in heavy rotation and may have been playing "Down Under" by the time we left. It was exciting enough for us to be in New York. But when I arrived, people would walk past me saying, "How you doin', Colin?" People would hang out of cabs, yelling out stuff. And that was because of MTV.

BRUCE DICKINSON, record executive: I was a product manager at Columbia Records, and the label had zero expectations for Men at Work. The first pressing was only 7,700 copies. But once "Who Can It Be Now?" went on MTV, things started to explode. Were they classic video stars? No. They didn't look like the guy in A Flock of Seagulls. They were offbeat, and the video got your attention. The album went to number one for something like sixteen weeks. That just didn't happen with a debut artist.

BOB SHERWOOD, record executive: Men at Work exploded because of their videos. That was a turning point. MTV knew how big and important they were. And record labels began to orient more towards the importance of a video. Now, it was a necessary promotion tool. And you'd better do it right.

GALE SPARROW: Acts like the Stray Cats, with no radio airplay, would tour MTV markets and sell out every club they played. Then bands would watch MTV while they were on tour and ask their labels, "How come we're not on MTV?"

GARY GERSH: I signed the Stray Cats to a U.S. record deal. The only thing that kept their album *Built for Speed* out of number one was Men at Work, and then *Thriller.*

CHRIS ISAAK: MTV played "Stray Cat Strut" endlessly. I mean, they wore that thing down. I couldn't believe it—a three-piece band playing rockabilly, and they're showing 'em *on TV.*

BRIAN SETZER, the Stray Cats: We were three brash guys from New York, living in England, when MTV started. We were told, "You're going to make a video. It's the latest thing." Okay, sounds good. We weren't popular until MTV came out. All of a sudden, we'd go to a place like Des Moines and play for a thousand people. Everyone was showing up in cowboy shirts and trying to look like Elvis.

JULIEN TEMPLE: I'd seen the Stray Cats and found them exciting live. They were quite cartoon-like, with their exaggerated quiffs and overdone '50s look, so I did a Tex Avery–like video for them.

STEWART COPELAND: In those days, the band had to look the part. Your haircuts and sartorial choices were very much a part of the product. And, led by Sting, we were good at it. We would tease Stingo that he couldn't walk past a mirror without primping. And he would say, "Fuck off, it's my job. And yours, too, by the way."

SIMON LE BON: MTV made bad haircuts look really cool for a while.

JERRY CASALE: Before I shot the Cars' "Panorama" video, Elliott Roberts, who managed Devo and the Cars, said to me offhand, "You know, Ric Ocasek's got a hairpiece." It had never occurred to me.

BRIAN SETZER: My hair was my speciality. If you don't have cool hair, don't make a video.

ANN WILSON: Put your hair up, take it down, rat it up, torment it, put some shit in it, make it bigger and bigger. It was never big enough.

NANCY WILSON: More mousse, more mousse, more hair dryers.

VICKI PETERSON, the Bangles: It wasn't just the hair that was big in the '80s. It was the shoulder pads, parachute pants, everything. For "Walk Like an Egyptian," I wore *four* pairs of false eyelashes.

RICHARD MARX: In a monologue, Chelsea Handler referred to me and my "fluffy mullet." The truth is, I absolutely had a fuckin' mullet. But I wasn't the first. Bono was before me. Mel Gibson in *Lethal Weapon* made it seem like a good idea. I remember watching *Lethal Weapon* and thinking, *I could totally rock that hairstyle.*

RICK SPRINGFIELD, artist: I was one of the first people to have my hair big and coiffed on top and long in the back. It was mullet-ish, but to me, the mullet was a Southern thing, super-short in front and super-long in the back.

SIMON LE BON: I had a mullet.

NICK RHODES: Our guitarist, Andy Taylor, had the king mullet to kill all other mullets, but I think we were probably all guilty at the time.

SIMON LE BON: David Bowie had the best mullet of all. And we were huge fans of his.

JOAN MYERS: One morning at work, my phone rang, and it was Stevie Nicks, calling from LA. She wanted us to play one of her videos right away so she could see how her hair looked in it. It was 9:30 A.M. in New York, 6:30 in LA. Les called the control room in Smithtown, and ten minutes later, they played the video.

MARTHA DAVIS: I remember going to award shows, and there'd be Cyndi Lauper, Dale Bozzio, and Terri Nunn. I was the only one with normal hair.

KATHY VALENTINE: I wonder how my life might have turned out different if I'd had a different hairstyle in the '80s.

OLIVIA NEWTON-JOHN, artist: I'd had long blond hair and when I went short brunette for "Physical," my haircut started a trend. The headband I wore also started a trend, which is hysterical, because it began as a way of keeping the hair out of my face. The record was number one for ten weeks. That was the last time I ever wore a white leotard. Once was enough.

JANE WIEDLIN: I have horrible '80s poodle hair in "Our Lips Are Sealed." But there's a simplicity and innocence to the video that appeals to me.

MICHAEL STIPE: The bands that were doing successful videos had big poofy hair and insane new wave costumes. I was jealous of their haircuts and their clothes. But we felt like we were the antithesis of that, and we should forge our own path.

VERNON REID, Living Colour: Very quickly, the video realm became about the young and the beautiful, or the odd and the quirky. If you weren't beautiful and hip, you had to be quirky in a particular way, like David Byrne of Talking Heads, or Ric Ocasek. In those Cars videos, Ric is just too tall and too thin, but that was the hook. He was a gangly scarecrow with great tunes.

JERRY HARRISON, Talking Heads: Our first video was "Crosseyed and Painless." But the band's not in it. David Byrne had befriended Toni Basil, and he did the video with her. They also codirected "Once in a Lifetime," which showed off David's quirkiness, with him borrowing the body language of Southern preachers and being in a sort of ecstatic state. And he's sweating a lot. "Once in a Lifetime" was about as successful as any early MTV video I can remember.

TONI BASIL, artist: When David and I codirected "Once in a Lifetime," we shot on a blue screen, because that was the only way to do things cheaply and without bringing in lights and sets.

"Crosseyed and Painless" started when Shabba-Doo—street-dancing star of *Electric Boogaloo* and *Breakin'*—called to my attention an insane dance group called the Electric Boogaloos, from Fresno, California. When they came to LA, I filmed them. That was the first time I saw Boogaloo Sam do the moonwalk, which is really called the backslide. Michael Jackson did *not* create the moonwalk! I showed the audition tape to David Byrne, and he wanted to use that style of dance for "Crosseyed and Painless."

JERRY HARRISON: We thought MTV was a little silly. A lot of the videos, like Duran Duran's, felt more like fashion shoots than films. David directed "Burning Down the House" with Julia Heyward, a conceptual artist, and the idea was that we had alter egos, including a little kid who climbs all over David. He had a tendency to cram a lot of ideas into those early videos, but the one for "Burning Down the House" was actually a hit.

TONI BASIL: On my "Mickey" video, I was the director, producer, choreographer, editor, singer—everything. I'd made very avant-garde 8mm and 16mm films, and hung out with Bruce Conner and Jonas Mekas, who were famous late '60s filmmakers. And I had been choreographing for television since the late '60s, so I certainly knew how to shoot for TV. I didn't have a calculated approach to "Mickey" of *Ooh, I'll wear a short skirt in the video because guys will like it*. If you don't like my talent, then fuck you. A European company signed me to make a video album, pre-MTV. I had to think of seven different concepts for the videos, and I'd been head cheerleader at Las Vegas High School, so I put a cheerleader concept into it. I used real cheerleaders, from Carson High School in LA. "Mickey" went to number one in Britain, and I got an American record deal just about the time MTV was starting, so the timing was great.

"WEIRD AL" YANKOVIC: On "Ricky," my parody of "Mickey," the budget was $3,000. We shot on video at somebody's house in the San Fernando Valley, very much like a porno. My friends were extras in the video. There was one scene where I'm supposed to be shaking maracas and nobody had bothered to get maracas. But we had a bowling pin. I thought, "Maybe if I shake it fast enough, it'll look like a maraca." Apparently, it was good enough for MTV.

RICK SPRINGFIELD: "Jessie's Girl" and "I've Done Everything for You" were so cheesy that now they're cool. "Jessie's Girl" was the only video where I had any real input. I storyboarded that and basically directed it with the camera guy. The big expense was smashing twenty-four mirrors. We wanted different takes, different angles. The scenes are so short, with split-second shots and fast cuts, there's no chance to do any real acting in them. Most musicians can't act anyway, even if they think they can.

BILLY JOEL: For "Uptown Girl," the director told me, "Look at the picture in your locker as if you're in love with this woman and then dance around with a wrench in your hand." I said, "Are you fucking kidding me?"

TOM PETTY: "You Got Lucky" was a real groundbreaker. There was a minute-long scene where we walk through the desert, uncover a dusty old boombox, and push play, and that's when the music begins. Michael Jackson called us, saying what an incredible idea that was. That video was terrific fun. We wrote the treatment ourselves and borrowed a ton from *Mad Max*, something we shared with many videos of that era. That was when we really saw MTV change our daily lives. Not only were teenagers spotting me on the street, older people would spot me, too. We knew it was big.

DON LETTS: I was in Texas with the Clash to shoot "Rock the Casbah," and Mick Jones showed up one day wearing red long johns, because he was in a mood. I said, "You really want to wear that for a video? If you look like a cunt on film, you'll look like a cunt forever." So he changed what he was wearing. I'd hit playback and the Clash would just go, go, go. They were like four sticks of dynamite.

Putting a Jew and an Arab in the video was just about breaking taboos. Yes, the Muslim in the video is drinking a beer. They pull into a petrol station and the Arab makes the Jewish gentleman pay for the gas. These days, with all the sensitivity towards religion, you wouldn't get to make that video.

MICK JONES: We were showing how people can get along—by drinking beer and going to Burger King. The idea of the video was about oil, really. We were in America, so we went to the oil fields in Texas. That was the subtext of it. I wanted to wear red long johns, but Don wouldn't let me. That's why I put a mosquito mask on my face, 'cause I was in a bad mood.

TODD RUNDGREN: At first, there was a more eclectic variety of videos on the air, because bands weren't yet making videos specifically for MTV. After MTV was recognized as being a great promotion vehicle, things got more formulaic: smoke bombs, scantily clad women, that sort of thing. There's nothing wrong with smoke bombs and scantily clad women the first couple of times, you know? Then you start to think, *Nobody has any ideas here, really.*

BRUCE ALLEN, manager: Loverboy wanted their videos to be sexier. It's all about sex. That's why I loved those videos like Duran Duran—what is it, "Hot Girls on Film"?

PAUL FLATTERY: We shot the Bryan Adams video for "Cuts Like a Knife" in the empty pool at Hollywood Athletic Club. Simon Fields was very proud of auditioning the girls. He'd have to see their breasts.

RAQUEL PENA, model: My modeling agency sent me to the audition, and there were hundreds of gorgeous girls there. I was shocked that I got chosen. Steve Barron wanted someone with really long legs, and I wore a black bathing suit that he liked. I wore the same suit in the video. That's how low-budget it was! I was twenty, but I looked like I was thirteen.

BRYAN ADAMS: The abandoned pool and a girl: that was the entire concept. A lot of people wanted to know about the girl—she became a bit of a cult figure. She ended up dating one of the guys at the record company, of course.

STEVE BARRON: I got some stink from *Rolling Stone* for the "Cuts Like a Knife" video. The song has a sexy vibe to it, so we made a sexy video, and we cast a very pretty girl in a swimsuit. And they wrote a big article about how videos like "Cuts Like a Knife" were bad for music because they were pushing sex.

DON LETTS: The record labels used to say, "We want this video to fit seamlessly with the video that's before it and the one after it." I'd think, *What the fuck are you talking about? I want my video to leap out of the screen.*

OLIVIA NEWTON-JOHN: The premise of the "Physical" video was to distract from the fact that the song was so sexual. I was freaked out about it: I had a good-girl image and the song was naughty. I called my manager and said, "We have to pull the record." But it was too late. The video plays against the lyrics by making *physical* mean exercise, not sex.

BRIAN GRANT: Olivia was coming off a massive flop with *Xanadu*, a dreadful film. I made fun of the lyrics by setting the video in a gym: She tries in vain to train some fat guys, then goes away, and when she comes back, they've turned into good-looking gay boys.

OLIVIA NEWTON-JOHN: Brian Grant threw in a twist at the end—instead of me walking off with a guy, the guys walk off with each other. Some people edited off the end when they showed the video. I always had gay friends. And as the choreographer, Kenny Ortega—we'd done *Xanadu* together—was gay, it seemed fine.

RUSSELL MULCAHY: Elton John's "I'm Still Standing" was super, super, super gay. There was no holding back. We shot in Nice, in the south of France. My costume designer was in charge of body-painting all the boys. Elton brought his suitcase of glasses and a thousand different colors of suits, and every scene he'd change his outfit and we'd use the painted boys in the shot. We had leather boys, and mimes, and kissing clowns. Bruno Tonioli, who's a judge of *Dancing with the Stars*, was one of our dancers. I think he played one of the traffic policemen dressed in leg warmers and a leotard.

Billy Joel's "Allentown" has homoerotic imagery, as well. There were shirtless construction workers. And there is bare assery. We had to pay the boys $500 each to show their asses. I think it was the first time bare ass had been shown in a video. Don't forget, that was 1982. There's been quite a cultural change since then. That was many years before I did the pilot for *Queer as Folk*, where the first day of the shoot I had a guy's tongue up another guy's ass.

BILLY JOEL: In *The Hangover Part II* they did a very profane and hilarious spoof of "Allentown." There was renewed interest in the video on YouTube, so I watched it the other day for the first time in a while. Now, Russell was a brilliant director. But I didn't realize until I watched it again how *gay* that video was. It's *really* gay! There's a shower scene with all these good-looking, muscular young steel workers who are completely bare assed. And then they're all oiled up and twisting valves and knobs. I'd missed this completely when I was doing the video. I just thought it was like *The Deer Hunter*. You know, guys go off to war, they come back, they're all messed up, and there're steelworkers who don't have jobs—okay, I get that. But did they have to be taking a shower with their bare asses hanging out? Maybe there's something artsy-fartsy about that, I don't know.

LOL CREME: We had a concept for Elton John's "Kiss the Bride" which was big, and big budget. He was all for it, but his manager John Reid got the budget and said, "Forget it." He'd recently gotten the bill for Elton's previous videos, done with Russell Mulcahy, and they spent God knows what in the south of France— most of it, I was told, on dinners, champagne, and coke.

BILLY JOEL: Russell directed my first real video, "Pressure." I put myself completely in his hands. I said, "What do you want me to do?" He said, "You're gonna sink into a pool of foam and disappear." "Okay." "And then you're gonna be in a chair raging at the sky." "Okay." "And then you're gonna walk down this bridge." "Okay." It was his movie, his vision. I didn't know what *any* of it meant.

BRIAN GRANT: Russell was probably the most successful director of that era. Everyone wanted him to direct their videos.

PAUL FLATTERY: Russell Mulcahy was so ahead of the curve. He invented the jump cut. He was the first to bring in glass shots, where you paint on a piece of glass and combine that with live footage to create a very elaborate appearance. He used it on Kim Carnes's "Bette Davis Eyes" and Fleetwood Mac's "Gypsy." He was the first to use dance in a meaningful way. He was the first to bring in body paint.

MARTY CALLNER, director: I was in bed one day, watching a pay cable station called the Z Channel, and a music video came on: "Bette Davis Eyes," directed by Russell Mulcahy. It broke every rule of what is and isn't allowed on television. It was the most creative thing I'd ever seen on TV.

RUSSELL MULCAHY: Steven Spielberg rang me up after he saw "Bette Davis Eyes." I was in a van in London, editing a video at two in the morning. An assistant came in and said, "Oh, there was a Steven Spielberg rang you. I told him to call back." I went, *"What?!"*

DANIEL PEARL, director of photography: Russell was a visionary. The whole genre was kind of his baby. I'd describe his directorial style as "organized chaos"; I'd use that phrase to describe most of the early directors, actually. Some things were planned, but some were happy accidents. There was a great sense of freedom. It wasn't anything like a studio film shoot. That's one of the things that made music videos unique from other kinds of filmmaking. We had a policy not to break the rules, but to *blow up* the fucking rules. There'd be a rule, like, "Do not shoot a person in black-and-white with a red filter, because it'll look all blown out." *Fuckin' cool.*

BRIAN GRANT: There was a lot of experimentation, some good and some bad. As a director, it was like somebody else was paying for me to attend film school. For

Stevie Nicks's "Stand Back," I dreamed up the idea of doing *Gone with the Wind* in three minutes. I wanted to direct feature films, and I thought this would help prove myself. When Stevie watched the video, she hugged me and said, "I look fat." And she redid the video with somebody else—a simple, boring, dance-routine video. Such is life.

STEVIE NICKS: "Stand Back" was my first and last foray into writing a video. I decided it was going to be a Civil War scene. It was insane—it didn't go with the song at all. It was so bad, it was almost good. I tried to act, which was horrific. We used a house in Beverly Hills that we accidentally set on fire. I almost got killed riding a horse; he went straight into a grove of trees and the crew in the car driving alongside screamed, "*Jump!*" So we watched it back and I said, "This can never come out. I don't care if it cost $1 million." Irving Azoff, my manager, said, "You're an idiot." We knew "Stand Back" was gonna be a big hit and we had to have a video, so we hired another director and I paid for two complete videos.

SHARON ORECK: The general rule was that video costs were 50 percent recoupable; so if a video cost $50,000, the band was in for $25,000, which would get deducted from their royalty payments.

DARYL HALL: I didn't pay attention to how much money was being spent, much to my shame and sorrow. I was too stupid to realize that all the stuff was charged to me anyway. People loved to spend my money. This is a good story: Somebody decided the "Maneater" video wouldn't be complete unless we had an actual panther, a man-eating animal, in the video. It appeared for a second and a half in the video and probably cost $10,000. This South American black panther was wired to the floor so it wouldn't attack everybody. Of course, it got loose in this gigantic studio in LA and went in the rafters, fifty feet up. Nobody could get it down. That's when I left the building.

RUSSELL MULCAHY: I collaborated on the storyboard for Bonnie Tyler's "Total Eclipse of the Heart" with Jim Steinman, who wrote and produced the song. Jim is fabulously, fabulously crazy. We would banter ideas over a bottle of red wine. I'd say, "Let's set it in a school and have ninjas in one scene," and he'd say "Let's have a choirboy with glowing eyeballs." We shot it in an old abandoned insane asylum in London. We had one sequence, which was Steinman's idea, where a shirtless young boy is holding a dove and he throws the dove at the camera in slow motion. Bonnie came around the corner and screamed, in her Welsh accent, "You're nothing but a fucking pre-vert!" And she stormed off.

There was nothing perverse intended. The imagery was meant to be sort of pure. Maybe slightly erotic and gothic and creepy, but pure. Anyway, the video went to number one, and a year later Bonnie's people rang up and asked if I would direct her new video. And I told them to fuck off, because I was insulted about being called a fucking pervert. And I was a little mad because *pervert* wasn't pronounced correctly.

PATTY SMYTH: Columbia had a full-blown video department by the time Scandal made "The Warrior." They all had to justify their jobs, and they were scrambling around to come up with what they thought were cool ideas. They found some French chick who did body-painting. And then they brought me to a haircutter who had some crazy vision for what I should look like, and she cut off all my hair. In retrospect, that chick must have hated me, because she made me look as bad as she possibly could. "The Warrior" was the biggest hit of my career, and no one recognized me in the video.

When I saw the video, I was crestfallen. I had no idea it would look like an off-Broadway version of *Cats*. I begged the label, "Please don't release that." I was so upset and embarrassed. But it turned out to be a Top 10 video. That Halloween, everybody dressed as the Warrior. People came to my shows dressed as the Warrior. And when I came to the "bang bang" part of the song, everyone in the crowd would shoot off their finger-guns, just like in the video. I prefer to think "The Warrior" was a hit because it was a great song. Because that video . . . oh my god.

DENNIS DeYOUNG: I'm still not sure what the "Mr. Roboto" video is about.

I wrote *Kilroy Was Here* like a screenplay: it's the story of a baby-boom kid who sees Elvis on *The Ed Sullivan Show*, then sees the Beatles and decides to form a band. The story revolved around censorship, the Big Brother idea of banning rock n' roll. The other guys in Styx were afraid of the idea. We'd sold out Madison Square Garden four tours in a row, so I was thinking, *What's next?* I decided we should make a short film.

The people who worked on the film were spectacular talents. I screened reels from a bunch of directors, and really liked Brian Gibson, who'd done an

English film, *Breaking Glass*. Brian brought Steven Goldblatt, who became a major cinematographer. They cobbled together three videos from the film footage. Stan Winston designed the masks in "Mr. Roboto," and he's regarded as a Hollywood legend. Michael Winslow, the guy who makes all the amazing sounds with his mouth in the *Police Academy* movies, played Hendrix in the long-form video. And you know who the goddamn choreographer was for the robot dancing in "Mr. Roboto"? Kenny Ortega, the same guy who ruined Billy Squier's career a year later.

I probably shouldn't have forced the idea on the band. Relations in Styx got really crappy after that, and Tommy Shaw quit at the end of the Kilroy tour.

STEVE LUKATHER: After "Rosanna" and "Africa," we did a horrible disco line-dancing video for "Waiting for Your Love," which MTV didn't play. MTV had turned against us. We were good enough for them when they launched, and then it was like, "Fuck you." So for the next album, *Isolation*, we decided not to even appear in our own videos. And one of them got nominated for a VMA, for Best Director! I have to say, I hated MTV.

Chapter 9

"POUTING AND SHOULDER PADS"

EFFEMINATE BRITISH BANDS SPREAD WEIRD HAIRCUTS ACROSS THE U.S.

FOR A HUGE MAJORITY OF PEOPLE IN THE 1980s, radio was the only delivery system for music. And radio had not evolved much—with few exceptions, American stations ignored punk rock, and hadn't changed their playlists in years. AOR (album-oriented rock) radio was based on tradition and legacy, and a belief that young audiences wanted to hear familiar music—Led Zeppelin's "Stairway to Heaven" and Lynyrd Skynyrd's "Freebird"—drawn from an unchanging canon. Rock was in danger of becoming as ossified as ballet, with its repeated repertoire of *Swan Lake* and *The Nutcracker*, and classical music, with its endless performances of Beethoven's fifth and seventh symphonies.

If there had been videos for Bad Company and Deep Purple, MTV probably would have played them—during the early days, they were still committed to an AOR playlist. But to fill time, they played new wave bands, mostly from England, who dressed in outrageous finery and adored the camera. "Video to us is like stereo was to Pink Floyd," Duran Duran keyboardist Nick Rhodes said in 1984. "It was new, it was just happening. And we saw we could do a lot with it."

When Duran Duran or Eurythmics videos aired in the same hour as Journey or REO Speedwagon, it was the Brits who seemed brighter, bolder, and more captivating. The lipsticked, cross-dressing audacity of these bands did not go unnoticed by an older generation. Bob Dylan, also in 1984, said, "I mean, now you can wear anything. You see a guy wearing a dress onstage now, it's like, 'Oh, yeah, right.' You expect it."

LIMAHL, Kajagoogoo: In the UK, we'd come out of a period of depression in the late 1970s. We'd had electricity strikes by the miners and it was a real anarchic atmosphere. There was a movement of punk and skinheads and violence. Punk was pain and spitting and swearing, and I didn't like it. When we arrived at new wave and the great synthesizer explosion, everybody wanted to forget the previous five years. New wave was optimism, color, escapism, and running a million miles an hour from reality.

MARTIN FRY: It's hard to explain to a younger audience, just how fucked up it was in 1982. You could get beaten up for wearing mascara, if you walked into a bar full of old guys playing dominoes, but that was part of the appeal. It was like saying "Fuck you." Long may that spirit exist.

ABC used to antagonize bands who wore leather jackets and leather pants. They'd say, "What the hell are you doing?" There was a war between bands who thought there was authenticity in wearing denim, and newfangled bands like Duran Duran, Eurythmics, and Culture Club. We were all children of Roxy Music anyway.

JOHN TAYLOR: In the first year or two, videos primarily were coming out of Europe, with a very sophisticated milieu. And they were dropping like bombs on the suburbs of Ohio and Texas, places that were so conservative. For people that were a little different—maybe they didn't yet know they were gay, or didn't know they were into art—the kinds of things that were on MTV were like life changers. All this stuff like Culture Club was the result of an underground, progressive, liberal, London art-school sensibility.

TOM BAILEY, Thompson Twins: A golden age of pop music had started in England. It began with the Human League and ended with Frankie Goes to Hollywood. Brits were using lots of electronics and synthesizers, and people in the American music scene were very suspicious of us.

ANDY MORAHAN, director: The American acts of that era wanted to wear what they normally wore, or be shot holding guitars. The British acts saw music video as a new art form in a way American acts didn't.

TOM BAILEY: English people found it easier to jump on the idea of videos and exploit them. Americans talk to each other readily, whereas we English people communicate by putting on our feathers. There's always been extraordinary street fashion in London.

DAVE HOLMES: All the men took dressing very seriously. I longed to dress like Spandau Ballet in those rich, burgundy suits and jackets with epaulets.

JULIEN TEMPLE: The New Romantics were all about looking at themselves in the mirror, so they absolutely adored the idea of someone sticking a camera in front of them.

HOWARD JONES, artist: It was a very liberating era. I felt that men are so tied up in a straitjacket of how they're supposed to look, so their sexuality won't ever be questioned. The '80s broke that down a bit. Just because you've got brightly colored clothes doesn't mean you're gay. Surely that's one of the functions of pop culture, to show people that there are many options out there and you can choose which one is right for you. MTV was socially progressive in that period.

LIMAHL: I loved making videos, 100 percent. "Too Shy" cost £30,000, which back then was a huge amount of money. MTV played it in quite heavy rotation. The girl in the video who plays a waitress, she's probably on camera more than any of us—her name is Ali Espley Miller, and she's now married to the American comedian Dennis Miller. I had a very identifying hairstyle. It seemed logical to stand out from the crowd. Yeah, I had a mullet. There was a book published called *The Mullet*, and they gave me a full page. I think they called me a "duo-toned spikey mullet man." In a way, it was theater.

JUDY McGRATH: I remember the first U2 video I ever saw, "I Will Follow." When it arrived at MTV, we gathered around the television like it was the invention of fire. I was like, *Oh my god, who is this singer in the mullet? And listen to that guitar!*

PAUL McGUINNESS, manager: U2's campaign in America pretty well started at the same time as MTV, and it became important for us extremely early on. There was a bit of snobbery about video—some rock acts thought it was tawdry. We liked making videos. And we didn't do it in any bashful way. We wanted to be on MTV, no doubt about it.

MEIERT AVIS, director: U2 wanted to be bigger than the Rolling Stones, and videos were a big part of how they set out to do it. We went to Sweden to make "New

Year's Day." There was a director of photography named Sven Nykvist, who was Ingmar Bergman's cameraman. We wanted to use him, but he was old and couldn't travel, so we went to Sweden. As it turned out, he wasn't well enough to shoot for us, so his camera operator shot "New Year's Day." We started in Stockholm and then went off looking for snow. We wanted big mountains, but Sweden's fairly flat, so we went up toward Norway. U2 was in the middle of touring, and they couldn't get insurance to cover them to ride horses in the video, so we got teenage girls to dress up as them and do their riding. You can't tell it's not them.

PAUL McGUINNESS: There are no members of U2 who can ride a horse. But in the end, it was a good little film. MTV was really quite a small organization, and you could get somebody to watch your video and have the pleasure of seeing it on air a few hours later.

BOB PITTMAN: Because we didn't have enough videos, we'd play unknown British acts: U2, Madness, A Flock of Seagulls, Duran Duran. We ushered in the second British Invasion.

MARTIN FRY: The record companies weren't pressuring anyone to look a certain way. That came later. For "The Look of Love" we wanted to cross the visual style of Benny Hill, a really crude slapstick comedian, with *An American in Paris*. I don't think Kurt Cobain would have ever put on a striped blazer and sung to a wooden crocodile. There's a parrot on my shoulder at one point. We were pushing it to the limit, seeing how embarrassed we could get. Art is what you get away with.

BRIAN GRANT: Martin Fry and I both loved old Hollywood movies. There was no *Look at us, we're a serious rock band*. They just wanted to have fun.

CLIFF BURNSTEIN: ABC never would have sold a record in America if it weren't for videos. Same was true for many English acts: Duran Duran, Tears for Fears, Thompson Twins . . .

SIR MIX-A-LOT, artist: Devo, Gary Numan, the Fixx—I liked all the new wave bands. But I didn't like any of 'em so much that I tried to style my hair like the guy from A Flock of Seagulls. And I never tried to hold one key on a synthesizer for as long as he did in "I Ran."

MIKE SCORE, A Flock of Seagulls: Frank, the bass player, and I were both hair-dressers. We were doing hair for models and photo shoots. We wanted to have a more distinctive look than every other band, so I created my particular hair-style. You want all the young girls to see you and go, *Ooooooh!*

The record company said, "We'll do your video on Wednesday." Like it was nothing. They didn't explain to us what MTV was. We had no idea what we were doing. "I Ran" cost £5,000. To us, that was a lot of money. I remember my manager arguing with the record company: "Who's gonna pay for it?"

They gave us money and said, "Get yourselves some clothes that will look good on-screen." The whole thing took maybe six hours—probably three of them in hair and makeup. The next thing we know, it's on MTV every hour. It put us in every living room from Kansas to Seattle to Miami. We were famous before we ever got to the U.S. Other bands immediately imitated the way we looked. There was one Flock of Seagulls and ninety-nine copies.

When we did gigs in New York, we would go in and do an interview with MTV. We'd talk about my hair, and talk about my hair, and talk about my hair. I was annoyed—we weren't really there to talk about the band and the music. We were there to talk about my hair.

GARY GERSH: MTV created a market in America for videos, so all of a sudden the quality went up. David Bowie, who had been making videos for a decade, was making more complex and expensive videos. We signed Bowie, and his first album for us was *Let's Dance*, which was gigantic worldwide.

DAVID MALLET: "Let's Dance" was Bowie's big comeback, pretty much a straight pop song as opposed to introverted, darker stuff. It was a superb gamble on his part and it paid off handsomely. He said, "I want to go to Australia and film videos." He came up with this concept of two Aborigines in the modern world who were a bit lost. The videos has these mystical red shoes—if you had them on, you could dance. He got that from the Emeric Pressburger film *The Red Shoes*, an early Technicolor film that's haunting and surreal.

We shot in a bar in the morning and it was one hundred degrees outside. The people in the bar hated us, absolutely hated us. We were faggots from some-where, and they were horrified that we had a young, attractive Aborigine girl in there, because they thought Aborigines were lower than dirt. She was dancing, and in order to show their hatred they started imitating her. I said, "Quick, film them." It looked as if they were enjoying themselves. Actually, it was a dance of pure hatred.

Why do the two Aborigines stomp the red shoes at the end of the video? People have asked me forever. I don't know! Because it's a music video, that's why. End of story.

NICK RHODES: I don't think videos have to make sense. They only have to be really cool-looking.

DAVE STEWART, Eurythmics: At the start of the Eurythmics, I became very ill. I had an operation because my lung kept collapsing. I had just gotten out of surgery, and they must've given me tons of morphine or something, because my head started to explode with the idea of visual imagery and making music. From then on, I was obsessed with videos.

Just before that, a weird thing happened: I was walking down the street in Australia and stepped on something quite hard. I looked down and it was a solid gold bracelet. I picked it up, and as I turned the corner, I saw a pawnshop. I swapped the bracelet for an 8mm cine camera. From that moment on, I was always filming. I started to understand about putting imagery together with music.

The first Eurythmics video is "Never Gonna Cry Again." Annie comes out of the sea backwards and I come out of the sand and there's a tea party on the beach and everything is on fire. It's totally surreal.

JON ROSEMAN, producer: Dave had a tremendous feel for images. People often ask me, "How did you come up with idea of the cow?" I tell them, "Dave just said, 'Let's have a cow.'"

DAVE STEWART: I drew the "Sweet Dreams" treatment in little blocks, like a comic book. Every scene, from beginning to end. I presented the treatment to the label, and they could not understand the bit with the cow. The cow *was* complicated, because we were in London, and the cow had to go down an elevator into a basement. The farmer who owned the cow was really agitated.

ANNIE LENNOX, Eurythmics: "Sweet Dreams" was shot in a basement studio in the middle of London. There was an elevator big enough to take the cow down from the ground floor. That was one of the most surreal moments I've had—being in a building with a cow walking around freely. In a way, the video is a statement about the different forms of existence. Here are humans, with our dreams of industry and achievement and success. And here is a cow. We share the same planet, but it's a strange coexistence.

During the scene where Dave is sitting at a prototype computer, tapping the keyboard, the cow's head came really close to him. I could see that happening and I thought, *Oh shit, what is the cow going to do?* It was almost nudging him. And Dave is so intuitive, he just rolled his eyes, so it looks like there was some kind of understanding between him and the cow. Like the cow had been told, "Right, so you do this and then Dave's gonna do this. And . . . ACTION!"

DAVE STEWART: "Sweet Dreams" prompted a big argument with the record company. They were pissed off when Annie and I turned up in matching suits, with Annie's hair cropped off. They wanted her to wear a dress. They were like, "We don't understand. Annie is such a pretty girl." Then MTV got the video and it just went mad. It didn't look like anything else. Annie's hair was so different, and the colors in the video looked amazing. It was shot on 16mm film, but it was very rich. It became a phenomenon.

STEVE BARRON: I believe Human League's "Don't You Want Me" was the first music video shot on 35mm. Everyone was shooting on 16mm; 35 felt like something that was only allowed for the movies.

At the time of "Don't You Want Me," I was really into the Truffaut movie *Day for Night.* I was intrigued by his idea of a film within a film, and I thought, *We have to go further. What about a film within a film within a film?* Phil Oakey was going out with Joanne Catherall at the time, the dark-haired singer. But it was Susan Ann Sulley who did the vocals, so she had to be the lead character. She walks into an editing room and hangs up her trench coat, and she's basically playing a girl I had a crush on, one of the assistant editors where I was working. That coat became iconic.

LIMAHL: Videos were so exciting. I remember watching Human League's "Don't You Want Me" and making no sense of it. It was just a lot of pouting and shoulder pads.

JEFF AYEROFF: I saw the "Don't You Want Me" video and said, "Who is this director? I want him to do all our videos."

CURT SMITH, Tears for Fears: When Steve Barron directed "Pale Shelter," that was the first time we worked with a serious director. The label said, "Steve Barron is the guy. He's doing all these great videos." And if I look back on it now, it's the cheesiest thing. The highlight of the video comes at the end, when a paper airplane lands in Roland's eye. That's the good bit.

JEFF AYEROFF: Joe Jackson ended up selling many more records than Elvis Costello did, mainly because of the videos he did with Steve Barron.

JOE JACKSON, artist: Music videos weren't even discussed when I made my first album in 1979. By 1982, there'd been a distinct shift. I made videos with Steve Barron for "Real Men" and "Steppin' Out," and by the time we got to "Breaking Us in Two," I said to the label, "I don't think this song should have a video." I was told I had to make a video, whether I liked it or not. "Breaking Us in Two" was a crappy video. I was embarrassed. So I decided in my great wisdom that not only would I no longer make videos, but I would write an anti-video editorial for *Billboard* magazine. I mean, I'm not such a miserable bastard that I won't admit that some videos are great fun. But I believed MTV was beginning to have a negative effect on music.

I'm well aware that refusing to make videos accomplished nothing whatsoever except—how should I put this?—to make my next record less successful. It damaged my career and it never fully recovered.

JOHN TAYLOR: One reason we were able to make the medium work for us better than a lot of our peers was Simon, who had a background in drama. He was much more open-minded and less self-conscious playing a role than, you know, Rod Stewart.

SIMON LE BON: I did a lot of commercials, a BBC TV program, amateur and professional stage work from age fourteen.

NICK RHODES: We shot "Hungry Like the Wolf," "Save a Prayer," and "Lonely in Your Nightmare" on a trip to Sri Lanka. When I arrived there, I was dressed from head to toe in black leather, because I'd come from London and it was cold. I felt this intense heat and thought, *I'm not really dressed properly, am I?* I see this guy holding a sign with my name on it, and I think, it's okay, I'll take the limo to the hotel and have a shower, it'll be fine. He leads me to a flatbed truck. It's about three hundred degrees and I said, "How far is it to the hotel?" He said, "Five hours."

We finally arrived and it was like a mirage—the most beautiful beach you've ever seen. As I was walking up to the hotel, an elephant passed me on the street, I thought, *It can't get any stranger than this.*

The people that look after the elephants were completely smashed. They drink this stuff called arrack. For "Save a Prayer," John and I were on an elephant, Simon was on one with Andy, and Roger was on one of his own. And they brought a female elephant who let out this enormous noise, which one of the guys in the crew was taping. He thought, *Oh, this will be funny,* and he played it back through the speakers. Nobody knew that it was her mating call. So the elephant with Roger on its back charges down the swamp and mounts this other elephant. Roger's hanging on for dear life, and all of the mahouts are rolling around, thinking it's hilarious. If he'd fallen off, he could have been trampled to death. It was funny as hell, but also quite hairy for a moment.

RUSSELL MULCAHY: In one shot, the band was standing atop an ancient fortress called Sigiriya. It's a sacred site, so they were in bare feet. It's about 140 degrees out, their backs are to the camera, and while the audio track is playing, "Save a prayer for me now," they're going, "Fuck you, Russell! *Fuck yooooooooou.*" Their feet were burning.

SIMON LE BON: As soon as Russell said, "Cut," we started hopping around on the hot stairs.

NICK RHODES: All three videos were made for something like $30,000. We pulled every favor we could from the Sri Lankan authorities. It was cheap to work there, but it was like a SWAT team. Simon and I got dropped from a helicopter onto the top of a monument, because they couldn't land the helicopter. I must have been entirely insane.

SIMON LE BON: "Hungry Like the Wolf" demanded a lot of acting. When other bands made videos with stories to them, you'd see them smirking and giggling. Whereas I acted as though I truly was being chased in the jungle. There's a scene in "Hungry Like the Wolf" where the rest of the band are chasing after me, and it's absolutely convincing.

JOHN TAYLOR: "Hungry Like the Wolf" had a vague plot. Simon was Kurtz in *Apocalypse Now*, going up the jungle. And we were searching for him. "Hungry Like the Wolf" was like *Apocalypse Now*, and "Save a Prayer" was like *Raiders of the Lost Ark*.

RUSSELL MULCAHY: We shot "Hungry Like the Wolf" in a city called Galle. The first shot was going to be set in the marketplace, with Simon coming through the market. The night before, Simon decided he wanted some highlights in his hair, but the girl did it all wrong, and Simon's hair turned bright yellow. He came out the next morning nearly in tears. Luckily I was wearing an Indiana Jones–type hat, and I said "Okay, stick my hat on him, and pull it down a bit." If you watch the video closely, when he's coming down the marketplace, his hair is bright yellow under that hat.

SIMON LE BON: I wanted to have blond highlights in my hair, as we did in the 1980s. The hairdresser bleached it orange. The first scene we shot that day was in a busy Sinhalese market—spices, vegetables, legs of lamb with flies buzzing around them. The locals had gathered around the camera in a semicircle. I'm striding along the market with real purpose in my gait, and one of the eaves on a roof caught the hat and knocked it off my head. And I'm not joking, this crowd of three hundred people took two steps back with a sharp intake of breath. I was scrambling to put the hat back on my head.

RUSSELL MULCAHY: After "Hungry Like the Wolf," an Australian producer rang me up and said "Do you want to do a horror film?" To which I answered, "Yes, absolutely. And what is it about?" That's how I came to direct my first feature film, *Razorback*.

JOHN TAYLOR: After a long tour, four of the five band members took off for Antigua and stayed next to one another in beach chalets. Paul Berrow called us and said, "Don't come home. We're coming down with Russell, we're going to shoot a video there." It was quite smart. We got the most significant visual of our career on that trip.

RUSSELL MULCAHY: We did "Rio" in Antigua because one of the managers said, "I want to go yachting in Antigua." So we wrote a video about yachts.

NICK RHODES: "Rio" was a day or two days of shooting. We were on the boat for possibly three or four hours. And that image is engrained upon a generation of MTV viewers. When we were making videos, we thought they would appear on *Top of the Pops* once in England, then get shown for a couple weeks on MTV. We didn't ever expect they'd be around thirty years later. It was hard to get away from the image of us in suits on the boat.

JOHN TAYLOR: When we were doing it, did we think, *This is going to be one of the defining images of the decade within popular music?* No. "Rio" was kind of our *Help!*, wasn't it? Think of the Beatles on those snowmobiles. I mean, they did some pretty stupid shit.

KENNEDY, MTV VJ: The first time I saw "Rio" was in the fifth grade at a friend's house. One look at those dudes in lipstick, dancing on a schooner, and I was hooked.

BOY GEORGE, Culture Club: Duran Duran were projecting an entirely different image than we were. They were selling champagne and yachts. When you're nineteen, you think you're in competition with everyone else, and your success depends on someone else's failure. And the '80s were all about the survival of the fittest and the richest. Simon and I are good friends now, but there was a rivalry between us.

JOE ELLIOTT: We got on well with Duran, but we were jealous of them, because they shot videos on yachts, with beautiful suits and women covered in war paint. We did ours at Battersea Power Station, and our women were caged. As much as they were all heterosexuals, you could understand why gay men would fancy them. Especially Nick Rhodes. I mean, even *we* fancied Nick Rhodes.

DAVE HOLMES: The clothes were beautiful, they were on a yacht. It was an escape to a beautiful place with beautiful people, which is what all of television is now. It blew my mind that girls were attracted to Nick Rhodes, because he was so feminine looking. It just didn't seem right. Up to that point, men hadn't been erotic.

NICK RHODES: Our videos became larger than life. People believed, *That's what they must do all day, hang out on yachts.*

SIMON LE BON: It was kind of quite annoying for a while, that suddenly we were put into that pigeonhole.

JOHN TAYLOR: The success of the *Rio* videos drove us crazy! Every interview we did would begin, "These videos of yours are really amazing! Whose idea was it?" The phrase "video band" started coming up, and it would set us off. We shot "The Reflex" video in Toronto at Maple Leaf Gardens—it was like, *Let's do a live video.* I think that was part of us saying, "Listen, we're not a fucking video band, okay?"

DAVID MALLET: When I made "White Wedding," Billy Idol was an ex–punk rocker from a silly band called Generation X. He was handsome and charismatic. So I did one thing only: I made him look good. He had one of the biggest star qualities since James Dean, in my opinion. No, it hasn't turned out right. But in those days, he was the greatest looker and mover since Elvis. Before "White Wedding," nobody would have admitted that was even possible. One look at that video and they got him.

PERRI LISTER: I said to David Mallet, "I'm dating Billy Idol. Can you do the video for 'White Wedding'? And don't charge what you usually charge. He hasn't got any money." And so David gave him a good price.

BILLY IDOL: We were thinking about how to create a nightmare wedding between a Goth and a straight girl, with crosses, nails being hammered into a coffin, and me as a vampire.

PERRI LISTER: I played the bride, and I came up with the idea for the barbed-wire wedding ring. Somebody asked Billy in an interview, "Don't you think that's sexist?" And he goes, "No, it was a girl's idea." We didn't have fake blood on the set, so when Billy slipped the ring on me, I said, "Cut my finger!" That's real blood you see in the video.

BILLY IDOL: Later on, some people made the inference that people attending the wedding make a Nazi salute.

DAVID MALLET: It's not a Nazi salute. It's just people sticking their hands out towards the bride and groom. Yes, I was playing with the power of crowd imagery, maybe a Nuremberg rally. And you'll immediately say, "The Nuremberg rallies were Nazi." Yes, but the Nazi side of it hadn't occurred to me.

BILLY IDOL: Perri and two of her dancer friends spank their own bums in time to the hand claps on the record. That's the kind of thing they love in England.

DAVID MALLET: Yes, the girls slap their own bottoms. Why not? It was a big laugh, a piss-take on soft-porn. It was an erotic satire of sexuality. It made me laugh and it made a lot of other clever people laugh. All the sexy videos I've done have been comedies.

ADAM ANT: My strategy for making videos was sex, subversion, style, and humor. I was the first person to put a star in a video—I cast Diana Dors, who was the British Marilyn Monroe, in "Prince Charming." The castle in "Goody Two Shoes" is a mental institution which housed Spike Milligan and Peter Sellers, a crazy, awful place. That's quite iconic, because it has Graham Stark, who was in the *Pink Panther* movies, and Caroline Munro, who was in the Hammer horror films. The bit where I'm sliding down the pole is an homage to Elvis in *Jailhouse Rock*. And "Strip" has an homage to the shower scene in *Psycho*. But things do burn out. You can't have a firecracker going off forever.

ROBIN SLOANE: Adam & the Ants went gold, largely because of MTV. So we threw a dinner party at Windows on the World for the MTV crew—Les Garland, Gale, Freston, Buzz Brindle, those people. I never told my boss about it until the day of the party. And I got fired. The next day, I got a job at Elektra as the head of video promotion. Elektra had a German synth-pop artist named Peter Schilling. I got "Major Tom" on MTV. Mike Bone, who was our head of promotion, said, "Hey, Sloane. You got Schilling into heavy rotation? Let's go." And he walked me down 52nd Street to a lingerie shop. He said, "Buy whatever you want." And I ended up with $500 of lingerie. That was the record biz.

THOMAS DOLBY: Because of the excitement around MTV, I wrote a storyboard for "She Blinded Me with Science" before I wrote the song. I also persuaded the label to let me direct it. I fancied myself a filmmaker; I specialized in splicing together discontinuous bits of film.

I was never going to be Simon Le Bon or Adam Ant. I needed a persona, and it wasn't a stretch to portray a young scientist. I was involved in synths and technology. My underdog persona was like the slight guy from silent films who wins the girl. I wanted a Japanese girl in the video, so I came up with the "good heavens, Miss Sakamoto" lyric. I was boldly ahead of the times in fetishizing Asian women.

My dad, a professor of classical archaeology at Oxford University, was one of the scientists in the video. And we had Dr. Magnus Pyke, a famous British TV personality and a bona fide scientist. When I saw him a few years later, he cursed me, because in America, people would walk up behind him in the street and shout, "Science!" He was a man of accomplishment, and he was annoyed by that.

DAVE STEWART: When we made "Love Is a Stranger," we hardly had any money. We had enough to hire a very plush car, and I was Annie's chauffeur. The apartment in the video is actually my mother's. Annie played a call girl calling on a client, but there was something very dark and sinister underneath. At the end she ripped off her wig and she had greased back hair. She looked like Mick Jagger in *Performance*.

JON ROSEMAN: In America, there was a huge furor. Everyone thought Annie was a transvestite.

BOY GEORGE: I can't imagine what people must have thought when they first saw me in America; it must have been mind-blowing. When we first went to the MTV offices, the VJs had really long hair, and not like how I had long hair. More like "rock n' roll" hair. Lots of perms. And they wore wide-collar jackets. Americans seemed quite '70s to me. One thing that really alarmed people about me was that they realized it wasn't a costume. It might have been for other artists, but that was how I lived 24/7. In fact, the look I had in Culture Club was toned down from what I normally wore.

Our early videos certainly didn't relate to the tunes, which tended to be love songs. Julien Temple was quite a well-known director, and we let him take control. The concept for "Do You Really Want to Hurt Me," if there was one, revolved around me as an outcast, being ejected from various, incongruous places throughout the twentieth century: the Gargoyle Club in the '30s, a swimming pool in the '50s. It played on the idea of me as an outsider, someone who wasn't part of normal society. There's a chorus of jurors in a jury box, and we had them done up in blackface. In the UK at that time, blackface was completely acceptable. Al Jolson–style entertainers like that were part of our "music hall" tradition. But in America, people got really upset. We didn't know it was a faux pas.

JULIEN TEMPLE: The popularity and hypocrisy of blackface had always fascinated me. During the early '60s, British TV programmers would air minstrel shows as primetime family entertainment while professing to be winning the battle against racism. "Do You Really Want to Hurt Me?" was about being gay and being victimized for your sexuality, which George was kind of emblematic of. It seemed appropriate to me that in the video he would be judged by jurors in blackface, to send up bigotry and point out the hypocrisy of the many gay judges and politicians in the UK who'd enacted anti-gay legislation.

HARVEY LEEDS, record executive: When I played the "Do You Really Want to Hurt Me?" video for people, they'd say, "Man, she's really ugly."

HUEY LEWIS: I went to Les Garland's office and he played me "Do You Really Want to Hurt Me." Everyone thought it was a chick. He said, "You believe this shit? It's gonna be huge."

BOY GEORGE: "Do You Really Want to Hurt Me" was prophetic; one of the first images people saw of me was that video, where I'm dragged away from a courtroom. I started my career in court, and also ended my career in court.

SIOBHAN BARRON: Boy George rang up and wanted my brother Steve or Julien Temple to do the video for "I'll Tumble 4 Ya." I told him that neither was available. And George called me a cunt. I'm still friends with him. He and [Culture Club drummer] Jon Moss, though, they'd fight all the time. They never came out of their dressing room until evening time. On one video shoot George stuck a hat pin through Jon's hand.

LOL CREME: Sting was a cocky bugger. On the very first video, he said, "Just keep the camera on the money," and pointed to himself. And we did. We're no fools.

ANDY SUMMERS, the Police: We made "Synchronicity II" on the outskirts of London. We had to wake up very early to get there, and we wore these kind of *Blade Runner* outfits. Godley and Creme had built a huge set with three scaffolding towers and gangplanks between them. The towers were way up in the air, probably twenty-five to thirty feet up, and we had to climb up with our instruments. Below, they'd created a sort of wasteland of debris, like cardboard boxes and stuff you'd find at a dump. And of course they had giant fans blowing dry ice every-where. Well, after several takes, the air in the room became extremely dry, and this fake wasteland spontaneously combusted and set Stewart's tower on fire.

LOL CREME: The fire alarm went off and the people on the stage started saying, "Clear everybody off the set." We said to the DP, "Keep rolling, *keep rolling.*"

STEWART COPELAND: There was a moment where I felt like King Kong, I was banging away on my thirty-foot-high pile of drums. I thought, *I'm stealing the video here.* You live and learn. The song isn't about King Kong climbing around a drum set. It's about a dragon and Loch Ness and Karl Jung.

LOL CREME: Sting was hanging from a rope, swinging like Tarzan, and he fell off. *Whoops, where's the star?*

STEWART COPELAND: My particular role was undignified. What's the drummer going to do? You jig along in time to the music, or else you try to look snarly and handsome. When the chorus comes along, you pretend to sing along even though you don't actually sing the chorus on the record. I felt like a dick.

LOL CREME: The first time I met Sting at his house, to discuss the video, he answered the door dressed up as Hamlet or something, and he'd been practic-ing in front of a mirror. We knew he'd be up for performing.

ANDY SUMMERS: Godley and Creme rocked. Those guys had an amazing part-nership. They both could draw incredibly well. They were both major dope smokers, too. They smoked a lot of fucking reefer.

KEVIN GODLEY: Most of the time, Lol Creme and I were stoned out of our minds. The first thing we'd do when we arrived on set was roll a reefer.

ANDY SUMMERS: "Every Breath You Take" is a complete rip of a much better 1944 film of jazz musicians made by a great Albanian photographer named Gjon Mili. Jeff Ayeroff showed us this film, and Godley and Creme basically copied it. But it certainly wasn't as good as the Gijon Mili one, which was much more artistic and a lot hipper. It's all these jazz giants—Lester Young, Jo Jones, Illinois Jacquet—playing in a nightclub with swirls of cigarette smoke, and it's a beautiful little five-minute film. Ours was a slightly watered down version, but of course very few people saw the original. A lot of people think ours is fantastic, but to me it's just okay.

RICHARD MARX: The first video I watched over and over was "Every Breath You Take." It was like seeing a Bergman film. Directors usually spelled out every word of the lyric in a video, but this was the first video I knew that didn't do that. It was abstract.

TIM NEWMAN: I admired Godley and Creme the most. I was a huge fan. Their ideas were amazingly original.

ANDY SUMMERS: I never much liked the idea for "Wrapped Around Your Finger." No, I was kind of pissed off about that one. I've never been much of a fan of that song, actually. Sting got to shoot his part last in that video and made a meal of knocking all the candles out. Fuck him.

WAYNE ISAAK, record executive: Sting was nervous for his closeup. He felt like he needed a couple of vodkas before his last take. I was in the greenroom, he did some shots and then did that scene where he runs through the candles.

DANIEL PEARL: The producer had rounded up thousands of candles and was nervous about how to set them up. She called Godley and Creme, who were still in England, and said, "You have to send me a diagram." So they faxed over a diagram, and—this was Godley and Creme's sense of humor—it was simply a drawing of one candle.

WAYNE ISHAM: When Godley and Creme made the Police's "Wrapped Around Your Finger" on the A&M lot, I was the electrician. This guy named Ron Volz, in the art department, he ran around with a torch and lit all those candles. And when they got knocked down, we set 'em back up. I was the guy who ended up scraping all the wax off the floor the next day. That was *my* gig.

DANIEL PEARL: After that video came out, I saw Sting in Los Angeles and he thanked me for how fantastic he looked.

KEVIN GODLEY: As they say, the camera loved him. Sting was very filmable, at any angle; slightly sinister, heavy on the cheekbones.

WAYNE ISAAK: Sting wouldn't be where he is, or where he was back then, without ambition. The Police were even competitive among themselves. Stewart and Sting fought like brothers on half of those videos.

ANDY SUMMERS: We dominated MTV that year. On the one hand you think, *This is pretty cool,* and the other you think, *This is bullshit.* Our music had sort of erroneously become extremely commercial. We looked right, we had the right songs—MTV was a perfect hookup for us. The band was a huge success. Everybody won. Everyone was making money.

JEFF AYEROFF: "Every Breath You Take" probably cost $75,000 to $100,000, and we sold over 5 million albums. With a good video, the return on your investment was phenomenal.

STEWART COPELAND: We joyfully exploited each other all the way to the bank.

ANDY SUMMERS: I don't like any of our videos. We were always made to look bright and inoffensive and appealing. As videos progressed, they started to move away from that: they got hipper, people started using Super 8 and handheld techniques, and everything got darker and more interesting. As a total film buff, I regret that we weren't around ten years later to make those kind of videos.

BOY GEORGE: I never liked any of our videos. They weren't glamorous or outrageous enough. Directors, management, and record labels wanted to make me look as normal as possible, whereas I would have preferred to have gone much, much further. When we did the "Karma Chameleon" video, out on a riverboat, I had the most amazing makeup and they made me look like I had none on. The lighting was really shit, and it was a miserable, gray English day. I thought, *I spent all morning getting ready and I look like this? What a waste of time.*

HOWARD JONES: Rock n' roll was a macho affair in the '70s. And us lot came along with brightly colored clothes and the haircuts. It was a real affront to the establishment. It rubbed so many people the wrong way. That whole explosion of MTV was quite significant in the sense that it gave the finger to rock n' roll.

MARTIN FRY: In the early '80s, a bunch of people imagined a world they wanted to live in. It was a more multiracial world, a less homophobic world. And it was a much more interesting world than the suburb where you lived. All those video clips were aspirational, you know. They're people's dreams. In a way, those dreams did come true, years later.

Chapter 10

"SHUT THAT DOOR!"

OFFICE SEX AND POWER STRUGGLES AT MTV

"WE WERE THE MEDIA OUTLAWS OF OUR TIME," John Lack says of MTV's original staff. "There was sex, drugs, and rock n' roll. We were creating new worlds. And when you're pioneers, half the world is going to think you're awful, and the other half can't get enough." There was a definite disparity among the MTV team—they looked like yuppies but partied like college freshmen. The biggest rock star on staff was Les Garland, an optimistic, amiable guy who seemed to know everyone in the music biz yet still hung out with interns.

LES GARLAND: We were approaching our first anniversary in the summer of '82. People had been working eighteen-hour days. Everyone was burned out. I went to corporate and told them we needed to have a major blowout for the staff. They said, "It wouldn't look good. We've spent too much money this year." I was pissed. So I called the department heads into my office. Because I didn't want Pittman to find out, I said, "This meeting never took place. If any of you ever say it did, you'll be accused of being a liar. We need to quietly organize a big blowout for the staff. And where the money comes from, I never need to know."

I decided the theme of the party should be gambling. If you won a certain amount of fake money—which, unbeknownst to me, became "Les Bucks," with my picture on it—you could buy one of the prizes, which were left over from giveaways and contests. We had a TV, I think we even had a motorcycle. There was a stage, where people could get up and jam, and a casino. The party was raging.

JOE DAVOLA, MTV producer: Les was basically saying *Fuck you* to Pittman by having this party. And it made him a hero to the staff.

ROBERTA CRUGER, MTV executive: We all overindulged that night. Gale and I got up onstage and did cheers for MTV: "Give me an *M*, give me a *T*, give me a *V*." We were acting like jackasses.

LES GARLAND: Around midnight, people were demanding a speech from me. I did a pretty good Bob Pittman imitation, so I got onstage and started talking like Pittman, and when I looked stage left, there was Pittman. I could not fucking believe it. I wrapped up within seconds and left. Because this could be trouble. I'd had some tequila, and this was not the time for a confrontation.

GALE SPARROW: Les was onstage when Bob walked in. Les said to me, "Hey, Bud, if we don't make it through this, we'll just start another channel." We all thought we'd be fired. I called Les the next day and said, "It's been nice working with you."

LES GARLAND: At 10 A.M., Dwight Tierney, the HR guy, phoned my office. I said, "Good morning, Dwight. Do I need my attorney?" He said, "We have one issue here: the prizes. Tell me where the prizes came from, because they have value and we can't be giving $25,000 motorcycles to people." So I told him. And he said, "There won't be another word about this. Happy birthday."

GALE SPARROW: Les was a great boss. Whenever we had a meeting with him, everybody felt good when they left, even though we were working around the clock and were completely burned out.

LES GARLAND: We were all kind of famous for not sleeping much. I'd be out until four or five in the morning, sideways from tequila, and I was in the office the next morning sending out memos at 9 A.M. I was pretty famous for my stamina. They were like, "How the fuck does he do that?" I tell people to this day, I invented tequila. I'm the guy that brought it into the rock n' roll business. I wasn't afraid to go rippin' and roarin'.

BOB PITTMAN: Les thought big and moved fast. He was one of the most creative people on our team. But Les was not very organized. At one point, Les became a senior vice president with no one reporting to him. But that turned out to be the right use of him.

MILES COPELAND: Les Garland talked a mile a minute. You were never sure which, ahem, "substance" was inspiring his volubility.

ALLEN NEWMAN, MTV staff: Rick Krim and I were referred to as "Garland's Boys." And although Garland was absolutely the poster child for *party*, it never took place in the office. I did something stupid—there were some illegal substances that showed up in the office—and I was absolutely reprimanded. Garland said, "You're young and stupid, and we're gonna give you a second chance. Don't do it again."

HARVEY LEEDS: Besides golf, the thing Les loved most was smoking dope. He'd call me in the middle of the day and say, "Hey, Bud, come on, let's go wash my car." We'd get in his car, drive up the West Side, smoke dope, and go to the car wash. It was great for me, because I'd have his complete attention for an hour.

STEVE SCHNUR: On my first day as an intern, Les said, "Hey, Bud, what are you doing for dinner tonight?" Two hours ago, I didn't know who this guy was. He said, "You're coming out to dinner with me and some buddies." And that night I found myself having dinner with the New York chapter of the Hell's Angels.

I came in the next morning and there's Garland, looking perfect. No bags under his eyes. That afternoon, he said, "Hey, Bud, we had a good time last night. Come over to my house later." My first impression was *Wait, what kind of creepy situation did I get myself into?* Anyway, I go to his house, and sitting there is the *Penthouse* Pet of the Year. This is unbelievable, right? We're eating this wonderful dinner, Les is chain-smoking and playing one great tune after another. I said, "Garland, I can't believe I'm getting college credit for this."

JOAN MYERS: My primary duty as Les's secretary was to juggle his girlfriends, which was nearly a full-time job in itself. I was the gatekeeper. He dated [actress] Maria Conchita Alonso for a while. One year, he brought her to my Passover Seder.

STEVE SCHNUR: Les never had a problem with the ladies. I'm a heterosexual and I've got to tell you, Les is one of the most handsome human beings I've ever seen.

RONALD "BUZZ" BRINDLE: I joined MTV as director of music-video programming. One year on Les's birthday, we were in a meeting and there was a knock on the door. Les's secretary brings in this woman in a gray business suit, carrying a boom box. She plays the boom box. And then she starts stripping. As she's taking her clothes off, Les starts taking his pants off. Next thing I know, she's topless and bouncing her breasts off my bald pate, while I'm trying to continue the meeting.

STEVE SCHNUR: I'd answer Les's phone, and it would be Huey Lewis or Grace Slick. They would say *hi* and ask for Garland. There were no barriers. We were completely accessible. Most of the programming MTV developed—like the first VMAs, with Madonna coming out of the cake—happened because of our relationships with artists, and that was because we spent time with them. We were fun to hang out with. And a lot of that, if not all of that, had to do with Les Garland.

RONALD "BUZZ" BRINDLE: Les Garland was in Eddie Murphy's hotel room, and he called and told me to play the "Axel F" song, from *Beverly Hills Cop*. I couldn't just throw it on the air. I had to research it—did we play the song fifteen minutes ago? But Les told Eddie he was gonna get it on the air within the next ten minutes, and he wanted it on. I can't say I wasn't annoyed.

MARK PELLINGTON, MTV staff; director: Les was larger than life. He'd walk out of his office with his shirt open and you'd think, "Was Les just fucking that girl in his office? That's a strong possibility."

KEN R. CLARK: There was a big MTV executive whose office was next to the VJ lounge. Missing Persons were in the building one day, and our studio manager walked to the VJ lounge and saw something he shouldn't have seen: Dale Bozzio fellating the MTV executive. The executive bellowed, "Shut that door!" I did not see this, but *everybody* talked about it.

BETH McCARTHY, MTV producer: I saw that. Mark Goodman asked me to go to his dressing room to get some notes for him—I was the assistant to the line producer, so I would do errands for the VJs. I ran to his dressing room, opened the door, and, um, Les was getting a blow job from Dale Bozzio. I saw this out of the corner of my eye and closed the door very quickly.

ALLEN NEWMAN: I can confirm that story—it happened in my office. I couldn't understand why the door was locked. I found out once I unlocked the door and went inside. Garland didn't even have permission to use my office.

DALE BOZZIO, Missing Persons: I don't have any comment. I appreciate your time, but I'm not interested in being interviewed, okay? I'd rather have nothing to say.

LES GARLAND: Dale Bozzio was one of the most beautiful women I ever saw. Very erotic. She was a dear friend, and, of course, Missing Persons were huge on MTV. But I never had sex with her in the MTV offices. Absolutely never.

ARNOLD STIEFEL, manager: One time Les Garland called me and said, "You've got to come over. I'm in a bungalow at the Beverly Hills Hotel. You're not going to believe this. I've got a hooker here. She can shoot six Ping-Pong balls out of her twat. I catch them in the trash can. Come over now." I swear.

STEVE SCHNUR: Through Garland, I became friendly with Rod Stewart. This was a typical night: I'm lying in bed at one, two in the morning, the phone would ring, and it'd be Garland: "Schnur!"—he always called me by my last name—"Schnur! What are you doing?" "I'm sleeping." "Rod and I are hanging, come on out! And pick up some cigarettes on the way." So I'd get my ass out of bed, go to the club or the bar, and there was Rod and Garland. Les would say, "Rod, you know Schnur, right?" And I'd met Rod a hundred times before. He goes, "Yeah, Schnur." See, Rod began to think that Schnur was my title and not my name. He though a "schnur" was someone you could call at one in the morning to grab cigarettes and show up at a club. One night we were all out and Rod turned to Les and said, "Garland, I've got to get me one of these schnurs."

LES GARLAND: One night, Rod and I went to the River Café in Brooklyn. It was the two of us, Rod's manager Randy Phillips, and four lovely ladies. We get there and we're feeling pretty good. It's Christmastime, everything's festive, everybody's tipsy, and Rod announces that we should play Truth or Dare. He says, "There are a couple of rules. You can only take two truths and you must take a dare. Also, there's another thing. We have to play with our pants down. And mine are already down." Rod was wearing a beautiful Versace suit. The lady sitting next to him reaches over and touches his leg and sure enough, she nods and say, "His pants are down." And next thing you know, we're all dropping our trousers down around our ankles. There was a tablecloth, so nobody in the restaurant knew we're sitting there with our pants down. It's kind of stupid, right?

One of the ladies would say "Truth," and Rod would ask, "Did you ever have sex in the backseat of a car?" Pretty soon, someone dared one of the ladies to ask the waiter where the ladies' room is, then grab his groin and walk off to the bathroom. And she did it. The waiter didn't know whether to laugh or cry. Pretty soon it comes around to the lady who was wearing a low-cut dress. She had a nice figure. Rod says to her, "I dare you to drop your dress straps and take your breasts out until the count of three." Boom, she does it. One, two, three. And she puts herself back together and the game goes on. Pretty soon, it was Rod's turn. There was a couple there who'd been gawking at him, checking him out, so someone dared Rod to go over there and say to the guy, "May I kiss your girlfriend?" He pulls his trousers up, goes over—a perfect gentleman—and the next thing you know, he bends her back like out of a 1940s romance film, sticks his tongue down her throat, and gives her a big kiss.

So now it comes around to the lady who had to drop her top, and she's gonna get even with Rod. She says, "Rod, do you have your trousers down?" He says, "I do." She goes, "I dare you to stand up and salute the Statue of Liberty." You can see the statue right outside the restaurant window. And damned if he didn't do it. By now, the game's been going on for a while. We're eating, champagne's flowing, tequila's flowing. We're not out of control, but we're close. Rod turns to me and goes, "I dare you to get up with your pants down, waddle over to the bar, get a shot of tequila, slam it down, and come back to the table."

RANDY PHILLIPS: Rod dared Les to take his pants down and walk around the restaurant with his "knob" showing. And Les did it. It just goes to show you, with Les Garland, there's no job too big—or in this case, too small—to keep an artist happy.

LES GARLAND: No one had refused a challenge dare yet, and I wasn't going to be the first. I stood up, waddled across the restaurant, walked up to the bar, ordered a shot of tequila, slammed it down, came back to the table, and sat down. The owner came over and said, "Gentlemen, this party's over." So we paid the check and left. I couldn't believe we got to stay as long as we did.

MARK GOODMAN: Garland and Sykes were living the life people thought *we* were living. We'd be in the studio at eight or nine in the morning, shooting, and

Garland would show up after having been out all night. "I was just out partying with Keith Richards." *That's great. I was in bed at eleven.*

STEVE BACKER, record executive: The greatest job ever invented was doing talent relations for MTV from 1981 to 1992.

JUDY McGRATH: The music department—Les Garland, Gale Sparrow, Roberta Cruger—they were the gods of the place.

TOM FRESTON: Gale Sparrow personified the spirit of MTV. She loved rock n' roll, she loved to party, she knew everybody. We would all get drunk at lunch, stagger back to work, sleep in the office, start drinking again later, then go out together at night. Sex, drugs, drinking—all that stuff was very much part of the company culture.

JOE DAVOLA: We worked a lot of hours, but we partied a lot, too. Gale Sparrow had an expense account, and she'd take us around the corner to Cafe Un Deux Trois. We used to shut that place down.

DEBBIE NEWMAN: I love Gale, but she's a complete lush.

JEANNE MATTIUSSI: Gale and I drank Sambuca on my expense account until we were sick. We also drank our fair share of champagne. And we enjoyed a good bottle of wine.

JUDY McGRATH: I'd be the first one in the office, and sometimes Gale was still there from the night before. She may have rested there overnight, shall we say.

JORDAN ROST: No matter how drunk and stoned you were at four in the morning, no one cared. But if you used that as an excuse not to show up at the 9 A.M. meeting, you lost a ton of points.

JOE DAVOLA: In the '80s, music companies had parties every night. We weren't getting paid a lot of money, but we were always able to go to a concert, and to eat and drink for free.

LES GARLAND: We were a bunch of fucking crazy misfits, but we loved each other. We looked out for one another.

RICHARD SCHENKMAN: MTV was like that scene in *Close Encounters of the Third Kind* where all those people are drawn together because they've all seen Devils Tower.

LES GARLAND: Bob and I both suffered eye injuries when we were young. So that became kind of a joke. "Pittman, between the two of us, we have two good eyes."

ALLEN NEWMAN: Have you heard the expression, "Bob Pittman—two t's, one eye"?

JOAN MYERS: When Les was a child, he was in an accident and lost the vision in one eye. They told him someday he might have to have it replaced. That day came when he was golfing in Hawaii. He had to take an emergency flight back to New York to have a glass eye put in.

HARVEY LEEDS: We all joked, "You'll do anything to suck up to Pittman. You'll even poke your fucking eye out."

ALLEN NEWMAN: I was up at Garland's apartment, watching Sunday football, and he calls me into the kitchen. He takes out the biggest knife in his drawer and sticks the knife in his eye. *Clink, clink, clink.* And he goes, "Bud, glass eye." I didn't know until he did that.

BOB PITTMAN: Les and Sykes managed relationships with the music industry. The wild and crazy ones dealt with Les, and the businesslike and analytical ones dealt with Sykes.

ABBEY KONOWITCH, record executive; MTV executive: John Sykes knew how to build relationships with artists. He was slick, and he got the Rolling Stones and Billy Idol and Tom Petty to do things for free, for a network that barely existed. He was great at getting artists to believe in the dream, and he executed his promotions so brilliantly that artists would say thank you to *him* when they were over.

FRED SEIBERT: John ran all our contests. As a kid growing up in Schenectady, New York, John entered *every* contest. He told us, "You know what the problem was? I never won anything." And so Marcy Brafman very smartly came up with the marketing proposition, "People Really Win on MTV." We determined that whenever we ran a contest, we would follow around the winner. Our first contest, "One Night Stand with Journey," was won by a Margaret Doebler. She was a typical older teenager—a little chunky, a little middle-American, with permed blond hair—and when we followed Margaret around, we proved the proposition: "People Really Win on MTV."

When we launched, we said we were in 3 million homes. We were not. We were only in a half million homes for at least the first few months. When we ran the Journey contest, we didn't know what to expect. When we counted the number of postcards, we had ninety thousand. That's when we knew we were good to go.

JOHN SYKES: For "One Night Stand with Journey," I wanted to put together the dream rock n' roll trip: We'd fly a fan anywhere in the world, they'd go backstage, hang with the group, fly home that night, and be in school or at work the next day. It was a fantasy, the ultimate one-night stand. Double meaning. And Bob loved planes. He said, "My friend Artie has a Learjet at Republic Airport on Long Island," so we went to Artie and leased his Learjet.

We wanted to make it look like it was *our* Learjet, so Fred made up a piece of Mylar with an MTV logo, and I taped it to the outside of the plane's door. The pilot said, "You know, that Mylar could get sucked into the engine and we could all die. You've got to take it off." So the camera shot the plane taxiing away, and once we got out of the camera range, the pilot stopped, opened the plane door, and we removed the Mylar logo. Then we'd land to pick up the contest winner, stop before the end of the runway, where like the local townspeople were waiting with their cameras, tape the Mylar back up, and taxi into view in the MTV Learjet.

ROBERT MORTON: John was a great hustler. We'd always say, "Oh fuck, Sykes has another contest." But years later, the business is now all about integration and contests, and doing things that cross over from the show to the Web. Sykes was aware of all that stuff early on.

CURT SMITH: Here's the thing about John Sykes: He's impossible to dislike. My wife and I were at his wedding in the Hamptons, at [*Rolling Stone* editor and publisher] Jann Wenner's house. MTV did a good job of hiring people who could meet, mingle, and be liked by everyone. Artists would do things for MTV they wouldn't normally do for other people, because you don't want to say *no* to your friends.

MICHAEL STIPE: John and I are still friends.

TOMMY MOTTOLA: Sykes was the ultimate promotion man, a royal pain in the ass who would not leave you alone until you finally gave in. He would call me relentlessly, twenty times, until I said either *yes* or *yes*.

JOHN SYKES: I made sure the trains ran on time. Les could go toe to toe with artists. But Bob was the genius strategist. One of the record company executives called him "the guy with the ten-thousand-pound brain."

JUDY McGRATH: Bob Pittman was very confident that MTV was going to be big, in spite of all evidence to the contrary. He made you want to paint the fence for him. He had the true sense of what this thing was going to be, and nothing was going to get in his way.

BOB PITTMAN: I was wildly passionate and naturally argumentative *and* incredibly inflexible. I was the programmer. I got to make the choices.

CHARLIE WARNER: If you talk with people who worked for Bob, you will find that some found him aloof, arrogant, and overly ambitious. The majority of them adore him.

MARCY BRAFMAN: I love Bob. I don't know that everyone says that.

ALLEN NEWMAN: The directors who were working for MTV went out on strike, because they wanted to join the Directors Guild of America. I got called into Bob Pittman's office, and he told me my new job was to run the studio while our directors were out striking. He doubled my salary from $11,500 to $25,000 a year. It was the first time I'd ever sat in the director's chair, and I had to learn on the fly. I was basically a scab, but I was a scab who had just doubled his salary, from the man himself.

FRED SEIBERT: Bob wanted the final word on everything. And when it came time for the credit, he would assume it as the biggest guy in the room: "Everything that happens under me is mine." The thing that drove me crazy about Bob was that when awards were handed out on a specific piece of work, he would collect it, rather than let the person who did the work collect it.

He had an incredible ability to drive you crazy on a project, but he knew when to back off. John Lack didn't always know how to do that. John would do things like mess with a typeface. Bob didn't know what a typeface was and didn't care. But that was John, all the way. I felt he was ultimately disrespectful to creative people.

SUE STEINBERG: John Lack was Batman and Bob Pittman was Robin. And ultimately, Bob became Batman.

JOHN LACK: Look, John Sykes will say he was the father of MTV. Bob Pittman will say he was. They're all saying it.

TOM FRESTON: Bob was the young star, he was the guy the press was attracted to. How could somebody that young be so articulate, smart, and committed? So Bob got a lot of ink, and that created dislocation and envy. I don't know for sure that John Lack felt that way, but he could rightly say that he was the father of MTV—it was his idea, he put the team together, he sold it to the board—yet the credit was evading his grasp. It was accruing to Bob. Bob would say, "I never took credit for having the idea, but I did make it happen." And in a way, Bob was right. Bob *did* lead the creative process for what MTV became. But *conceptually,* it was John who had the idea to do it.

BOB PITTMAN: John Lack fell out of favor with the board of directors. We'd projected $10 million in ad revenue, and we'd done $500,000. The ad agencies would buy national programming only when it had a two-thirds reach of the country and a 3.0 rating. Cable networks don't even have that today. The board began to get nervous. It all got crazy, at which point I came close to leaving. Barry Diller, the CEO of Paramount, was wooing me to leave MTV. David Geffen tried to hire me to become president of the Geffen Company.

An old-line Hollywood film producer named Marty Ransohoff said, "Why should *you* have to leave? MTV's *your* idea. *You're* the one doing it. If you have a fight, *you* don't have to leave." So I stuck it out.

Drew Lewis, who'd been President Reagan's secretary of transportation and was famous for firing all the air traffic controllers, came in as chairman and CEO of Warner Amex Cable Communications [in February 1983]. Drew pulled me aside and said, "Look, you're gonna take over MTV eventually. But only if you fix this thing. And if you can't get us to break even by the end of the year, we're shutting it down."

TOM FRESTON: He'd fired the air traffic controllers. He would have had no problem firing forty hippies who were working out of some dump.

JOHN SYKES: Those were bumpy times for MTV. Drew Lewis was really pressing us to cut costs. Cable was a more expensive business than anyone at Warner Amex had anticipated. It was expensive to wire neighborhoods. And we were still just getting going. The buzz was getting bigger and bigger, but the cash wasn't coming in like it did later. We were very much the Facebook of our time. Every kid loved us, but the financial model wasn't quite working yet.

JOHN LACK: Jack Schneider came into my office one day and said, "John, we're consolidating. There's only room for one of us and it ain't gonna be you." So I left MTV towards the end of '83. The Movie Channel had just about gotten to break-even. MTV wasn't making money. Steve Ross said, "We're spending millions. We can't do this shit anymore." They paid me big dough to go away, paid me for the three years left on my contract. I exercised all my stock options. I was richer than I should have been at thirty-five years old, so I wasn't too upset with Jack. When you're playing in big-boy land, the air gets kind of thin at the top. I learned that you can't stay too long at the party when the party's over for you. And a year later, Schneider got fired. When I left, Schneider promoted Pittman to take over some of my functions; he didn't give him Nickelodeon to program, but he made him executive vice president of MTV and The Movie Channel. Now, Bob Pittman was the smartest guy I ever met. He believed MTV was his dream, too. Unfortunately, he tried to make it his own dream by taking credit for it when I left. The world finally said, "Bob, weren't you an employee hired to do this?" If I was the architect, he was the general contractor.

JACK SCHNEIDER: John Lack was an enormous disappointment. I was very disappointed in his conduct and development. He wasn't a good executive. I think John has always represented himself as being a bigger player in this than he was.

JOHN LACK: When I left, Bob did an even better job than I did, but he didn't invent the thing. He was great at implementing the vision. But it wasn't his vision. After I left, he took the vision and went left and right with it, God bless. That's what all good executives do. But he was married to a strange, upwardly-mobile lady by the name of Sandy. A famous, controversial character. She was obsessed with building his image as a media giant. They lived above their means in an apartment they couldn't afford. She was a social climber. They're long divorced now.

CHARLIE WARNER: A lot of people expected, when somebody did a story about MTV, for Bob to say, "Well, it wasn't my idea, it was John Lack's idea and he gets all the credit for hiring me." And when he didn't, people were angry at him. But that's the game. That's how you get ahead.

ANDY SETOS: Bob tried to climb over everyone to the top, even though he was but one of the people who contributed to the enterprise. He took credit for everyone else's work. And that put a bad taste in people's mouths. People were grumbling about Bob as early as 1982.

JORDAN ROST: It's disgusting that anyone would take credit away from John Lack. It shouldn't be a controversy. I was in the room after we got an okay from the board, and Schneider said to Lack, "You're in charge. You've gotta make this happen." But Bob was very savvy in working with the press and managing his career. When people interviewed him and attributed him as the creator, he let it lie. He never dissuaded anyone or said, "No, you got that wrong." Silence can be telling.

CAROLYN BAKER: MTV was John Lack's idea. He hired Bob Pittman. But there is no way this would have been achieved without Bob. He had that killer instinct. Nobody worked harder than Bob. He worked so hard that I thought he was going to drop dead.

STEVE LEEDS: John Lack is the unsung hero. Most people go, "Oh, it's Bob Pittman." No, it's John Lack and Michael Nesmith.

MICHAEL NESMITH: The word *invent*, it's inapt. There's not one moment where you flip the switch and it starts running. It's a gradual coalescence of different things, a confluence of energies. It's one of those ideas that nobody really thinks up. It's like justice. Or kindness. Nobody thinks that up.

Chapter 11

"THEY FIGURED OUT
A WHOLE NEW PERSONA"

HOW THREE GNARLY OLD DUDES
BECAME UNLIKELY VIDEO STARS

NOT EVERY STAR ON MTV WAS BEAUTIFUL, OR EVEN young. When ZZ Top released *Eliminator* in 1983, the three band members were a combined ninety-nine years old. They'd been recording since 1971 and, in the course of seven albums, had built a sturdy career as a touring band, mostly in the Midwest and South. Texans who wore cowboy hats, boots, and jeans—two of whom had grown long beards—they were unlikely video stars. But these shit-kickers were not stodgy (singer Billy Gibbons adored Depeche Mode), and *Eliminator* suddenly propelled them to pop stardom, selling 10 million albums, as director Tim Newman paired their deadpan cool with much-younger women in sheer clothing. ZZ Top's success cemented the video meme of shapely females used as decoration.

Newman, whose family was a Hollywood dynasty, and who'd come to music videos from the world of commercial directing, became baffled by the economics of videos. A smart director could make a band rich—why shouldn't the director get rich, too? The story of what happened after *Eliminator*, and how Newman was replaced as director without the band's knowledge, illustrates the struggles that continuously emerged between bands, directors, and record companies—usually over money.

TIM NEWMAN: I met a girl who was dating Jerry Casale from Devo, and she had a VHS tape of her favorite videos, including Devo and Duran Duran. I was a very successful commercial director, and when I saw "Girls on Film," I thought,

I would like to do this. For someone who did ads for airlines and detergent and cereal, this looked like a lot more fun.

I come from a musical family: My father Alfred and uncle Lionel were screen composers, and heads of the music department at 20th Century Fox, and my cousin is Randy Newman, who had signed at Warner Bros. Records. So I called Lenny Waronker, the president of Warner Bros. Records, and said, "What's this music-video deal?" Lenny had been friends with Randy since they were boys.

Jo Bergman at Warners said, "You direct commercials, and we don't spend much money on these things—maybe $50,000." Even in those days, that was hardly any money. But I got a call to do the video for my cousin Randy's song "I Love L.A." We did a day of camera-car work and I wanted to do a lot more. It turned out to be about as much fun as I had ever had filming, probably to this day.

JO BERGMAN: "I Love L.A." became a classic video, so we had Tim direct ZZ Top's "Gimme All Your Lovin'." He was responsible for reinventing the band. That key chain? The girls? That was Tim. On the day of the shoot, their manager was looking at the models, who were neither made up nor in costume, and he said, "I don't think these are the right girls. They're not sexy enough." When they came out of the trailer all dolled up, there were smiles everywhere.

TIM NEWMAN: The creative brief from ZZ Top's manager, Bill Ham, who was kind of a Svengali type, was "Use the car and put some girls in it." *Yeah, I can work with that.* By then, music video was on everybody's lips—there was a cover story in *Time* magazine.

BILLY GIBBONS: Tim was the hands-down favorite, because his reel showed commercials he had done for Coca-Cola. If you can do it in thirty seconds, then three minutes is an epic tale. Many of the same elements—cars, pretty girls—felt right for what ZZ Top is: loud, raucous, a good time.

TOM PETTY: ZZ Top were brilliant at transitioning into the MTV era. They figured out a whole new persona.

BILLY GIBBONS: Let me brag on Tim, because directors are rarely credited in the public's perception. When we speak of the early days, support from the label was scant. Tim said, "If we do this as a union shoot, we'll chew up the budget in the first hour." To avoid falling into the union's hands, we started at 6 P.M. on a Friday, when union hours close, and that gave us until Sunday at 6 P.M. We drove to Palmdale, California, in the high desert, and there was a stretch of road with an abandoned gas station. It was freezing cold. Tim assigned three guys to hold big Mexican blankets to wrap the girls up, because they were so scantily clad.

The little red car was a 1933 Ford three-window coupe. I bought it in 1976, and it had only just come off the finishing line in 1983. When the car was finally completed, there was an outstanding balance, which I didn't have. All told, the coupe cost well over $250,000. I was in debt, but my accountant said if I used the car as a business expense, I would get a tax deduction. So it became the focus of the *Eliminator* album cover. On the day the shoot took place, I was able to go to the bank and borrow the money I owed to pay off the car. Not only did the car become a celebrity, thanks to Tim placing it front and center in the videos, it was a milestone vehicle in the hot-rodding world.

When I saw the girls Tim picked, I said, "Gosh, you've got the eye." And he said, "Yeah, I've also got the *Playboy* modeling booklet." There was Daniele Arnaud—she was French and could barely speak English—Jeana Tomasina, and a third girl who mysteriously disappeared. She never came to collect her money. It was just weird.

DANIELE ARNAUD, model: I was born in Nice, in the south of France, and I didn't know ZZ Top. I'm the blonde one who shows the garters. I come out of the car, put my leg up on the hood, and I put my money in the garter.

JEANA TOMASINA KEOUGH, model: People recognize me now only if they know me from *The Real Housewives of Orange County*. I'm the only brunette in "Gimme All Your Lovin'." When Tim asked me, I said *no*. It was against the union—the Screen Actors Guild and AFTRA—to do those things, because videos didn't pay residuals. And I'd never heard of the band. All their songs sounded alike to me. Not paying attention to music hurt me a lot, because when I had a chance to audition for a guy named Prince in Minneapolis, for *Purple Rain*, I refused to go. I said, "There's no prince in Minneapolis, they must think I'm stupid."

TIM NEWMAN: Even though ZZ Top look wild, they're not crazy guys. I was thinking, *What the fuck am I going to do with these guys?* The song seemed to be about a horny, yearning kid. So I had the idea to base it around a guy who worked at a gas station in the middle of nowhere. I would not be making a huge demand on ZZ Top's acting ability if I cast them in the role of mythological characters. If you've read Joseph Campbell, you know there are classic mythological themes in our culture, and the details change but the story remains the same.

JEFF AYEROFF: After "Gimme All Your Lovin'," people said, "Yeah, that video's great. But we're not doing another one." I'd just gotten to Warners, and I said, "Not only are we doing another video, we're gonna do the same video! And we're gonna spend more money, and it's gonna be even better."

TIM NEWMAN: When they asked me to do another one, the idea that you would do a sequel in a form that isn't even a form struck me as funny, in a very insidery way. The intention was to keep everything the same: same three guys, same car, same key chain.

BILLY GIBBONS: The continuity was steadfast. There were so many lucky moments—at the end of "Sharp Dressed Man," when the cars are racing into the heat waves, a tiny bunny rabbit came and sat down in the middle of the road, watching the car leave.

DANIELE ARNAUD: In "Sharp Dressed Man," we had to show ourselves off to the camera, almost like in those nightclubs where women try to get money from the men.

TIM NEWMAN: For "Sharp Dressed Man," Warner Bros. had made a deal for product placement. Not openly, because MTV was against that. Schlitz, I think it was, offered to put up a bunch of money and my job was to figure out how to work Schlitz into the video. When MTV saw it, they said, "You've got to take that shot out." Now the label is mad at me because they're not going to get money from the brewery. It left a bad taste in my mouth, so I said, "Fuck you, I'm not doing this anymore."

The videos made them bigger than life. When we started, they were a hugely successful Midwestern touring band. By the time we were done with those videos, they were international. I was capable of being a loudmouth, and I said, "I would love to have some upside, some form of profit participation—points." Video directors should have had points in those days. Jeff Ayeroff said, "We're going to straighten everything out. We won't give you points"—because that would have been precedent-setting—"but we're going to give you X dollars for every 250,000 albums sold over a certain amount." So we did the "Legs" video and it worked out quite well for me, financially. I said, "Why not make the main character a girl?" and that allowed me to do one more *Eliminator* video. Plus we had the spinning fur guitars. But they're all the same video.

BILLY GIBBONS: Kym Herrin was the tall blonde in "Legs." Kymmy's this groovy hippie chick from Santa Barbara, and I still talk to her quite frequently.

TIM NEWMAN: I dated a girl I cast in "Legs," Wendy Fraser. She's the one with the glasses who's kind of mousy and afraid. She wasn't my girlfriend when I cast her. Look, you spend time with these people. What can I tell you?

When ZZ Top finished their next album, I came in to talk to Jeff Ayeroff about directing a video for "Sleeping Bag." Shortly thereafter, Mo Ostin, who ran Warner Bros. Records, stepped in and rescinded the deal. And I refused to work with ZZ Top. I said, "Fuck it, why do I need this?"

BILLY GIBBONS: I was not part of any decision-making, nor was the band. When we showed up to do "Sleeping Bag," we said, "Where's Tim? Where's Jeana?"

We used to refer to our audience as our "sea of dudes." However, videos made us more acceptable to the females. I still sign autographs for girls who say, "I was just thirteen and I couldn't wait to dress up like the girl in 'Legs.'"

Chapter 12

——————

"GIRLS BELONG IN CAGES"

METAL TAKES OVER THE AIRWAVES

I F YOU WATCHED MTV WITH THE SOUND OFF, YOU MIGHT not have been able to tell the difference between Duran Duran and Def Leppard (except that women in Duran Duran videos weren't in cages). In both cases, a hairdresser and makeup artist were the uncredited video auteurs. MTV didn't play only new wave bands with outrageous style, they also played hard rock bands with outrageous style. Early videos by Twisted Sister, Def Leppard, Ratt, and Mötley Crüe marked the start of MTV's uneasy romance with metal, and initiated the careers of Wayne Isham, the video director who most closely emulated a rock star, and Tawny Kitaen, a self-described "serious actress" who a few years later became the first video star who couldn't sing. "Until then," Kitaen says, "girls weren't the focus of videos—the bands were the focus. I came along and changed all that."

DAVE HOLMES: Videos were very European at first. Then things started to get less Euro and more big-titted and American.

DAVID MALLET: It started with a British sensibility and then the American sensibility took over—i.e., money.

DEE SNIDER, Twisted Sister: MTV needed acts that knew how to present themselves in a visually interesting way. And they noticed metal bands: "Oh my god, these bands are very theatrical." Anyone who wasn't theatrical was done. Videos inspired a resurgence of metal—heavy metal has never gone away, but it had a really big moment in the '80s. Metal owes MTV for that. But MTV owes metal.

LARS ULRICH: I remember all these strange dudes from England with funny haircuts. But then you'd see a Saxon video. That was what kept me glued to the TV.

STEVE ISAACS, MTV VJ: I didn't see MTV until I was fourteen. At that point, they were putting a lot of boobies in the videos. That was the one good thing about shitty metal. For a teenage boy, MTV really yanked you through puberty.

DAVID MALLET: AC/DC's "You Shook Me All Night Long" is one of the funniest videos ever. I based the singer, Brian Johnson, on Andy Capp, a hugely popular cartoon character who was an English institution and never did any work. He was always in the pub. Brian follows a trail of underwear up the stairs in a little house, and it all opens out into a huge set with girls in rubber, riding stationary bicycles and mechanical bulls.

ROBIN SLOANE: Culture Club's "Do You Really Want to Hurt Me" video had a scene with a jury in blackface. At the same time, we had a video from some godawful rock band, and the video was totally degrading to women. I was in a marketing meeting, and somebody said, "I'll play two videos. One is really offensive and the other is really good." The one they thought was offensive was Culture Club. As a woman, I was thinking, *You have got to be kidding me.*

RIKI RACHTMAN, MTV host: The first video I saw on MTV was Mötley Crüe's "Live Wire." They were wearing red leather and Nikki Sixx set his legs on fire.

NIKKI SIXX, Mötley Crüe: We shot "Live Wire" and two other songs just down and dirty, to give away to fans, inspired by shows like *Don Kirshner's Rock Concert* and *Midnight Special.* When MTV came along, we did "Looks That Kill," and MTV also played "Live Wire."

What I liked and respected was, MTV played all kinds of music, which is what FM radio used to be when I was growing up. You'd wait to see videos by bands you were into, but you sat through other bands and you'd go, "Hmm, that Duran Duran band's not bad." MTV broke down those barriers, to the point where I actually bought a Thompson Twins album.

ROBIN SLOANE: The first video shoot I ever went on was Mötley Crüe's "Looks That Kill." Bob Krasnow, who ran Elektra, decided I should go to LA and oversee production of the video. I walked onto the set, went up to Mötley's guitarist,

Mick Mars, and said, "Hello, I'm Robin Sloane from Elektra." And he goes, "Fuck you, who cares?" *Okay, then.*

STEVE SCHNUR: I kept telling Les Garland that MTV should be playing Mötley Crüe's "Looks That Kill." "This is where we should be, Les. It's got to be about rock n' roll."

SEBASTIAN BACH: "Looks That Kill" was all blue and silver, and it looked striking. That was my favorite video back then. I love the outfits: platform boots and makeup.

NIKKI SIXX: The '70s were about fashion and music; it was a merging. Fashion designers hung out with rock stars. We said, "Let's top it. Let's go even farther." At times it was ludicrous, but wonderful. To be honest, I can't remember the concept for "Looks That Kill." If you strip it down, it's only about being over the top.

JOE ELLIOTT: When we were kids growing up in Sheffield, there were only two types of clothing shops—men's and women's. And you were never going to find stage wear in a men's shop. So nearly everything we wore, from the waist up, was female. Blouses and T-shirts with loud patterns, designed for big ladies.

PHIL COLLEN, Def Leppard: Girls liked us. We were like Duran Duran, if they played hard rock. We were the same age as Duran, from the same era. We were a rock band, but we didn't want to look like other bands who had greasy hair and greasy jeans. Our girlfriends let us borrow their clothes.

DAVID MALLET: Def Leppard's "Photograph" looked different from anything at the time. Different colors, mood, visuals, editing, photography. It's hard to believe now, because it looks like every heavy metal video ever made. But nothing had ever looked like that before.

JOE ELLIOTT: When we did "Photograph," we went mental. Phil wore a polka-dot top. Steve wore all white. The day before the shoot, I had £25 in my pocket, and I went down Kings Road in London to get some clothes. I found a pair of black pleather trousers that were too short by about four inches, so I bought them, and some leg warmers, which I'd seen in the TV show *Fame*. When I was done buying the pants and the effeminate leggings, I had £8 left. I walked past a punk rock shop and they had a red-white-and-blue Union Jack shirt in the window for £7.99. It was all I could afford, and it was loud. After that video, the shirt became so iconic that we sold almost 100,000 of them on tour that summer. We couldn't *wait* to the make videos. The morning we shot "Photograph" is when I frosted my hair for the first time. When "Photograph" came out, I was a blond bombshell.

David Mallet was hilarious. He called everybody "dear boy." He was very posh, very theatrical. When we turned up to shoot "Photograph" at Battersea Power Station, he'd built that whole set. There was gridding on the floor with lights underneath. It was fantastic. The girls in the cages have become a little dated, but at the time, it hadn't been done so much, so it worked fine.

DAVID MALLET: Why did I put the girls in a cage? Girls belong in cages, come on.

JANI LANE, Warrant: I was a junior in high school, and when I saw "Photograph," I was like, *Oh my god.*

DAVID MALLET: With David Bowie, we'd been thinking about surrealism. With Def Leppard, we were thinking about comic books. A huge influence on me was Bob Kane, who drew the early *Batman* comics. On "Rock of Ages," I was satirizing sword-and-sorcery movies and comic books.

JOE ELLIOTT: "Rock of Ages" was a laugh. I wield this giant prop sword through fiery hallways and then the sword magically turns into a guitar. It's very *Spinal Tap.* When I sang "All-right," which sounded a bit like "Owl-right," Mallet put an owl in the video at that moment.

PETER MENSCH, manager: Def Leppard put me in "Rock of Ages." I'm the hooded figure playing chess, and I lip-sync the words *"Gunter glieben glauchen globen."* That video was set in a quarry or something, where female bodybuilders were knocking buildings down. It made no sense at all.

JOE ELLIOTT: "Foolin'" was a three-day shoot somewhere on Long Island. David had me running down a tunnel with explosions going off, and my arms caught fire. All the hair burned off and I stank like burning flesh for a week. The smell was fucking rotten. And there's a fantastic scene when I'm chained to a pyramid and I break out of the shackles. I sit up and look at the camera and sing, "Is anybody out there?" And if you look at the video—which I suggest you do, because it's quite funny—you can see that underneath my white trousers I have on tighty whities. I wasn't wearing them on the first take. Mallet watched that scene back through the lens and said, "Dear boy, I can see your wedding tackle. You need to put some underpants on. They'll never show this on the telly if we don't clean it up a bit."

I spent the entire third day riding a horse on a beach. I'd never been on a horse in my life. My ass was fucking killing me by the time we finished. Turned out, not a second of that footage got used in the video.

PERRI LISTER: I was in "Foolin'." I had a mask on my face and was playing a harp. And they set fire to me. I saw my life flash before me: "Girl Burns to Death in Rock Video; Nobody Helped Her."

TAWNY KITAEN, actress: My first love was Robbin Crosby, the guitarist from Ratt. We met in high school. He had a dream of being a rock star, and I had a dream of being an actress. I eventually broke up with Robb, and started dating Pete Angelus, Van Halen's lighting director. It was so goddamn fun. Eddie Van Halen was with Valerie Bertinelli. I remember walking arm in arm with Pete after a concert, behind Eddie and Valerie, and saying to myself, "One day, I am going to be an actress and I am going to be married to the lead singer."

David Lee Roth and Pete and I became the Three Musketeers. We would travel everywhere together, and then we'd come home and Dave would sleep on our couch. I was with Pete for three years. But we broke up when I got my first movie. I started dating Tommy Lee, before he met Heather Locklear. That was really weird, because Nikki Sixx was Robb's roommate, and he wasn't thrilled that I was dating Tommy.

PETE ANGELUS: I met Tawny Kitaen when she was seventeen, maybe eighteen, at a Van Halen concert in San Diego. She was very attractive, outgoing, and we started dating. I invited her up to LA, and we were living together. I photographed her and sent her to the Elite modeling agency, so that was her entree into the entertainment business. That was before she started dating O.J. Simpson and before she married David Coverdale.

When she moved to LA, I think she was dating Robbin Crosby from Ratt. I discovered she was dating a lot of people, but I was on the road, so what could you do?

ROBERT LOMBARD: I became part of the inner circle of Van Halen. I had carte blanche at their offices on Sunset. I ended up living across the street from Dave. We would go out and chase girls. And do drugs. And drink Jack. I had my own bodyguard. When Dave walked in a club it was—and I don't like to use religious terms—it was like God parting the waters. One night we went to the Troubadour to look for girls and there were no open tables, and they told people they had to leave so we could sit down. Girls would come to our table, lift their skirts up, pull their panties down, and throw 'em at David. Or undo their tops. No one had the charisma David Lee Roth had. He had midgets all over the place who hung out to drink. At that time, I drove a 924 Porsche with a hatchback, and the midgets used to sit in the trunk.

MARK GOODMAN: I interviewed David Lee Roth at the U.S. Festival in 1983. He was drunk and coked up, laughing at every joke he made. Dave was the greatest interview.

ROBERT LOMBARD: Once Van Halen got into the MTV mode, they got *into* it. Dave was glued to that TV. He threw something through his TV set one night because they'd dropped in rotation on MTV. He cut an artery and ended up in Cedars-Sinai Hospital. Blood's spurting out of him and he goes, "I'm David Lee Roth. I could buy this place." The nurse told him, "Just sit down and shut up." They were obsessed. It was like a new drug.

MARSHALL BERLE, manager: Those videos Pete Angelus and Dave Roth created were the best I've ever seen.

PETE ANGELUS: When I was in high school in Connecticut, I had a teacher who allowed me to make Super 8 films rather than take tests. That was 1973. I moved to the West Coast to go to UCLA film school, but my parking tickets started to exceed the cost of tuition. So I ended up on the Sunset Strip, and I interviewed with a gentleman named Mario who owned the Roxy and the Rainbow and the Whiskey A-Go-Go. He gave me a job at the Roxy, probably in 1975. Van Halen asked me to travel with them—I'd designed their merchandise and worked on their album packages and logos, then I designed their productions and their lighting—and when MTV reared its ugly head, I thought well, okay, the full circle has come back to me, so I'll direct the videos.

ROBERT LOMBARD: "Jump" is where the drama really started. During the production of "Jump," we had a high-end DP. Pete Angelus operated one of the cameras, but we never used any of his footage, because he didn't know how to operate a 16mm camera to save his life. Dave wanted the performance video intercut with him doing crazy shit, like driving his chopped Merc hot rod and hanging out with midgets and girls in maids' outfits. So we shot hours of footage.

PETE ANGELUS: Rather that doing something bigger than life, which is how Van Halen was perceived, we wanted something very personal. Let's see if we can get Edward to smile. Of course, we also had to appease Dave, who wanted to throw his karate tricks into the equation.

MICHAEL ANTHONY: There was getting to be a little bit of tension between us three and Dave.

ROBERT LOMBARD: I told the band, "I'm gonna shoot in sections." Alex would show up, we'd do some drum segments, then bass, then guitar, then David. I didn't shoot them together until the end of the day. I was trying to keep peace, because I felt tension amongst them. David thought he was bigger than the rest of them.

I was in post-production with a rough cut of the video. I knew that if they kept it as a straight-on performance video, they would have a number one single. So I took the rough cut to Eddie's house up in Coldwater Canyon and played it for him and his brother Alex. I said, "Guys, I'm taking a stand here. If you put in this crazy footage"—which later surfaced in "Panama," after I was gone—"the video isn't gonna have the impact it should have." Eddie and Alex said, "We agree with you, one hundred percent. We're not gonna release this video unless it's done this way."

Two days later, I got fired. Noel Monk, their manager, said, "You don't do that—you don't go behind Dave's back. Here's your check, never want to see you again." That video won the award for best performance video at the first VMAs. And I still don't have my award.

PETE ANGELUS: I think we spent less money making "Jump" than we did on having pizzas delivered to the set of "Hot for Teacher."

ANN CARLI: The legend was that "Jump" was a $5,000 video. David Lee Roth's swinging on a rope, but he's also playing right to camera. Nobody did that. That was a groundbreaking video, and it had an impact on how everybody looked at making videos.

DON LETTS: There was a period of six months or so when I was living in LA and working for Limelight. They had juice. The original director Ratt were going to use for "Round and Round" got ill. I was around. Guys with permed hair and spandex pants weren't my thing, but I enjoy a challenge. When that band walked into Limelight, black as I am, it was like a Mexican standoff for a second. They must have been thinking, *What the fuck?*

I just wanted to meet Milton Berle. I love having any connection to old-school Hollywood. Milton was funny. He called me a Persian rug—he was talking about my hair. He took total control on the set. "Right my boy, this is how we're going to do this." He directed me. I would have done anything he asked.

WARREN DeMARTINI, Ratt: Milton Berle was our manager's uncle. It was quite a juxtaposition—this television legend in a bombed-out building in some condemned area of downtown LA, some place that didn't require permits.

MARSHALL BERLE: I put my uncle in the video because I thought it might get some press, like *What the hell is he doing in a hard rock video?* I had the idea for him to play two roles, because he loved dressing up in drag. He showed up with his valet, and he brought his gown, his wig, and his jewelry. Milton's an old-school guy—started in vaudeville, made silent pictures—and he took over. He was telling the cameraman what to do, telling the director what to do. No, we didn't pay him. He's my uncle.

STEPHEN PEARCY, Ratt: Milton just took over, you know? Like, "I'll have control, thank you." It was all new to us, and we didn't know what to do. He was known as "Mr. Television."

WARREN DeMARTINI: There was only one chance to do the scene where I crash through the ceiling and destroy everything on the table. There was no cleaning it up and doing a second take. I had to stand on the table and jump up in the air as high as I could, and there were people standing off camera with big trays of powder, to get the effect of dust flying around. Oh, I nailed it.

DON LETTS: That girl in the video was kind of hot. Not that I'm into putting hot girls in videos, but I was willing to go with that. She was easy on the eyes.

MARSHALL BERLE: I wanted to show that Ratt didn't take themselves seriously, that everything they did was a party.

STEPHEN PEARCY: Milton told us, "Keep it tongue in cheek," and that stuck with us. You shouldn't take yourselves seriously when you're doing a video. Most of our videos have humor; we didn't do videos with castles and demons, or the devil and pentagrams.

MARSHALL BERLE: It was a big deal that MTV had anyone of Milton's stature in a video, it got into heavy rotation, and that first album sold 4 million copies.

WARREN DeMARTINI: We went from struggling to get decent bookings at LA clubs to opening for ZZ Top.

STEPHEN PEARCY: Milton Berle came back for more in our video "Back for More." Tommy Lee and Nikki Sixx from Mötley are in the video, beating up Bobby Blotzer, our drummer. We used to hang out, and we started a street gang, called "The Gladiators." Robbin was *King,* Nikki was *Leader Six,* and Tommy was *Field Marshall.*

Robbin and I created "The Three P's": *pussy, party, paycheck.* That was the decade of decadence. We lived and breathed it

MARTY CALLNER: I'd been working at HBO, directing their music and comedy specials. I'd done Steve Martin, George Carlin, Diana Ross, Liza Minnelli, you name it. I was making a lot of money. I went to see Ahmet Ertegun and said, "I want to try a music video. I have a feeling I'm gonna be good at it." Atlantic Records had signed a Long Island band they didn't know what to do with, Twisted Sister. They had a song, "We're Not Gonna Take It," and because of my comedy and music background, they seemed like the perfect hybrid for me.

"We're Not Gonna Take It" is based on the rebellious nature of Road Runner cartoons. I wrote the spoken-word part at the beginning. And we cast Mark Metcalf, who had just come from a hot movie, *Animal House.* "We're Not Gonna Take It" was big, it was bright, it was colorful, it was funny, it was rock n' roll. And it went on to become a classic video.

DEE SNIDER: Marty and I hit it off. He's originally from Pittsburgh, and I was a rube from Long Island. The first time I met him, at the Palm, I ordered a shrimp cocktail, and they brought out incredibly huge shrimp. I'm like, "Oh my god, I'm used to eating at places where the shrimp is the size of a pea." And Marty calls to the waiter, "Hey! Bring out a bowl of these things, will ya?"

MARTY CALLNER: Dee was 100 percent ham. Delicious.

MARK METCALF, actor: Dee is just so ugly. It's like God made the ugliest guy in the world, and then He hit him in the face with a shovel.

DEE SNIDER: Me and my four brothers were constantly quoting lines from *Animal House*. I told Marty, "You know Neidermeyer from *Animal House*? Someone like Mark Metcalf would be perfect to play the father." And Marty goes, "Why don't we get Mark Metcalf? What's he doing, working on a cure for cancer?" I couldn't fathom the idea of getting Mark Metcalf, but apparently for $2,000 and a round-trip coach ticket, we could get Mark Metcalf. When it came time to pick him up at the airport, they were gonna send a PA, and I was like, "Oh no! I'm picking up Mark Metcalf." I drove to LAX and I stood in baggage claim with my big hair and platform shoes.

MARK METCALF: They paid me a day's wage, the Screen Actors Guild minimum, which I think was $360 at the time. It was a non-SAG picture. I had a girlfriend in LA who I wanted to see, because I'd left some stuff at her apartment, so I took the free flight and slept on Marty Callner's couch that night. When Dee met me at the airport, he was so excited, like a little kid. He loved Neidermeyer so much.

DEE SNIDER: Les Garland hated the video. Somebody told me his quote was "This isn't a rock video. This is method acting." MTV even tried to cut Mark's famous rant—"You call this a room? This is a pigsty. You are a disgusting slob." That video was like nitrous oxide on a hot-rod car. A great video will fuel-inject your career. And as huge as that video was, it was never in heavy airplay, because Garland didn't like it. Now it's a classic. It makes every list of the Top 100 videos of all time.

We followed "We're Not Gonna Take It" with "I Wanna Rock," which was the sequel. We turned the Neidermeyer character into a teacher. In the intro, we paraphrased the *Animal House* dialogue where he's yelling at Flounder. We even brought in Stephen Durst, who played Flounder, to do a cameo. It was a long day on the set, and we were so bored that we made Stephen recite lines from *Animal House* over and over again. "Say 'The negroes stole our dates!' Say 'The negroes stole our dates!'"

MARK METCALF: I got a letter from the Screen Actors Guild after "I Wanna Rock"—they caught on because it was so big on MTV. They said, "If you do this again, we'll throw you out of the union." I also got letters from Universal Pictures' lawyers, saying, "We own the character Neidermeyer. You have no rights to the character." They didn't go any further than that because in the long run, it was good publicity for the movie.

MARTY CALLNER: The labels did not know what they had with music videos. I actually owned the copyright on "We're Not Gonna Take It." It's probably the only time a director ever owned a video.

DEE SNIDER: "We're Not Gonna Take it" changed music videos. Everyone, metal bands in particular, started embracing story lines. You don't have Mötley Crüe's "Smokin' in the Boys Room" or Van Halen's "Hot for Teacher" without "We're Not Gonna Take It."

BETH BRODAY: Marty Callner didn't care about production rules. He did everything his own way. And he made stars, God bless him. But he charged a lot of money. A *lot* of money. I'd never seen anybody charge that kind of money. I love Marty, but he took direction from no one.

MARTY CALLNER: I always tried to make videos sexy without being sexual. I did a video for the Scorpions called "Big City Nights," and MTV rejected it because there were too many girls in bikinis. So I added seven more shots of girls in bikinis and sent it in, and they aired it.

PAT BENATAR: When we made "We Belong" with Marty Callner, I was throwing up constantly between takes because I was pregnant. He was very generous and sweet, even though he was crazy. He was like an eight-year-old with money and a video camera. He wore big jewelry—big enough that I could lift it for weights—

and he had big hair and a beautiful Israeli wife who ordered him around all the time.

NEIL "SPYDER" GIRALDO: Marty was a maniac. The first time Patricia and I met him, it was 80 degrees out, and he walked into a restaurant wearing a giant fur coat. On the set of "Ooh Ooh Song," I said, "Hey, Marty, get me a monkey." And he said to his assistant, "Let's get a monkey in here." So the monkey was *my* idea. I don't know whose idea it was to have a mime in the video.

RUDOLF SCHENKER: When we were on tour in America, I was watching MTV every day to see who was the right director. We were very careful about choosing. Billy Idol, who is the guy directing him? Oh, David Mallet, he's great. David saw us live and was smart enough to get the essence of the Scorpions into "Rock You Like a Hurricane." He said, "Don't be serious, let's get crazy." That video is about attitude, craziness, and sexuality. That's how we survived into the video generation.

DOC McGHEE, manager: Nobody else could come up with "Rock You Like a Hurricane." You have to be German to come up with shit like that.

DAVID MALLET: The Scorpions are very funny. "Rock You Like a Hurricane" has the girls all shaking their cages.

NIKKI SIXX: Didn't Scorpions have a video that showed women in cages? In our minds, we think we have the power, but we never do. We can't keep them in that cage.

SEBASTIAN BACH: In hindsight, having girls in cages was pretty "Smell the Glove."

MIKE RENO: For "Hot Girls in Love," we sang on top of these giant kegs of TNT. Or maybe kegs of whiskey. There were always pretty girls in our videos. There's nothing wrong with a pretty girl in the video.

PAUL DEAN, Loverboy: How are you going to take a song like "Hot Girls in Love" and do a serious treatment for it?

STEVE BARRON: I did a terrible video for Loverboy: "Hot Girls in Love." Absolutely dreadful.

MIKE RENO: Loverboy made horrible videos. We still get teased about 'em today. They were really obvious, schmaltzy videos that were probably great for our careers.

BRUCE ALLEN: Nobody's going to say a Loverboy video was brilliant, but it gave the people what they wanted. What is your audience? Good-looking broads lifting their tops up and a bunch of guys with their fists in the air. You didn't need a rocket scientist to make a video; just get some sexy babes. They're falling out of the trees in Hollywood.

DEBBIE SAMUELSON, record executive: I can't remember which video it was, but I definitely saw Loverboy stuff socks down their pants before the cameras started to roll.

GALE SPARROW: MTV binged and purged on heavy metal. In the beginning, we played it to death, and then we pulled way back on it. But research told us we might be losing an audience, so we started a heavy metal half hour in the middle of the afternoon.

ALAN NIVEN, manager: My first substantial encounter with a video production company was on a Great White song called "Stick It," and it was less than happy. They arrive with half-baked clichés of what rock n' roll is, spend a lot of your money, then walk off and do another video while you have to live with what they've done. If you pull up this video, you'll see it's unfortunate and cheesy, and the best shot was the 1970 Cadillac Eldorado I drove at the time. I was still learning that making videos is a beastly contract with the devil, and it should be as much about the band as possible.

DOC McGHEE: With all the bands I managed—Mötley Crüe, Bon Jovi, Scorpions, Skid Row—I wanted to see them play themselves, not playing characters. Every video director was a Fellini back then. They'd have an idea like, *Let's have Nikki stand by a hot dog stand.* It was bullshit. They don't stand by hot dog stands. *We'll have Vince Neil riding on a horse through the weeds.* The fucking guy doesn't ride a horse. He's at the Rainbow until four in the morning. What does a horse have to do with Mötley Crüe? They're a menacing rock group, that's what you have to show. Most of my videos were done with a live kind of feel to them. To me, the video was an informercial for our live show. MTV was the

Guthy-Renker of the '80s; they were infomercial kings who sold millions of records for people.

WAYNE ISHAM: Mötley Crüe shot "Looks That Kill" on the A&M soundstage. I was the stage manager. During the shoot they came up to me and said, "Dude, can you get us some Jack Daniel's and keep it in your office?" I go, "Yeah, sure, no problem, man." Unbeknownst to me, they weren't allowed to drink at the time. So I bought a bottle of Jack for them, and between takes they'd stroll into my office with all their makeup on, do a big hit, and go back to the set. A couple years later, I did my first video with them, "Smokin' in the Boys Room." When we met, first thing I said was "Hey, remember me?" And they laughed: "I *do* remember." We had an immediate affinity.

ROBIN SLOANE: I went to Mötley Crüe's manager, Doc McGhee, and said, "I think this dude Wayne is totally happening. Let's give him a shot." So we made "Smokin' in the Boys Room" and Wayne became a huge superstar director.

TOMMY LEE, Mötley Crüe: Whatever we were doing, Wayne Isham was doing. If we were partying, he was partying. If we were doing drugs, he was doing drugs. He'd wake up at 8 A.M., hungover, and direct the video. He was like the fifth Beatle.

VALERIE FARIS, director: Wayne could party as hard as any of the bands. They felt so comfortable with him because he was one of them.

DOC McGHEE: Wayne is Mr. MTV. He did most of my stuff, because he was crazier than the bands. Wayne was low IQ, high RPM. He had no dimmer switch.

WAYNE ISHAM: I was never really was a big Jack drinker until I met Mötley. I went to an arena in Houston to shoot "Home Sweet Home." Which is a great live video, in all honesty. I'm setting up the cameras, and I'm told that the band wants to see me in their dressing room. I walk in, and they shout, "You're late!" Even though I wasn't. I go, "What are you talking about?" They're like, "That's it. Double bubble!" I go, "What the fuck does 'double bubble' mean?" Turns out, "double bubble" meant I had to hold the bottle of Jack Daniel's by its handle, and drink until two bubbles go up. I explained that I had to shoot their video in a few minutes, and "double bubble" wasn't such a good idea. But they kept saying "double bubble, double bubble." So I double bubbled.

I look back now and can't believe we rocked so hard and still got so much work done. I'd grab a camera, they'd grab their guitars, we'd see the sun rise and think, *How the fuck did we just do that?* We drank, we did coke. I have no qualms about saying that.

CURT MARVIS, producer: Wayne and I named our company The Company. We'd make up T-shirts where we'd print the words "The Company" in the logo style of a brand near and dear to Wayne: the Stolichnaya vodka label, the Harley logo, the Corona logo. But the most famous one had the words "Where's Wayne?" on the back. Because the most enduring phrase about him on any set was "Where's Wayne? Has anybody seen Wayne?" Wayne would be off doing shots with the band at a bar across the street, or finding a "clean shitter" somewhere.

NIKKI SIXX: Wayne knew the band, he hung out with the band, he partied with the band, he was friends with the band, so he was able to get inside our heads and take it over the top. We were traveling around the country in tour buses, the show's going up and the show's going down, and we wanted to capture it in "Home Sweet Home." We wanted to capture what it's like to be on tour. None of that was staged. It was just this honest moment.

DOC McGHEE: "Home Sweet Home" showed Tommy playing the piano. It gave Mötley a little more credibility.

TOMMY LEE: MTV played "Home Sweet Home" so many times, I honestly started to get sick of seeing it.

DOC McGHEE: I'd just starting to manage Bon Jovi when we did the video for "Runaway." There's a chubby girl who's a runaway, but she has laser eyes, and the band is playing in a warehouse that's burning. In the '80s, every video had to look like *Escape from New York*. Something had to be on fire, and you had to be in an alley that was wet, or else you couldn't shoot a video. Then "In and Out of Love" was done like a scripted movie, where the band is on the boardwalk, girls chase after them, and they hold newspapers in front of their faces to hide. Terrible.

LEN EPAND: For "Runaway," we used a commercial director named Michael Cuesta, who had no music-video experience. After that, we shifted to Masfin Kahan, who did a few Bon Jovi videos. I wasn't there, but I was told that he offered an illegal substance to one of the police officers assigned to the shoot for security. He was taken away before the shoot was done.

DOC McGHEE: I was there when he got arrested. Some cop saw him doing blow in the middle of the Jersey boardwalk, and they arrested him. It wasn't a hard case for the police to solve. We just kept shooting the video.

Chapter 13

"THAT RACISM BULLSHIT"

MTV'S AOR FORMAT COMES UNDER FIRE

N 1983, *TIME* AND *ROLLING STONE* RAN COVER STORIES on MTV, almost simultaneously. MTV was finally being noticed by the mainstream press, and the mainstream press was unimpressed. Both articles took disapproving tones. *Time* sniffed that "the majority of clips now in circulation are labored ephemera with heavily imitative associations," unfavorably compared Duran Duran ("an affable, uninspired British band currently aglow with success") to Beethoven, and concluded, "the pervading silliness is worrisome."

Steven Levy, writing in *Rolling Stone*, unfavorably compared "superficial, easy-to-swallow" acts such as Adam Ant to Bob Dylan. To bolster his accusation that "heavy-metal pounding" videos were dangerously violent, he quoted Dr. Thomas Radecki, chairman of the right-wing National Coalition on TV Violence, who a year later testified to Congress on behalf of the PMRC (Parents Music Resource Center) and served on their board of directors. (Radecki also routinely claimed that Dungeons & Dragons was "causing young men to kill themselves and others." His reign at NCTV lasted until 1992, when his medical license was revoked for "engaging in immoral conduct" with a patient.) MTV, Levy wrote, "makes the musical energy and optimism of the Sixties seem a thousand light-years ago." He called the network "the ultimate junk culture triumph," and concluded, "Unlike the activist '60s rock coalition, the MTV coalition is essentially passive. Their function is to sit still, watch the commercials and buy the products, not change the world." In other words, the pervading silliness was worrisome.

Criticism of MTV was not unique throughout the decade. Feminists, including Naomi Wolf, deplored the depiction of women in videos. Conservatives like Allan Bloom saw peril in the loose morality of videos, which contained "nothing noble, sublime, profound, delicate, tasteful, or even decent"—and in which, he claimed dubiously, "Hitler's image recurs frequently enough in exciting contexts to give one pause." Ted Turner called MTV's programming violent, degrading to women, and "Satanic." Criticism was even more pointed within the music industry—at a 1983 convention, Chris Strackwitz, founder of a small label that released blues and Cajun records, asked MTV programmer Buzz Brindle, during a panel discussion, "How can you justify showing twenty-four hours of garbage?" Even video directors sometimes expressed disdain, including John Scarlett-Davies, who in 1984 memorably dismissed the work of his colleagues as "masturbation fantasies for middle America. They just sit there with their cans of beer, tossing off while all these scantily-clad girls do this and that with men with their big electric guitars like prick extensions."

One accusation proved stickier than others: MTV showed few black artists. Buzz Brindle told a reporter, "We'll air black artists who play rock," which ignored the fact that MTV aired videos by plenty of white artists who didn't play rock. Bob Pittman and Les Garland defended their policy (which caused grumbling even within the company's offices) by saying that black artists weren't excluded because they were black, but because they didn't play rock n' roll, which was MTV's format. Both had been trained at AOR radio, where music was narrowcast to a small population that liked rock, and only rock. MTV, Andrew Goodwin later wrote acutely, "denied racism, on the grounds that it merely followed the rules of the rock business (which were, nonetheless, the consequence of a long history of racism)." And Jordan Rost, the vice president of research for MTV, believes that Pittman, in creating the format that excluded most black artists, misunderstood and misapplied the network's research. This rejection of black pop did harm to MTV—the network needed to constantly evolve, and its dependence on new wave and heavy metal limited that ability—and it took remarkable circumstances for them to finally give a black singer the kind of attention that had been reserved for Men at Work and Twisted Sister.

JOE JACKSON: And another thing: MTV was racist.

LES GARLAND: The worst thing was that "racism" bullshit. There were artists of color on MTV: Joan Armatrading, Eddy Grant, the Bus Boys, even Prince. But there were hardly any videos being made by black artists. Record companies weren't funding them. *They* never got charged with racism.

Rick James singled me out in an interview, and it pissed me off. I have nothing bad to say about Rick James. The mistake he made was calling me a racist and not knowing me. "Super Freak" was a booty video in a swimming pool. We couldn't play that shit.

CAROLYN BAKER: It wasn't MTV that turned down "Super Freak." It was me. *I* turned it down. You know why? Because there were half-naked women in it, and it was a piece of crap. As a black woman, I did not want that representing my people as the first black video on MTV.

LES GARLAND: I ran across Rick James one night in a club. I went up to him and said, "My name is Les Garland. Does that mean anything to you? You called me a fucking racist. You don't even know me." He said, "Dude, I'm sorry." He apologized, I accepted it, and we became friendly. You remember the Eddie Murphy video "Party All the Time"? Rick wrote that song. And I'm one of the two white guys in the video.

JUDY McGRATH: The music department was the driver of the programming, but people in the halls were starting to rise up and say, "I get the format you want to follow, but this is incredible music and these are unbelievable artists." The staff was ready for revolt.

TOM FRESTON: Bob wanted a rock n' roll format. But there was a lot of pressure building up, because all of sudden people wanted to be on MTV. Because of his Mississippi background, Bob was thought by some people in the business to be racist. But it did bother me that we had to have this format. There were a lot of people at the network saying, "We should broaden this out."

JORDAN ROST: The original research study for MTV showed that playing a few, specific urban artists would turn off a lot of the core audience. I remember thinking, "Oh, Bob is remembering that first study." But he translated the research in a way that wasn't ever studied, and he created a rule from it that was erroneous, as opposed to saying, "Let's do another study in six months, with different artists." It shows how quickly you can create a mold, even if it's a faulty one.

CAROLYN BAKER: I said, "We've got to play James Brown." And Bob said, "The research says our audience thinks rock n' roll started with the Beatles." I came through the civil rights movement. I was a member of SNCC. I believe in opening doors. The party line at MTV was that we weren't playing black music because of the "research." But the research was based on ignorance. I told Bob that to his face. We were young, we were cutting edge. We didn't have to be on the cutting edge of racism.

GEORGE BRADT, MTV staff: It's worth remembering who had cable at that time: white suburbanites, mostly. MTV was playing it safe with the audience. My first job there was call-out research, four to nine every weekday, for minimum wage. We were given phone books from areas with a lot of MTV coverage, and randomly called people. Once we found regular viewers, we'd call back every few weeks and ask about videos. I don't remember many, if any, recognizably black or Latino voices on the phone. That research drove a lot of the music decisions, and let's just say it wasn't exactly a sophisticated research operation.

The people at the top had all come from radio stations. They were old-school, white radio guys with an AOR mind-set, probably because in the world of '80s radio, AOR was cool. MTV was slow to realize that they didn't have to think of themselves as "the rock channel"—they were the *only* channel.

MARK GOODMAN: I did an interview with David Bowie, and he asked me why there were so few black faces on MTV. I was in an odd position, because I couldn't diss the company. So when Bowie started in with me, I tried to explain the rock format idea. And Bowie was not having it. I was fumpfering around for something to say, and the interview felt like an eternity.

The fact was, J.J. and I had been talking about this. He pointed out to me that he was initially down with the rock format, but once MTV started to play Spandau Ballet and ABC—basically, white R&B acts—he felt there was no reason not to play black R&B acts. He was like, "What the fuck is up with that?" He told me he talked to management about it. I don't for a minute believe Pittman was a bigot—we were a rock station, the programming made absolute sense to me.

JEFF AYEROFF: I was one of the first people to point out that MTV didn't play videos by black artists. But the people running MTV weren't racist. Part of the problem was the quality of videos. If you look at the Michael Jackson videos before "Billie Jean," even those were just him backlit by lasers.

RALPH TRESVANT, New Edition: We didn't have any budget to make our first video, "Candy Girl," so we had to go home and get our own clothes. Those are our school clothes we're wearing. We shot "Popcorn Love" and "She Gives Me a Bang" the same day in London, while we were on a promotional tour. We shot "Cool It Now" and "Mr. Telephone Man" on the same day, too.

BOBBY BROWN, New Edition: The first time I saw a music video wasn't on MTV, it was on BET. When I saw New Edition's video on BET, I was thirteen, and I felt like a star. Everybody saw it in Boston, so we was the shit in the hood. People were impressed we were on TV. Didn't matter why. We could have robbed a bank . . .

LISA COLEMAN, Prince and the Revolution: We were on tour when "Little Red Corvette" started doing well on radio, so we squeezed in a video. A director flew in, we set up our gear at the venue in Jacksonville, and Prince threw together some choreography.

ANN CARLI: When I came to Jive Records, only one video had been made in the U.S. office, and that was Whodini's "Magic's Wand." It was awful. The guys in the group just ride up and down escalators—that was the video. Barry Weiss, who managed artist development at Jive, said to me, "I'm never going to make another video, because I almost got fired over that one." I thought, *Yeah, I can see why.*

DON LETTS: Once MTV came onto the scene, a corporate mentality came into play: "We don't want any radical ideas, nothing political." For directors like me, who were smart enough, you learned to be subtle. I did a video for Musical Youth, "Pass the Dutchie," five little black guys playing a reggae track. I placed them in front of the House of Parliament, which is a postcard shot of what England is supposed to be. Instead, I replaced it with my vision of London. It was a subtle way of acknowledging the importance of black culture in the UK.

People often say "Billie Jean" was the first black music video on MTV. "Pass the Dutchie" was first. Because they were little and spoke in funny British accents, Musical Youth were deemed as nonthreatening, and therefore non-black.

DENNIS SEATON, Musical Youth: Kelvin was the youngest, eleven years old, and I was the oldest, fifteen. In our first four videos, which Don Letts directed, the band was always skipping and jumping. You just see the innocence of youth. We didn't see MTV until a year after "Pass the Dutchie," when we recorded our second album in LA.

DON LETTS: I'm in New York, and I get a call from MTV. They want to interview me about making videos for the Clash. When I get to the studio, everyone looks at me like I've shit myself. After an embarrassing five minutes, a guy sits me down and says, "I don't know how to tell you this, we can't do the interview. We didn't realize you were black."

DONNA SUMMER, artist: When I began, people focused on my sexuality. I started my career with "Love to Love You Baby," and when I used to do that song, pandemonium would break out. They would body-slam the stage. But I'd pulled away. I was always trying to have more dignity. I wanted people to focus on the music.

I don't know if MTV knew what to do with me, because "She Works Hard for the Money" wasn't your typical rock n' roll video. It takes you to where people work hard, where lives are tough, maybe thankless. All these different characters who've had to struggle, the waitress and the nurse, are saying, "I've succeeded." That's why they dance at the end. As a black woman, that might not be the easiest thing for my record company to sell. I don't say this as a racial slur. Because I was black, they just couldn't understand me having that level of creativity. Even though I was forward-thinking, I didn't get the opportunity to do something that, say, Madonna did. That's just pure, institutionalized racism.

BILL ADLER, record executive: The first so-called "hip-hop" video MTV played was Herbie Hancock's "Rockit," which was great, but there are no human beings in it, except once in a while you see Herbie on a little TV screen. It's a way of programming black music to white youth without any scary black people in it.

KEVIN GODLEY: The brief we were given for "Rockit" was to find a way to get Herbie onto MTV.

HERBIE HANCOCK, artist: Godley and Creme explained to me what was going on in the video. It was about our fear of machines taking over. In the video, robots have replaced humans. At the end of the video, when I come on the TV, it gets thrown out the window, because robots are afraid of humans. Or something like that.

DEBBIE NEWMAN: I sent a two-line description of the video: "Herbie Hancock appears on a television screen in a room full of robots. $35,000." Nobody thought this would ever get played.

LOL CREME: Our concept was to put the robots in a domestic situation, like a family. I had to explain it to the video genius at CBS. She said, "Are you sure you can make robots interesting for three and a half minutes?" That was the kind of fabulous mind in charge of videos.

KEVIN GODLEY: They were hydraulically powered and unstable robots, and there were arms flying around, legs kicking, bits falling off. They were quite danger-ous, like something out of *Texas Chainsaw Massacre*. There was one robot hav-ing a wank under the bedclothes, which you could not get away with now. It was strange and grotesque—that was something I hadn't seen on MTV yet.

NICK RHODES: "Rockit" was a landmark.

GALE SPARROW: Godley and Creme came to the studio, supposedly for an inter-view. I set up all our studio interviews, and we had nothing scheduled. They said, "Oh, sorry . . . Well, as long as we're here, we'd like to show you some-thing." They'd made this mistake on purpose, to play me the Herbie Hancock video. And I was blown away. I said to Les Garland, "We have a problem. Because this is the most fabulous video, and I think we've got to play it." Word came back from CBS Records that Godley and Creme told them they'd get Her-bie Hancock on MTV, and if they didn't, CBS didn't have to pay them. And they did. We played the hell out of it.

HERBIE HANCOCK: I saw the final product in a screening room in London, and I'll admit, I had no idea what I was looking at. We played it for Columbia Records in London, and they went insane. They were congratulating me, telling me how great this was. And I said, "It is?" MTV started the video in light rotation, and the response was so incredible that they sent it to heavy rotation. It just blew up.

I remember being on *The Phil Donahue Show*, and even he asked me why they didn't have videos of black artists before me and Michael Jackson.

ABBEY KONOWITCH: MTV adhered to a rock format, and record companies accepted formats. That's how radio was programmed. We never thought an R&B artist would get played on MTV. It didn't enter our minds until "Billie Jean."

Chapter 14

"I'M NOT LIKE OTHER BOYS"

MICHAEL JACKSON SAVES A STRUGGLING NETWORK FROM ITSELF

CBS RECORDS AND MTV BOTH PROFITED IMMENSELY from the success of Michael Jackson. But neither party can agree on how it happened, and each, in effect, says the other is lying. MTV says they loved "Billie Jean" and were happy to play it; CBS says MTV turned down the video and played it only after the label threatened to pull its videos, which comprised a substantial part of MTV's playlist.

"The MTV version of the story is bullshit," says a former CBS executive who asked to not be named. "Walter Yetnikoff loved to fight. So did David Benjamin. They both relished a fight, and there was a sense of justice about it, too." If key CBS executives are lying, it's to exaggerate their power and importance. If MTV executives are lying, it's to disguise the fact that they had to be forced to play a singer who more or less saved their network. Also, if they did reject "Billie Jean," it's consistent with Bob Pittman's often-stated commitment to maintaining a rock n' roll playlist.

This much is inarguable: MTV did not immediately play "Billie Jean." By the time MTV added it, the song had been out for more than two months and had reached number one, and *Thriller* had ended Men at Work's long run at the top of the album chart. A *Billboard* article in March 1983 observed that "some time elapsed between when the tape was submitted [to MTV] and when it was aired," and writer Paul Grein added in the article, the "decision to add a mainstream black music smash, even if its mass audience appeal is by now rather obvious, is significant."

At first, MTV added "Billie Jean" in medium rotation, with two to three plays per day. It was bumped into heavy rotation a month later, only a week before MTV began to play "Beat It." For eight weeks, both songs were in heavy rotation. Then "Beat It" dropped out, and after four more weeks, so did "Billie Jean." By early summer, Michael Jackson was off MTV, even as *Thriller* remained at number one. Medium rotation for "Billie Jean," eight weeks of rotation for "Beat It": This is strong but not overwhelming support.

At a point when it seemed *Thriller*'s run was over, Jackson released the "Thriller" video—strategically, just before the Christmas buying season. The upper range of a video budget was $50,000; Jackson spent $1 million. It was the most elaborate video ever made, and this time, MTV was fully behind it. The decision, and the success it brought MTV at a time when staffers worried daily about the network's survival, effectively ended the policy of playing only rock artists.

BOB PITTMAN: Rick James made the claim that MTV wasn't playing any black videos. I figured, "That's ridiculous, people will watch MTV and know it's not true." I learned my first great PR lesson there. The press ran with MTV PLAYS NO BLACK VIDEOS, ALLEGES RICK JAMES. All of us realized, "God, we'd better work extra hard to find some black videos." And the problem was not just black videos. *No one* was making videos yet. But people got paranoid about it, and it began to be a problem. So we looked for artists. And when the guys saw "Billie Jean," they said, "This is it."

ROBIN SLOANE: I was at Epic when the "Billie Jean" video came out. MTV refused to play it under the guise that it was not an AOR record. It became a huge battle. Those negotiations were mostly handled by Freddy DeMann and Ron Weisner, who were managing Michael. Michael paid for the video himself. He owned it. We had nothing to do with it. And our head of pop promotion, Frank DiLeo, got involved as well.

JEFF AYEROFF: Quincy Jones called one day and told me to come to his office and meet Michael. He asked me who should do Michael's video. I played them the Human League "Don't You Want Me" video and said, "That's who should do the video."

STEVE BARRON: Michael Jackson liked "Don't You Want Me," so his management contacted me. They said he had a new song coming out and he wanted something cinematic. I got the track and loved it. I had this flash to do something magical, where he'd have a Midas Touch, and everything he touches lights up. I'd had a similar idea for a Joan Armatrading video that never happened, and as soon as I heard "Billie Jean" I went back to that idea.

SIMON FIELDS: Steve originally wrote a *Wizard of Oz*–ish concept that cost way more than we could afford.

STEVE BARRON: Michael really liked the treatment I wrote. And the budget was set at somewhere around $55,000 for a two-day shoot. Then he had an idea that would have required a choreographer and dancers and another $5,000. Simon Fields called CBS, and CBS said, "No way. *No. Way.*"

Michael was lovely. Really sweet, soft-spoken, and excited about this next step in his career. He felt like he'd grown up, even from *Off the Wall*. Freddy DeMann called me and said Michael had been practicing dance moves in front of the mirror, so it would be good to save some of the video for him to dance. There's an interview somewhere with Michael where he says the director on "Billie Jean" didn't want him to dance. Which is completely and utterly untrue. Can you imagine me saying, "Sorry, Michael, I don't want to have dancing in your video"?

DANIEL PEARL: Steve Barron and I brought in a guy from England named Eric Critchley. He did matte paintings. We didn't have much money, so we built a small set and faked the rest. We'd set up a shot where the set might occupy only a third or a quarter of the frame. Then we'd put a piece of glass between the camera and the set, and Critchley would paint an extension of the set on the glass. And we'd fill up the whole frame with the blend of the actual set and Eric's painting. For example, there's a scene where Michael is walking down the sidewalk and you see a wide shot of the sidewalk and the buildings. In reality, only the sidewalk and the first floor of the storefront existed. Above the first floor, the buildings were painted on glass. But it looks like one big set.

RAQUEL PENA: I had posters of Michael Jackson on my wall when I was a kid, and then I spent fourteen hours alongside him for "Billie Jean." They took my picture and superimposed it on a big billboard, and they put me in bed right next to him. He got in and laid down, and we both giggled. He was the gentlest guy, hiding and playing on the set, just having fun. His brothers came—I think he had six or seven siblings there.

WAYNE ISHAM: I worked on several Michael videos in those days. Years later, when I directed "You Are Not Alone," I said, "Michael, I've worked with you before." And he goes, "Really, Wayne? When?" And I go, "Dude, I'm the one who picked up the tiger's shit from 'Billie Jean'!"

PAUL FLATTERY: While we were making "Billie Jean," MTV called and said, "We don't want 'Billie Jean' first, we want 'Beat It.'" Because "Beat It" had Eddie Van Halen playing guitar on it. We didn't have any control over which videos the labels were going to make, or in what order. But MTV was green when they started out. They thought we owned the videos.

GALE SPARROW: We wanted "Beat It" to be the first *Thriller* video, because Eddie Van Halen was on it. But "Billie Jean" was fabulous. We started to realize that we had to open up the playlist a bit. We realized we had a broader audience than we'd thought.

LES GARLAND: We got a copy of "Billie Jean." I had huge speakers in my office. I mean, I'd rock the fucking building. And so we popped in the video and invited everybody in, and it became a party. And from the first shot, I was mind-blown. It was like the first time I saw "Hungry Like the Wolf." We got it on the air as quick as we could.

SUSAN BLOND, record executive: In those days, we usually had a messenger bring a new video to MTV, but in this case, we realized it was special. I brought them this amazing video, and they said, basically, "This doesn't fit onto our network." I first met Michael when he was a kid, and he was obsessed with the Osmonds— they were getting more coverage than the Jacksons, because Michael was black. This had been a major thing with Michael—his whole life, he had been excluded from the media because he was black.

BRUCE DICKINSON: All I can tell you is what I heard Walter Yetnikoff say. I was sitting in Bob Sherwood's office while Walter was talking to Don Dempsey, who was the head of Epic Records, and Sherwood, the vice president of marketing for Columbia Records, who was there because what Walter had to say affected both labels. Walter goes, "If they don't play this, I'm going to pull all the CBS videos." That's the way Walter was. He liked to fight. MTV would always say, "Well, it doesn't quite fit our format." They'd use every euphemism for "He's black!" It was really sick stuff.

DAVID BENJAMIN, record executive: I was vice president of business affairs for CBS Records. I helped negotiate our contract with MTV, and there was a clause that allowed us to pull all our videos on twenty-four hours' notice. This was for our own protection, in case we hadn't negotiated the proper clearances with our acts to supply their videos to MTV. We hadn't intended it, but that clause gave us a heavy hammer to wield.

The "Billie Jean" video came in, and it was brilliant. Susan Blond was doing video promotion, and she came back from MTV and told me they didn't want to play it. I knew Bob Pittman well, so I called him. He didn't take the call. Then I called Les. He didn't take the call. Eventually, I got Sykes on the phone. I said, "The fickle finger of fate points at you, John. If you don't play 'Billie Jean,' we're pulling all our videos off the air." We were CBS. You didn't fuck around with us.

After I hung up, I walked around the corner to tell Walter Yetnikoff what I'd done. When I got there, his secretary Bonnie said, "He's on the phone with Bob Pittman." Walter waved me in and he was laughing. He said, "It's your friend Bob Pittman. Bob says they'll play 'Billie Jean.'" And let's face it, that video *made* MTV, right? Because all of a sudden they started playing black videos. We integrated MTV.

JOHN SYKES: That's David's recollection of what happened. I've heard that before. But I don't remember having that conversation with him. And I wouldn't be the person to get that call. Discussions about "Billie Jean" would have come down to Bob and Walter—not even Bob and David, but Bob and *Walter*.

CAROLYN BAKER: I don't know if Walter ever talked to Bob directly, but I think that's exactly what the hell happened: CBS threatened to pull its videos, and Bob and Garland tried to cover that up. MTV was a white boy's trip. That's what it was.

RON WEISNER, manager: We submitted "Billie Jean" to MTV, but they didn't add it that first week. We were not only appalled, but surprised, too, because production-value wise, it was a great video, especially for the times. If you looked at "Billie Jean" versus everything else that was out there, there was no comparison. It was a different animal. But then what happened was, the video sort of leaked out; people saw it and were raving about it, and then MTV jumped on it. They were getting beat up because they weren't playing black artists, so we became a test case for them.

RON McCARRELL, record executive: When Ron Weisner brought in the video, we all flipped out, because it was ground-breaking. But he told us he'd run into some resistance at MTV—they were playing Journey and Van Halen, and said Michael Jackson wasn't "right for our audience." Our position was, *How can you not play this?* Ron told me his next stop was Walter's office. Then Walter called me and said, "I just spoke to MTV and they're gonna add the Michael Jackson video now." I heard this directly from Walter, and also from Ron Weisner.

Pittman and Garland are friends of mine, and they have a different version of it that's almost dismissive: "I don't know what you're talking about, we loved that video, we put it right on." I believe our version of the story. There's a mountain of circumstantial evidence that to me, proves it beyond a reasonable doubt.

FREDDY DeMANN, manager: Ron Weisner and I were comanaging Michael Jackson when "Billie Jean" came out. I had a good relationship with MTV, and I pitched the video. They said, "No, we can't play it." We all called MTV. We persevered like crazy. I went to Walter. Walter was very colorful. He called MTV and made the appropriate threats. "Billie Jean" was just too great a song not to. And it worked. They acquiesced.

WALTER YETNIKOFF: My recollection about "Billie Jean"—and I was drinking and drugging a lot during that period, so my memory's a little spotty—is that I called Pittman and said, "You have to play this video." He said, "We're a rock station, Walter, we don't play black music." I said, "That's great. I'm pulling all my stuff. Then I'm gonna tell the whole world what your attitude is towards black people." Then I said, *"And* I'm calling Quincy Jones." Quincy produced *Thriller,* of course. But just as important, Quincy was close to Steve Ross, who ran Warner Communications and was part owner of MTV. If Quincy called Ross to complain about MTV, that would be that. And Pittman said, "All right, all right, we'll play it." Now they say they played "Billie Jean" because they loved it. How plausible is it that they "loved it"? Their playlist had no black artists on it. And at the time, Michael Jackson was black. So what is this bullshit that they loved it? They were forced into it by me.

LES GARLAND: I love him dearly, but I believe Walter Yetnikoff cooked up that story about threatening to pull CBS videos if we didn't play "Billie Jean." I got more grief from Walter for not playing Barbra Streisand!

BOB PITTMAN: If anybody at CBS thought that we weren't going to play Michael Jackson, they were out of their minds. Walter Yetnikoff claims that he made us play the video. That's such a typical Walter trick, to make himself seem important to his artists. Quincy Jones, Michael's producer, is my oldest son's godfather. He and I often laugh about Walter.

RONALD "BUZZ" BRINDLE: We may have declined it initially. It seems to me CBS threatened to pull their videos. My reaction was "Great, go tell your rock acts they're not getting exposed on MTV because we're not gonna play Michael Jackson's video." There was a confrontation.

LARRY STESSEL, record executive: I heard from some fellow executives at CBS that Walter was out of his mind about "Billie Jean" and was going to pull all of our videos at MTV if they didn't play it. The story I heard—I don't know if it's true—was that Walter called Pittman. But even if MTV didn't play black videos, they were going to play "Billie Jean." It's one of the most perfect songs ever made. It's like "I Want to Hold Your Hand"—how can you not like it? It's "Billie Jean," for God's sake.

JOHN SYKES: Michael Jackson was the reason MTV went from big to huge. He put us at the center of the culture.

SUSAN BLOND: Eventually, when "Billie Jean" went on the air, someone from CBS sent champagne to MTV. I thought that was disgusting, because they'd given us such a hard time and been so awful.

TREACH, Naughty by Nature: Are you kidding me? The "Billie Jean" video was major. I rocked a red pleather jacket, can't lie. I wasn't too hardcore for that.

RALPH TRESVANT: When "Billie Jean" came on the TV, I lost my brains.

PAUL FLATTERY: Steve Barron was initially hired to do both "Billie Jean" and "Beat It." I think his "Beat It" was going to be set on a slave boat.

RONALD "BUZZ" BRINDLE: For the "Beat It" clip, Michael originally wanted to do it on a white slave ship with him as the slave master. I heard that from a director in Roberta Cruger's office.

SIOBHAN BARRON: CBS originally wanted Steve to direct "Beat It" as well, but they didn't like our concept. It was more political. It had something to do with a slave ship. All the Americans were flipping out.

PAUL FLATTERY: Michael was very mercurial, and he saw something by Bob Giraldi and asked him to direct "Beat It." And it was fantastic, obviously.

BOB GIRALDI, director: I was disappointed. "Billie Jean" had been the track I really wanted to direct.

STEVE BARRON: I have friends who say "Billie Jean" changed their lives. But "Beat It" quickly came along and stole a lot of the thunder, because it was harder and edgier.

FREDDY DeMANN: Bob Giraldi was *the* hot commercial director. His reel was phenomenal. He found a dilapidated area in downtown LA. Michael went up to the apartment where we were shooting interiors, jumped on the bed as if it were his own bed, in his own room, in his own house. He became part of it. The beat and melody of "Billie Jean" are phenomenal, but "Beat It" was a better visual. It brought out who and what Michael really was.

RON WEISNER: For "Beat It," Michael and I spent a lot of time trying to define exactly what we wanted, and to find somebody who could translate that. I looked at hundreds of demo reels, and the one that stuck out was Bob Giraldi's. He had a PSA on his reel for a free clinic or something. It was very street, and that's what we wanted: we wanted to do a contemporary version of *West Side Story*.

BOB GIRALDI: Everybody says "Beat It" was taken from *West Side Story*. It's not true. I had no idea what *West Side Story* was. My inspiration was the streets of Paterson, New Jersey, where I'm from. I listened to the song over and over, and realized it was about all the Italian hoodlums I grew up with—everybody trying to be tougher than they are, but really, we're all cowards at heart. The budget was $200,000, which was unprecedented. The art form, if you want to call it that, was not clear yet. It was sort of like, *What is this?*

Michael was beautiful. His complexion was stunning. Don't forget, I knew him as young Michael, not the getting-older, let-me-destroy-myself Michael. He had a gentle way. He didn't like me using the F word and told me so. "You use the F word too much." He was a gentle soul who exploded when he performed. Why did he do "Bad"? Why did he grab his crotch? Why did he do "Smooth

Criminal"? Most of his stuff was about being macho. This is the psychiatrist in me: I think Michael suffered a bit from being too androgynous. There was always a contradiction going with Michael.

On the first night, I came this close to walking off the set of "Beat It." Michael had the idea of getting the Crips and the Bloods for the video. We were shooting the pool-hall scene and the Crips and Bloods got rambunctious. They started smacking each other around. They didn't love being directed. I lose it when I direct, and they looked at me like they'd never been talked to like that in their lives. Everybody was scared to death. The cops came and they were going to shut us down.

So I called over Michael Peters, the choreographer. Michael was a legitimate Broadway dancer who'd choreographed major Broadway shows. It was a two-night shoot and we were supposed to dance on the second night. I said, "Let's shoot the dance scenes right now." He said, "We're not ready." I said, "Get ready."

Michael Peters and Vince Patterson, the guy with the toothpick in his mouth, came at each other with a rubber knife. Michael and Vince were living together at the time. They were lovers. On the second take, I gave a real switchblade to my AD and told him to quietly substitute it for the rubber knife. He said, "That's illegal." Michael and Vince are backing away from the knives—really backing away—because they were actually afraid. Once they started dancing, I must tell you, it was the most glorious moment of my directing life, as the macho, killer Crips and Bloods watched their brothers, most of them gay, dance in a way they never could.

"WEIRD AL" YANKOVIC: People became intimately familiar with every nuance of a video, which made it easy to do a parody. I could tweak something a bit and people would get the joke. Michael Jackson was the biggest artist in the world, and I thought it would be great to parody "Beat It." As it turned out, Michael had a great sense of humor and he personally signed off on "Eat It," which blew my mind. All of a sudden, if a manager gave us static, we could say, "Michael Jackson gave his permission, so I guess you feel like you're more important than Michael Jackson." As soon as "Eat It" went into heavy rotation, my life changed. It was overnight fame.

BOB GIRALDI: I hated that "Weird Al" video. It made fun of something serious and valuable to me. I felt it was a put-down.

HARVEY LEEDS: Jay Levey, "Weird Al"'s manager, wanted to make a video for "Eat It," but the president of Epic, Don Dempsey, was scared to ask Michael. Walter Yetnikoff had to call Michael, who thought it was flattering and hilarious. That video cost something like $27,000, and it launched Al's career. MTV loved Al. Because every time he parodied a video, it only served to reinforce the power of MTV.

BOB GIRALDI: All of a sudden, I'm a star in the video world. I went to London to work on "Say Say Say." It was a story about con artists, Paul McCartney and Michael Jackson. Paul said to me, "Let's go for a walk." He took me in the woods of the Santa Inez Valley and got me high. He tried to get me to promise I wouldn't make him dance next to Michael Jackson, because that would be suicidal.

While I was doing "Say Say Say," a reporter calls me and says, "How does it feel to work with Michael and Paul?" I said, "There's only one star on my set: me." Brilliant. The next day, Michael calls: "How could you say such a thing?" Paul was pissed. Everybody was pissed. They were going to fire me, they were going to hang me. How many times can you apologize?

JOHN LANDIS, director: Michael Jackson saw my film *An American Werewolf in London* and was taken with the special effects makeup by Rick Baker, especially the transformation. He contacted me and said he wanted to turn into a monster. That was the inspiration for "Thriller": "Can I turn into a monster?" I didn't even want to make a rock video. I felt they were just commercials to sell records. But what was interesting to me was Michael's ginormous celebrity. I thought, "Shit, I could exploit this, and maybe make a theatrical short." An old-fashioned two-reeler, fifteen minutes long, like the old Little Rascals or Laurel and Hardy shorts. I wanted to use Michael's stardom to bring back the theatrical short.

George Folsey was my partner and editor, and we figured out what it would cost to do a fifteen-minute union shoot. We had expensive ticket items: Up until Tim Burton's *Planet of the Apes*, I think "Thriller" was the largest makeup call in movie history. Rick Baker designed the zombie look—I wanted Michael to look like Michael Landon in *I Was a Teenage Werewolf*, but Rick suggested that because of Michael's features, we make it more catlike. I had Bob Paynter shoot it as we would a movie, as opposed to a down-and-dirty music video. I insisted that the dancers get at least ten days' rehearsal. The initial budget was about $500,000, which was a lot of money.

I'll never forget when Michael called Walter Yetnikoff with the budget. He was still living at his parents' house in Encino. He said, "Walter, I'm here with John Landis and George Folsey and we want to do this . . . ," and he explained it and said, "Well, they say it's gonna cost $500,000." Pause. "John, Walter wants to talk to you." And I pick up the phone, and it was like a cartoon, where my ear blows, my hair blows. He was just, "You motherfucker! If you cocksuckers think you're getting half a million . . ." I never met the guy, but could he scream. He went on and on—"Go fuck yourself," basically. He said, "The album's over, anyway. Tell Michael to work on a new album." He kept screaming. Michael asked, "What did Walter say?" I said, "Well, Walter said *no*, Mike." And Michael said, "Well then, I'll pay for it." And I said, "No, you're not putting your own money in." So George Folsey said, "Why don't we create an hour-long program, *Making Michael Jackson's "Thriller,"* with a forty-five-minute documentary on the making of 'Thriller' plus the fifteen-minute 'Thriller' video, and sell it to a network?" George and I referred to it as *The Making of Filler*—you'd see us rehearsing a scene, then you'd see the clip from the video; then us rehearsing, then the actual clip. Well, none of the networks wanted it. HBO didn't want it. Showtime was new, and they paid us something like $250,000 for a short window of exclusivity. When MTV heard that, we got a call from Pittman, screaming. Very upset. We said, "But you turned us down." Because they said they would never pay for a music video. Well, they ended up paying a little over $250,000 to show it second, which in truth was the real window, because Showtime was in less than a million homes. So that's how we got our $500,000.

WALTER YETNIKOFF: Jon Landis and Michael said they wanted to do a video, very expensive, about monsters. *That's* the part that made me crazy. I don't think it was the money. A video about monsters? What are you, nuts?

BOB PITTMAN: The only video we ever paid for was "Thriller." CBS had decided they were going to make only two videos per album. We wanted another Michael video after "Billie Jean" and "Beat It," but we didn't want to set a precedent of paying to produce videos. So we paid to produce *The Making of "Thriller,"* but the money went to pay for "Thriller." And it turned out to be the single most successful video in the history of MTV.

LES GARLAND: I gotta give it to Pittman, he came up with it. I said, "If this thing ends up airing somewhere else, it's gonna be so embarrassing." He goes, "Garland, I've got an idea. That's not a video. That's a short film. We can buy a short film and not change our precedent of paying for music." I go, "That's fucking brilliant."

JOHN LANDIS: Bob Pittman, Michael's lawyer John Branca—those guys always claim they made "Thriller." The reality is, it was a vanity video. Everything that happened on "Thriller" happened because Michael wanted to turn into a monster. None of it was planned. I want to make that clear, because there was a course taught at the Harvard Business School on "Thriller," and it was complete bullshit.

LES GARLAND: I was on the set for "Thriller." Michael was so pure and lovable. I got there and was invited into his trailer. So I'm sitting in the living room section, talking to two women who work for Michael. Pretty soon, from the back of the trailer, a pair of socks come bouncing across the room and land right by me. One of the women said, "That means Michael is ready to see you." I go, "That's unique."

I walk back, and it's pitch dark. And I'm like, "Michael?" He says, "Come over here." I go, "You're gonna need to smile or open your eyes real wide." And that got a little chuckle. He was laying down resting and I sat in a chair. He goes, "Garland, I can't thank you enough for everything you and MTV have done for me." I said, "Michael, this is backwards. It's me who should be thanking you."

JOHN LANDIS: One of the reasons people liked "Thriller" so much is because it's a little movie. When I say a little movie, I mean it was made like a motion picture as opposed to a commercial. It's a funny story with "Thriller": The song was five minutes long, and I needed it to be twelve minutes long for the video. Bruce Swedien, who engineered *Thriller*, and Quincy Jones, who produced it, would not let me have the master tracks. So Michael and I went to the recording studio at three in the morning. We walked past the guard—"Hi, Michael." "Hi"—put the tracks in a big suitcase and walked out with them. Then we drove across Hollywood, duped them, and put them back. And if you listen to "Thriller" on the video and on record, they're very different. I really cut it up and changed things. One of my guilty pleasures is that when I see a group of people try to do the "Thriller" dance using the record, they have to wander around like zombies waiting for the goddamn music to start, because the recorded version begins with all these sound effects that aren't in the video.

LARRY STESSEL: I saw "Thriller" for the first time at Michael's house, in his screening room, with his brothers Tito, Jackie, and Randy. When Michael said, "I'm not like other boys" in the video, Jackie and Randy started laughing. Jackie put his mouth to my ear and repeated the line: "He's not like other boys." Michael said, "Shut up, Jackie, that's not nice."

HARVEY LEEDS: Michael had a little movie theater upstairs in his house, with all these people watching an Elizabeth Taylor movie. I was being really quiet, and then I realized those weren't people—they were mannequins.

RALPH TRESVANT: The first time we saw "Thriller" was at Michael's house. We played with his llama, spent the whole day with him. Michael's mom was there, both his sisters were there, all the animals.

BOBBY BROWN: His sisters was running around and everybody was slapping asses. That was their thing. They would slap each other on the ass all the time. Michael would smack Janet and LaToya on the ass. They'd say, "You bad, you stop it!" And I was sitting there, thinking, "Oh boy, I would love to slap that ass, too."

CEE LO GREEN, artist: I was terrified of "Thriller" when I was a kid. I ran from the room when it was on. Michael Jackson was someone we all held dear—we lived vicariously through his ability, his light, his love. So you could associate with becoming a monster. If he could be possessed, then I *damn* sure could be possessed, because Michael was so much stronger than I.

ROZONDA "CHILLI" THOMAS, TLC: Oh my god, I loved Michael Jackson. When his videos came on, I'd run over and kiss the TV. Remember the close-ups in "Beat It"? There was one in the beginning when he was lying down on the bed, then he sat up and turned his head, and the camera came closer. I kissed him there. And when he was walking through the pool tables in the bar, and he did that heavy breathing? He went "*HUH-HUH-HUH*"? Ooh, I was all over the TV. I loved that heavy breathing.

JOHN LANDIS: Michael wanted "Thriller" to have a proper theatrical premiere. So we had a premiere at the Crest Theater on Westwood Boulevard in LA. I've been to the Oscars and the Golden Globes and BAFTA. I've been to Cannes. But I've never been to anything as star-studded as that. Everyone from Diana Ross to Warren Beatty. Mike had an insane range of acquaintances. He was a passionate Hollywood film buff. Everyone knows about his friendship with Liz Taylor, but he was also close to people like Spanky McFarland, from *Our Gang*. We had the strangest people visiting the set of "Thriller." Walt Disney's widow, Lillian. Fred Astaire came to a rehearsal. Gene Kelly came to a screening, and so did Fayard Nicholas of the Nicholas Brothers. Jackie Kennedy came to the set. It was three in the morning in East LA—which is not a very nice place—and Michael's Japanese assistant said, "Michael would like to see you." I knocked on the door of his Winnebago, and as I stepped up into it, Michael goes, "John, do you know Mrs. Onassis?" And there's Jackie fucking Kennedy.

BOB PITTMAN: We were playing it every hour, and announcing when it would air: "'Thriller' is one hour away," "fifty minutes away," "thirty minutes away." Ironically, we probably would *not* have gone that far, nor would we have gotten that involved, had it not been for Rick James's criticism that we didn't play black artists. "Thriller" brought people to MTV for the first time, and it made them stay and watch it again and again. Now everybody was into MTV.

ED LOVER, *Yo! MTV Raps* host: MTV didn't play black videos. So why would I watch? When "Thriller" got on MTV, we started checking it out. It was like whoever you knew had MTV, however you could you get to MTV, you had to see it. Movie theaters showed "Thriller." Any nightclub, any spot you went to, if they had "Thriller," they showed it.

LES GARLAND: We were averaging a 1.2 ratings share, but the rating would spike when "Thriller" aired.

DAVE HOLMES: My family went on a ski vacation to Breckenridge, Colorado, and I skied for forty-five minutes a day, just to get my folks off my back. MTV was showing "Thriller" every hour—so twenty minutes of every hour was devoted to "Thriller." And I watched it every time.

TOM FRESTON: "Thriller" was the *Jersey Shore* of its day.

FREDDY DeMANN: I was blessed to manage two of the biggest and best artists of the twentieth century—Michael Jackson and Madonna. The camera was kind to both of them, and they loved the camera. Did MTV make them or did they make MTV? I think it was a happy combination. I owned the '80s.

CLIFF BURNSTEIN: Things started to turn around in 1983. A more positive spirit enveloped the country, and that was reflected on MTV. The videos were flamboyant, over-the-top, happy, bright, colorful. 1983 was the year of *Pyromania*, Michael Jackson, the Police. These were all ten-million sellers. I think 1983 was really the beginning of the '80s, in many ways.

JOHN LANDIS: "Thriller" made MTV. "Thriller" created the home video business. "Thriller" created so many things.

LEE MASTERS: Bob Pittman came from a radio background, and radio formats tend to be very specific. One thing we learned, one thing Michael Jackson did teach us, was that MTV is not a radio station.

DONNA SUMMER: Michael tended to be outside the box, and he was not going to allow anybody to constrain his creativity. He saw himself as more of an actor, in some ways. A musician, but also an actor. I mean, until today I don't think I've seen any more intensely passionate, well-directed videos.

USHER, artist: His dancing was his magic. He was able to comingle current movement with a classic understanding of choreography. Michael Jackson made three different dance styles—jazz, hip-hop, and show—all work together. He wanted to know what the kids were doing in the street, but he also kept it theatrical, out of respect for dance tradition.

TONI BASIL: When he danced, he looked like he walked on water. He took Fred Astaire footage and steps taught to him by street dancers like Casper and Cooley from *Soul Train*, who taught him the moonwalk, and made it into his own quilt. He's the greatest dancing pop star ever. Only Tina Turner and James Brown came close to the rank of equals.

MC HAMMER, artist: "Thriller" blew the roof off. When Michael is dancing in the middle of the street, that was *West Side Story*, and then we had a horror film going on, too. That went beyond the song and gave a bigger vision than what we would have seen in our heads.

LIONEL RICHIE, artist: When MTV started, it wanted nothing to do with black artists. They told me that my music didn't fit. I admit I was a little offended. MTV was such an innovative company, and I thought, *Wow, are we gonna miss out on* this? But then I gave them "All Night Long," after Michael had broken down the door. And from then on I was on MTV.

JOHN TAYLOR: For our first two albums, Duran Duran shot on video and worked very cheaply. After Michael Jackson, when American artists got a sense of the potency of a well-thought-out video, they started shooting on film, and everything became much more expensive.

RICK SPRINGFIELD: Michael Jackson had taken hold of the video form and shown everyone what you're supposed to do with it. We all thought, *Oh, okay—dancing.* Thank God I only danced in that one video, "Affair of the Heart," because it was abhorrent.

BRYAN ADAMS: Michael's videos stand up today. The guitar bands suffered because they weren't innovative—just, you know, standing on a rock cliff with a wind machine blowing your hair.

JANET JACKSON: My brother was always trying to do something different, fresh, exciting. Something that had never been done before. George Michael did a wonderful job at that. Madonna did a wonderful job, too. My brother, though, did it the best.

Chapter 15

"THE TWO M'S"

MADONNA TOUCHES MTV FOR
THE VERY FIRST TIME

MICHAEL JACKSON WAS THE FIRST VIDEO ARTIST; Madonna was second, and she's the one who created the idea that video could be a forum for provocation and exhibitionism. Who else could stir the Vatican to condemn a music video? After a few low-budget, undistinguished clips, she found her footing, in part by teaming with director Mary Lambert. Madonna filled the frames of her videos with images of burning crosses, interracial kisses, gay kisses, lavish jewels, crucifixes, wedding dresses, S&M toys, Keith Carradine, Danny Aiello, zoo animals, cleavage shot from above, and cleavage shot from below. Her appearance at the first Video Music Awards in 1984 was the award-show equivalent of Abraham Lincoln's Gettysburg Address—the ideal against which all successors would be measured. She treated MTV as her canvas and, later, her bitch.

But at first, her interdependence with MTV ("You believed in me when I was chubby," she said in a filmed tribute to their tenth anniversary) was a source of contempt within the rock establishment. She, like MTV, was viewed as a passing fancy. "Madonna will be out of the business in six months," a *Billboard* editor pronounced, because "her image has completely overshadowed her music." This quote is the "Dewey Defeats Truman" of music video, disproven by Madonna's seventeen consecutive top ten hits. She did this not by making her image secondary to her music, but by combining them until they were inseparable.

LES GARLAND: Freddy DeMann had managed the Jacksons and Michael, but he got fired by the dad, Joe Jackson. So Freddy wasn't really doing anything for about a year, if not more, and he was a good friend of mine. One afternoon he phoned and said, "Gar-Man? I got one that's gonna be huge. She's gonna be bigger than Michael." I go, "Dude, you've got big balls. Big balls, Freddy." "Trust me, Gar. Her name is Madonna." He showed up a few days later and played her video, "Burning Up." It sounded very disco to me. But all right, we'll put it on.

SUSAN SILVERMAN: Madonna came into our office on a skateboard, all sweaty and dirty. I was like, "Shit, what's with this girl?" She went to see Bob Regehr—a big product manager at Warner Bros.—and left a note on his bulletin board that said, "Sorry I missed you, because I'm gonna be a star."

BOB GIRALDI: Freddy DeMann brought Madonna to my studio, and we talked about me maybe directing her first single. I said to Freddy, "I'm not sure she's going to amount to anything." *Good job, Giraldi.*

STEVE BARRON: I didn't like "Burning Up." Not at all. But my partner, Simon Fields, said, "We've got to do this because it's Warner Bros. and they think she's gonna be massive." I went to New York to meet her, begrudgingly, and showed up at an address in SoHo, which turned out to be a squat, basically. Madonna was scantily clad, working out to a massive disco track. She was charismatic. She kept putting her head down on the table and talking to me, very flirtatious, and that gave me the idea for the scene in "Burning Up" where her face is on the road, and the camera's really low and close.

JEFF AYEROFF: I introduced Madonna to Steve Barron. I don't think that's one of his best videos.

GALE SPARROW: "Burning Up" was too disco for MTV. Simon Fields arranged a dinner for us to meet her. Madonna wore a black *schmatte*, and it had green on it—I thought it was mold. She had on purple lipstick and was very sweet. A few days later, she called the office and said, "Are you gonna play my video?" I said, "It's not quite our format, but we'll play it." So we played it at three in the morning.

STEVE BARRON: Madonna had a fling with my partner Simon. Before we shot the video, she said, "Come on, we gotta go to Trashy Lingerie"—which was across from Simon's flat—"and get some stuff for me to wear." So she tried on lingerie for us. "Do you like it?," that kind of thing. A week after the video, I rang up Simon at his flat. He had an answer machine, and the message said, very English: "This is Simon Fields, leave a message after the beep." But this one day, the voice on the machine said, "Hi, this is Simon's phone"—it was Madonna's voice—"if you're a guy, leave a message. If you're a girl, *fuck off.*"

SIMON FIELDS: I had gone to London for the weekend, and I told Madonna she could stay in my apartment while I was gone. She changed my outgoing phone message to something crazy, like, "If you're a girl and looking for Simon, you can go eat pigeons on the roof."

DANIEL KLEINMAN, director: Simon Fields and I used to share a house together. Simon has an edge of wheeler-dealer about him, but he's also the most charming man in the world, which is quite a good quality for a producer. I had the looks and no charm, and he had the charm and no looks. I thought he had a face like the back of a bus. I mean, how he got Janice Dickinson into bed, I do not know. That was the end of our sharing a house together.

STEPHEN R. JOHNSON, director: I used to say, "Simon Fields is a snake. But I want him to be *my* snake." When I arrived at Limelight, I was made aware by Simon that he had slept with Madonna. Then I bumped into two more guys who said they'd slept with Madonna. One was her mixer, I think, and one was a record executive. At first I thought she was just anther floozy trying to fuck her way to the top. But I sat back and watched as she played them like a fiddle, and I realized she was a genius. She was using what she had and was getting way more out of those guys than a piece of tail.

SHARON ORECK: When I got into the video business, I didn't actually know what a video was. I hadn't seen MTV because I was too poor to afford cable. I went to film school, then worked in the independent film industry, which prior to music videos was the only place you could get experience if you weren't in the union. It was all karate movies and horror films. Then in 1983, I produced a short film that got nominated for an Academy Award.

I kept getting phone calls from a friend of mine, a camerawoman who was working on a video called "Borderline" for some chick named Madonna. She kept calling with questions like "Where do you get a generator?" "How does film flashing work?" "What do you do when you don't have lights?" Basic film questions. I said, "What are you doing?" And she said, "I'm doing this thing called a video for Madonna." And I was like, "Don't you have a producer? Don't you have someone who gets the stuff for you?" And she's like, "We do, but he doesn't know what to do." So I said, "Well, I'll help you this time, but next time you should hire me, and I'll produce it."

TONY WARD, actor: Since I was a kid, when I first saw "Borderline," I was really obsessed with Madonna. I was like, "That's my lady and I'm gonna be with her someday." I knew it. But I wasn't obsessed with her music. I was into black music, and then Oingo Boingo.

MARY LAMBERT, director: I studied film and painting at the Rhode Island School of Design in the late '70s. Tina Weymouth and Chris Frantz of Talking Heads were two of my closest friends at RISD. After college, I moved to LA and got a job in the fledgling special effects business. I was on the fringes of the film industry, directing special effects commercials for washing machines, going to punk clubs, and making weird films. And then, in like, '82, I saw a music video: Rickie Lee Jones's "Chuck E.'s in Love." I thought, *Wow, this is kind of like my films. I should do music videos.* I had no concept of the industry, actually. I thought I was going to be an artist and make short abstract films. I was really stupid.

I asked Tina and Chris if I could do a music video for them, which was "As Above, So Below," for their other band, the Tom Tom Club. When I took it to Warner Bros. to show Jeff Ayeroff, he said, "This is great, but it's useless, because we're not promoting the album anymore." But he did give me a job directing a video for a new artist named Madonna. She'd released a couple of disco-pop singles, and Jeff wanted to position her with a little more integrity and depth. He gave me the song "Borderline" and bought me a plane ticket to New York to go meet her. I had no idea what she even looked like. When I heard her music, I thought she was black.

First I had to track her down—this was before cell phones—and she wasn't easy to find. She was living in a bare-bones apartment on the Upper East Side. It didn't look like anyone lived there, to tell you the truth. There wasn't any furniture. But we hit it off. We bonded on the level of just being girls. I came away thinking that she was a piece of work, and that this was going to be fun. She had four or five different boyfriends at the time. One of them was a record producer, Jellybean Benitez, but he was really, really jealous of everybody. Of every*thing*.

He was the prototype for Sean Penn. He was convinced that she was seeing other guys and that he wasn't going to be able to control her. And he was completely right, of course, on both accounts.

We talked for a couple of days about "Borderline." She was really into Hispanic boys, and she wanted the video to be about having an affair with a cute Hispanic boy who was part of the street scene. She wanted to be involved in casting the cute Hispanic boy. She was going to be in LA, so we decided to make it into a real LA video. I knew the downtown LA area really well, because there were a lot of artist bars there.

There was no formula. We were *inventing* it as we went along. When I screened "Borderline" for Madonna's manager, Freddy DeMann, he was hysterical that I had combined black-and-white footage with color footage. Nobody had done that before. He made me screen it for all the secretaries in his office and see how they reacted, because he felt I had crossed a line that shouldn't be crossed.

JEFF AYEROFF: MTV jumped on "Borderline," and that was it. Away we go.

CINDY CRAWFORD, model; host, *House of Style*: Madonna was the first person on MTV whose style we tried to emulate. I was a freshman at Northwestern University and my roommate from New Jersey was a huge Madonna fan. The way she mixed things—lace and skirts, gloves and boots—I didn't know what to make of it, but there were elements I could relate to.

MARY LAMBERT: She works with a lot of different stylists and costume designers, but nobody really dresses Madonna except Madonna. The whole trashed-out lingerie street-look—where your dark roots and bra strap are always showing, and there's holes in your stockings—that was all her.

DEBBIE GIBSON, artist: Madonna paved the way for all of us, and may we never forget it. "Lucky Star" was my favorite video, because it was all about her and the performance. Those early Madonna videos were about her energy, and what she was wearing, and how she was dancing. When I was fourteen, I won two tickets on WPLJ radio to see her in concert, and my cousin and my sister were upset that they couldn't go, because I had to take my mom. And so in a very cocky manner, I said, "Well then, I'll win two more." And I did. The four of us dressed like Madonna and went to the concert.

JEFF AYEROFF: I made "Lucky Star" for $14,000 with a friend who was a pot grower from Bolinas, California. We'd released "Everybody," "Burning Up," "Holiday," and "Borderline" as singles. And Madonna didn't want to release "Lucky Star." Around the same time, she was getting sued and needed money. I said, "Let me release 'Lucky Star,' and I guarantee you'll sell enough records to pay that off." "Lucky Star" broke the first album wide open.

WAYNE ISHAM: Jeff Ayeroff gave his friend Arthur Pierson a video to direct, and I ended up as the director of photography on that clip, "Lucky Star." And Madonna was so pissy. We start to do a shot and I realized I was using the wrong lens. I said, "Sorry, I have to change lenses." And she was *angry*. Didn't want to wait. I said, "Dude, I can't just *shit* a lens." Everybody was freaking out. Maybe I could have said it in a *different* way.

MARY LAMBERT: For "Like a Virgin," Jeff Ayeroff said, "We want to do something outrageous." I said, "Let's do it in Venice!" The idea of Madonna singing in a gondola was the most outrageous thing I could think of. And Madonna dug it, because she has the whole thing with the Catholic Church and her Italian heritage. It turned into a huge party. One night, we were waiting to take a ferry back to where we were staying. Everyone had been drinking, and somebody bet the photographer Larry Williams that he couldn't put his fist in his mouth. He did get it all the way in his mouth, but then it got stuck and he couldn't get it out. He won the bet, though.

Madonna stayed at the Hotel Cipriani, partly because she was avoiding Simon Fields, who still wanted to sleep with her—so did everybody else, for that matter—and partly because there was a pool there, and she swam every morning as part of her exercise routine. The rest of us stayed at a sleazebag hotel on Lido, a little island just outside Venice. There were 3 million mosquitoes and the mattresses were stuffed with rocks. Shooting in Venice was definitely excessive. We shot during the day, ate in little cafes, and partied with Madonna at the Cipriani at night.

JEFF AYEROFF: By that point, Madonna was on the cover of *Rolling Stone*. So we went to Venice, like a bunch of fucking whack jobs. I don't know what we spent—$150,000? $175,000?—but it was way more than we'd ever spent on a video. Simon Fields was having an affair with Madonna, Mary Lambert was having an affair with somebody else. What did I do on the shoot? I sat on the back of the barge and yelled "*Duck*," so Madonna didn't smack her head on the bridges.

MARY LAMBERT: There's this famous yearly Carnival in Venice where everyone wears elaborate masks. I loved that idea, of things not being what they seem. Madonna's love interest in the video wore a lion mask, and that gave me the idea to get a real lion. I wanted to have the guy in the lion mask turn into an actual lion. Nobody else liked the lion. Madonna went along with it.

SIMON FIELDS: The lion started to get crazy around Madonna. No one else. And then we found out that you can't have a lion around a woman when she's on her period.

MARY LAMBERT: You can't be in Madonna's presence, ever, without feeling the raw sexuality and sensuality she exudes. And that's something I encouraged in all the videos we did. When you're near her, and she turns that charm on you, it's like somebody switching on a spotlight. The camera sees it.

SHARON ORECK: I was on the "Material Girl" set when Madonna first met Sean Penn. They were so perfect for each other—she was an extraordinary beauty and a rebel princess, and he was a young god of cinema and also clearly the James Dean, rebel type. The PA on the video, Meegan Lee Ochs, had been Sean's assistant. She was Phil Ochs's daughter, and Sean met her when he was trying to make a film about Phil. So she said to either Mary Lambert or me, "My ex boss really wants to meet Madonna." The crew knew he was coming and everyone was super excited and giddy. We were shooting the musical sequence where she's in the pink halter dress. So he met her when she was in her Marilyn Monroe finery. We all knew they were going to fall in love and get married.

Madonna's breasts are super perky, so they tend to pop out when she dances. In the "Material Girl" video, she's wearing a pink outfit, and I guess it didn't have a bra, so whenever she'd go upside down, or lay back with her arms in the air, one or two of her boobs would come out.

FREDDY DeMANN: People often misunderstand the "Material Girl" video. The idea was that Madonna was a Marilyn Monroe–type actress playing the role of a gold digger—a "material girl"—in a musical, but off-camera she was a good person. She chooses the poor guy in the shitty car instead of the rich guy. But everyone assumed Madonna was identifying with the material girl, not the good girl. The title stuck to her, and that bothered her. She never liked that handle.

MARY LAMBERT: Madonna's always had a dual personality. A lot of her early videos—"Borderline," "Material Girl," "La Isla Bonita," perhaps "Like a Virgin" and "Like a Prayer"—are largely about her straddling two different worlds.

DANIEL KLEINMAN: After I shot Madonna in concert on the "Like a Virgin" tour, she came to look at the footage while I was editing, and to tell me what I'd done wrong. She was going out with Sean Penn, and she used to take cuts home and show him, and she'd come back with notes from Sean Penn. The editor and I would tear our hair out.

ADAM HOROVITZ, Beastie Boys: The first time we went to LA as a band was when we opened for Madonna. That was the greatest. Kids were literally in tears when we were playing. It was one of the most punk rock things we've ever done. And Madonna is the best. After the first night, her manager, Freddy DeMann, said, "These guys suck." "No, seriously, they suck. They need to go home." And Madonna was like, "These guys are staying." She put her foot down. We didn't realize until later that the audience's hatred for us worked in her favor. When she got onstage, they couldn't have been happier to see her.

TOM FRESTON: Madonna once said that we grew up together. We sort of did. It was the two M's, Madonna and MTV. She created what a modern artist could be, and how you could reinvent yourself, or reinterpret yourself, with music videos.

MARK GOODMAN: I interviewed Madonna a couple of times. Once when we were in Miami, talking backstage, I said, "I don't know if you remember, I'm Mark Goodman. I interviewed you at MTV before you were 'Madonna.'" And she looked at me and said, "Mark, I was *always* Madonna."

Chapter 16

"YOU GOT CHAR-AS-MA"

PRINCE, BRUCE, BILLY IDOL, AND THE GODS OF 1984

THE FIRST PHASE OF MTV—NAIVE, EXPERIMENTAL, low-key, low-budget—had come to an end. Skeptical record executives, watching Michael Jackson and Madonna, now had inarguable proof that an expensive video could be a wise investment.

For the record business, this was the first good news in years. Between 1975 and 1978, record sales had grown from $2.4 billion a year to $4.1 billion, a 71 percent increase in three years. By 1981, when MTV launched, sales had recessed to $3.9 billion. Ten years later, annual sales were at $7.8 billion. Rarely has an industry benefitted so well from an innovation it rejected.

The average budget had been $30,000 to $40,000, but videos now became more sleek and elaborate—and so grueling that *three different people* went temporarily blind. As more cities were wired for cable, and more cable operators began to carry MTV, the network also benefitted from a fluke of timing: 1984 was a fantastic time for pop and rock music. Prince, Billy Idol, Cyndi Lauper, and Van Halen all became superstars that year. Even Bruce Springsteen, the spiritual leader of rock's anti-video movement, relented, though his first big video was one he didn't like.

BOB PITTMAN: Until Michael Jackson and Madonna, we didn't have an act who was truly a video artist. We, without shame, flogged Michael Jackson videos, because we wanted other artists to see how you *should* do a video. We wanted to advance the art form. If you look at videos prior to "Thriller" and after "Thriller," there was a marked change. Every artist wanted to do *that* kind of video. Three guys standing on a stage began to look pretty lame.

PAUL FLATTERY: Before MTV, bands used to break out regionally. And then MTV became the national radio station, with pictures. It became the tail that wagged the dog.

ABBEY KONOWITCH: I feel like a really old guy when I say this, but back then, the industry could make a hit. Clive Davis at Arista, Donnie Ienner at Columbia, David Geffen—if they decided something should be a hit, it was a hit. And if MTV decided a song was going to be a hit, it became a hit. Today, the consumer makes that decision. There is no gatekeeper with that kind of power.

JOHN SYKES: 1984 was our tipping point. It was an incredible year for music: Bruce Springsteen, Michael Jackson, Prince, Madonna, Van Halen. All of a sudden, we began to feel the wind at our backs. Artists were selling tens of millions of records, in no small part due to video. And finally, *finally*, after three years, people understood what we'd been pitching them.

GALE SPARROW: John Sykes and I went to an international video conference in St. Tropez. Every record-label person that dealt with video was there. Elton John's manager, John Reid, had a boat, so he'd have unbelievable cocktail parties there. The guy who put together the conference went to jail because he owed so much money to the hotel we stayed at. Everything was comped: our rooms, all our food and alcohol. We drank St. Tropez dry. They ran out of Cristal champagne. On the last night, Harvey Leeds decided there was no way we could drive from St. Tropez to Cannes and make our flights, so he hired three helicopters to take us. We were living like millionaires.

TIM NEWMAN: This St. Tropez event was a great deal of fun with a lot of really bad behavior. You felt like you belonged to this interesting, crazy little club.

LIZ HELLER, record executive: We stayed at an incredibly grand hotel, Les Mas De Chastelas. John has always been healthy and fit, really into exercise, and one night I said, "So what are we gonna do tonight?' And John very seriously said, "Well, it's a health night. I've got to be in bed by 5 A.M."

TOMMY MOTTOLA: Sykes got friendly with John Mellencamp, so we put together a big promotion. We were trying to get in everybody's good favor at MTV, so we'd get as much heavy rotation as possible.

JOHN SYKES: I met John Mellencamp performing in New York. I think he was John Cougar at the time. We were playing "Jack and Diane" over and over again. And he was a smart guy. He said, "Okay, I'm gonna do business with you guys." I asked if he wanted to do a promotion for us where we'd give away a pink house. I said, "We'll buy it in your hometown, and we'll have a big party if you'll play in the living room." He said, "I'll do that."

MARCY BRAFMAN: We went to the Russian Tea Room, and there was a certain amount of vodka being drunk. Bob Pittman said, "You know what we should do? We should buy a house somewhere and blow it up." We're like, "Yeah! Let's do that." And we did, pretty much. We got college kids to spray-paint it pink, and then Mellencamp drove his motorcycle through the house and out the door.

JOHN SYKES: The response turned out to be huge. We bought the house, a little shack, I think we paid $20,000 for it, after which I get a letter from John, asking, "Did you see *Rolling Stone* this week? The house you bought is across the street from a toxic waste dump. You gotta get another house." So I got on the plane and went to Indiana to find another house. I pulled up in the car, and a woman came out with cookies to give to me, because she really wanted to sell her house, this poor single mom with her kid. I didn't even get out of the car. I said, "We'll take it." And that first house stayed on the books for MTV through, like, 1992. They couldn't sell it, because it was across the street from a toxic waste dump. They finally wrote it off.

JON LANDAU: John Sykes wanted us to do an MTV contest. I said, "You know, we're not really the contest types," but they came up with the idea of being a Bruce roadie for a day. It was an enormous success in terms of the number of people who entered, and some nice kid won a signed guitar, and they filmed a little reel of him pretending to do different tasks. That promotion probably had the impact of a couple of videos.

MILES COPELAND: As MTV became the primary outlet for pop music, everybody started putting as much effort into videos as they did into recording a song. Other acts came along, doing more adventurous videos, so you had to keep up. You could no longer just have a guy standing there strumming his guitar.

BOB GIRALDI: "Love Is a Battlefield" was about a runaway. I give Pat Benatar credit, because she was not a dancer, at all. But she almost pulled it off.

PAT BENATAR: The choreographer on "Love Is a Battlefield" was Michael Peters, who worked with Michael Jackson. And I have two left feet. That *five, six, seven, eight* style of dancing? Are you fucking nuts? I can't do that.

So there I was, like, "Oh good Christ, what have I gotten myself into?" I hated it so much. I was crying, and Michael Peters is like, "Come on!" I'm happy I did it, but I can't say there was one moment when it was pleasant. When I do the song live now, I go back by the drums and do the "Battlefield" dance for like eight seconds, and the crowd goes nuts.

SINEAD O'CONNOR, artist: I thought "Love Is a Battlefield" was quite good, with the threatening gang of dancing women coming toward the camera. I also liked all of Cyndi Lauper's stuff. She was unconventional in terms of how she looked, so it was encouraging to those of us who were young women at the time.

CYNDI LAUPER, artist: I wanted "Girls Just Want to Have Fun" to be an anthem for women around the world—and I mean *all* women—and a sustaining message that we are powerful human beings. I made sure that when a woman saw the video, she would see herself represented, whether she was thin or heavy, glamorous or not, and whatever race she was. It was about representing as many different women as I could. And I cast my mother, to be honest, because I just wanted to hang out with her. And you know what? She was a natural.

AL TELLER: MTV compounded the possibility of overexposure. I think Cyndi Lauper got caught in the MTV trap. Her image became frozen because of MTV. Which is unfortunate, because she's a very talented artist. She should have had a stronger career. If Madonna hadn't been a marketing genius and reinvented herself from album to album, she would have been toast many years ago.

CYNDI LAUPER: Funny, my manager, she now says that maybe my image became so big that my talent got hidden. I can see that now, but we put our energy into making videos because I got more love from MTV at first than I did from radio.

GEORGE MICHAEL, artist: I think I picked up on how the business worked really quickly. The way people in record companies respond when they see someone who genuinely knows what he's doing is unbelievable; they never say *no*. It starts with what to do for videos, then it becomes what singles should be released.

JAZZ SUMMERS, manager: Wham!'s "Wake Me Up Before You Go-Go" is a bit camp. Two young boys dancing around in shorts. I thought it was tacky, and I said so. I tried to talk them out of it, but my management partner, Simon Napier-Bell, was more camp than a row of tents. He thought it was lovely. And MTV really got behind it.

JON ROSEMAN: "Careless Whisper" was a fucking disaster. We shot it in Miami. After the first day of shooting, George told me he didn't like his hair.

ANDY MORAHAN: Wham! went to Miami to shoot "Careless Whisper," and they didn't like what they shot, so their manager, Jazz Summers, called me. Jazz had managed my college band, Havana Let's Go—Tim Pope was supposed to do our first video but we couldn't afford him, and since I'd studied film at college, I made it instead. Jazz said, "I need a favor. We screwed up the video, and I'd like you to reshoot it." By then I'd developed a small reputation as a director. "Careless Whisper" is basically George Michael performing in an empty theater, the Lyceum in London. It's probably best known for how much George's hair resembles Princess Diana's.

JAZZ SUMMERS: MTV was pounding Wham! videos. It was like Wham! TV. George and Andrew Ridgeley were dancing on the carpets of 22 million homes, fifteen times a day. In cities where MTV was big, we were selling loads of records. I sat down with Simon Napier-Bell. I'd stopped drinking and he was still drinking, so he got drunk. He said, "Wham! should be playing stadiums." Then he got even more drunk, and said, "Fuck it, let's do something interesting. Let's go to China." I thought it was a great idea. We could get national and international press by being the first pop band in China.

So we went to China and made a film, and took footage from that to make the "Freedom" video: George and Andrew walking around the Great Wall of China, a bit of concert footage, and it starts with a minute and a half of the Chinese countryside, and zillions of people walking over a bridge and riding their bikes. MTV were chomping at the bit for it. They said, "We want an exclusive on it. But we don't want to air the bit on the front of the video." I said, "In that case, you can't have an exclusive." And I went back to England.

MTV needed this video. So John Sykes and Les Garland flew to London with David Hilton, their top negotiator. Hilton set up the Fox network years later. We went to an Italian restaurant, and he said, "We'd like to play the video six times a day." I wanted nine times a day, and I wanted it in peak-viewing time. He said, "I'm not sure we can do that." I said, "You can do whatever you want. You can show it once an hour if you want. In fact, *that's* what I want; I want you to show it once an hour every day for the first ten days, *with* the introduction on the front, and after that, you can take it off." And he said, "Deal!" David Hilton has been one of my best friends ever since.

Everybody said I was crazy when we did the stadium tour, but we picked cities where MTV was on. We had 60,000 people in LA, 40,000 people in Miami. We didn't play Chicago, because MTV wasn't strong enough there. Ticket sales in a city were directly proportional to the strength of MTV in that market.

DEBBIE GIBSON: Being a gay-boy magnet even at fourteen, I was in love with George Michael. I'd come home from school and turn on MTV—and there was "Wake Me Up Before You Go-Go." There were a lot of people dressed in white, dancing. I thought all thirty people were members of Wham! George Michael had a million-watt smile and a tan. There was a Wham! camp and a Duran Duran camp, and I was in the Wham! camp. For me, Duran Duran were sort of dark compared to Wham! They probably had more songs in minor keys.

BRIAN GRANT: I made Duran's "New Moon on Monday" because Russell Mulcahy wasn't available. I wasn't the first choice. We attempted to make a little movie, and I'm not sure we succeeded. We shot in Noyers, a village northeast of Paris, and the former Miss France was in the video. The band was instrumental in casting her, I recollect.

NICK RHODES: "New Moon on Monday" is my least favorite of our videos.

JOHN TAYLOR: Russell optioned the William Burroughs book *Wild Boys*, and he was in development with the film. The film fell through, which we benefitted from because Russell took all the crazy, fantastic ideas he'd developed for the film and jammed them into the video.

RUSSELL MULCAHY: *Wild Boys* is a hard novel to read. Very homoerotic. One day I was on vacation in Greece and I ran into Simon Le Bon and Nick Rhodes. Their yacht pulled up next to our rented yacht.

SIMON LE BON: I had taken a sailing boat and Russell had brought his boyfriend on another boat.

RUSSELL MULCAHY: We started talking about *Wild Boys* and they asked to write a song for the film. They spent a lot of money on the video, around $1 million. Sting was next door filming *The Bride*, and he came over to the set and went, "Holy fuck." It was a four-day shoot, and celebrities kept turning up to gawk at this extraordinary set, with a giant windmill that had poor Simon strapped to it. The windmill would spin around and Simon's head would go underwater into this chilly tank. It did break down at one point, and people had to jump in and lift his head out.

PERRI LISTER: "Wild Boys" was outrageous. That went on for two weeks at Shepperton Studios. There were all kinds of freaks in that video. I think they had the tallest man in England, and a guy who was twenty-four but looked like he was two hundred. There must have been twenty-five dwarves as well. One of the girls had a terrible fear of dwarves, and every time they came near, she'd start gasping and palpitating. Russell had me topless, painted gray from head to toe, and my hair was painted white. At 6 A.M., they would stand there and spray-paint us. We'd all been up most of the night. There was one scene where a guy flew across the ceiling, and everyone heard this ghasly sound—*KA CHUNK*. I think he broke his collarbone.

RUSSELL MULCAHY: There's a scene where we put Billy Idol's girlfriend Perri among all the dystopian, *Mad Max*–looking boys prancing along. I asked her, "Can we see a tit? One tit?" She said, "Darling, at this price, you're gonna get two!"

JEFF STEIN: I was dragged into making Billy Idol's "Rebel Yell." Bill Aucoin, Billy's manager, had been KISS's manager. He was a marketing genius. Bill lived it up—you could lose brain cells by osmosis being with him. He was the most full-tilt character I knew, besides Keith Moon. Bill knew I had done the Who documentary *The Kids Are Alright*, and he kept saying, "We're getting lame concepts for the video." I said, "If I were you, I'd do a live performance." He said, "Great. Can you do it tomorrow?"

It was the holiday season, so all the equipment houses were closed and we had nowhere to shoot it. Somehow we organized getting the Capitol Theater in New Jersey the next night. We bused kids out of New York to the theater. Of course, we had a lot of beer and wine on the buses, which nowadays you could not do. Everyone was well soused. I put the hot-looking girls with the big tits up front. We had a mosh pit—my cameraman had the footprint of a Doc Marten boot in his cheek for a week after that gig.

Even though it was a triumph, it was a hair-raising experience. About an hour before the "Rebel Yell" world premiere, we got a phone call from MTV, telling us to remove a shot of a kid in the front row holding a Budweiser can. So we got the master tape and had to find a shot to slug in, right? We need one more shot of hot-looking girls with big tits. We ran it over to MTV ten minutes before the world premiere, or there would have been 4:50 of black. That's what it was like in those days.

Billy went from playing to fifteen hundred people to playing the Oakland Coliseum in six weeks. That was the power of MTV.

BILLY IDOL: That tour, we went from playing in clubs to playing in theaters to playing in arenas, over a ten-month period. Videos were gigantic in putting across, in images, what I was about. You almost didn't have to say much, because the video espoused what you were about.

JEFF STEIN: The look of "Rebel Yell"—that backlighting, the purple, the smoke— was totally mimicked in *Purple Rain*. My video influenced a lot of live videos that came down the pike.

JOHN DIAZ: On "Eyes Without a Face," I brought in Tony Mitchell as DP—that was one of the first videos he shot. David Mallet directed, and David always shot in 16mm. I said, "I don't care what else you do, but we have to shoot this in 35mm and Billy has to look like a beauty queen."

BILLY IDOL: The video was super-important because we had large hopes for "Eyes Without a Face." We poured into it not only ideas, but also money and time. For three days, I didn't see anything but dry ice, smoke, fire, and naked bodies. We hardly slept.

JOHN DIAZ: Bill Aucoin brought some new contact lenses for Billy. I said, "You can't give them to Billy, they might redden his eyes during the shoot." Well, he gave them to Billy. David Mallet liked to use lots of dry ice in videos. So Billy was laying in dry ice for quite some time, *and* he was really tired, and his eyes dried out. The contact lenses fused to his eyeballs.

BILLY IDOL: We'd been up all night finishing the video and got straight on a plane to do a gig in Arizona. It was boiling hot so I laid down on the grass outside the venue, and when I woke up, a sheriff was standing with his gun drawn. I'd never really had a gun barrel in my face.

I almost couldn't think because of the pain in my eyes. I'd fallen asleep with my contact lenses in, and they were dried out from being on set, then on an airplane. I said, "I'm with the band that's sound-checking inside that building." My eyes were tearing, pouring water. So we got inside and the sheriff made my road crew line up. He said, "Who is this?" And they said, in unison, "The boss." So he left me alone. Then they had to take me to the hospital because I'd scraped the cornea so badly. I had my eyes bandaged for three days, until the cornea grew back. It was stupid, really; I should have known. But I wasn't thinking too much, I was just trying to get the video done.

PERRI LISTER: On "Flesh for Fantasy," Billy and I had a terrible fight. We were screaming at each in one of the dressing rooms, and I stormed out. When I slammed the door, it made the door of the next room open, and all the dancers were peeking through a hole in the wall, trying to see what we were fighting about. Between the drugs and the drama, it's amazing that video ever got finished.

JOHN DIAZ: "Flesh for Fantasy" was the most difficult video I ever produced. Jeff Stein didn't direct that—Howie Deutch did—but Jeff's the reason it was a disaster. My whole crew was working for Jeff on another video that went way over deadline. I had to push our shoot back and charter a LearJet to fly the crew back. On the day he was supposed to light the set, my DP, Tony Mitchell, arrived at 4 P.M., totally wasted because he hadn't slept in five days. Our first day ended up going thirty-six hours. The second day went about twenty-four hours. The final setup was a long dolly shot, and Tony said to me, "Johnny, you gotta do this shot." I said, "*What?!*" He goes, "I'm blind." He couldn't see anymore. The pace of the last six days had wrecked his vision.

HOWIE DEUTCH, director: I don't know if I was qualified to direct that video. But Billy liked that I'd worked on the *Apocalypse Now* trailer. I wasn't used to staying up for days. I wore contact lenses, and I was awake for so long directing the video that when it was done and I fell asleep, my lenses stuck in my eyes. I couldn't get them out. That's my biggest memory.

ROBIN SLOANE: I found Jeff Stein for the Cars. He'd done "Rebel Yell," one of the best live videos ever made. He showed me footage from a company called Charlex that he really wanted to work with. They'd been doing *National Enquirer* commercials with weird cut-and-paste animation. So I hired Jeff and Charlex to work together on "You Might Think." Then it got complicated.

JEFF STEIN: After "Rebel Yell," Robin Sloane wanted me to do a video for the Cars. They had a reputation for being completely boring live, and I said, "I'm not interested." I had worked with the Who, the greatest live act *ever*. I'd done it. I was going to turn in my badge. Charlex was doing a campaign for the *National Enquirer* that had animated cutouts and photographs of celebrities, big heads on bodies that moved a little. I heard the Cars' "You Might Think" and thought I could make the first cartoon with real people, which I think we did.

One of the worst parts of the video process was pitching ideas to the band. I met the Cars and told them, "The band's in the medicine chest, and then on a bar of soap, and Ric's a fly," and one of them said, "Why don't we all just play on a turd in the toilet bowl?" That was the prevailing attitude.

I wanted them to make fun of themselves and be self-effacing. I put together all this pop-culture imagery, from Ric as King Kong on the Empire State Building through B- and Z-movies: *Incredible Shrinking Man* and *Glen or Glenda*, the Ed Wood film, because Ric changes from a dude to a lady in it. It was the first music video put in the permanent collection of the Museum of Modern Art.

ROBIN SLOANE: Charlie Levy and Alex Wild, who owned Charlex, shut down their company to do the video, so they had no income coming in, and it took months to make. Animation takes a long time and no one had ever done anything like this. Everyone was up all night, every night, for months. Jeff was difficult to deal with, and he ended up in a huge fight with Charlex: Whose name is going to go first? Is it Jeff Stein and Charlex, or Charlex and Jeff Stein?

We had to finish the video without Jeff there day to day. When Charlex finished, they came up to Elektra and wouldn't let us have the video. They wanted more money. One of the guys who worked for Charlex had the video in an attaché case handcuffed to his wrist. I kid you not.

Ric hated "You Might Think." He thought it made fun of the way he looked. The original version ran on MTV without the fly part, because the video wasn't finished when it was scheduled to world premiere, so we had to give them an unfinished version, then replace it. But that video completely changed their image. It took a band that was not visually dynamic and made them incredibly visually dynamic. "You Might Think" won the Video of the Year award at the first VMAs.

JEFF STEIN: "You Might Think" was nominated for so many awards, eight or nine, and we'd lost all of them. So I was asleep in the audience at Radio City Music Hall when Eddie Murphy announced the Cars for Best Video of the Year.

TIMOTHY HUTTON, actor: In 1984, you couldn't have a conversation about a song without someone saying, "Did you see the video?" I was a twenty-three-year-old actor living in New York, and the manager of the Cars played me their new album. I especially liked the song "Drive," and Ric asked to talk about me directing the video. I wanted to direct—who doesn't?

I called a casting director and said I needed an attractive, exotic woman who has something fierce about her. Paulina Porizkova walked in toward the end of the casting session. It was before she became a supermodel. I rented a hotel suite to rehearse, and asked them to imagine they'd had a fight that was escalating. We rehearsed for a whole day, and neither Ric nor Paula wanted to stop. They said, "Give us another situation to play." Little did I know they would end up married.

DARYL HALL: Jeff Stein directed "Out of Touch," which was maybe our most significant video because of its look: the huge bass drum and my costume, which made me look like a Dalmatian. It's visually arresting, for sure. Jeff did psychedelic cartoon versions of songs, that was his trademark. He loved anything connected to the circus. If there's one thing I hate, it's the circus. Later on, Jeff wanted to do a video on Martha's Vineyard in December and have me stand in the surf. He said, "No, it's all right, we'll have towels, we'll have heaters." I said, "No, Jeff, it ain't gonna happen. I'm not part of the Polar Bear Club."

PAUL FLATTERY: Jeff Stein did some good stuff, but he bankrupted our production company, Picture Music International. Every video went over budget. The Jacksons' "Torture" video is legendary. The shoot went on so long that band members stopped showing up.

JEFF STEIN: The Jacksons' "Torture" video: an experience that lived up to the song title.

JOHN DIAZ: Michael Jackson was at the first meeting we had with his brothers for "Torture," and he said, "I want to do this, I want to do that." And then, of course, Michael didn't show up to the shoot. I had a feeling he wasn't going to show, so I found a wax museum in Nashville to make a dummy of Michael. And that's what you see in the video. We placed it in different positions: sometimes with its hand up, sometimes with it down at its side.

Perri Lister was the choreographer on "Torture." She was Billy Idol's girlfriend and choreographed many videos I produced. But Jackie Jackson kept saying, "She's not right for us." And I had to fire her.

PERRI LISTER: I love Jeff Stein. He's a great director and a sweetheart. "Torture"—so aptly named. Jeff wanted me on board as choreographer, but I had to get approved by the Jacksons first. It was like I was joining the CIA. I've never been through more security checks in my life, to get to the inner sanctum of the Jacksons sitting in their hotel room. I finally get there, and they're all there but Michael, and they each had their own lawyer. And manager. Anyway, they liked my reel and they hired me.

A few days later, Jeff says, "Listen, I've got a slight problem. Jackie's girlfriend wants to be in the video. He says she's a dancer." I'm like, "Let her come to the audition, and if she's okay, we'll put her in the video, and if she's not, I'm sorry, I'm not putting her in." She comes to the audition, and she's a little shorter and a little plumper than most, but I figured if I hired some other girls that were the same size, she wouldn't stand out. The first day of rehearsal comes and she doesn't show up. So I thought, *Never mind her, I'll keep the other short girls.* So we rehearsed for a week, and the day comes to show the routine to Jackie Jackson. I see this girl come in and stand with Jackie. I'm like, "Oh my god, it's the girlfriend." Afterwards, Jeff Stein said, "I'm sorry, Perri, but, um, Jackie's girlfriend has decided that she wants to choreograph the video." I said, "Well, as long as you give me my check, Jeff, I'm fine with that." So they gave me my check and I left. And the girlfriend was Paula Abdul.

JEFF STEIN: I'll take the blame for many things, but not for that video. We were constantly waiting around for everybody to be ready. It was endless. I don't even know if there was a budget. I mean, it was not my company, I was not the producer, I did not make the deal. I have no idea what it ended up costing. For certain videos, I remember the cost only in terms of human lives. One of our crew members lost control of her bodily functions while we were making the video. The crew motto used to be "Death or victory." I think that was the only time we ever prayed for death.

I had a gut feeling Michael wasn't going to show up. So I had the foresight to get a wax figure from Madame Tussauds to double for Michael, and that proved to be a good decision. That wax figure was put through the ringer. Its head ended up in the salad bowl at lunch one day.

PAULA ABDUL, choreographer; artist: Michael couldn't make it, so they ended up using a wax dummy stand-in. I was so young and naive, I just figured this is what they normally do on music videos.

JEFF STEIN: The Jacksons were Jehovah's Witnesses, I believe, and I was told there could be no drugs or alcohol on the set. So I gathered the crew and told them I expected everybody to adhere to those instructions carefully. We were ready to shoot a sequence, and I couldn't find two key members of my crew. I was frantic. I turned around and behind the cyclorama I saw two silhouettes of my missing crew guys, the size of Godzilla and Rodan, shoveling something into their nostrils. The silhouette was thirty feet high. I ran the length of two football fields, kicked out the lights, and nobody ever saw it but me.

JON LANDAU: When it came time to announce the release of Springsteen's *Born in the U.S.A.* in 1984, we gave MTV a spectacular live version of "Rosalita" we'd shot in 1980 to warm things up. Then Bruce bit the bullet. He said, "Well, I guess we've got to." He understood we had to do a video for "Dancing in the Dark."

We both loved Jeff Stein and went to him first for "Dancing in the Dark." Jeff had a particular idea, a no-frills way he wanted to shoot Bruce, and we were all for it. We had a couple of days' shooting planned, and after the first day, we knew it wasn't working. It was just a misfire.

DANIEL PEARL: Jeff Stein's idea for "Dancing in the Dark" was to get a Louma crane, the original remote-controlled crane with a camera on the end of it, put Springsteen in an all-black stage—black floor, black walls, no set—and fly the camera around Springsteen as he performed. This would be the first real Bruce Springsteen music video, and he was concerned about everything. When he arrives at the Kaufman Astoria studio in New York, he looks like a '50s rock n' roller: He's got sideburns, a day's stubble, a wife-beater T-shirt, and tight sharkskin pants. And he's ripped. He's been working out.

He starts telling me how to light him. "I want a big silk over the camera. Throw a big light through it and front light me all flat." I go, "No way, man." He goes, "What?" I go, "That's how we light Stevie Nicks. That's for lighting women. I want to light you hard, I want to show the ripples of your muscles." So I lit him much harder than he wanted. I figured we'd do one take and then talk about it. He performed one time, we cut the camera, and he walked off the fucking set and didn't come back. No explanation. We stood around for half an hour, people scoured the building looking for him, and we finally realized, *Oh my god, he's gone.* Jeff had no real idea for the video, anyway. Black and dark? That's a concept?

JEFF STEIN: Bruce and I were friends; my brother and I played on his softball team, the E Street Kings. But I did not want to do a video with him, because, due to scheduling, it couldn't be done as a performance video. And Bruce comes alive onstage—along with Jimi Hendrix and Pete Townshend, he's one of the greatest rock n' roll showmen of all time. It was definitely the video everybody wanted to do, and I got talked into it.

We came up with one epic concept, which was a spoof of "Thriller" with elements of *The Wizard of Oz*, *Close Encounters of the Third Kind*, and *A Midsummer Night's Dream*. Then I came up with the idea—which hadn't been done at the time—to shoot Bruce doing the song in one take. And Daniel Pearl took forever and ever to light the set. It took way too long. And I think Bruce got restless. If you knew Bruce, you knew when he was into something or he wasn't into it. It was probably the worst experience in my music-video career. It was traumatic. But it was not my fault. I'd take the blame if I should, but Daniel should take the bullet for it. I know there are copies of our camera rehearsals on YouTube.

It didn't ruin the friendship, thank God. Bruce gave me a muscle car, a 1969 Ford XL convertible that his mechanic rebuilt for him. We were driving around, he wanted to play me the *Born in the U.S.A.* album in the car. "Rock n' roll always sounds better in the car." We got back to his house and there was a car in the driveway with one flat tire. He said, "I've got to get rid of that." I said,

"I'll take it." I was joking. He said, "Okay." And he went in his kitchen and got the keys.

JON LANDAU: I happened to be a very good friend of Brian De Palma, who was a wonderful director, and I said to him, "We took a shot and it really didn't work. You got any ideas?" At this point we were pretty much up for anything. Brian came to the first night of the "Born in the U.S.A." tour in Minneapolis with his crew, and he shot us performing "Dancing in the Dark" in the afternoon a couple of times. He lit it fantastically, found Courteney Cox, and created a little vignette where Bruce pulls her onstage from the front row.

AL TELLER: Bruce didn't like the idea of videos, and I wasn't enthusiastic about his doing them, either. When I saw "Dancing in the Dark," I almost winced. Bruce pulling Courteney Cox onto the stage, that struck me as very contrived.

JOHN SYKES: Before 1984, Springsteen hadn't done anything with us. He did a video for "Atlantic City," from *Nebraska*, but he wasn't even in it. I met with Jon when they were rolling out *Born in the U.S.A.*, and he was ready to play. And it was huge for MTV for Bruce to make the "Dancing in the Dark" video. Les went to the video shoot in Minneapolis. He flew in the CBS jet. I missed the flight.

LES GARLAND: I flew on the CBS private jet with Walter Yetnikoff to the taping of the "Dancing in the Dark" video. Landau was there, and we said *hi* to Bruce before showtime. Bruce grabs a young girl from the audience and pulls her up onstage. We didn't know she was a plant. He plops her back down into her seat, and that's when Bruce told the crowd, "We're shooting a video tonight. We gotta make sure we get it right, so we're gonna do that one again." I think he did it three times.

JON LANDAU: When Bruce looked at it, he had mixed feelings. He knew Brian and was very appreciative that he'd bailed us out. But the whole thing was slick and high gloss, not a typical Bruce Springsteen thing. On the other hand, because it was commercial, it helped us go after a younger audience. It was controversial with fans, but it broadened Bruce's appeal, especially with women and teens. Bruce would be out on the Jersey Shore and kids would come up to him and start imitating his dance moves from the video.

"Cover Me" was the next single, but we couldn't figure out what to do with that, so we skipped making a video for it. And then we hooked up with John Sayles for "Born in the U.S.A." Bruce and I both liked John's work; Bruce gave John permission to use his music in his film *Baby It's You*, which Bruce never did. When we got to "Born in the U.S.A.," I said to John, "The big thing is, Bruce doesn't want to do anything special for the video. You can film him onstage. You can build a story around that. But he's not going to act, and he's not going to lip-sync." So John filmed Bruce doing the song, then tried to match the recorded version with Bruce's live performance. And then John shot some lovely documentary footage to go around the concert. We loved the video. So John became our guy.

JOHN SAYLES, director: The mandate I got from Springsteen was "I've made one of these videos and it did its job. And this song needs something gritty." I was able to say, "Well, I do gritty." I shot it in 16mm, so it would have a little bit of grain. I said, "Let's include some concert footage and some documentary stuff of images that are suggested by the song." So artistically, it was a kind of free association on the images from the song. Not the Ronald Reagan version of the song, but the song the rest of us heard. The character in the song is talking about tough things. There's pride in it, and stubbornness, and disappointment.

We shot in a Vietnamese neighborhood in LA, we went down to the Stone Pony in Asbury Park, New Jersey, where Bruce started, and shot there. Ernest Dickerson, who had already shot for Spike Lee, was our main guy, and for the concert stuff we shot in LA, I used Ernest and second camera was Michael Ballhaus, who later shot *Goodfellas* and a few other films for Martin Scorsese, and shot most of Fassbinder's movies.

We said, "Bruce, we're going to shoot you in concert, do you want to lip-sync?" And he said, "God, I hate to lip-sync, especially with this song." So he wore the same outfit every night for three or four nights, and I got a bunch of different camera angles. If you look at the video, a couple things are slightly out of sync. At one point, he turns away from the microphone and his voice stays right there. Whatever its technical roughness—some of that was on purpose, some of it was the best we could do—it kept that emotion.

So it is gritty, and it is kind of guerrilla filmmaking. The cutting is more frenetic than other rock videos, there aren't any dissolves, and you keep coming back to the concert footage and Bruce's energetic performance. It was right about the time that Ronald Reagan had co-opted "Born in the U.S.A." and Reagan, his policies were everything that the song was complaining about. I think some of the energy of the performance came from Bruce deciding, "I'm going to claim this song back from Reagan." He made it mean something.

JON LANDAU: When John Sayles did "I'm on Fire," Bruce's confidence level was high enough for him to try some acting.

JOHN SAYLES: He was going to play a character from one of his songs, and not Bruce Springsteen. It's a short song, and the intro we did, before the music starts, makes it a normal-length video. I wanted to give him an entrance. I figured, in the context of the song, he should come from underneath a car with a little grease on him. It's the car Suzanne Somers drives in *American Graffiti*. You never see the woman he's talking to, but you know she's a classy dame. The two characters know it's going to be a big mistake if they get together, but the sexual longing is there and they can't ignore it.

For the next video, "Glory Days," Bruce had a basic idea about a character who's a mix between the guy telling the story and the guy he's telling a story about, the guy who can't stop talking about his baseball days. That's the bittersweet part of the story. My first question was "Bruce, can you pitch?" He said, "Well, we get to do more than one take, right?" His pitching was okay. When we shot that sequence, we placed a big board behind home plate, with a cutout for the lens, and the DP was looking over the board. I said, "Put a helmet on." The first pitch, *boom*, hit right off his helmet. There's a cutaway shot of him toeing the mound, and Bruce said, "Oh shit, I don't want to endorse the sneakers." He took some dirt and rubbed it on the sneakers.

Making the video was complicated by how famous Bruce had gotten. When our little caravan was going to find the ballpark, there were radio-station helicopters following us. "They're heading left on Route Three . . ." There was a big crowd outside the bar where we were shooting the band, so we pulled a car up and my assistant editor ran out with his coat over his head, so people would follow him and we could take the band out through another door.

JON LANDAU: The most important component of the success of *Born in the U.S.A.* was the quality of the songs. Second was the tour. We played to five million people on that tour. If it wasn't the biggest tour of all time, it was very close. It was a magic time for us. Everything we did worked. The videos were a component, too, but I don't think any of us who worked on the project would say that the videos were the key element.

SHARON ORECK: The first video I was hired to work on was Sheila E.'s "The Glamorous Life." I was immediately drafted to go to a meeting with Prince on the Warners lot in West Hollywood, to discuss important things about the video. Mary Lambert was introduced and told everyone what she had in mind. She said, "We'll shoot performance footage, and she'll be bathed in colors and light, and she'll look stunning, and we'll also do a little narrative and Sheila will explore her sexuality and life and love . . ." It was mostly horseshit—that's what you did, you said this kind of stuff. When she was done, everyone was like, "It sounds great." And then, quietly, almost in a whisper, Prince said something that sounded like "Sheila should have drumsticks on her." But no one could hear him. The table went silent. Steve Fargnoli, Prince's manager, who's this super-handsome Italian guy, huddled with Prince and said, "Prince says Sheila should have drumsticks on her pants." And they got up and left. Prince was there for ten minutes.

After he left, I was like, "Do they mean real drumsticks taped on her pants?" We figured out that he meant fabric drumsticks sewn into the pants. And of course, Jeff Ayeroff from Warner Bros. said, "Mary, she better not be wearing fucking drumsticks on those pants." We're like, *You tell him!* That's how things worked around Prince. No one ever said *no* to him. And she ended up with drumsticks on her pants, I'll tell you that. They were the silliest pants I've ever seen.

MARY LAMBERT: I met Prince when I was hired to do Sheila E.'s "The Glamorous Life." He had two stylists named Louis and Vaughn. When I was introduced to them, it looked like they'd made their entire wardrobe out of chenille bathroom rugs and toilet-seat coverings. They were the most bizarre clothes I'd ever seen. The weirdest thing, though, was that they designed a wardrobe for Sheila E. that could barely fit a Barbie doll. They were itty-bitty-teeny-weeny. She's small and thin, but these clothes weren't going to fit *anybody*. On the day of the shoot, she tried them on and couldn't even get her legs in them. They had to put extenders in the pants. We never did zip them up.

SHARON ORECK: When we cast "Glamorous Life," we hired a really handsome black guy to play Sheila E.'s love interest. A short while later, we heard back from Simon Fields that Prince's camp didn't like him, and we couldn't hire him. Mary Lambert said, "Why don't they like him? Is he too tall? Too short?" And finally Simon said, "They don't want a black guy." We were like, "What are you talking about? She's black!" We were told they wanted the record to cross over, so there needed to be a white boyfriend. Mary and I were appalled.

SIMON FIELDS: I produced most of Prince's video between 1980 and 1990. He hardly talked to me for the first year; he was very shy. Then he grew to trust me. Which sometimes meant having to fire directors before they'd even started. We'd fly in a director and Prince would whisper in my ear, "Get rid of him." So I would, and Prince would direct the video himself.

I hired Larry Williams to direct "When Doves Cry." Before the first shot, Prince said to me, "He doesn't have to be here." So I gave Larry some magazines and he sat outside and did some reading.

SHARON ORECK: Prince was cuckoo paranoid. When I produced "When Doves Cry," I didn't know what the concept was until the day of the shoot. The director, Larry Williams, had worked with Prince on some still photographs. I'm like, "Well, what do you want me to do as the producer?" He said, "Just get a stage, a crew, a bunch of cameras, a bunch of smoke, and some doves." A crapload of smoke, and a crapload of doves. The day before we're going to shoot, I was told, "Paint a room purple and get a bathtub and some candles." And the bathtub wrangler had to get three bathtubs, so Prince could choose. We were finally told that Prince would be in the bathtub naked, then crawl around on the floor. The day of shooting, he got there six hours late. He'd tell Steve Fargnoli to put this here and that there, then Steve would tell Simon Fields, then Simon would tell me, then I would tell someone else. At one point Prince told Steve, "Tell Simon to get me a pair of woolen underpants." So we got him this teeny-weeny size of long underwear. He had the wardrobe person snip them down into a tiny little banana hammock for him, and then dye it purple. And that's what he wore when he was in the bathtub.

LISA COLEMAN: Prince basically directed all of his videos. He'd get help from people on the technical side, but he didn't let anyone else have creative control.

It was part of his megalomania. He didn't trust other people to translate his vision.

RANDY SKINNER: I was editing a Prince video with Albert Magnoli, who directed the *Purple Rain* film. All of a sudden, Albert says, "Prince is coming." The rule was, Don't look at Prince, don't talk to Prince. So I huddled in a corner thinking, *Oh God, what do I do?* He came in, walked right up to me, said "Hello," and put out his hand. I was thinking, *Oh shit! Do I look at him, do I shake the hand, do I not shake the hand?* So I shook the hand. And he was lovely, actually.

LISA COLEMAN: "When Doves Cry" was the first time the band had to perform choreographed dance steps. Prince tortured us in rehearsal. He said, "Everybody come to the front of the stage. Let me see you walk." And of course, he started making fun of us. "That's not sexy. You don't have a sexy walk." I said, "Let me see *you* walk." And then he walked like George Jefferson. Total swagger.

HOWARD WOFFINDEN, producer: I was dispatched from Limelight to Minneapolis, where Prince was rehearsing for a tour, to meet with him about a video concept. I sat in the arena watching rehearsals for three days before somebody came and told me, "You should go home now."

SIMON FIELDS: For "Raspberry Beret," we filmed a whole video, then Prince got a Japanese animator to do a completely different video and we mashed the two up. He would mess with directors. He would give them the impression that they'd be in charge of the video, then halfway through he'd go, "Thank you," take what he liked, and edit it himself.

LISA COLEMAN: Here's a good piece of trivia: Pat Smear from Nirvana and Foo Fighters was an extra in "Raspberry Beret." I met him years later and he said, "I'm such a huge fan, I was in the video." Look closely and you can spot him, in the front.

DAVE GROHL: That's when Pat had dreadlocks all the way down to his butt. He gets to the auditions at a rehearsal space in Los Angeles, and everyone has to do a synchronized dance. Pat can't dance. So they sent him home. He starts walking down the hallway and hears, "Hey you!" He turns around and there's this big bodyguard standing next to Prince. And Prince whispers in the bodyguard's ear. The bodyguard says, "You can stay. He likes your hair."

HOWARD WOFFINDEN: A few of us traipsed to Prince's house in LA about 11 A.M. to meet with him about a video. Someone lets us in and we're sitting in the living room, waiting. Eventually Prince comes in, dressed in silk pajamas, with a blue stiletto on his right foot and a yellow stiletto on his left foot. He sits down and we launch into our spiel. He listens politely for a minute and says, "Uh, hang on." He disappears for another thirty-five minutes or so. Again, he wanders out, and now he's got the blue stiletto on his *left* foot and the yellow stiletto on his *right* foot. He sits down and says, "Now, what were you saying?"

SHARON ORECK: There was a story told at Limelight about an early Prince video. Supposedly, there was a shot where Prince wanted doves released into the air, but the production manager decided not to work with an animal trainer because it was too expensive, so he bought some doves from a local pet store. When it came time to throw the doves into the air, he literally *threw* them from the stage, and they were immediately sucked into a giant fan, chopped up, and then sprayed around the room and all over the band. That was one of the first rock video legends.

MICHAEL ANTHONY: The Van Halen approach to videos was, like, this is the party, you're in our living room, come on in and join the party.

PETE ANGELUS: I'm not sure I ever understood why it was necessary for Van Halen to fly across the stage while drinking beers in "Panama."

MICHAEL ANTHONY: They said, "Mike, why don't you go first?" They strapped me in a harness under my clothes, and it was totally—how would you say?—I mean, it almost castrated me, the way it was wrapped around my legs and groin. My nuts were, like, in a vise. These straps were coming right around my ball sac. As soon as I did it, then you got Al swinging and drinking a beer, and Eddie swinging while Al and Dave yank on him.

PETE ANGELUS: The harness didn't fit Mike very well. I wasn't doing any testicular inspections, but I do remember him gripping his groin and complaining.

RANDY SKINNER: The director who started out on "Hot for Teacher" ended up not finishing it. Things weren't going the way the band wanted, and Pete was a little bossy, so he took over.

PETE ANGELUS: I had an idea to have young kids portray the four band members. Once the kids spent a little time with the band, they started to assume different personalities. It was weird. Like, the little Alex became very argumentative and difficult to find on the set. The little Edward was shy, and of course the little Dave started running his mouth. I also had an idea of seeing the band members thirty years later, based on their personalities. Alex, that was a nobrainer: He was a gynecologist.

MICHAEL ANTHONY: The kid who played me looked pretty similar to me. The kids who played Eddie and Dave, they wore wigs. I think Alex had his guy drinking a Schlitz Malt before the end of the shoot. When the teacher jumps on the desk and whips off her dress, the little kids were hooting and hollering. We said, "Just go for it, guys. You're going to enjoy this."

DONNA RUPERT, model: I was first runner-up in the Miss Canada 1981 pageant, then I moved down to LA and signed with the Wilhelmina modeling agency. I lived in a motel on Sunset Strip for a month, until I could find an apartment. It was a sleazy business, but I was too naive to know how sleazy it was. I did forty or fifty national commercials, from Camay to Toyota to Tab, and the agency almost didn't let me do the Van Halen video. They said, "It's not a good image for a model to do a rock video."

At the audition, there were five of us standing there for what seemed like forever, turning around in our bikinis, in a room with Van Halen and the director. I thought, *Kill me. I can't believe I have to do this.*

MICHAEL ANTHONY: The thing I'll never forget about that day is, I got up early, and my wife got up along with me, and my oldest daughter, Elisha, was conceived that morning.

PETE ANGELUS: We had a great time casting the women. I'd love to tell you there was some talent or skill that went along with it, but there wasn't. We spent a day looking at women in bikinis. A few years later, I read in *Fortune* about some billionaire who had accomplished many things, and he said the only thing he hadn't done was to be the casting director in a Van Halen video.

DONNA RUPERT: This is something I don't think anybody knows: There are two girls, two blond teachers, in the video. I was the one wearing a tiara and dancing with David Lee Roth. There's a second girl, who drops to her knees on the desk, wearing a white wife-beater, and does the stripper dancing—that wasn't me. But it transitions quickly to me again, so you think it's me through the whole thing.

I think I made $2,500 for the video.

MICHAEL ANTHONY: In the final scene, all the kids come out of school and jump in Dave's hot rod. And Dave never could drive a car that well. Sometimes I feared for my life because he just could not drive. They got in the hot rod with him, and he took off and almost crashed the thing. It was like, "Oh my God! Dave is going to kill these kids!"

PETE ANGELUS: At the time, there was a lot of choreographed dancing on MTV. It was kind of appalling that everybody had dancers. We felt it would be humorous to have Van Halen do their own dancing. The worse it got, the better. Alex was having a lot of difficulties. I said, "Let's do another take," with the intention of seeing how bad it could actually get.

MICHAEL ANTHONY: One of the dancers in "Beat It," the white guy, he choreographed the little dance moves we did. Alex Van Halen, he's the drummer, he's gotta keep the beat, he's the guy with perfect rhythm—but if you watch the video, he's a half beat behind everybody else. I remember him asking me to help him with his dance steps minutes before we did it.

DONNA RUPERT: Phil Donohue showed "Hot for Teacher" as an example of what your kids shouldn't see.

RANDY SKINNER: I remember watching various scenes get filmed for "Hot for Teacher" and thinking, *Oh my god, this is never going to get on MTV.*

PETE ANGELUS: There was a big to-do in the press from women's groups about how the teachers were disrespectfully represented. I didn't see it that way. It was a fantasy that every boy goes through in school.

ADAM DUBIN: I saw "Hot for Teacher" when I was in college. The dorm had a TV in the lounge area, and most often, it was set to MTV. So I saw "Hot for Teacher" with a group of people, and we loved it. There was an excitement about music videos, a buildup to seeing them, and then discussions afterwards about what it meant. I was already in film school, but "Hot for Teacher" made me want to direct music videos.

PETE ANGELUS: Dave didn't change his mind-set for his solo videos. He was the biggest proponent of more, more, more. Bigger. More exciting. He enjoyed the over-the-top characters. In "Just a Gigolo," he's the Dave-TV talk show host. I like the idea of "Gigolo" quite a bit, of Dave hosting a television program and bouncing his way into different TV studios and interrupting video shoots. He was thrilled by creating a different character, an obese producer, in "Goin' Crazy." Later on, in "Eat 'Em and Smile," we had him in a prosthetic fat suit. What made "California Girls" enjoyable was the idea of Dave being a tour guide, through ridiculous scenarios involving women. I think the women made it popular. But I hope the sense of humor contributed. Dave looked like he was having fun—and he *was* having fun. He liked being around the set, he always came into the edit bay with me. He'd be sitting there with his sunglasses on, usually doing something to anesthetize himself, going, "That's doesn't look bright enough to me." *Really? Maybe you wanna take off those fucking sunglasses and give it a look.*

HUEY LEWIS: Dave's videos were off the charts, just brilliant. I still use that line from "Just a Gigolo": "You got char-*as*-ma."

PETE ANGELUS: After I delivered "Just a Gigolo" for Dave's solo project, Warner Bros. said, "Do you think it's a good idea, really, to be electrocuting Billy Idol or punching Boy George in the face?" I said, "I think it's great." And that was the end of the conversation. It was the biggest budget I'd done with Dave, but I don't think it exceeded $300,000. I think we got a phone call from Cyndi Lauper, that she enjoyed it quite a bit. But I didn't hear from Billy Idol, "Congratulations for electrocuting me."

Chapter 17

"HE'S GOT A METAL PLATE IN HIS HEAD"

MTV AND VAN HALEN TEAM UP TO NEARLY KILL A SUPER-FAN

KURT JEFFERIS, MTV viewer: How many people can say they smoked a fatty with David Lee Roth, man? It was a high point, a once-in-a-lifetime experience, for a kid from a little town in Pennsylvania to win a national contest.

RICHARD SCHENKMAN: We ran a contest, "Lost Weekend with Van Halen." I wrote the copy for the promo spot. There was a trashed hotel room, girls, David Lee Roth, and the pitch was that if you win, you won't remember the weekend. In fact, there's a chance you might not survive.

David Lee Roth, God bless him, loved it. He wanted to push it as far as possible. I hired two gorgeous models for the promo, and I'm pretty sure he slept with both of them.

The promo was a big hit. For the first time, we got over a million postcard entries. So when it came time to do the Lost Weekend event, it was a no-brainer that we were going to film what transpired.

KURT JEFFERIS: I was allowed to take one person as my guest. My best friend Tom said, "Are you gonna take me?" But I was thinking about taking my girlfriend. Tom said, "C'mon, you're gonna take your girlfriend to something like that?"

JOHN SYKES: In the promo for the "Lost Weekend with Van Halen" contest, David Lee Roth said, "You won't know where you are, you won't know what's gonna happen, and when you come back, you're not gonna have any memory of it." It was a takeoff on the old movie *The Lost Weekend*, with Ray Milland, about an alcoholic. And then the guy who won—we didn't know this—turned out to have a metal plate in his head.

KURT JEFFERIS: Thirty days after I started college, I had a bad head-trauma accident. I fell down a staircase, from the seventh floor to the sixth floor. I was in the hospital for three months, with a blood clot on my brain. If that had never happened, I don't think I would have ever won the contest, because I was home recovering and had lots of time to mail postcards to MTV.

JOHN SYKES: We fly to Detroit with Van Halen and the contest winner, and they're putting him through the ringer. Dave—not us, Dave—locked the kid in a room with an exotic dancer. They set him up with drinks. They brought him onstage and presented him with a big sheet cake, then they slammed it into his face and doused him with champagne.

MICHAEL ANTHONY: I probably remember more of what happened than the guy who won the contest. Because boy, I'll tell you, he jumped in, full-on. I guarantee, he had a great time. I think he almost ended up in the hospital, from drinking too much. He got laid. He drank. He did everything. He hung out with the band, but I think he got into more trouble hanging out with our crew.

KURT JEFFERIS: They gave me a "Lost Weekend" T-shirt and a hat. I met Valerie Bertinelli when I was backstage smoking a joint and drinking Jack Daniel's. They brought me onstage and smashed a cake in my face, then about a dozen people poured champagne on me, including two midgets. After the show, we went backstage and they brought in a girl for me. She was a stripper in a short black leather skirt. David Lee Roth said, "Kurt needs to meet Tammy." They put on some music so she could dance and take her clothes off for me. David told her to take me into the shower. And I had Tammy in the shower.

RICHARD SCHENKMAN: I'd brought Don Lenzer—an award-winning documentary cameraman—to shoot the event with a real documentary crew. After the show, they sent the kid to the inner sanctum of their dressing room, to take a shower with a groupie. Obviously I didn't film that. I wasn't allowed in, but I understand they rubbed egg salad all over her. I could hear him howling from where I was sitting.

JOHN SYKES: And later, the kid goes back to his hotel and loses it. I was in Detroit that night, taping a Pretenders concert, and Richard Schenkman called because the kid was freaking out. His friend said, "He's got a metal plate in his head. He shouldn't be drinking." At the hotel, it was just insane. The band's having a huge party, they're saying, "Get the kid out of here." We had to lock him in a room, and one of our producers stayed with him. Van Halen *poisoned* everybody that night. It turned out to be one of our greatest promotions ever.

RICHARD SCHENKMAN: I go back to my hotel, go to bed, and I get a call that there's a problem with the winner. His friend said, "You know, he has a plate in his head, and he's not supposed to drink." *Thanks for telling us now.* There was a coked-out asshole who worked for Van Halen's management, and he called John Sykes, because the winner was throwing up and freaking out. The crazy coked-up guy was breaking glasses and plates into the phone, and saying to John, "You see what you did to me? I'm breaking glasses. That's how upset I am." John's assistant had the job of sitting up all night with the winner, to make sure he didn't swallow his tongue or anything.

TOM FRESTON: They gave cocaine to the guy who won the contest. It turned out he had a plate in his head.

KURT JEFFERIS: I blacked out the first night. I don't remember going back to the hotel. Really, I don't know what happened that night. I'd been on an antiseizure medication, Dilantin, since I had my head trauma. The next morning, I had one of the worst hangovers of my life. On the second night, Alex Van Halen handed me a sixteen-ouncer and said, "You're not leaving this spot until you drink that beer." I poured it out in a trash can.

RICHARD SCHENKMAN: To add insult to injury, John sat down with the asshole from management and went through my footage frame by frame and let him dictate what we could and couldn't use. I had a strenuous objection to that. I said, "John, we're MTV. A band doesn't get to tell us what we can or can't do." And he said, "Yeah, but if we don't have a good relationship with the bands, there is no MTV."

KURT JEFFERIS: I'm in an Anonymous program now. I was drinking oil tankers of booze, smoking plantations of marijuana, snorting coke and meth, and heading to buried. My parents gave me an ultimatum: Get help or move out.

I now work as a facility manager at a school, doing maintenance and that. I've had surgery on my eyes three times. I'm legally blind in both eyes, my balance is off, I have diabetes insipidus. I don't have a wahoo life. Someone said, "Kurt, you got your fifteen minutes of fame." I said, "Dude, it lasted a little longer than that."

Chapter 18

"WANNABE CECIL B. DEMILLES"

EVERYTHING—BUDGETS, IDEAS,
HAIR—GETS BIGGER

A S 1984 ENDED, *ROLLING STONE* RENEWED ITS ATTACK on MTV, even in a year when their cover stars included Duran Duran, Madonna, Culture Club, Cyndi Lauper, the Go-Go's, Huey Lewis, Tina Turner, and David Bowie—all staples of MTV. In a barbed essay, film critic Kenneth Turan (a baby boomer born in 1946) described music videos as "Orwellian" and complained that filmmakers were being forced to keep up with MTV, which was "creating a generation of gratification-hungry sensation junkies with atrophied attention spans." He also saw a societal threat in "the non-stop video parade of pouty cuties wearing low-cut leather bikinis or skin-tight skirts, their bodies sometimes chained but always concupiscent," adding, "videos offer nothing *but* sexual stereotypes."

By 1985, the record industry's recovery was clear, as evidenced by headlines in *BusinessWeek* (THE RECORD BUSINESS IS SOLID GOLD AGAIN) and *Variety* (RECORD BIZ MAKES A STRONG COMEBACK: BUYERS RESPOND TO NEW MUSIC). A *BusinessWeek* reporter wrote, "Much of the credit for the turnaround may belong not to the industry itself—or to better product—but to the popularity of Music Television (MTV)." In *The Washington Post*, CBS Records president Walter Yetnikoff said, "MTV has been a shot in the arm for the record business. If somebody had asked me three years ago, 'What do you think of an idea like MTV?' I would have said they were crazy. Fortunately, nobody asked me."

PETE ANGELUS: Videos changed the music business completely. It brought the business back to life. It created stars out of people who normally would never have been seen. Because the revenue streams increased dramatically with labels, more money was handed out. That doesn't necessarily mean something is going to be more creative, it just means that more money is handed out. Some artists took advantage of that and did memorable work. There were some exceptional videos, and some fucking car accidents. And sometimes a car accident cost as much as an exceptional video.

LES GARLAND: I got word that Pepsi had bought the first spot in the 1984 Grammy telecast and they were gonna play a new Michael Jackson Pepsi ad. I'm like, "Michael Jackson belongs to MTV, not the Grammys." I wasn't gonna let it happen. So I called Roger Enrico, the head of Pepsi, and said, "Roger, I've got a major problem. This Pepsi Michael Jackson spot that's gonna run in three weeks on the Grammys? That should run on MTV first."

"Well, Garland, I've already made a deal with the Grammys." I go, "Wait a minute. You know how we do world premieres of videos. What if I world premiere the commercial? And what if I give you twenty-four promos a day for two weeks leading up to it? Would that interest you?"

He goes, "How much do you want for this?" I said, "Nothing." He goes, "What? You're telling me you would promote a commercial twenty-four times a day for two weeks before playing it? Garland, I like your style. Done." So it played for the first time on MTV.

BOB GIRALDI: I got the ad campaign for Pepsi, because I had a relationship with Michael. The money was big, but I really don't think he wanted to do it—the father had signed the Jacksons to it. I believe they were embarrassed to do television commercials. I didn't like the Pepsi people telling me what to do. "Tell the Jacksons to take their sunglasses off." *You made the deal, you go tell them.* The vibe on the set was brutal, with everyone trying to get a piece of the biggest superstar in the world.

When we did "Beat It," Michael came in the van with us to scout locations. I remember saying, "I'm hungry, let's stop for a pizza." Michael said, "Oh good, I've never had a pizza." This is a twenty-five-year-old man who'd never had pizza. Now he wasn't accessible like that. He was a superstar, but then he became a deity.

There was an explosion on the set. Sparks hit him, ignited the pomade in his hair, and went traveling down his body. Am I responsible for the accident?

Yes, as the director, I guess so. Did he blame me? I think so. His bodyguard, Miko Brando, blamed me and we went at each other. I feel bad for the pain it caused him. There was a little relief for the pain because the next day, *Thriller* returned to number one.

TOM MOHLER, manager: We did talk at one point with Bob Giraldi about doing a Billy Squier video. His fee was over $100,000. We all said, *I don't think so.*

BOB GIRALDI: For Lionel Richie's "Hello," I came up with the idea of a blind girl and Lionel as a teacher. "Hello" is one of the top videos ever, still to this day.

LIONEL RICHIE: I just figured that the video would be a simple love story. And then Bob leveled me to the floor when he said, "Here's my big pitch. You're a teacher, and you're gonna fall in love with a blind girl." I admit, I hesitated for a moment. But you don't hire Picasso and then tell him how to paint.

The funniest story about "Hello" is that I kept going back to Bob over and over again, saying, "Bob, that bust of me does not look like me." "Bob, the bust does not *look* like me." Finally, Bob came over to me and said, "Lionel, she's *blind.*"

BOB GIRALDI: With Lionel, we used to have day shoots. He would show up at 9 P.M. I'd say, "Rich, you know how much money I just spent waiting for you?" "Oh sorry, Bob. I overslept." *Overslept? Until nine in the evening?* I wasn't very patient with that.

DEE SNIDER: By the time we made "I Wanna Rock," Mark Metcalf was on his high horse. He cost more money, he had more demands, and he showed up coked out of his brain. He'd been up all night—he was wired, on edge, and in a lousy mood. After he messed up a take, Marty Callner said to him, "Listen, we gotta do this again. You gotta stop screwing up." And Metcalf said, "Or what? You don't look so tough." Now Marty is a pit bull, a tough little motherfucker. He said, "Really? Let's go outside." Everybody went quiet on the set. They're all looking at Metcalf, wondering if he was going to take on Marty. And Metcalf, smartly, backed down.

Marty yelled, "Action." And that moment, when you see Metcalf screaming at the fat kid in the classroom, and spit is flying out of his mouth? That was immediately after he had backed down in front of the entire cast. Of course, he took it out on the poor kid. He was on fucking fire. And Marty goes, "Cut! That's the one." We got a historic performance out of Metcalf. People have been talking about the spit flying out of his mouth for thirty years now.

MARK METCALF: The line "What do you wanna *do* with your life?" was Dee's work. People still come up to me and say, "Do the line, do the line," and they're not happy unless I spit on them.

GREG GOLD, director: I got a gig with Bill Parker, who had a monopoly on producing and directing R&B videos. I was hired as an assistant director, and Dominic Sena was the director of photography. Bill's vision was always greater than his budgets. He had a thing for transportation: Every video had a huge party in a zeppelin, or on a boat, or on a train. We did one for Rick James and Smokey Robinson, "Ebony Eyes," that started out in a plane in a storm, so I had to get a vintage plane and have the grips shake it. Rick and Smokey are in a flight and they get shipwrecked on an island. Of course, Bill picked the hardest beach to access on the West Coast, El Matador Beach in Malibu. We pitched tents for Rick and everybody to hang out in. I'm not going to comment about what went on in those tents, but I will say that part of our budget went toward a case of Cristal champagne.

DOMINIC SENA, director: I'd shot a million videos between '81 and '83, and I was carrying a lot of these directors. Some of them would fall asleep in their trailer, and I'd keep making the video without them. Finally I said to an AD named Greg Gold, "We might as well do this ourselves." So we raised $25,000 and made a video, and got representation from Beth Broday at Fusion Films. We said, "Let's go to Istanbul!" So we wrote a concept that revolved around Istanbul and went there for a week. Videos were great excuses to travel.

GREG GOLD: We wrote a treatment for an English group, Vitamin Z—the idea was, they're in Istanbul to write their next song, and they go to a cafe filled with men smoking from hookahs, and some kid steals their wallet. They chase him through the city, only it turns out the kid was returning their wallet, not stealing it, and they see the poverty the kid lives in.

We got to Istanbul, and after we'd scouted locations, we got called into a meeting with the head of the local production company. He said, "In order to get permission for you to come here, we had to rewrite your script." *Midnight*

Express had made the Turkish people look like animals, and they were paranoid about Westerners shooting there. So we read the treatment he'd submitted: "Vitamin Z arrive in beautiful Istanbul, have tea at the beautiful cafe, and walk in the beautiful park." We were so punch-drunk from traveling, we just started laughing. We refused to do anything different than we had written.

DARYL HALL: Videos began to attract wannabe Cecil B. DeMilles, who had almost unlimited budgets and did whatever they felt like. "Adult Education" is a perfect example. We brought in a director I didn't know [Tim Pope], who was newly hot. He didn't have a clue what to do with the song. The plot? I couldn't tell you. It's some sort of primitive de-virginizing ritual. Everybody was dressed in kind of faux primitive war paint, John Oates shook some kind of magical stick, and there was a virgin laying on a table. That's all I know.

KEVIN GODLEY: Some video directors made little versions of movies. I never felt that worked; it's not an ideal medium for telling a story. We saw it as something that existed outside cinema, with its own set of unknown rules. You don't have to tell a story. You don't have to abide by any rules at all.

AIMEE MANN, artist; 'Til Tuesday: The director of "Voices Carry" really loved a scene in *The Man Who Knew Too Much*, the Alfred Hitchcock movie—there's a scene at a symphony concert at this big moment when somebody's going to get assassinated. The video is about a girl who's trying to be heard and has to suppress her feelings because her boyfriend's an asshole. The director had an idea to emulate Hitchcock, where I'd get up and make a scene in public at the symphony. It certainly resonated with women, even though it was done in broad strokes.

PHIL COLLINS: "Against All Odds" was a nightmare. I was standing in two inches of cold water, in my Wellingtons. The shoot started at 6 P.M. and was supposed to finish around midnight, but the crew had a problem with the tracking for the camera. Come 6 A.M., I was still there, still standing in two inches of cold water.

BETH BRODAY: The Cars shot "Magic" at the Hilton family house in Beverly Hills. Kathy Hilton rented us her house. I think Paris was in school. In the video, Ric Ocasek walks on water across a swimming pool. "Oh-oh, it's magic." Get it? We built a Plexiglas platform that sat under the surface of the water, so

Ric could walk out to the center of the pool and back. On the first take, he walked onto the platform and it collapsed. It took *hours* to rig the platform to hold him. I thought somebody was gonna decapitate themselves, because the platform was clear and you couldn't see it. I was scared to death the whole shoot.

DAVID ROBINSON: My own mother saw "Magic" and said I wasn't in it. I had to play it for her, pause the video, and say, "Look look look, *that's me.*"

VALERIE FARIS: A lot of bands would get what we called shot counters—that's our phrase—where every guy in the band counts how many shots he's in and there's a whole negotiation: "I'm only in fifteen shots and you're in twenty."

BRUCE ALLEN: Guys would sit there with stopwatches to make sure they got enough camera time. The drummer wanted as much camera time as the front man.

STEWART COPELAND: I grew to understand that videos were mainly about getting our singer's face out there. Because it was so pretty. That's the way it goes. Drummers learn that lesson pretty early in life. Guitarists never quite learn that lesson. Drummers and bass players, we're over it.

JERRY CASALE: It got to a point where the contract would say, "You shall feature the lead singer 35 percent of the time in medium close-ups or close-ups." And when you're hiring extras, you might be told that the singer's girlfriend didn't like the girl you're putting in the video because she's too pretty. She's jealous and thinks the singer's gonna screw her, so you can't have that girl. Or, if you put guys in the video, they couldn't be better looking than the band. These are all things I was told.

KEVIN GODLEY: I gave a vitriolic speech at the 1985 VMA awards, slamming the fact that everything was becoming predictable, and saying we must hang on to this beautiful thing we'd created and not bow down to commercial pressure. Big music videos were starting to look the same. It wasn't as quite adventurous as it had been. I wouldn't say the rot had set in. But the beginning of the rot had set in.

NIGEL DICK: When I worked at Phonogram Records, I commissioned a video for Tears for Fears called "Mothers Talk." The band *hated* the video. Just hated it. Their next single was "Shout," and we all decided that I'd direct it. The label was happy I was now producing *and* directing, because they didn't have to pay the 15 percent production company fee or the 10 percent director's fee. I made "Shout," and the U.S. label rep hated it. He said, "Well, this is a piece of crap, isn't it? We're gonna have to remake this for America." As you can probably deduce, that never happened. It became a big hit.

CURT SMITH: The downside of videos is, they're a reminder of all the bad fashion you went through. Our videos are kind of embarrassing, especially "Shout," but they're an endless source of amusement for my children: "Oh my God, you've got *braids* in your hair!" They laugh hysterically. It's not like we looked worse than anyone else. There were people who looked even worse than we did. So on a scale, we were somewhere in the middle.

"Everybody Wants to Rule the World" was like an American driving song, one of those things you'd hear on the radio. So we went to LA, to the desert, we got a car—an Austin Healey 3000—and we drove. That's pretty much the whole concept. The shoot was a disaster. I remember Nigel being in tears on the second night. He had to lug equipment around. He couldn't get anyone to clean the car, so he was there with a sponge cleaning the Austin Healey.

I slept in a camper bus out in the middle of nowhere for a couple of nights, and I had to be up at 4 A.M. so we could get the sunrise shot. We had an accident while we were filming the dirt bikes and four-wheel off-road vehicles, and one kid flew off and smashed his head. He was out cold. The video producer, an American girl, stood there and chanted some Buddhist stuff. We're frantically trying to find an ambulance while she's chanting.

NIGEL DICK: Roland Orzabal told me what he envisioned for "Head Over Heels": "I see myself in a library, there's a beautiful girl, we'll grow old together, and there's all this random stuff like a rabbi and a chimp." And I'm rapidly scribbling on a piece of paper: "Chimp. Rabbi."

CURT SMITH: When Roland pulls out the drawer and all the cards fly out at him? That was a ripoff of *Ghost Busters.* We were in the middle of a huge tour, and the album was getting more successful. I remember I was asleep in the dressing room and someone woke me up to say that "Everybody Wants to Rule the World" had gone to number one in America. Then we finished the video. It was hard to find time to celebrate.

DAVID MALLET: The Queen video where we really nailed it was "I Want to Break Free," where they're in drag. We didn't stop laughing for three days. We were ill from laughing. Freddy Mercury was desperately shy. It was a hell of a job to get him out of the dressing room. I'd say, "Come on, Fred, don't be silly, let's go." He'd say, "All right darling, all right." He called me Mistress Mallet. He used to shout, "Come on girls, Mistress Mallet's here."

MICK KLEBER: David Mallet is one of the top video-makers of all time. He directed Heart's "What About Love?," which was a *huge* video with a lot of killer imagery—big explosions, cauldrons pouring molten steel into molds while Nancy Wilson played a guitar solo.

ANN WILSON: David Mallet had a nickname: Miss Mallet. He was a perfectionist, and he wanted things his way. I think that video may have been the moment when the idea of feminine naturalness was at an all-time low. The heels were at an all-time high, the corsets were at an all-time tightness. That was when we got our first hair extensions. The idea was to transform us into porn kittens.

NANCY WILSON: We took our clothing cues from *Purple Rain* and from *Amadeus*, which we watched a million times. I was rocker-cising on top of a fiery spiral staircase. We had so much hair and hairspray, and there's fire coming at us. It's like, *Why did we say yes to this again?*

LIMAHL: I'm going to tell you something, but I'm not going to name names. In one of my solo videos, the director came to my hotel while I was in Sydney, to discuss the video, and we ended up having sex. He was a famous director and he was considered very important. I was thinking, *Oh my God, I'm having sex with him.* I mean, at that point I was pretty famous all over the world.

Of course, when he was directing me on the set with lots of people around, there was a twinkle in his eye, and in mine, because we knew what had happened a few nights before. The video was great.

KEVIN CRONIN: "Can't Fight This Feeling" was directed by a guy who married my seventh-grade girlfriend, Sherry. Her husband, Kevin Dole, was an aspiring video director and she suggested that he contact me. Kevin had been doing commercials and was very into pixillation. All the big-name directors wanted this video, but I wanted to give him a shot. Everybody around me was like, "Oh great, you want to hire your first girlfriend's husband to do this huge video?" When I saw "Can't Fight This Feeling," I was mortified by my hair. I was like, "We can't release this. I'll be a laughingstock." There was casual footage of us at the piano, in T-shirts and jeans, and they used that for the video.

KEVIN DOLE, director: "I Do' Wanna Know" was a fun song, so I wrote a goofy video in which all the REO members dressed in wacky outfits, acting as the family of a loony kid—who, for better or worse, Kevin asked me to portray. So I shaved my head, donned makeup, and did my best. It turned out to be a big hit on MTV.

LOL CREME: We wanted to give the Go West singer an image for "We Close Our Eyes." He had a great voice, great presence, but terrible teeth. We said, "You have to get your teeth fixed." We were brutal. We thought this was the sort of thing despot directors did. He fixed his teeth, we styled him, gave him a grease-monkey look, and it helped enormously.

HOWARD JONES: When I was playing clubs as a one-man synth band, I had a mime, Jed, who danced onstage. That's about as un–rock n' roll as you can get, really. Jed's in the "Things Can Only Get Better" video, doing a Charlie Chaplin character, and I also had a magician—people had never seen *that* before.

JERRY CASALE: The best story is the Jane Siberry video I directed, "One More Colour." She wanted to walk a cow on a leash. This was her demand. So we went to a cow wrangler in Simi Valley, California, and settled on one cow she seemed comfortable with. The location was way out in Saugus, where they shot Roy Rogers westerns. It's time for the cow to be there and the guy doesn't show up. He's MIA, nowhere to be found. We're pissed off. Suddenly we see dust in the distance of a long dirt road, he's driving very fast, and his truck has an animal trailer hitched to it. He jumps out of the truck and he's really mean, like, "Don't even fuckin' talk to me." He's sweating and he looks crazed. As a guy who had done coke myself, I knew he was totally coked up.

He goes to the trailer and at least thirty of us are watching him. We see him looking into the trailer, and he goes, "Fuck! Goddamn it! Fuck! I lost the fucking cow!" And he jumps back into the truck. When he'd turned off the highway, into the dirt road, the cow flew out the back of the trailer. Eventually he comes back with the cow, and the whole left side of it is skinned and bleeding from pavement burns, like if you had a bike accident. He goes, "It'll be okay. Just shoot the cow from the other side and the blood won't show."

ANTON CORBIJN, director: I had a low opinion of music videos. I had no desire to make them. Photographing musicians was my first love. But bands said, "You do our photographs and our album covers, why not do this, too?" U2 had done a video for "Pride" with Donald Cammell, who was a proper filmmaker. The band was afraid it was too cinematic, almost too devoid of street vibe. So Bono asked me to have a try. I had to do it near Heathrow Airport, before they boarded a plane to Japan. I was given a couple of hours in the basement of a hotel. I did it in one shot, mostly close-ups of their faces. It's terrible. Island Records sent it out and then recalled it. And the manager, Paul McGuinness, swore that I would never be allowed near U2 again with a film camera.

PAUL McGUINNESS: Anton made one video where he shot U2 in a photographic homage to the cover of *Meet the Beatles*, where the band are lit only from the side. When we looked at it, we immediately realized it was really terrible.

BRYAN ADAMS: "Heaven" was Steve Barron trying to be sci-fi, I guess. Televisions represent people sitting in seats, stacks of video monitors represent each member of the band. Everything I did with Steve was kind of nonsensical. They didn't have the computer technology we have now. It was, like, a couple of carpenters and an electrician.

The whole budget for the "Run to You" video went into building a tree. Lightning was supposed to hit the tree, and create a big, long lightning storm. Imagine the shock and horror on set when the fucking thing burns in about a minute. We stood there, looking at this tree up in flames. And Steve Barron's going, "Oh. *Shit.*" That is probably my worst video.

STEVE BARRON: I worked with Jeff Ayeroff when he was commissioning videos at A&M, on Bryan Adams and a couple of other things. When Jeff got to Warner Bros., the label had released a single called "Take on Me," by a new Norwegian act A-ha. The song had failed miserably: No radio play, no MTV play. Jeff said to me, "I need an amazing video for these guys. You can have as much time as you'd like. And I'm going to give you £100,000 to do it." Which was an unheard of amount, especially for an unknown act.

JOHN BEUG, record executive: I came across an animator named Michael Patterson, who was studying to be a medical illustrator at the Chicago Circle campus of the University of Illinois but decided he wanted to become an animator instead. He'd made a short film called *Commuter*. I showed it to Ayeroff, and eventually that film turned into a-ha's "Take on Me.".

JEFF AYEROFF: *Commuter* was great. I paid Michael Patterson $2,500 to give me a six-month exclusive on his services, so I'd get to use him first. Soon after, I heard a-ha's "Take on Me" and fell in love with the song. Then I saw a picture of the band, and it was like, *Do people actually look like this?* Morten Harket was one of the best-looking men in the world.

STEVE BARRON: I'd been obsessed with animation from an early age—I loved all the Disney films—and I decided to do frame-by-frame animation for "Take on Me." No video director had ever had the time or the money to do that. I was in a hotel in New York, working on a Toto video, and I had an image flash through my mind of an animated hand reaching out of a comic book. I literally got a little tingle.

RUSSELL MULCAHY: Steve Barron's a-ha video was absolutely groundbreaking. Just extraordinary. Probably the most creative video I'd ever seen.

STEVE BARRON: The technique we used is rotoscope animation. In rotoscope, you shoot everything first as a live-action film, and then it's reanimated, frame by frame. The animator, Michael Patterson, did eighteen hundred drawings.

A-ha were grateful to be given this big shot. They were all quite young, and Morten, the singer, was sort of sweetly naive. His first real relationship was with the girl in the video, Bunty Bailey. When we started shooting, I told him I wanted him to take her hand and lead her into the comic world. And by about take four, they would carry on holding hands even when we'd cut.

CONAN O'BRIEN: That a-ha video was huge when I came to LA. I was feeling detached; am I going to make it in show business? And then there's a guy being chased by World War I motorcyclists. I didn't understand what was happening.

STEVE BARRON: A-ha didn't want to be known as the "animation band." They loved the video, but they wanted to be known as a band with a great body of work, not a band with that one video.

MICK KLEBER: Jeff Ayeroff's team at Warner Bros. made a significant number of top-notch videos. He had control over the entire image of an artist: videos, photo shoots, album covers. He had access to a very impressive talent pool. I mean, who else got Mondino to do a video for them? Warner Bros., along with Columbia, ruled the roost.

JEFF AYEROFF: Jean-Baptiste Mondino was a graphic artist who could barely speak English. He sent me a video he'd done for a French singer, Axel Bauer. The song's called "Cargo de Nuit." It was the best thing I'd seen since "Every Breath You Take." I told him to come to California and direct videos for me. I brought him to Don Henley's house, and we had a completely wacky meeting. I could see Don's head kind of going, *What the fuck is going on?* But somehow Don, in his infinite wisdom—because he is one of the smartest men I know—goes "All right, I'm gonna go with it." And "The Boys of Summer" is one of the best videos I ever made.

JEAN-BAPTISTE MONDINO, director: We were all the children of Andy Warhol. I was a frustrated musician who was doing photography rather than guitar. Video was a way to celebrate music with imagery. For me, it was a very weak period for music. Music had never been so bad as during the '80s. The packaging was more interesting than the music itself.

I was not really into California music. I was living in Paris, and we were into a new era, more modern. But I couldn't refuse to go to LA—it was like a dream. When I got there, I was very disappointed, because there's a big difference between what I saw when I was a kid in the beautiful old Hollywood movies, and what LA's actually about. When I listened to "Boys of Summer," there was something nostalgic—he was looking back, talking about something that he's leaving behind. The '70s were dying.

ANDY SLATER, manager: I showed the Axel Bauer video to Henley, and he said, "Call that guy and send him the song." Some video makers come from technical backgrounds—Mondino was a visionary and an artist. There's a mysteriousness to the video, an eerie abstractness. I thought of it very much as a film noir. Until that point, videos were more Hanna-Barbera. "Boys of Summer" was closer to something Godard would have made than to Hanna-Barbera. Its success opened up the possibility of doing videos that were not lowest-common-denominator, that didn't pander.

I brought Les Garland to the recording studio, and we played the record for MTV before it was even delivered to the record label. They got to know Don, and I think that served him well.

RANDY SKINNER: Don Henley did not like making videos. And he didn't enjoy making "Boys of Summer." Don's not a trusting kind of guy, either, God bless him. What Don said at the VMAs that year when he won all those awards was true: "I had no idea what they were doing, but it worked. They made Southern California look like the South of France."

JEFF AYEROFF: They used to call me the king of video. It wasn't that I was so fucking smart, I just had good taste and I understood the medium. I even helped get Chicago a hit video on MTV, "Stay the Night." They weren't exactly a current act. I thought that if I could create a car chase in their video, and the car got wrecked, how could MTV not play it? And it worked.

STEPHEN R. JOHNSON: If it wasn't for Jeff, I wouldn't have had a career in music video. I made a stop-motion animated film at USC Film School that won a bunch of awards, and Jeff saw my film. He commissioned me to direct my first video, for a god-awful band called Combonation. The singer was a great friend of mine from Kansas who I'd talked into moving to LA with me. He was the only other guy in a four-county area of Kansas who knew who Jimi Hendrix was.

Then I made the "Walk of Life" video for Dire Straits. Two videos for that song had already been made and discarded. I went on tour with them to shoot live footage, and Mark Knopfler told me he wanted the video to have sports in it. So I wrangled all this funny sports footage, with bloopers and the like. Mark's other edict was that he didn't want to be photographed from the side, because he didn't like the fact that he had a prominent proboscis. Everyone in the crew was running into each other, trying to avoid that angle.

SIOBHAN BARRON: Dire Straits' manager, Ed Bicknell, asked me one day what I thought his band needed to do to get on MTV, because they weren't selling in

America. I said, "Get Mark Knopfler to write an MTV-able song. And then let us make the video." And they did: They wrote "Money for Nothing," with the famous "I want my MTV" hook, and my brother Steve made a great video.

LES GARLAND: I loved Dire Straits. In 1985, they had the *Brothers in Arms* album, and they'd released "So Far Away" as the first single and video. Pittman and I were meeting with Mo Ostin and Lenny Waronker, who ran Warner Bros., and I said, "Talk to me about Dire Straits. I'm not sure that track you guys have out now is the right one. But I think that song that mentions MTV is a smash." They go, "You weren't offended?" I go, "Offended? *Flattered* might be a better word."

STEVE BARRON: Mark Knopfler didn't like doing videos. Dire Straits had done them before, but they showed the band playing, and Dire Straits weren't all that interesting. Jeff Ayeroff told me to go meet the band in Budapest, where they were on tour, shoot some live footage, and somehow convince Mark to do a concept video. I really wanted to use a new computer animation technology called Paintbox, which was used to do colorization in commercials and to create logos for corporations. Mark and his girlfriend and I had dinner together, I'm trying to broach the idea that MTV should be shaken up a bit. I can see he's going to say no. And luckily, his girlfriend, who was from the States, said "Wow, you're so right about that. That's exactly what MTV needs."

"Money for Nothing" starts with Sting singing "I want my MTV," and the song is damning to MTV in a way. That was an ironic video. The characters we created were made of televisions, and they were slagging off television. Videos were getting a bit boring, they needed some waking up. And MTV went nuts for it. It was like a big advertisement for them. It won Video of the Year at the 1986 VMAs. That was the same year as a-ha's "Take on Me," which won Best Director and a bunch of others. I think a-ha was probably the better video.

ADAM ANT: In its initial form, video was a revolution. Then MTV became worse than the record companies, and that's fucking saying something. That's harsh, but it became very decadent, like ancient Rome in a way. It was all about who you knew, and how many bottles of champagne you sent them. It began as a tough, groundbreaking, sexy, subversive, stylish thing with a sense of humor. Then it became all business.

I think the golden era ended with Michael Jackson, ironically. You got John Landis in, and you can't compete with that, because that was *big* fucking money.

Then groups started to hire slick, adept filmmakers. Dire Straits was a turning point, because you had a group that visually was like a Quaalude. They didn't have a clue, so they hired someone to do an animated film, which is even *more* expensive, and that set another barrier. When Michael did videos, he was the talent, so I've got no problem with that. But when the band aren't even in it? Like that Swedish group, what are they called? A-ha. That's all postproduction.

Chapter 19

"WHY DON'T I JUST TAKE $50,000 AND LIGHT IT ON FIRE?"

THE BACKLASH AGAINST MTV

MTV, EVERYONE AGREES, HELPED MUSICIANS AND their record companies make a lot of money. But not everyone who benefitted felt gratitude toward MTV. Pretty soon, record executives began to look at the channel not as a partner, but as a leech. And they picked a fight—over money, of course—MTV bosses knew they couldn't win.

MARK MOTHERSBAUGH: MTV changed the architecture of being an artist. In some good ways, because all of a sudden, bands were forced to think about images. Some of them were doing great films.

The bad thing about MTV is, they decided early on that the most lucrative avenue was to let their palms be greased by record companies. They promoted whatever crap record companies put money into. It became a lot of mindless baby pictures. And it changed the way artists worked, because music got punished in the trade-off. There was a one-two punch: MTV was swiftly followed by CDs, and all of sudden instead of a well-crafted album of ten songs, you had to put all your bets on one particular song, and that's what people saw or heard from you. The rest of the CD was filler. So MTV created the all-or-nothing syndrome in pop music that made for CDs full of *shite* with, like, one strong song.

Bands had to go for gold right away. MTV got all the money you were making. They got all of your advance, because it went to a video. So you were paying for MTV's programming, instead of surviving for a year as a band. It's no accident the term "one-hit wonder" is centered around the '80s. MTV destroyed the idea of a band being able to do an album or two before they made their big opus, or before they made their strong statement. Videos changed the economics of the industry.

RICK RUBIN, record executive: In some ways, MTV hurt music, in that it changed what was expected of an artist. The job changed. It became a job of controlling your image. Part of it was being camera-ready and having good concepts. Then you started to see artists break who may have been stronger visually than they were musically.

PAUL McGUINNESS: There were a lot of artists for whom MTV didn't work. They would have large sums of money spent on their videos, and if MTV didn't like them, their labels would drop them and they'd have a very short career.

DEE SNIDER: While MTV exposure accelerated your sales, it also shortened your shelf life. Bands had long careers in the '70s. They came to town once a year and there was no way to experience them unless you went to the show. But with MTV, you could sit in your living room and watch rock bands. MTV created an environment where a three- to five-year career was the norm.

PAUL FLATTERY: On the one hand, MTV was genius. On the other, it could be seen as the great rock n' roll swindle. The record industry pours millions and millions of dollars into videos. Meanwhile, the artists, for the most part, pay for the videos. And then MTV gets them for free.

PAUL McGUINNESS: They had designed a brilliant business, where they got free programming, paid for by record companies and artists, and they sold the advertising and made a lot of money. I mean, it was wonderful—for *them*. There was widespread resentment of their business model, which was regarded by many people as parasitic. But look, for U2, the bargain was fair, otherwise we wouldn't have gone along with it.

JEFF AYEROFF: People who whined about the cost of music videos weren't sophisticated enough to understand that the better the video was, the more likely it was to get on MTV. The more valuable the video became to MTV, the greater the likelihood that your act could build a brand with MTV, and MTV would continue to support that brand. The greater the likelihood they supported the brand, the greater the likelihood that radio would play your act, and you'd sell lots of records. It's a simple equation, but record executives spent years not dealing with the visual side of the business.

STEVE LUKATHER: MTV convinced artists and labels to give them videos for free under the guise of "We can't afford to pay you anything, and we're great promotion for you." Everybody said, "Fine, this is never gonna work anyway." Next thing you know, it blows up into a massive thing and they don't even pay royalties to the artists or songwriters. We got nothing, and they got to decide whose careers lived and died. We spent millions on shitty videos and they'd never get shown. It's like, *Why don't I just take $50,000 into the backyard and light it on fire?*

JOHN SYKES: We got 90 percent of our content for free. Which made our margins huge.

TOM PETTY: I never thought it was fair. MTV was getting programing for free. I was going in the hole *millions* because I had to deliver videos to promote my singles, and they weren't giving anything back. They looked at it like airplay was your payment, but you weren't guaranteed that airplay.

JOE ELLIOTT: We'd spend up to $750,000 making videos to promote an album, and MTV didn't pay us a royalty for playing our music. I always thought it was wrong, and I always will think it's wrong. We get paid for having our songs played on the radio. When, say, *The Drew Carey Show* gets rebroadcast, actors get paid residuals. When MTV played our videos hundreds and hundreds of times, we didn't get *anything.*

TOMMY MOTTOLA: They built the biggest music enterprise in the history of the world off of our backs, off of our money, off of our sweat. Very cagey, very shrewd. As they began to become a powerhouse, they had the big stick, you know? We all went in and said, "Look, we're spending a lot of money on videos, and you guys are generating millions a year in profits. We need something back." So we negotiated a big contract with them, and all the other record companies did the same, where they would pay us X amount of money.

BOB PITTMAN: At a certain point, the labels wanted to get paid for their videos. I sat down with our lawyer, Allen Grubman, and figured out that if MTV could get something out of it, I'd pay. So we asked to have an exclusive window on a certain number of their videos for our world premieres, which at that time was important to us. In exchange, we gave them money, some spots on the air, and gave them some "puts," which meant they could actually put a certain number of videos into rotation on MTV, even if we didn't want to play them. Because for the first time, there were more videos than slots to play them in.

ALLEN GRUBMAN: Bob Pittman was at my house in the Hamptons. By this point, the record companies wanted to be compensated for their videos, so we came up with a concept that we would pay each record company a sum of money every year for the exclusive right to play certain key videos for a period of thirty days. That gave MTV a big leg up against their competitors.

AL TELLER: When Pittman went around to the record companies to negotiate exclusivity deals, I laughed at him. I said, "Bob, I'm not going to give you an exclusive." I had no interest whatsoever in seeing MTV become a monopoly for music videos. I thought that would be a disaster for us. But they were clever; they offered multimillion-dollar deals to each of the major labels in exchange for an exclusivity period that was clearly designed to kill off their competitors. Warner Bros. and CBS were profitable, but RCA wasn't profitable, PolyGram wasn't profitable, Capitol wasn't profitable. So when MTV came to them with a check, they couldn't resist. MTV played its cards well. I was overruled by my boss, Walter Yetnikoff, and we ended up making the deal. The music industry has a long history of doing incredibly stupid things at important moments in its history.

TIM NEWMAN: The record industry is in fairly deep trouble today, of their own doing. Music video was a tremendous way to promote music, and they let themselves become captives of MTV. Early on, MTV would take any video and be happy to run it. When the tables turned and there were more artists making videos, MTV could pick and choose. The labels tried to fight back, which wasn't successful. They delivered themselves into a situation where they did not have control over promotion. They had a partner, in MTV, that had a different agenda. The record business is an old-fashioned industry that's had a low level of success in adapting to change. They were shortsighted. They never, ever took the long view—instead of embracing MTV, they should have done everything in their power to create competition for MTV, so there would be more than one outlet for their videos.

JAZZ SUMMERS: There was a standoff between record companies and MTV, over who had more power. The record companies were paying for MTV's free programming. And they're thinking, *Shit, what are we doing that for?* But their free programming was selling a zillion records. After the mid-'80s, MTV knew they had the power. That's when the record companies said, "Please play our record!" instead of "Why should we give you our record?"

Chapter 20

"DON'T BE A WANKER
ALL YOUR LIFE"

"DO THEY KNOW IT'S CHRISTMAS?,"
"WE ARE THE WORLD," AND LIVE AID

Bob GELDOF LEARNED ABOUT THE DISASTROUS famine in Ethiopia while watching TV, and he resolved to raise money to feed starving Africans. Geldof was not a music star—his band, the Boomtown Rats, is remembered mostly for the crazy-assassin ballad "I Don't Like Mondays"—but he knew England was full of pop phenoms, and he gathered them to record a song he cowrote, "Do They Know It's Christmas?" The success and attention led to "We Are the World," an American all-star answer record to "Do They Know It's Christmas?" But Geldof wasn't done exploiting celebrity to raise money for charity. Working relentlessly, using persuasion, negotiation, guilt, and manipulation, he organized Live Aid, a daylong concert held in London and Philadelphia on July 13, 1985, and broadcast around the world.

In the U.S. Live Aid was broadcast live on ABC and MTV, whose VJs hosted the event—quite badly, almost ineptly. ABC's audience was much larger than MTV's, so the VJs' inexperience was seen by millions, including TV critics who hammered the fives faces of the network. "The MTV video jockeys should hide their heads," *USA Today* wrote. Live Aid raised close to $300 million, and Geldof was knighted, but the countdown began on the MTV careers of Martha Quinn, Nina Blackwood, Alan Hunter, Mark Goodman, and J.J. Jackson.

NIGEL DICK: At Phonogram, I'd made two videos for the Boomtown Rats, when their career was on the way out and the band had no money. One day my boss, Tony Powell, said, "Bob Geldof's gonna make this charity record over the weekend. You need to shoot a video and figure out how to do it for free. And it needs to be ready by Monday evening." I had five days to plan, shoot, edit, and complete a video for a song which had yet to be recorded. Which actually had yet to be *written*.

When I showed up on Sunday morning to begin filming "Do They Know It's Christmas?" nobody was there apart from Geldof and Trevor Horn, the producer. We had two cameras, so I set up one outside and one inside. People started arriving around noon to do the chorus, and during the day people sang their various parts. All the artists were very focused. At some point, somebody asked, "Hey, Bob, where's the food?" And he completely lost it. He said, "This is a fucking charity record and people are starving. Go buy your own fucking lunch."

GEORGE MICHAEL: The musicians in England had been slagging each other off all year, and everyone kind of forgot about it for the day. The only person who didn't succumb to the charitable nature of the day was Paul Weller, who decided to have a go at me in front of everybody. I said, "Don't be a wanker all your life. Have a day off."

BOY GEORGE: I had just got off a flight from New York and I was tired. I'd done a show the night before, and I looked like I'd been beaten up. Cameras were shoved in your face from the minute you got there, but because it was for charity, you didn't complain. Everybody was really, really friendly—I think Simon Le Bon came up and gave me a hug. In front of the press, of course.

BOB GELDOF, artist: The '80s were characterized by greed, in effect. But you must understand, I missed that. To me, the '80s were characterized by overwhelming generosity and kindness. Prior to Live Aid, people had been participating in this phenomenon for months. "Do They Know It's Christmas?" was sold in butcher shops all during Christmas. They weren't selling turkeys or partridges. For whatever reason, this song—not a particularly good song—tapped into a groundswell of compassion. We never said we'd eliminate world hunger, but we could draw attention to a monstrous human crime, a moral and intellectual absurdity. It worked.

JON LANDAU: "We Are the World" had a huge impact on Bruce Springsteen's career, especially internationally. I couldn't be there the night the thing was filmed. But I was in California a little while afterwards and went to see Ken

Kragen, who had organized the thing. Ken says, "Let me show you this." And when Bruce's bit comes up at the end, juxtaposed with Stevie Wonder, I couldn't believe it. I was so excited. That video arguably had as much impact as any of Bruce's own videos, and it was completely unplanned. And that also became the Bruce that Joe Piscopo and everybody loved to parody.

CHIP RACHLIN, MTV executive: I called a concert promoter I knew, Harvey Goldsmith, who had aligned with Sir Bob. He said, "We're trying to feed the starving in Africa. What do you bring to the party?" I said, "Well, I *do* have a twenty-four-hour music channel playing most of the artists on that song. Why don't we start there?" So I talked to Garland and explained that if we made some sort of commitment to give them inventory on the air, we could get the exclusive on the video. And that led to us broadcasting the Live Aid concert. I did that deal. About six weeks before the broadcast, Gale Sparrow and I left to form a new company.

CURT SMITH: We'd been touring for a year, really hard work. We had five days off and planned a holiday in Hawaii. Then Bob Geldof announced that we were playing Live Aid. He never asked us. Geldof thought he was so powerful that if he announced it, we'd have to say *yes*, or we'd look like bad people. I was pissed off. Whether we played or not wasn't going to make a difference to the amount of money raised. So we went on holiday, because that was the only break we had.

BOB GELDOF: I didn't lie or blackmail very much. I had to announce the gig, and I realized that talking on the phone to a band was one thing, but unless their names were in the paper, they weren't going to commit. Once it was in the paper, they couldn't back out. Bryan Ferry rang me up and said, "Listen, I haven't agreed to do this." And I said, "Well, it's cool, Bryan, if you want to pull out, that's fine." Of course, really, he couldn't.

DARYL HALL: It was an unforgettable experience backstage: "Hey, Jimmy Page." "Look, Madonna." Jack Nicholson was passing joints around.

ALAN HUNTER: I wish Jack had tapped on my shoulder.

MARTHA QUINN: I said to Jack Nicholson, "I'm Martha Quinn from MTV." And he goes, "I know who you are." That's when I realized I was a celebrity.

DAVID ROBINSON: The Cars had a lot of technical trouble. It was way too hot. We seldom played in the daytime, so that was disconcerting. The electronic drums weren't working when we started "Drive," and I had to yell, "Shut off all the electronic drums." There was a rush to get bands onstage and off. I just remember being nervous and hot, and not really liking it too much.

JUDY McGRATH: I was standing in mud up to my knees for what felt like twelve hours, feeding the producers copy and trying to make sure we had our facts straight. I was exhilarated beyond belief.

MARTHA QUINN: Everybody lambasted the VJs for our Live Aid coverage, because the production truck cut to us while Paul McCartney was singing "Let It Be." How do *we* know what they're doing in the truck? That's not *my* fault.

ALAN HUNTER: Kurt Loder called us airheads in *Rolling Stone*. That was a little mean, but he was not far off.

JOHN TAYLOR: Duran broke up in '84 and there was a rift. Andy Taylor and I were touring with Power Station in America, and Simon and Nick were working on the *Arcadia* album. We met in Philadelphia and did several days of rehearsal, and it was not a friendly or happy situation. The only time we were able to get in the same space together was when we did the photo for the program. Live Aid was the last time the band played together for a few years.

RICK SPRINGFIELD: Eric Clapton asked to meet me that day. I was a big fan. But I was stressed out and I blew him off, which is kind of embarrassing. He probably thought, *Oh, what a dick.*

TOM BAILEY: That show was mayhem. We were announced, the curtain went up, and as I walked towards the mic stand, I realized my guitar cable wasn't long enough to get there. It was a shambles.

On the bus back to the hotel, I sat next to a corpse who turned out to be David Crosby. He looked white as a sheet and he was unconscious. It was a bit like the final scene in *Midnight Cowboy.*

There was a big party afterwards, but I went back to the hotel with Nile Rodgers and we played Scrabble. Nile was very good at Scrabble.

HOWARD JONES: U2 established themselves as a global band that day. And Queen established themselves as probably the best band of all time.

JOE DAVOLA: I told the people I worked with, "I wanna get onstage at some point today." They were like, "You're full of shit." When they were singing "We Are the World," the finale, security had fallen apart. I found Doug Herzog and said, "Follow me." I ran up to the microphone, got between two guys in Duran Duran, and started singing. That was the MTV attitude: You might as well go for it. No guts, no glory.

Chapter 21

"A WHOPPING, STEAMING TURD"

THE WORST VIDEO EVER MADE

BILLY SQUIER, artist: I came up with "Rock Me Tonite" on holiday in Greece, swimming off Santorini. I came out of the water and said to my girlfriend, "I've got a hit for the next record."

MICK KLEBER: "Rock Me Tonite" is often ranked as one of the worst music videos of all time.

RUDOLF SCHENKER: I liked Billy Squier very much, but then I saw him doing this video in a very terrible way. I couldn't take the music serious anymore.

STEVE LUKATHER: Billy Squier was a cool guy. I worked on one of his records. But that video killed his career.

PHIL COLLEN: The first big tour Def Leppard did in the States was in '83, as the opening act for Billy Squier. A year later, Squier learned the hard way that rock singers shouldn't skip through their bedroom, ripping their shirts off. That's in the first chapter of the rock handbook. You should know that straight off the bat.

BILLY SQUIER: I had an idea for the video, based on the ritual of going to a concert. If we admit it, when we're getting ready to go out, we're checking our clothes and our hair. So I wanted to show me doing that in my apartment, then cut back and forth with kids getting ready to go to a Billy Squier concert and sneaking out of the house. In the last chorus, they get to where they're going, I get to where I'm going, we're all in it together.

The first person we went to is Bob Giraldi, the biggest video director in the world. I sent him the song, he loved it, we had a meeting, everything was good. Three weeks later, he called my office and said, "I'm out." He decided it wasn't something he'd want his kids to see. I was like, "*Huh?*"

BOB GIRALDI: Having seen the video, he was right: I should have been the director.

MICK KLEBER: Giraldi said he was routinely turning down projects that were underfunded. He was interested, if we could enlarge the budget. Compared to other labels, Capitol budgets were conservative. Bob understood and politely bowed out.

BILLY SQUIER: So we regrouped and went to David Mallet. I told him the idea and he came back a few weeks later with storyboards. The first thing he showed me was a scene of me riding into a diner on a white horse. I was like, "Get rid of him." That was the end of that.

MICK KLEBER: Capitol had worked with David on clips for David Bowie, Iron Maiden, Queen, and a Tina Turner video, "Let's Stay Together," which demonstrated her comeback potential. But David wasn't sold on "Rock Me Tonite" as a song. He may have submitted a treatment out of professional courtesy.

BILLY SQUIER: Now we're in trouble—this thing has already been scheduled for an MTV world premiere. I'd had two huge records, huge tours, everything is set up. We're running out of time.

MICK KLEBER: We talked to MTV about moving back the premiere date, but they were reluctant to change and couldn't guarantee a world premiere at a later date. I passed this on to Billy's manager, Tom Mohler.

ARNOLD STIEFEL: Bullshit, MTV's already given them a date. Fuck MTV, they can wait. But Billy's a sweet, gentle guy. I don't think he had anyone fighting for him.

BILLY SQUIER: David Mallet had been using a choreographer named Kenny Ortega, who is considered a great choreographer. Kenny was a friend of my girlfriend, Fleur Thiemeyer, who was a costume designer. Kenny rang up and said, "I would really like to direct this video. I love Billy."

TOM MOHLER: Stewart Young and I started comanaging Billy in 1980. We absolutely did not endorse Kenny Ortega and did not want it to happen. Stewart fought diligently to get rid of him.

BILLY SQUIER: The idea Kenny pitched was "I've seen you perform, and you have great moves onstage. Let's go onto a soundstage, you take the guitar off, and do stuff you would do onstage."

I wanted it to look like *American Gigolo*: grainy textures, somber colors. I was very clear about this. Kenny made a reference to the Tom Cruise scene in *Risky Business*, where he's playing air guitar. I said, "Absolutely not. This is not a pop video." We shot on a soundstage in LA, only a week or two weeks before the world premiere. There wasn't much time left. I come to the set and see all these pastel colors, a comic-book city backdrop, smoke machines, a bed with satin sheets. This is not what we said we were going to do. And Kenny says, "No, trust me. When it goes onto film, it'll look the way you want." "So this is gonna look like *American Gigolo*?" "Yep." I didn't like the sheets, but I trusted the guy.

I mean look, Kenny is gay. And this is the way he saw me. He abused my trust, I really feel that. He did not do what he said he would do.

PETE ANGELUS: Let me stop you right there. What could the director have said? "You're going to dance around like an idiot and don't worry, we'll cut around it?" There's no finger-pointing in that regard, Mr. Squier. I don't care if the director was lying dead on the floor, you shouldn't have put on a fucking pink T-shirt and danced around like that.

MICK KLEBER: Kenny Ortega has since become famous as the director of the *High School Musical* series and the Michael Jackson documentary *This Is It!* At that point, he had directed a few videos—most notably the Pointer Sisters' "I'm So Excited"—but he had no experience with rock singers. Capitol frowned on artists meeting directly with video directors, but Billy was determined to control the process. By going around the label, he had thrown down the gauntlet. And although the concept seemed questionable to us, and we were somewhat alarmed about the idea of the video, Billy was completely sold on it.

ARNOLD STIEFEL: Duran Duran videos were pretty light in the loafers, for straight men. But did Billy not notice the pastel satin sheets? I mean, I don't know that Barry Manilow ever did such a gay video. Billy was dancing like Donald O'Connor and Gene Kelly in *Singin' in the Rain*. It's more than swishy. He was jumping on beds and ripping off his shirt. He's the world's most horrible dancer. This is the great Kenny Ortega. How could he have allowed such a thing?

TOM MOHLER: I was at the shoot, and I asked Kenny only one thing: "Please make sure you film the entire song with the band." I wanted coverage so we could cut away to the band. He said, "No problem," and that never happened. He did not do that. I was tremendously disappointed. Stewart and I wanted footage of Billy with a guitar, and if we'd had that, we could have re-edited Kenny's video.

I saw the video in my apartment in Beverly Hills. I was speechless. I asked the label if we could just *not* put out a video. And Jim Mazza, who was the president of Capitol, said, "We need optimal visual support." I wish we'd had the balls to say to the label, "We're not putting it out."

MICK KLEBER: When the rough cut arrived at Capitol, the immediate consensus was that Billy's performance was disturbingly effeminate. "Is this supposed to be funny?" "Is Billy okay with this? He looks totally gay." "A pink shirt? What was he thinking?" "It wouldn't be so bad except for all the skipping." "Maybe we should call it 'Cock Me Tonite.'" "Maybe we should kill it right now." "But Billy's already approved it." "Fuck it. It's only a video."

ROBERTA CRUGER: It was a pretty bad video. In fact, it was a very bad video. At MTV, we all said, "Oh my god, what were they thinking?"

BILLY SQUIER: When I saw the video, my jaw dropped. It was diabolical. I looked at it and went, "What the fuck is this?" I remember a guy from the record company saying, "Don't worry about it, the record's a smash." I wanted to believe it would be okay. My girlfriend said something like "This is gonna ruin you." This is where I'll take responsibility. I could have stopped it. I found out subsequently that Springsteen had shot a video and hated it, so he scrapped it.

The video misrepresents who I am as an artist. I was a good-looking, sexy guy. That certainly didn't hurt in promoting my music. But in this video I'm kind of a pretty boy. And I'm preening around a room. People said, "He's gay." Or, "He's on drugs." It was traumatizing to me. I mean, I had nothing against gays. I have a lot of gay friends. But like it or not, it was much more of a sticky issue then. At that point, I told my manager, "Pull the video. Just get it off TV." I was a mess.

The video had a deleterious effect on my career. The tour before, I was selling out arenas faster than Sinatra, and as soon as that video came out I was playing to half houses. I went from 15,000 and 20,000 people a night to 10,000 people. Everything I'd worked for my whole life was crumbling, and I couldn't stop it. How can a four-minute video do that? Okay, it sucked. So?

Kenny Ortega didn't get hurt by this; I did. That's ironic. Nobody said, "I'm not gonna hire him, look what he did to Billy Squier!" He just moved on. The only person who got hurt by it was me. If you want to get really dramatic, you could say the guy crippled me.

WARREN DeMARTINI: We were on the road with Billy when "Rock Me Tonite" wasn't being received well. We were on the sidelines for that bombshell. I couldn't figure out why Capitol Records didn't pull the video and make another one.

MICK KLEBER: The budget for "Rock Me Tonite" was perhaps the most money Capitol had ever spent on a video. When you compare the production value to other clips, it was a rip-off. Creatively it was a clunker. And from an artist development standpoint, it was a tragedy. The enterprise was a whopping, steaming turd just about any way you look at it.

BILLY SQUIER: This was so traumatizing, it led to me firing Stewart Young and Tom Mohler in September 1984, after three and a half years together, and hiring Arnold Stiefel, who manages Rod Stewart.

TOM MOHLER: I heard from Billy's road manager that we were no longer the managers. I think Billy blamed us, to a certain extent. We should've been stronger. That's what managers do.

This was a dark time. I mean, we had it all. Billy was selling records, tickets, and merchandise. It was personally devastating as well. Billy and I were very close. He'd been the best man at my wedding in February that year.

ARNOLD STIEFEL: Fleur Thiemeyer did Rod Stewart's stage clothes, so I sort of knew her. She said, "Billy's in trouble." We met him in Philadelphia, and I said, "This video is terrible for you. It's going to cause you horrible problems. You ought to get it pulled off the air immediately." I thought maybe I could help, but it was too late. He finished the tour and then he became a recluse for a bit.

BILLY SQUIER: It really points to a seismic shift in music. You weren't listening to music anymore, you were seeing it. I think MTV had a negative effect on music. Video directors were guys who made commercials and used videos as a kind of stepping-stone to movies. There are instances where it worked well. I mean, I'm sure Duran Duran was happy with it, you know?

I think videos changed how record companies acted. It's a force, so you're going to look for bands that are videogenic. I would never point a finger at MTV and say it's the Evil Empire. It was a good idea. But then MTV became the biggest radio station in the country, and the most influential. It became this monster.

Aside from this, I don't really talk about the video. I want to tell the story so people get a better idea of how this machine worked. It's like "Rock Me Tonite" is the MBA course in how a video can go really wrong. On a lesser level, this stuff goes on all the time. I just get to be the poster boy for it.

The wounds have healed and the scars aren't that deep, because my life has evolved in a good way. I left the music business when I was forty-three. I don't have to work. Look who's smiling now! That video is a bad part of a good life.

MICK KLEBER: The lessons from "Rock Me Tonite" are that fame can be oddly fleeting in show business—and that rock stars should always think carefully about wearing pink.

ARNOLD STIEFEL: I mean, lordy lordy lordy. Everybody must die when they talk about this video, right? I saw it last night on YouTube, and I almost peed. I had to keep watching it over and over. All I could do was call friends and say, "You must go to YouTube right now." The response was extraordinary. "You mean, this was on television?" I said, "It was on television. I promise."

Chapter 22

"A WEDDING DRESS WITH NOTHING UNDERNEATH IT"

MADONNA TAKES—AND POPS OUT OF— THE CAKE AT THE FIRST VIDEO MUSIC AWARDS

MTV REJECTED MOST NETWORK TRADITIONS: THE cheerful morning shows, the sitcoms, professionalism. But the awards show was an old idea MTV couldn't resist. To launch the Video Music Awards (VMAs), they enlisted Don Ohlmeyer, a TV power-house who has had significant roles at ESPN, *Saturday Night Live*, and *Monday Night Football*. The VMAs immediately became more interesting than the Grammys or any other music awards, and the ratings highlight of MTV's year. But where the Grammys celebrates itself, and the Tonys honor theater, the VMAs celebrated MTV with a display of the channel's growth, influence, and taste for scandal.

ALAN HUNTER: Nina Blackwood and I were waiting for a cab one day, and a woman in her sixties, shouted, "More Van Halen!" Everybody was watching MTV.

JOHN SYKES: Come 1984, we were finally big enough that we could throw our own awards show. Artists who only two years ago wouldn't give us interviews or even make videos would show up. Les got Bette Midler and Dan Aykroyd to host, I got the Police to appear, and we were on our way.

BOB PITTMAN: Don Ohlmeyer, who had a business relationship with Nabisco and was one of my old NBC television guys, gave me the idea for the VMAs. We'd been thinking about an awards show, so it was in the back of my mind, but I didn't know how to do it. Don said, "Look, I'll finance it through Nabisco advertising, and I'll produce it. We'll be partners in it." So that's the way it started. We weren't in enough homes to make it work for national advertisers, so we had to simulcast it on broadcast TV for the first couple of years.

CHIP RACHLIN: Garland called me before the first VMAs and said, "I'm having a little problem with ZZ Top. I don't care how you get them on the show, just get them." Their manager, Bill Ham, was quite a challenge—he was a good ol' boy from Texas. I called and told him to set a VCR to record MTV from midnight Tuesday to midnight Wednesday, and that we would talk on Thursday. For leverage, we'd removed all ZZ Top videos from the air. Bill called me early that day and said, "I looked at those tapes, and for twenty-four hours we weren't on MTV." "And you'd like to fix that?" "Yeah, we'd like to fix that."

RANDY PHILLIPS: Les convinced me that Rod Stewart should play the first Video Music Awards. Rod was the intro to the show, and Ronnie Wood performed with him. Later on in the show, Rod and Ronnie were going to present MTV's first Lifetime Achievement Award to Quincy Jones, honoring Quincy's career as a musician, arranger, producer, and humanitarian. So Rod and Ronnie perform, after which they head back to their dressing room and wait for their turn to present. Unfortunately, there was a bunch of booze in said dressing room. When it came time to present this solemn award to Quincy Jones—the greatest producer of all time—the two of them were *completely* soused. When they walked onstage, Rod was wearing the lampshade from the dressing room, and Ronnie was carrying the ironing board. They were drunk off their asses, and they totally bollixed up the introduction to Quincy Jones. Did I mention that Quincy was best friends with Steve Ross, the chairman of Warner Communications? The calls I got the next day from Les and Pittman were unbelievable. Rod actually had to apologize to Quincy.

BOB PITTMAN: The show was a wicked undertaking. We'd never tried to put on anything of that scale before. And we had never tried to organize an industry event. We made a terrible error the first year; we put VIPs in the first few rows. Industry people are totally jaded, so whenever we cut to a crowd shot, you'd see a bunch of deadpan old people. After that, we always put fans in the front rows.

CHIP RACHLIN: We booked Madonna for the first VMAs. You'd think that at this early stage of her career she'd have been head over heels to be part of it, but that wasn't the case. She was a bit difficult from the word go. She didn't want to perform one of her hits. She wanted to sing a new song, "Like a Virgin."

LES GARLAND: We're getting closer to the show, we're building sets, and Madonna had no idea what she wanted to do. I'd call her and say, "Look, we've really got to know." She called me the next day and says, "I've got it. I want to sing 'Like a Virgin' to a Bengal tiger."

"What?" She goes, "A Bengal tiger." And I go, "You mean like a baby one?" "No, no, full-grown." "You want a full-grown Bengal tiger?" "A white one." I go, "You want a white, full-grown Bengal tiger onstage at Radio City Music Hall? If it gets loose and kills Walter Yetnikoff, I've got a fucking problem. Come up with something else." And she came up with the cake idea—she burst out of a wedding cake. So we had a seventeen-foot cake built.

It's rehearsal the day before the show, and it's time for her to do her number. She comes out in a wedding dress with nothing underneath it, and up the ladder she goes. I'm standing below and looking up. She figures out what's going on, looks down, and says, "How do I look from down there?" And I said, "Pretty good to me!"

CHIP RACHLIN: I was standing next to Garland. We thought we were out of her sightline. She calls down, "How do my seams look?" Garland shouts, "They look good to me, honey!" To which she replies, "Fuck off!"

FREDDY DeMANN: Madonna was quoted as saying, "My manager was losing his mind," regarding her performance of "Like a Virgin" at the VMAs. Her dress was splitting open! But she had no doubts, no concerns.

LIZ ROSENBERG, record executive: People were stunned and speechless that Madonna behaved in such a shocking fashion. People came up to me and told me her career was over before it started.

NICK RHODES: She came onstage in a wedding dress and rolled around on the floor. Afterwards, everyone knew she was going to be a *big* star. There was a confidence about her, an energy and a charisma, that really came across.

LES GARLAND: I thought she was very hot. Who didn't? A few weeks after the show I said to Freddy DeMann, "Do you think I have a shot?" He says, "Go ahead, but I think you might be too late." So I'm on the phone with her and I kind of threw it out there. And she laughed and goes, "Garland, don't think I haven't checked you out. I heard you like to talk." I said, "It's true. If anything happens between us, I'm telling everybody." I knew I was doomed.

HUEY LEWIS: We played at the Video Music Awards and I saw Madonna for the first time. She was fantastic. After the show, she got a hard time from the press about being so sexual. I said, "Hey, wait a second. I'll tell you why Madonna is here. She makes great records." Which was true.

FRED SCHNEIDER: I went to the awards when Madonna did "Like a Virgin," and Cher was there. I was excited to meet Cher. And Madonna comes up and says, "Do you think that was too shocking?" It didn't seem shocking to me. Having lived in Athens, Georgia, you see a lot of crazier stuff. But some punk comes up to Cher, and says, "Hey, Cher, where's Sonny?" And without missing a beat, Cher goes, "He's home, fucking your mother." That's the sort of story you remember.

HERBIE HANCOCK: At the first Video Music Awards, "Rockit" vied with "Thriller" for the same awards. We got more than anybody else. We got five, and Michael Jackson got three. At one of the parties afterwards, Michael pulled me off to the corner and asked me, "How did you put that song together?" I have a photograph of Michael and me from that night behind my desk in my office.

TIM NEWMAN: I won Best Director for "Sharp Dressed Man." I was engaged in some bad behavior in those days which renders memories less clear than they might otherwise be. I partied with Godley and Creme. They were prodigious smokers. We used to get so high that you just sort of drifted through wherever you were. I didn't dance on any tables. I didn't make out with Madonna in the bathroom. Or if I did, I don't remember.

BOB PITTMAN: The first year, it was everything we could do to get talent to come to the event and fill the seats. By the *second* year, every act wanted to be on the bill, and we didn't have nearly enough tickets to go around. That's when we knew we had a franchise—something we could go back to year after year and didn't have to build from scratch. In TV, that's nirvana.

Chapter 23

———

"NO CABLE NETWORK IS WORTH $500 MILLION"

MTV GETS NEW OWNERS; THE FOUNDING TEAM TRASHES A HOTEL, THEN HEADS FOR THE EXIT

I N 1984, HELPED ALONG BY "THRILLER"-MANIA, MTV HAD its first profitable quarter, which was a triumph for a network that had faced the possibility of financial failure. But MTV's two owners were distracted by much larger financial issues.

American Express had begun a high-end shopping spree: They bought up other financial services companies, including Shearson Loeb Rhoades in 1981, Lehman Brothers in 1984 for $360 million, and a few years later, E. F. Hutton, for almost $1 billion. For Amex, MTV's profit was loose change. The original vision of selling financial services via interactive cable had not panned out and clearly never would. And a company that managed financial portfolios for millionaires was uneasy about being affiliated with Van Halen videos—or with Warners, where executives, the government alleged, were involved in bribery and racketeering. One was convicted, another pled guilty. Amex decided to get out of cable TV.

Warner Communications had astutely anticipated the rise of not only cable TV, but also the home computer, via an investment in Atari that looked brilliant: The Atari 2600 Video Computer System was the first must-have video game console, the top item on every kid's wish list. Atari sold 25 million consoles, and millions of Space Invaders and Missile Command game cartridges. This success created "a kind of corporate euphoria" at Warners, Connie Bruck later wrote, adding, "There had probably not been another company, in the history of American business, that grew as large, as fast, as Atari."

But Atari's collapse was as rapid as its ascent—the company was "hemorrhaging money," John Lack says. Atari released some bad games (its version of Pac-Man was widely despised, as was its E.T.), and the industry went into pre-Nintendo doldrums. Dragged down by Atari, Warners tallied a combined loss of $1 billion in 1983 and 1984. The stock price dropped from $63 to $17. "One of my buddies was the head of investor relations at Warners," Jordan Rost says, "and after the Atari failure, he started getting death threats." Warners had amassed huge debt and needed to raise cash. With a little nudge from Pac-Man, MTV was about to get a new owner.

MTV went up for sale, along with Nickelodeon and half of Showtime/The Movie Channel, as MTV Networks, and a bidding war erupted. One competing party was MTV's own senior management, who tried to buy control of the network. They failed, losing MTV over what is now a minuscule amount of money. As a result of that failure, and new management that didn't care for the staff's rock n' roll attitude, many of the people who'd made MTV a cultural phenomenon began leaving as though the building was on fire.

BOB PITTMAN: In 1984, we decided to take the company public. Warner Amex needed to reduce debt, so Jack Messman, the CFO, pitched the idea that we could sell 20 percent to the public and use that money to reduce the debt. Everything was going swimmingly, but before the public offering they decided to replace Jack Schneider with David Horowitz as CEO. Which was great for me, because David had always been a big supporter of mine.

JACK SCHNEIDER: Steve Ross didn't like me. Which is okay, because I didn't like him either. He was an uncultured slob. You wouldn't want your sister to marry him. He wasn't a class act. And I conveyed my appraisal of him to him on several occasions. I knew I was toast. But it didn't bother me. I had a life before MTV, and I've had a life after it. I don't want it on my epitaph. MTV was just a gig.

BOB PITTMAN: Originally, MTV had started off advertiser-supported, which means we didn't charge cable operators to carry us. But now we needed money, so we had to go back and tell them, "Pay us or we're going to go out of business." If we hadn't gotten those fees, MTV probably wouldn't be profitable today. John Malone, chairman of the biggest cable provider, ATC, decided he didn't want to pay us a lot of money, and he needed negotiating leverage, so he got Ted Turner to start the Cable Music Channel. I'm not sure Turner realized he was the stalking horse, but he was.

And the day we went public, Turner announced CMC, right on top of us. So we went into the war room and decided a couple of things. We were going to go see John Malone at ATC and try to cut a deal. But first, we were going to start a fighting brand. A fighting brand is: Let's say you produce coffee, and it's a great coffee, and somebody starts a competitor. The best thing for you to do is start competitive coffee to fight with the new competitor and keep your big brand out of the fight. HBO started Cinemax as a fighting brand against The Movie Channel. Whatever The Movie Channel would do, Cinemax would do. And that really knocked the legs out from under The Movie Channel.

So we came up with the idea for VH1. Turner was going to be family-friendly, he was going to sell his spots cheaper, he was going to be free to the cable operator. So we came out with VH1 and we said, "*We're* gonna be free to the cable operator. *We're* gonna be family-friendly. *We're* gonna sell our spots cheaper." Whatever he was, *we* were gonna be. I think VH1 cost $5 million. It was the cheapest network ever done. I didn't care if it got beaten up and its teeth knocked out in the fight. I just wanted to keep my baby—MTV—out of the fight. We didn't care a bit if VH1 was good.

PETER BARON, record executive: When VH1 launched, I made a Kenny G video for $30,000. People began walking into record stores and asking for the album by "that sax player on the beach."

LES GARLAND: In the beginning we actually tried to make VH1 bad on purpose, because we didn't want it to hurt MTV. We'd play a country video into an R&B video.

TOM HUNTER, MTV executive: When Lee Masters was hired to run VH1, Pittman gave him two rules to follow. One, stay within your budget. And two, don't be successful in the ratings. Because the cost per thousand we could command for an ad on MTV was double that of VH1. So if VH1 succeeded and people advertised there, MTV would lose money.

BOB PITTMAN: VH1 was there for one reason: to get rid of Turner. And thirty-four days after VH1 launched, CMC went off the air. After that, David Horowitz and I saw Turner at some cable conference. And he pulled out a white handkerchief and got on his knees in front of David and started waving the white flag.

JAMES D. ROBINSON III: The cable industry had changed. After we formed Warner Amex, it went from simply getting the franchise in an area to having to competitively bid against other cable companies and promise local officials you'd put in a gymnasium, plant trees, do a whole host of things. You were dealing in multimillion-dollar bids to get the franchise before you even put a shovel in the ground or a wire on the poles. Also, it quickly became clear that cable was going to be an entertainment medium, and not a platform for interactive services. And while MTV was a great asset, it scared some of our directors. They wondered how this psychedelic noise fit with the profile of a financial services company. So rather than continue, we agreed to sell our stake. We sold too early, but from American Express's standpoint, Warner Amex had been deemed to be not only nonstrategic, but something of a distraction.

BOB PITTMAN: Jim Robinson had a whole plan about getting into this new cable world in order to retail their services. It did not pan out. So cable came to be viewed as a non-core business. Plus there was a lot of capital expenditure in cable. It ate cash. American Express reevaluated Warner Amex and decided to get out, and they sold their stake to Steve Ross. But the collapse of Warners' Atari business had made them financially vulnerable, too. They needed money. So the Warners board approved the purchase with the provision that Steve had to sell either MTV Networks or half of the cable franchise business. We were on the inside, so we knew Steve had to sell something. That's when David Horowitz and I decided to try a leveraged buyout for MTV. We'd lead it, and take the senior managers with us, and we'd all share in the equity. We were introduced to the private equity firm Forstmann Little: Teddy Forstmann, Nicky Forstmann, Brian Little and Steve Klinsky. Steve was a young guy and he championed us. He got Fortsmann Little to commit.

TOM FRESTON: This was at the height of the LBO mania. We each had a little money, although the way the stock options were distributed—Bob got something like 100,000, David had 100,000 or 200,000, everyone else got between 1,000 and 10,000—raised a lot of eyebrows.

BOB PITTMAN: Not long after David and I met with Forstmann Little, Steve Ross called me in to his office. He said, "Listen, Bob—I've made a deal with Viacom to buy MTV Networks, and I want you to be part of it." Viacom was a television syndication company that owned half of Showtime/The Movie Channel; Warner Amex owned the other half. At that moment I was Mr. MTV; if Viacom tried to purchase MTV and I didn't stay, they wouldn't get their financing. Now, Steve had been very good to me. He was a father figure. I said, "Steve, of course I'll stay, because I owe it to you, but I'm going to ask one thing first: Please listen to Teddy Forstmann before you say yes to Viacom." Teddy came in and pitched Steve. He offered a lot of money for MTV: $475 million. And Steve said yes. He accepted our offer. David and I brought together Sykes, Freston, and the whole inner group, and told them we had a deal. We actually began working out how we would divvy up the equity.

JOHN SYKES: We were preparing to take ownership. We were going to have to carefully manage overhead and increase revenues, but this was a long-term play, and we knew the business had barely scratched the surface of its potential. The night our offer was accepted, I took some of the Forstmann Little people to a Bruce Springsteen concert in New Jersey to celebrate. The LBO had gone through! We had a press release written. We were having a great time.

BOB PITTMAN: Steve Ross was a great trader. And as we were drawing up the papers, he was whittling away at the conditions—changing terms, trying to get more and more out of Teddy. At a certain moment, Teddy blew up at Steve. I forget what about. But things got heated between them. And at that point Alberto Cribiore, who was Steve's dealmaker, went across the street to Viacom and told them, "You pay us $525 million and buy our half of Showtime/The Movie Channel, and we'll sell you the company."

I was having dinner with Teddy and Nicky at a restaurant on the Upper East Side when I got a message that Steve Ross had called. I had no idea what was happening. I walked over to Nicky's apartment to use the phone. And that's when Steve said, "I'm not going to do the deal with Forstmann. I'm going with Viacom. It's done." I went back and told Teddy. Teddy said, "Well, I'm not gonna pay any more. That's it."

JOHN SYKES: We told Forstmann Little that if we matched the offer, Steve would do the deal with us. And Forstmann's quote was, "No cable network is worth $500 million. We're out." We ran into a brick wall. Fortsmann Little were very disciplined about their deals. Once they put pen to paper and figured out a valuation, they weren't going to budge from it. They weren't emotionally caught up in the deal like we were. Our feeling was that this company could be worth a lot more than $500 million. And it turned out we were *right*, of course. Years later, I said to Ted Forstmann, "My God, if you had made that deal, you could have a multibillion-dollar company." And he said, "If I had to do it all over again today, I'd make the same decision." That's just the way these guys run their companies.

BOB PITTMAN: MTV Networks sold to Viacom for $525 million. Teddy Forstmann's brother Nicky was a pal up until he passed away, and years later I'd periodically tell Nicky, "MTV's now worth $2 billion . . . $3 billion . . . $5 billion . . . $10 billion." We'd laugh about the fact that we cared about $50 million back then.

JOHN SYKES: Virtually overnight, we went from thinking we were going to own our company to becoming salaried employees of an outside corporation. We felt blindsided. We were all in our twenties. We didn't have enough experience to know that this was the way business sometimes went. We were demoralized. We'd built this company from day one—we had been in the room when the logo was sketched, when we named it, when we went on the air with a handful of videos. We built it cable system by cable system. We'd put our *lives* into this startup, and we felt like it was taken right out from underneath our noses. It wasn't all bad—we cashed out our stock when Viacom bought the company. But it was really a consolation prize.

And that was the beginning of the end for the original group of MTV executives. Within the year, Les, Bob, and I all left MTV.

BOB PITTMAN: It was very tough to lose out on the LBO. But I felt I owed Steve, so I agreed to stay on and work for Viacom. David Geffen called me and said, "Listen, disappear from town. I'll negotiate your deal. Steve should pay you $10 million or $20 million to go to Viacom." I said, "I can't do that." I think I got $3 million or $4 million out of the deal. By the way: $3 million or $4 million? A lot of money to me at that age.

JOHN SYKES: When Steve Ross sold to Viacom, that's when all the fun stopped. In the fall of '85, MTV Networks held an offsite at Gurney's Inn in Montauk. This was the first time most of us were meeting the new owners. Terry Elkes, who ran Viacom, landed on the property in a helicopter. That didn't make such a good impression. He spoke to us, and it wasn't a well-received speech. He basically said, *This is how we're going to do things from now on,* and then got back in his helicopter and flew back to Manhattan. MTV Networks get-togethers were always kind of wild, but this one turned a notch crazier. We were frustrated that we had been bought out by a hostile opponent and then to talked to like children by a company that, in our minds, made widgets. So the offsite turned into an Irish wake.

TOM FRESTON: All the top MTV Networks management was at Gurney's. The night before we met our new owners, we stayed up drinking tequila. I remember people grabbing fish out of the aquarium and throwing them everywhere. We were tossing around six-foot palm trees. Chairs were overturned. We trashed the hotel. And then into this very hungover group walks Terry Elkes for this lunch meeting. And about the first thing he says is, "We know that many of you have stock options"—because the *only* silver lining of this Viacom deal was that our meager options would accelerate and vest. "Well," he said, "I just want you to know that we don't intend to honor that." This was the coldest possible water you could have thrown on this crowd. We were dumbfounded that this was their opening gambit. They did end up paying us our options. But a feeling of dread and pessimism was cemented right there.

BOB PITTMAN: Every year I hear another story about that offsite, so god knows what went on.

TOM FRESTON: Viacom was not a major player back then. It was run by Terry Elkes and Ken Gorman, and they owned a few TV stations and cable systems, some radio stations. Their big asset was a syndication company that distributed *The Cosby Show.* Terry and Ken were smart guys, but they were more the financial engineering types. They had a reputation for being very cheap. It would be impossible for them to look at a business and not think there was a lot of fat to be trimmed. When they saw that Bob had two assistants, they said, "Two assistants is not the Viacom way of doing things. We're a one-assistant or a split-assistant company."

BOB PITTMAN: Terry Elkes and Ken Gorman's business philosophy was one-hundred-and-eighty-degrees different from Steve Ross's. They were former finance guys who'd been in syndication sales. They were very stiff. They were not at all like the people at Warners or MTV.

ALLEN NEWMAN: It started to become about profit and programming. All of a sudden, there was hierarchy and bureaucracy. The attitude changed. The fun had gone out of it. When Viacom came in, it just started to become corporate.

MARCY BRAFMAN: It wasn't fun anymore. Our ideas were getting rejected. I could feel the tectonic plates shifting.

TOM FRESTON: People started heading for the exits.

LES GARLAND: When the company was sold, Pittman signed a long-term deal with Viacom. He was a cheerleader for the new company and talked about how we needed to make this work. Finally, in the middle of '86, he came to me, one-on-one, and dropped the news that he was leaving. I shouldn't have been surprised, but I admit it, I was like, "*Oh. My. God.*"

BOB PITTMAN: David Geffen had a huge impact on me. When MTV became wildly popular, he'd said, "Are you just going to be a one-idea guy?" You know when somebody says something to you and it just picks at you? That question picked at me and picked at me. I was thirty or thirty-one, and I had a lot of other ideas I wanted to try. I'd come out of radio, where every year or so I moved to another station. Plus, as a preacher's kid, we moved every two or three years. I've got it in my blood; always on the go. But it was tough, because I felt like I was leaving my family. MTV was my baby.

It was a very difficult decision. But at a certain point, I realized that Viacom had taken my company and my heart wasn't in it anymore. People would offer me jobs, and my attorney would say, "No, not that one." Finally, Sid Sheinberg at MCA said, "Why don't you start your own company? We'll finance the company and split it with you fifty-fifty." My attorney said, "You should take that deal." So I left MTV and started Quantum Media.

TOM FRESTON: I think Bob was getting a sense that the bloom was off the rose for MTV. And Bob very much wants to be associated with success. I believed the bloom *wasn't* off the rose. Hell, five years earlier I was living in fucking Afghanistan. Who was I to complain?

LES GARLAND: One of the terms of his exit from Viacom was that Bob wasn't allowed to poach people, but I can admit now that he and I had some conversations. We decided that the move had to take place in two steps. First, I had to resign. There was a great going-away party at the China Club; David Bowie's band played, and I got up and did "Secret Agent Man" with them. We blew it out, and I said good-bye to MTV. I went on vacation for a while. When I surfaced a month or so later, I took an office over at Quantum Media. Nothing was official. We let it go real slow like that, and ultimately MTV allowed it to go down.

Quantum developed TV shows, we had a music company, we had publishing, we were gonna do magazines, we wanted to do films. We'd come off a home run, we were ambitious guys, and my recollection is that there were no budgets. We launched *The Morton Downey Jr. Show*, which was huge, until Downey claimed someone painted a swastika on his forehead in an airport bathroom.

JOHN SYKES: When Viacom took over, I checked out. There was nothing there for me emotionally. I left in the summer of '86 to go work for Mike Ovitz at CAA. Bob went to work for MCA. Les left with him. The dream was over. We cashed in. We didn't make the kind of money guys make now when they cash in, but we all made more money than we ever thought we would.

TOM FRESTON: I was the general manager of MTV and VH1 and had been for some time. When Bob left, he anointed me to be his successor. He made me copresident with a fellow named Bob Roganti. I was the president of MTV Networks Entertainment, and Roganti was the president of ad sales and operations. When I took over, a lot of people were leaving the company, not just because of the change in ownership, but because they were burned out. Our ratings were eroding, and as they slipped, the perception grew that MTV was a flash in the pan, that this downward trend was irrevocable, that we'd burned hot and bright, and now we were going to crash.

Chapter 24

"GACKED TO THE TITS"

TWENTY-FOUR STORIES ABOUT DRUGS

STEVIE NICKS: "I Can't Wait" is one of my favorite songs, and it became a famous video. But now I look at that video, I look at my eyes, and I say to myself, "Could you have laid off the pot, the coke, and the tequila for three days, so you could have looked a little better? Because your eyes look like they're swimming." It just makes me want to go back into that video and stab myself.

Was I doing drugs on the set of my videos? Absolutely. Which videos? All of them. I knew only two people from that era who didn't do drugs. And one of them did drugs, but never very much.

BOB GIRALDI: I had a meeting with Stevie Nicks where we sat on her bed. I've never seen a woman that stoned in my life. She was so wasted, we couldn't even communicate.

DOMINIC SENA: I did Fleetwood Mac's "As Long As You Follow." Christine McVie had the lead vocals, and I was focused on her, then drifted over to capture Stevie Nicks sitting on the arm of a couch, and there was no Stevie there. She had fallen off the couch and onto the floor. I said "Jesus Christ, would somebody please pick Stevie up and put her back onto the sofa?"

JEFF STEIN: My crew and I had a thirty-six-hour day once. It was for the Vinnie Vincent Invasion. I can't remember the name of the video—would *you*?

BETH BRODAY: There was never enough money or time to fully execute the ambitious visions of directors and artists, and we would end up shooting twenty-four-, twenty-five-, twenty-six-hour days. I would have to keep my crews happy and awake by providing them certain substances beyond coffee.

DAVE GROHL: My father-in-law used to help bands make videos in the '70s and early '80s, back when they'd just pay you in cocaine. "The band's gonna be here, you have them for one hour, just set something up quick." They'd get a bunch of VHS tape and cocaine, and you got yourself a video.

MICK KLEBER: I certainly saw a lot of eight balls being consumed on set, especially when a video would run long. *Bump up and go.* I heard a lot of records in those days where we'd go, "That's the cocaine mix." All brittle treble, no bottom end.

PAUL FLATTERY: Toto were known as David Paich and the New Crusty Nostrils. But then again, everyone was doing coke. Lawyers. The record company execs. Everyone.

STEVE LUKATHER: Everybody was gacked to the tits for a decade. There was piles of coke everywhere. Some of us dabbled, some of us became drug addicts. It started out fun, and then people got hurt. We had to fire our singer because he disappeared into drugs. That whole period was just a nightmare, let's face it.

SHARON ORECK: One of the guys in Toto kept sending a PA out to get coke. And while he was snorting, he told me he'd been saved by the Lord from hard drugs. I said, "Well, what's that going in your nose?" And he's like, "That's just cocaine." In the early '80s, there was still this bizarre impression that heroin was a drug, but cocaine was like a cigarette. Pretty much every person in the music-video industry was doing cocaine, except me. And I wasn't doing cocaine only because I'd finished with it in the '70s. It was beyond pervasive. Everyone was high. I never heard the term "rehab" until 1985 or so. And then, all of a sudden, I started hearing it a lot.

BOB GIRALDI: I smoked a lot of dope. We were always high. We were never straight.

LOL CREME: The crew was as stoned as the rest of us. Early on, a lot of them were paid in drugs, since there were no real budgets yet. They'd go overtime and they got paid a little bit more coke or grass. The crew were delighted to do these shoots, and they did great favors to us, because they were so bored with doing advertising or movies. This was the spirit of rock n' roll, as far as they were concerned.

DARYL HALL: I'm sure the cameramen were doing blow. That's pretty much the '80s. The artists were high, but not as high as the crew.

JERRY CASALE: Nobody thought coke was bad for you. We thought it was great. Executives at Warner Bros. used to break it out at meetings.

ROBERT LOMBARD: Cocaine in those days was just something to get laid with. If you give cocaine to girls, they're gonna pull their clothes off.

JOHN DIAZ: Coke was all over the place. The excuses were the long hours and the hard work, but I don't know if the drugs were the result of that or the cause. The coke didn't make anyone more aware or help them get things done more quickly. It just made them want more coke.

ROBERT SMITH: Drugs and alcohol were the fuel for many of our videos.

SIOBHAN FAHEY, Bananarama: The "Cruel Summer" video was just an excuse to get us to the fabled city of New York for the first time. It was August, over one hundred degrees. Our HQ was a tavern under the Brooklyn Bridge, which had a ladies' toilet with a chipped mirror where we had to do our makeup. When we repaired to the tavern for lunch, we met a bunch of dockworkers. They were intrigued by us and started chatting, and they all had these little vials of coke. I'd never done coke—I was aware of its existence, but I didn't know anybody who could afford it. We were exhausted and they gave us very generous bumps. That was our lunch. When you watch that video, we look really tired and miserable in the scenes we shot before lunch, and then the after-lunch shots are all euphoric and manic.

BOY GEORGE: There was one video when Jon Moss and I had this *massive* fight, and as he was about to go on set, I dropped a vase of flowers on him. By that point, we were pretty messed up on drugs. That affected everything, not just the videos—that affected life, full stop.

BRYAN ADAMS: Sex, drugs, and rock n' roll, that comes with the territory. I mean, it's a lot of guys in film and music, getting together and partying. What do you expect?

LES GARLAND: John Belushi was a dear friend, and when he died of an overdose, I said, "That's it. I'm done with coke." My buddy Glenn Frey, of the Eagles, nicknamed it "the enemy."

TOM PETTY: There was a lot of coke on the sets of music videos. I found that coke made all the waiting around even more painful. I didn't do it much. But the crews, they were cocaine-powered. Nowadays, I can't bear to look at one of my music videos. I can't stand 'em. I feel like I can taste the cocaine, smell the arc lamps.

NANCY WILSON: Jeff Stein was a really fun director to work with. He probably was not on cocaine, unlike everybody else at the time. Including us.

ANN WILSON: Of course, including us. Otherwise we never would have done some of these videos. In the '80s, we drank a lot of champagne, we did a lot of blow, and made a bunch of videos.

Chapter 25

"THEY DISS THE BEATLES"

RUN-DMC AND THE BEASTIE BOYS
SMUGGLE RAP ONTO MTV

IF MTV DIDN'T WANT TO PLAY RICK JAMES, JUST IMAGINE how much they didn't want to play Kool Moe Dee or Roxanne Shante.

The black artists MTV embraced were mostly nonthreatening figures, like Lionel Richie and (no matter how much he *tried* to look tough) Michael Jackson. Not for the first time, MTV was accused of racism for ignoring hip-hop. To be fair, from the time it emerged in New York City, rap was dismissed as a passing fad by record labels, radio stations, newspapers, and magazines as well. But with MTV, there was an added chicken-and-egg dilemma: MTV rejected videos by rap pioneers like Kool Moe Dee and Roxanne Shante because they didn't look very good, and labels wouldn't invest more money to make rap videos look good because MTV wasn't playing them. Recognizing this obstacle, Public Enemy refused to even make a video for their first album.

The cycle was broken by Run-DMC, who were first in many things, including the first rappers to get significant MTV support, and then by the Beastie Boys, whose Def Jam label—founded by Rick Rubin and Russell Simmons—overcame MTV's fear of rap by making striking and original videos that couldn't be ignored. On the contrary, they were often the best videos on MTV.

DMC, Run-DMC: When we did "Rock Box," everybody at Profile Records was like, "Yo! The video's on MTV! That's the first rap video on MTV!" They were so excited. We was like, "What the hell is MTV?" We wanted our videos on *New York Hot Tracks* and *Video Music Box*.

LIONEL MARTIN, director; TV host: Ralph McDaniels and I DJed at parties. We were hip-hop kids. I grew up in Queens, New York. Russell Simmons lived down the street from me. Ralph worked for a TV station, WNYC, which is like a public-access station. In 1984, he came up with the idea to do *Video Music Box*. I mean, we didn't see rap videos anywhere else. I don't think we did it because of MTV. It was to fill our thirst. Our show came on at 11 P.M., but it became so popular that we got an afternoon slot. Kids would come home right after school and watch *Video Music Box*.

VERNON REID: They were real pioneers. I saw my first hip-hop videos on *Video Music Box*, because no one else was playing them.

YOUNG MC, artist: *Video Music Box* was my MTV, to an extent. I lived in Queens, and my neighborhood didn't have cable. It was mostly two-family homes, and it took a long time for that area to get wired.

DMC: Making "Rock Box" was weird. We weren't into it—it was just something we were told to do. And the director had the idea to have some little boy chasing after Run-DMC, to show that we had appeal to the younger generation. A little white boy, too.

"Rock Box" was the first rap-rock record. It took Eddie Martinez's rock guitar to get us on MTV. Our producer, Larry Smith, came up with the idea. People forget about Larry Smith, but Larry Smith owned hip-hop and rap. He produced our first two albums, and he produced Whodini. The rock-rap sound was Larry Smith's vision, not Rick Rubin's. Rick changed history, but Larry was there first. Actually, me and Run was against the guitar. We did two versions of "Rock Box" because we didn't want the guitar version playing in the hood. But when DJ Red Alert played it on his radio show, black people loved the guitar version more than the hip-hop version.

EVERLAST, artist: The first video that blew my mind was Run-DMC's "Rock Box." It was like when some kids heard punk rock for the first time.

BILL ADLER: DMC came up with the concept of "King of Rock." It's not "King of Rap," you know? Alien as it seemed to the average white person, our guys always thought of it as rock. You *rock* the mic. You *rock* the bells. In the video, Run-DMC bum-rush a Museum of Rock n' Roll, and they're blocked at the doorway by a guy from David Letterman's show, Larry "Bud" Melman, playing a smirking security guard: "You guys don't belong in here." They push past him and shoulder their way into the museum. They diss Michael Jackson. They diss the Beatles. It's all bullshit to them. There's an exhibit in the museum with a video monitor. They look at a clip of Little Richard. *No.* Jerry Lee Lewis. *No.* Then they see their own first video, which was "Rock Box."

Twenty-five years later, they were inducted into the Rock n' Roll Hall of Fame, which didn't even exist at the time. So not only did they imagine something that didn't exist, they imagined themselves as part of it!

DMC: We loved the fact that we walked into the Museum of Rock and got to pull the plug on a TV showing Jerry Lee Lewis, and step on Michael Jackson's glove. We were sick of journalists asking, "Do you think hip-hop is a fad?" "Where do you think you'll be in five years?" We felt disrespected. You're goddamn right we wanted to cuss out the Beatles. We got a lot of grief for that video. They wanted to hang us for dissing Michael, because Michael was god. But let me tell you something—we met Michael a couple of times, and he thought it was the coolest shit ever. He said to us, "Run-DMC, I think you guys are the greatest. I love the way you stepped on my glove."

GEORGE BRADT: *Thriller* had already happened, but in general, the reaction to black artists at MTV was still *That's just not our format.*

ANN CARLI: The only rap videos they would play were by Run-DMC. MTV were comfortable playing Run-DMC because they weren't threatening; they dressed like cartoon characters, in the hats and the jackets. They came out with a song, "King of Rock," to try and get themselves on MTV. A lot of their videos had a cartoon quality, and that was an easier fit for MTV.

RICK RUBIN: I was friends with people who worked at MTV, including Peter Dougherty, and it was a constant fight and struggle to get rap music on the station. I was lobbying them to play our stuff.

PETER DOUGHERTY: This goes back to MTV's history of racism—almost everybody who worked there, from Gale Sparrow to the VJs, came from FM rock radio. I don't think they knew how segregated things were. The only soul music we played was Hall & Oates.

JOE DAVOLA: We still weren't playing black music. I wanted to put Cameo on the New Year's show—I loved that song "Word Up." My bosses were like, "There's no fucking way you're doing it."

CHUCK D: Around that time, *Night Tracks* was on TBS, late on Friday nights, and they debuted rap videos. MTV had to pay notice to that buzz. How could they not? The motherfuckers were based in New York, the birthplace of rap. Either they were totally blind to the fact, or they were racist. And if they were blind to the fact, then they were racist anyway, because they chose not to acknowledge what was happening.

ANN CARLI: We told MTV, "This is incredibly racist, that you're not playing rap." As Russell Simmons used to say, "It's not limited to African-American youth, it's teenage music." Boy, did he get proved right.

KOOL MOE DEE, artist: Ann Carli and Russell Simmons deserve credit for believing hip-hop artists should be treated like mainstream artists. We were aware that there was one video budget for an R&B or hip-hop act and another budget for a pop act. We had to fight to even *have* a video budget in our contract. The record label would tell us we could do one video, and if our single sold 250,000 copies, we could potentially get a second video. Labels didn't believe in spending money on hip-hop videos.

LIONEL MARTIN: After hosting *Video Music Box*, I got an opportunity to direct my first music video, by Roxanne Shante—"Roxanne's Revenge." The budget was $400.

DMC: Jam Master Jay, our DJ, had been sampling "Walk This Way" for years. We didn't even call it "Walk This Way." We didn't know who Aerosmith was. We just knew that in Jay's crate there was an album cover that said *Toys in the Attic*, and it had a picture of a toy chest and a teddy bear. We'd say, "Get *Toys in the Attic* and play number four."

When we were making *Raising Hell*, we wanted to put something old-school on the album, and Jay was like, "Yo, let's do *Toys in the Attic*," because that beat is real B-boy. If it had been up to us, our version of "Walk This Way" would have just been the beat, a couple of the guitars, and me and Run bragging about how great we are. But Rick Rubin came into the studio and was like, "What are you listening to?" We said, "This is *Toys in the Attic*." He was like, "No, the name of the record is 'Walk This Way' and the name of the band is Aerosmith." Then he said, "It would be really great if you guys remade this song with Aerosmith. Not just sample it. Actually do the record over."

Jay, being a visionary, goes, "Whoa, great idea." Me and Run turned to Jay like, "What the fuck you talking about?" Rick took the record off the turntable and handed it to me and Run. He said, "Go learn this song." We was like, "Nah, that's bullshit." We took the record home to the basement, dropped the needle, and we hear Steven Tyler sing "backstroke lover always hidin' 'neath the covers . . ." We got on the phone with Russell Simmons: "Yo, this is hillbilly gibberish"—we couldn't even *understand* what this guy was saying. We definitely didn't know it was about a dude having sex. We just knew we completely hated it.

Russell was screaming at us, "Y'all stupid motherfuckers, you gotta do this record!" And we hung up the phone on him. For six hours we sat in our basement in Hollis, Queens, letting the phone ring, me and Run looking at each other, like, "*You* pick it up." "No, *you* pick it up." We *know* it's Russell and Rick, and we ain't doing this record. So finally I pick up the phone, and it's Jay. Russell's in the background, screaming, and Jay tells Russell, "Shut up, man. You know they stupid little kids, you keep screaming at 'em, they ain't *never* gonna do this."

Jay says, "Yo, don't bug out, Rick went and got Aerosmith, they're here in the studio, Steven's doing his vocals and he's busting your ass." Jay was using psychology. But me and Run, we're crying, "Jay, this song's gonna ruin us! We already done 'Rock Box' and 'King of Rock.' We're taking this rock-rap shit too fucking far." So Jay said, "Do it like a Run-DMC record. Switch off. Run, you take a word, then D, you take a word." We went back to the studio and tried it like Jay wanted. And it worked. That record changed our lives. It changed theirs, too. Aerosmith were going through a rough patch in their career when we did "Walk This Way." That video got them motherfuckers a new $40 million record deal. They should have given us 10 percent of that.

RICK RUBIN: I don't think it was hard for me to get Aerosmith to record the song, or to make the video. They were going through a down period. They'd reformed, put out one album, and it flopped. The record and the video had a huge effect on both groups. It opened the door to Run-DMC's full suburban cross-over, and it reminded people how great Aerosmith was.

DMC: The video was amazing. We shot it at an old theater in Union City, New Jersey. My favorite part is when Steven takes a mike stand and busts a hole in the wall. That was prophetic. It showed our worlds coming together. And that's what happened when MTV played the video. It went into all sorts of living rooms, and as soon as people saw it, they were addicted to rap.

BETH McCARTHY: I was a PA on the New Year's Eve show when the Beastie Boys' *Licensed to Ill* had just come out. Mark Goodman almost got into a fistfight with them because they were rude to his wife.

ADAM HOROVITZ: "Fight for Your Right (to Party)" started as a joke. The goal was "Let's write a stupid frat song. *That*'ll be funny." Then people liked it. So Rick said we had to make a video.

RIC MENELLO, director: I was a desk clerk at the NYU dorm from midnight to 8 A.M. I knew a lot about movies. Rick Rubin used to come by. Russell Simmons used to come to the dorm. The Beastie Boys would come by, especially Adam Horovitz, because his dad was a playwright and a screenwriter. You pop by Menello at the front desk, bullshit a little, then split. One day, Rubin said, "I think you should direct the next Beastie Boys video." That was "Fight for Your Right (to Party)." I was like, "No." 'Cause directing is sacred to me. I knew I would feel bad if I fucked it up.

ADAM HOROVITZ: I used to cut school and hang out at Rick Rubin's dorm room, and Menello would be there at four in the morning, working the desk. We said to Rick, "*That* guy's gonna direct the video? Okay, if you say so."

RICK RUBIN: Menello knew more about film than anybody. Why did I think he could direct a video? I thought *anybody* could. Because it was more about the idea than about technical ability. Concept was king.

RIC MENELLO: Rubin said, "You're going to do it." ("I'm not doing it.") "You're going to do it!" ("All right, I'll do it.") We were two loudmouths and we had knock-down, drag-out yelling sessions. I decided to use Adam Dubin, Rick's roommate, as a codirector, so if it went bad, I would blame him.

ADAM DUBIN: "Fight for Your Right (to Party)" caught fire on radio, and MTV said, "We're holding a spot in heavy rotation. If we don't have a video two weeks from now, we're moving on." It was an ultimatum. What Rubin specifically did not want was any of the slew of video directors who, on any other day, were directing Coca-Cola commercials. So Rubin called Menello. Now, Menello is a great character. He's ten years older than me, and he knows more about film than anybody you know. He's like an idiot savant of film, and he would preside behind the desk of Weinstein dorm. He would tell you about Orson Welles for four hours, and imitate him as he's doing it.

I'd graduated NYU film school in May of '86, and I'd produced and directed my own student films, so Menello brought me in. He hit on the look and the feel of the video by saying, "It's going to be like the party scene in *Breakfast at Tiffany's*," which is really just a long series of gags. In fact, we stole some of the gags from director Blake Edwards, particularly having a guy with an eye patch. We'd known the Beastie Boys for years, and they were knuckleheads. We said, "Who are these guys? They're the guys who come to the party and drink all your beer, steal your girls, wreck the place, and then leave." We gave that image to them.

We had $20,000 for a two-day shoot, which is insane. It was just a wing and a prayer.

ADAM HOROVITZ: We shot at our friend Sunny Bak's loft, a block away from the movie theater on Nineteenth and Broadway. The premise was Rick Rubin's: a party that turns into a food fight. Just about everyone in the video was a friend of ours. My two best friends to this day—Cey Adams, who did a bunch of artwork for us, and Nadia Dajani, who I met in elementary school—were pie throwers in the video. The nerds at the beginning were our old friends Ricky Powell and David Sparks. My favorite thing about that video is that we made it with our friends, and I'm still friends with many of those people.

TABITHA SOREN, MTV reporter: I'm in that video, with dyed blond hair. I'm still close friends with Rick Rubin, and they needed extras for the video. I worked hard at not getting any pie goo on me, because there was no money for the budget, so they went to the back of a supermarket, and from the garbage, they grabbed whipped cream that had expired and was rancid. The smell in that room, when everybody was done throwing pies, was like rotten eggs. You wanted to throw up.

RICK RUBIN: If you put a lot of whipped cream in a hot room for a few hours, it ends up smelling horribly bad.

RIC MENELLO: We wrecked the place. We threw pies, we kicked in the door to the bathroom. The idea of the video was infantile rebellion. Some people, like frat boys, didn't see the satire of it. It's not so much satire as a kind of blanket, cartoonish rejection of anything adult. It was stupid, but stupidity did not preclude intelligence around the edges. The style was rigorous and exact. It was influenced by Jerry Lewis, the Three Stooges, and silent movies. I played off the song—when the lyric goes, "Your mom busted in," then I busted in as the janitor. I wanted to be crude. I wanted to raise a fist against videos being very slick.

RICK RUBIN: It was rooted in Hal Roach's slapstick comedies, especially his *Our Gang* films of the '20s and '30s. Years later, those three Beastie Boys characters are iconic. People know who those three guys are; they know those characters like they would know cartoon characters.

ADAM DUBIN: Adam Yauch grabs a guitar and smashes it, which is a gag we stole from *Animal House*. And it ends in a Three Stooges pie fight, where it suddenly ropes in everybody. Rick Rubin got a pie in the face, and the first one hit him in the chest, so Ad-Rock ran through and tried to stuff another pie in his face. That's the footage we used.

RIC MENELLO: When I saw the rough cut, I cried. I thought it was the worst thing I had ever seen. To make myself feel better I turned on PBS and *Gigi* was on, by Vincent Minnelli. So I cried again. "He did *Gigi*, I did *this*." I showed the video to Rubin and the Beastie Boys. They were like, "This is really good! It's kind of like a porno film."

MTV interviewed me about the video, and I told complete and utter lies. I said it was shot in France.

ADAM DUBIN: The minute MTV ran that video, my parents knew who the Beastie Boys were. They were like, "Wow, my son did the most popular video on MTV right now."

RIC MENELLO: The video was a mammoth hit. It was the most requested video on MTV. I quit the desk job.

ADAM HOROVITZ: People loved that video. *Instantly.* Which was super-weird, because as much as I was dying to be a celebrity—I'd turn up anywhere I could be recognized—the video wasn't a planned, big-budget, marketing-team thing. We just made a video with our friends, and people were drawn to it. Then we had our *become-what–you-hate* moment. We were making fun of a fratboy mentality, and suddenly we were the thing we were making fun of.

PETER DOUGHERTY: I directed three Beastie Boys videos—"Hold It Now, Hit It" and then two live ones, "Rhyming and Stealing" and "She's Crafty," when they had a girl dancing in a cage. Rick Rubin made me get a shot of a girl lifting her top up in "She's Crafty." In the dressing room, I gave out mayonnaise and honey. Ad-Rock was taking whole six-packs and throwing them against the wall. DJ Hurricane was pouring honey on this girl in the dressing room. A couple of the Beastie Boys had serious girlfriends, who got very mad at me.

CHUCK D: We totally rejected the idea of making a video for our first album, because there was no clear-cut place where our video would be seen on a regular basis. We made an album for $17,000, so a video would cost more than our album—and half of the cost would be recouped against us anyway. People like Fab 5 Freddy and Forest Whitaker came to us with ideas. But why would we spend our own money that we ain't got?

RICK RUBIN: I didn't care that Public Enemy didn't want to make a video, not at all. Even though there weren't that many videos in those days, there were too many bad videos already. I didn't like the idea of a video as a marketing tool. I liked it as its own artistic piece.

I never believed in doing a video for the sake of doing a video, or promoting our new single. The idea had to be first. The reason we didn't do a video from the first LL Cool J album was, there never was a great concept. Jean-Paul Goude, the fashion photographer who did the Grace Jones video, had a unique enough visual style to separate LL from everyone else who made rap videos, all the guys with the gold chains. I thought, *If we can get him, then we should do a video.* But he never responded.

ADAM DUBIN: For "No Sleep 'Til Brooklyn," the record company wanted a video in the style of "Fight for Your Right (to Party)." Nobody wanted to mess with the formula. *Licensed to Ill* was tearing up the charts. There were eight guys from the record company at the video, because suddenly, the Beastie Boys mattered. Menello and I wrote all the gags, again, which we mostly took from Bugs Bunny cartoons. We had $70,000 this time, so we shot on 35mm instead of 16mm and got a better crew. We did a prologue, where Menello was the club owner and he's like, "Where are your instruments?" And then they come back as the band, wearing heavy-metal gear. Simone Reyes, the receptionist at Def Jam, was in the video—she's the girl holding a can opener. Simone was pretty, so a lot of people flirted with her, and I think she dated Yauch at one point.

I played the gorilla. If there's a gorilla suit on set, I'm in it.

We had Kerry King from Slayer, who played the guitar solo. Rubin wanted Kerry to appear to be fifty feet tall, like David Fincher later did on the "Love Is Strong" video for the Rolling Stones. The Beasties weren't pleased about that, because then Kerry is exalted in the video and they were just the putzes. They were miffed. But I think they were missing the joke. See, the bloom was off the rose by that point. The good feeling that was on the set of "Fight for Your Right (to Party)" was not there on "No Sleep 'Til Brooklyn." We got through it, but it was a tough set. I could feel the tension.

ADAM HOROVITZ: Rick Rubin was into metal and classic rock. None of us were into that, and he was always pushing this metal thing on us. He had us wearing metal wigs and outfits, and that was supposed to be funny. I didn't know anybody who dressed like that. It just wasn't what we were into.

RIC MENELLO: At one point, Rubin wanted me to get involved with a David Lee Roth video. His offer was "You work for free, I'll put you up at a nice hotel. You can eat great food and I'll give you a hooker."

ADAM DUBIN: I always give the Beastie Boys a lot of credit, because nobody in the record business, even people who knew them, would've given you two cents for their chances down the line. Everybody thought they were a one-hit wonder, certainly a one-album wonder. But they were smart guys.

FAB 5 FREDDY, *Yo! MTV Raps* host: LL Cool J's "Going Back to Cali" is one of the best hip-hop videos. It was cinematic, and it felt like the song.

RIC MENELLO: "Going Back to Cali" was supposed to look like a French New Wave film, 1960s art-house cinema. Not Truffaut, I hate Truffaut, more Claude Chabrol, Godard, Antonioni. Also a little Fellini—I watched *8½* and stole two shots from that. The video has a lot of stern, rigorous imagery, overheated.

RICK RUBIN: It was meant to be like a European art film, almost like a James Bond film, as done by Antonioni. It shows that good taste can translate to the mainstream. You don't have to dumb down something good, if you expose it the right way.

My role on set was usually supporting Menello—or yelling at Menello, depending on what was going on.

RIC MENELLO: I told LL Cool J, "This is not a video. This is a movie. You're a movie star." Rick Rubin got upset about the shot where LL's hand goes over the girl's stomach, 'cause it was his girlfriend, Melissa Melendez. She was a porn actress. Very nice girl. Since I didn't drive, she drove me everywhere.

The theme was alienation and sterility. It was about hot people looking at each other and not seeing each other. The girls all like LL, but he rejects them. "I'm so bored"—that's the Antonioni influence. I shot two people up against a wall: LL and Martha Quinn, who I'd been good friends with at NYU. He looks at her, she looks away; then she looks at him and he doesn't look at her. Camera pans up the wall. That's a quote from an Antonioni movie called *The Passenger*, except they're in bed and it's Jack Nicholson and Maria Schneider.

MARTHA QUINN: Blink and you'll miss me. My boyfriend during most of my MTV years was the cinematographer for that video. You can barely see me, but it did give me a heavy amount of street cred.

RIC MENELLO: The cinematographer was Adam Kimmel, who has since shot *Capote* and *New Jersey Drive*. He used to come visit Martha when she lived at the NYU dorm. I kept pushing Kimmel to make the first part of the video look sun-baked, and I told him to overexpose the opening shots. Kimmel later took as much credit as possible for the look and shots, which were mine. He got a blow job from some hot blonde who was an extra. She drove him to the transfer, so we could look at the footage, pulled over to the side of the road, and suddenly went down on him. He told me the whole story. This is typical. Cinematographers get all the ladies.

It turned out that one of the girls we signed to dance was underage. We'd done low-angle shots of them dancing on phone booths, which look great, and she was incredible. She was wearing a miniskirt, and she's like, "You can't see my panties, can you?" And I'm like, "No." But actually, I could. Little polka-dot panties. Her mother threatened to sue, so we edited part of her out. Rubin was like, "Can you cut her completely out?" I said, "No, she's too good."

Chapter 26

"WE PUT FINCHER ON THE MAP"

RICK SPRINGFIELD, CHRISTOPHER CROSS, AND THE HUMBLE BEGINNINGS OF A GENIUS

VIDEO DIRECTORS WERE UNSUNG, UNSUPERVISED, and probably underpaid. Most loved their jobs. A few were miserable, but continued nonetheless. There were no union regulations to dictate scheduling, so they could march a crew like Napoleon's army, advancing past bravery into foolishness. Their names were rarely mentioned: George Michael and Guns N' Roses thanked their directors when accepting Video Vanguard awards at the VMAs, but Madonna and David Byrne didn't. Michael Jackson thanked his fans, but not any of his directors.

David Fincher—the greatest video director of his era—grew up in Marin County, California, and lived two doors from *Star Wars* and *Indiana Jones* creator George Lucas, which made Fincher feel that Hollywood was nearly his neighbor. At nineteen, he began working at Lucas's visual effects company, Industrial Light & Magic. "Then all of a sudden there's this thing called MTV," he later said, "and I'm going, Fuck, I know how to do that." Fincher worked on a grand scale (as he did later in his films *Seven*, *The Curious Case of Benjamin Button*, and *The Social Network*) and gave his videos a European stylishness, as though he was always filming in the lobby of a boutique hotel, though he was also slyly funny in a way that anticipated his movies. In Paula Abdul's "Cold Hearted Snake," he made a video about making a video—a computer plays a pre-recorded track as Abdul auditions a routine for stuffy record-company geeks, one of whom looks alarmed when told the video will be "really, really *hot*." "Yeah, but tastefully," an underling quickly adds. "It's tastefully hot." Fincher exploits seminaked dancers and close-ups of brassieres to his advantage, while making fun of an industry that's built around the exploitation of seminaked bodies and close-ups of brassieres. He made sexy and smart indistinguishable. He also shot Madonna crawling on her hands and knees, and drinking from a saucer of milk. But before Madonna, he had to work his way up from the bottom—which in this case, meant Rick Springfield.

SIMON FIELDS: Video budgets started to blow up around '86. When MTV paid fees to the record companies, they started to spend more money. In the meantime, MTV got bigger, their distribution grew, they had more power. Everything got bigger and bigger.

JOHN DIAZ: In 1985, a successful music-video director might earn somewhere between $100,000 to $125,000 in a year. Same for a top producer.

JEFF STEIN: We did very well. The director got 10 percent of the budget, but I was also a profit participant in the production companies. There were signing bonuses and so forth.

CURT SMITH: Most video directors are big and brash and larger that life. They need to control the set, so they tend to be loud, they scream at people, they can be abrasive and pushy. I guess that's how they get things done.

DAVID MALLET: A director has to be slightly bossy if he's going to direct anything, doesn't he?

DANIEL KLEINMAN: I'd gone to art school, not film school, so for me, music videos were a fantastic training ground. The music itself was secondary to me. Which is a bit selfish, but I saw videos as a means to an end, which was learning the craft and experimenting with different film techniques. I tried my best to make them as brilliant as I could, but whether they helped make a record a hit was a matter of indifference to me.

AIMEE MANN: You get assigned a director, and you try to have some say, and then you're steamrolled. It's not fun. It doesn't feel good. It's awkward. You know it's not going to look great. It's also way out of your hands, and everybody's putting pressure on you to go along with it, and it could not be less comfortable, and could not be less of an artistic representation of you.

BOB GIRALDI: Directors get uptight, no question about it. I yelled at the talent, the crew. I remember shooting Jermaine Jackson's "When the Rain Begins to Fall" in Italy. The Italians said to each other, in Italian, "If that director yells at me one more time, I'm going to kill him."

MEIERT AVIS: It was very competitive between directors. You'd be bidding on a job, and you'd know exactly who you were bidding against. I've never seen directors palling around with other directors. It's war.

MATT MAHURIN, director: You'd get a call for a video and they'd say, "Oh, you're up against a couple other directors." You'd send in a treatment, then get a phone call: "The drummer's girlfriend didn't like it." Or, "Oh, we never called you? We shot that video two weeks ago." As a director, you had all this responsibility, but zero power.

SOPHIE MULLER, director: To this day, I have never gotten a job by writing a treatment. The only time I get a job is if I talk to an artist, and they say, "I wanna work with her." I don't like the competition. It's horrible, and there's no other situation like it, where you work to come up with an idea and don't get paid for it. The treatment is the hard work, the filmmaking is the easy bit. No matter what your body of work is like, you have to compete for the job. That doesn't seem right to me. Even now I'm like, *How did this happen? Where's our union?*

TIM NEWMAN: You couldn't get any closer to being in a band than being a music-video director. You're sort of the extra member of the band. It was a wonderful job.

JEFF STEIN: At that time, I don't think there was a better occupation on this planet than being a music-video director. The only thing better would be being a rock star.

ANDY MORAHAN: A director typically earned 10 percent of the video budget. But when a video grew from three or four days into seven days, the director was the only person who didn't get paid extra.

ANTON CORBIJN: I never took 10 percent. I had a fee. Whether that's 20 percent of the budget or 5 percent of the budget, it was a set fee.

DOC McGHEE: There's a saying: "You never get what you deserve, you get what you negotiate." I believe a video director was more influential to the success of an artist than the producer of the record. And it's standard to pay royalties to producers, but not to video directors. If I had been repping Wayne Isham and about five other ones, they would've gotten royalties. Record companies are as cheap as they get, and artists are maybe even cheaper. And managers are the cheapest of the three, so just by the food chain, directors got fucked.

JEFF STEIN: Music videos were the bastard offspring of the hideous music business and the heinous movie business. And music-video directors were the crazed midwives that brought that mutant howling into the world.

TAMRA DAVIS, director: It's embarrassing, how many videos I made—somewhere between 100 and 150. Sometimes I'll see videos I did, and it's like guys I slept with that I have no memory of.

JEAN-BAPTISTE MONDINO: I used to spend two weeks with a musician, to come up with an idea for the video. And little by little, videos became like an industry, so they were calling you, "Could you do a video next week with this artist from London who's coming to LA?" I was saying, "But what am I going to do with somebody I don't know?" When I was making three videos, the other guys were making fifteen. Everybody was in a hurry.

PAULA GREIF, director: Cutting Crew, I don't even remember that video. That's so awful, but I heard their song "(I Just) Died in Your Arms" on the radio the other day and thought, *I think I did the video for this.* Couldn't even remember what it looked like.

MEIERT AVIS: Making videos is a horrible pastime. I'm serious. It's about the most difficult thing you can possibly do. It's grueling. It's physically hard. You've got to make four minutes of material in a day's worth of shooting, which is a lot of productivity. The stress is high. Then you've got band issues to deal with, and record company issues. It's extremely unpleasant. Half the time you don't know what you're doing, but you have to pretend you do, because everybody has to believe there's a plan and an outcome in mind. You have to create that belief, even if you don't believe it yourself.

JEFF STEIN: It was a great excuse not to have to work for a living. I had the world's greatest crew. There were a lot of beautiful girls. We traveled all over the world to exotic locales. Worked with influential people. And created a new form of entertainment that rocked the world.

LOL CREME: The producers are the unsung heroes. Lunatics like me or Brian Grant would phone up and say, "I need four dwarves and a rhinoceros," and no matter what you asked for, it would be there. The producers, these women—it was almost exclusively women—they were unbelievable.

PAULA GREIF: A lot of the producers were women. There weren't a lot of women directors. And there still aren't, even in television commercials, which is what I do now.

BETH BRODAY: There weren't enough women directors. There was Mary Lambert, Paula Greif, and that was about it. But women ran the business. Women made good producers because they were used to taking care of things and making sure everything got done.

SHARON ORECK: The biggest nightmare I ever had was on Janet Jackson's "Control." Janet was splitting with her father, Joe, as her manager, and he was angry and taking it out on everyone. In the video, Janet was supposed to sit on a trapeze. Joe said if I put her on that trapeze, I had to take out $1 million worth of insurance on her. I went to the record company, and they're like, "Don't tell Joe Jackson anything, but don't tell him *no* either. We don't say *no* to Joe Jackson." So I didn't tell him anything, and he threatened to kill me or maybe break my legs—it was something bad. Mary Lambert went to the record company and said, "We're both quitting unless you tell Joe Jackson that you're going to cover the insurance."

We went on an urban radio station in LA and said, "Come watch Janet Jackson perform at the Shrine Auditorium." Thousands of people showed up for what they thought was a free concert. And what we gave them was fifty takes of Janet lip-syncing "Control." None of them knew they were going to be free extras in the video. And they were unruly even before it started, because we were running late. We're finally ready to go, and the record company said to me, "We need white people in the audience." There were white people scattered throughout the crowd. They're like, "No, bring the white people to the front." At first I tried to pretend I was doing some minor rearranging: "You in the red jacket, can you move forward a bit?" But by the third time, the audience started to figure it out. So I had a nervous breakdown and started crying. I said to the man from A&M Records, "This is fucked up. If you want it, *you* go onstage and make the announcement." And he agreed.

Crying helped sometimes.

KEVIN GODLEY: I was making a video with U2 and decided we needed an elephant. I told Ned O'Hanlon, the producer, "We need an elephant by tomorrow." Not many elephants in Dublin. Poor Ned somehow managed to fly an elephant from Belgium to Dublin.

SIMON LE BON: The thing about videos is, they're awfully long days. At midday, a big glass of whiskey or a fat line of coke seems like a great idea. But come 8 P.M., when you've been on set for hours, it's *awful*. You can see which Duran Duran members were getting too high. They're usually covered up with sunglasses.

JOHN TAYLOR: When we did the "View to a Kill" video, I don't think there's any shot of us all together. You couldn't get us in the same space at the same time. I wish I could say, "We loved being famous and we had even more fun together than when we started." But it wasn't like that.

PAULA GREIF: Duran Duran saw Steve Winwood's "Higher Love" and wanted to meet with us. My partner, Peter Kagan, said, "Put us on the Concorde and we'll do it." So they did. We flew to London and back on the Concorde to have a meeting in one afternoon. Those were the days!

TOM BAILEY: Godley and Creme spent a lot of the budget for "Don't Mess with Doctor Dream" on a Learjet. Instead of buying stock footage of clouds, they went up in the sky and spent all day filming clouds. That's kind of rock n' roll madness. It shows how out of control the industry was in those days.

There's a shot that comes out of the sky and into an open grave. That was done with a helicopter; these days, you'd do it with CGI, I suppose. A helicopter with a camera underneath was straddled across an open grave in a churchyard and then did a vertical takeoff as fast as possible, and the footage was played in reverse. The plan was that if it went wrong, we would all dive into the grave. That's what passed for health and safety.

The whole thing was supposed to be a critique of heroin abuse. And it was so dreamy and fantastic that everyone thought it looked like an advert for heroin.

LOL CREME: It was banned because it was so trippy—MTV said it would turn people *on* to drugs, not *off*. They never aired it.

TOM BAILEY: Lol was also in trouble around that time for having done a Howard Jones video which featured static on the screen. No one would play it, because it looked like your TV was breaking down.

HOWARD JONES: The point of "Life in One Day" was that the video is like a malfunctioning TV, skipping channels every thirty seconds. It switches to a Swedish TV show, the news, adverts, a religious program, and I keep appearing as different characters. At the end, the screen goes to snow and white noise. Nobody had ever done that. It's just so innovative and brilliant.

KEVIN GODLEY: People had showed us medical cameras, endoscopes, boroscopes, and so on. We were looking for an excuse to use them, and the Huey Lewis video "Hip to Be Square" seemed perfect—put a camera inside someone's mouth, inside the saxophone, attach it to drumsticks.

HUEY LEWIS: Godley and Creme had a fabulous camera that did all this weird stuff. We performed two feet away from the camera, three or four times, and that was it. It was all done in postproduction. They were fantastic, they really knew what they were doing. And they were stoned the whole time.

BETH BRODAY: Everybody wanted to direct music videos. It was like a drug; there was instant gratification. You could write a concept, sell it to a label, spend two weeks putting it together, two or three days shooting it, a week cutting it, and in under thirty days, it would premiere on MTV. Compared to features and TV, it was so instant. It was intoxicating.

CLIFF BURNSTEIN: We always wanted to find new directors, because they weren't as expensive as established ones.

RICK SPRINGFIELD: "Bop' Til You Drop" was the first video David Fincher did. He was just a pasty-faced kid who had come off doing special effects on *The Empire Strikes Back*. I'm a big science fiction fan, and he came up with a *1984/*

Star Wars theme. He stood out as a guy with a great imagination and a great eye. He made it look almost movie-esque. He was making videos, but his sights were on getting into movies, and it shows.

BETH BRODAY: David Fincher walked into my office one day with his reel. He'd done a video for Rick Springfield. I could see he had a good feel. When I listened to him talk about filmmaking, I knew he was a star. I signed him on the spot. *On the spot.*

I had to beg record labels to even *look* at him. Debbie Samuelson was the only one who got it. I had to *beg* Jeff Ayeroff to consider working with him.

JEANNE MATTIUSSI: Debbie Samuelson and I started David Fincher's career. He had done Rick Springfield videos for RCA. Then Deb and I made him the de facto in-house director at Columbia. Columbia and Warner Bros. were the two biggest labels, and fierce rivals. Directors who worked for Warner Bros. didn't necessarily work for Columbia. We were jealous of Warner Bros. because they had better artists and they didn't have Al Teller to deal with. Al Teller hated MTV. He hated everything about it, and we never had any budgets to speak of. Jeff Ayeroff and Warners gave directors monster dollars to work with, and we could only give them $75,000.

ANNE-MARIE MACKAY, producer: Jeanne Mattiussi, Debbie Samuelson, Randy Skinner, Robin Sloane: those women were visionaries. They would go to bat for a director if they believed in him. Without them, the careers of David Fincher and others would never have taken off.

JEANNE MATTIUSSI: We put Fincher on the map. Deb Samuelson got him to do the Outfield, Loverboy, Patty Smyth, Wire Train, and the Hooters. I got him to do Eddie Money's "Endless Nights" and a pop group called the Stabilizers.

Eddie Money was an idiot. He was a drug addict. He was loaded all the time, and he acted like a shit. Then he had half his face paralyzed. He was not a happy camper. For "Endless Nights," we were in this horrible alley in downtown LA that Fincher had art-directed beautifully, with washer lines and clothing. I think it upset him when he had to shoot the actual performance.

MICK KLEBER: I think I did the second-ever David Fincher video, for the Motels' "Shame." He grew up in northern California, lived a couple houses down from

George Lucas, so as a young kid, he worked on *Neverending Story*. Look in the credits, you'll see Dave Fincher in the visual effects department. I never saw anybody rehearse camera moves as much as he did. When you're shooting models for Industrial Light & Magic, that's what you do. You do it over and over, until you get it exactly right. Those videos for the Motels were very stylish. He met Martha Davis's daughter on the set, and they were an item for quite a while. They were a very attractive couple.

MARTHA DAVIS: Fincher was hilarious, wonderful, funny, sweet. Just an absolute doll. My daughter Maria was doing my wardrobe. They were both born on 8/28, so it was the 8/28 Club. She was nineteen, and he was her first love. They were adorable. It's too bad, because it didn't end well.

JEFF AYEROFF: This Motels video for "Shame" had billboards with images of Martha Davis that came to life. I was like, *Who the fuck did this?* I called Anne-Marie Mackay at Propaganda. She said, "Ah, you've got to meet this kid. His name is David Fincher. He never went to film school, he's a genius!"

The first video I had him do was for Christopher Cross, "Charm the Snake." Christopher was a perfect example of "video killed the radio star." He was a good singer, but he wasn't very exciting visually. He liked driving Formula 1 race cars, though, so Fincher did a video that revolved around Christopher and race cars.

RANDY SKINNER: We were all like, *This guy's really talented and he's doing Christopher Cross?* There were race cars and a snake. It didn't go well.

DOMINIC SENA: We'd heard of a young guy named David Fincher, who had done one Rick Springfield video and a television commercial with a smoking baby. Greg Gold and I went out for a drink with Fincher and said, "Maybe we should start our own company." We discussed who would raise money, and we thought of Steve Golin and Joni Sighvatsson. They were associate producers on a movie called *Hard Rock Zombies*. That was their calling card. They asked if they could bring in Nigel Dick. And the six of us—me, Greg, David, Nigel, Steve, and Joni—founded Propaganda.

BETH BRODAY: The guys who founded Propaganda were my guys. Joni was my producer. Greg Gold, Dominic Sena, David Fincher, they were my directors.

But I'd had enough. I was burned out on videos, and I didn't want to produce commercials, which was where things were headed. I said, "You know what, guys? I gotta go."

JONI SIGHVATSSON, producer: We started the company with $100,000: Steve and I invested our own money, and the other $75,000 came from people in the garment business. We all shared the same goal: We wanted to make movies. Music videos and commercials were a means to an end.

NIGEL DICK: Steve and Joni said, "All six of us will be equal partners in the company." I should have recorded that conversation, because that turned out to be a bunch of hooey. They said, "Don't worry, our lawyers are working on the formal agreement." After about eighteen months, I said, "Um, where's my agreement? Because I'm hearing rumors that you've given a big chunk of the company to Fincher." "No, no, no, no, no." We all shared the same lawyer, so I had to get my own. I told him, "The agreement is that I get a sixth of the company." He said, "You can't have a sixth of the company, because there isn't a sixth of the company left." Here's the huge lesson I took from my experience at Propaganda: GET IT IN WRITING.

DOMINIC SENA: I came up with the name Propaganda. It was desperation, because Joni was starting to say, "Why don't we call the company Blue Ice?" Fincher and I said, "We gotta come up with a better name than that." I thought, *That's what we're doing, we're selling propaganda.* David had a friend named Bobby Woods, and he came up with the Russian constructivist logo. We were very much into the idea of Propaganda being a collective.

PAUL FLATTERY: The turning point for the video industry came when Propaganda was formed. Propaganda was the first company to sell the record labels a brand. A video wasn't a David Fincher video, it was a Propaganda video. They had a level of financial backing no one else had, and they discovered great talent. They spelled the end for us.

DOMINIC SENA: For the first year or so, Propaganda worked out of a loft that we shared with other companies. Finally, we hired architects and took over a warehouse in Hollywood as our headquarters. We installed a cappuccino bar, which was unheard of in 1986.

As soon as one Propaganda director would finish a video, the other directors would check it out and you'd get feedback. It was very competitive. We always gathered around the cappuccino machine, sharing stories and picking each other's brain. Editors and cameramen would hang out there. We were growing up and making mistakes and having breakthroughs together.

JONI SIGHVATSSON: Our directors were the first generation to grow up watching MTV. They had film backgrounds. That's what distinguished us from Russell Mulcahy and Julien Temple. Don't get me wrong: Russell, Steve Barron, David Mallett, these were seminal video directors. But their stuff was dated by the mid-'80s. And if you look at their résumés, now they don't compare to those of the directors that came out of Propaganda.

ANDY MORAHAN: I won an MTV Best Director Award, but that didn't count for shit at a commercial production company. They thought video directors were the bottom of the food chain. It took the Finchers of this world to change that perception.

ANNE-MARIE MACKAY: David directed a Loverboy video, "Notorious," that got a lot of commercial agencies interested. There were young men on the street, a beautiful girl walks by, a boy pretends to faint, and his friends catch him. The agencies looked at that and said, "Wow! This would be a good way to sell beer." They were captivated by what they were seeing on MTV and they wanted to duplicate it. They wanted in on the youth market.

DOMINIC SENA: If a music video cost $150,000, you'd make $15,000. Commercials were a quantum leap. One of my first commercials was a perfume ad with Liza Minnelli. They paid me $35,000.

GREG GOLD: David broke us into commercials, because he was able to read that market. He was very supportive creatively. On the business side, though, he was tough and strong-willed. He knew what he wanted and stuck to his guns. There was no defense against him.

PAULA ABDUL: On the set, David's very meticulous, cool and quiet. He doesn't raise his voice. He knows he's good, so he doesn't have to yell. He has an inner strength that's very sexy.

JEANNE MATTIUSSI: When I got to RCA, I weaseled Fincher into doing the Patrick Swayze "She's Like the Wind" video, from *Dirty Dancing*. What a horrible song. I think that was the last time I worked with him.

JEAN-BAPTISTE MONDINO: For me, David Fincher was the boss. He was the one. When you have a small budget, you have less pressure, and you can feel more free. But David could deal with pressure and be as free as if he was dealing with a small budget. He was not afraid to embrace big shooting. And graphically, his videos were incredibly well done.

JEFF AYEROFF: Fincher was smarter than anybody I'd met in a long, long time. There were a few directors who were like that. Fincher. Mondino. Mark Romanek. And Stephen Johnson. Johnson was this Midwest whack job. His hand has been severed and sewn back on. He'd been addicted to painkillers, and who knows what else.

JERRY HARRISON: David Byrne had directed two videos for our previous album. Tension started to rise up in the band, because we felt David was making a grab for excessive credit. I said to our manager, "We need to have equality in the band. This can't be something only David does. Tell Warner Bros. they're going to pay for each of us to direct a video." Our budget was $35,000, but Warner Bros. secretly pumped more money into "Road to Nowhere."

STEPHEN R. JOHNSON: David Byrne was struggling to come up with an idea for the Talking Heads's "Road to Nowhere" video so Jeff Ayeroff got us together. I think Jeff thought of me because David and I both wore button-down tab collar white shirts. The video concept was very collaborative. But the bizarre thing was that, when the band was about to arrive, David took all my storyboard pages and redrew them in his own hand, so the band would think he had done it all himself. I had a long talk with him later. I said, "You're not one of *those* people, are you?"

JEFF AYEROFF: The "Road to Nowhere" video turned out to be genius. There's one section, about halfway through, where David is seated on a throne and wild stop-motion animation is happening all around him. I showed Peter Gabriel the video and said, "I want you to work with Stephen Johnson on 'Sledgehammer.'" It turned out to be one of the great videos of all time.

STEVE BARRON: Stephen Johnson's "Sledgehammer" was amazing.

STEPHEN R. JOHNSON: I didn't even like the song, frankly. I thought it was just another white boy trying to sound black. But Peter Gabriel took me to dinner, got me drunk on wine, and I agreed to do it.

I have a brain anomaly, and animation comes easily to me. We all have a retina-to-frontal-cortex connection that results in what is known as "persistence of vision," which is usually a tenth of a second. It allows us to view a series of still images as a continuum of motion. I see discrete images at six times that, so I can see individual frames as they fly by. I also have an eidetic memory, more commonly known as a photographic memory. I try to avoid using this word—I grew to hate it—but I was deemed a genius.

Peter wanted to work with a British animation studio called Aardman. Another friend turned me onto the Quay Brothers, and I loved their work. I threw them together and came up with a new way to do animation. Not to get too technical, but I shot a blueprint for the video on an old Beta machine that let you advance, or reverse, frame by frame. The words to the song and the time code were prominently displayed, so at any given time, the animators could tell right where they were. No one had ever thought to do that. The Quays were twins and animated like one mind with four hands. As I saw them constructing a locomotive that circled Peter, with bits of cotton for smoke, I was impressed.

I got the idea for the dancing chickens during a trip to Harrods, the department store in London, where they had every form of fowl that existed. Poor Nick Park, from Aardman, was working with the chickens. We didn't have enough time or money to build armatures, which are metallic mechanisms you insert into the thing you're animating. Instead, we did it the poor man's way and put aluminum wire into two chickens. That shot took longer than expected, and we were all about to puke. Nicky said, "Would it be all right if they don't perform the dance you described and instead do a minuet?" I said, "Yes, just get it done and get the stench out of here."

Upon the first meeting on "Sledgehammer," I learned that one of Aardman's team of workers had just lost his brother. I explained to him that when I was nineteen, I'd severed my right hand, mid-wrist, in a spectacular car wreck in which I rolled a van end over end five times, into the bottom of a ravine. After climbing out of the van, my right hand was attached only by a skin flap. Arcs of blood shot nearly four feet, coming from my radial and ulnar arteries, as my hand and fingers dangled. I had been premed, so I reached inside my wrist, found the arteries, and pinched them off. I was in Loveland Pass, Colorado, and had to climb a mountain and hitchhike to a hospital, where I was clinically dead from loss of blood. I flew out of my body, saw my whole life, and headed to a luminous, sparkly door. Just as I reached the door, I heard the words "We've got him," because I'd been shocked back to life. After eleven operations in less than a year, I was the only person in the world with a complete set of silicone-dacron plastic tendons which work. I used to wear a shiny high-tech glove made from fabric engineered by NASA, because I had chronic coldness in my undervascularized hand. The car wreck gave me a belief in some form of continuation of consciousness beyond death. I told this story to comfort the guy who'd lost his brother, and I vowed to include something about my "seeing the light" in the video we were going to make.

Mid-shoot, the chief cinematographer and lighting director David Sproxton rigged a Christmas-tree "suit" for Peter to wear. He put it on and danced around in a wild herky-jerky motion. We thought he was goofing off, but we realized that Peter was being electrocuted, so I put the idea aside. Later, David discovered that Scotchlite tape, when illuminated with a small light source just above the camera, shows up very brightly. Peter agreed to go overtime and everyone cut up tiny pieces of Scotchlite and covered everything, including Peter. I believe a big reason for the success of the video, aside from the silliness, was that end shot, which took it to another level. This was all done in one week flat. Simply put, we arrive as a random speck out of the random cosmos and there is where we return, with some fun and some work in between.

SIMON FIELDS: Stephen Johnson was crazy, but fun. He had a bad back, and he was taking painkillers. He was paranoid. He'd directed some episodes on the first season of *Pee-wee's Playhouse*, and he kept talking about how Pee-wee's management was trying to drug him and take control of the show.

STEVEN R. JOHNSON: The year "Sledgehammer" won all those Video Music Awards, they structured the show so that I didn't get to say one word of acceptance. I think they realized they couldn't have directors being idolized as well as music stars. So they'd just announce, "Okay, and another award for Stephen Johnson."

The "Sledgehammer" video flung me into worldwide notice, which I didn't want. I was overwhelmed with offers. Kids would look me up in the phone book and drop off presents—like sheets of windowpane acid, something I'd given up by 1970.

JIM YUKICH, director: The Genesis video "Land of Confusion" was enormously popular on MTV, and we were up for something like seven Video Music Awards that year. Stephen Johnson and "Sledgehammer" won every award.

GEORGE BRADT: While I was doing music research, the best "testing" artist of all was probably Phil Collins. Research showed that viewers never got tired of his videos, so they were played regularly, months or even years after they were hits. Phil Collins's management actually called MTV and asked us to play his videos *less*.

PAUL FLATTERY: I've done twenty-three videos for Phil Collins and about fifteen for Genesis—we never once had a contract between us. Just a handshake agreement on the budget. They never, ever stinted. Which didn't mean they didn't complain. If you look at "Land of Confusion," which is their favorite video because they didn't have to *be* in it, you'll notice Tony Banks playing a cash register. That's because he was always complaining about how much videos cost.

JIM YUKICH: There was a big TV show in England called *Spitting Image*, with life-size puppets. I mentioned to Phil's manager, Tony Smith, that we should use the puppets for a video. It took a while to get the *Spitting Image* creators, Peter Fluck and Roger Law, onboard. For "Land of Confusion," each puppet cost $10,000 to make. Not just the Genesis puppets, but the Reagan puppet, the Michael Jackson puppet, the Gorbachev puppet. And there had to be five different Reagans: one with the president's brain missing, one where he was crying, and so on. They were so big, we needed two guys to operate each one.

The video was very politically charged. But the only image that caused a stir was the pope puppet playing bass. Tony Smith called and said, "Can we back off on the shots of the pope? We don't want to piss off the Catholics."

PHIL COLLINS: The only Grammy Genesis ever won was for the "Land of Confusion" video. Which, it's worth noting, we weren't even in. "Sledgehammer" won all the VMAs that year. That was a trailblazing video. No one had seen anything like that. Ours was more blatantly humorous, and Peter's was more artistic. I still have one of the Phil Collins puppets at home.

Chapter 27

"THERE I AM, WITH MY RACK"

THE RISE OF THE SUPERDIVAS, MALE AND FEMALE

VIDEO DIRECTORS NO LONGER CAME FROM THE ranks of the outcasts—fashion photographers, including Terence Donovan, Jean-Baptiste Mondino, Rebecca Blake, Herb Ritts, and Stéphane Sednaoui, entered the field. They were accustomed to working with models, and their work tilted videos in the direction of *Vogue* fashion spreads. "I love music that is like perfume sprayed into a room," Mondino said. For Heart, this aesthetic meant discomfort and shame. For Robert Palmer, it meant the instantly iconic "Addicted to Love," which was a satire, but also a pure embodiment, of video's obsession with looks.

MARTY CALLNER: In Heart's "Never" video, which was very successful, I featured Nancy Wilson, who had never been featured in a video before. Everybody told me how much they loved her tits in that video.

ANN WILSON: That was his niche. Marty was a princess.

NANCY WILSON: There I am, with my rack. I got relegated to the bombshell department in videos. It's a blessing and a curse at the same time. Everybody was like, "It's sexy! *Sexy!* Sex-ayyy! Sexy's *good!*" Videos were instrumental in giving us a second career, after the late '70s. I realized it had gotten completely out of hand one day when I was in a store and someone said, "I love your videos. Do you really play guitar, or is that a prop?"

ANN WILSON: When I watched them objectify Nancy, it broke my heart. When they loaded her into a harness with her guitar and shoved her off a cliff in the

"Never" video, I burst into tears and had to leave the room. Each video had to outdo the last video. "Alone" was really over-the-top. Marty Callner got Nancy to ride a horse. It was a pretty obvious idea—get a woman to straddle something, with her breasts bouncing.

NANCY WILSON: It seemed like everybody else got to make cooler, more artistic videos than we did, like the Police, or the mind-blowing stuff Peter Gabriel was doing.

ANN WILSON: It hurt our feelings, and we felt jealous. The guys didn't have pressure to be sex kittens.

SINEAD O'CONNOR: There was a great band called Heart—I used to love this band—and they had a singer who was quite overweight, who in videos they shot only from the neck up. Prince's sister, Tyka Nelson, made a great fucking record called "Marc Anthony's Tune." She was an enormously fat woman, and her label insisted she become skinny if she was going to get on MTV. So a) there were no black people on MTV, and b) there were no fat people.

MICK KLEBER: Ann Wilson's weight was a big issue. People had this perception of what she looked like from the "Magic Man" era, when she was slender. And now that she wasn't, each video presented a challenge. There were a lot of different tactics that were used, with technology and lighting. You didn't have to be a genius to figure out that we were sort of hiding her in different ways.

On one shoot, David Mallet blasted a huge amount of backlight and had reflective panels sewn into the sides of her dress, so the light would blow off and create sort of an artificial waist. In other clips, they stretched the video in postproduction to make her appear slimmer. As for me, I'd been in the Marines before working for Capitol, so I said, "Why don't we just get her in shape?" Her management were insulted that I would suggest that, even though they were keeping her in full-length coats and shooting her from the neck up. They would rather spend $100,000 extra in video production costs to hide her weight instead of putting $35,000 into fitness.

ANN WILSON: The videos were stretched at the request of management. I never liked it. I've always felt that the effort to disguise a flaw is worse than the flaw. And I had to answer questions about it; if you didn't look like a porn star, everyone was like, "What's wrong?" People said horrible things about me.

DOMINIC SENA: I was doing a video for Anita Baker, and we made sure she picked out the wardrobe she wanted to wear. A few days later, we were shooting some other footage while she got ready, and they came to me and said, "She doesn't like her wardrobe." I said, "She liked it a few days ago *when she picked it out!*"

"Well, she doesn't like it now and she doesn't want to shoot." My stylist frantically made some calls—it was Sunday, no less—and got designer shops to open. She came back with racks and racks of the hippest, coolest clothes, gathered in a few hours. Anita went through all *that* stuff, and didn't find anything she wanted to wear. It turned out that she felt fat and didn't want to go in front of the camera. So I never shot a single frame of her.

ANN CARLI: We signed Samantha Fox—she was one of the biggest Page Three Girls in England. Page Three Girls pose topless in the *Sun*. She was fairly young, and extremely buxom. RCA wanted to do pinup calendars and take a real skanky approach. I wanted her to be more of a girl next door, so that was a big fight. Ultimately, I was right—guys liked her videos and girls bought her records.

Samantha was a great girl. But she would drink early in the day. She wanted champagne right from the beginning of the day. I made sure her drinks got watered down. At one video shoot, she was constipated. She was bloated and wearing a midriff costume. I had to get a doctor. This is kind of a disgusting story. I don't want to know what the doctor did, but the problem was solved.

JEANNE MATTIUSSI: Barbra Streisand tortured me on a daily basis. She used to call at the crack of dawn. She was intent that she belonged on MTV. The directive to get her "Somewhere" video played came from the top, from Walter Yetnikoff and Al Teller. Walter used to call me the "dago broad on the West Coast." That's the only sign I had that he knew who I was. And Al threatened me if I didn't get the video on MTV.

RONALD "BUZZ" BRINDLE: The song was not an MTV song. It was a Barbra Streisand song. Dom Fiorvante was one level above Garland and I was sitting in Dom's office when he was on the phone with Walter Yetnikoff. All I could hear was f-words. I guess Barbra was emphatic in terms of her desire to get a video on MTV.

DAVID MALLET: Everybody around her was terrified of Diana Ross. I didn't know that, so when she asked me, "What are we going to do for the video?" I said, "I'm going to dress you in a wig and make you look like an idiot, like you did on a '60s TV show." There was a terrible silence in the room. And she said, "Oh, I like that. I'll do that." There's a scene in "Chain Reaction" where she crawls on the ground, that's always a good thing to do when you're desperate. She had a huge hit, and it was regarded as a seminal video.

PETER BARON: Whitney Houston was the first breakthrough for Arista Records at MTV. We didn't spend a whole lot of money on Whitney's videos; she didn't have the charisma and personality of a Madonna or Prince. She was a churchgoing, gospel-singing teenager who rarely left the house. And she had two old Jewish managers—one named Gene Harvey and the other, I'm not making this up, named Seymour Flics. They were two *alter kockers* who didn't know anything about videos. Clive Davis was barely involved. He didn't even have a TV in his office for the first five years of MTV.

I went to to England to supervise "How Will I Know." The day before the shoot, my phone rings, and it's Don Ienner, who was a VP at Arista. He says, "Peter, we need a favor with Whitney. I'm going to have Tommy Mottola call you." I said, "Fine." *Ring, ring.* "Peter, how you doing, I hear great things about you." I was like, *Oh, that's a setup.* "One of my dearest friends is in England, and I was wondering if there's a way you could hook up"—he used the phrase *hook up*—"an introduction between him and Whitney. He's in the UK working on a movie called *The Mission*." I said, "Well, who is it?" He said, "It's Robert De Niro."

Two seconds later, *ring, ring.* "Hey, Pete, it's Bob De Niro. What are you guys doing tonight?" When I told Whitney, she dropped a fork out of her hand. And said, "No fucking way," or something along those lines. "He's really been coming after me. He keeps sending me flowers and calling my dad." So I had to blow off Robert De Niro. He said, "Maybe tomorrow night?" I go, "Yeah, maybe." And he called me the next day and about three or four more times, before he understood that it wasn't going to happen.

CLIVE DAVIS, record executive: Whitney was so young and fresh and beautiful in "How Will I Know." That video took her album to a different level. We'd established a good base at R&B radio with the first few singles, but "How Will I Know" established Whitney as a star.

BRIAN GRANT: Women always looked good in my vids. That reputation followed me around. Some directors just didn't put a lot of effort into it. Russell never got women, because he never spent any time making them look good. Also, I always operated the camera myself, because I felt it was crucial to make them feel safe and comfortable. There's a close-up in Whitney's "How Will I Know" video where she looks absolutely stunning. You become a still photographer for a short period of time, and it's just you and the artist. It becomes very personal.

MARTY CALLNER: I saw situations where one shot would make a star, like with Susanna Hoffs and "Walk Like an Egyptian." That thing she did with her eyes made her a star.

SUSANNA HOFFS, the Bangles: We used Gary Weis because we'd been huge fans of the Rutles movie he codirected. It was a two-day shoot in New York. You really felt like you had arrived when you had a two-day shoot. Part one was a live performance in some warehouse filled with contest winners from a radio station. The DP was using a long lens way back in the crowd. There was a close-up on me toward the end of the video, when I sing my section, but because the camera was so far away from me, I had no idea how close up it really was. Back then, when we performed live, I'd pick a friendly face in the middle of the crowd and then someone to my left and someone to my right, and I would sing to them, using them as focal points. That's what I was doing in that part of the video. I wasn't aware it was such a tight shot. People always ask me, "Were you trying to do something with your eyes there? Was that a thing?"

TONY WARD: If you're a model and you're working in music videos, you're an extra—just cheap talent, a nobody. They moved you around like cattle and sometimes worked you twenty-four hours straight. It was quite murderous.

MAK GILCHRIST, model: When you do music videos, you usually get pages and pages of production notes, detailing what emotions and feelings you should be conveying. With Robert Palmer's "Addicted to Love," there was a paragraph on a single sheet that said, "Look like showroom mannequins. Easy on the personality, girls, we're selling sex here."

JULIA BOLINO, model: When I did "Addicted to Love," I'd never heard of Robert Palmer. I was eighteen—I'd been modeling for two years—and I was more into Blondie and people like that.

MAK GILCHRIST: I was twenty-one and had to be persuaded to do it. Music videos were something you did on the side from your modeling career. "Addicted to Love" was shot in a basement studio in London. I got paid a quarter of my normal day rate.

JULIA BOLINO: When we got to the set, the director, Terence Donovan, told us each to pick an instrument. I happened to pick lead guitar. I'm glad I didn't pick drums. Poor Kathy Davies, she didn't get much screen time. Then we went into hair and makeup, which took quite a long time as you can imagine. The makeup was ladled on. I could barely talk because my lip gloss was so heavy.

MAK GILCHRIST: I was really into funk, and I thought, *I get to be the funky bass player who slaps the bass.* As you can see, I insisted on slapping the bass, even though the song had no slapping bass whatsoever. In fact, I'm not even dancing to the tune that's playing. I am not in rhythm with anybody or anything.

If you're looking at the video, from right to left, Julie Pankhurst is the keyboard player. Patty Kelly, the guitarist, is next, standing on Robert's right. I'm the bassist, and Julia Bolino is on the far right. She's the one with what we called the autonomous breast, the girl whose boob is swinging to its own tune. And behind us is the drummer, Kathy Davies. Julie Pankhurst is the one whose legs get a close-up.

We girls were sitting together on lunch break, and Terence slammed a bottle of wine on the table and said, "Right, you lot, get your chops around that." I got a little tipsy. In fact, I got rather drunk. After lunch, my ankles began to wobble in those heels. My ankle sort of clicked over and I lost my balance. The neck of my bass hit Robert in the back of the head, and his head hit the microphone. That would have been a hilarious outtake.

JOHN TAYLOR: Robert Palmer wasn't comfortable doing videos. "Addicted to Love" exemplified how he felt about it—it's a video commenting on itself. He's making fun of it. He didn't really step outside of that. He did "I Didn't Mean to Turn You On" and "Simply Irresistible," and they're both variations on "Addicted to Love." He was a bit too old and self-conscious by the time videos became important.

JULIA BOLINO: Robert Palmer was very polite, very professional. His wife was there, so perhaps he had no choice.

MAK GILCHRIST: None of us felt we were being exploited in that video. That was a shock to me, when people said the video was demeaning to women. I thought the opposite; I thought we looked strong and quite scary.

JULIA BOLINO: The dresses were by Azzedine Alaïa. We had no idea they were see-through. It was only when I saw the video played back that I was like, *Oh my God, you can see my boobs.* I've always had quite big boobs.

MAK GILCHRIST: I kept it quiet that I was involved in the video. It did not appear on my résumé. When the video comes to the point where you see me licking my lips, I would go crimson and leave the room. I remember walking into bars, and if it was on TV, I'd turn around and walk back out. I was horrified. My best friend Gil would introduce me to his male friends and say, "This is the one from the Robert Palmer video." And the guy would look at me in a way that made me want to wash my hands straightaway.

BRUCE ALLEN: You had to have great-looking babes in your videos. And the biggest arguments, of course, were over who got to pick the girls.

JOEY ALLEN, Warrant: Once you picked a director, you'd get a book of the two hundred hottest women in LA: models, video girls, actresses, Playmates, *Penthouse* Pets. We'd say, "Who in the band is single?" And that guy got to pick.

SIMON LE BON: I had one on-set romance, and I'm sure Nick had at least one. Sheila, who turned into a cat in the "Hungry Like the Wolf" video, she became the girlfriend of our manager Michael Berrow for a year after that.

BRIAN SETZER: I asked out the girl in the "Stray Cat Strut" video and she said *no*.

RICK SPRINGFIELD: When I was shooting "Affair of the Heart," I pulled an extra out of the crowd and took her in a back room. It was pretty quick. That went on all the time. I was a big extras person, to be honest. Extras were great.

TOM PETTY: We didn't go for the sexy video girl thing. I knew it would cheapen our long-term play. I wasn't happy the way videos started to exploit women. I thought, we're all better than this, and that the music should do the job.

HUEY LEWIS: We had some attractive women in our videos. The woman in "Stuck with You" is Keely Smith, Pierce Brosnan's wife. And the gal in "Heart and Soul" and "I Want a New Drug" is Signy Coleman, who later was a regular on *The Young & The Restless*. I'd like to tell you that I chose the women in my videos like Diamond Dave Roth did, but I didn't.

STEPHEN PEARCY: I was looking through *Playboy* when I saw a photo of Marianne Gravatte and said, "I want her." Our manager said, "We'll get her." We got her for the "Lay It Down" video. I don't think I got her *that* way, but I probably tried. Now the girl in "You Think You're Tough," that one I got ahold of. But I couldn't tell you her name to save my life.

DON BARNES: Julianne Phillips was in "If I'd Been the One." She was Bruce Springsteen's future wife; supposedly, he first saw her in our video. Mercy. It was hard to keep your eyes off her, or even think about anything else in the shoot.

CAMILLE GRAMMER, *Club MTV* dancer: I did a few videos, including David Lee Roth's "Sensible Shoes." I was one of the two blonde—what did they call them?—oh yeah, "video vixens." I remember some tabloid calling me that when I started dating Kelsey Grammer. I was in Colin Quinn's "Going Back to Brooklyn," which was a parody of LL Cool J's "Going Back to Cali." Ben Stiller directed that. I did a Kool Moe Dee video, a Manitoba's Wild Kingdom video, plus a few others I can't even remember. I played a prom queen, a bride, a nun. It ran the gamut.

ANNE-MARIE MACKAY: On one shoot, we had to wait around because the artist—I won't say who it was—wouldn't come out of his trailer until his management arranged to fly in—from another country!—some young women he knew. We waited and waited, and eventually these gorgeous women arrived. It was one of those moments where you realize, some people have completely different concepts of what making a video is all about.

REBECCA BLAKE, director: When Prince's manager called and asked if I would direct "Kiss," the first thing out of my mouth was "I'd like to speak to Prince first, and I'm not doing it unless I can bring in my own hair, makeup, models, and choreographer." A few minutes later, Prince called me. He was charming. The conversation was brief and there was a lot of giggling on his end.

I was on a heavy vampire kick—I was into Anne Rice very early—so that's where the black veil on the dancer's head comes from. Prince was brilliant in terms of dance and choreography. You could show him something and three seconds later he could do it perfectly. He's also funnier than people know. I'd put him next to a six-foot-tall model and he would give me an expression like, "Are you kidding? Where's my apple box?" He was the one who decided at the last minute to use Wendy in "Kiss." They had great chemistry, and they were funny together. Her facial expressions in that video were perfect.

LISA COLEMAN: At the last minute, Prince asked Wendy Melvoin to be in "Kiss." Wendy and I were living together, and he called her: "I'm shooting the video today. Why don't you come down and play guitar?" As it turns out, the stuff with Wendy playing guitar stole the show. She ended up being more of the focus than the hot female dancer with the see-through scarves. When Prince dances up to Wendy and sings "You got to not talk dirty, baby / If you wanna impress me," and Wendy smiles and shrugs? There was something special about that. But I admit, when I saw that video, I felt a little left out and jealous.

JEFF AYEROFF: Rebecca Blake was an outlandish, powerful woman. Both she and Prince were over the top. It was a fusion of over-the-top-ness. She directed "Kiss," which was the most elegant Prince video.

REBECCA BLAKE: Prince would not talk to anyone but me. *No one.* Five years after "Kiss," when I was working on his "Cream" video, a producer said, "I'm gonna tell Prince this and that." I said, "No, you're not." He said, "Yes, I am. I'm gonna talk to Prince." A few days later, he said, "You're right. I'm never talking to Prince 'cause he won't let me."

TIM CLAWSON, producer: When I worked at Limelight, I routinely flew to Minnesota for meetings with Prince. We'd get a call from Steve Fargnoli—"Prince has an idea for a video"—and I'd meet him the next day. My favorite Prince pitch was for a video that never happened, for a song on *Lovesexy.* He was describing a scene where he'd be in bed with a girl, and beside the bed would be a neon sign that said "Lovesexy." He said, "We can do that at my house." I said, "We'll build the sign on the set and have it transported over."

And he said, "We can do it at my house." And I thought, *Ohhh, I get it: You have a neon sign in your bedroom that says "Lovesexy." Right.*

ROB KAHANE, manager: You've seen the Wham! videos—two guys running around in shorts, jumping around onstage. The purpose of the *Faith* videos was to wipe out that image. Starting with "I Want Your Sex," George Michael looks very masculine in videos. He wanted a kind of throwback, James Dean vibe.

And "Faith" is one of the top 20 videos ever made, in terms of launching and executing an image.

ANDY MORAHAN: "I Want Your Sex" was George doing his version of Prince's "Kiss." The girl in "I Want Your Sex" was Kathy Jeung, who was his makeup artist and traveled with him all the time, and people assumed there was something going on between them. She was a useful foil. I think he was terrified about coming out. The blindfold, and the writing with lipstick on Kathy's body, that was George's idea. He was one of the first artists pushing sexual imagery on MTV. Personally, I find the blindfold and lipstick to be embarrassing—it was a bit obvious, even at the time—but George was exploring the boundaries of what he could get away with. It was his first solo video and he was trying to make an impression. He knew what was going to push people's buttons. Like Madonna and Prince, he had a better understanding of his career and the marketplace than his record company did.

ROB KAHANE: George was very involved in the editing of his videos, to the degree that he would do a complete re-edit of what the director had done, or sit with the director every day in the editing bay. He was very savvy when it came to videos.

ALEX COLETTI, MTV producer: An associate producer got fired because he said there was a transvestite in "I Want Your Sex." He wrote it in a script and either Mark Goodman or J.J. Jackson said it on the air, and the producer took the fall for it. That's when I was hired on a trial basis, to work with the VJs.

LOU STELLATO, MTV staff: The APs were held responsible for what VJs said. Allie Eberhardt was one of the first floor producers for the VJs, and there was a rumor that he got in trouble because Mark Goodman said the British press was reporting that the woman in "I Want Your Sex" video was a transsexual. Allie was the producer of that segment, and George saw it and called. It was a big deal. It was insane how big a deal it was.

JOHN DIAZ: Andy Morahan made a man of George Michael. George never exuded any, um, manhood prior to working with Andy. Andy toughed him up, made him look like a ladies' man.

ANDY MORAHAN: George's sexuality was kept quiet. He had armies of girl fans, and people used to think it was important to keep it a secret. But I'll put it this way: The way he looks on film, you'd be hard pressed not to pick up on it.

ROB KAHANE: *I* didn't pick up on it. I had no idea he wasn't heterosexual, and he lived with my family and me half the time. Maybe I was naive; my wife knew more than I did. He had a girlfriend, Kathy Jeung, and she spent many nights at my place. They slept in the same room. But I didn't want to know, because I did not want to lie. So I was probably one of the last people to find out.

While his mother was alive, George did not want to come out. As soon as his mom passed, he became a different person. He was really unhappy, and didn't give a shit about a lot of things.

ANDY MORAHAN: George wanted to be taken more seriously, so it fit for him to harken back visually to an icon like Elvis Presley. George was very aware of what he was doing. "Faith" was a dry-sounding record, so we wanted something more 2D than 3D. That's why we kept the background white, and shot the juke-box very flat. A lot of people were getting flashy and clever with their videos, whereas "Faith" stripped everything away. It was so successful that a dozen people have claimed they styled George for it. The truth is, he didn't like any of the clothes a stylist picked out, so we drove down Melrose to a shop called Leathers and Treasures and found a leather jacket. Then we walked across the road to a pawnshop and found an acoustic guitar. George barely even played guitar. When we got back to the shoot, he added pearls to his jacket. He says now that he was giving out clues to his sexuality.

The girl in "Father Figure," Tanya Coleridge, was the girlfriend of the director Tony Scott. She had a sophisticated look, kind of harsh, very Helmut Newton, and that fit the provocativeness of *Faith*. In the video, George is basically stalking her, which was a risky part for a huge pop star to play. He also doesn't lip-sync in the video. He had sold something like 8 million copies of *Faith* by then, and the label was terrified by the video. George was braver than they were.

We staged a runway show for the video, and that sequence has been ripped off God knows how many times. I think "Father Figure" stands up really well. I mean, apart from the way George looks.

ROB KAHANE: A few years later, when George came out to me, I was in Brazil with him, to do Rock in Rio. He said, "I need you to come to my hotel as soon as possible." He never called me like that. So I raced to his hotel, and he walked out of the bathroom with his entire head shaved, like a Freddie Mercury haircut. He'd cut off all those beautiful locks, and we were about to go on national television. He said, "You hate it!" I said, "Wait a second, I need to get used to it." Then I go, "Yeah, I hate it." At that point, he indicated to me that he was gay. I said, "Okay. Now on to phase two."

Chapter 28

"THE LEGION OF DECENCY"

CENSORING VIDEOS, FOR FUN AND PROFIT

A MOTHER WAS WATCHING TV WITH HER YOUNG daughter when Van Halen's "Hot for Teacher" came on. The six year old, demonstrating a precocious ability to follow plot, soon asked, "Mom, why is the teacher taking off her clothes?"

The mother, Tipper Gore, was married to United States Senator Al Gore, and as she spoke to her circle of friends, many of whom were also married to politicians, she discovered a shared fear: Music videos were corrupting their children by exposing them to stacked blondes in bikinis, dancing on school desks. But it wasn't only sexuality they feared. On another occasion, Gore and her six year old saw Tom Petty's "Don't Come Around Here No More" video—some other parent, having gone through the "Hot for Teacher" incident, might have learned a lesson and banished MTV from the home—and the girl was "disturbed," Gore said, "because the last scene showed [an actress] turning into a cake and being sliced up."

Gore and her friends formed the Parents Music Resource Center (PMRC), and for a few months they wrote articles and gave interviews denouncing what they called "porno rock." In September 1985, Senator John Danforth, also married to a PMRC member, convened a congressional hearing to discuss the excesses of rock music in the age of cable TV. And that is how the Commerce Committee of the 99th Congress of the United States, like millions of other Americans, watched "Hot for Teacher" and Twisted Sister's "We're Not Going to Take It" when they should have been working.

"Graphic sex, sadomasochism and violence, particularly toward women, are rampant on MTV," Tipper Gore testified. MTV had been asking bands to edit and tone down videos ever since "Girls on Film." By the time of the PMRC hearings, the network had created a formal system of review, in which a (one-person) standards and practices department examined every video before it could air. Officially, MTV had a policy against excessive sex or violence—though to the delight of most viewers, the policy proved to be pretty flexible.

TOM PETTY: Dave Stewart and I wrote and produced "Don't Come Around Here No More." We were talking about the video while we were in the studio, and he said, "I've always wanted to be the guy sitting on a mushroom with long nails and a hookah. You know, like in *Alice in Wonderland*." And I said, "That's it. We'll do *Alice*."

Jeff Stein just had a big success with the Cars' "You Might Think," and he really caught on to our idea and took it forward. When I saw the set, I went, "Oh man, we killed it." We didn't use any special effects. Everything that's big was big, and everything that's small was small. It was a two-day shoot, and each day was fourteen hours, *way* into the night. Even for musicians, those were challenging hours. But we knew while we were doing it how shit-hot it was.

The girl who played Alice was named Wish. Stan Lynch, our drummer, dated her for years. And our bassist, Howie Epstein, had a kid with one of the other girls from the video. Videos were a great place to meet really hot women.

WISH FOLEY, actress: When I went to the audition, there were fifteen or twenty girls coming in at the same time. They were models, in skimpy leather outfits with short skirts. Boobs everywhere. It was kind of gross, they would stand in front of a mirror and do their "come hither" look. And here I am, dressed up like Alice in Wonderland.

I was twenty-one years old, strictly an actress. I did close to fifty commercials before that, starting at age six, and I was picked for the TV series *Family* over Helen Hunt. I'd also been the original Joanie on *Happy Days*. But *The Brady Bunch* had just gone off the air, and after I shot the pilot, they said, "We're sorry, she looks too much like Cindy Brady."

JEFF STEIN: Wish Foley definitely suffered for art. We built a giant teacup out of an aboveground pool. The doughnut was a giant inner tube. I asked for the water in the teacup to be warm, and it wasn't. She was in cold water on an air-conditioned stage for quite some time, and never said anything. When she came out, she had hypothermia.

WISH FOLEY: It was 7 A.M., after twenty-four hours of shooting, and the water was ice cold. If you look closely, you can see me shivering. They bundled me up and shoved me into an emergency-wash shower.

JEFF STEIN: There's a scene with a pig in a baby carriage, wearing a bonnet, which means we had to hire a pig wrangler. The guy brings out his piglet, and maybe there was pork roast in the catering truck that day, but the pig took off. Maybe he thought he was lunch. Ever try to catch a pig in a sound studio?

TOM PETTY: For the last shot, where we cut a piece of Wish's body and eat, we had a giant cake made in the shape of her body, and Wish slipped her head from underneath. That must have been uncomfortable as hell. There was only one cake, so we had one take to get it right. When MTV saw that shot, they said one of my looks down at Wish was too menacing, like I was enjoying it too much. I thought that's what the character would do. He was pretty scary. They asked us to pull that shot. We used a different one where I looked a little less menacing.

WISH FOLEY: I was under the cake for four and a half hours, with my head flipped all the way back. When people said that the cutting of the cake promoted cruelty to women, I had to laugh that people took it so damn seriously.

JEFF STEIN: For laughs, I asked them to fill the cake with strawberry jam, so when they started hacking it up, jam was squirting all over the place. There was a big stink about the cake cutting. I was cited by a parents-teachers organization for promoting cannibalism.

SCOTT KALVERT, director: Jeff Stein had a great sense of humor. He was the first director who took it to a different level. "Don't Come Around Here No More"? That was brilliant.

TOM PETTY: I thought the problem with Jeff was that he was a little bit off the rails. But he did great by us. I was *knocked out* when I saw the final cut; I played it thirty times in a row. "Don't Come Around Here" kicked the barn doors off for us. We hit the moon with that one.

LIZ HELLER: Everyone stayed up all night finishing the video to get it ready for an MTV world premiere, which was scheduled for the next day. We were going to send it directly to MTV's studios via satellite, and because of the time crunch, MTV's standards and practices wouldn't get to see the final edit. At the end of the video, Alice turns into a cake, and Tom Petty and his band cut up the cake. It was a crazy, drugged-out image, and for those days, it was pretty extreme. Standards and practices was completely panicked.

MICHELLE VONFELD, MTV executive: I was executive assistant to David Horowitz, who oversaw the cable and recorded music divisions of Warner Communications, and when David became CEO of MTV Networks, he asked me to go with him. He saw that no one person was overseeing the network's standards and practices. I became the one-person standards and practices department.

JEFF STEIN: "Don't Come Around Here No More" is the video that led to the formation of the PMRC. Tipper Gore's daughter saw the video, and the cake-cutting freaked her out.

Around that time, a parent-teacher organization picked the five most offensive music videos, and two of them were mine: "Don't Come Around Here No More" and the Jacksons' "Torture." That was probably my career highlight in music videos.

LES GARLAND: We had the PMRC up our ass.

DEE SNIDER: Twisted Sister's "We're Not Gonna Take It" was on the "Filthy 15," the PMRC's list of songs they felt were most objectionable. They rated "We're Not Gonna Take It" *V* for Violence. When I testified before Congress, I said, "These lyrics are no more violent than the Declaration of Independence."

MARTY CALLNER: Tipper Gore and the PMRC called "We're Not Gonna Take It" the most violent video of all time. Which is pretty funny, because there was no blood in it, no *anything*.

MICHELLE VONFELD: We actually met with the PMRC early on, because some of the things they accused us of playing were either videos we didn't play or videos we played in an edited form. Tipper Gore was at the meeting. I think she was surprised to learn that we had standards at all.

SAM KAISER, MTV executive: We secretly called Michelle Vonfeld "The Legion of Decency."

MICHELE VONFELD: Each video they wanted to air, I watched frame by frame. I often heard the criticism that our policies were inconsistent. But we felt we were being consistent with a product that was inconsistent. No two videos were the same.

Here's an example: To the best of my recollection, the Dire Straits "Money for Nothing" video ran unedited—even though the word "faggot" is used—because of the context in which the word appeared. It wasn't a slur against gays; it was part of the artistic makeup of the song. But the following week, if I'd been brought a video where somebody's being called "a dirty little fag" in a mean, disrespectful way, it was not going to air. If somebody wants to interpret that as inconsistent, well, then, *yes*.

GEORGE BRADT: We played "Money for Nothing," with its prominent use of "faggot," about a billion times. That still pisses me off.

MICK KLEBER: MTV's standards and practices were totally malleable. If you were David Lee Roth or Madonna or Michael Jackson, you could grab your crotch all day long. If you were a baby act like Poison, MTV would make you take that out. And we'd say, "Wait a minute, look at Van Halen. They're doing that." And their answer was really bald-faced: "When Poison get to be as big as Van Halen, then we'll see."

CHRIS ISAAK: There was a list of things MTV said *no* to. It was a big list, like Hollywood had the Hays Code rules starting in the '30s. "You can't have a gun in the video. You can't have somebody smoking in the video. You can't show part of a woman's body. You can't show *only* her legs." But believe me, you can find a video with every one of these things in it. They made exceptions, if you were connected right. They were politically correct with the people they felt they could push around. And the people on top of the heap did whatever they wanted.

JEFF STEIN: MTV's standards and practices were the same for everyone, except Madonna.

ROB KAHANE: We always said, there was the Madonna rule, and then everybody else's rule.

TOM PETTY: Standards and practices always found something I hadn't even noticed. In the video for "Yer So Bad," they swore there was a girl sniffing cocaine in one scene. To this day, I still can't see that.

MICHELE VONFELD: We had four constituents we were trying to please: the cable community, the advertising community, the creative community, and the consumer. We devised a two- or three-page document, our standards document. It wasn't a list of words you couldn't say on television. It was more our philosophy. It talked about not glorifying violence, it discussed sexual matters, issues of taste, things that could be hurtful to other people.

DAVE KENDALL, host, *120 Minutes*: There was a sense that MTV was naughty and decadent, because it was giving people cheap thrills and instant gratification. The network played on the idea of excess and debauchery. We had promos like, "Too much is never enough." But that's kind of a myth. I don't think MTV, in that sense, was anything new. The allure was always very sexualized. People think of MTV as a new cultural phenomenon, when all it did was merge archaic desires: the sex drive, the desire to be better than one's peers. MTV's newness was not so much cultural as technological. There was suddenly a new platform, cable television.

JEFF STEIN: I did a Quiet Riot video, "The Wild and the Young," as an allegory about the PMRC. We shot in Pasadena, California, at an old power station. I had two old dames who were friends of mine, a lesbian couple, playing fascist brain police. I got Wink Martindale, the game-show host, to be Big Brother. Together, they were like the anti–rock n' roll gestapo.

PATTI GALLUZZI, MTV executive: When I was hired as director of music programming, I was in charge of picking the videos we played, and getting them approved by standards became my job, too. In the beginning, it was hell. It could take ages. Michelle Vonfeld had a lot of power. Often she just didn't understand something, so she wouldn't clear it, and we would waste days going back and forth with the record company, requesting lyrics. Eventually I wised up and went, "Okay, nobody can submit a video to MTV without sending us the lyrics."

Our goal wasn't to "censor" videos—we wanted to play videos in a way that preserved as much of the artist's integrity as possible while not warping the minds of America's youth. We were desperately trying to avoid glorifying guns. If it was a superstar, like Madonna, obviously we wanted to premiere the video, so we'd be on the phone with the label or the manager, trying to clear it up quickly. Everybody would be desperate to get a Madonna video on the air, and people didn't care so much about a Nice & Smooth video.

And obviously, we wanted to be sure to play the videos of musicians we wanted to book at the VMAs.

Chapter 29

"HICKORY DICKORY DOCK, THIS BITCH WAS . . ."

BACKSTAGE AT THE VIDEO MUSIC AWARDS

WHAT PEOPLE REMEMBERED FROM THE FIRST VMA broadcast wasn't Herbie Hancock's five victories for a mind-twisting video, it was the sight of Madonna humping the stage in a wedding dress. That set the tone for every VMA to follow—the point wasn't to be honored for excellence in your field, but to cause a commotion, even if it meant showing off your lumpy buttocks, as Howard Stern did in 1992. The show reinforced MTV's reputation as a place for edgy behavior, even when presenters insulted the network—as comedian Eddie Murphy did on the second VMAs, shortly after *Beverly Hills Cop* made him a Hollywood superstar: "They came to me about six months ago and said, 'Eddie, host the MTV awards,'" Murphy declared, on a live broadcast. "And I'm an actor, so my first reaction was, 'Fuck MTV.'" The crowd loved it. So did MTV.

LES GARLAND: Eddie Murphy and I became good buddies, and I got him to host the second VMAs in 1985. He was the biggest star in the world at that point. The night before the show, rehearsal is set for 9 P.M. We had a great rehearsal. And I gave him careful instructions about what he could and couldn't say on TV. The show was being simulcast on Metromedia, which is Fox before it became Fox. I said, "Listen, you have to control the four-letter words, you can't say *shit*, like you do on pay TV, okay? Promise me?" And he goes, "Don't worry, Garland."

So next night, he comes out—"Ladies and gentlemen, EDDIE MURPHY!"— and right after he says hello to everybody, he goes off script.

GEORGE BRADT: He walks out and goes, "A year ago, I would have said, 'Fuck MTV.' But now I got a video, so I kiss their ass." This was when you could still swear on cable.

LES GARLAND: He takes a left and just keeps going. Starts talking about how loose the women are in rock n' roll. "I'm not gonna say I got a disease, but all I know is there was flames coming out of my dick." This is live. There's no seven-second delay. Pittman comes running across Radio City Music Hall: "Garland, stop him!" And I'm like, "What do you want me to do? Go onstage?" I'm taking the heat, of course, because I put Eddie on the show. And stations are pulling the plug on us left and right. But this is the anarchy of MTV, this is what it was all about. Eddie finishes the monologue, we go to commercials, he comes off-stage, and I grab him and go, "I can't believe you did that. I told you, you can't say that stuff." He goes, "No, you told me I couldn't say *shit*."

BRIAN DIAMOND, MTV staff: Once the cat was out of the bag, the show spiraled from there. It was the year after Live Aid, and we gave a special award to Bob Geldof. They introduce him, he gets a standing ovation, and the first words out of Geldof's mouth were "I find it amazing in these times you can say *fuck* on national television." Glenn Frey also said *fuck*. We weren't on a tape delay—nobody did that back then. Needless to say, there were several bottles of champagne sent to cable operators in the next day or two.

ROBERTA CRUGER: It was my job to seat everyone at the VMAs. That became very complicated. I had to keep Van Halen separated from David Lee Roth, after they broke up. They had to be in different sections, but one couldn't have a better seat than the other.

PETE ANGELUS: David Lee Roth was nominated for a lot of awards in 1985 and lost every single one. I met James Brown that night, who said, "Man, you got fucked." To me, that was better than any award. Joe Davola handed me a Moonman statue and said, "The crew and I feel horribly about what happened." So I have a Moonman for the most losses ever.

JOE DAVOLA: They made cases of these things. I ripped off a Moonman, walked out with it, and gave it to Pete the next day. I was like, "Dude, you got robbed."

SUSAN SILVERMAN: "California Girls" and "Just a Gigolo" were nominated for Video of the Year, and lost to "Boys of Summer." After the show, David Lee Roth and I went to a party, and he got wasted. You know how someone sort of pins you against a wall at a party and you can't escape? Well, Dave was in my face for forty-five minutes about how he really should have won Video of the Year.

RUSSELL MULCAHY: Duran presented me with the Video Vanguard award at the VMAs, and while I was walking onstage, the ass of my suit pants ripped open. And so I'm standing there giving my speech, and I'm completely fucked because all I could think about was the breeze going up my ass, and hoping my jacket was long enough so that it wasn't caught on camera.

WISH FOLEY: I went to the VMAs the year "Don't Come Around Here No More" lost to "Boys of Summer." I got hit on by Jon Anderson, the singer of Yes—he was short—and by "Weird Al" Yankovic, which I loved.

DEBBIE GIBSON: I was supposed to perform on the VMAs one year, but here's one of the perils of being a teen star: My wisdom teeth acted up, I got an abscess, and I couldn't sing. My face was all puffy and swollen. That was my hottest year, too. After that, no invites. Oh well.

ARSENIO HALL, TV host: Sam Kinison was a friend of mine, and one night at the Comedy Store in LA, he told me he was gonna host the 1988 MTV Awards. Then I got a call asking if I was interested. I said, "I was told that Sam Kinison is hosting." And they said, *"Are you interested?"* And I said, "Yeah, but before you pull the trigger, me and Sam should talk." And they never gave me that opportunity. Sam called me and just said, "Fuck you, bastard," and he hung up.

Eddie Murphy and I were friends, but friends can be competitive. At that time, he had the prettiest woman, the most money, and the nicest house. But MTV only called him once to host. I hosted four years in a row. Every year I'd say to Eddie, "Yeah, MTV called me again, they want me to host that shit one more time. How many times did you host it?" "Once." "Well, maybe it didn't work out that good." That was the only thing I ever had on Eddie.

My first year, I spent some time hanging out with Cher. A little kid came over and said, "Could I have a picture of you all?" And the picture ended up on the front page of the *Globe*, with the headline CHER'S NEW BOY TOY. It would have been cooler if it had paid off and I got the punani from Cher. I could tell my grandchildren, "See that lady with the feathers on her head? Daddy rocked that."

At the time of my second VMAs, I was going out with Paula Abdul. John Landis had hired her to choreograph the African dances in *Coming to America*. I teased Landis about that: "So, apparently, all the African choreographers were busy?" He said, "Are you complaining?" I told John, "If she comes here, she's mine." And that's when we hooked up. She was the biggest thing in pop music. It felt like life was perfect. Paula's taking *all* the trophies home, I'm *in* the "Straight Up" video, that's my girl, and I'm the host. *Can life be any better?*

PAULA ABDUL: Me and my sister have a habit of peeing in our pants when we laugh too hard. If you touch us on the side of our ribs, we will pee. It's not a fun thing. When I was hanging around Arsenio and Eddie Murphy, I had to have a change of clothes with me all the time. Arsenio always made me laugh.

JOEL GALLEN, MTV producer: I was supervising producer of the 1989 VMAs, which was the last year of MTV's contract to have Dick Clark Productions oversee the show. There was talk about Jerry Seinfeld hosting the show, but everybody was like, "He's not big enough yet." So we brought back Arsenio. After that year, I came in as executive producer and said, "We can't allow lip-syncing anymore. Let's emphasize live performance." Of course, that's all changed now. It's one big lip-sync.

JUDY McGRATH: Bobby Brown had a moment on the VMAs that year. It's on YouTube. If you freeze the video, you can see that he dropped a vial of something while he was performing. It could be any number of things, I suppose. But it probably wasn't Splenda.

BOBBY BROWN: That was my diamond bracelet falling off my wrist. I know everybody says it was a package of coke or some shit. They can say what they want. I know what happened. Anyway, why would I pick it up if it was coke? "Wait, wait, my shit fell?!" No.

TRACEY JORDAN, record executive: Oh, I was there for that. I was with Bobby—I've known him since he was like thirteen years old. He was dancing around the stage and all of a sudden, something flew out of his pocket. Then he did this elaborate dance step to pick it up and put it back in his pocket. And I'm like,

"What the hell was that?" I have my suspicions. It was probably something to, ahh, lift his spirits.

JOEL GALLEN: Bobby Brown dropped his coke vial onstage. The show always runs a bit long, so they want us to take out ten minutes and clean things up for rebroadcast. When I started editing, I was like, "Wait a second—what's going on?" He was dancing a thousand miles an hour. There was a close-up of Bobby, who looks panicked, then you see a little thing in the foreground—which is definitely a coke vial—then it cuts back to Bobby looking around, like, "What should I do?" Bobby picks it up, puts it in his pocket, and keeps singing. If you look at the clip on YouTube, it's pretty hilarious.

TOM PETTY: I played the VMAs with Axl Rose and Izzy Stradlin from Guns N' Roses—we did "Free Fallin'" and "Heartbreak Hotel." I thought it was kind of a shaky performance. We didn't get a lot of rehearsal time, because Cher was doing a big production number and there wasn't much time for us.

As we finished "Heartbreak Hotel" and walked offstage, Vince Neil from Mötley Crüe came running out of the wings and decked Izzy, hit him right in the face. Our sound guy, Jim Lenahan, was walking off the stage with us, and Lenahan was like, "I don't even know this Izzy kid, but he's with us," so he decked Vince Neil. Izzy was getting a lot of black eyes those days. I think he already had a black eye before Vince hit him.

SEBASTIAN BACH: I was on the side of the stage when Vince punched Izzy. Vince's gold bracelet flew off his wrist as he cracked Izzy. It was a big chunk of gold. Vince was huffing and puffing, and I was like, "Dude, I've got your bracelet." He's like, "You can have it, man." In the day, if somebody said something bad about your band, you were obliged to punch him. It was considered totally appropriate.

ALAN NIVEN: Izzy and I were walking offstage when Vince came out of the darkness and whomped Izzy on the face, at which point I threw Vince to the floor and put my left hand around his throat. I cocked up my right arm to bury in his nose, and had a moment of lucidity where I looked at his rhinoplasty, said, "That's too expensive," and let him up. Then Axl ran all over the building, trying to find Mötley and extend the dialogue further. It was very timely that Nikki had jumped into a limo and fled the scene.

TOM FRESTON: When Neil Young's "This Note's for You" won Video of the Year at the 1989 VMAs, that was our audience saying, "Fuck you, MTV." And we deserved it.

BOB MERLIS, record executive: "This Note's for You" was a parody. Neil was at war with the way the commercial world had co-opted music and turned it into a vehicle for shilling products. The look of the bar in the video is a parody of the Michelob commercials Eric Clapton did. A Michael Jackson imitator's hair catches on fire, and a Whitney Houston impersonator puts out his hair fire, presumably with a can of Coke. It was the era of selling out, and Neil was an iconoclast.

JULIEN TEMPLE: Beer companies and the like were beginning to take over music. A lot of beer ads were using rock musicians. It felt like the line between videos and commercials was blurring, and "This Note's for You" was a great opportunity to make a piece about that. MTV was making lots of money from those advertisers, so anything that made fun of them was going to be incendiary in MTV's eyes. We managed to get banned from MTV *and* win the Best Video of the Year award. That was the peak of my video-making career.

TOM FRESTON: People thought we banned it because the video spoofed us. But that wasn't the reason. Our ad salespeople said, "If we have products in videos, advertisers aren't going to bother to buy time anymore. They'll just put their products in the videos." And I went along with them. Neil Young made a big stink about it in the press. We looked like a bunch of pussies. We *were* a bunch of pussies. That's a fact. Not playing "This Note's for You" was the biggest mistake I made at MTV.

JOEL GALLEN: In 1989, Andrew Dice Clay was the hottest comedian on the planet. He was racy and edgy, MTV was racy and edgy, so we wanted to roll the dice with him, so to speak, and give him a spot. He was fine in rehearsal. Night of the show, the stage manager said to him, "We're running long, you gotta trim your act a little bit." And he didn't react kindly to that. He started saying things he shouldn't say. The Dice incident was fantastic for the VMAs. We wouldn't admit it at the time, but controversy is great. You want people to talk about the show. You want it to be a show where anything can happen, and there's spontaneity and danger.

LEE MASTERS: I asked Doug Herzog, over and over, whether Dice would keep it clean, and Doug kept saying, "He's gonna keep it clean, he's gonna keep it clean." And so Dice starts doing his act, and he's keeping it clean, but no one's laughing. I was five rows back and I could see it in his eyes: He was bombing and he knew it. And he launched into "Hickory dickory dock, this bitch was sucking my cock." Or whatever it was. Freston went nuts, and John Reardon, who ran affiliate and ad sales, went nuts

ARSENIO HALL: Dick Clark was producing the show, and he and I were standing in the wings. He had a headset on and I didn't, so I didn't know what Dice was saying. Then I saw Dick throw his headset on the podium. He suggested I pull Dice off the stage. I said, "That's not what I do. I do jokes." I saw Dice last month, and told him I was given the assignment of pulling him off, and we laughed our asses off. I think Dice knew what he was doing. You remembered him the next day.

TOM FRESTON: It was a scene. It was one of those moments you hoped for at the VMAs. Barry Kluger, who ran communications, said to the press, "We're banning him for life from MTV." Which was crazy. Barry had one of those Al Haig moments.

LEE MASTERS: The VMAs were high stress, so every year I'd go on vacation immediately after. That year, I was feeling pretty good. VMA ratings were the highest they'd been since the first one. I said to my wife, "For the last four years, every day I went to work I felt I could get fired. I don't feel that way anymore. I feel safe." I went back to work on Monday, and I got fired. If you ask people, they'll say no, but John Reardon wanted to be president of MTV, and he used the Dice Clay thing as a catalyst to get Tom Freston to push me out.

Two days later, I got an offer to run what was then Movietime, which we turned into E!, which made my career. And a year after he fired me, Freston fired Reardon. To this day, Tom will say, "That was the worst business decision I ever made, when we let you leave." And I say, "Tom, you didn't *let* me leave, you *told* me to leave!"

ABBEY KONOWITCH: Don Henley was an edgy guy, but we got on. In 1990, I got Henley to come to the VMAs, when "End of the Innocence" was up for a few awards. But this was the year of MC Hammer. Hammer won everything. About halfway through the show, I got bored and went for a walk backstage. I went upstairs in the offices of the Universal Amphitheater, and there's Don Henley, Don's manager Irving Azoff, and his wife Shelli. They're watching a monitor.

This will be shocking for some people to hear, but I knew that in ten minutes, Henley was going to win the award for Best Male Video. And when that award was presented, he couldn't be up in this office. I said, "So how long you gonna stay up here, Don?" He goes, "For the rest of the night. Hammer's winning everything. It's embarrassing for me to sit in the audience and lose to Hammer."

I said, "Don, it would be helpful to me if you were in your seat when the Best Male Video award comes up." He goes, "No. I'm not going to. I don't want to be embarrassed."

Then I said to Irving, "It would make me feel good if Don could be in his seat." He goes, "Ab, he's not gonna do it!" I said, "Irving, can you please *tell* him to go sit in his seat." All of a sudden, Don realized why I needed him in his seat. He fixed his shirt and tie, went downstairs, and accepted the award for "End of the Innocence."

SINEAD O'CONNOR: It was funny, when we won the award for "Nothing Compares 2 U," Madonna was raging about it, because she had her "Vogue" video nominated also, and we *fucked* her. She and Sandra Bernhard had been really nasty about me in magazine interviews, based on how I looked. As if being blond and having big tits and a big ass was more important. Which it is, if you're Madonna, because your records aren't great, so all you have to sell is tits and ass. So yeah, I was very pleased to beat the shit out of her that night.

TABITHA SOREN: Whenever I covered the VMAs, they said, "It's a party, Tabitha. Don't ask the rock stars anything serious. It's supposed to be light." I always thought, *What a waste of time.*

ARSENIO HALL: One year I was in the host dressing room, and next to me was Madonna; next to her was Janet Jackson. Madonna's door was cracked open and I heard her talk about Janet, not in a positive way, and one of Janet's people heard it, too. It was always a soap opera.

CINDY CRAWFORD: I loved doing the VMAs, because everyone was there. One time, Todd Oldham loaned me a dress to wear, and I was sewn into it. Only later did we figure out that there was no way for me to pee. It was 5 P.M. until 12:30 A.M., when I could get the dress off. That was a long night.

VAN TOFFLER, MTV executive: I was the guy who got Pee-wee Herman to open the 1991 VMAs. I spoke to his manager for months. When he said yes, I danced on Doug Herzog's desk.

JOE GALLEN: Pee-wee Herman had been arrested a few months before the VMAs, for masturbating in a movie theater. This became the object of jokes on every late-night talk show. Dana Friedman, who nows runs Fox Television production, was his publicist, and I started conversations with her about Pee-wee appearing on the show. After the arrest, he had basically gone into hiding. The first line we pitched him was "Heard any good jokes lately?" We pitched a few other ideas back and forth, but we never could beat that one. His appearance was a big secret. I had to put him in a special dressing room in the basement. We had to make sure it was forty-five degrees in there, because otherwise his makeup would start coming off.

ARSENIO HALL: Pee-wee Herman upstaged my monologue. They told me Pee-wee was gonna open the show, and I'm like, *You know what? No monologue can beat that.*

BILLY IDOL: I was trying to figure out how I could make presenting an award a bit of fun, not just open an envelope and announce the winner. The pants I was wearing had a large zipper. So I realized I could stick the envelope inside my trousers, zip up, then pull it out of my crotch and read it. When I thrust my hand into my trousers, you could hear a gasp from the audience. I can imagine the director going, "For Christ's sake, don't show his balls! If he gets his dick out, cut to anything else." I love Jane's Addiction, so I was proud to give them an award.

DAVE NAVARRO: Billy Idol announced our song as "Been Caught Wanking," because that was on the heels of Pee-wee Herman getting caught masturbating in a movie theater. I accepted the award. This was my first time on live television. I'm saying "Thank you very much," but in my head the dialogue was "Get the fuck out of here, because there's drugs at home." I was a big junkie. I went onstage, took the award, got in the car, and left. Within fifteen minutes of leaving the podium, I was in my cousin's house, shooting dope.

The next morning, I went to score drugs and the dealer recognized me. He's like, "Hey, man, I saw you on TV last night." And he gave me a few extra bags of heroin. At that moment, I realized the power of MTV.

BRET MICHAELS: CC DeVille was completely hammered the night of the VMAs. At rehearsals, he'd yell, "Fuck this, I'm going solo!"

Our original plan had been to play "Something to Believe In," but it was too long, so we agreed on "Unskinny Bop." That's what we rehearsed. By showtime, CC was annihilated. And I'd had a couple of drinks. I'm not innocent here either. So we ran onstage and launched into "Unskinny Bop." We didn't realize the show was in a commercial break. We're up there playing, and MTV is screaming at us to stop. By then we'd already played the song! We didn't know what to do. All of a sudden CC goes, "What the fuck, let's go into 'Talk Dirty to Me.'" He starts playing it, we follow along, and the whole MTV crew is waving for us to stop. But at this point we're already in. And then CC's guitar cord came unplugged. He didn't even know it. I walked over to him and said, "CC, your fucking guitar cord is out of your guitar, no one can hear you." He's like, "Oh shit!" And he reaches over and plugs it back in. You can watch it on YouTube, it's hilarious.

When we came offstage, I walked one way and CC walked the other, and he made a few comments to me that I won't repeat. I said, "Go fuck yourself." He said, "Fuck you." I'm not a guy to back down, so I'm like, "Wait a minute, if you want to talk, let's talk right now." He shoved me, I shoved him, and *bing bang boom*, we were on the ground, kicking and punching each other. We fought on the side of the stage, in between Eddie Van Halen and Cindy Crawford. Then MTV bitched us out like crazy for the performance. They crucified us. It wasn't like we were trying to be malicious. It was an innocent mistake.

ARSENIO HALL: I was standing in the wings and I saw Prince pass me with no ass in his pants. That shocked me, and I thought, "He has hair on his ass." So I picked up a yellow pad and started to write no-ass-in-pants jokes. When a man from Minneapolis has no ass in his pants, the jokes kind of write themselves. A week later? A black-and-white suit with no ass in the pants was delivered to my office, from Prince and his tailor. I still have it.

MICHAEL STIPE: The VMA awards for me are like weddings and funerals. It's such high-pitched emotion coming off of everyone in the room that I can barely breathe. And so I tend to just kind of black out.

With "Losing My Religion," 1991 was our year at the VMAs. Dennis Hopper presented to us, and I kind of rushed him. I came out from the side, wide-eyed and yelling, and I scared the life out of him. He looked at me like, *Who the fuck are you?*

TARSEM SINGH, director: The evening of the VMAs, I went to the restaurant where I'd worked as a busboy two years earlier. And the cook said, "You've got to show people your heritage. Here, wear my turban." So I walked into the MTV awards wearing a turban, which I'd never worn in my life. I went up to accept an award wearing the cook's turban from Bombay Palace.

People don't know how to treat you when you wear a turban. They think you're a holy man, not a foul-mouthed moron. Dennis Hopper bowed and said, "Namaste" to me. He's a hero of mine, and I was like, *If I open my mouth, he's going to call me a cunt,* so I bowed back.

CINDY CRAWFORD: I was a Midwestern girl, thrown into this rock n' roll world. We were backstage at the VMAs looking for people to interview, and Chris Robinson of the Black Crowes was there, wearing cool suede pants with leaves embroidered on them. I asked him, "What kind of leaves are those?" He's like, "Cannabis." Then it was like, *beat beat beat . . .* And I said, "That's pot, right?" I wasn't playing the ingenue, I really didn't know.

At the Freddie Mercury Tribute Concert in London, they said I was going to interview Def Leppard, and a whole group of guys was walking over. I asked, "Which one is he?" They're like, "It's a band, you idiot." I wasn't Kurt Loder, and I didn't have to be.

ALISA MARIE BELLETTINI, MTV producer: *House of Style* always did shows from the VMAs. One year, Anthony Kiedis from the Red Hot Chili Peppers came up to Cindy at the end of the night like he was on fire. He picked up her underarm and said, "I want to lick you." I pulled her arm down and said, "Get the fuck out of here." It was invasive.

CINDY CRAWFORD: My kids love the Red Hot Chili Peppers. Anthony Kiedis and I both live in Malibu, and I see him a lot. I tell my kids, "He tried to lick my armpit once." Those moments only happen at the VMAs.

Chapter 30

"I'D LIKE TO THANK MY CHEEKBONES"

JON BON JOVI AND TAWNY KITAEN TAKE HAIR METAL TO THE TOP

MANY PEOPLE AT MTV HAD A LOVE/HATE RELA-tionship with metal; they hated the way women were depicted in the videos, but loved the ratings generated by the music's rabid fans. Metal, rock critic Deborah Frost wrote in September 1984, was "more popular than ever," and she attributed the success to MTV, where approximately a third of all videos were by hard rock bands: "Suddenly, rock's most extreme fantasy genre looked bigger, brighter, more *fantastic* than ever before," she wrote. "And MTV is in the fantasy business."

Seven months later, Bob Pittman suddenly announced that MTV was deemphasizing metal. "We want to play music that's on the cutting edge," he said, dismissing heavy metal as "a quick, crass, easy buck for record companies." Ironically, metal outlasted Pittman at MTV. Once he left, a new set of programmers gorged on hair metal bands whose male singers were nearly as pretty as the girls in their videos. In this era of MTV, you might see Great White, White Lion, and Whitesnake consecutively. And having outlasted criticism from the PMRC, hard rock bands grew more brazen than ever, creating a pantheon of video absurdity, usually involving explosions and cleavage.

With the survival skills of a cockroach, metal kept on. As for Pittman, by 1988 he and radio consultant Lee Abrams had started Radio Lisa, a twenty-four-hour heavy metal radio network with a "party atmosphere." Metal, Pittman now declared, "has real appeal and deserves its own format." Crass was in.

DEE SNIDER: Marty Callner told me MTV had decided to cut back on metal videos. They didn't need us anymore. I said to Marty, "What the fuck? Metal has a loyal audience." I told him to tell MTV to give me a show: Metal fans will tune in, just like they do for midnight metal shows on radio stations.

STEVE CASEY: In '85, I came up with the idea for a metal show, with Dee Snider hosting. We had done a focus group in Atlanta, where there was a local UHF music-video program playing metal, and teen males were nuts about it. It seemed like a no-brainer. And *Heavy Metal Mania* did huge ratings.

DEE SNIDER: *Heavy Metal Mania* got huge ratings, as I knew it would. At first I did it for free. But the workload started getting heavy, so I was like, "All right, time for me to get paid." To which the response was the same they gave every-body: "Oh, this is great promotion for you." I'm like, "I'm the most recognized face in heavy metal. Everybody knows who I am. My career is starting to floun-der because I'm over-fucking-exposed. I want some money!" "Well, we really can't do that." "Well, then I really can't do the show anymore." So I left.

LEE MASTERS: Metal was always divisive at the network. Young men watched MTV the most, so if we played more hair metal, we'd get higher ratings. But that ran counter to the cool, cutting-edge image we were presenting. Judy McGrath and the on-air promotion people were creating fabulous promos, talking about how hip and edgy we were, and then we'd play White Lion.

SAM KAISER: When I got to MTV from Atlantic Records, the channel was play-ing 100 to 110 current videos and was all over the place. I wanted to trim the playlist and focus more on the mainstream American kid who leaned towards rock. Because rock was on fire, with Mötley Crüe and Bon Jovi. I came in right during the hair metal surge.

DOC McGHEE: I mean, MTV was playing so much Mötley and Bon Jovi, I'd have to tell them, "You're overexposing my artists. If you don't take them off the air, I'm not going to give you another video." I was fighting to get less airplay, not more.

STEVE CASEY: I also started *Dial MTV*, which set records for ratings. Count-down shows were huge. Mötley Crüe's "Home Sweet Home" went to number one and we couldn't get rid of it. We had to change the rules or it would have never come off. It would probably still be number one today.

ALAN NIVEN: What a cockamamie idea. How fast do you think bands and labels tried to jack that? You could hire people to phone in and request your band's video. You could pay your way onto *Dial MTV*, totally. My ex-roommate Don Dokken said, "You gotta get on this." I didn't want to pay people all across the country to be phoning MTV to get our clip played. There was no integrity to that at all. I mean, if you don't trust your own programming judgment, go sell shoes somewhere.

CURT MARVIS: Other metal bands saw Mötley Crüe's "Home Sweet Home" and said, "I want a video just like that." Doc McGhee was managing Mötley and Bon Jovi, and Jon was dead-set against using Wayne Isham. The last thing he wanted was to use the Mötley Crüe director. But Doc said, "You've gotta use these guys."

DOC McGHEE: Jon said, "Why can't we have our own guy?" And I go, "Because you've done bad videos. Sorry, we're not standing on the boardwalk like the Beatles. We're a fucking rock band." I wanted their videos to be like Mötley Crüe, but fun. Let's see Johnny's million-dollar smile. That's what sold Johnny.

ALAN NIVEN: With Jon, you had a reasonably talented individual who was extremely good-looking and very much liked by the camera lens. His sidekick, Richie Sambora, most people would agree, has a better voice. But Jon had star quality. I'm not sure how well that band would have done before MTV. One track off their first album worked, "Runaway." Their second album was not good. Had it not been for Jon's good looks, I'm not sure Bon Jovi would have been allowed to make a third album. Wayne Isham was at least as important to that band as Jon Bon Jovi.

WAYNE ISHAM: Doc McGhee called me about meeting with Bon Jovi. It was Jon's birthday, and I met him at a bar, and he was not into me doing their videos at all. He looked at me, like, "Who the *fuck* is this crazy guy?" I wasn't the serious auteur he was hoping for.

Jon had his own ideas for "You Give Love a Bad Name." He wanted chicks in low-cut tops mud wrestling. That wasn't what I was about. I know it sounds funny, coming from the guy who directed Mötley Crüe's "Girls Girls Girls," but there's a world of difference between the burlesque in "Girls Girls Girls" and mud wrestling.

TOMMY LEE: When Wayne started doing Bon Jovi videos, we gave him all kinds of shit. "How can you *do* that, man?"

NIKKI SIXX: My problem with Bon Jovi was that Doc McGee had started managing them, and without a doubt, they were poaching on our success. When we would see Bon Jovi do a knockoff of what we did, we didn't like it. Go think of your own shtick! It's just disrespectful, and it's all about the money at that point.

WAYNE ISHAM: I shot "You Give Love a Bad Name" at the Olympic Auditorium in LA. It had been closed down forever, so we opened it again and hung the lights, built the stage, brought in the fans, and created our own mock arena. I painted the Bon Jovi logo on the stage floor. I told the band they couldn't check out the stage until I had the lights working and everything ready to go. I made them wait outside, then I opened the big doors. They came in and were blown away. Because this was *their* show. *Their* rig. *Their* stage with *their* name written on it.

Right before that video came out, Bon Jovi were on the road opening for .38 Special. After a few weeks on MTV, they were headlining.

RICHIE SAMBORA, Bon Jovi: Our success had a lot to do with timing. I guess there was a hole—there was a need by the people for a Bon Jovi. Just a good-time entertainment band, you know? A bridge between Phil Collins and Whitesnake.

WAYNE ISHAM: We went back to the Olympic Auditorium and re-created the stage for "Livin' on a Prayer." Jon wanted to fly over the crowd. So Joe Branam— he's the best stage rigger on earth—came up with a kooky harness, where you pull really hard on a rig and it flies out and swings back. Jon loved it. After those Bon Jovi videos came out, everybody wanted *that* video. Everyone wanted that live energy. Def Leppard wanted it. Whitney Houston wanted it. The Rolling Stones wanted it.

PETE ANGELUS: With all due respect to Bon Jovi, they copied a lot of things Van Halen had already done. I've seen this before, my friend. I know your hair is more poofed up, but still it's the same thing. Don't kid yourself; it's not a genius concept.

LARS ULRICH: Maybe my favorite video of the '80s was "Wanted Dead or Alive." Wayne Isham brilliantly captured the other side of rock n' roll, the pictures of

Jon Bon Jovi staring out the plane window. Wayne was by far the number one guy in rock videos.

ADAM DUBIN: Wayne Isham is one of the best live directors there is. That video, about the tribulations of being on the road, seemed very real. Lars was friends with Wayne and he asked me, "How long you think it took them to shoot that?" I guessed two weeks. Lars said, "No. Seven months."

TOMMY LEE: Every video started to look like "Home Sweet Home." "Wanted Dead or Alive" looks just like "Home Sweet Home." Except ours is on a bus and Bon Jovi's is on a plane.

DOC McGHEE: They're the same video, pretty much. Listen, everybody steals from everybody.

RICHARD MARX: My video "Right Here Waiting" is very similar to "Wanted Dead or Alive." Except I was wearing more eyeliner than Jon Bon Jovi. The makeup person said, "You don't understand, you're not gonna see it on camera." Sure enough, I saw the dailies and went, "Motherfucker!" I look like a drag queen.

LEN EPAND: Once Bon Jovi established a winning style on "Bad Name" and "Livin' on a Prayer," we pulled their prior videos out of circulation. They were all deemed embarrassing, or at least not the right image. We notified all video outlets, including MTV, that they were no longer licensed for use. I doubt they ever appeared on broadcast again.

MICK KLEBER: Marty Callner and Wayne Isham were better than anyone at shooting a crowd. The crowd is a huge part of the concert experience. Marty would get great shots of girls reverently looking up at their heroes onstage. And Wayne's Bon Jovi videos had the same.

DOC McGHEE: The concept is simple: show people what you want them to believe you are. So I showed them crazy rock bands, with chicks everywhere, and people staring up at the stage in awe.

SAM KAISER: MTV and Bon Jovi went to a resort called Hedonism II in Jamaica and broadcast from there [in April 1987]. It was called Hedonism Weekend. Bon Jovi's manager, Doc McGhee, invited me to come with him and the band to a little place called Miss Jenny's Teas and Cakes. I'm not going to say who in the band partook. It definitely wasn't Johnny. Johnny never got involved in the nonsense.

Miss Jenny's Teas and Cakes was a tumbledown shack with a chain-link fence over it. And Miss Jenny had a special set of teas and cakes, if you know what I mean. Doc walks up to the Jamaican woman behind the counter and says, "Give me a gallon of tea and that whole pan of cake." She goes, "You crazy, mon." And we were off and running. I have never laughed so hard in my life. I recall trying to go to bed at 3 A.M. and still hallucinating at 8. That next morning, I somehow got dressed and walked down to the breakfast area, and everyone is wearing sunglasses. Everyone is moving slowly. One guy is standing in front of the scrambled eggs, staring at the serving spoon. And it dawned on me, *Holy shit, the crew is tripping, too.* A couple of years ago I ran into Richie Sambora at the ASCAP awards, and he said, "You almost got me killed in Jamaica."

DOC McGHEE: We flew contest winners down to be in this resort with Bon Jovi. All the heads of MTV came. I'm pouring them psilocybin tea and serving pot brownies, and nobody's getting high. We drank all the tea and drove back to the resort, eating more brownies. When we pulled up, we were flying. They found one MTV executive at 5:30 A.M., sobbing on the lawn. I slept by the pool, because I couldn't move and it would've looked bad for the manager to be dragged to his room on a fucking golf cart.

MARSHALL BERLE: The guys in Ratt were party animals. We shot "Dance" at the Whiskey in LA and Stephen Pearcy showed up late. We did one take, he said "I'm done," and he was gone.

We shot "Slip of the Lip" in New Orleans and Shreveport. My head of security was an ex-policeman, and he's in the video, wearing a cowboy hat. He was more trouble than the band. The morning after we made the video, the manager of the hotel asks me to come to the fifth floor. He opens the door and there's my head of security, handcuffed to a bed, stark naked. He says, "I was partying with a couple of girls and they stole my wallet, my gun, my badge, all my clothes, and left me here."

DANIEL KLEINMAN: Ronnie Dio was a funny little guy. I made a video called "Rock n' Roll Children" for him. He had two huge minders with him. Because

Ronnie was very short—about five-foot-four—they told us we weren't allowed to allude to his height. But there's a type of spotlight in America called a "midget." It's a very small spotlight, and it has a different name in England. We were getting ready to do a take and the gaffer shouted, "All right, bring on the midget!" The minders thought we were referring to Dio. They went out of their minds.

KEN R. CLARK: Vinnie Vincent was briefly the guitarist for Kiss, and then formed the Vinnie Vincent Invasion. He came to the studio one day totally done up, with the makeup and the wig. And he ended up locking himself in the janitor's broom closet in the hallway. His management and record label people were outside the door desperately trying to coax him out, but he wouldn't come out of the broom closet.

NIGEL DICK: Vinnie Vincent had an astonishingly great head of hair, but felt it necessary to wear a wig. I said, "Vinnie, what the fuck are you doing? What's wrong with your real hair? It's great." I will totally confess that I did Vinnie Vincent Invasion videos solely for the money. Musically, they were bereft.

STEVE SCHNUR: Don Dokken had hair issues. His hair was long and stringy, with a big ball of sunshine on top.

MICK KLEBER: When the pop-metal aesthetic took over and hair bands reigned, Capitol Records spent an insane amount of money on extensions and hair plugs. For Great White alone. But it paid off. "Once Bitten, Twice Shy" was a huge moneymaker for Capitol.

ALAN NIVEN: Jack Russell and Mark Kendall of Great White spent the money as a personal choice, for their own self-confidence. They went to the same guy as Don Dokken, who also suffered an early hair recession. Jack used to hide his stash under his weave, by the way, which took me a little time to figure out.

MARTY CALLNER: Whitesnake were signed to Geffen Records, and they couldn't get arrested. David Coverdale was dead broke. He was living at the Mondrian Hotel, but he couldn't pay the bill. He couldn't drive his car because he couldn't afford insurance. He was making money singing seltzer commercials. We went to lunch and he had $5 and a condom in his wallet. He said, "I'm sorry, but I can't even afford to pick up my share of the lunch." Now I'm feeling really sorry for this guy, and I know that this is his last shot, so I got really passionate about doing the video for "Still of the Night."

JOHN KALODNER: Making the Whitesnake album took more than a year, but we finally finished. For the first video, "Still of the Night," Marty Callner was a real auteur: director, writer, creator. The band you see in that video wasn't a band. David had fired the rest of Whitesnake, so I assembled a great bunch of musicians for his new band. That video was the first time they met one another.

MARTY CALLNER: We had $125,000, and we made a performance video for a six-minute song. As I'm editing the video, I start to realize it's a piece of shit because the guys in the band aren't communicating. And the reason they're not communicating is because they'd just met. It was like Milli Vanilli. I called their manager, Howard Kaufman, and said, "This is not gonna work." Luckily, Coverdale had marched through my house the previous Saturday night with a girl named Tawny Kitaen, who at the time was having an affair with O.J. Simpson. She was drop-dead gorgeous. I asked if she wanted to be in a music video, and she said *yes*. So I told Kaufman I needed $35,000 more to shoot Tawny and re-edit the video, and he said, "Fuck Coverdale. I'm not giving him the money." Geffen said the same thing. I had to personally lend Coverdale the money to finish the video.

TAWNY KITAEN: I remember it as if it were yesterday. Like, I don't remember yesterday, but I remember *that*. David was in debt to Geffen to the tune of $2 million. He was pretending to be a rock star. One night, I went with David to Marty Callner's house. They were shooting "Still of the Night" the next day. The second I walked in, Marty went, "Fire the chick we hired—you're gonna do the video!" And I said, "I don't do videos. I'm a professional actress." But Marty said, "No. You're the girl. You're the one who's going to make this video."

SAM KAISER: We introduced a spot on our playlist called "Hip Clip of the Week," where a video would get played six or seven times a day for four weeks. I mean, we pounded the daylights out of it. John Cannelli came and played Whitesnake's "Still of the Night." I'm like, *Oh man, this is spot-on*. It was brilliant and we made it "Hip Clip of the Week." As soon as it got on air, Jeff Ayeroff at Warners called me: "I can't believe this! That's not hip!" I said, "Maybe not to you and me, but it is to Joe and Janie out in Iowa."

EDDIE ROSENBLATT, record executive: Even though it was a six-minute track, MTV must've played it fifty times a week.

MARTY CALLNER: David Coverdale became a megastar. Tawny and David made three videos together, and ended up falling in love and getting married. That was never going to last. Tawny relished the exposure. She was cute, sexy, sassy, charming. It was the good Tawny Kitaen. She wasn't the girl on the rehab shows yet. She was young and rock n' roll and fun.

The cars that Tawny gyrates on at the beginning of "Here I Go Again" are my Jag and David's Jag. We didn't have enough money to rent cars. Paula Abdul choreographed that scene for me. I said, "Will you stage this dance on the Jaguars for me?" And she did.

PAULA ABDUL: Tawny started doing cartwheels on top of the Jaguars. With rock videos, you can do whatever you want. It doesn't even have to make sense.

TAWNY KITAEN: I got on top of the cars and started doing cartwheels and splits. I'd been a ballerina and a gymnast until I was fifteen. I was very limber.

LADY GAGA: I don't know a person in the universe who didn't melt when Tawny got on the top of that car. That was one of the greatest moments in video history. I mean, I wish I could steal that moment every day. If I was Paula Abdul, I would do that choreography by myself all the time.

SAM KAISER: When we got the video for "Here I Go Again," I told Marty, "It's a little too aggressive. There's too much breast in one scene, and too much butt in another." He argued, but I said, "Marty, just take care of it." When the new version came back, I called and thanked him. He said, "Oh, there's still something edgy in there. But you have to find it." I brought it to Michelle Vonfeld in standards and practices, and it passed muster with her. One day, we're sitting in a programming meeting, and the channel was playing in the background, and Rick Krim goes, "Oh my god, I just saw Tawny Kitaen's tit." We called the studio in Smithtown, Long Island, to pull that clip. And sure enough, in one frame, Marty had left Tawny's tit completely exposed. I called Marty right away, and he goes, "You found it!"

TAWNY KITAEN: There's nothing slutty about anything I wore. But the public's perception is that I dressed like a slut. Apparently, you can put me in a brown paper bag and I will still be sexier than some chick with nothing on. When I looked lustfully into the camera, it wasn't in an *I want to fuck the whole world*, "Cherry Pie" way. I was looking at my husband. I wanted to fuck my husband, and that translated to anyone watching.

MARTY CALLNER: I got lots of criticism for the Whitesnake videos. There was a class at Santa Monica College about my videos. Taught by a lesbian. Isn't that funny? MTV pretended to give me guff. They said "Oh no, Marty, you can't do that." Yet they wanted me to go as far as I could.

JO BERGMAN: With all the girls in the metal videos, you had to be careful about nipples. I was on constant nipple watch.

TOM HUNTER: *Dial MTV* was our highest-rated video show, yet it was the same ten videos in the same order at the same time every day. I had to change how we tabulated positions, because some videos would just live forever. People would vote for them again and again. Whitesnake's "Here We Go Again" was one of those.

JOHN KALODNER: Tawny was a beautiful, smart, flamboyant, controlling woman. At the beginning, she was great for them. But for the long-term career of Whitesnake, she was terrible. The rest of Whitesnake grew to hate her. She tortured the other wives and girlfriends. Coverdale's career was ruined because he was pussy-whipped by Tawny.

TAWNY KITAEN: David and I were the Elizabeth Taylor and Richard Burton of rock n' roll. John Kalodner used to call me Yoko Ono. I was arguing about which single to release. I was picking the photographer for album covers. At concerts, people would hold up signs saying, "We Want Tawny." I was more famous than the band.

I was truly, truly in love with David. We became filthy rich. I was spending $75,000 a month. I think I was compensating for growing up in poverty, and David didn't know how to stop me. It's like David had married a teenager. So we broke up. I got the house in Beverly Hills, he got the house in Tahoe. I never saw him again. I have never burned a bridge with anybody, but David won't speak to me. I have only great memories of him. But in my case, absolute power corrupted absolutely. I do give myself credit, though, for the fact that "Here I Go Again" has over 11 million views on YouTube.

SOPHIE MULLER: We didn't have MTV in England. I yearned to watch it. When I came to America, it was on 24/7 in my hotel room, and you had to sit through ghastly videos like Whitesnake, just to watch something you wanted to see. The lighting was horrible, the art direction was crass, and it was offensive to see a woman sprawled on a car with a short skirt and big hair.

ALAN NIVEN: In making Great White's "Rock Me," I wilted to pressure from the label. "Got to have a girl in the video, mate. Look at Tawny Kitaen on top of the Jaguar." For the moment, that became the ideal of rock videos. "Rock Me" is a safe, cliché-ridden video.

MICK KLEBER: Compared to many managers, Alan Niven was very hands-on at video shoots, scrutinizing each shot and offering intelligent input. I conceived the notion of staging Great White on platforms surrounded by water patrolled by sharks, intercut with a sexy "shark goddess" who would strip to her torso of fish scales and fire a phallic spear. This proved to be too expensive for our budget. I proposed to Propaganda that I would recommend Nigel Dick to Great White as director for the "Rock Me" video on the condition that Propaganda absorb the difference between the actual production costs and the allotted budget. They agreed to make an investment in the development of Dick's career, so the video was made based on the original idea. Dick shot footage of small sharks in a tank, but they were unconvincing and rejected. Fortunately, the model cast as the shark girl provided plenty of high-quality cutaway eye candy.

JOE ELLIOTT: The original video we did for "Pour Some Sugar on Me" might be the worst video of all time. The idea was that we're inside a house that's being demolished, and we're trying to play the song while the building falls down around us. MTV said, "We can't play this. It's crap." When we released our videos on a VHS compilation, we called that one a "rare UK version." It *was* rare, because it rarely got any airplay.

CLIFF BURNSTEIN: Def Leppard's *Hysteria* cost a fortune to make, about $7 million, and it didn't sell all that well. "Pour Some Sugar on Me" was the fourth single. We made a concept video that didn't work, and we had to scrap it. The song was a stiff at radio. The label said, "Look, it's over." As a last-ditch attempt, we decided to shoot a live version of "Sugar" in Denver. Wayne Isham found twelve of the best-looking girls in town, we stuck them in the audience, and went at it. And boom, the video just went nuts.

JOE ELLIOTT: That's when *Hysteria* went mad.

CLIFF BURNSTEIN: Wayne was a rock star. Watching him shoot a live concert was worth the price of admission. He'd be in the truck, directing, yelling out the camera moves, and he would have obscene nicknames for every camera op. He'd be in a frenzied state for an hour and half. He'd yell to the cameraman, "Get right beside that fucking whore!" He was better than the show.

JOE ELLIOTT: Wayne was a bottle rocket, an absolute lunatic. He was on caffeine overload twenty-four hours a day. Nothing was big enough, fast enough, wide enough, or tall enough. He was always saying, "We need more of that."

CURT MARVIS: Ron Jeremy showed up to many of our video shoots. He was friends with a lot of the metal guys. You always knew things were going to get bad when Ron showed up with a couple of porn stars.

WAYNE ISHAM: I'd never been a strip club guy. But hanging out with Mötley, I became a strip club guy. And they wanted to shoot "Girls, Girls, Girls" in a strip club. So I went to every strip club in LA and scouted locations. This is one reason I love my wife. I could tell her that I was going out to location scout at strip clubs, and she trusted me.

ROBIN SLOANE: During "Girls Girls Girls," I had to go all these strip clubs with the band. Vince's girlfriend came up to me and warned me: "You stay away from my man." *No problem.*

STEVE SCHNUR: Mötley loved making videos. They loved showing off. I'm not saying they were the first, and they certainly weren't the last, but nobody knew how to play to the camera better than Mötley Crüe. I never had a problem getting their videos played on MTV.

TOMMY LEE: All of us rode motorcycles except for Mick. He was only into guitars. So in the video, you can see us on our bikes, riding around, and Mick was sitting on a motorcycle strapped to a trailer, pretending to ride. It looks so cheesy and obvious. I laugh every time I see that video.

CURT MARVIS: Mick didn't know how to ride a motorcycle, so we put his bike on a rig and towed it. We struggled for hours with the camera angles. When we finally got one that worked out, we had to figure out how to keep Mick's wig from blowing off.

WAYNE ISHAM: Pole dancing was new, so we found a girl who knew how to pole dance. At a certain point though, we realized the strippers couldn't really dance, so we had to hire professional dancers who could actually move in time to the song. If you look at "Girls Girls Girls" now, it seems pretty innocent compared to the stripper videos of today.

TOMMY LEE: I went home with one of the girls in the video, the dancer with the dark hair. We shot the video, then we had an afterparty, then one thing led to another, and she went home with me. I was like, *Dude, I can't believe I'm having sex with this girl, she's so fucking hot!*

DOC McGHEE: Tommy *never* went home without one or two of the dancers. That's every strip club we ever went into! I'm surprised Tommy or Nikki can remember making the video, but that's okay. They may have heard about it from somebody else.

ROBIN SLOANE: Les Garland and I went through "Girls Girls Girls" frame by frame, to see if there was any exposed breast. I couldn't believe that was my job.

STEVE SCHNUR: One time, Mötley Crüe played Providence, Rhode Island. I was in the limo with them, leaving the gig, going back to the Biltmore Hotel, and there were tons of girls outside, screaming "Take me up to the room" and taking their shirts off. And Nikki Sixx said to this sea of girls, "Who wants to come up and fuck me?" *Bedlam. Mayhem.* And he goes, "You got to go through Schnur." I looked at him as if the messiah had arrived.

Nikki was the sane one in the band, believe it or not.

RICK KRIM: Mötley was in town once and we went out to a dive bar called Alcatrazz, on Eighth Street and Avenue A. I met a couple of people from work there, plus Heather Locklear and Tommy Lee. I still got off on that; hanging out with them made me feel cool. Heather was a little wary about going to this place, and I said, "It's really mellow, no one will hassle you." We walked in and the first guy she sees looks at her and goes, "Heather Locklear! I used to jerk off to you all the time when you were on *Dynasty*."

BRET MICHAELS: Wayne Isham was supposed to do "Talk Dirty to Me." And this is no diss to Wayne, but he had bigger fish to fry. He was getting $300,000 budgets to do videos, and we had $8,400. So instead, he sent his DP and camera guy to do it. Luckily, they were so energetic and young that they helped to make it a mega fucking hit. We all got hammered, we handed out some beer to the audience, everyone had fun. We shot it in half a day. My motto has always been "If you can't do it right, do it anyway."

MICK KLEBER: I was Poison's video guy at Capitol Records for a long time. We had issues where Bret would have some drinks on set, which is a no-no for a diabetic, and he'd get violently ill.

BRET MICHAELS: Watch "Talk Dirty to Me" and you'll see our drummer Rikki fall off the back of his drum stool. That wasn't a stunt. He liked to jump up when he played, and we didn't have enough money to get a big drum riser, so he had his drums on a small riser. When he stepped back, he fucking bit it. We had to shut down for a half hour while we made sure he didn't have a concussion.

Bobby Dall, our bass player, had a firm grip on how our record deal was structured, and we were very good at making sure we got a bang for our buck when it came to videos. Instead of spending a million dollars on a video, we'd shoot one for $150,000, work a little harder, and still be competitive with the big-budget videos out there.

CURT MARVIS: If one hard rock group made a video with ten explosions, the next group had to have twenty explosions. If one had a lighting rig with five hundred lights, the next wanted a thousand.

MARTY CALLNER: I was in great favor at the Geffen company, because I had made Whitesnake. Geffen had been in trouble and now they were rolling. I saw the Aerosmith video with Run-DMC. I called Geffen and said I'd love to do a video with Aerosmith. Starting with "Dude (Looks Like a Lady)," we went on to do something like ten videos together. They put themselves in my hands.

Steven Tyler is a great performer, and he has a rubber face. He can do comedy. Joe Perry is a sexy guitar player. And, you know, the LI Three are the LI Three. The Least Interesting Three. But those two together had a powerful dynamic.

JOHN KALODNER: The first album I made with Aerosmith was *Done with Mirrors*. It stunk. David Geffen wanted to drop them. So for the next album, *Permanent Vacation*, we were gonna do it my way. Steven Tyler still hates me for it. He tells people I ruined his career by making him sing "I Don't Want to Miss a Thing," which Diane Warren wrote.

STEVEN TYLER: I'd been living at the Gorham Hotel, on twenty dollars a week that my manager gave me, splitting a twenty-dollar bag of heroin with my girlfriend. When we crawled out of the ashes, we barely got a record contract. I said to John Kalodner, "Wouldn't it be nice if I knew somebody I could write lyrics with?" He said, "I know some people." So yes. We used other writers to help us get out of the hole, and I did a lot of lame things. Like "Magic Touch," for *Permanent Vacation*: "You've got the magic touch, don't you know, I've got a feeling, and I can't let go." I'm so embarrassed. I did that.

JOHN KALODNER: Tyler put me in a wedding dress in the "Dude (Looks Like a Lady)" video as a sort of *Fuck you*. Marty Callner directed "Dude." It was an instant hit. He was the force behind all those Aerosmith videos: "Dude," "Angel," "Rag Doll."

NIGEL DICK: I met Marty Callner at some video conference. Somebody said, "Marty, do you know Nigel Dick?" He shook my hand and said, very condescendingly, "So, *you're* the poor man's Marty Callner."

RUDOLF SCHENKER: Marty Callner was open for any crazy ideas. So I said, "Marty, why don't we put two girls' asses into the bass drum?" And that's what we did on the "Rhythm of Love" video. There are two butts in the bass drum. Marty was more fun than fun.

JUDY McGRATH: The hair metal bands loved MTV and they had a huge number of fans. But their videos promoted the objectification of women. There were years here when it was hard to be a woman. I had a conversation with Jeff Ayeroff about the Sam Kinison video for "Wild Thing." He said, "I understand that you have to play it. But did you have to make it a hit?"

MARTY CALLNER: Sam Kinison's "Wild Thing" was the nastiest video I ever made. That was the misogynistic, evil side of rock n' roll. I loved it.

JOHN CANNELLI, MTV executive: Many of the standards and practices conversations revolved around the portrayal of women in videos. "Wild Thing" was a tough one. We didn't want to play it, but we were in our hard rock period.

SAM KAISER: MTV had a lot of hits with Great White. They had one video, though, "Save Your Love," that we weren't quite sure of, so we put it into medium rotation. Capitol was busting us because they wanted heavy. Around this time, I was in LA for the Super Bowl. When I walked into my room at the Four Seasons Hotel, it was filled, from floor to ceiling, with inflated condoms. And every one of the condoms was embossed with the Great White logo and the words "Save Your Love." This was a big suite, mind you. We're talking thousands of condoms. I respected the balls and the creativity it took to break into my hotel room. A week later we put the video in heavy rotation.

RIC MENELLO: Danzig's "Mother" was about silent movies and horror movies—Fritz Lang, *Nosferatu*. Hot girls, shot in black and white.

We had a chicken sacrifice at the end. We didn't kill a real chicken. It looks like Glenn Danzig is ripping it apart, but he lets go and I did an Eisenstein, a hidden edit. MTV was like, "This is Satanic. You killed a chicken." They went through that video with a fine-tooth comb.

So I made the changes they asked for. But I sent them the wrong cut. For a whole weekend, the original version was on the air. Rick Rubin got one hundred people to call MTV, "Yo, I want to see that video where they sacrifice the chicken." On Monday I got a call from MTV—"Get the edited version to us by five o'clock or we will never show this video again." So it showed in a butchered form. It was one of the few videos Beavis and Butt-head liked.

RICK RUBIN: "Mother," wasn't that the one with the chicken in it? That was a good one. We definitely wanted it to look like we killed the chicken, as you would in a horror movie. It worked a little too well—it didn't get much play.

WAYNE ISHAM: I was the director and the DP on Ozzy's "Miracle Man." The song was about the hypocrisy of organized religion—this was around the time of the Jimmy Swaggart scandal—and Sharon wanted to do something different, so we set the video in a deconsecrated church, with Ozzy as the preacher, and dozens of pigs as the parishioners. I'd just bought new $300 Nike Airs. And the first guitar riff Zakk Wylde played was so loud, every pig in there shat. They freaked out. My brand-new shoes were covered in pig shit.

KIP WINGER, Winger: The first video treatment we got for "Seventeen," the guy wanted to put us in a theater and have a goat swinging upside down. We were like, *What are you talking about? We're a rock band, get a hot chick and put us onstage.* It was the era of big rock music. I wanted to make it. When I met Reb Beach, I said, "I'm going to sing at the top of my register, and you play guitar as fast as you can." Yeah, we had poofy hair. That was the formula.

Rick Krim was a huge Dixie Dregs fan, and our drummer had been in the Dregs. Tom Hunter, the president of MTV, was from Denver, and I'm from Denver. Those two things helped them put our first video on the air. And then Abbey Konowitch was really into "Seventeen." His quote was "This is the video Van Halen should've made."

RICK KRIM: Yes, I championed Winger, and I still champion Winger. They were my discovery. They were brilliant musicians who wrote really good songs. Kip was the pretty boy with chest hair who posed for *Playgirl* and danced ballet moves in a video, so they got unfairly maligned. They became the poster boys for fake metal.

KIP WINGER: I starved myself for a week before the first video, trying to be skinny for the camera. MTV changed my life overnight. It's rock n' roll, there are a ton of perks, especially women. I mean, it was a two or three a day when we were on tour. And we did 250 shows a year, so you do the math.

RICK KRIM: I was with Kip in LA the night he met Rachel Hunter. He'd seen her in *Sports Illustrated*, she'd seen him on MTV, and they connected. One time I went to his house and she was there in her underwear. That was pretty cool.

KIP WINGER: On "Seventeen" and "Headed for a Heartbreak," MTV played us every fifteen minutes. Then we did "Hungry" and thought, *Enough chicks, let's try to give it a little meaning.* I had an idea for a mini-movie: a guy is in love with his girlfriend, they get married, and they're driving in the hills, his brakes fail, and he drives off the cliff and she dies. So we spend $200,000 on the video, but the car didn't really go off the cliffs. We had to push it over. This is total *Spinal Tap*. And here we are dressed in what I consider to be our worst clothing choice—I'm in a velvet coat with studs on it and denim chaps—jumping up and down on police cars. It was ridiculous. Guns N' Roses stole a couple of our video ideas and that was one of them. When they drove a car off the cliff, it was way cooler, because they had more money.

JOEY ALLEN: Warrant filmed its first video, "Down Boys," on December 16, 1988. I remember because I got pulled over the night before with Jerry Dixon, our bass player. A female sheriff pulled me over, and we had a six-pack on the floor. She asked if I had any outstanding tickets, and I had a warrant out for my arrest, for bad registration tags. She said, "Are you guys in a band?" I said, "We are. Believe it or not, the band's name is Warrant." She let me go.

JANI LANE: We were told by the label how to dress, how to have our hair done, the whole nine yards. For "Heaven," we wore white leather outfits. Looked like a bunch of Elvis impersonators. We were pegged as a fluff band.

JOEY ALLEN: We'd seen the Poison video for "Every Rose Has Its Thorn," where they had tour footage, and we wanted to copy it for "Heaven." Because the formula worked. In our genre, once there was a winning formula with one band, the others would follow. There weren't any hair metal bands winning Video Vanguard awards, that's the best way to put it.

JANI LANE: Donnie Ienner, the president of Columbia Records, called and said, "Jani, give me something like 'Love in an Elevator.' Sex sells." I wrote "Cherry Pie" in two or three hours.

JOEY ALLEN: The Tom Petty "Don't Come Around Here No More" video was brilliant, which locked us into hiring Jeff Stein for "Cherry Pie."

JANI LANE: There was so much pressure to sell sex. Pressure from MTV, from the label, and from the consumer. I was trying to fight that. I have three sisters and a mom.

BOBBIE BROWN, model: Jani and Tommy Lee were on tour together—I guess Warrant was opening for Mötley Crüe—and they were watching an episode of *Star Search* on TV. When I came on, they were both, like, "Hey, she's cute." Or maybe they were like, "She's fucking hot." Then Jani called my agent.

JEFF STEIN: I wanted to cast Josie Bissett, who ended up on *Melrose Place*, but I was overruled by Jani, who may have been right for a change. Bobbie was perfect for that role. What did I tell her? "Do more of *that*. Shake it up until it hurts." She followed instructions carefully.

BOBBIE BROWN: The director told me it was gonna be sexy, but he didn't say, "We're gonna take a fire hose and blow your face off." Let me tell you, that hose had some power behind it. You can see me turn my head really quick, because it was physically uncomfortable. I ended up fighting a little with the director, 'cause he was kind of a dick. He wanted me to get in a tub full of cream. I refused to do that, by the way.

JOEY ALLEN: Jani was turning on the charm. Bobbie was dating Matthew Nelson at the time, and he came to the shoot.

JANI LANE: I had a horrible time. The rest of the guys shot for eight hours and went home. I was there for twenty-four hours straight, in the middle of summer in Hollywood, and the stage was about 125 degrees. I think I took eight showers that day. I'll give Bobbie Brown credit, she was there with me the whole time.

BOBBIE BROWN: During the video, Jani was being flirtatious, making it very obvious that he liked me. Was there an immediate attraction? Not for me. Jani sent me flowers and kept calling. He went on Howard Stern and said, "I'm gonna marry Bobbie Brown one day." I was like, *Oh my god.* He went as far as going out with my roommate and showing up at my house. He was constantly pursuing me, and I go, "Hey, I have your number. If I want to use it, I will." After we got married, he said, "I was devastated when you said that."

But then I broke up with Matthew, because he was jealous over the success of "Cherry Pie." I called Joey Allen's wife and told her, mostly to piss off Matthew and rub it in his face, and within five minutes, Jani called me.

JANI LANE: I had broken up with my girlfriend, who moved on to Richie Sambora. I called Bobbie, because I heard she wasn't happy with her boyfriend, and said, "I was wondering if you wanted to go to Disneyland." She said, "I have your number, if I want to call you, I'll call you." Then she broke up with her boyfriend and wanted to come out and see a show. We hit it off for a while, not very long. She got pregnant, we got married.

BOBBIE BROWN: The video made me a weird icon in people's minds. I didn't take advantage of my opportunities the way I should have. I was supposed to be in *Casino* with Robert De Niro—I was going to play Sharon Stone's part—and have an interview with Steven Spielberg for *Hook*. I was somewhat of a fuckup—I got a huge ego, and I was fucked up on drugs. I'd walked into a club and the owner would shake my hand and give me drugs, for free. I never had to pay for it. Even my agent, if I had to lose weight, would give me drugs. I try not to dwell on it, but it really sucks. I have a lot of regret.

JEFF STEIN: I thought "Cherry Pie" was the perfect music video. The concept meshed with the song. This is going to sound full of shit, but I wanted to do a parody of sexism in music videos. And instead, I was accused of creating a sexist video. So I don't know, if you parody something and people think it's real, have you done a good parody or have you failed?

The band knew exactly what they were. They did every hair band pose. That's one reason the video was perfect. There were bright colors, very bold, in your face. It was like pop art without the art.

JOHN CANNELLI: We had an internal controversy over the video. Judy McGrath was offended by a woman being hosed down.

ABBEY KONOWITCH: There was a time when the liberal feminists on MTV's staff were unhappy with the music programming. We were playing "Cherry Pie," that kind of thing. It was awkward, because our job was to play the hits of the day.

JOEY ALLEN: Spraying down a girl with a fire hose? It's rock n' roll, give me a break. It was just shock value. "Let's put this hot chick in here and sell as many records as we can." *Rolling Stone* called it the most tasteless video of the year. It also sold over a million records for us, real fast.

JANI LANE: From that point on, I was the "Cherry Pie" guy.

JEFF STEIN: I'm sure Jani felt he was a great songwriter. If I were him, I'd rather watch "Cherry Pie" than "Heaven," which is an anthem for eunuchs. Come on! Strap your balls on, Jani! And if you don't like the video, give me your platinum record!

BOBBIE BROWN: Jani has a love/hate relationship with the song. Yes, it's the one song that's keeping his name alive, and people remember him for. But in his mind, as a writer or an artist, it's not his best work. It's a song he wrote in the bathroom, in five minutes.

ADAM LEVINE, Maroon 5: "Cherry Pie" was metaphor-free. It left nothing to the imagination. There's a scene where a piece of cherry pie falls into her lap, and you're like, *Really?* Even at twelve years old, I thought, *Wow, how tacky.*

BRET MICHAELS: Our "Flesh and Blood" video didn't pan out. CC wanted his girlfriend—Tammy was her name—to be in the video. I said, "CC, the video is basically softcore porn. We're playing Adam and Eve and we're going to be half-naked and sucking face. Isn't that gonna be weird for you?" He goes, "Don't worry about it—she's a model, she wants to do it. She's a professional." So we shot the video, and let me put it this way, it didn't go over well with CC But hey, if I saw a buddy doing that with my girlfriend, I wouldn't be happy either. It probably led to our fistfight at the VMAs. One of many.

SEBASTIAN BACH: We made a conscious decision to not objectify women in Skid Row videos. It didn't feel good, it wasn't a good thing to do, and every single video had chicks in it. Not that we don't like chicks, but it was overplayed at that point. We wanted our videos to follow the lyrical content of the song, intercut with beautiful, slow-motion hair twirling. And I think we achieved our goal.

Dude, when they talk about "hair metal," whose hair do you think they're talking about? I've still got it. I'm looking at it right now. And it's so flaxen!

WAYNE ISHAM: For Skid Row's "18 and Life," about a kid who runs away from an abusive family and ends up getting drunk and shooting his best friend, I knew we were going to have problems with the guns. There was a scene where the kid spray-paints a drippy bullet hole in the middle of his forehead—like a third eye—and MTV made me remove that. You couldn't predict what they would or wouldn't allow.

DOC McGHEE: "18 and Life" was a big video. I mean, you had a kid, Sebastian Bach, who if you put a set of tits on him, he could run for Miss Texas. One of the best-looking guys on the planet at that time.

SEBASTIAN BACH: I was upstairs with my girlfriend Maria, fucking her on the floor in the video studio. She was riding me and they knocked on the door: "Sebastian, it's your scene." She dismounted me, I pulled up my pants. Maybe that had something to do with the video's success, too, having just got fucked. My hair is tousled.

Then I saw Nine Inch Nails' "Head Like a Hole" and thought it looked amazing, so we hired the same company to shoot "Monkey Business." Michael Schmidt made the tight leather pants I wore. It's all about the cock, baby. It's framed perfectly in that video.

When Rick Krim liked your band, he got your videos on MTV. Here I am today, standing in my huge house with platinum records all over the wall, and I owe that to two things: Rick Krim and my cheekbones. Though my lips had a lot to do with it, too. So I'd like to thank my cheekbones, my lips, my hair, and Rick Krim. And my crotch.

Warner Cable executive vice president John Lack, in 1979. It was Lack who came up with the idea for MTV. (Courtesy of John Lack)

MTV creative director Fred Seibert and MTV programming chief Bob Pittman, in 1982. (Courtesy of Fred Seibert)

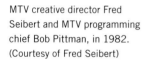

MTV director of promotions John Sykes and creative consultant Alan Goodman prepare for takeoff in the MTV Learjet for the channel's first promotion, "One Night Stand with Journey," in October 1981. (Courtesy of John Sykes)

The original five VJs (clockwise from left): Nina Blackwood, Mark Goodman, J. J. Jackson, Martha Quinn, and Alan Hunter. (Mark Weiss/WireImage/Getty Images)

Director Steve Barron and Michael Jackson on the set of the momentous 1983 video "Billie Jean." (Credit Sam Emerson/Polaris)

R&B artist Rick James, MTV executive vice president of programming Les Garland, and MTV's John Sykes, in 1984. (Courtesy of John Sykes)

Van Halen's David Lee Roth
and MTV VJ Mark Goodman,
at the 1983 US Festival.
(© Roger Ressmeyer/Corbis)

ZZ Top and friends on the
set of the 1983 video "Gimme
All Your Lovin'" (from left):
Jeana Tomasino, Frank Beard,
Danielle Arnaud, director Tim
Newman; (front): Billy Gibbons,
unknown model, and Dusty Hill.
(Credit David Blayney)

Put 'em up: Twisted Sister's
Jay Jay French and Dee Snider
with Martha Quinn and Mark
Goodman at the MTV studios.
(Courtesy of Ken R. Clark)

Madonna, after performing "Like a Virgin" at the inaugural MTV Video Music Awards, held at New York City's Radio City Music Hall, September 14, 1984. (Time Life Pictures/Getty Images)

Wet T-shirt Contest! Duran Duran's Simon Le Bon and John Taylor, on video location in 1983. (Express Newspapers/Hulton Archive/Getty Images)

Bruce Springsteen and director John Sayles on the set of the 1985 video "Glory Days." (Courtesy Bob Marshak)

Bon Jovi pose with "Hedonism Weekend" contest winners and VJ Alan Hunter (middle row, left) at Hedonism II resort, Jamaica, 1987. (Courtesy of Doug Herzog)

Arista Records' Peter Baron and Whitney Houston on the set of Houston's "I Wanna Dance With Somebody (Who Loves Me)" video, 1987. (Courtesy of Peter Baron)

Yo! MTV Raps' cohost Ed Lover, creator/producer Ted Demme, and cohost Dr. Dre, 1988. (Getty Images)

R&B artist Bobby Brown, host Arsenio Hall, and VJ "Downtown" Julie Brown, at the 1989 Video Music Awards, Los Angeles. (Courtesy of Ken R. Clark)

Someone in this photo got jobbed at the 2011 Oscars . . . Propaganda Films staff, circa 1987 (from left): head of production Tim Clawson, cofounder Steve Golin, head of music video Anne-Marie Mackay, cofounder Joni Sighvatsson, director Nigel Dick, director David Fincher, director Greg Gold, head of commercial division Bill Curran, and director Dominic Sena. (Courtesy of Nigel Dick)

Stephen R. Johnson, director of Peter Gabriel's acclaimed "Sledgehammer" video, poses with his bounty of Moonmen from the 1987 Video Music Awards. (Courtesy of Stephen R. Johnson)

MTV VJ Adam Curry, center, with the Beastie Boys and Darryl "D.M.C." McDaniels at the Montreux Rock Festival, Switzerland, 1988. (Courtesy of Adam Curry)

It's a living: MTV vice president of music programming Tom Hunter (left) and senior vice president of artist and talent relations Abbey Konowitch (right) receive programming advice from stripper Kitten Natividad, who was sent to the MTV offices by Elektra Records to promote a new release. (Courtesy of Rick Krim)

Comedian and MTV VJ Pauly Shore. One MTV executive refers to Shore as "the first VJ who had nothing to do with music." (Courtesy of Pauly Shore)

Comedian Chris Farley, MTV VJ Karen Duffy, and *You Wrote It, You Watch It* host Jon Stewart, 1993. (Courtesy of Karen Duffy)

Big Guns (top row, from left): Guns N' Roses' Duff McKagan, MTV general manager Lee Masters, vice president of programming Doug Herzog, Abbey Konowitch, vice president of production Jock McLean, Izzy Stradlin, Axl Rose, vice president of artist and talent relations John Cannelli; (bottom row, from left): Slash, Tom Hunter, Guns N' Roses manager Alan Niven, and Steven Adler. (Courtesy of Doug Herzog)

At the taping of MTV's 10th anniversary TV special, broadcast on ABC: (from left) MTV Networks chairman/CEO Tom Freston, MTV executive vice president/creative director Judy McGrath, Abbey Konowitch, Michael Jackson, Doug Herzog, and show producer Joel Gallen. (Courtesy of Doug Herzog)

Judy McGrath and U2's Bono, at the singer's house in Dublin following the "Zoo TV" tour, 1993. (Courtesy of Judy McGrath)

MTV vice president of artist and talent relations Rick Krim and Pearl Jam's Eddie Vedder at the 1993 Video Music Awards, Los Angeles. (Courtesy of Rick Krim)

Nirvana in their backstage trailer at the infamous 1992 Video Music Awards, Los Angeles. (FilmMagic, Inc.)

Chapter 31

"THE ISLAND OF MISFIT TOYS"

120 MINUTES AND THE RISING UP/SELLING OUT OF ALTERNATIVE ROCK

MTV's CENTRAL RELATIONSHIP WAS WITH ROCK stars—making them famous, interviewing them, playing their videos, keeping them happy. But they also delved into the weird corners of music, where videos were still made on minuscule budgets, often with startling or innovative results.

The Cutting Edge was a beloved showcase for freakiness, made by I.R.S. Records and licensed to MTV, which kept it hidden on the last Sunday of every month, playing videos from upstarts like R.E.M., Red Hot Chili Peppers, and the Minutemen late in the night, giving weirdos a good reason for showing up to work tired on Monday mornings. "For those of us out in the sticks, it was a lifeline," musician and newspaper editor Kate Messer wrote years later, "an encyclopedia to certain strata of 'underground' culture."

In March 1986, MTV introduced *120 Minutes*, a two-hour weekly show airing on Sunday at 1 A.M. *120 Minutes* went through a number of hosts, largely because it was an unglamorous job that no one wanted to keep. Except, eventually, Dave Kendall.

VALERIE FARIS: *The Cutting Edge* was an hour-long show that aired once a month, on Sunday night. It was hosted by Peter Zaremba, the singer of the Fleshtones. Peter is a music lover and historian, so he lent some credibility to the show.

PETER ZAREMBA, host, *The Cutting Edge*: It was MTV's alternative music show, the precursor to *120 Minutes*. As host, I got paid $1,000 a show, which was a lot of money for me. We'd air offbeat videos MTV wouldn't show. We played Madonna before MTV put her videos in rotation. And we'd film artists playing just for us—we'd go to a sound check, or invite R.E.M. to some interesting location, and they'd do acoustic versions of their songs. The Red Hot Chili Peppers' first national TV appearance was on *The Cutting Edge*. We had the Replacements, the Minutemen, Hüsker Dü, Alex Chilton, Jonathan Richman, and we also had Willie Dixon, Jimmy Cliff, and Tom Waits. Iggy Pop wanted to be filmed up in a tree. Morrissey insisted on no interviewer, because he didn't want to be sullied by talking to a host.

JONATHAN DAYTON, director: It was bands that otherwise might not appear on MTV. This was the one place where you could see Henry Rollins reading his poetry. We filmed Morrissey in his bathroom at a hotel, and gave him a stack of envelopes, each with a single word inside. He would open the envelope and talk to a little camera. The word might be "beauty," so he'd talk about beauty. There were no VJs or happy talk. It was very homemade. No one was making much money, so in exchange you were given a lot of freedom.

PETER ZAREMBA: Two of the show's producers, Valerie Faris and Jonathan Dayton, went on to become big-deal directors. They did lots of music videos, and later they directed *Little Miss Sunshine*. They were very mellow. They put up with a lot of junk.

MICHAEL STIPE: Everyone I knew would find a television set, have beers, and watch *The Cutting Edge*. It was like *The Island of Misfit Toys*. All the miscreants and the outcasts and the punks and the fat girls and the kids with bad skin and the queers could gather together around this universe. Pre-Internet, and before the instantaneous sharing of information and knowledge about music or about art, that was it. That was for the Lee Renaldos and the Kim Gordons and the Courtney Loves and the Michael Stipes.

DAVE HOLMES: MTV helped create the trench coat–wearing, Cure-loving, zine-reading kid of the '80s. Echo and the Bunnymen came to St. Louis and there were all these kids dressed the same who knew every word, but the band wasn't getting played on the radio. Somehow, they'd all gotten the same message, and it was from watching MTV late at night.

DAVE KENDALL: I was cleaning a woman's apartment the first time I saw MTV. She felt bad for me, a young kid having to clean apartments to pay the bills. So she said, "Hey, we've got MTV!" And I was like, "What's that?" I'd come to New York from London on a student exchange.

To be honest, I wanted to work for any company that would allow me to stay in the States legally. I was getting laid for the first time in my life; that's probably why I stayed. I would've worked for a burger stand if they could've gotten me a work permit. I was a music journalist, writing for *Melody Maker* in England, and Judy McGrath hired me to write *120 Minutes*. Then I started producing it as well. There was a parade of hosts: J.J. Jackson, then Mark Goodman, Martha Quinn, Alan Hunter, Kevin Seal—whoever was available. Hosting the show wasn't a plum assignment.

But *120 Minutes* was culturally important, because there was nowhere else to find this music in 1986, so I felt a sense of satisfaction. These were the days when VCRs were available, so people started to tape the shows and watch them later. MTV was always conceived to be both an art and a business. There was a desire to cater to a smaller audience that was not the lowest common denominator.

RICK KRIM: The first times I met Bruce Springsteen and Bono, the conversations were about *120 Minutes*, because they both loved that show.

MARK GHUNEIM, record executive: *120 Minutes* was the Pitchfork of its time.

DAVE GROHL: On *120 Minutes*, you'd see a video that was made with a Pixelvision camera and Super 8 and bad lighting. I found it endearing. Like, *This band made their own video? That's pretty fucking cool.* Like in R.E.M.'s "Driver 8," where they have images projected on their faces and they're shaking the car to make it look like they're driving. I'd much rather see a school play than a Broadway musical.

DAVE KENDALL: I started hosting *120 Minutes* because I wrote myself into the script. I did record reviews on the show, then Kevin Seal went away and someone suggested I fill in. And I did it for three and a half years. I had a fairly grating persona. I mean, I annoy myself. So I took great pleasure in annoying my public, by being brash and sarcastic. Being on television was not a natural thing for me.

KEN R. CLARK: We used to kid Dave, usually behind his back, about his hair. He wore a really bad rug. People used to joke about the dead cat on top of his head. John Lydon from Public Image came in the studio and his focus was completely fixated on the top of Dave's head. Dave asked a question, and John said, "Dave, I have to ask—are you wearing a wig?" The entire studio exploded in laughter.

DAVE KENDALL: I used to wear a hair weave, the so-called dead cat on my head. I'd come from the New Romantic era, so why wear a subtle hair weave when you can have something totally ridiculous? John Lydon turned to me at the end of a segment and said, "Is that a wig?" And of course, that didn't air.

Alternative music grew, and *120 Minutes* assumed a higher profile, in terms of advertisers and sponsors. There was more press attention, more label attention. *120 Minutes* was attractive to people who had a sense of being different, but they also had a sense of violation when a video crossed over into regular rotation. They felt something had been taken from them, part of their identity had been co-opted. They felt a sense of loss and anger, because the uncool people started to like Depeche Mode or the Cure.

ROBERT SMITH: MTV played our videos because they set other videos into relief. We were their pet alternative UK band for a while. I was pleased that they did play us. But I also knew that if MTV stopped playing us, it wouldn't be the end of the world.

PAUL WESTERBERG, the Replacements: When MTV came on, I would defiantly avert my eyes. I found it scary and weird. I thought they were the enemy—the antithesis of what the Replacements were, a living, breathing entity you had to see live to understand. We certainly made some awful videos, like the rest of the sheep. "I'll Be You," that was one of the good ones. At one point, I was drinking gin out of a dog's dish.

MICHAEL STIPE: Our disdain towards MTV videos culminated in "Fall on Me," which I shot at a rock quarry in Indiana. There's not a single edit in it. I took a piece of film, turned it backwards, flipped it upside down, and put the words of the song on top of it in red lettering. I was following Andy Warhol's idea of the camera being a passive observer. And MTV played the living shit out of it, which was profoundly shocking. The video for "It's the End of the World as We Know It" was also radical. And MTV played that. We were in a position of power for a long time; we could make weird videos, and MTV would feel somewhat obligated to play them. We got immense joy from that. It became a way to bring our brand of fringe art into people's homes and living rooms. MTV was an amazing tool to be able to do that.

By 1987 I had started my first film company, with Jim McKay, and we were experimenting with music videos and public service announcements and short experimental film. I was spending a lot of time with visual-art people. Robert Longo was one of the premier painters coming out of New York. We wanted to upset the visual language of videos, and that's what we got with "The One I Love." He was referencing Renaissance paintings, rather than Madonna. I saw the video he did for New Order's "Bizarre Love Triangle"—he interrupts it about two-thirds of the way through with a scene out of a movie, where a woman stands up at a table and says, "I refuse to believe in reincarnation, because I will not come back as a bug or an insect," and a guy goes, "Well you're a real up person," and then it slam-cuts back into the song. I don't think anyone had ever interrupted a song, cut to something, and then cut back to the song.

KEVIN KERSLAKE, director: It was a point of honor among bands on *120 Minutes* to *not* show up in regular rotation on MTV. They wanted to be the bad kids on the block, who showed up for those two hours on Sunday night and ran riot. At that point, indie rock was thriving. You had great underground labels like SST and Rough Trade, and they'd give you complete freedom. I wanted to do something totally new. I'd shoot on Super 8, and play with the color palette to make it more psychedelic. The punk rock ethos really drove the visual content, even if you weren't working with punk bands. My first music video—"Shadow of a Doubt," for Sonic Youth—used horrible quality, super-grainy performance footage. It was fantastic.

PETER HOOK, New Order: We weren't at all interested in self-promotion, so traditional music videos didn't make sense to us. Often, we didn't even appear in our own videos. To my knowledge, we were the first band to do that. We thought of video as its own art form. We didn't use them to push our faces down people's throats. We met Michael Shamberg when he filmed us playing in New York, and we gave him more or less complete artistic freedom to do the videos. Michael's a big producer now—he did *Pulp Fiction* and *Garden State*—and he introduced us to interesting directors: Robert Longo, Kathryn Bigelow, Philippe Decouflé,

Robert Frank, William Wegman, and Jonathan Demme. Jonathan directed "Perfect Kiss," which was a live performance video. I think he captured the awkwardness and the edginess of the group. It was quite an artistic statement.

MATT MAHURIN: I had no film experience; I didn't even have MTV. I'd never held a film camera before. I knew nothing about the process. Sharon Oreck taught me how to be a filmmaker. Her office was in an old refurbished motel, and we had production meetings in one of the bedrooms. "Okay, Matt, this is what we call a production meeting. And now we're going to put you in a car, and this is what we call a location scout."

I was already a painter and a photographer, and I had a distinct look to my work. Jeff Ayeroff, the head of creative at Warner Bros., and a brilliant guy, said, "Do you want to direct a video?" There were a lot of people starting to do slick things, like David Fincher—cinematic, controlled, very art-directed, pristine. I wanted something edgier, darker, moodier. I could add emotional weight to something. I used lighting, film grain, shadows, to make things ethereal and dreamy. I wanted everything I did to have some truth to it. I had no desire to fake anything or deceive anybody, or turn artists into computer-generated sex symbols. I didn't like blowing stuff up; I didn't like to build sets.

VALERIE FARIS: Matt Mahurin brought a new angle to music videos. Before that, they were fairly conventional in terms of photography and lighting. He took it into a more sophisticated visual world, and brought a new visual language.

JONATHAN DAYTON: Matt would take a single Arcan light and shine it on an artist, and it would become ghoulish or blown out. He let things burn and get very orange and hot. It wasn't a perfect image—he let them degrade.

MEIERT AVIS: I was hired to do U2's "With or Without You." I'd seen Matt's work, and he was very Man Ray–influenced, and I'd stolen a lot from Man Ray, so Matt seemed like a good fit to assist. He was working with Sam Bayer, who also ended up being a great music-video director. So they shot Super 8 footage, which I edited and transferred to 35mm and projected onto the semitransparent scrims. That was one of those shoots where everything was right. But the weak link was the transfer from film to video, because in those days the telecines weren't great, and it was being transferred onto standard-def videotape. I wish one day they'd remaster all the great videos to HD, because the image on the 35mm film in "With or Without You" is spectacular. We were shooting through three or four layers of gauze with different projections on them, it was beautiful. But now, especially when you see it on YouTube, you can't even tell.

SAMUEL BAYER: Matt Mahurin was my teacher at the School of Visual Arts in New York. I was a painter and I needed money, so when I got out of school in 1987, he let me work on some music-video sets as a PA. God bless Matt, I was a really bad PA.

MATT MAHURIN: Bono asked if I wanted to work on U2's "With or Without You." Meiert Avis had a big production going with 35mm and dollies and a Luma crane and track laid out. He shot the band performing, and then I shot a bunch of b-roll or second unit stuff that was atmospheric. He'd shoot a band member, send him to me, and I'd have ten minutes. I didn't have any crew helping me, so I took a light and strapped it to the end of a broomstick and dug it into my hip, and I was pivoting this light around.

There's one background image of a white, ghostly figure jumping naked into a wave—that's me at my house in Long Island.

Bono really is like the savior of the world, but he's also like the devil. He's the king *and* the court jester. He's got that duality to him. You'd be drinking with the band at their local pub and he was a wild man. He could be comfortable with the Dalai Lama or George W. Bush; he could adapt. He could put on any mask; it was a very real mask, but he could turn on a dime to get what he wanted.

MEIERT AVIS: Nothing with U2 happens by accident. They study. If you want to be the biggest rock band in the world, you'd better do your homework. Take advantage of what worked for other people. The rooftop video we did for "Where the Streets Have No Name" was the Beatles' idea first. They did it for their last concert.

You can't tell from the video, but we got proper permits to shoot on the rooftop of that liquor store. The police got the worst of it in the video. Contrary to what you see, they tried their best to help us. They just got frightened as more and more people streamed into downtown. Which is exactly what we wanted. Every beat of that video is exactly what was planned. The band played five or six songs, then we did three or four live takes of "Streets," and then two or three playback takes. What you see is a mixture of playback and live and then shots from other songs altogether. There was a lot of editorial work, but it was the easiest job I ever did in terms of shooting. There were seven cameras, the band looked great, the location was great, and you just let it go. It was easy.

There was one moment during "Streets" where the police pulled a fuse out of the generator. We were in the middle of a take, and the cops pulled out the fuse to shut us down. Bono's up there singing, he's flapping his lips, but no sound's coming out. We'd planned this for months, though, and we had a backup generator on the roof. So we flipped the switch, and that was that.

PAUL McGUINNESS: Jon Landau refers to Meiert Avis as "U2's gift to Bruce Springsteen." Bruce obviously liked the films Meiert had made with U2, and he hired Meiert to make quite a number of videos.

JON LANDAU: Meiert had directed some U2 videos Bruce Springsteen and I liked. We were looking for something fresh for "Brilliant Disguise," and we met with him and we really liked him. Meiert had a great intuition about how to work with Bruce. And once Bruce finds somebody he can communicate with and feels comfortable with, he likes to stick with that person. He doesn't like to jump around. We loved the "Brilliant Disguise" video. Meiert used a great cinematographer, Carlo Di Palma. And it was Meiert's idea for the video to be one long take. We got a lot of respect for that video, especially considering that Bruce is not fundamentally a video artist. And so we continued on with Meiert. We did "Tunnel of Love," "One Step Up," and "Tougher Than the Rest" with him.

MEIERT AVIS: Jon Landau asked if I'd meet Springsteen. That was an insane phone call to get. He was coming off the *Born in the U.S.A.* album and tour, which had turned him into the biggest artist in the world. And he had a new album, *Tunnel of Love*, that was the opposite of that. The first single was "Brilliant Disguise." Bruce told me, "Whatever you do, I don't want a huge music video. I want something personal."

He said, "If you can look someone in the eye and lie to them, that's the brilliant disguise." So I felt the right way to do the video was to do as little as possible. Initially I wanted to have just a still close-up of his face. But after really listening to the song, I pictured the narrator downstairs while his woman is upstairs in bed, and it's, like, three in the morning and he gets up and has a revelation. I wanted him to be in a kitchen, so you felt that there was another life upstairs. The video became one long push-in that revealed the setting, and ended with an extreme close-up. It's a single take. There were no cuts, no lying, no subterfuge. Even though the song is all about subterfuge. We did the vocals live, which was a thing I'd come up with for the Waterboys, because their singer, Mike Scott, wouldn't lip-sync.

Getting the kitchen for "Brilliant Disguise" was a fucking nightmare. I'd scouted a bunch of stuff in New Jersey and eventually found a kitchen big enough to shoot in. It belonged to a banker who was away on business, and his wife gave us permission to shoot. Four o'clock in the afternoon, the day before the shoot, I get a call from the wife: "My husband has come back and he doesn't want a film crew in the house." The trucks had already left New York with all the equipment. I was in a phone booth in pouring rain off the New Jersey Turnpike, begging the husband—literally on my knees—saying, "Today is my birthday and this is the most important job in the world. If I don't have somewhere to shoot tomorrow, my career's over, this is my dream come true . . ." And he hung up on me.

So we decided to call the National Guard. I figured, this is New Jersey, and it's for "The Boss," let's call the army. The National Guard happened to have an officer's house on an empty base in northern New Jersey that was built in the 1950s, and it had a perfect '50s kitchen. They let us use it, because it was for Bruce Springsteen.

Making that one-take video was absurdly expensive. You'd kill yourself if you knew the number. I feel embarrassed. It looks simple, but I had Woody Allen's cameraman, Carlo Di Palma. It's actually a complicated shot—it starts high and drops down and pushes in and remains in focus right up to the close-up. The live audio didn't make it easier, because there was a recording session going on as well. That video won an editing award, even though it's all one take. Can you imagine?

MATT MAHURIN: I sent my portfolio to Elektra Records, and they said, "Your work is a little too dark. But we have this new artist, Tracy Chapman . . ." I said, "Just let me shoot her. If you don't like what I do, you can pay me $5 for the film." She came to my apartment, and she was so shy. When I shot "Fast Car," I wanted it as simple as possible. I put the camera on eight feet of dolly and went back and forth for several takes. I projected some photographs on the wall behind her, to add different textures. I had a minimal crew, and kept everybody out of her eye line.

Then a buddy and I went on a road trip for a couple of days with a 16mm camera and no storyboard or ideas. I did many videos like that, where I'd shoot the working man—cobblers, ironworkers, bicycle messengers. I loved the truth that was imbedded in their lives. I loved the juxtaposition of the music with these raw bits.

When they sent "Fast Car" to MTV, it was almost like, "We dare you to not play this video. This is not Michael Jackson, this is not Lionel Richie." She was undeniable.

LENNY KRAVITZ: The original "Let Love Rule" was done by Matt Mahurin, who made a lot of great videos. It's dark and beautiful, with the same feeling as "Fast Car." But I was a hippie, and I felt "Let Love Rule" needed to be more colorful and open and outdoors, so I didn't use Matt's version. He wasn't happy with me about that. My then-wife, Lisa Bonet, directed the version of "Let Love Rule" everyone knows. She shot it in Woodstock and Central Park. No one wanted me to use Lisa. Everyone thought we were becoming John and Yoko. Or that she was Jeanine, the girlfriend in *Spinal Tap*, who said, "You don't do heavy metal in Dolby." But I believed in her. And it became a classic.

SINEAD O'CONNOR: I shaved my head after I signed a record contract. Two guys from the record company wanted me to wear miniskirts. They described their mistresses to me, and said I should look like that. I didn't want to be pushed as some kind of pretty girl, so my way of answering was to shave my head. I didn't want to be governed by a load of middle-aged blokes.

It was a time when you hadn't really come across angry women. I wasn't standing there with blond hair, saying, "Oh baby, do me." The way I looked caused a lot of opinions. Madonna did an interview at the time, saying, "Sinead O'Connor has about as much sex appeal as Venetian blinds." I was an unusual character in all kinds of ways, and I suppose from the boring desks of MTV, I must have looked interesting. I didn't conform visually, and that's part of the reason MTV were attracted to me.

I often look quite serious, when in fact I'm not that serious of a person. But there was a fucking camera in my face, and I didn't know what I was supposed to do. On videos, my job was just to fucking turn up and let everyone do whatever they wanted to me. The phallic-looking flowers in "I Want Your (Hands on Me)," that's the director, John Maybury. John was obviously obsessed with penises.

MICHAEL STIPE: Our contribution to MTV—and I'll use a term that was not really around in the 1980s—was very queer. And purposefully so. If you saw a beautiful woman wearing not much in "The One I Love" video, then you were also going to see a man wearing not much. There are a lot of shirtless men in R.E.M. videos. I shot and edited "Finest Worksong" and basically called all my hot, male friends and said, "Okay, everyone take your shirt off and get sweaty." I shot from a particular angle that was taken from Russian Constructivist art, where everyone looks like a god or goddess.

I wanted our videos and our songs to appeal to guys and girls. And that exactly reflected my sexuality, actually.

MATT MAHURIN: When I met with Michael Stipe to discuss "Orange Crush," he said, "We don't want to be in the video." The band had a kind of androgyny, so maybe I picked up on that. It's about a soldier going off to war, and there were things in the video that could be perceived as sexy. It had a youthful virility— the shirtless soldier with the dogtag, the military theme, the physicality. The VMA award it won was "Post-modern Video." I'm fifty-one years old, and I still don't know what *post-modern* means. But I've got the little Moonman to prove it.

MICHAEL STIPE: Peter Buck hated doing music videos. He adopted a curmudgeonly "I'm miserable, and I don't want to be here" attitude. That provided an interesting tension, because I was trying to do something different and cool, and there was Peter with his arms crossed, standing in the back and not really wanting to participate. It was an almost cartoonish persona, and he did not step out of character. At the end of "Stand," he looks totally miserable. It's hysterical.

RANDY SKINNER: Peter always read books while R.E.M. was making videos.

KEVIN GODLEY: Lou Reed didn't want to be in his own video. We came up with the idea of creating an animatronic version of Lou for "No Money Down," and having the robot lip-sync the song. We figured people wouldn't quite suss what was going on. "Is that Lou Reed? He doesn't look well." We did three takes, then wondered what would happen if the robot started to tear its face off, but kept performing. It's a bit *Terminator*, actually.

TAMRA DAVIS: I went to Lou Reed's dressing room at Radio City Music Hall, and I was nervous. He hadn't done a music video in years. He was standing, I was sitting, and he's like, "I'm not making this music video, fuck you." He was just yelling at me. Screaming. I tried to stand up so I would be at eye level. I said, "Whatever you want to do, we'll do." He's like, "I'll give you two hours at a concert next week in Detroit." He showed up on set wearing a shirt covered in swear words. I had a PA tape up every letter. I shot him live, doing "Busload of Faith" with a full band. Then I said, "I have fifteen minutes left. Would you do the song alone, just you and the guitar?" I set up two cameras, and it became an amazing video.

PETER HOOK: Most music videos are so narcissistic. The singer has to be on-screen the most, etc. It is so fucking boring when people do that. If I was watching one of our videos and it had just been just Barney Sumner's face, it would not entertain me.

SINEAD O'CONNOR: The close-up of me singing "Nothing Compares 2 U" was supposed to be only one part of the video. But the song reminded me of my mother, who had died three years previously. Everyone thinks it's about some bloke, but if you notice where I start crying, it's at the lines, "All the flowers that you planted, mama, in the backyard / All died when you went away." I made an emotional connection, which I was not expecting—it didn't hit me when I was recording the song. It only kicked in when I was being filmed. So I was sitting there, thinking about me mother, and trying hard not to bawl my eyes out. I had one little tear. That became the whole video. But it wasn't supposed to be. The video was massive, and it changed my career. What was funny, when the video won an award, John Maybury said, "Thank you to the plate of onions," saying it was onions that made me cry.

PETER HOOK: The American record company hated every video we ever made. That always cheered us up. Later on, we set some sort of record with "Regret" for spending the most amount of money on a video that featured the least amount of a group. That video cost something like £750,000 and we were in it for about twenty seconds. The record company went fucking berserk.

DAVE NAVARRO: The record company put Jane's Addiction together with a director who gave us his take on "Mountain Song," and when we saw it, we were very unhappy. It didn't represent us on any level. So we decided to reshoot it on our own. They ended up using black strips over the genitalia. The nudity was so brief that putting black bars over it called attention to the nudity. It was like shooting off a flare, saying, "There's something edgy and dangerous in this." So it worked to our advantage.

We shot "Been Caught Stealing" in a supermarket in Venice, California. By that time, we had an aversion to being on MTV. We saw bands—Bullet Boys, for instance—who had a cool song and a cool video, and were enormous for a minute, then you never heard from them again. I wasn't convinced there could be any longevity around an MTV band unless it was pop music. We were one of the first bands asked to do an *Unplugged*, and we turned it down. I think we upset some people over there. MTV would come to Lollapalooza and cover every band on the festival except us—and we were headlining! It started to feel like a power play, like, "Play ball with us or else."

FLEA, Red Hot Chili Peppers: Stéphane Sednaoui had made some videos we liked, so we met with him and he came up with a treatment for "Give It Away." We didn't really understand it. The only thing we got was that we were going to be painted silver. So he takes out a picture from a magazine—it was a picture of a girl lying on a rock. He goes, "You see zis? Zis picture of zis girl on zee rock?" We're like, "Yeah." He goes, "It's not like zis." We made another video with Stéphane for "Breaking the Girl," also in Joshua Tree. Stéphane got real mad at the crew at one point. He was frustrated and he yelled, "Everybody! Get in your position!" But with his French accent, it sounded like "Get in your fuzzy sham." Our drummer Chad's e-mail address is still Fuzzy Sham.

ANTON CORBIJN: For Depeche Mode's *Music for the Masses*, the videos had been in black and white, so for *Violator* I decided we'd go to color. On "Personal Jesus," I took a sexual approach, and shot in a little brothel in the south of Spain. There was one shot I had to take out, the horse's tail. The record company said it was too suggestive of sex with an animal. Nobody objected to the brothel.

It was a massive hit in America and I got more offers, but I was very focused on Depeche. On "Enjoy the Silence," I had this idea of a king with a deck chair, walking all around the world and finding peace. They didn't like the idea and asked me to think of another one. I couldn't. They said, "Just make it, then." We shot in Portugal, Switzerland, Scotland, and a garage studio in London, over somebody's house. There's a lyric, "Words are very unnecessary," and it's the only line Dave sings.

It was really cheap. I filmed everything, we didn't use lighting, we had one girl for makeup, a producer to help me carry stuff, and Dave Gahan. Four people. Tiny budget, but the video was massive. Massive. It did a lot for Depeche Mode.

I re-created the video in 2008 with Coldplay. Chris Martin had written "Viva La Vida" about "Enjoy the Silence"—it was his favorite video, so he wrote the song about a king without a kingdom. I re-created the video with Chris dressed as a king. I got the same outfit as we did with Dave Gahan. Then the song became so big that EMI dismissed the video; they said I made Coldplay look like an indie band, and they wanted them to be seen as the biggest band in the world. They commissioned some American guy [Hype Williams] to make another video for the song. Oh, it's dreadful.

Chapter 32

"MARTHA WAS HEARTBROKEN"

MTV FINDS A NEW, MOUTHIER SQUAD OF VJs

BC, CBS, AND NBC HAD ALWAYS BEEN IN THE BUSI-
ness of making stars, but when a show became a hit, and the stars
were indispensible, the networks had to pay whatever it cost to keep
them. At MTV, the network was the star. Bands and videos were popular for a
few months, then dismissed as new ones came along. The one constant was the
VJs, and in order for the network to evolve and grow, executives felt they needed
not only new talent, but someone respectable. The second wave of VJs—notably
Downtown Julie Brown, a brash, foul-mouthed British fashion plate and disco
dancing champion, and Adam Curry, an opinionated, confident, fluffy-maned
American raised in the Netherlands—brought ample egos with them, creating
conflicts that hadn't previously existed at the network. For a news anchor, MTV
turned to *Rolling Stone* writer Kurt Loder, an unlikely choice. Loder was disdainful of MTV, which he made clear by shoehorning digs into his articles,
whether he was interviewing Bruce Springsteen or writing reviews of Cyndi
Lauper ("more than just MTV overnight wonder") or Huey Lewis and the News
("mere MTV fodder"). In February 1988, this opponent of MTV became an
employee of MTV, to the displeasure of VJs on their way out of the network, as
well as those who'd recently arrived.

STEVE LEEDS, MTV executive: Tom Freston once said to me, "VJs are like fruits
and vegetables—they're perishable, and you have to know when to toss them
out." So one of the not-fun things I had to do was find new VJs.

MARK GOODMAN: Bob Pittman was about keeping the VJs down. He didn't want us to get too famous, he didn't want us getting other TV shows, or films. He wouldn't allow it. There were huge fights about this. People were contacting us to do commercials and things—all the things you saw the second round of VJs doing—and Bob wouldn't permit it. Bob's thing was always, MTV is the star, and if MTV is big, you're big.

JOHN SYKES: When I got oversight of the VJs, I told Mark he had to get his hair cut. He had really big hair. I said, "Mark, big hair is over." And he said, "I can't cut my hair. It's my signature." So I said, "Go wherever you want, I'll pay, I'll fly you anywhere, just get your hair cut. You look like the guy from *Welcome Back, Kotter.*"

So one day, I'm in my office and I get a call from Mark: "John, I want you to talk to somebody." And this guy says, "Hello? This is José Eber." Jose Eber was famous, he was Cher's haircutter in Beverly Hills. And José says to me, "I cannot cut this man's hair. It is beautiful." I said, "Look, José, just do *something* with his hair." And he goes, "I will try, but you are ruining a masterpiece."

NINA BLACKWOOD: You could feel the corporate reins tightening. They sent us all to a voice coach, which was good. And they got more restrictive with what we could say on the air. We were no longer allowed to announce which VJ was coming up next. They didn't want us to become stars. We were approached for lucrative commercial and endorsement deals. But our contracts prohibited any outside work. We were signed exclusively.

Procter & Gamble wanted me for a skin product. Merv Griffin wanted to do a music show and was dead set on having me host. MTV gave us the go-ahead. We shot the pilot, then my manager got a call reversing the decision. I could have broken my contract, of course. But the thing was, we all loved MTV.

MARTHA QUINN: I was offered a gig at *The Today Show* to do music reporting, in addition to MTV. Bob Pittman wouldn't let me do it. I thought, *That's okay, MTV wants me to be theirs.* I thought I was going to be Mrs. MTV my whole life. He was the great Bob Pittman, the legendary Bob Pittman. Whatever Pittman wanted, I would do. Pittman *über alles.*

ALAN HUNTER: I had an offer to be in a movie called *Girls Just Want to Have Fun,* and Bob said, "Alan, I'm happy for you, but I don't think this is the right opportunity..." I was trying to interject: "*Er... Uh... Bob...*" He did not want the five originals to get too big for our britches. By this time, doing my job didn't make me nervous anymore. And one night, I definitely transgressed. I went out partying and used whatever stimuli I needed to stay awake. At about 7 A.M., I thought, *I've got to go on the air in an hour. I'll just stay up!* I wasn't even coming down at the time. The director saw I was sniffing and wheezing and sweating. I was practically incoherent. They kept saying, "You're doing great. Just read the teleprompter." We weren't working the hardest job ever. We weren't rocket scientists.

DOUG HERZOG, MTV executive: At that point, *MTV News* was basically the VJs ripping out articles from *Billboard* and reading them. Then it started evolving. Our genius promo department came up with the *MTV News* open, with the graphic and the bass line from Megadeth's "Peace Sells."

DAVE MUSTAINE: MTV scammed me. They never paid for using the bass line from "Peace Sells" as the *MTV News* theme. I wrote that music.

DOUG HERZOG: A lot of the more credible rock stars—the Springsteens and Bonos—did not want to talk to VJs. They had reps as lightweights. Martha was a good interviewer, but Alan was not a big music-head, J.J. was seen as past his prime, and Nina, who was totally into music, had an airhead rep. Linda Corradina, who succeeded me as news director, had the idea to bring in Kurt Loder, who was writing for *Rolling Stone*.

ALAN HUNTER: When I saw Kurt, I said, "Joined the enemy, did ya?"

NINA BLACKWOOD: Kurt Loder, who slimed us in *Rolling Stone*, took a job at MTV. There was no upward growth for the VJs. I was ready to leave, and then contract time came and my contract was not renewed. I wasn't going to renew it anyway. I took a deal from Paramount to do two shows, *Entertainment Tonight* and *Solid Gold*, and did a deal for a syndicated radio show as well. MTV had me under a gag order, and they put out a press release saying my exit was solely their decision. They said that they had declined to renew my contract and J.J.'s contract. That was painful.

KEN R. CLARK: Nina was the first to leave. That was shocking. Then J.J. was next.

JULIE BROWN, MTV VJ: They gave me a dressing room and I started putting my stuff in there. Unfortunately, Nina hadn't quite moved out. It was revolving doors—I walked in and she walked out.

KEN R. CLARK: Julie Brown hit that place like a ton of bricks. She had an enormous, enormous personality. She was a loaded cannon. You didn't know when it would go off or which direction it would be pointing. She was by far the most volatile VJ we ever had. At that point, I was manager of on-air talent. And the MTV executives' mandate to me was "Keep her the hell away from us."

ADAM CURRY: I grew up in Holland, where there were only two TV stations, because it was all government-run. I was hosting the music show on Sunday night, presenting videos, and half the country watched it. I was a national celebrity. All the rock stars wanted to come to Amsterdam, of course: "Yay! Hookers and blow!" I spoke fluent English, so I could have a conversation with Mick Jagger or Boy George. Somehow a tape of what I was doing got to Steve Leeds. He called and said, "Would you like to work for us in New York?" Maybe six weeks later, I was on a plane.

My first day was Halloween, 1987. From day one, I was a misfit in the organization. Carol Robinson, who ran the press department, arranged an interview with *TV Guide*. They go, "What do you think of Madonna?" And I go, "Well, she's kind of a bitch." Everyone at MTV shit themselves: "You can't say that about Madonna!" They were not happy with me. But I was really good at being a VJ. I was fired many, many times, and they'd hire me back the next day.

LOU STELLATO: The rumor was that Adam was paid a lot of money to come to America, because he was huge in Europe. He had a lot of confidence. I got along with Adam, but he could be a dick.

VAN TOFFLER: MTV needed to send the signal that we would evolve, and not grow old with our audience. And that meant new talent, new faces, and new music. We said good-bye to a lot of musicians who were relevant in the early '80s, like A Flock of Seagulls.

CAROLYNE HELDMAN, MTV VJ: I was the music director at a rock radio station in Aspen, Colorado, when I saw a full-page ad looking for MTV VJs. It said something like "Is rock n' roll your life?" I was like, "I don't know. Kinda? Maybe?" I didn't even have MTV at the time. When I got there, Nina and J.J. had already left. Alan, being from the South, was super open and nice. Mark was very big-brothery to me. Martha was not overtly friendly or welcoming. I started in September, and she was let go in January.

BETH McCARTHY: All the original VJs were getting fired. It was pretty traumatizing. Martha was heartbroken.

ALAN HUNTER: When they let Martha go, we all thought the sky was falling.

LOU STELLATO: Martha seemed to embody MTV. On her last segment, she said good-bye on camera, and Beth McCarthy was crying.

MARTHA QUINN: I was devastated when MTV let me go. I thought I was going to be there forever. Sometimes people ask if I can see myself having an opportunity like that again. That's like asking Buzz Aldrin, "Can you ever top being in the first moon landing?"

TABITHA SOREN: VJs came and went. I can't even remember half of them.

ALAN HUNTER: Mark and I said to each other, "Are we gonna be VJs for the rest of our lives?" I had another two years on my contract. Mark and I left of our own volition.

MARK GOODMAN: Alan and I quit on the same day. Most people think the original VJs were fired, but Alan and I chose to go. They had hired Kurt Loder, and I knew Kurt would be doing a lot of the interviews I'd been doing. Which annoyed me, because whenever Kurt reviewed a record for *Rolling Stone*, he would find a way to slag off MTV. But when he was offered a job, it was, "What? You're gonna pay me how much? I'm there!" And he never, ever, ever made great television.

DAVE SIRULNICK, MTV executive: I'd been a segment producer at CNN, and I went to MTV to help develop and create *The Week in Rock*. Adam Curry and Carolyne Heldman became the hosts of the show, but we wanted somebody who could really add to the level of credibility.

ADAM CURRY: I lived for hosting *The Week in Rock*. It was the *Entertainment Tonight* of MTV. But everyone said, "We need Kurt Loder, because he has credibility." "We need credibility on the channel." "Kurt brings us credibility." What the fuck? He wrote a book with Tina Turner—big deal. All of a sudden, this old dude with a bad haircut came in to host the show. It was insulting.

DAVE SIRULNICK: Kurt's audition was a little sweaty, but he had a confidence in himself. I asked him to talk about the first concert he went to. He said, "I've been to millions of concerts and can't remember the first one. That's not really who I am." And we're like, *We love him.* There were various attempts at giving him a wardrobe, and Kurt would say, "Get away from me. I don't want to deal with you people. Let me wear what I want to wear."

ALEX COLETTI: At his audition, Kurt Loder sweat so much, it was running down his shirt. I was like, "This poor guy is just not made for TV." And of course, Kurt outlived us all there. He was awesome to work with. On Fridays, he'd make margaritas for everyone.

ADAM CURRY: Kurt liked to drink. He would bring a blender to the studio and make margaritas. He'd have at least one margarita before he went on the air.

KEN R. CLARK: Adam and Julie were the biggest stars of the second wave of VJs, and they did not get along at all. They would insult each other and take jabs at one another on air. I remember Julie opening a fan letter, asking what she wanted for Christmas. She said with a smirk, "Maybe a blow-dryer, so I can look like Adam Curry." I tried to arrange the schedule so they wouldn't be in the studio at the same time. VJ life had become very different then. It was about sending limos as opposed to people showing up in sweatpants. Most of my time was spent negotiating with their managers and agents about whether or not, say, Julie's makeup artist could fly first class to Spring Break. That's what that era became about.

JULIE BROWN: Adam Curry didn't like me. I probably annoyed him. He's cool and calm, and I was a bit buzzy and wacky. You either get along or you don't. So Adam continued getting his hair done by his wife, and I continued disco dancing.

ADAM CURRY: The evil Julie Brown. Oh, I hated her. The crew hated her. She was never on time and was always bitching.

JULIE BROWN: I could understand if people thought I was a bitch. I'm very British and to-the-point. If I'm in Ralph's supermarket, I go to the front of the line.

I don't have time to wait! I made one wardrobe girl cry. When new clothes came in, I'd go, "Okay that's mine, that's mine, and that's mine." She got a little overwhelmed and started crying.

ALISON STEWART, MTV reporter: I was hired as an assistant to the VJs, putting Downtown Julie Brown's wigs in her dressing room, autographing pictures for her. She got a lot of mail from prisoners. She could be a diva. One time, she wanted me to keep her company at some event in Westchester. I thought, *Oh, this is a nice thing—older black woman asking a younger black woman to go someplace with you.* No. When I got there, she told me I had to stay in the car. I think I was there until 3 A.M. That was pretty rotten.

GEORGE BRADT: Julie Brown was a nightmare. She was always unprepared. The night before taping, VJs would get a script for the next day. To prepare, they'd need to read the script for an hour or two. She did nothing, ever. She'd show up at the studio, usually late, rifling though her script. We didn't have a lot of time to fuck around. It had to be really bad for us to say, "That sucked, do it again." When we did, she would get upset. And the crew would get pissed off, because it meant we were gonna be late for lunch break. One day we came out of a video, into a commercial break, and she said, "Take a Valium and we'll be back in a few minutes." She didn't understand why that was a problem.

ALISON STEWART: It's almost like she was born to be a VJ, almost like they made this network around her. Because she had a look and an attitude and she wasn't really afraid of much. I think she was older than she said she was. She kept saying, "Do I look okay? Do I look fine?" I always felt bad for her. "You look great. You've got a rocking body, why are you so insecure about aging?"

KEN R. CLARK: She called John Cannelli a cunt. I'll never forget that. "Oh shut up, you fucking cunt." Her favorite expression was "Kiss my clit." The control room would say, "Julie, you need to redo that segment." And Julie would say, "You can come out here and kiss my clit. I'm not redoing it." She could be horribly offensive, but she was also one of the most caring people you could ever meet.

ALEX COLETTI: Julie would flash people if the energy on set was lagging. And the energy was always lagging. I can't tell you how many times we saw her knickers.

LOU STELLATO: Julie Brown was a handful. Two handfuls. Oh my God. She could be so cunty. But I was lucky, because I could make her laugh. I would ask her to do things and if she wasn't in the mood, she would just tell me to kiss her clit.

BETH McCARTHY: Julie Brown was a piece of work. A lot of people did not get along with her. She would throw fits in her dressing room and refuse to come to the set. If she did not like you, she made your life a living hell. But she liked me. She always called me "Barf Bag," as a term of endearment.

Julie was in a tumultuous relationship with a jerk named Chris. He was also British. He was always, "I'm gonna open a nightclub," and she would fund his hobbies. And he cheated on her all the time. She caught him in bed with Mariah Carey once, before she had a career, before she hooked up with Tommy Mottola. He was a leech. And when Julie was having a problem at home, she would come in and take it out on everyone at work.

JULIE BROWN: When I came from England, I was engaged. That lasted a long time, like five years or so, until I broke up with my fiancé.

BETH McCARTHY: Julie and I would go to the China Club on the Upper West Side. There'd always be big athletes hitting on her. Lawrence Taylor, who played for the New York Giants, hit on her. She dated John Salley, the basketball player. She called me from his house one night because she was freaked out about how big he was. She's like, "I don't know what to do." I said, "Julie, I'm hanging up."

JULIE BROWN: I called my mum and said, "I've got a date with Billy Idol." And she said, "Well, you only live once." I don't kiss and tell, but I will say Billy makes a good cup of tea in the morning. I think I bored him—I'm not a rock n' roll chick, I don't party all night.

BILLY IDOL: We were quite serious for a while, but in the end, she married some German bloke. We just weren't 100 percent right for each other. I was a bit of a drug addict, and that was probably the height of my drug addiction. I wasn't fully committed to anything or anybody.

STEVE LEEDS: Julie was hired to be our diva. Lee Masters felt that VJs needed to be seen as stars. You couldn't have Julie Brown be a star on television and then see her flying coach. And mind you, we were now paying VJs a hell of a lot of money.

JULIE BROWN: Being on MTV, you never paid for anything. There were limos, first-class flights, clothes—it was the first time designers had a big outlet for fashion on TV, so things came in free, from jewelry to shoes to handbags. I was dressing in Gaultier, Dolce & Gabbana, Donna Karan, Nicole Miller. I had a crew of press people taking care of me, backstage passes to everything. MTV ruled. That's when life was good. Some of the other VJs struggled, apparently, but MTV did me the right way. I had a very nice contract. They did Adam Curry much better, I believe.

KEN R. CLARK: When MTV started, the VJs didn't have assistants, and they got paid $40,000 to $50,000 a year. Man, how that changed. Everybody ended up with stretch limos, their own makeup, some people had private security.

ADAM CURRY: I had a two-year contract when I came in: $150,000 the first year, $175,000 the second year. I was the highest-paid VJ. However, no one got first-class airfare. So I'd bitch and moan to get an upgrade: "I'm a star, man, I can't be flying in the back of the bus."

BETH McCARTHY: I never got along with Adam. Other people loved him. I found him arrogant. We butted heads a lot.

ADAM CURRY: The people in charge were idiots. They had no idea how television worked, no idea how cool it could have been. I felt so restricted. They would not let you say or do anything crazy or wacky or edgy. You couldn't make jokes about the artists, you couldn't do anything off key or a little blue. And there's a reason for it: The packaging of cable channels had just started, and a "basic package" came with MTV, regardless of where you were. We had broken through to 40 million households. That was huge. And it brought about a complete clampdown. You weren't allowed to say "VMAs"; you had to say "Video Music Awards." I called MTV "the big M." Nope, can't say that. I thought that was genius of me. After I did a take, the director would say, "That's truly funny, man, but you mentioned pubic hair. That's a burn." *Burn* meant we roll back the tape and tape over that segment. It was very annoying. It was television being made poorly, with a lot of politics involved.

When they fired me, it was usually about the hair. "Cut your hair." *No.* "Well, then we don't want you anymore." *Okay, fuck you.* I had big, poofy hair. With short hair, I look like a penis. And the hair made me famous.

KEN CLARK: The person behind Adam's hairstyle was his wife Patricia. She was a famous Dutch singer and television star. Patricia would wake up early and set his hair in hot rollers. She did his makeup, his wardrobe, his hair. And Adam's hair just kept getting bigger and bigger.

ALISON STEWART: On the back of Steve Leeds's door, there was a nude poster of Adam Curry's wife. Adam knew it was there—he may have given it to Steve.

STEVE LEEDS: Adam's wife, Patricia Paay, was a big celebrity in Holland. She was a singer, and she posed for *Playboy.* The poster was a blowup of her centerfold. Adam and his wife insisted I hang it there. He was proud of her and often brought celebrities to my office to show it off. The whole scenario made me very uncomfortable, and many times I asked Adam if I could remove it. I hung it on the back of my door, so most folks would never see it.

ADAM CURRY: The VJs worked all year, doing the interviews, and on the big night, the VMAs, we wouldn't even get tickets to sit in the crowd. Kurt Loder was doing the backstage interviews. Like, "Fuck you, you motherfucker." It was very annoying.

TOM HUNTER: Judy McGrath said, "Let's face it, viewers don't care about the VJs." So we stopped showing the VJs before commercial breaks. Judy, who'd been promoted to creative director, also took the VJs out of the studio and put them in all crazy locations. The VJs hated these new initiatives, of course. Julie Brown stormed out of a VJ meeting. I said, "We'll have a better meeting without her." Some people didn't want change.

CAROLYNE HELDMAN: Julie Brown thought of me as this odd bird who didn't care about fashion, or any of the things she cared about. She realized we had nothing in common, so she didn't pay me much mind.

KEN R. CLARK: Carolyne was a hippie. She didn't shave her pits, she didn't shave her legs, she had bad eyesight, and wore nerdy glasses. She liked frumpy, flowered dresses, and MTV wasn't having it. There was an ongoing battle to get her to shave her legs, to wear contacts, to look sexier.

CAROLYNE HELDMAN: I did an interview with Robert Plant once. I'm a huge Led Zeppelin fan; I still consider them to be the greatest rock band of all time. We were seated right next to each other on little bar stools, and the lighting was very stark. It was very intimate—our legs kept touching—and he flirted shamelessly with me. I held it together—I did a good interview with him—but I was smitten, just smitten with the man. After the interview, Robert said, "My manager and I are going to a comedy show tonight, would you like to join us?" And I said, "Oh sure, I'll go," as calmly as I could. So I got myself together and went to the comedy club, and there he was, as advertised, sitting at a table. I took a deep breath, walked over to his table, and said, "Hello Robert, how are you?" And he's like, "I'm sorry, dear, who are you?" That was a huge blow to my ego. But it was also a valuable lesson: These guys are pros. They know exactly what they're doing. They know just how to charm the hell out of a naive young journalist.

BETH McCARTHY: MTV loved that Carolyne was earthy and different, then all of a sudden, some executive saw her and said, "Why is she on the air?" She appeared on the air in shorts once, and they saw that she didn't shave her legs. They freaked out.

CAROLYNE HELDMAN: I wore shorts on the air once, and I got into big trouble. They sent me a memo afterwards: "You will never wear shorts again, you violated the terms of your contract."

STEVE LEEDS: They were like, "Steve, you've got to get rid of her." I have a master's degree from the Newhouse School of Public Communication at Syracuse, and I had to have a conversation with Carolyne Heldman about shaving her legs.

ADAM CURRY: Carolyne got fired because her legs were too fat. That was kind of fucked up. She was hired as the girl-next-door type, and she insisted on wearing shorts. Steve Leeds said, "Please wear long pants." She refused. And they fired her for her thunder thighs.

STEVE LEEDS: I was always on the lookout for new VJs. A production guy handed me a tape of Daisy Fuentes, a smoking-hot weather girl from the Spanish station in Newark. She became the host of a countdown show on Telemundo, called *MTV Internacional*, and I put her on MTV sporadically in the middle of the night. One afternoon, Judy McGrath walked into my office and said, "Who is this bimbo you have on in the middle of the night? Get her off. She's not connecting with the music." I said, "We're working on that." And eventually Daisy became a regular VJ on MTV. She filled the hot-babe slot.

Any time a VJ was giving me attitude, I would pull in this NYU college kid to fill in. I'd say, "Adam, you want to make $300? Can you be here this afternoon at four?" That was Adam Sandler. He was doing comedy around town, and he was a fill-in VJ. We also hired Dweezil Zappa, who was a smart-ass. One time, he came out of a hair band video where the hero gets hung, and said, "Kids, don't try that at home. Unless you're a Young Republican. Then it's okay." I told him, "You can't do that." Dweezil said, "Stop telling me what I can't do. Tom Freston said I can do whatever I want. And I'm not redoing it." So it went on the air. Judy McGrath said, "Steve, what the fuck? I'm getting angry phone calls." I said, "I asked him to redo it, and he refused." Well, that was the end of Dweezil.

We did a big search at colleges for VJs, all over the country. Kevin Seal's roommates at the University of Washington decided to audition, and Kevin went along as a goof. His audition was amazing. He had no intention of actually becoming a VJ.

KEVIN SEAL, MTV VJ: The University of Washington women's crew team was racing the Russian national crew team, and I was looking forward to attending that, but it was raining terribly that morning, so instead I went with my friends to the MTV tryout. I don't know what skills I brought to the job, besides frantic gesticulation, near-inchoate ravings, and a palpable distaste for Duran Duran. People assumed I was high all the time, probably because I was all squinty and raving. I think I may have represented the segment of viewers who were high, which was not inconsiderable.

KEN R. CLARK: Kevin was an engineering major, a total nerd. There was nothing rock n' roll about him. The story goes, he was tripping on mushrooms when he tried out.

KEVIN SEAL: People assumed that somebody behaving the way I did must be on drugs. But it's just a neurological disorder of some kind. Though I was a fan of 'shrooms, so it was not implausible. Not long after I got the job, I did half a hit of acid while we were taping in Philadelphia for Fourth of July weekend. That was the one time I was tripping on the air. I remember feeling it come on at Betsy Ross's house. I thought I could discover something, but it was just like, "This is Betsy Ross's house. *Rross. Rrrosss.*"

ALISON STEWART: Kevin Seal was sort of the accidental VJ. Once in a while, he'd spend the night in his dressing room. He seemed uncomfortable with the attention, like he thought it was a joke and he was in on the joke. Kind of like how Jimmy Kimmel is in on the joke of hosting a late night talk show.

KENNEDY: My favorite VJ was Kevin Seal. I loved his irreverence and wit, and his willingness to look silly. I've never heard a bad word uttered about the guy.

KEVIN SEAL: I was uncomfortable when people would see me on the street and hoot, "MTV, dude!" Since I was not, myself, MTV, I'd shrink from it. I was a fan of David Letterman. Also, as in the Eastern Bloc countries, there was a sense that there are certain things you're not allowed to say, so you would allude to them obliquely. In that tiny way, Vaclav Havel and I were both struggling within the system.

DAVE HOLMES: Like Kurt Loder, Kevin was brainy, but in a biting, sarcastic way. A little disdainful, like a David Letterman for the younger generation. In the late '80s, irony was suddenly the cool worldview. You had *Spy* magazine, you had Paul Rudnick, you had smart people writing snarky things. Now everybody's snarky; even socialites are snarky. It's tiresome, but at the time, it was fresh.

KEVIN SEAL: I'd take record albums and wing 'em down the hallways, see if I could get them to lodge in the ceiling tiles. Steve Leeds would patiently pull me aside to say, "How would you feel if you were Don Dokken, you came through this hallway, and you saw a broken album cover stuck in the ceiling, like trash?" I got the sense that money in the music business was corrupting, and the music was cynically devised. I'm thinking of Winger, immediately. I wrote long letters to fans who would chat to me about smirking at one video or another, and I'd write, "Forget about recorded music. These bands are just a product that's promoted to get your money. What you need to do is buy an accordion. Go stand on the street corner with your friends and do some clogging." I don't think I was smirking, actually. I looked at some old tapes recently, and I appeared as though

I was having a seizure, like I was about to leave language behind. I was fidgety. Almost everything else except the pay, I could have done without.

ALEX COLETTI: Kevin Seal was so much fun. One day he came to work with a box of caffeine pills and decided we should do an experiment. So we ate handfuls of pills and drank black coffee. I called him at 3 A.M.: "I'm still awake!" He's like, "Isn't it great?!"

KEVIN SEAL: Interviewing John Lydon was a high point. I loved the Sex Pistols, and he blew his nose on the stage floor. It's not often your heroes live up to your picture of them. And another time Exene, the singer in X, called me "a little shit." She had appeared in a movie I intended to see, but it was gone from the theater before I had time. I mentioned that, probably in an insulting way, though I meant to commiserate with her, and she said, "Well, he is a real little shit isn't he?" I loved X, so I was flummoxed. Steve Leeds pulled me aside, showed me the clip, and suggested that was the kind of thing we didn't want to have happen, whereas I thought, *No, that's the kind of thing I would like if I was watching.* It was good TV. But he had a different agenda.

ADAM CURRY: Kevin Seal would get on a tangent, and even though he knew it would never air, he'd go on for three minutes, and we'd be peeing our pants. He was a Bill Murray–like genius, but he didn't like what he was doing. He didn't understand show business.

KEVIN SEAL: For a while, Carolyne Heldman and I did the news at the *MTV News* desk. I did one show with no pants on. I'd seen TV anchors sitting at a desk, and assumed, *You'd do that with no pants, if you could.* And so I did. At the end, at that moment when in regular news shows they roll the credits and the two anchors pretend to talk to each other, Carolyne leaned over and said, "I can see your penis through your fly."

KEN R. CLARK: Kevin came to New York with nothing but a duffel bag, and he probably left the same away. I don't think he ever owned an alarm clock. I had to dispatch an intern to his apartment to wake him every morning, or he wouldn't show up. He never did research, he never prepped. But the reason he was so funny was that he just didn't care. He didn't want a career in television or music.

KEVIN SEAL: For a lot of people there, it was a career. You do it because it's your job, and maybe you'll get a raise or a bonus. But the people who thought MTV was the coolest thing in the world, I didn't drink that Kool-Aid. And then I didn't have a career either.

ALAN HUNTER: All the original VJs got pigeonholed. What were we going to do after MTV? A lot of times, we competed for the same jobs. One time, I showed up for a game-show pilot, and the script said MARK GOODMAN. "Oh, sorry, we gave you the wrong script."

Two years after I left MTV, I was cohosting a show called *Malibu Beach Party* with a sixteen-year-old Alyssa Milano, and we were doing most of the show in a hot tub. I thought, *This is either the great thing ever, or I've sunk really far.*

Chapter 33

"A TRUE TELEVISION NETWORK"

THE NEW BOSS ORDERS UP A RIOTOUS SHOW THAT FOREVER CHANGES THE NETWORK

HERE'S THE UPSIDE OF BUILDING A BUSINESS around a product you get for free: The profit margins are huge. And here's the downside: You don't control your own inventory. Years earlier, music stars had released two or even three albums a year, but now, because of videos, and the expansion of the record and concert industry, and the greater ease of international touring, the biggest acts routinely went three or four years between albums. In a year like 1984, full of great music, MTV's ratings were way up. But in other years, the network's core artists were inactive, and ratings went down.

Even in the first two years, MTV's schedule had other programs besides videos—Saturday-night concerts with the Police and Journey, the Sunday night shows *Liner Notes*, *Fast Forward*, and *MTV Extra!*, as well as movies like *Phantom of the Paradise* and *Reefer Madness*. After that came *The Cutting Edge* and *120 Minutes*, *Headbangers Ball*, and episodes of *The Monkees* or the British comedy *The Young Ones*.

But the MTV brand—the core of their huge business—was videos. Now key executives—most notably Tom Freston, Doug Herzog, and Judy McGrath—wondered if the network was big enough to untether itself from record labels and rock stars.

TOM HUNTER: My first official day at MTV was June 1, 1987, six days before Sumner Redstone bought the network. He won the takeover battle with Gorman and Elkes, and he got it on June 6. The company's name was pronounced

VEE-a-com. But Sumner Redstone said *VY-a-com,* so suddenly the entire world called it *VY-a-com.* We thought that was hysterical. He owned 85 percent of the stock, so he could call it whatever he wanted.

JOHN SYKES: Sumner Redstone said to Tom, "Stay with me and you're gonna be my guy." And it became Tom's place.

BOB PITTMAN: Around six months after I left MTV, Sumner Redstone called. He'd been buying stock in Viacom and wanted to take it over. I had a couple of meetings with him and gave my opinions of what was going on at the company. A little later, he asked if I could see him at the Carlyle Hotel. He says, "Listen, management told me they're going to walk out if I take over the company." So I called Freston and Gerry Laybourne, the head of Nickelodeon, and said, "You should come have dinner with Sumner." And Tom says, "Are you crazy? Viacom would fire me in a second if I met with Sumner." I said, "Look, here's the logic. Right now, you're the outsiders at Viacom. You're never going to be on the inside. But if you throw your lot in with Sumner, he'll owe you forever. You're going to have a lot of power." And so Tom and Gerry went to see Sumner and agreed to support him. Based on that, Sumner bought the company. And Tom Freston and Gerry Laybourne became the center of the empire.

TOM FRESTON: At first, the Viacom guys said MTV was an advertising-based business, and I didn't know anything about advertising. So they made me co-president with Bob Roganti. He was president of ad sales and operations, I was president of entertainment. Then there was a battle for control of Viacom, and Sumner Redstone took over in an LBO. He hired Frank Biondi, who had been head of HBO, to be CEO. We had breakfast at the Warwick Hotel in the summer of 1987. By the time I was finished, he says, "You're now CEO of MTV Networks. Go fire Roganti." I walked out of the Warwick, bouncing down the street.

If Sumner hadn't prevailed in his battle for Viacom, I don't think that MTV Networks would have gotten the financial resources that it needed to grow. Even though Sumner assumed a lot of debt to buy the company, he was eager to spend money to make money. He invested in programming. I don't know that the Terry Elkes regime would have been as generous. Elkes had an aura about him that said *The end is near.* Those guys thought that we had peaked. When Redstone took over, I thought, "Man, I don't know this guy, but he's *got to* be better than these guys we have."

JUDY McGRATH: When Bob Pittman left, it was unsettling. There was a period after that where we had copresidents, and a revolving door at the top. At different times it seemed like distribution was more important, and then advertising was more important. But Bob, John, Les, and Fred had already established the DNA of the place. The main rule was that there were no rules.

MARK PELLINGTON: Freston was the guy who'd come into your office and say, "Hey, what are you listening to?" and rifle through your albums.

RICK KRIM: Everybody will always love Tom. Until the day he left, the culture of MTV emanated from him. He was a music guy who believed in doing the right things for artists. The fact that he'd been at MTV from day one had resonance for almost everyone who worked there, even if they'd started ten days ago.

JON LANDAU: Tom Freston was the fucking best. If you were to call him and say, "Could you take a look at this video that we sent over there?," even though he was running the network and not programming it, you always got a straightforward response. I called him when he got fired [in 2006]. I said, "Tom, if there was ever a 'no good deed goes unpunished' moment . . ." I don't know Sumner Redstone, but my feeling is that he must have been jealous, because he was not a popular or well-loved guy. And people loved Tom.

ALLEN GRUBMAN: Tom Freston is the best-loved guy I've ever seen in the music business. People who worked for him loved him, and people at record companies loved him. Even in the heat of a negotiation, where it got hairy, nobody ever had a bad word about Tom.

ADAM CURRY: He took the subway to work, he didn't have a limo, and he really didn't know what the fuck was going on at the channel, which kind of made him cool. He always looked drunk. That's the kind of CEO MTV should have, a disheveled-hair-looking guy who was hanging out with Bono and all the superstars.

TABITHA SOREN: He's a genius, a good person, a colorful character. He's the reason there's MTV Asia, MTV China, MTV Europe—it's all Tom Freston.

CHIP RACHLIN: Freston was the most down-to-earth, unpretentious guy. In a movie, he'd be played by Ted Danson. I don't think any of us assumed he had the ambition to become the wealthy, wealthy man he became.

TOM FRESTON: MTV and Nickelodeon went from the smallest part of Viacom to the biggest. Back then, Sumner was learning the business from Frank Biondi and others. He was a theater operator. He'd sit through meetings for six, seven hours and not say a word. He was like, "If you make your numbers, we'll leave you alone."

Problem was, people started to feel they'd seen it all with regard to music videos. And this was a period when music wasn't especially vital in the culture. It became clearer and clearer to me and others that when you're programming ten three-minute programs every half hour, it's hard to grow ratings. Prior to MTV, no network had pursued a young audience. Then Fox came along and took aim at eighteen- to thirty-four-year-olds with cutting-edge scripted fare. And we saw that as a threat.

Doug Herzog, Judy McGrath, and I would talk about "What if MTV wasn't just about music?" We looked at *Rolling Stone*, which had repositioned itself to be more about popular culture—they had comedians and movie stars on the cover. We knew nothing about developing programming, and we couldn't afford to have stuff made somewhere else, so we came up with simple ideas. We did *The Week in Rock* and got into the news business. We had shows about movies. We ran old episodes of *The Monkees*. Eventually we had Cindy Crawford and *House of Style*. But the real breakthrough was a show called *Remote Control*.

TOM HUNTER: We'd gone from a 0.9 rating in 1983 to a 0.5 on some days. We were going like crap. A tenth of a ratings point was worth millions in revenue. Everyone still believed music videos could sustain the network, if only we could find the right balance and combination. Judy always said, "Music is our first name, and our first, second, and third priority." It was a great line, we all used it. But in reality, we were now in a multichannel universe. Barry Diller had launched Fox, so there was another channel on television that kids were noticing.

LEE MASTERS: I tried every single trick that had worked successfully for years in radio; I narrowed the music selection, I changed rotations, I changed the VJs. None of it worked.

I don't know what other people are telling you, but the idea to do long-form programming—and it's really strange to give them credit—the idea came from the ad sales department. The sales guys started pushing the idea internally that we needed to do shows. They didn't know what the shows should be about; they didn't have a clue.

TOM HUNTER: We batted around the idea of purchasing established network programs and rerunning them. Lee Masters became obsessed with the idea of running repeats of NFL football games. He was very attentive to research that said we were young, male, teen, and affluent. The other ideas were *Letterman* and *Saturday Night Live*. We thought we could cut up *SNL* episodes and sprinkle in videos. We played with all those ideas. And I give Judy McGrath a lot of credit. She said, "It doesn't make sense to take network programming and put it on cable. It doesn't have the integrity of authorship that we think our brand reflects. We should take what we have and change everything up."

LES GARLAND: Bob Pittman, John Sykes, and I had been against long-form programming. We were okay with non-music-video programming, so long as it had a music foundation or was in the spirit of MTV. We were doing countdown shows, and stunts like *Amuck in America,* where we sent some guys across America in vans. Nobody had ever done anything like that on TV. We made it wacky and sent some rock star to meet them in the middle of Texas. But we hadn't sold ourselves on the fact that music doesn't work on television. That's the line we'd never cross. This was music television. I'm sure if I had stayed, I would have been the last soldier still fighting to do music television.

DOUG HERZOG: The marching orders were specific: "We're going to do a dance show, a game show, and a news show." *The Week in Rock* was our weekly news wrap-up. *Club MTV* was the dance show. *Remote Control* was the game show. I embraced it. I thought it was the right time to become a true television network.

JUDY McGRATH: When *Remote Control* came on the air, people were ready to egg the building, because it wasn't music. But it began to position MTV as being about pop culture, in addition to music.

MIKE DUGAN, MTV writer: The MTV attitude was irreverent and a bit fed up with buttoned-down society. Judy was good as realizing that MTV was more than just playing videos—it was a lifestyle.

TOM HUNTER: We lived in a *TV Guide* world. People decided what to watch by looking at the programming grids in *TV Guide*. MTV had a slot in the grid, but all it said was "Music Videos." And the next hour it would say "Music Videos." And the next hour. *Remote Control* made us a TV network. It was the first time we acknowledged that we lived in a television universe and not in a music universe. People didn't turn off MTV and turn on the radio; they turned off MTV and put on *Married with Children.*

DOUG HERZOG: *Remote Control* was controversial within MTV. There was a lot of Sturm und Drang about whether we should be doing a show that wasn't about music. "What are we doing to the brand?" "This isn't what we set out to do." Yadda yadda. Doing a game show on MTV was heresy. Game shows were *The Price Is Right.* Of the three new shows we started, *Remote Control* was the most transformative.

LEE MASTERS: *Remote Control* was extremely controversial. The research department was adamant that we couldn't do a game show. *Adamant.* They would ask focus groups, "Should MTV do a game show?" And everybody would answer, "No. That's stupid." When Doug Herzog assigned Joe Davola to develop the show, Davola said, "You're gonna ruin my fucking career." Those were his exact words. And of course, it went on to make his career.

JOE DAVOLA: One day, Doug Herzog brought me in with two other producers and said, "You guys are in charge of putting new shows together." I was told to figure out a game show. *Remote Control* was a standard game show, with the MTV attitude.

MIKE ARMSTRONG, MTV staff: Doug Herzog hired me and John Ten Eyck as writers. I was completely unqualified for a job on a game show. I'd been a speechwriter for Dan Hill, who was ombudsman for the province of Ontario. But Doug and I had gone to school together, and he knew Ten Eyck and I were both half-crazy, and we probably embodied the spirit of MTV at the time.

It was strange, because offices are usually filled with adults, but this place was overrun with kids. I kept thinking, *Who's running this thing? Where are the authority figures?* A writers' meeting would devolve into lunch, or watching *Club MTV* and discussing which dancer you lusted after. Given how unprofessional we were, it's a miracle the show ever got on the air. From the writers to the cameramen, it seemed less professional than a college production. Everybody was having so much fun that the work was an afterthought.

My impression was that people inside the network were rooting against us. They were predicting, first, that it would be a big bomb, and second, that when it bombed, it would be a good thing for MTV, because it had to stay true to its original purpose, and we were a bad precedent. Before the show went on the air, all the writers were saying, "Who knows if this is gonna work?" We felt like the best thing about the show was giving a *fuck-you* to the people at MTV who didn't think it was a good idea. That was our motivating factor. None of us had much respect for traditional television. We'd grown up on it, and we were addicted to it, and now it was time to make fun of it, to attack it. That was *Remote Control*'s job.

DOUG HERZOG: One reason we did a game show was because Nickelodeon had put on *Double Dare*, which was a huge success. And the Nickelodeon people were smug about it. We really wanted to one-up them. And we were very pleased when we did.

TOM FRESTON: *Remote Control* was a cheeky send-up of a game show. Ken Ober, a comedian, hosted. It cost $15,000 an episode, and became an instant hit.

DOUG HERZOG: Danny Bonaduce auditioned to host *Remote Control*. He almost got the gig. We offered it to Ben Stiller, who auditioned and then turned it down.

COLIN QUINN, comedian: Ken Ober and I were embarrassed to be on a game show. I was this hip comedian, and we were afraid our comedian friends were going to look down on us, because *Brady Bunch* jokes were for hacks. We thought that was beneath us. From day one, I had an attitude.

DENIS LEARY, comedian/actor: Anybody who knows the standup world from that time will tell you, Colin and Kenny were absolute originals. On *Remote Control* they were flying by the seat of their pants, and they were brilliant at it. Smart people could watch for the banter between those two guys, and dumb people could watch it because they thought it was just a stupid game show.

JOE DAVOLA: Ken and Colin weren't sure what this was gonna do for their careers, and they were bitching a bit during the first season.

MIKE DUGAN: They started to change their tune once women were throwing pussy at them. Then they said, "You know, it's not so bad, being on a game show."

COLIN QUINN: One night I went through a particularly bad rant with Kenny. I was like, "This show is fucking bullshit, man." The next day we were taping a show, and a girl came over and took out her tits. A beautiful girl. She said, "Will you sign my tit?" Kenny was signing somebody else's ass. He looks over at me and says, "What do you have to say now?"

BETH McCARTHY: I was an AD on *Remote Control.* MTV was non-Guild, so I was directing when I was twenty-five years old. In the real world, I would never be directing at age twenty-five. We got paid no money and worked ridiculous hours. The studio started at eight-thirty in the morning and there were days that we were there until midnight. But we were all there together, we were all friends, and we learned a ton.

COLIN QUINN: The money was horrible. I got $100 a show to start. I'd already made $4,000 for a Burger King commercial, so I was like, "These motherfuckers are ripping me off," which of course they were. I was angry the whole time. When I read ad copy, I was obnoxious and insulting, I'd mispronounce the names of advertisers: Chrysalis, Mitsubishi. The companies were complaining: "He's insulting our product." I was like, "What am I, a fucking shill for your product? Fuck you." MTV wanted to fire me. Doug Herzog was like, "This guy is a prick." I wanted out from day one. We didn't give a fuck, which the kids loved, of course.

MICHAEL IAN BLACK: *Remote Control* was a comedy show much more than a game show. It was an excuse to do jokes. *Remote Control* was deconstructing game shows in the way that David Letterman, in the early days, was deconstructing talk shows. It was kind of a meta exploration of the form. Now everything is so meta and self-referential, but back then, it wasn't. There was nothing else like it on television.

As a viewer, MTV felt like a place that fostered an anarchic spirit, run by people who maybe didn't know what they were doing. In a good way. It was a place to throw shit against the wall, similar to what CollegeHumor does now, or Funny or Die.

JOE DAVOLA: We knew Colin was a horrible singer, so we started a bit called "Singalong with Colin."

COLIN QUINN: I had an easy job. I just had to smoke cigarettes, do "Singalong with Colin," and be my miserable self.

MIKE DUGAN: Did Colin talk to you about how much he showed people his penis? Oh, he loved showing people his dick. It came out at all sorts of occasions. We were having dinner one time at a fairly fancy restaurant, and he said, "I'll take it out right now." And he actually put his dick in Lauren Corrao's chocolate mousse. It was just an average-sized dick. I mean, for an Irishman, it wasn't bad. I probably saw it twenty times. We did a Christmas show, and I played the Three Wise Men, along with two of the writers, Chris Kresti and John Ten Eyck. Kresti was strapped into one of the chairs and he couldn't move until the stagehands removed him. Colin told the stagehands to leave him in the chair, and he took that opportunity to take out his dick and slap it against poor Kresti's head while he was strapped into a chair, upside down. There were no adults whatsoever. Colin would drum with his dick against the metal locker to a beat, and say, "Hey, Kari, guess what song I'm playing."

COLIN QUINN: Kids would come up to us on the street, as young as eleven years old, screaming. Kenny came to me two months after we shot the first bunch of episodes, and he goes, "We are fucking famous." We went to Spring Break at Daytona Beach in '88, and one night we went to a strip club. The strippers ran from their customers, paying customers, and surrounded us.

KARI WUHRER, actress: I used to roller-skate from my apartment on East Eighty-second Street to the studio at Seventy-fourth Street. Ken and Colin walked me to the back door, where there was a huge group of fans waiting. They held the crowd back so I could get a head start. It was awesome. MTV sent us to Puerto

Rico for a media event, and as we drove through San Juan, kids attacked the limo. It was like Elvis.

COLIN QUINN: I smoked on the first season, then they said I couldn't anymore, which was fine. I had kids come up to me and say, "You're the reason I started smoking."

MIKE DUGAN: After the first season, we started getting really ridiculous. We wanted to do something called "Roll the Pope," and our legal department told us we couldn't, because there's only one pope, and it's offensive to people, and who knows, the pope could sue. So we turned it into "Beat the Bishop." We had a guy come out dressed like a bishop, he would run around the audience, and contestants had to figure out a math problem before he got back. "Beat the Bishop" was a euphemism for jerking off, which standards and practices apparently didn't know.

We got tired of doing "Beat the Bishop," so we did "Beat the Bologna." One of the writers dressed in a giant bologna suit, and he'd run through the studio while audience members threw mayonnaise on him. By the way, I don't know if I mentioned this before: We didn't know how to make television. Amateurism was part of the appeal of the show.

KARI WUHRER: I was a born-again Christian, getting baptized in the Holy Spirit and speaking in tongues. My audition for *Remote Control* was April 28, 1988—my twenty-first birthday. I wasn't watching MTV because I was living a sort of biblical life. I talked to Ken and Colin about Jesus. Once I started at MTV, that lasted six months.

I was wearing a sherbet-colored spandex tank top every day, without a bra. Not that I needed one. Even though I didn't have a voluptuous body, I unabashedly used it. I didn't really understand the power of it at that point.

What was I? I was fluff. My career launched on fluff, and of course, it dissipated in the wind.

COLIN QUINN: Every guy was obsessed with Kari. She brought sex appeal to *Remote Control*. To this day, everyone talks about her stomach. She had great abs.

MIKE DUGAN: Basically, Kari was there to keep the boys in the audience interested.

KARI WUHRER: I got paid about $10,000 a season. If you worked for MTV, you were MTV's bitch. This is before they committed to making any one person a star. Now everybody who appears on MTV has their own conglomerate.

BETH McCARTHY: I think there was a fistfight between two girls in the talent department who were both dating Ken Ober.

KARI WUHRER: Oh my god, women were crazy for Ken and Colin. Ken got most of it. He had an on-off girlfriend, so Colin picked up the slack.

MIKE ARMSTRONG: I became best friends with Ken, and he remained my closest friend. He turned into a rock star. For a short period, Ken and Colin were Elvis and Jim Morrison, only on a smaller scale and to a specific audience of college kids. And Ken took advantage of the situation. He had a great girlfriend, Sue Kolinsky, a New York comic, and I don't think his hosting gig helped their relationship in any way, to put it mildly.

KARI WUHRER: I kissed Ken once. We were drunk, we went back to his apartment, and I kissed him. The *Deliverance* theme played in my head.

MIKE DUGAN: The story I heard is that Kari, Ken, and Colin were in a hot tub together, and she kissed them both. I heard that from Kenny.

COLIN QUINN: There was always some sex going on. Sometimes we'd have sex between tapings. It was crazy. There were always girls coming over to us. I used to tell girls, "I need to see your ID, I'm sorry."

JOE DAVOLA: There was a bet about who would come back after work and have sex on the Craftmatic bed in the middle of the stage. I think maybe Kenny won.

MIKE DUGAN: As far as I know, Davola's the only one who had sex on the Craftmatic bed. After we found out about that, nobody else wanted to have sex on the Craftmatic bed. How did I hear about it? From Joe. He was very proud of it.

DOUG HERZOG: I went to the Comic Strip on the Upper East Side, to see a comedian named Rhonda Shear. Adam Sandler was one of the opening acts. He was still a student at NYU. He got onstage in a T-shirt, sweatpants, and sneakers. He was incredibly charming and funny. This was the time of the Beastie Boys, and

I thought he was part Beastie Boy. My favorite bit, which he did for years, was "Here's my imitation of Wilt Chamberlain's teammates the night he scored 100 points: 'Hey, Wilt! I'm open!'"

MIKE ARMSTRONG: In the second season, they made me head writer. Doug sent Sandler to my office, He was doing a character that he wanted to do on the show, called Stud Boy, and in a thick Spanish accent, he was seducing an old woman. I didn't get it, and I wasn't sure anybody would laugh at it. Then I stood off to the side in awe as I saw kids go nuts for him.

LAUREN CORRAO, MTV producer: When we took *Remote Control* on tour to colleges, guys were screaming Sandler's and Colin's names. They were quoting lines from Sandler.

COLIN QUINN: Sandler had a character called Bossy Boy—he'd wear a fast-food uniform and they'd put freckles on his face with an orange Magic Marker. It was deconstructionist comedy, way before anybody else, like he was mocking the idea of doing a character, but he'd still commit to it. It was absurdist, Ionesco humor. It was so fucking funny it made me cry. I couldn't help it.

KARI WUHRER: I thought Sandler was an idiot. An annoying, skinny twerp. And I thought, "Colin's an amazing comedian, why's he laughing at this guy?"

COLIN QUINN: We all knew Denis Leary. We brought him on the show as my brother, and the two of us fought every time he came out. We were two guys in their twenties, like, "Hey, fuck you. You're not gonna get the better of me."

DENIS LEARY: They kept saying, "We want you to play some characters on the show." And I was like, *Yeah, whatever.* I don't think Colin was a big fan of the show, but it made him and Ober big stars, kind of overnight. They hit the jackpot, and I was a broke, out-of-work actor and a barely working comedian, so the phone call was very welcome. They said, "You're gonna play Andy Warhol, Keith Richards, and Quinn's brother." I was like, *I don't care who I'm playing.* I needed the money.

KARI WUHRER: We shot down in Florida during the third season, and Britny Fox were on the show as contestants. It was the height of hair metal. I hit on their singer. The next thing I knew, I was getting tattooed and I was on tour with them. He was so dumb, my father called him "the house plant." As soon as the tour ended, I never heard from him again.

JOE DAVOLA: When the show ended, ratings were still high. But MTV had this philosophy of "We'll die if we don't keep changing." So after three years, they took it off the air.

COLIN QUINN: By then, it was time to go. We did so many shows, so many *Brady Bunch* questions. I was like, "Shit, didn't we ask that last season?"

MIKE DUGAN: MTV wanted to keep doing new things. That thinking has changed; now the mind-set is "If it's working, we're not changing it." *Jersey Shore* will stay on the air until it stops getting ratings.

MIKE ARMSTRONG: After *Remote Control*, Ken had mixed success. He did a sitcom called *Parenthood*, and he hosted a few other game shows. *Remote Control* remained his calling card. He was a journeyman comic and had a very dark sense of humor. One of his funniest lines was on the twenty-fifth anniversary of the JFK assassination. He popped his head into my office and said, "You know who was really responsible for that? The guy at the airport who bumped him up to a convertible." I talked about this at his memorial.

Ken had some bad habits that he had to give up. And he did. He stopped doing drugs, he gave up drinking, he lived a straight life. But he'd had some surgery involving his spine, and then he had two cornea transplants, because the first one didn't take. He joked about how the wheels were starting to come off. But I talked to him almost every day, and it didn't seem like he was in bad health. The last time I called him, he said he had a horrible headache and was really in pain. The next day, November 14, 2009, I got a call that he'd died. It was determined he'd had a heart attack. We had a great memorial for him, with everyone who ever knew him, it seemed; Ray Romano, Adam Sandler, and Larry David were there.

DAVE HOLMES: Everything is snarky now, everything is pop culture–based now. But pre–*Remote Control*, it wasn't cool to know all the spin-off shows from *Happy Days*. That meant you were strange.

DOUG HERZOG: Michael Dugan and Joe Davola are two lifelong friends of mine. We had the time of our lives making *Remote Control.*

TOM FRESTON: *Remote Control* stabilized our ratings. And it was a turning point. The idea of a game show on MTV would have been anathema five years earlier. When we had shows, we got better ratings.

DOUG HERZOG: There were still a lot of music videos on the channel. It wasn't the MTV you know today. But the naysayers either left or shut up.

Chapter 34

"THAT'S WHAT HYPE CAN DO TO YOU"

CLUB MTV LAUNCHES THE "UPSKIRT SHOT" AND A POP SCANDAL

DISCO NEVER DIED—IT HID, MUTATED, AND RETURNED. The era of hair metal was also a gala period for dance music, which fulfilled MTV's need—dating back to Michael Jackson—for vivid, fast-stepping videos. By the summer of 1987, dance music had earned its own daily show, *Club MTV,* guided by a pervy director who shot dancers, male and female, like they were strippers. The show thrived not only due to its displays of gyrating flesh, but also as a measure of what was topping the charts. Paula Abdul became the breakout star of 1989, despite a flimsy singing voice, because she was an expert dancer (and was also willing to duet with a cartoon feline who "rapped," MC Scat Kat). And in 1990, *Forbes* reported, the highest-paid act in music was New Kids on the Block thanks to sales of lunch boxes and dolls and a Saturday-morning cartoon.

No act was more silly than Milli Vanilli, a name that has become synonymous with fraud. The music was created by Frank Farian, a German producer in his mid-forties who'd had success across Europe with the disco group Boney M. His first U.S. success came with "Girl You Know It's True," which was sung by generic American session singers living in Germany. The success of "Girl" and subsequent Milli Vanilli singles surprised Farian, who unexpectedly needed the nonexistent "group" to perform in clubs and on TV. He assigned the job—possibly under duress—to Fab Morvan and Rob Pilatus, whose dancing had made them minor celebrities in Munich. The fraud deepened as the album sold 7 million copies in the U.S., "and then," Farian said, "it was too late." After he admitted the Milli Vanilli hoax in November 1990, he predicted, "in five or ten years, Rob will see it wasn't so bad. Then he'll be thankful." It didn't work out that way. Less than eight years later, Rob—who, since Milli Vanilli was exposed, had made multiple suicide attempts, gone to prison, and been estranged from Fab—died of a drug overdose in a hotel room. His death was ruled accidental, though Fab has his doubts about the official cause of death.

JULIE BROWN: A lot of great dance music was popping up: Janet Jackson's *Rhythm Nation*, Cameo, Taylor Dayne, Jody Watley. MTV took the dance-music niche and created *Club MTV*. It was a hip-hop, rocking, dance, nonstop, energizing show. It became a phenomenon, didn't it?

TOM HUNTER: *Club MTV* was *American Bandstand* with dance music and hot girls. It got great ratings, but just as important, it showed people we weren't merely a hair band channel. I was hell-bent for leather to try to defeat that notion.

JULIE BROWN: We shot *Club MTV* two days a month and did between fifteen and nineteen shows in a weekend. I went out with the crew to choose dancers for the show. I chose beautiful girls and great-looking guys. The boys had their shirts off, the girls had their skirts short and tight, and they danced on top of podiums, so the cameramen could shoot up to the dancers, and make it hot, but not disgusting. I always wore two pairs of underwear, just in case the camera took a slight detour in the wrong direction.

KEN R. CLARK: Julie would come out of her dressing room in those outrageous outfits and say, "Can you see my cunt through this thing?"

LOU STELLATO: We would shoot fifteen shows in two days, at the Palladium in New York, and then they would run the hell out of those fifteen shows. One of the dancers was Camille Donatacci, who ended up being Mrs. Kelsey Grammer.

CAMILLE GRAMMER: When I tried out for *Club MTV*, I was nineteen years old, going to college, and working as a dental assistant. I was on *Club MTV* from the first episode to the very end. The pay was $35 a day. That barely covered parking and lunch. We basically did it for free. We would get to the Palladium at nine o'clock in the morning and we would dance until nine o'clock at night. MTV would always say to us, "This is great exposure for you."

BETH McCARTHY: I was in Tampa with Ted Demme and Colin Quinn for one of our Super Bowl shoots. They thought it would be hilarious to take me to a strip club. I'm like, "I'm not going." So they took me through what I thought was the back door of a club, and it ended up being a strip club called the Dollhouse. All of a sudden I hear, "Hi, Beth!" And there's one of the strippers waving at me. She was an ex–*Club MTV* dancer. The guys fell down laughing.

MIKE ARMSTRONG: There was a horrific incident when they were taking the *Club MTV* dancers by bus to Daytona for Spring Break. As they approached a toll-booth near Baltimore, someone was trying to lower the shade, and the bus driver got distracted and plowed into cars at sixty miles per hour. People were killed. It was on the news. At the end of the day, a friend of mine who was on the bus approached two *Club MTV* dancers and he overheard one say to the other, "After all we've been through today, your hair looks great." I've been telling that story for twenty-three years now.

ALEX COLETTI: Not only did I segment produce on *Club MTV*, I performed on *Club MTV*. There was a group of people from MTV—me, the producer Bruce Gilmer, and Troi from the mailroom, who later became Star from the radio show *Star and Buc Wild*—who played various instruments. When artists would come and lip-sync on *Club MTV*, and they couldn't afford a band to pretend to play behind them, we'd back them up. My brother played percussion. We backed up Roxette, Robbie Nevil, Rick Astley. I mimed a great guitar solo in Astley's "It Would Take a Strong, Strong Man."

LOU STELLATO: I was very involved in *Club MTV*. I was Julie's floor producer. I wrote the scripts for Julie. Yes, there were scripts for *Club MTV*.

BETH McCARTHY: I still see one of the dancers from *Club MTV*, Laura B, because she's now Tina Fey's stand-in on *30 Rock*.

CAMILLE GRAMMER: At the end of the first year of *Club MTV*, I had a breast augmentation. I came back for season two and everybody was like, "Huh! Wow!" I don't know if I got more camera time, but I definitely got a lot of fan mail.

BETH McCARTHY: Camille was a pretty girl who started doing stuff to herself that made her not as pretty. I had a problem with her because I didn't like the way she treated my friend Milt. Milt was a director at MTV. Camille was friends with Milt, and when she didn't have a boyfriend, she would date him a little bit. Except that he took it to mean they were totally together.

ALEX COLETTI: I knew Camille very well. She used to date Milt Lage. Milt and I went to London to do the Oasis *Unplugged* in 1996, and we had adjoining hotel rooms. We turned on a baseball game, and there was a shot of Camille and Kelsey Grammer at the game. That's when he found out they were dating.

LOU STELLATO: Milt Lage invented the *Club MTV* upskirt shot.

CAMILLE GRAMMER: The cameramen knew what they were doing. The girls wore miniskirts, and then we realized it would be a good idea for us to wear bike shorts underneath, for those upskirt camera angles.

LOU STELLATO: For some reason, they booked the Dead Milkmen to perform on *Club MTV*. And the band didn't take their performance seriously. During the interview they handcuffed Julie, either to a mic stand or to one of the guys in the band. She tried to keep it together, but it got ugly. And when we faded, she ran back to her dressing room. They were cracking up in the truck as it was happening. She was on the stairwell at the Palladium, with snot running down her nose, saying, "I can't fucking believe it!"

JULIE BROWN: The Dead Milkmen handcuffed me. I got a bit pissed about that.

DEBBIE GIBSON: Everyone at my school watched *Club MTV*. I wanted to be on that show. But one thing I never liked; they made you lip-sync. I was more petrified of lip-syncing than singing live, because if you messed up live or your voice sounded edgy, so what? But if you're lip-syncing and you forgot a riff, then you looked like an idiot. Then you're Milli Vanilli. And I was already in a genre people didn't seriously.

FAB MORVAN, Milli Vanilli: Milli Vanilli made dancing a focal point in our videos. We didn't have much budget, right? We didn't have access to those top directors in Germany, we didn't even have a stylist. I did all the choreography. Because when we did "Girl You Know It's True," the first video, no one thought it would become so successful. You can see the difference in our third and fourth videos, "Girl I'm Gonna Miss You" and "Blame It On the Rain"; we were selling records, so those videos had a little more like a real story.

ABBEY KONOWITCH: Steve Leeds and I were at the *Club MTV* tour date [July 21, 1989] when Milli Vanilli got busted for lip-syncing. I thought they were charismatic onstage; it was like a gymnastics show. Steve brought it to my attention that they weren't singing. They would lip-sync, and between verses they'd say something like, "Yeah man! All right!" They could barely speak English! It was hysterical!

BETH McCARTHY: The first time Milli Vanilli came in to be interviewed, we were all thinking, *There's no way these two guys are singing those songs. They don't even speak English.*

CLIVE DAVIS: Milli Vanilli was the brainchild of Frank Farian, a German record producer. He was probably the number one record man in Europe. When Arista licensed the record for U.S. release, I had never seen the group. I didn't even meet them until they'd sold 2 million records in America. Frank Farian furnished us with the videos. We had no idea Rob and Fab didn't sing on the record. We were as shocked as the public. It turned out they were paid union scale; they weren't even getting royalties. Farian took the position that this was done all the time in Europe.

FAB MORVAN: My response to that is very simple: If a pin drops in the company, Clive Davis will know about it. That's all I have to say.

KIM MARLOWE, manager: The singers Frank Farian used were very unattractive, older—one of them was fat, one was skinny. I don't mean to disrespect them, but they didn't have stage presence. They had decent voices, but you still have to be a great performer, you have to be able to rip up those stages and control an audience. You're either a star, or you're not a star. Rob and Fab *were* stars. They had a great look and a great image.

Frank Farian is a very talented producer, but he is an unbelievably despicable human being, period. Because he gets young talent, signs them to contracts, and then gives them a small amount of advance. Rob and Fab didn't sign a lip-syncing deal. He brought them back many months later and told them what they were gonna do. "And if you don't, you have to pay the money back."

FAB MORVAN: We were not hired, we were trapped. You sign a recording contract with a big producer, and you get your little advance money. "Cool, we're gonna get some food, some clothes, take care of the trademark—the hair." Then he said, "You have to lip-sync. If you want to get out of the contract, pay us back all the money we paid you." And at this point, what can we do? The only way we can repay the debt is to work, to do what they asked us to do.

So we do it, and then you get addicted to the lifestyle, to being a rock star. Who doesn't want to be a rock star? But in the end, when the party's gone and you're all alone, you face the reality: "Damn, I didn't sing on the records." And that hurts. That's one of the reasons we ended up hanging out with the night. You know, sex, drugs, and alcohol gets down in the night. The night is your best friend, because you want to escape the pressure, and once you start selling more and more records, more is demanded from you. You have to make sure you hide this very heavy secret.

I think we grossed $250 million. Out of that, we got pretty much nothing.

STEVE LEEDS: The track they were lip-syncing to skipped. They freaked out, threw their mics down—BOOM!—and ran offstage to their tour bus. Julie Brown said, "Holy shit, what are we going to do? We've got to fix this." I went back to their bus with Julie and she convinced them to go back onstage. Two dates later, the same thing happened.

PAULA ABDUL: I headlined the *Club MTV* tour with Milli Vanilli—they played right before me. "Girl You Know It's True" came on in the dressing room, and all of a sudden we heard, "Girl you know it's—girl you know it's—girl you know it's . . ." Everyone jerked to a halt, like, "Oh my god. *Oh* my god." Of course, we knew they used backing tracks, but lots of acts, myself included, sang along to backing tracks during parts of their shows. And we'd heard whispers that maybe they didn't sing all the vocal parts on their album. But we didn't know they weren't singing *at all*.

The next thing you know, they're getting booed, and they run offstage and lock themselves in their trailer. Downtown Julie Brown had to bang on their door for them to come out and get back onstage. To their credit, they went back out. But word spread pretty fast after that. I felt bad for them. I mean, how do you recover from that?

KIM MARLOWE: If you've seen the clip, Rob ran off the stage. Fab did not, until he finally went, "Fuck, he ain't coming back, I've gotta go get him."

JULIE BROWN: I was backstage in my trailer, in the bathroom to be honest with you, and someone knocked and said, "You've got to get onstage, the track is stuck." It kept repeating "Girl you know it's—girl you know it's—girl you know it's . . ." Quite a few artists at the time were lip-syncing, and the boys were caught with their pants down. But who's to blame, really? Is it the record company? Is it the producers? Before that moment, they did a great job of selling it.

It was difficult to calm them down—especially Rob, God rest his soul. He worked so hard at pretending to be a superstar, and it hit him harder than it should have, and yeah, he lost his life. That's what hype can do to you.

I didn't know they were lip-syncing and I didn't care. There were all these songs that were done by pseudo people: "It's Raining Men" by the Weather Girls, and Black Box.

BILLY JOEL: Milli Vanilli were *crucified* for not singing in concert. But most people knew them only through their videos, and *everybody* lip-syncs in their videos. I guess Milli Vanilli died for our sins.

ARSENIO HALL: When it all blew up, I did a joke in my monologue: I sang, "Girl, you know it's true / Ooh, ooh, ooh, you are through."

KIM MARLOWE: The VH1 *Behind the Music* episode made it seem like that show was their downfall, but that's a fabrication. They went on to win the Grammy after that. Their downfall was Frank Farian announcing, "They didn't sing," then leaving Rob and Fab bleeding in the streets. He's partly responsible for Rob's death, in my opinion.

Rob and Fab couldn't take it anymore and were tired of living a lie, feeling like shit, and making no money while everybody else got rich, then constantly wondering who was gonna tell on them. So they decided, "Let's go ahead and destroy it so we can get out of this thing that makes us want to kill ourselves." They wouldn't continue on with the second Milli Vanilli record.

FAB MORVAN: Rob is dead as a result of excess, acquired via the rock-star life. I'd known Rob Pilatus for years. We lived together, traveled together, shared the same hotel room at first. I know Rob's habits. The minute Rob got to a hotel room, he would destroy the room—open his bags and throw his things everywhere, all right? Rob was found in a room that was clean. No mess. That makes no sense. I'm not saying he was murdered. I'm just saying it's shady.

To this day, I'm the poster boy for lip-syncing. But we didn't invent it. And what I did back then is no different from what people are doing today. With the audio tools we have, Auto-Tune and Melodyne, you can take anybody off the street and make him sound like a beautiful bird. We can enhance someone's performance, enhance someone's looks, we can enhance *everything*, and create something that *appears* to be, but is *not*.

For years, everyone tried to crucify me and make me suffer for "not being authentic," and I'm like, "You're making me laugh now." There's so many people that came before me, and that came after me, and that will come after and after and after. Authenticity? No, it's about entertainment.

Chapter 35

"THE FIRST TIME
I SMELLED FREEBASE"

MTV PARTIES DOWN AT SPRING BREAK

ADAM CURRY: MTV needed to get alcohol companies to advertise on the network. It was a big deal. We needed beer; we were doing Skittles. A lot of Skittles. That's how Spring Break was born. It's not like someone said, "Hey, let's go film Spring Break." It was like, "How do we get Budweiser on the network? Let's go to where Budweiser is." And Budweiser was at Spring Break. That was a turning point for MTV ad sales—once we had the beer market, because that's where all the money was.

JOE DAVOLA: I produced the first Spring Break in Florida. We were live eight to nine hours a day, so we had a Best Body contest, this contest, that contest. We were usually staying at a crap-hole hotel, going to work every day, and we'd go out every night. Once we traveled outside New York, we really saw the power of MTV. People went nuts.

BETH McCARTHY: Beginning in 1986, I went to Spring Break for nine years straight. It was horrific. Everything was disgusting. We'd work all day and night, and then walk back to a disgusting sleazebag hotel at 1 A.M. It was hilarious, but *ugh*. Our executives would flash their MTV IDs and whore around with college girls.

JOE DAVOLA: During commercial breaks, we'd throw T-shirts to the crowd and tell girls to take their tops off. Bars around the country had satellite TV, so they didn't get the commercials, just the live feed. And we started getting complaints about nudity on the channel.

ALAN HUNTER: I was in the middle of one thousand beer-drinking frat boys at Daytona, talking to the Hawaiian Tropic girls while the guys chanted, "Hunter's got a woody." I repeated it out loud on the air, then realized what they were saying. I don't think I had a woody. I think they did, and they were projecting.

NINA BLACKWOOD: Spring Break was a miserable experience. People running around half-naked and drunk, and I couldn't get a decent meal. Everything was served on paper plates. I came back and said, "I'm never doing one of those again." It was sponsored by some beer company, so there I was hawking beer for MTV, after all the stuff they wouldn't let me do. I remember slamming copy on the table and saying, "I'm not reading this. Give it to Martha, she'll read anything." Because she would. She was such a darling.

JOHN CANNELLI: I booked Sam Kinison to come to Spring Break. He was in his hotel with his girlfriends, Malika and Sabrina, running around the room, jumping on the couches, barking like a dog.

ALEX COLETTI: One Spring Break there was an epic poker game in Sam's hotel room. Marjoe Gortner was there. He's a famous preacher who was in some bad '70s films, like *Bobbie Joe and the Outlaw*, with a naked Lynda Carter. By the end of the night, half the talent department was in the room. Gilbert Gottfried and Sandler were there. There were lots of drugs, and Gilbert, who probably has never done a drug in his life, kept walking up to people and making them sniff him: "Am I clean? Am I clean?"

STEVE BACKER: I walked into Sam Kinison's room by accident during Spring Break and smelled the foulest shit I ever smelled in my life. That was the first and last time I smelled freebase. Spring Break was just ridiculous.

MARCY BRAFMAN: MTV's Spring Break coverage really bothered me. I mean, wet T-shirt contests? Even with all the rock n' roll mayhem at the network, we'd never had a sexist outlook. Of course, a lot of that had to do with the fact that there'd been a lot of women running the network. MTV didn't objectify women back then.

DOUG HERZOG: Daytona was a miserable place. It seemed like it poured rain the entire time we were there. We stayed at the most miserable hotel, the Pagoda, which the MTV staff referred to as the Abe Vigoda. Just the most disgusting place, with shag carpeting in the rooms, and filled with kids who were puking and partying. At the same time, there was lot of fun to be had. We would take over the town. Joe Davola became an instant local celebrity. We started doing a series of spots about him, called "Joe Davola, Hardworking Producer."

JULIE BROWN: Spring Break, oh my gosh. I wore the highest platform shoes and it still didn't help me tread through the vomit in Daytona. That was the wildest of MTV. We had the sexy girls, the guys, and you mix that together with booze, and trust me, you've got a party.

ADAM HOROVITZ: We did an amazing stunt for Spring Break in 1986. It was a contest where the Beastie Boys would kidnap the winner and bring him down to Daytona. We're like, "This sounds really stupid. What? We're gonna get free beer? This sounds really awesome!"

I'd just turned twenty. I didn't go to college, so I had no idea what frat life was like. I was like, "How do you people get the money to party like this?" It was just drink drink drink. It was totally nasty. But don't get me wrong: I loved it. There's nothing wrong with nasty. I'm a fan of nasty.

My favorite part was going to a party thrown by Ron Rice, who owned Hawaiian Tropic. We're like, "Party at a guy's house who owns a suntan lotion company? Let's go!" We walked into the house, and as we were checking out the scene, we saw a super-drunk guy in his midsixties, wearing a captain's hat, like a broken-down Charles Nelson Reilly. He turns to a security guard and shouts, "Security? Throw me out!" That's still a running joke. Any time I have a couple too many, I'll say to my friends, "Security? Throw me out!"

Each thing we saw at the party was weirder than the previous thing. Weirdest of all was when we opened one door and there was a huge room with rows and rows of bunk beds, like an army barracks. That was where the Hawaiian Tropic girls lived.

ALEX COLETTI: The Red Hot Chili Peppers played on *Club MTV* at Spring Break. They had to lip-sync and they just weren't feeling it, so toward the end of the song, Chad Smith got up from his drum kit, and he and Flea dove into the crowd. Flea picked a girl up, smacked her on the ass, and maybe pulled part of her bathing suit down. The cameras cut away as soon as they stopped lip-syncing. The cops came and looked at all our tapes and the Chili Peppers were put in lockdown. That was a bad incident.

FLEA: We were totally against lip-syncing, so when we were faced with a lip-sync situation, we never just stood there and pretended to play. I'd play bass with my shoe and then jump into the audience, something like that. So we're onstage in Daytona, and the song starts, "Knock Me Down." And about halfway through, I leave the stage with the song still playing and leap into the crowd. The first thing I see is a girl in a bikini standing in front of me. She's jumping around, having a good time. Woo-hoo! So I grab her and pick her up over my shoulders. While I was spinning her around, Chad ran up behind her and spanked her on the butt. I didn't realize it. The girl and I both fell onto the sand, and she started yelling at me. I yelled back at her, "Well, fuck you, then." About twenty minutes afterwards I hear this girl is really upset. I was like, "Can I apologize?" I still had no idea that Chad had spanked her.

The next day, the local newspaper runs a picture on the front page of this girl, cowering in fear with me standing over, with the headline FLEA ATTACKS GIRL. I've always been crazy on stage, but the last thing I would want to do is hurt someone's feelings. We go to the next town in Florida, and after our show, Chad and I walk offstage and bam!, a cop places us in handcuffs and takes us off to jail. And that's when I find out that Chad had spanked her. We were in jail overnight, but the case dragged on for months. We settled it, but the words *Flea* and *sexual assault* went out across the national press. What I did was wrong—I shouldn't have touched her. But to claim that it was any kind of sexual thing was completely wrong.

JULIE BROWN: I swore on the air at Spring Break. I got punished for it, which people don't know; I was taken off *Club MTV* for a couple of days. I was wearing a green Lycra dress—very thin, of course—and we were live. One of the dancers, in his little swimsuit, started rubbing up behind me. I told him to fuck off, basically. I don't like people touching me.

CAMILLE GRAMMER: Jean-Claude van Damme was at Spring Break and he was hitting on me. Julie pushed him away. One of his people jumped in and said,

"Excuse me, but that's Jean-Claude van Damme." Julie said, "I don't give a fuck who he is."

JANET KLEINBAUM, record executive: I went down for many Spring Breaks. Couldn't wait to get out of there. Hectic, crowded, freezing cold, filthy beaches. It always looked better on camera than it did in reality.

KEVIN SEAL: They set up huge klieg lights around the pool, so it looked like it was sunny, and kids pranced around in their bathing suits every time a floor manager cued them. We'd cut away to some video and they'd stand there, shivering. It was a bacchanal. The Daytona Police converted a Safeway parking lot into a temporary jail, with chain-link fences. Scores of kids in zip cuffs stood around, shouting at their friends. There were reports in the paper about kids who plunged off a hotel balcony and hit the deck. I dreaded it.

There was the sense of young lives being wasted, which was sort of a pall that hung over my time at MTV, generally. Not only with the audience, but perhaps in my own life as well.

DOUG HERZOG: Mister Mister played Spring Break, and their record company sent them a package via FedEx, which was mistakenly delivered to the room of an MTV executive, who saw it on his bed and ripped it open, thinking it was for him. He found . . . well, something meant to keep the band awake and happy for several days.

VANILLA ICE, artist: My Spring Break show must have been the most-skipped school day in history. Some principal actually showed up at the concert and busted a bunch of kids.

TREACH: I met my ex-wife, Pepa, at Spring Break. I was a Salt-n-Pepa fan; I had pictures of them on my wall. I loved Pepa before she even knew me. I saw her at the airport, and she had a gang of bags and I helped her carry them. I was the biggest star out of everybody, so she was looking at me like, "Oh, the biggest star out here is concerned about me." We ended up going bungee jumping in a park in Miami. She dared me. I couldn't back out.

PEPA, Salt-n-Pepa: I had my son with me, and after our show, I was gonna leave. Treach was like, "Stay and watch my show tomorrow." I was like, "Stay? Just like that? Okay." And then he leaned in and gave me a little peck.

TREACH: We stayed in the same hotel, but nothing popped off down there. I wanted to, but she was like, *Nah*. She wasn't fast with it. We had one kiss, when I was taking her to her room. A couple of weeks after Spring Break, Pepa and I got together. We were together for ten years. MTV was a matchmaker, for sure.

GERARDO, artist: I had a foot fetish, so my road manager, Nick Light, would stand the girls against a wall and see who had cute feet, or who had them polished all nice, and the girls that had those and other qualifications came to my room. Nick was a great road manager, because he would start the party somewhere else, and he'd get rid of anybody under eighteen. By the end of the night, he always knew the right girl for me, and only then would he bring her to my room. My wife knows all about this. This isn't going to be getting me in trouble. And she has very beautiful feet.

ALLEN NEWMAN: We'd had a lot of success with Spring Break, so we did a live Mardi Gras broadcast. And I was given very specific instructions from Doug Herzog: Avoid showing any breasts. Because the big expression at Mardi Gras was "Show us your tits."

We were shooting a segment at the corner of Bourbon and Royal in New Orleans, and I've got my eyes peeled to make sure there are no naked women in the background. The phone rings, and it's Herzog, yelling at me: "What are you doing? How could you let this happen?" I look at the feed—there are no tits. Except there was some guy standing behind Mark Goodman and Alan Hunter, holding an eight-foot black dildo.

PAULY SHORE: I was sitting at my mom's house in 1988, watching Spring Break and going, "I've got to be there, because I want to get laid." I was like any other kid thinking the same thing, just wanting vagina.

DOUG HERZOG: Pauly flew himself down to Spring Break, and hung around, and annoyed everybody. We didn't know who he was.

LENNY KRAVITZ: I showed up to Spring Break in a loincloth. I'd grown a beard and was living in the Bahamas like a fucking jungle man. I just did not care at all. I got on a private plane and came in a loincloth, man. I sat there and got interviewed and people were like, "What is wrong with this guy?" Pauly Shore was there. Every time I see him, he talks about that loincloth.

PAULY SHORE: I was desperate to be on MTV. Next Spring Break, MTV gave me an opportunity, and I did a couple little tosses to a video, but people didn't know who I was. Me and Christian Slater sat in his hotel room, going, "This sucks," because we weren't famous and Corey Feldman was getting all the girls. But that didn't last long.

Chapter 36

"I BROUGHT SNOWBALLS TO THE DESERT"

SUCKING UP TO MTV'S LADDISH NEW POWER BROKER

MTV'S SHOWS ALL HAD CONNECTIONS TO MUSIC, even if it was only *Remote Control*'s questions about song lyrics and appearances by "Weird Al" and LL Cool J. In 1988, the network began a slow breakup with music by debuting *The Big Picture*, a show about movies; the *Half Hour Comedy Hour*, which introduced the wicked wit of future VMA host Chris Rock; and *Way USA*, an annoying travelogue show which—well, it's enough to know that it ended after two episodes, twice what it deserved.

These changes upset and confused some employees, so in October 1988, Lee Masters, MTV's general manager, wrote an internal memo to explain the "aggressive and risky moves" of MTV's "new programming strategy." Videos, he explained, "aren't the novelty they once were" and were available on other networks. Soon, MTV would have a nightly talk show, and a daily soap opera "with an MTV spin." (Neither program evolved as quickly as Masters predicted.) And he answered the question MTV staffers were asking one another: "Is MTV moving away from music? Absolutely not." MTV would have nonmusic shows, he wrote, "but music must always be the base" of the network.

And Top 40 songs were increasingly the base of MTV's music, thanks to new VP of programming Abbey Konowitch. A few years earlier, when he worked at Arista Records, Konowitch was "really bothered about sitting with my eleven-year-old son and seeing a girl in a garter belt" on MTV, he'd told a *Christian Science Monitor* reporter. Once he joined MTV, garter belts were in heavy rotation, driving up ratings and profits. More than any MTV executive since Les Garland, Konowitch had a big ego and a bawdy reputation. And he didn't hide his music philosophy: "I like hit songs," he declared. "We want to get behind those that will be *big stars*."

ABBEY KONOWITCH: When John Sykes left to work with Mike Ovitz at CAA in 1986, I thought, *That's going to be my next job*. But no one from MTV approached me. They hired Sam Kaiser, who was friends with someone there. I was a little bummed about that. Now, I had a great job at Arista Records. I was senior VP of artist development and video, which was essentially the head of marketing. I was part of the inner circle of a very successful company. But Sam Kaiser didn't last long, he was there for about thirty minutes, and suddenly that job was available again. And still, they didn't call me! I couldn't believe it!

So I talked to a friend who knew people at MTV, and asked him why no one had called me. He came back to me and said, "No one's called you because they don't want to piss off Clive Davis, and they don't think you would take the job." I said, "Tell them I'd take it." They called the next day, and soon thereafter Lee Masters offered me the job.

When I got to MTV in July of 1988, ratings were down. MTV's first half-life was over. They were looking for a way to regain their mojo, and they'd started to develop long-form programming. MTV was morphing. By 1988, any thirty-minute program got a better rating than the highest-rated half hour of videos. Even in 1988, videos were already old news. I brought snowballs to the desert. I had a fresh view in a place that had become stale, because no one knew what the fuck to do.

ALEX COLETTI: Abbey's first day, he had the music way too loud. I'm like, "Who the fuck is this guy?" And he started calling me Axl, because Guns N' Roses was happening and my name is Alex. I thought, "Oh, I'm gonna hate this dude." To this day he still calls me Axl.

MC HAMMER: Anything MTV needed me to do, I would do it. I never told Abbey *no*. If I was in the middle of a tour and MTV was doing Spring Break, but Abbey said, "Hammer, baby, this is important to us," I'd say, "Okay, I'll do this, but when my next video comes out, I'm gonna need you to turn it up." It was a partnership.

TOMMY LEE: Mötley Crüe was always trying to push the boundaries of what MTV would play. "Okay, we'll pan up the girl's chest and show her boob, but cut away *right* before the nipple. How's that?" Then Abbey Konowitch would call and say it didn't pass standards and practices. It's hard to imagine Abbey as an enforcer of moral values, but it's true.

ADAM CURRY: There was continuous wheeling and dealing, collusion between MTV programming and the record industry. It was very clear: If you give us a certain video premiere, we'll throw this other piece-of-shit band you have into the Buzz Bin. Buzz Bin was a big joke. It was so obvious that Konowitch was a shill. He was very open about it: "Shut up, we're playing this video." He was doing all the deals.

STEVE BACKER: When Living Colour came around, it was a head-scratcher. "Cult of Personality" seems like an obvious hit now, but let's face it, four black guys doing rock n' roll wasn't your everyday thing. The reaction from MTV wasn't so much resistance as confusion: "What do we do with it?"

VERNON REID: When I saw the playback of "Cult of Personality," I was like, *America isn't ready for this.* There's footage of SS troops, shots of Mussolini. It's very confrontational.

STEVE BACKER: The fact is, I got Living Colour on MTV by threatening to withhold a new Michael Jackson video. I called Frank DiLeo, who'd worked at Epic and was managing Michael. The "Smooth Criminal" video was about to come out, and we had to decide who'd get the world premiere. I told Frank, "I'm having trouble getting Living Colour on MTV. Can I tell them they're not going to get Michael unless they deal with Living Colour?" Frank was our former head of promotion. He understood. He said, "Do what you gotta do. I'll back you up."

So I went to see Abbey, whom I didn't know well. I was ridiculously nervous. I had Living Colour in one hand and Michael Jackson in the other. Abbey said, "Backer, this is not how we do business." And I said, "It's exactly how you do business." They put "Cult of Personality" into rotation.

COREY GLOVER, Living Colour: We owe most of our career to Michael Jackson.

GEOFF TATE, Queensrÿche: We put out an album called *Operation: Mindcrime,* and it sold exactly what all our other records had sold, about 250,000. We'd been on tour for nine months, and then we began the process of making a new record. A month later, our managers called and said, "This guy at MTV, Abbey

Konowitch, really likes the band. He's interested in playing a video from you." We made a nice video with Marc Reshovsky for "Eyes of a Stranger," and it went to MTV. Within a couple of weeks our sales were up to 500,000.

JANET KLEINBAUM: MTV wielded a lot of power, and Abbey enjoyed that position very much. He had a reputation as a crazy man. There was partying, long dinners, lots of drinking, girls, foul language—that was the norm. I didn't have to participate; I think I had to play along, I had to not be offended and have a good sense of humor and show them I could keep up. Any promotion for a metal band would involve scantily clad women and lots of alcohol. And that sometimes breeds egotistical behavior.

The men had a very different style of promoting than the women did, and they had advantages over us. The guys would go off golfing for a weekend. Those things didn't happen often with the women. Who were we gonna take out? There weren't any women in powerful positions at MTV. The women who worked there were managers, directors, and assistants.

PATTI GALLUZZI: Abbey would say sleazy, inappropriate things all the time. He'd be about to leave my office after a meeting and say, "Just show me your tits one time. Come on, just once." And I'd be like, "Oh, get out of here." It wasn't the culture of MTV to talk like that, but it was the culture of the music business, and I was used to it. I'd had [Geffen Records executive] Marko Babineau pinch my ass at a convention when he didn't know me from Adam.

I have two points to make about Abbey's behavior. The first is, he never made me feel uncomfortable. He would also say similar things to Tom Hunter. We'd be in a boring meeting, and he would mouth to Tom, "Blow me." And Hunter and I would both crack up.

On the other hand, this was before Anita Hill. Honestly, the Anita Hill hearing made a lot of us go, "I've had that happen to me millions of times." So my second point is, in retrospect, because I was complicit with his behavior, I might have been enabling him to also say those things to assistants and secretaries. I feel bad thinking that maybe he was saying these things to people who weren't in a position to say, "Oh, Abbey, fuck off."

LINDA CORRADINA, MTV executive: Boys are stupid, what can I say? A lot of the guys were known for hitting on girls, especially younger girls. There were men—married men—who didn't have boundaries, absolutely. But girls can make their own reality. You put up with it, or you don't. If you're intimidated by it, you should report it. I can't say it ever bothered me.

GEORGE BRADT: MTV was hardly the tolerant environment you might imagine. When I was an associate producer, we were preparing scripts to promote a benefit concert for AIDS charities with Jimmy Somerville and other gay and gay-friendly British artists. A female director said, "Who knows something about this concert with the faggots for the faggots?" It's a little horrifying that people spoke like that in New York, in a supposedly creative company.

I was in a relationship with a male staffer who was also not out. Among the people I knew, I can think of eight who were gay, but only one who was out. There was a female couple—a writer and an administrative assistant—who went to great lengths to hide their relationship at the office. This did not stop someone in the news department from referring to the assistant as a "bulldyke."

JOHN CANNELLI: I wasn't out when I worked at MTV, but I didn't go out of my way to hide my sexuality, either. I had gay friends and partners. I didn't mix the personal with business. I was dealing with artists in an industry that was still somewhat homophobic. MTV could be a bit like high school, and jokes were made that today would be considered insensitive. But my reluctance to be more open was a personal choice. Did I think coming out might hurt my ability to get things done on behalf of the network, or that people would think differently of me? Maybe it was in the background, but that was my own issue.

TOM HUNTER: Abbey and I ran the Monday acquisitions meeting in a giant conference room, so we could hear from young staffers who went out to hear music all the time. One Monday, the conference room's double doors burst open. Everybody turned around, and through the doors come six super-hot girls, blondes, wearing yellow rain slickers, fireman helmets, and very little else. And they were carrying a stretcher. Someone's lying on the stretcher, covered by a blanket. The girls drop their rain slickers and they're wearing little teddies. It's practically pornographic. They put the stretcher down, and all together they pull off the blanket. And out pops Gene Simmons!

He sits up and says, "Sorry to distract you guys, but it's hard to get your attention. I started a record label, and I brought a video to play you. I really want it played on MTV. I brought my kneepads. So who do I have to blow to get some spins?" Everybody starts chanting, "*Hun-TER, Hun-TER Hun-TER*." Gene says, "Who's Hunter?" They point at me. Gene drops to his knees in front of me and simulates a blow job. The room was total chaos. People were pounding on the conference room table. Gene goes, "All right, who else?" Everyone goes, "Ab-BEY, Ab-BEY." So Abbey got the same treatment from Gene. One of my favorite moments of all time.

RICK KRIM: Elektra Records sent over a stripper once. A Mexican porn star. Kitten Natividad was her name. She had been in a bunch of Russ Meyer movies, and she was in the Georgia Satellites video "Shake That Thing." She showed up at one of our weekly music meetings in a fishnet bodystocking. I remember her jiggling herself all over Tom Hunter's head.

JOHN CANNELLI: People tried all kinds of things to get our attention. I had a corner office that overlooked the Marriott. And I got a phone call from someone at a label, saying, "Look out your window!" They'd booked a room opposite my office and hired a stripper to perform for me. That's how they would promote an act.

STEVE BACKER: We signed a band called Danger Danger. Just the worst of the fucking hair bands. They were dreadful. But our label president, Dave Glew, was obsessed with a song and video of theirs, "Bang Bang." I could get five videos onto MTV and it didn't matter to him, because Danger Danger wasn't in rotation. "Bang Bang" was going to be a smash record if it killed him. So he came up with this awful idea: The entire staff of Epic would put on hard hats—because hard hats symbolized danger, get it?—and walk to the MTV offices. I'm talking about the entire label. When the receptionist announced that Steve Backer had arrived for his 11 A.M. meeting, I've never been more mortified in my life. I still cringe when I think about it.

MARK GHUNEIM: MTV hated Toad the Wet Sprocket. Hated them. The hardest work I ever did was getting that band into rotation. I bought a dozen toads, put them in boxes with little airholes, and sent them to everyone in Abbey's department. They were horrified. *Horrified.* I understood. It was cruel to the toads. But I would do anything to promote an artist.

ABBEY KONOWITCH: My detractors said I was power hungry, and I took credit for everything, and my ego was out of control. I wasn't power hungry. The power came to me. I had a problem thanks to my friend John Sykes. John wanted to do me a favor. When *Entertainment Weekly* was doing its first list of the 101 Most Powerful People in Entertainment, in 1990, he convinced them that I was the most important figure in the music-video industry. Which I hated. It wasn't fair to my staff, and it was damaging for me personally. Everyone from David Geffen to Tommy Mottola wanted to kill me. David Geffen said to Tom Freston, "Why would you let this guy have power over me?"

But I was the MTV guy. I mean, let's be honest. I'm not giving you any bullshit. I was the MTV guy. I never thought for a moment that this shit was real. It was so surreal it couldn't be real. But I had a really good time with it.

Chapter 37

"PEOPLE IN THE HOOD RUSHED TO GET CABLE"

HOW TED DEMME DID, DIDN'T, MAYBE DID, AND ABSOLUTELY DID CREATE *YO! MTV RAPS*

IF IT HADN'T BEEN FOR MICHAEL JACKSON, WHOSE MUSIC didn't fit MTV's format, the network might have gone the way of the Betamax and other quickly failed inventions. In one sense, MTV learned a lesson: Black pop became an integral part of its programming. On the other hand, MTV had a show about movies before it had a show about hip-hop. As black pop transformed from Lionel Richie to Run-DMC, the network concluded that rap didn't fit their format, once again prompting accusations of racial discrimination. ("We didn't know if rap would fit MTV," Lee Masters bravely admitted, after *Yo! MTV Raps* was a hit.) And for the second time, a form of music excluded from the network ended up saving the network—rap was MTV's escape route from hair metal. *Yo!* started only through the relentless efforts of Ted Demme, a twenty-three-year-old underling whose bosses reluctantly made a concession that changed the network's future, and sped Demme on his way to being a Hollywood director.

SCOTT KALVERT: The first big video I directed was "Parents Just Don't Understand" by DJ Jazzy Jeff and the Fresh Prince. I had the idea of doing a human cartoon, because the song was so funny. People were hesitant, though. They said, "They're rappers. You've gotta put them on the street."

ANN CARLI: The video had almost a Marx Brothers feel. And I would say it was a tipping point in hip-hop. Will Smith was a middle-class suburban kid from Philly, and what he rapped about was accessible. He wasn't pretending to be from the hood.

DJ JAZZY JEFF, DJ Jazzy Jeff & the Fresh Prince: The first video Will and I did was "Parents Just Don't Understand." That was also Will's first time in front of a camera.

ANN CARLI: Will was a scrawny kid. He was seventeen, he usually had pimples, he wore baseball caps because he didn't like to do anything to his hair. He was a bit awkward. So I was surprised when we saw the rough footage after the first day of shooting. Scott Kalvert and I said to each other, "Oh my god, this kid's a huge star. The camera absolutely loves him." I wanted to make a movie with Will. So I called Russell Simmons and said, "He's going to be a movie star. He's going to be as big as Eddie Murphy." And Russell said to me, "He may be the next Malcolm Jamal Warner, but he ain't no Eddie Murphy." I still bug Russell about that.

BILL ADLER: "Parents Just Don't Understand" was an important video. They were young, suburban-seeming kids from Philadelphia. Will Smith was not a scary black man. He was handsome, charismatic, good-humored, sexy. Not scary. And yet, he's rapping. Okay, MTV programs it, and boom, their phones light up. If there was a tipping point for rap at MTV, it was the success of that video.

DJ JAZZY JEFF: That video introduced a lot of white kids to hip-hop.

JANET KLEINBAUM: There was definitely a lot of jealousy from other rappers towards Will. "What is it about *him*, why don't they like *me*, what are you doing for him that you're not doing for me?"

KOOL MOE DEE: We shot "Wild Wild West" at an "Old West" park in New Jersey. I used to go there in fifth grade on class trips. It had wagon wheels and make-shift western scenes. We shot it in the middle of February, in freezing cold, and we were there for the better part of ten hours. I was numb. I told Scott Kalvert I was done shooting, and he acted like I was being uncooperative. But I was freezing cold.

MTV wouldn't play the video. Even when "Wild Wild West" got to number four on the pop charts, they wouldn't play it. Over and over, we'd hear, "It's not our format." I was no Rick James, but I made a lot of noise about MTV not playing hip-hop. Shortly after I spoke out, they played Jazzy Jeff and the Fresh

Prince's "Parents Just Don't Understand." It felt like, "Yeah, we're gonna play rap, but we're not gonna play you."

A lot of people don't know "Wild Wild West" is part of why *Yo! MTV Raps* was put on the air. Ted Demme told me that once "Wild Wild West" made it onto the pop charts, rap was hard to overlook.

FAB 5 FREDDY: Russell Simmons was going to BET and begging them to put some kind of rap show on the air, and they wouldn't. The look, the attitude, the swagger—at the time, rap was a complete affront to what black music had been.

PETER DOUGHERTY: Ted Demme was an assistant in my department, the promotions department. We had nothing to do with producing shows. We were into hip-hop, and Ted was very keen to do a rap show. He used to put a note under Judy McGrath's door every week. I think they looked at the idea and said, "Is it going to scare our core audience away?" Little did they know hip-hop kids would become the core of MTV's audience. Ted was essentially telling the music department, "You don't have a clue what's going on, you're missing the next wave of music." They didn't want somebody from another department telling them how to do their jobs. But that's the way Teddy was. You could say, "Oh, he's a runaway train," or you could say, "What a cuddly bunch of energy." Luckily, MTV found his enthusiasm endearing.

When "Parents Just Don't Understand" became huge, that cleared the way—we were given the green light to do a pilot. I hooked up with Revolt, an old graffiti artist, and we did the logo together. We shot an hour-long pilot in Texas with Run-DMC as the host, plus Jazzy Jeff and the Fresh Prince, and JJ Fad.

TOM HUNTER: Here's how *Yo!* happened. An independent promotion guy bought me lunch one day and said, "Do you know what's going on with rap? It's huge, and MTV should play it." He told me about *Video Music Box*, the Manhattan cable show hosted by Ralph McDaniels. So I started to look at rap sales numbers and became convinced that we should do a show.

I'd bring it up every week at my meeting with Lee Masters, and his argument against it was consistent: "We're white, suburban, male, affluent. That's who we are." When Pittman left the channel, he told Lee to pay attention to that audience profile. Finally, I got desperate, and I said, "Lee, give me from 2 to 3 A.M. on Tuesdays and let me put rap there." He still said *no*. I said, "Okay, how about we do a one-off, two-hour rap special, and you let me air it between noon and 6 P.M. on either a Saturday or a Sunday?" He finally said *okay.* Then Judy brought in Peter Dougherty and Ted Demme.

We got the highest ratings in the channel's history. I walked into Lee Masters's office the next day and said, "Do you believe me now?"

ABBEY KONOWITCH: When I started at MTV, I was full of piss and vinegar. I could do anything I wanted! Ted Demme and Pete Dougherty came to my office and said, "We have an idea. We get no ratings on Saturday night. We want to play an hour of rap videos in that time slot. It's gonna be a smash." To me, it sounded like the stupidest idea ever. I said to Lee Masters, "What do you think?" He goes, "Who's gonna watch *that*? The audience for rap would never be home on a Saturday night." I said, "Let's have them at least put a budget together." When Ted put a budget together, we said, "Go ahead and try it. We got the ratings first thing Monday morning, and it was the highest-rated show MTV ever had.

STEVE LEEDS: When I worked at Channel 68, we had a Saturday afternoon show called *Fresh Rap.* Then when I got to MTV, I said to Lee Masters, "We should be playing more urban videos." He didn't believe there were enough rap videos to do a show, so I brought him a couple of air checks of *Fresh Rap.* He agreed to try a one-off weekend special. Ted Demme got wind of that, and he became the producer.

LEE MASTERS: What's the expression? "Success has many fathers." There are conflicting stories about who was truly the creative forced behind rap on MTV. I have to tell you, it was Ted Demme.

Ted came into my office and pounded on my desk. And this part of the story is embarrassing for me, but when we okayed the show, I called him to my office and said, "I'm glad you're doing it, but this show will not get ratings, okay? I don't want you to be bummed out about it, and I don't want you to feel like you're a failure." Of course, we got the ratings in, and it was stupid how successful it was. So I called Ted back in and said, "Can you do another one next weekend?" Then we got the ratings in again, and I said, "Can you do a daily half-hour show?" Ted was the front guy. He was so gregarious and persuasive; he basically charmed me into letting him do it.

DJ JAZZY JEFF: Jazzy Jeff and the Fresh Prince were on the very first episode of *Yo! MTV Raps*, which Run-DMC hosted. We were on tour with Run-DMC, Public Enemy, a bunch of us, when "Parents" started getting big on MTV. Both Will and I remember the cheers getting louder for us night after night. One night before the show Will said, "I'm gonna try something." He was going to rap a verse of "Parents" and ask the crowd to chant the next one. I'm sitting there with my fingers crossed, hoping this works. Will's up there and raps, "I remember one year my mom took me school shopping," and twenty thousand people sang back, "It was me, my brother, my mom, oh, my pop, and . . ." When the tour started, we were going on second. After about two weeks, somebody says, "Okay, you guys go on third." Then, "Okay, you guys go on fourth." Before the tour ended, we were going on right before Run-DMC. And that was all because of the success of "Parents," and mostly due to the video.

ALEX COLETTI: We did a *Yo! MTV Raps* weekend to launch the show, with a whole week of VJ segments with Will Smith and DJ Jazzy Jeff. Will and Jeff came up from Philly by train every day; we didn't put them in a hotel.

PETER DOUGHERTY: Hiring Fab 5 Freddy as a host was a no-brainer. He was involved in the art world, in the hip-hop world, the graffiti scene, he had been in Blondie's video "Rapture." And he was not a gangster. The way he dressed—he was not a typical b-boy. He could float through different worlds, highbrow and lowbrow, and not be out of place.

FAB 5 FREDDY: My on-air persona was an extension of my character in the movie *Wild Style*, who was a hip, cool, knowledgeable guy. Essentially, I'm a cool nerd, if you will.

Being on MTV was nowhere on my radar. I'd become restless with painting in the late '80s, and started thinking about music video. I'd learned the rudiments of filmmaking when I was in *Wild Style*—it was my idea to combine break dancing, graffiti, rap, and DJing. Prior to that, these things weren't on the radar of pop culture. Ann Carli at Jive said, "I've got a video for you to direct." It was "My Philosophy," by KRS-One. I used images of Malcolm X, Louis Farrakhan, Marcus Garvey, and Hailie Selassie. My father was active in social change; he marched on Washington, he was in the room when Malcolm X was assassinated. My grandfather worked with Garvey. I was from that ilk of conscious black folks.

When we were shooting "My Philosophy," people were asking, "Yo, Fab, you think this will get aired on MTV?" I made an announcement: "Nobody else ask me that. I'm making this video so black, that's not even a question. I am not trying to get on MTV." And then "My Philosophy" was the final video on the pilot for *Yo! MTV Raps.*

When they hired me, I was adamant about not being cooped up in a studio like the other VJs. Things were emerging from other parts of the country, so we talked about what's going on in Philly, we had Too Short and Ice-T from LA, Luke from Miami, Texas with the Geto Boys. We would jump at opportunities to travel and show this culture. Rap was spreading like Ebola.

DMC: Until *Yo!*, Run-DMC was the only hip-hop kids saw on MTV. Once *Yo!* started, they got to see Eric B & Rakim, Public Enemy, the Geto Boys, LL Cool J, De La Soul, Leaders of the New School, X-Clan. *Yo!* showed the diversity of hip-hop. And everyone was dope as hell. When you went on *Yo!*, it wasn't about your video, or your clothes, or your money. You had to perform live, and you had to be *better* than your record and video.

MC HAMMER: Fab 5 Freddy launched my "Turn This Mother Out" video in Times Square. That's the show where I had Jennifer Lopez as one of my backup dancers. *Yo!* said, "You have to get to New York." My dancers were in Florida, for my next show. They go, "Don't worry, we can get some dancers from New York to do it." When I get up to the dance studio to pick out dancers, J.Lo is there. She stood out, even then. There were tons of girls in that room, but her energy, her look, and her disposition got her in all the shots. I'm sure I flirted with her.

FAB 5 FREDDY: MC Hammer debuted on my show, in a famous episode that was also J.Lo's television debut. I had something to do with that. A casting director rounded up a few dancers. I came into the room and saw her and said, "Yo, Ted, put her front and center." MC Hammer offered Ted Demme a Corvette. In a joking way, but serious, and Ted was like, "Nah, man."

MONICA LYNCH, record executive: All these little white kids in middle America sat on the edge of their seats, waiting to see what Fab 5 Freddy, Ed Lover, and Dr. Dre would say or wear or play, or who they're gonna have on their show, so they could try to live that lifestyle themselves. The white homeboy nation arose, and *Yo!* had a lot to do with that.

SCOTT KALVERT: Eric B. & Rakim's "Follow the Leader" was the first gangsta rap video. We modeled it on *The Godfather*. We wanted to do something street and gangster, but without being contemporary, so we went period. There were lots of machine guns. Everyone was like, "It's never gonna get played." And it was the first video ever played on *Yo! MTV Raps*.

DON LETTS: The irony is, *Yo! MTV Raps* ended up being the highest-viewed program on MTV. And that made me realize that in America, it ain't about black, it ain't about white, it's all about green. If you're making money, you are accepted instantly, no matter what color you are.

FAB 5 FREDDY: Ted sat me down and said, "This shit is blowing up. MTV wants to do the show daily." They asked me to host the daily version, and I refused, because I didn't want to be overexposed. People grew to hate a lot of VJs.

ED LOVER: I met Ted when I was fifteen or sixteen. I used to go on religious retreats, just to get the hell out of Queens. My church fellowshipped with Ted's father's church in Rockville Center, Long Island. We'd be at the religious retreat smoking weed and drinking communion wine out in the woods. And Ted knew a lot about hip-hop. I stayed friends with him throughout high school and college.

Yo! became extremely popular when it debuted, and when I saw Ted's name on the credits, I contacted him about how I could get on the show—I thought I knew everything there was to know about hip-hop. When Fab turned down the daily show, Ted contacted me. Dre and I didn't know one another—I met him for the first time when he came in for his audition. Ted was the one who had the foresight to give a different look to the daily show and put two guys together. Early on, people might say to me, "Who's the white dude?" And I'm like, "This is Ted, who knows more about hip-hop than you probably do."

Freddy was all serious and cool. He was a downtown hipster wearing sunglasses. Dre and I made it funny. We were the dudes next door that were in love with hip-hop. You were in the basement with me and Dre. "Oh, we got a big foam cowboy hat on the set. I'm gonna wear it. Now I'm country-western hip-hop," and Dre would follow me.

FAB 5 FREDDY: Ed is a comic genius. He and Dre developed an Abbott and Costello–Laurel and Hardy kind of slapstick routine.

ED LOVER: Whoever was in the MTV studios doing other things, we would ask them to come on. We had Carole King on as a guest. Mel Gibson was in the studio doing something else, so Dre and I knocked on his door. He knew exactly who were were, and he came and did the show. I remember he liked "Rapper's Delight" and "It Takes Two" by Rob Base.

Dre and I had to split the money. The salary was $1,000 a week. It was like, "I'll take $500, you take $500." I was a school safety officer, working for the Board of Education, making $732.96 every two weeks. $500 a week for me was great. But I kept my job at the Board of Ed because we didn't have a contract.

No assistants, no writers, no dressing room. Did we have MTV's full support? Hell no. They had no idea what it was, no idea it was going to be that big. They didn't think the show would last. We knew MTV was gonna be changed forever. We knew the power hip-hop had. White kids already thought hip-hop was cool. MTV didn't understand that hip-hop had crossed over. There were white kids at Big Daddy Kane and LL Cool J concerts.

MC HAMMER: I was a huge fan of *Yo! MTV Raps*. They played so many of my videos, I shouted them out in a song: "Ted, Dre, or Ed Lover / Fab 5, homeys, won't you help a young brother?"

SCARFACE, Geto Boys: We watched *Yo! MTV Raps* every friggin' day at four-thirty, religiously. We were so excited to see videos from our favorite groups. "Wow, look at Public Enemy!"

B-REAL: Hip-hop was the lowest member on the pole to get any love within all of the musical genres, and here came *Yo! MTV Raps,* which said "This shit is serious. This shit is real. And we ain't going anywhere."

CEE LO GREEN: *Yo!* in the afternoon, that's what we were rushing to get home from school for. I had a friend who was staying around the corner from me, he was a little older, so he'd be out of school first, and he would record the show. You can hear how animated my voice becomes; I remember like it was yesterday. That was a big part of my day, to get home and see *Yo!*

This way we could identify the new trends coming through, and who wore the new jogging suits. LL Cool J really took on Troop—they gave him his own Troop suit. There was this one dude in the eighth grade, and you could tell he was getting some street money, because he had the red-and-blue suede LL Cool J Troop suit. He set the school on fire with that suit.

HANK SHOCKLEE, music producer: A rock video was about, What kind of guitar is he playing? What's the attitude of the singer? With a rap video, it was a different aesthetic: Were there any cars in the video? Any fly chicks in the background? Were any of my homies in it? Rap videos came out in that context—the stars and their posses, and then trying to squeeze in some storyline. A video could redefine what was hot. "What kind of sneakers has he got on? Is that a hoodie? Yo, he's rocking the crazy hoodie." It's these different aesthetics that represented real life for us.

CHUCK D: We didn't make our first true video until 1988, with "Night of the Living Baseheads," from *It Takes a Nation of Millions to Hold Us Back*. What changed my mind about making videos? *Yo! MTV Raps* is the only thing that changed, because now we knew the video would be seen.

B-REAL: My favorite hip-hop video is "Night of the Living Baseheads." When I saw it for the first time I went ape-shit. I liked dark, aggressive, in-your-face shit like that.

HANK SHOCKLEE: If Public Enemy was going to do a video, we wanted something outside the norm. My thing is, I hate literal translations. The video should always tell you what the lyric doesn't.

LIONEL MARTIN, director: I didn't even know who Public Enemy was.

HANK SHOCKLEE: The song was about drug addiction, especially crack. The crack epidemic was destroying the black community. Everybody I know, including myself, had close family members who were on crack or trying to recover from it. The fact that the song was disjointed gave us the impetus to create skits within the video. I didn't want to make light of crack, but a video needs to have entertainment value.

LIONEL MARTIN: They had some crazy ideas. Hank Shocklee said, "Could we stop the music and insert a commercial?" Flavor Flav was a mess. He was full of surprises, like when he said, "Kick the ballistics." He was always late, and he would disappear for drugs or for girls. He was just a crazy dude.

CHUCK D: "Baseheads" was brutal. It was my first video, it took a long time, and we had a lot of different locations. We knew we had to go over and beyond, make something that had never been seen before.

LIONEL MARTIN: When you're in telecine doing color correction, there's a term you use: "crush the blacks." I like my blacks to be dark and deep and rich. Flavor and Chuck were in the room and I kept telling the colorist, "Crush the blacks, crush the blacks." Flav jumped up and said, "What the fuck are you talking about? Yo, Chuck, I got a problem with this dude." So I explained it to them.

JAC BENSON, MTV producer: I studied finance in college, at Hampton University, and sometimes we would, like, maybe not go to class, because we wanted to watch *Yo!* In addition to the videos, it provided an environment for artists to be themselves. The show was fun, it was smart, it was all these things. Every day there was a new video or a new artist. The only real reference point I had for MTV was Michael Jackson, and it was questionable how black he was.

PETER DOUGHERTY: It was like a runaway train. The show aired fourteen hours a week at one point; the daily show was on twice a day, then the Freddy show was on twice a day on weekends.

FAB 5 FREDDY: I remember Ice-T telling me how in LA, in the hood, people were rushing to get cable to see my show.

ED LOVER: We went from a half hour to an hour. Then we went to six days a week.

KOOL MOE DEE: Rap videos were segregated into an hour-long segment of the day, but we were definitely glad to have it.

FAB 5 FREDDY: The first show I did with N.W.A, a lot of people say that's their favorite show. Ted was like, "Eazy-E has a new group, they're called Niggaz With Attitude." I'm like, "The group is called *what*?" We were standing by the "Welcome to Compton" sign, setting up a shot, and guys were riding by looking at me. So I threw up the peace sign. Ice Cube said, "Fab, I know that's the peace sign back east, but out here it's a gang sign." I didn't get how serious the gangs were.

SIR MIX-A-LOT: Freddy came to Seattle and thought it was a place where everybody rode horses and drank coffee. When he got here, nine gangsters showed up in my group, holding guns. Freddy stood there like, "What the fuck is this?" I think he was surprised at how much juice showed up.

FAB 5 FREDDY: Our trip to Jamaica was weird. We got free accommodations at a place called Hedonism. I knew what the word meant, but I didn't realize I was staying in some fucking free-love swingers hotel. There were ugly people walking around in togas, naked in the hot tub. The concept is, you're safe from the native people. I was like, "Money, I want Jamaican food *now*, I want jerk chicken, motherfucker. We are leaving." They were like, "We don't recommend that." I was like, "Motherfucker, I'm from the hood, I'll see you later."

I interviewed a whole litany of Jamaican artists, including Ziggy Marley, who recognized me right away. This was in the first year. He was like, "We are watching *pon* satellite dish." When I'm out of the country, whether it's Nigeria, Brazil, Spain, Israel, people talk about what the show meant to them. If they didn't get it directly, tapes were passed around. It really sparked and inspired hip-hop around the world.

B-REAL: If you were an up-and-coming rapper, one of your goals was to get on *Yo! MTV Raps*, to visit Ed Lover and Dr. Dre and see Ed Lover do that crazy dance he used to do on Wednesdays. That was every rapper's dream. I mean hey, even Notorious B.I.G. mentioned it in one of his raps.

EVERLAST: It was a big deal to be on *Yo!* It was like doing the Johnny Carson show.

ED LOVER: We did a Big Daddy Kane day, played five of his videos, and at the end of the show I started spitting some of his rhymes. And I was like, "Kane, you know you stole them rhymes from me, you old flat-top-wearing sucker ass." It was a joke, but his guys took it seriously. So later I'm at Queen Latifah's birthday party and these guys come threaten me. "We're gonna fuck you up." One of them had a straight razor. Ice-T protected me and got me to my car safely. I knew where they were from. That night we strapped up, me and Live Squad, the dudes Tupac used to run with. We went out to Brooklyn and chased them niggas down the block shooting at them. I believe somebody got hit, but it didn't come from my gun. That's all I'm gonna say.

The next day, Lyor Cohen came to the set to talk to me, and he squashed everything. Kane and I cleared the air, he let me know he had nothing to do with that. We're great friends to this day.

BIG DADDY KANE, artist: Keep in mind, in the late '80s it was still difficult to get rap songs on the radio. A video gave you nationwide exposure. If you hear a song, it's like, "Yo, did you hear what he *said*?" But if you see a video, now dudes say, "Where can I get that jacket? Yo, I need those glasses." You've got girls saying, "I'm going to fuck the shit out of him whenever he comes to this state." It helps build your fan base, because they get to *see* you. If you're a man, women get a chance to fall in love with you, and men get a chance to try to dress like you and *be* you. Whether they're saying, "Kane had on the most incredible outfit," or "Kane had on some ridiculous bullshit," they're talking about you.

Yeah, I wore some ridiculous bullshit. One of Chubb Rock's boys was cracking on me about what I wore in Heavy D's "Don't Curse" video—a purple paisley shirt with matching purple paisley scarf. He told me I was dressed like a bullfighter. One time I wore a sheer purple outfit, straight-up see-through, and I intentionally had on leopard drawers. I was on some Gentleman GaGa shit.

DJ JAZZY JEFF: My family was from Virginia, and to people in Virginia, Philly might as well have been Mars. I'd go back home when I was younger, and people would be like, "Wow, you guys dress like this?" After MTV started playing rap videos, I went down to Virginia for my family reunion. I walked into a 7-Eleven, and there was a kid with a box haircut and parts in his hair. He looked *exactly* like he was from Philly. That's what MTV did. It changed fashion, it changed culture.

PETER DOUGHERTY: In '88, you couldn't find anybody at MTV who wasn't white, except in the mailroom. I was very insistent that we get black people to work on *Yo!*, and I was met with "Why? You think that's necessary?" And I was, like, "Yeah. I don't think it should be run indefinitely by a couple white people."

JAC BENSON: When I got hired at MTV, my job was in production management. I lasted a whole week. *Yo! MTV Raps* was celebrating its third anniversary with a special show, and production management was handling the logistics, prepping for a shoot. I was running to get more food for catering, that kind of busy stuff. I was introduced to Ted Demme, and as the shoot was wrapping up, he said, "I'm thinking about hiring a PA for *Yo!* Let me know if you're interested."

He told me the rate and I did the quick math. I was like, "Well, that's $75 less per day than I'm making now." Ted Demme gave me the opportunity to work for him for less money.

One of my jobs was to take Fab 5 Freddy his check every week. No one else wanted to do it, because Fab liked to *talk*. But the shit he was talking about was fly.

FAB 5 FREDDY: We were astute enough to smell a phony. "Rico Suave"? No, we're not doing this.

ED LOVER: I'll tell you right now who tried to bribe us. Somebody from Vanilla Ice's label offered a couple hundred thousand dollars, cash, to play "Ice Ice Baby" regularly. I refused. I hated Vanilla Ice.

JAC BENSON: Tupac and Ed were friends. We were in the studio, and the week before, Tupac had a fight with these directors, the Hughes Brothers. I think they pressed charges. He comes to *Yo! MTV Raps*, and when Ed asks about the incident, Tupac just *goes*. He's bragging about what he did, then he challenges the Hughes Brothers to a boxing match. Those tapes ended up being subpoenaed by the court.

FAB 5 FREDDY: Tupac was a crazy dude. He could have an intelligent, substantive discussion with you, then flip on a dime and be the illest street guy that doesn't give a fuck. This one particular show, he was like, "Yo Fab, I just got this new tat, let me show you." And he lifts up his shirt to show the Thug Life tattoo, but there's a pistol in his waist which we can clearly see. So we huddle with his manager and say "Should we retape it?" Tupac was like, "Nah, fuck that. Let it air." So it aired.

ED LOVER: My favorite episode? We went to Mike Tyson's house in Vegas. Ted decides we're going to shoot on a golf course in the backyard. When we're done, Mike can't find a key to the back fence. It's six feet high. The crew gets over the fence, then Ted, then Mike Tyson. Don King says, "No fucking way I'm jumping over this fence." I jump over the fence. Now we're waiting on Dre. Tyson says, "Dre, jump over the fucking fence, you fat motherfucker." Dre's holding on to an eagle that's built into the cement and it snaps off. Tyson goes ballistic: "Look what you did to my fence, you fat piece of shit."

Finally we shoot the segment, and Mike says, "I'm a Brooklyn guy, I've always had this lisp, when I was young everybody laughed at me." And I go, "We got more *Yo! MTV Raps* coming up. Mike Tyson is talking this Brooklyn crap. Let me tell you, I'm from Queens, and there ain't never no punk had nothing from no dude from Queens." And Mike runs up behind me and hits me in the rib cage. All the air just left my body. And Mike stands over me and says, "Oh, Ed Lover is gonna sue me now." That's the first time he punched me. It wouldn't be the last time.

JAC BENSON: Ed was the star of the show. This is no disrespect to Dre, but Ed was going to be the comedian. He would make a fool of himself, in a good way, playing different characters. We would be doubled over in laughter and pain. You'd plan a forty-five-second segment and it would run two minutes, and then there wasn't time to show the videos.

KEN R. CLARK: The town car bills for Ed and Dre were outrageous. They'd stop the car twenty-five places on their way home.

JAC BENSON: Trust me, every day Ed and Dre would remind me that they were the highest-rated show on the channel.

ED LOVER: I was in a rap group called No Face—we were doing fun, 2 Live Crew–type of parody stuff. MTV made me choose between doing my music or being on MTV—so we took my face off the No Face album and my name off the credits. They said it was because of a morals clause in my contract, and because we had the lyric, "I'm gonna wake your daughter up, we wanna fuck." "Fake Hair Wearing Bitch" was one of our records. Yet after that, Jenny McCarthy posed naked in *Playboy* while she was at MTV, and morally, that's okay?

MTV had no late-night television show. Our ratings were great, but they didn't want to do a late-night show with me and Dre. Jon Stewart comes right after us and they give him a late-night show. What the fuck? It's race. That's all it is. We were treated different than white talent, absolutely. There was no problem paying Adam Curry. All them dudes was making way more money than us, and we were out-rating them every single fucking day. We were killing Adam Curry and had to fight for our money. We had Lyor Cohen negotiate our deal in '91, and he got us each $250,000 a year. We had to threaten to leave the show. And from $250,000, we went up to $500,000 apiece. Then we were doing radio and MTV at the same time, and I was clearing almost $2 million a year.

FAB 5 FREDDY: For the first three years or so, we were kind of untethered and could do whatever we wanted. Then the network became overly sensitive, because it was black content. There was a constant pressure to edit videos: The gun has to come out; that FUBU T-shirt was okay before, but now we can't show it because we're getting pressure from advertisers. We weren't debuting all the hottest stuff like we were before. BET and The Box were playing this shit in every major city. That became problematic.

JAC BENSON: Rap videos exploded on MTV. You'd see Ice Cube and Tupac played outside of *Yo! MTV Raps*. So that thing we held close to our hearts and kept authentic, it was starting to grow beyond its boundaries. Ed and Dre and Fab would say, "We used to program the show ourselves and do what we wanted." And at that point, there was more of a channel involvement in it. Patti Galluzzi programmed all the shows, from *Headbangers Ball* to *Yo! MTV Raps*. Videos were getting caught up in bullshit, getting caught up in standards. They got pushed back to the record labels: "You've got to make these edits, change this language, bleep this, back-scratch that, before we can play the video." We were early in the beginning, then we became late. Rap had grown bigger than the show. Michelle Vonfeld in standards and practices, I maybe saw her once or twice. It was like the Wizard of Oz that you hated.

ABBEY KONOWITCH: All of a sudden, we went from a network that played a little R&B to a rap network. I didn't know anything about rap. Lee Masters had no idea. Judy McGrath was terrified. So Patti Galluzzi became our expert. She played me a song called "O.P.P." and said, "It stands for 'Other People's Pussy.'" I go, "What?! You're telling me we should be playing this?!" And of course it became one of our biggest hits.

TREACH: "O.P.P." was a phrase in the hood: Other People's Pussy. It was a funny concept, so we made a song about it. "You down with O.P.P.? Yeah, you know me!" Ed and Dre took "O.P.P." and made their own video, "Down with MTV." They rerecorded "O.P.P" with new verses from Ed and Dre, and we did the hook. "You down with MTV? Yeah you know me." All the VJs were in the video, Queen Latifah was in the video, MC Lyte, Marky Mark. It was a family thing.

JAC BENSON: There was a line in a Heavy D video, "I'm not your H-E-R-B, I'm your H-E-A-V-Y." *Herb* meaning nerd. But Michelle Vonfeld was like, "*Herb,* that's a weed reference." I'm like, "No, no, *no*." Rap was a very smart and cunning language. That was a higher level of thinking, of wordplay. But it got boiled down to a weed reference and the video was held back. I don't think Michelle understood black culture, forget about just hip-hop.

PATTI GALLUZZI: One time Michelle said there were derogatory terms about homosexuals in a video. I was like, "What are you talking about?" She said, "He's constantly calling this guy a *homey*." Which I thought was pretty funny. Michelle was a little square. A rapper would call somebody a "Herb." She'd go, "That's obviously a reference to marijuana." And we'd go, "No, Michelle, if you're a 'Herb,' you're a nerd." MTV's system for standards was poorly equipped for understanding rap, and most rap videos had a much higher amount of logos, product mentions, drugs, alcohol, guns, overt sexuality, and objectification of the female form than your average Bon Jovi video did.

ED LOVER: They took the power of programming away from us. We were told what videos to play and on what date. They knew the power the show had. We always argued with Patti Galluzzi about clearing videos. She'd say, "You can't play that, it's on hold." It meant a video wasn't cleared to be played yet. It took a while to get "Fight the Power" off hold. We never played "Straight Outta Compton" on *Yo!* I love Patti, but we used to *argue*. Because *Yo!* had to be at the forefront of what was happening in hip-hop. That was frustrating as fuck, yo. And it absolutely hurt the show.

PATTI GALLUZZI: We argued pretty much every week. Never in my years at MTV did I fight with anybody as much as I fought with those guys. Their goal was, "Let's play ten brand-new videos." And my goal was to play three or four new videos, and also some videos that were recognizable. The Box would get rap videos at the same time we did and put them on the air the next day, while we were still arguing. The one time I really pissed off Judy McGrath, I wrote a scathing memo saying, "We need to stop holding up videos just because we don't understand some of the words." Judy was like, "I'm the one who put this show on the air, so why am I suddenly the racist here?"

ED LOVER: People talk about what Russell Simmons did with hip-hop and the level he took it to. Nobody says this: Ted Demme is the one dude who is absolutely responsible for hip-hop being a multimillion-dollar genre of music, because *Yo! MTV Raps* took it international. I've been to Holland, to Japan, and in all these places they said they learned to speak English by watching *Yo! MTV Raps*. Hip-hop has blown up all over this globe because of Ted Demme, and that's the God's honest truth.

SALT, Salt-n-Pepa: Ted had a crush on me. I was going out with Herbie, our producer, at the time. Ted must have liked black girls, I know that. He used to look me up and down. I was a little hood back then, so maybe he liked that.

DENIS LEARY: Teddy is the only guy who could get gangster rappers on television and make them laugh. The first time I met him, I was shooting something connected to *Yo!* and he was the cue-card holder. I said, "What the hell are those?" And he said, "Those are your lines, *sir!*" I said, "I don't need those." And he went, "These are gone, *sir!*" and he threw them in the air. I went, "Who the fuck is this guy?" He made me laugh about ninety times, so he stuck in my head.

PETER DOUGHERTY: You know that Beastie Boys line from *Paul's Boutique*, "Sneaky pouch time bomb"? "Sneaky pouch" was coke. They got that phrase from Teddy. He just had a taste to party too much. I was at Ted's wake and his funeral, and it was all about partying and partying. In front of Ted's family and his kids, Denis Leary had people doing shots at the funeral. I was just appalled. Partying is what killed Ted.

ED LOVER: Ted was jovial, smart, fun, caring, considerate, and loyal. When he died of a heart attack, in 2002, it ripped out a big part of me. At his funeral, Michael J. Fox was sitting next to me, Bernie Mac, Eddie Murphy, Natalie Portman, Denis Leary, Johnny Depp—all of these people Ted had worked with when he went on to be a movie director.

ALEX COLETTI: Ted was the biggest personality. He lit up a room. Ted was just a thousand-watt bulb every day.

EVERLAST: Our manager, Amanda Scheer, wound up becoming his wife five or six years later. Ted was one of our first champions at MTV—that's how they met. He was a funny cat, a life-of-the-party kind of guy, laughing and talking a lot of shit. He was a big, jolly dude.

AMY FINNERTY, MTV executive: I loved Ted. I was a bridesmaid at his wedding in 1994. Ted got into a scuffle outside the party, and somehow I got in the middle of it and got punched in the face. Who knows who he was fighting with? Everybody was drunk.

TONY DiSANTO, MTV producer: I worked with Ted on a live afternoon show, *Hangin' with MTV*. For me, being a good producer was about preparation, so nothing can go wrong. Ted wanted surprises. It was the antithesis of everything I'd learned. He was in the control room and I was out on the floor, and he was always in my earpiece saying, "Shake up the audience! Get them fired up!"

JAC BENSON: Because I made no money, Ted would give me cash out of his own pocket on Friday, to make sure I had some for the weekend. Everyone loved Ted Demme. I don't know anyone that would tell you a different story.

FAB 5 FREDDY: It was a fresh, buoyant, diverse time for this music. That period is now referred to as the golden era of rap. It wasn't about me. I know I was cool and all that, but I was just a vehicle to lead you into this shit.

BILL ADLER: Rap integrated MTV, to the benefit of rap and MTV. If MTV had continued to play Genesis for ten years, they might not have seen their tenth anniversary.

Chapter 38

"WE'VE *ALWAYS* LOVED GUNS N' ROSES"

CHICKS AND A SNAKE, *HEADBANGERS BALL*, AND THE RETURN OF HARD ROCK

THERE WAS PLENTY OF IMITATION IN THE 1980s; WHAT was Whitesnake but a hugely successful Led Zeppelin tribute act? But many of the decade's biggest stars were unique, sounded like no one else when they appeared, and were not predicted to be Next Big Things: Madonna, Prince, Beastie Boys, U2, Metallica, Dire Straits, Tracy Chapman—even Kenny G, who was unique in a bad way.

No one was a bigger underdog than Guns N' Roses, five scuzzballs from LA whose caustic notion of hard rock had little to do with Poison or Bon Jovi. As with rap, MTV was afraid of the band. The network relented only under pressure from David Geffen, one of the titans of the record business, and ironically, Guns eventually became so prominent on MTV—in his memoir, guitarist Slash called MTV "a channel that helped us out, but that we didn't care for"—that the network hired a new VJ mostly because he came recommended by the band.

JOHN CANNELLI: I was taking a ride through Central Park on my ten-speed, and I put the Guns N' Roses cassette on my Walkman. When I heard "Welcome to the Jungle," I almost fell off my bike.

SAM KAISER: I had two right arms in the department. One was Rick Krim and the other was John Cannelli. John maybe had the best eyes and ears in the place. He was soft-spoken and dry, but he had a knack for picking stuff. When John spoke up, you listened. He brought us a video by Guns N' Roses, "Welcome to the Jungle," and I fell out of my chair.

TABITHA SOREN: The news department was a less important area in the scheme of the channel. MTV was just discovering Guns N' Roses, and they traded exclusive access to some A-list video for an interview with the band at CBGB. Nobody wanted to do it, so they sent me, with a crew. I was nineteen, and Axl said, "Are you even old enough to be in here?" It was so exciting. Then I went home to my dorm room and went to sleep.

NIGEL DICK: I was strictly known as a pop guy. But I was a huge fan of Led Zeppelin, Rory Gallagher, Bad Company, and Free, so getting to direct a Great White video was a breakthrough for me. And I was on my second Great White video when Alan Niven, their manager, said, "I've got this new band called Guns N' Roses. They're hugely difficult, they don't want to work with anybody, nobody wants to work with them. Would you do their video?" I turned him down. A week later, Alan said, "Look, I can't find anybody to do it. You *have* to do me a favor." So I thought, *What the heck, I'll make some extra money.* I shot the second Great White video on, say, a Thursday and Friday, and shot "Welcome to the Jungle" on Saturday and Sunday. I honestly preferred Great White's music.

STEVEN ADLER, Guns N' Roses: At the time, *nobody* wanted to have anything to do with us. They were afraid one of us was gonna die, or kill somebody. Even recording *Appetite for Destruction*, we had ten different producers who said, "No way, I already heard about those guys." And then, of course, they all regretted it.

ALAN NIVEN: The budget that Geffen afforded for "Jungle" was insufficient for us to realize the storyboard we wanted, so we piggybacked it onto a Great White shoot, so we could have a four-day rental in equipment and staff.

NIGEL DICK: The video for "Welcome to the Jungle" was Alan Niven's idea. He told me, "Axl will step off a bus, then he'll be sitting in a chair watching TV, and there will be all this horrible footage on the TV." The hardest part of a Guns N' Roses video was waiting for Axl to show up. He was always late. He had to be in the right vibe, and you couldn't get too pushy. You were always worried he'd have a tantrum and leave. After we did the close-up of him on a stage, he hid in the dressing room for two hours. He couldn't handle the shiny boards and the lights and the bounce cards. Suddenly, instead of a bunch of hot girls at his feet when he's singing, there were a bunch of aged film people with light meters. It freaked him out.

DOUG GOLDSTEIN, manager: Nigel was quiet and soft-spoken. If Axl was running two and a half hours late, Nigel was like, "Well, he'll get here when he gets here."

ALAN NIVEN: Everything of worth in a video is stolen from somewhere, so I stole from some cool movies. Axl's character is a corollary to Jon Voight in *Midnight Cowboy*, who comes to a city that's a cauldron of false dreams. That plays beautifully into the scene from *The Man Who Fell to Earth* where David Bowie is in a motel out in the desert with a pile of TVs, trying to absorb information about the planet he's landed on. Then there's the scene from *A Clockwork Orange*, when they're made to watch all these insane images on TV.

STEVEN ADLER: Believe it or not, we couldn't find any girls to be in the video. It was one night out of forever when no girls were around. So I called my roommate—her name was Julie, I couldn't tell you her last name—and she's the girl laying in bed with me while Axl watches the TVs. There was an X-rated part where I was making out with the girl, rubbing and licking her neck, her boobs were out and everything. When we went to Japan, I saw the video and they didn't cut out that scene. It was so great!

TOM HUNTER: When they submitted "Welcome to the Jungle," we accepted it for *Headbangers Ball*, which was typically what we'd do with a video that extreme. Axl was twitching in an electric chair!

DOUG GOLDSTEIN: MTV wasn't interested. Their response was "We'll play it two times overnight and see how it goes."

ALAN NIVEN: MTV didn't give a damn. Didn't care.

NIGEL DICK: Initially, they wanted to play it only once or twice after midnight. Then we had to re-edit it, because there was a brief moment when a red soda machine appeared, and MTV said it could have been perceived as a Coca-Cola sign.

JOHN CANNELLI: There was controversy over how much to play "Welcome to the Jungle." Our GM, Lee Masters, thought we were playing too much hard rock. Lee and Tom Hunter, the guys with radio backgrounds, were afraid of the video.

Tom got some pressure from Geffen, so we put it on the overnights, and all of a sudden we started getting requests. Then we played it in the afternoon, and from there it went through the roof. And I became GNR's guy at the network. We did one of Axl's first MTV interviews at my apartment in Chelsea.

EDDIE ROSENBLATT: We had sold a couple hundred thousand albums and they still wouldn't play the video. I sent my weekly sales report on the album to Lee Masters, and I got on the phone and made him read it with me.

DOUG GOLDSTEIN: The interesting thing nobody knows is that we'd been touring for a year and three months and had sold 150,000 units. Eddie Rosenblatt took Alan Niven to lunch and said, "Great first album, it's time to record another one." But Alan begged for the money to make the "Sweet Child O' Mine" video.

ALAN NIVEN: I looked at Eddie with total disbelief and said, "What do you think might happen if we got MTV's support?"

DOUG GOLDSTEIN: Axl was frustrated that "Jungle" wasn't getting played. He and Cannelli were great friends, so he couldn't understand why they wouldn't play it. He knew that, in order to be one of the biggest bands in the world, they'd have to be played on MTV. Axl loved Cannelli. He didn't care John was gay, that didn't bother him at all.

GARY GERSH: David Geffen and Eddie Rosenblatt didn't spend much time listening to people bitch about what they weren't getting done. We all courted MTV, from David on down. It was different at Geffen—we didn't have a central video promotion person. It was like, "Get your fucking ass in there if you want your video played."

TOM FRESTON: The programming group decided to put "Welcome to the Jungle" on *Headbangers Ball* for starters. Not in regular rotation. It was getting played a couple of times a week. David Geffen called me and said, "Every time you guys play this thing at 3 A.M., our sales light up. Please leave it on." Normally, I would never tell the programming guys what to put into rotation. But this was David Geffen. And the song kicked ass. Guns N' Roses broke out.

TOM HUNTER: Freston called me and said we had to play "Welcome to the Jungle" in regular rotation. I said, "Have you seen the video?" He said, "One of the pieces of advice I got from Pittman was: When David Geffen calls, pay attention. And Geffen called me."

ALAN NIVEN: I love the euphemistic quality of that statement. In other words, David is an incredibly powerful person, don't piss him off.

TOM HUNTER: If we added it into regular rotation, we'd get shit from other managers and labels whose hard rock videos we wouldn't play. So I handwrote it into the programming log—that way, the add wouldn't appear in trade magazines. I gave it two plays a day in regular rotation. It got an amazing number of calls right out of the box.

NIGEL DICK: On the second Guns N' Roses video, "Sweet Child O' Mine," all the girls from the Geffen office wanted to be in the video. There's a scene with a guy on a dolly, pulling focus or something. He worked at MTV. Alan said we needed to put him in the video because he was part of the team that could make sure the video got played.

There'd been two previous attempts to shoot "Sweet Child O' Mine." We had the location and the crew booked, but the band was unable to appear because they were "ill." I was quite happy, because I got paid each time.

DOUG GOLDSTEIN: Axl left some of the best of 'em waiting. He left the Rolling Stones waiting for a sound check. In late '89, Niven took Axl to do a pay-per-view show in Atlantic City and he kept banging on Axl's door. Axl said, "The longer you pound, the longer I'm gonna take." Two hours later, Axl walks onstage and Mick Jagger is staring at him. And Keith Richards says, "I slept inside of a chandelier last night. What's your excuse?"

JOHN CANNELLI: I'm in the "Sweet Child O' Mine" video. I was there when they shot it, and they asked me to be in it. I'm like, "I can't be in your video. People already accuse me of being on your payroll." So they put me on a dolly and shot me so you can't see my face. I have a clear recollection: It was the same day we shot Cher for the final "I Want My MTV" ad campaign, and she won the Oscar for *Moonstruck*.

DOUG GOLDSTEIN: "Sweet Child O' Mine" is about Erin Everly, so it was important to Axl to have her in the video. He didn't want to cause any shit with the rest of the guys by excluding their girlfriends: Angie, who was Izzy's girlfriend;

Mindy, who was married to Duff; and Cheryl Swiderski, Steven's wife, are also in the video.

STEVEN ADLER: The girlfriends and wives, they didn't demand to be in the video, but it was something that wasn't said and had to be done. Everybody's got a wife or a girlfriend in the video—except Izzy, who's there with his dog. Or maybe that *was* his girlfriend.

NIGEL DICK: The idea for "Sweet Child O' Mine" was simple. After the first couple of takes, I thought, *God, this is awful. It's so dull.* Some execs from Geffen were standing behind me, going, "This is so fucking cool." I'm thinking, *I'm shooting a bunch of guys playing guitar. What's special about this?* But for whatever reason, people thought it was the hottest thing in the world. There's nothing remarkable about the video at all, except, of course, for the band. Which is exactly how it should be.

DOUG GOLDSTEIN: MTV liked "Sweet Child O' Mine" a lot. Cannelli was on-site, which he seemed to be for most of our videos in the early days. He said, "It's a great video, Doug. We're going to play it." And the label relaunched "Jungle" after that. So they had two songs being played regularly on MTV. And it just took off.

NIGEL DICK: Soon everyone at MTV was like, "Yeah, we've *always* loved Guns N' Roses!"

ALAN NIVEN: On the first video, Axl didn't have confidence in his ideas or how they could be applied. But once he'd done "Jungle," now he was David Lean. For "Sweet Child," he had an incredibly involved story line that he wanted to apply with his microscopic sense of myopic detail. So I asked Nigel Dick to give me a thumbnail budget, and he said it would be at least $250,000. I told Axl and said, "By the way, we've got $35,000."

Nigel came up with a brilliant idea. Anyone on the set who had a spare five minutes could grab a windup Bolex camera and shoot B-roll. He had one of his staff sit there all night long, loading the Bolexes with 16mm film. Then we did two different edits of the video, so when "Sweet Child" took off and the first video reached burnout stage, I dropped version number two to Cannelli and extended the life of the song at MTV. The first version was a mix of color and black-and-white, and the second was entirely black-and-white except for the final shot, when Axl fades into color.

JOHN CANNELLI: There was an element of danger with Guns N' Roses. They seemed fragile; there always seemed to be a crisis. But God, when you saw them perform . . . I booked them for a concert called *Live at the Ritz*, and the show was amazing.

STEVE BACKER: Guns N' Roses gave MTV a second wind. Dana Marshall produced a live show with Guns N' Roses from the Ritz. I went to MTV and there must have been twenty people hunched into her office, just to watch her edit raw footage of Guns N' Roses.

ALAN NIVEN: MTV had a conflicted relationship with mainstream America. They were club-dwelling, Manhattan-living aficionados who were more comfortable with music coming out of London than with what played in Peoria or Birmingham. They played hard rock only because they wanted to pay the bills. It was selling records hand over fist at the time.

NIGEL DICK: "Paradise City" was the biggest video I'd ever done. It cost $200,000, $45,000 of which was a payment to the unions at Giants Stadium. They got $45,000 for carrying a hundred camera cases thirty yards from a parking lot into the stadium.

ALAN NIVEN: We went from $35,000 to a $250,000 budget, shooting with six cameras at Giants Stadium in front of 77,000 people. I wanted to show the scale of the band's phenomenon. I needed the audience. And Axl is resplendent in his brand-new white leather jacket.

PETER BARON: There's an "It's So Easy" video we never released. It had Erin Everly, Axl's wife, in bondage. She had a ball-gag in her mouth. It was a bad look for them.

STEVEN ADLER: I never saw that, but I'd like to. Erin was a fox.

RIKI RACHTMAN: Sometimes you can find it on YouTube. It was a great video, filmed at the Cathouse in black-and-white, with Erin shaking her butt. I have no idea why it wasn't released. Maybe it was the ball-gag.

PETER BARON: The first Guns N' Roses video I commissioned was "Patience." Alan Niven sort of codirected those early videos with Nigel Dick. We shot the conceptual part at the Ambassador Hotel, and the performance in Hollywood. Of course Axl showed up about seven hours late. And Izzy was screwed up. Coke was dripping out of his nose, but he didn't realize it because his whole face was numb.

NIGEL DICK: Mostly what I remember about that video is a shitload of chicks and a snake.

ALAN NIVEN: Izzy, who was in the depths of a cocaine habit that was destroying him, sat in a dark corner while we were filming. When we looked at the footage, Nigel and I agreed to minimize Izzy in the video, because he looked wretched. He got sober not long thereafter, but that video represents the nadir of Izzy's cocaine habit. There were other moments when Slash was in dire condition, and moments when Steven was in dire condition. Those were the three that had the biggest problems with excess.

STEVEN ADLER: I was sitting there rolling joints. That was my whole gig in that video: light incense and roll joints. As for Izzy, if you look at the cover of *Rolling Stone* when we were on it in 1988, he's sitting on the ground, and if you look at his wrists, you can see the track marks. He was doing drugs longer than anybody, but he ended up getting it together better than anybody, and then he left the band because he got clean and couldn't be around us.

JOHN CANNELLI: One night, I was hanging out with Slash and his girlfriend in their hotel room. It was late, we'd been drinking, and she asked if I wanted to spend the night with them. I'm pretty sure she meant more than just sleep on the couch. Now, as far as I know, she was speaking only for herself. There's no reason to think Slash was in on the offer. But I said, "Gee, thanks very much, but I think I gotta go now."

DOUG GOLDSTEIN: When you're dealing with two heroin addicts, a cocaine addict, and a bipolar lead singer, every day is mayhem. Well, three heroin addicts, actually: Izzy, too. But Izzy cleaned up midway through the Appetite tour. Rehab wasn't working for some of the other guys, so I decided to sit in a hotel room for two weeks with Steven and give him sleeping pills, and clean up his puke and excrement. We went to the Orange Tree Resort in Arizona, and Steven is doing good, he's about four days clean and sleeping until 4 P.M. because of the pills. I decide to go golfing, and when I get back to the hotel, there's four ambulances, two fire engines, about fifteen cop cars, and three hundred people standing in a circle. Slash is there, naked. And bleeding. He'd come in overnight, to bring Steven heroin, I think. I told my security guy, "Earl, go to my room and get my briefcase." I used to carry between $30,000 and $50,000 at all times, just for situations like this.

So I go, "Did anybody see anything here?" And a guy goes, "Yeah, I did." So I walk away with him and he goes, "I saw him throw a maid to the ground." I'm thinking, *Okay, this is not good.* I said, "I notice you got a little blood on your shirt. That's, what, a $2,000 custom shirt?" He goes, "No, no." I said, "Trust me, I know clothing. That's a $2,000 shirt." I bring out $2,000 and give it to him. "Think you're okay going on with your day?" He said, "Yeah."

The cops are cracking up because they can see I'm paying people off. I grabbed the hotel manager and said, "Give the maid $1,000 and an apology from us, please. What about the damage to the hotel?" He goes, "I'd say it was $700." I said, "So another $2,000 will take care of that. Do you feel like pressing charges?" He goes, "No."

This whole time, Steven is on his balcony, yelling at Slash: "You stupid heroin addict!" We got in the car as quick as we could and boogied. It probably cost $10,000, but I kept 'em out of jail.

TOM HUNTER: We'd had a show called *Heavy Metal Mania*, a weekly, hour-long dumping ground for metal videos, airing at 1 or 2 A.M. Then we started *Headbangers Ball*, made it a two-hour show, and ran it at midnight.

KEVIN SEAL: I hosted *Headbangers Ball* for a few months. I wore a leather jacket from wardrobe. These heavy metal people who try to induce concussions inside their own brains, I have a respect for that. But I'd never buy a record or go to a show. It made sense to have Adam Curry replace me. He had his own leather jacket.

ADAM CURRY: This is the big secret: Metal musicians were always professional, courteous, and gracious, happy that they were getting played on MTV.

GEORGE BRADT: I became an associate producer, and *Headbangers Ball* was one of my jobs. The metal bands were like businessmen. They were so excited to be on MTV, they'd do anything we said. No matter what the band's reputation, they were nice and professional.

ADAM CURRY: If I'm recognized in public now, it's always about *Headbangers Ball*. Sure, we had to play Bon Jovi videos. But Saturday at midnight, for three hours, we'd play Metallica, Anthrax, Iron Maiden . . . It was a little niche when you could show crazy stuff, and I knew everyone was drinking beers and stoned. I would be on newsgroups, talking with fans. I always got asked, "Hey man, why are you playing Bon Jovi? This is *our* three hours."

TOM HUNTER: The real genius happened when Doug Herzog had some of his guys take a look at the show. They wanted to get a host who had credibility with the audience. We needed a tattooed guy who hung with bands. And poof! We got Riki Rachtman.

TONY DiSANTO: I worked on Adam's daily afternoon show *Full Tilt*. Adam used to call me his "boot-lickin' lackey." But it was all in fun. I also worked with him when he hosted *Headbangers Ball*. He'd wear a blazer for *Full Tilt*, and when it was time to tape *Headbangers*, he'd take off the blazer and put on a leather motorcycle jacket. Adam was bummed when they brought Riki on board to do *Headbangers*. Adam and Riki never became friends.

ADAM CURRY: I loved *Headbangers Ball* so much, and I was destroyed when Riki Rachtman took my job. He did his audition with Axl Rose. I was gone within a second.

I thought Riki was a douche bag, because I didn't think he could do the job. He wasn't a TV guy. I bumped into him years later at LAX. I was running a publicly listed company which I started. I had seven hundred employees; he was managing a porn star. I kinda felt good about that.

RIKI RACHTMAN: Put it this way, if you said "Riki Rachtman," you thought *Guns N' Roses*. If you said "Adam Curry," you thought *Bon Jovi*. You wouldn't picture Adam waking up in a gutter, but you knew I did. You wouldn't picture Adam getting arrested, but I did. I was living the rock n' roll lifestyle without ever picking up an instrument. I opened a club called the Cathouse in September

1986, a mile or two from the Sunset Strip in LA. I hate saying it, because I'm patting myself on the back, but it was the most important rock club of that era. Everyone played there: Guns N' Roses, Faster Pussycat, Black Crowes, Pearl Jam, Alice in Chains. I didn't see *Headbangers Ball*, because the chances of me being home on a Saturday night were nil. On Saturday, we got hammered.

I was with Guns N' Roses when they got their record deal, all the way up to recording *Appetite for Destruction*, when all of a sudden they became the biggest rock band in the world. We'd see Adam Curry, and it didn't make sense for him to be on *Headbangers Ball*. So Axl said, "Do you want to be a VJ on MTV? I'll make a call." I walked into my audition with Axl. Would I have gotten the VJ job without him? I doubt it. I had no TV experience—I had drinking experience, that's all I had. I started hosting in January 1990—I wore a Motorhead shirt and a studded leather jacket with a blue circle for the Germs, because I wanted to hold on to my punk roots. I still don't feel comfortable saying the word, but that show made me kind of famous.

I never had any say in what we played, and there were many videos I hated that did not belong on *Headbangers Ball*: Bon Jovi, Winger, Warrant, Slaughter, Firehouse, all the pretty, long-haired boys. I mean, we were even playing their ballads.

JOEY ALLEN: Riki was a bandwagon guy. Once you weren't in vogue anymore, he was the first to say, "Oh, I hated that band." That guy's got no backbone.

JANI LANE: I had a good relationship with Riki, until grunge came along, and there was a huge backlash against hair metal. It wasn't cool for his image to be palling around with us.

DAVE MUSTAINE: I had a good time as a correspondent for *Headbangers Ball*. But there was a sad sack hosting the show, this sap named Riki Rachtman. For some distorted reason, this guy liked for me to pick on him. And I didn't know him well, so I couldn't pick on him with any real fondness. I felt uncomfortable when I would do it, because I didn't dislike him. I just wasn't one of his friends, like a lot of guys who would come on the show.

Off the air, he seemed genuine. But on the air, he took on a kind of self-deprecating, slapstick approach, and I didn't dig it. Towards the end, they took pity on us and let us do the show without Riki, since he had become a caricature of himself.

RIKI RACHTMAN: Dave had fun picking on me and putting me down, and I don't mind being the butt of a joke. But the feud wasn't real—I mean, he invited me to his wedding, we went skydiving together. Except for one time when he said onstage, "Why doesn't Riki Rachtman just kill himself and put us out of the misery?" He did apologize, and then we were good friends.

LARS ULRICH: I've always liked Riki Rachtman. He was one of the kings of the LA nightclub scene, so there was a tremendous amount of respect. He was one of us. I mean, he made it easy to poke fun at him, but it was a nudge-nudge, wink-wink type of thing.

CURT MARVIS: Metallica famously wasn't interested in making videos, but Q Prime, their managers, asked if we could help Lars and James edit footage for a long-form home video called *Cliff 'Em All*. So they were constantly in our offices. Lars and James would buy a case of this shitty beer called Meister Bräu, for $4. And they would go through a case of beer in—I'm not kidding—an *hour*. Then they'd go across the street and buy another case. I never saw them eat.

CLIFF BURNSTEIN: Metallica were anti-everything. That whole positive social mood of the '80s? Fuck that. It was embodied in their attitude toward videos: We're not going to make videos; that's for fuckin' posers.

LARS ULRICH: We had a lot of contrary energy. And we were fueled by a lot of booze and spunk. We'd had conversations about videos for "Fade to Black," "For Whom the Bell Tolls," "Master of Puppets." We were trying to keep the band mysterious, and we felt there was an underlying purity to the whole thing that would be compromised by making a video.

But we were on tour in Paris, in a dressing room with our managers Cliff and Peter, and they started talking about the song "One," and about the movie *Johnny Got His Gun*, based on a book by Dalton Trumbo. And we thought *that* might be an idea worth embracing in a video. We'd use the movie footage, and then intercut band performance—but without really showing our faces. If you watch that video, there are a lot of shoulders and arms. We were proud to have struck the right balance between our own feelings about video and the commercial demands. We didn't think of it as a particularly accessible video.

WAYNE ISHAM: I'd been a Metallica fan since *Ride the Lightning*, I thought they were fucking awesome. I kept begging Robin Sloane to let me do a video for them. The opportunity came with "One," but I couldn't figure out how to combine the footage from *Johnny Got His Gun* with performance footage. I choked.

ROBIN SLOANE: At the "One" video, James Hetfield had a sticker on his guitar that read, F-U-K BON JOVI. I said, "You have to cover that up, or MTV will not play this." He looked at me, like, "Who the fuck are you? Give me some beer." He refused to cover it. So I told the director, Bill Pope, to shoot in a way that no one can see the sticker.

CLIFF BURNSTEIN: We gave MTV a seven-minute video. It was totally outside what they would normally play, so we asked for just one play, at night, but promoted. Like, "Metallica's never made a video before, it's seven minutes long, and we're going to show it at a certain time." We had only $25,000 invested in it. They played it once, at night, and the next afternoon, it was their second-most-requested video.

JULIANA ROBERTS, producer: Peter Mensch and Cliff Burnstein are geniuses. They still fly coach. Cliff's suitcase is a plastic bag. And he's the smartest person I know.

LARS ULRICH: The rise of "One" was amazing. We were in San Antonio in February of '89. It was a Monday and we had a day off. Monday was the day that MTV's countdown show—was it called *Dial MTV*?—would air that week's newly eligible videos. "One" had been played once or twice over the past weekend. And that day, "One" entered *Dial MTV* at number one. We were stunned. We knocked off Bon Jovi. It was like we landed on another planet.

I'll say it hand on heart: We became MTV whores.

STEVE SCHNUR: When Metallica made their video for "One," they had really never been on more than seven or eight radio stations across America, but they filled arenas. This was when MTV used to do the Top 10 countdown in the afternoon. I remember calling Abbey Konowitch and saying, "I'm going to deliver you Metallica's first video. And I'm telling you right now, as cocky as this might sound, it will be your number one most requested video before you even play it." And Abbey was like, "What are you talking about?" To make it even more difficult, the video barely even had Metallica in it. He wouldn't add it at first, even though, as I predicted, it was MTV's most requested video. Metallica was too scary. MTV looked weak, just playing it in the overnight, at 2 A.M. And inevitably "One" became the number one video in the countdown.

CLIFF BURNSTEIN: After seeing what the "One" video did for them, Metallica were just as interested in making videos as everybody else was.

LARS ULRICH: When we started working with Bob Rock on *The Black Album*, and making records that sounded bigger, we wanted to widen our horizons and move on to more established directors. And Wayne Isham was by far the number one guy in rock videos. Some of these video directors are failed film guys, and they can be pretty full of themselves, pretty aloof, pretty contrived. Pretty full of shit, generally. But Wayne had this childlike excitement that just makes you want to go at it together.

WAYNE ISHAM: For "Enter Sandman," we all sat around a hotel room talking about our worst nightmares. Cliff Burnstein had the nightmare of being naked in front of a roomful of people. Mine is always about falling. And the video just went from there.

LARS ULRICH: Running on the edge of a building, I think that was my nightmare. I'm not comfortable with heights.

ADAM DUBIN: I was on the set of that video. Videos serve a purpose. They're actually sales pieces for the band. You cover that up with as much art as you can, but still, it has to be serviceable. "Enter Sandman" was a new sound for Metallica—a shorter song, very catchy—and it's basically about nightmares, so it's not as intricate as some of James Hetfield's other lyrics. Wayne delivered a straight-ahead video, with people falling and trucks coming at you. It works.

WAYNE ISHAM: There were two stunt kids on the set. Troy Robinson was the kid who was in bed and then starts running to get out of the way of a truck. He was just incredible. His dad was Dar Robinson, one of the most famous stuntmen in history, who'd been killed on a set a few years earlier. When Troy's running out in front of the speeding truck, and he leaps out of the way just in time? His father's stunt friends were right there running with him.

LARS ULRICH: Peter Mensch came up with the idea of documenting the making of *The Black Album*. We ended up making this film called *A Year-and-a-Half in the Life of Metallica*.

ADAM DUBIN: I was told I had to convince them to do it. I felt like a lamb to slaughter. These guys were tough. They were the anti-MTV band. James Hetfield plopped down in a chair—he's tall, he's big, he's Viking Lord Hetfield—and it's almost like the way Lincoln's sitting in the Lincoln Memorial. I start to explain how important it is that they document what they're about to do. James just laughs, like a fuck-you laugh. He's glowering at me. I realized I was getting shoved out the door, so I said, "Look, let me get a camera and shoot. I'll show you the footage. If you don't like it, I'll go home."

I started filming in November of 1990. The record was supposed to be done in February. With Metallica, nothing is by schedule and everything costs twice as much. So I wound up living in recording studios with those guys for ten months.

LARS ULRICH: We were pretty obnoxious back then. A guy named Lonn Friend, who ran the metal magazine *RIP*, was chronicling the making of *The Black Album* for his zine, so he was hanging around us a lot. *RIP* was owned by Larry Flynt, and every time Lonn would come down to the studio he'd bring us tons of *RIP*s, tons of *Hustler*s, tons of *Barely Legal*s and *Over 45*s, and different fetish and gay magazines. We were a bunch of twenty-four-year-olds. So we'd rip out pictures and pin them to the walls of the studio. Some dude with a fourteen-inch cock would go up, and then some naked forty-five-year-old woman. And on an impulse, a picture of Kip Winger ended up on the studio dartboard. Adam Dubin was there shooting, and it ended up in the *Year-and-a-Half in the Life of Metallica* documentary and in the "Nothing Else Matters" video.

KIP WINGER: My guitarist was like, "Hey, have you seen the new Metallica video? They're throwing darts at your poster." And I thought, *Wow, that really sucks.*

LARS ULRICH: I've heard over the years from a number of people that Kip Winger didn't think that was particularly funny. I didn't have an issue with him personally—but he represented the opposite of what we were. And we were very much an "us vs. them" band. To me, they represented image before music, looks before credibility. It certainly wasn't personal. It was never *Kip Winger's a fucking cunt.* It was more *Look at this guy's hair.*

Chapter 39

"THOSE HAREM PANTS CAME OUT OF NOWHERE"

RAP BUSTS A MOVE INTO THE MTV MAINSTREAM

OON AFTER *YO!* DEBUTED, TV WENT BLACK: START-
ing in early '89, comedian Arsenio Hall's talk show darkened the
complexion of late night and regularly gave a spotlight to rappers; *In
Living Color* introduced the idea of a black *Saturday Night Live* (complete with
a token white cast member) and brought hip-hop dance and graphics to prime
time; and Will Smith, whose charming disposition had helped ease rap onto
MTV, became a bigger star via *The Fresh Prince of Bel-Air*. Rap hadn't just
entered the mainstream—it had taken over.

TAMRA DAVIS: Tone-Lōc's "Wild Thing" was my first rap video. Matt Dike, who
co-owned the Delicious Vinyl label with Mike Ross, was my best friend, and he
wanted to rip off the Robert Palmer video "Addicted to Love."

MIKE ROSS, record executive: "Wild Thing" is a comedy about trying to get a chick
into bed. Matt came up with the idea, and Tamra was willing to make a video
really cheap. We'd never shot a video before. The idea was to put Tone in a suit,
the way Robert Palmer's in a suit, with the hot zombie chicks all around him.
But he wouldn't do it. I mean, he was a real gangster—a Rollin' 60 Crip from Los
Angeles. So he put on a Delicious Vinyl shirt, and it was the right move. All of a
sudden, when the lights were on, Tone was funny and charismatic—a natural.
We didn't know he could turn it on like that.

TAMRA DAVIS: We had no idea that Tone-Lōc was, like, a superstar. He had
charisma. We hired some girls we knew from clubs—Cat, who's a very famous

English model; Annabella, a beautiful French model; Jade, who was Matt's girl-friend; and Lisa Ann Cabasa, who's Hawaiian and Puerto Rican. Matt and I were in a club and we saw Lisa Ann dancing, and she had the best ass we'd ever seen. She dated Adam Yauch of the Beastie Boys for a while, and then she was with [surfer] Kelly Slater for five years.

MIKE ROSS: Jade's playing bass, Annabella's playing guitar, Kat's on keyboards, and Lisa Ann's on tambourine. Tone's DJ, M-Walk, wouldn't do the close-up shot of the DJ scratching a record, because he thought we were clowning him. This other guy we were working with said, "I'll do it." So two different guys play Tone-Lōc's DJ in "Wild Thing." The budget was around $450, which probably went into catering and weed. Everything else was free. No one got paid.

TAMRA DAVIS: I used three rolls of 16mm film and two rolls of Super 8, so my budget was $200. In those days, videos were ruled by money. I shot it myself on a handheld Bolex camera, and I did a double exposure that was right out of film school.

We got a call from MTV, and thought for sure we were in trouble. Nobody had seen black and white people mixing together like that, especially black men. Matt said, "There's no way MTV is going to show a black guy pumping up against a white girl." But it was the most played video of the year, hands down. Every kid knew that video.

MIKE ROSS: It didn't look like anything else on MTV. We'd seen six rap videos on MTV, and four of them were by Run-DMC. To us, MTV was hair metal and Haircut 100 videos. So that wasn't our focus. But all of a sudden, here's a small label on the West Coast that out of nowhere has a video in heavy rotation. We were a couple of white guys in a dingy studio on Santa Monica Blvd. who'd gone global in the blink of an eye.

YOUNG MC: We knew there was some importance to my "Bust a Move" video, because Tone-Lōc had such success with "Wild Thing." The idea was to have me in the foreground, narrating the song, like Rod Serling from *The Twi-light Zone*, and in the background to show the characters as I was speaking about them. It was one of the most literal videos ever shot. "Bust a Move" was a juggernaut. It was on the charts for forty weeks, which was pretty much unprecedented.

MIKE ROSS: "Bust a Move" isn't as good as "Wild Thing." It was almost a year later. You can never recapture that initial energy. Young was a little awkward in front of the camera, so we created a lot of action around him. And there was some drama on the set—Lisa Ann, who was dating Adam Yauch, was the star of that video, but she was crying hysterically. Yauch was on the phone with her, and they weren't getting along—I think he wasn't happy that she was in our video, or he wanted her to be in his video.

After "Wild Thing," MTV wanted to start spiking hip-hop videos. And we gave them black artists they could play. Our videos weren't super-safe, like "Parents Just Don't Understand," but it's not anything they were gonna take shit for playing, like N.W.A.

TAMRA DAVIS: This was before I directed *Billy Madison* and *CB4*, but I was already trying to work on comedy. Yes, the girls are in short skirts and I'm filming up their dresses, but they're having a good time. The shot of the girl in the hot pants is straight out of *Starsky & Hutch*.

MIKE ROSS: Cindy Leer is wearing the stop-go shorts, like a little version of Marilyn Monroe. She was in the Ramones video "I Wanna Be Sedated," and was a local LA phenomenon.

YOUNG MC: Flea is wearing pants that look like they're adorned with a child's toys. I wasn't there, but the story was that he bobbed his head so much that he threw up. He was really going at it.

MIKE ROSS: Flea's standing on top of a truck, going berserk and violently rocking his bass. I don't know if he was hungover or what, but he blew chow in between takes. This was before the Chili Peppers had really busted out. That's the beauty of Flea—he's all or nothing.

ADAM HOROVITZ: When it came time to make a video for *Paul's Boutique*, we got to pick a director. I liked a couple of videos from They Might Be Giants, so I said, "Let's find that guy," and that's how we got Adam Bernstein to direct "Hey Ladies." We threw in every stupid '70s reference we could think of. Mike's dressed as John Travolta. I give Bella Abzug a high five.

We were living in a house on Mulholland Drive that we'd rented from a Hollywood filmmaker couple, Alex and Marilyn Grasshoff. The Grasshoffs had a huge walk-in closet that was locked, so we picked the lock, and inside were all Marilyn Grasshoff's clothes from the '70s. I mean, it was a gold mine: fur coats, fur hats, crazy leather pants. So we were wearing her clothes in the video.

SHOCK G, Digital Underground: The shoot for "Doowutchyalike" was a true and real party first, a video shoot second. We rented out a hotel in downtown Oakland—the entire hotel—and threw a wild three-day party, Friday though Sunday. To give you an idea of how much fun it was, it wound up costing twice the approved budget to finish. Every time we ran out of dough, the video rep who was on the scene would call the label and say, "This is gonna be bananas! You gotta send more money and let us finish!"

"Doowutchyalike" was voted number forty on MTV's Top 100 video countdown of 1989. Then "The Humpty Dance" was a hit with MTV, but damn near every other sentence was bleeped out, anything with a sexual reference. We were baffled, because there's not a single cuss word in the entire song. Meanwhile, songs that boasted mad violence and murder were left uncensored—which makes perfect sense when you think about it. It's not robbers and killers that make the world unsafe, it's all those dang 69 rear ticklers. The even-more-backwards thing was, the bleeps made it seem more offensive. "I once got busy in a Burger King bathroom" became "I once got busy in a muthafuckin' bathroom" after your mind filled in the blanks.

RUPERT WAINWRIGHT, director: When I started, I didn't really like rap. I was like, *God, this is annoying.* There weren't many black directors around. And almost exclusively doing black videos. For two or three years, people thought Rupert Wainwright was some black dude, until I got better known. At first, my friends would go, "You're doing a rap video? Oh, I'm sorry." They thought I was a nerd because I wasn't directing Whitesnake videos. Six months later, all the white boys on the West Coast suddenly became black.

We got a call to do a band I hadn't heard of, N.W.A. I listened to "Straight Outta Compton," and it had a good beat. For the video, I came up with the idea of a revolution in Compton, panic in the streets, stuff like that. Then I listened to the song a little harder. And I realized, this could actually cause a riot. So I flipped the idea on its head, and we shot a police sweep, which made N.W.A look like the victims of police brutality.

We were shooting in the LA River, a concrete culvert about a hundred meters wide and twenty meters high, where four inches of water travels through. Three hundred people were watching from the overpasses and bridges. It was a hot day, and I said to Eazy-E, "Do you want to change what you're wearing? You must be kind of hot. Do you want to take the jacket off?" And he pulled down the top part of his jacket, revealing a bulletproof vest. I wasn't wearing a bulletproof vest. So I realized, I needed to dress appropriately when around Eazy.

Here's what would typically happen with N.W.A: We would meet at Jerry's Famous Deli for, like, three hours while I went through the video concepts. I'd get a sense of consensus and then there'd be a quiet voice from the corner: "No, man, it's wack." I'm sorry, I didn't hear you. "It's wack." And everyone else would turn and go, "Yeah, man, it's wack." *But five minutes ago you all loved it.*

Then Eazy would get up, throw the bill at me, and say, "You pick it up, white boy." I probably would have picked it up anyway, but I didn't need it thrown in my face. And Dr. Dre was always the one who'd come along and say, "I'm really sorry, he's just a bit tense right now." Dre had the best manners and was always kind of apologizing for Eazy.

Nobody in N.W.A fucking coughed or farted without Eazy's permission. It was weird. Dre was the musical genius of the group. Ice Cube was a great rapper. But the group was totally in Eazy's control. He'd make a decision and bang, that was it. There was no dispute.

TAMRA DAVIS: "Wild Thing" and "Bust a Move" led to working with Eazy-E. I met him in the office of the president of Capitol Records. He was like, "I wanted to show you how important I am. I kicked that motherfucker out of his office so I could impress you." And I was like, "It's working." That was my first meeting with him.

N.W.A, those guys all wanted to act. They all wanted to be De Niro, or Rudy Ray Moore. They loved it, because it's all an act anyway. I mean, they really had to live the life of being gangsters, and part of it is intimidation and acting and pushing it. So they loved building the myth.

DJ JAZZY JEFF: Every hip-hop group in the business asked Mike Tyson to be in their videos, and they'd set up shooting days, prepare everything, and he'd never show up. For "I Think I Can Beat Mike Tyson," we were allowed to do a video at his training camp in Ohio, and he showed up.

ANN CARLI: That was a horrible experience, I'll tell you right now. Mike Tyson was very big at the time. Russell Simmons knew Don King and he was able to get this video together. We couldn't believe our luck. It was an expensive video for us, especially in hip-hop, probably $100,000, maybe even $150,000. As soon as we got to Tyson's training camp in Ohio, Mike gets Jeff and Will in his car—a gold Mercedes with actual diamonds—and he takes off, driving very fast. We're on a schedule and we don't know where they've gone.

DJ JAZZY JEFF: Mike said, "Hey, I want to show you guys my house." And he grabbed me and Will and put us in his car and we drove for an hour, looking for his house. He couldn't find his house. He pulled over—this was in the country, in rural Ohio—and asked somebody, "I'm Mike Tyson. Do you know where I live?" And the guy was just like, "Yeah, you live right up this road."

It was funny, because on the one hand he was doing us a huge favor by being in our video. But on the other we needed to get back. We were trying to tastefully say, "Mike, this is cool, you know, but we really need to get started."

ANN CARLI: Don King was saying, "Don't worry." Will told me afterwards he said, "Mike, let's go back," and Mike was saying, "Fuck them, they have to wait for you." Will was like, "Well, but it's my money I'm wasting."

JOHN DIAZ: Tyson was a train wreck. He accosted every girl on the set. He grabbed them in the most lascivious way you could imagine. He was menacing. I had to send all the women away. Also, Mike would hit anybody that got into the ring. He hit me. He punched Scott Kalvert in the arm so much, Scott lost all feeling for three or four days. He hit the cameraman. The cameraman wanted to brain him with one of his cameras.

SCOTT KALVERT: Tyson cracked me in the ribs, thinking it was funny. He almost killed me. I was a big boxing fan, so it was pretty cool.

ANN CARLI: There were times when Tyson seemed lucid, and other times he was abusive. I was on the pay phone when everybody broke for lunch and Tyson stayed back. When I hung up the phone, he pushed me up against a wall and lifted me off my feet. I don't know where I got the nerve, but I said, "If you don't put me down right now, I'm going to have to hurt you." He started laughing, and when he dropped me, I ran into the lunchroom.

DJ JAZZY JEFF: That was Mike back in the day. He wasn't a model gentleman.

ANN CARLI: Tyson had already said to me, "I want to fuck you." He had a massive knot of bills secured by rubber bands, with condoms on the outside. In front of everybody, he held it up and said, "I'm going to use this on you." Russell Simmons told him, "She's a big executive at the record company, chill."

DJ JAZZY JEFF: Don King was cool. He kept trying to get Russell Simmons to sell him Def Jam.

ANN CARLI: At one point, Will said to me, "I'm sorry this is happening, and if it was up to me, I'd beat the crap out of him for what he's doing to you. But I also know you want to get this video done as much as I do."

DJ JAZZY JEFF: One of Mike's friends was at the shoot, and he said, "If Mike likes you, he's gonna throw a lot of punches at you." And every time Mike was around me, he was throwing punches. He'd pull his punches an inch away from my face. My life would flash before my eyes. But Mike was cool. He stayed for a while, did two or three scenes, and then said, "Ahh, I don't feel like doing this no more. I'm done."

ANN CARLI: Will and Mike were fake sparring. Mike's hitting Will, not hard. Will taps him on the cheek and Mike grabs his face and goes, "Ow! Ow!" And Tyson walked off the set. We were told by Don King that Will had cracked Tyson's tooth, and he had to go to the dentist. This was the only time I've ever felt in actual danger at a shoot.

HANK SHOCKLEE: I thought Public Enemy's "Fight the Power" was gonna be in *Do the Right Thing* for maybe a minute. I had no idea Spike Lee was gonna use the song in the entire movie. Once we saw that, Spike said, "I want to direct a video for it." His idea was to stage a rally in Brooklyn and film it. And I was like, *Wow, that's ambitious.*

CHUCK D: To me, every video was a pain. And "Fight the Power" was convoluted, because of the magnitude of it. It was big, and there was no room for error. We had about four thousand people in a one-block area. Plus, it was raining.

HANK SHOCKLEE: Spike contacted schools and youth organizations in Brooklyn. We were driving out to Brooklyn, early in the morning, and the energy level was amazing. By 8 A.M., people started coming in. Then more and more people started coming in. By 9 A.M., the streets were mobbed. I didn't know there were that many people on the planet. It was massive.

CHUCK D: Spike was trying to remember the legacy of the past, the present, and the future of black people in America, all in one video. The marriage of film and rap music had never been planned that distinctly. That wasn't the first rap video, but it was the first time it was planned to be a significant statement in culture and art.

HANK SHOCKLEE: The set design people made banners. Public Enemy performed "Fight the Power" at the end of the rally, and Spike made it look like something out of the '60s, like a cross between the Black Panthers and Martin Luther King's march on Washington. And the video created a groundswell for the movie. From that perspective, it was brilliant. Spike was doing branding at a level people are only starting to get on today. He took the hottest underground group at the time and shot a huge video that shows a massive rally in the heart of Brooklyn. People said, "I want to know more. This is a soundtrack? To what? *Do the Right Thing*? What's that about? We want to do the right thing. Should we rally? Should we protest? I want to go see this movie." It was about something bigger than the song.

It was the only video that captured the energy and spirit of black youth at that moment, when the black community was on the borderline of hopelessness. When you saw the energy of those kids, it's a contagious thing. You're feeding energy to an energy source, because kids' energy is off the charts. Whatever the video lacked from an artistic level, Spike bottled the spirit of a revolution and put it in a three-minute video. That solidified not only Public Enemy's growth and appeal, but also the movement of rap music and its influence. Look, rap hasn't slowed down yet. This video helped spark that.

MC HAMMER: My idea for "U Can't Touch This" was a celebration to counter the darkness I was seeing in Oakland, because of all the crack. All of a sudden, guys were cutting heads off—literally. Instead of shooting someone once, they'd shoot 'em thirty times. Uncles started pimping their nieces for crack. It was stuff you'd never seen before. I wanted a visual that would give you a form of escape and joy and fun.

MICK KLEBER: With "U Can't Touch This," we knew we had a hit on our hands, and we needed to step up and spend some money. I'd been reading a bunch of books on Fred Astaire, and Astaire never let himself be filmed any way other than head to toe. All his little in-between movements were the hallmarks of his artistry, and Hammer felt the same way. So when we did "U Can't Touch This," we focused on filming continuous sequences of Hammer performing his dance moves, with no cuts.

Those harem pants came out of nowhere. When I first saw them I thought, *This will either go down as the most brilliant wardrobe idea in the history of music video, or a total laughingstock.* But once you saw him move in them, against a white backdrop, you knew it was going to kill.

RUPERT WAINWRIGHT: Mick Kleber got a little frustrated, because Hammer and I—I'm not saying we ran our own show; Mick was creative and smart, but Hammer couldn't pick him out of a lineup of one. The classic thing that would happen is, my phone would ring about 4 A.M. "Yo, Rupes, wake up. It's Hammer. I'm in Detroit, and we want to do a shoot on Saturday." Oh, great. Well, whereabouts? "Yes, so Saturday, Detroit, all right?" Click. I would fall back to sleep, wake up four hours later, and go, *Did I dream that?* Then I'd call Capitol Records and say, "So, great news, we're doing a video on Saturday." "Oh," they'd say. "Tell us more. We haven't heard from Mr. Hammer about this. Did he mention which song we're doing a video for?" I'd jump on a plane and get out there, pull a producer, start booking crew. And then Friday, Capitol would go, "All right, it's confirmed, you're doing a shoot."

MC HAMMER: I never let the label hire my directors. I was firm in my belief that you didn't want a director who was already vested in his approach to making videos. Rupert Wainwright had the perfect personality to counter mine. We could argue, we could fight, we could insult each other, and then we could hug and love each other. I'd take my time to get into what I call "I'm ready" mode. I understand a dancer's mentality, so I'd keep the crew loud and wild, and it would always interrupt something Rupert was trying to do.

RUPERT WAINWRIGHT: I was always putting my foot in it, because the racial terms in England are different to the racial terms in America. I was onstage with Hammer, trying to get a rehearsal going—we were shooting a concert the next day, and he was also rehearsing his live show. I'm quite pushy on the set. And I was like, "We've got to get focused here," and he's ignoring me. I said something like, "Just get over here, boy." And there was total silence. Like, two hundred people went, *Oh my fucking God.* Hammer looked at me good-naturedly and said, "I'm not your boy. You're my boy." Somehow I knew I'd said the wrong thing, but it just slipped out, and I didn't quite know how it was the wrong thing.

MC HAMMER: Showing my dancing was most important to me. Boogalooing, roboting, it began in Oakland, California, in 1968, Fremont High School, 6 P.M. one night in between a high school basketball game. The first guy did what we called a robot boogaloo move, and then it took off from the Bay Area and went to LA and jumped all the way to New York. In '75, disco came, and San Francisco was one of the epicenters for disco. Disco dancing incorporated modern and jazz and tap. I mastered that style. Most video choreography was Broadway style, and I brought synchronization with street moves. My videos catapulted that style of dance to the world.

RUPERT WAINWRIGHT: On "U Can't Touch This," they wanted to totally re-brand Hammer as a full-on pop star, instead of being a rapper. So we shot it with lots of pretty colors, and at the same time, I was shooting a movie of the week, *Dillinger*, with Mark Harmon and Sherilyn Fenn. I had to go back on location, so I gave the video footage to the editor. Hammer watched it and said, "This is no good. You can't see my dance moves." I'm like, "Hammer, I love you, but trust me, nobody in America wants to watch you jiggle from one side of the stage to another for twelve seconds." He's like, "Listen, Rupe, let me sit here with the editor and work with him." I had to go back to Ohio and finish *Dillinger*, so I said, "You guys play with it and send me a copy when you're done." I got a FedEx package, and when I watched "U Can't Touch This" in my hotel room, I said, "Oh God, my days of directing music videos are over. I'll never work again." It just looked so slow.

Guess what? Hammer was right! It's one of the most popular videos of all time.

MC HAMMER: I introduced a new style of cutting videos, which video editors, after this, called "The Hammer Cut." It was the completion of a dance move without interrupting the move. I learned this from Michael Jackson; Michael would sit in on the editing of his videos. He'd make sure editors did not mess up his dancing with their editing. I wanted to keep up with the energy of the record: a dance move, then cut to the story, then cut to some color, more energy, then jump back. I had to come up with a faster cut. I would tell the editor, "Oh no, no, no. This is all wrong. Let's start over."

RUPERT WAINWRIGHT: I was shooting a video with Hammer and we were doing a club scene in a bad part of LA, on Olympic Blvd. Hammer was kind of in hiding, because there was a certain guy, who shall be nameless, who was basically kidnapping people. Bobby Brown had gone back to Atlanta because his mother had been kidnapped. This guy was trying to get to Hammer and shake him down.

So we were doing a scene in a nightclub during the day, and a prop guy said to me, "When are we shooting the scene with the Uzi?" I said, "We're not shooting a scene with an Uzi." He said, "Well, a couple of guys in the back have got Uzis." I went, "Oh fuck." We called the police and got everybody out of the club, out onto the sidewalk. Three cop cars turn up. We explain what's going on. The cops don't even turn their engines off. They said, "Send everybody home now, and get out of here." That should have happened on the N.W.A shoot, but it happened on a Hammer shoot.

RIC MENELLO: Russell Simmons asked me to direct "Children's Story" for Slick Rick. And Russell wanted midgets. We shot in Central Park and put a bed there. Slick Rick is reading a bedtime story, and two girls were in bed with the midget, Little Jimmy. There were supposed to be two midgets. But one midget was a horrible guy. He'd done a lot of porno. He wouldn't sign a release. I said, "All right, get the fuck out of here. We'll use one midget." Little Jimmy walked out about three-quarters of the way through the video. He kept saying, "I want to dance." So I had him dance on the bed. Suddenly he goes, "You're making fun of me!" He jumped up, landed on the bed, belly flopped off, and walked away. Slick Rick's DJ, Vance, followed him, yelling, "Yo, midget dick! Don't ever show your face again."

BILL ADLER: The song is a ghetto tale, it's dire and heart-wrenching. If you represented the story in a video, MTV wouldn't go anywhere near it. So instead, Rick played it for laughs.

RIC MENELLO: One of my assistants was holding Slick Rick's coat, and she put it down on a bench. I'm like, "When I tell you to hold the coat, hold it." She goes, "There's a butcher knife in it." I don't know, I got along with him.

LIONEL MARTIN: On "Just a Friend," I came up with the idea to make Biz Markie look like Mozart. We put a wig on him. We put him at the piano. The funny thing was, he told me that in the studio, he played all the instruments. And it just looked off to me. I was like, "Biz, didn't you say you played the piano when you recorded the song?" He said, "Yeah, but the keys were numbered." You knew he was lying to you, but he was just so colorful.

He was really late to the shoot. He called and said, "Lionel, I'm on the Long Island Expressway and I got a flat tire." He called an hour later and said, "I fixed the flat, and now the other tire is flat."

BIG DADDY KANE: Fab 5 Freddy was sick of me the day he directed "Erase Racism" for Kool G Rap. He was trying to keep everything on schedule, and he had the scene set up in a graveyard, basically saying that racism can result in death. But we got there and I was like, "I'm not going in no graveyard." If it was up to me, I'd miss my own funeral. So we had to find a new location to shoot my scene. He was hot about that.

EVERLAST: There's no better way to do a video than the way House of Pain did "Jump Around," because it wasn't even work. This was the era of Afrocentric black power, and we have Irish lineage, so we went to the St. Paddy's Day parade in New York. We were drinking at five in the morning. We went to the parade and acted crazy, and we were still drinking at five the next morning.

We didn't get permits, we just went to the parade, bounced in and out, got kicked out, filmed fights happening on Madison Avenue. People drunk, fighting, puking, and it captured the insanity and stupidity. That's all real shit, man. We knew what was going to happen: drunken fighting. Do you know any Irish people? Fighting is like the peak; that's when you know they're having the most fun, when they're fighting.

The success of "Jump Around" put me off MTV for a minute. I was like, I'm glad it's happening, but how many times do I have to watch my own video? I couldn't believe how many times they played it. Later on, we were spending

$100,000 or $200,000 on videos, and I was like, "The one we made for $10,000 was better."

SIR MIX-A-LOT: In "Baby Got Back," we were making fun of videos. Black men have always liked voluptuous women. I got tired of seeing skinny girls in videos. Rick Rubin and the director, Adam Bernstein, decided the video was gonna be about a bunch of hot chicks doing their thing with a big Sir Mix-a-Lot scaffolding across the screen. I expected to see a butt about the size of a Volkswagen. Instead, it was probably twenty-five to thirty feet tall, and twenty feet across the butt cheeks. I was kind of in awe. I had done a couple of videos on an independent label, and we didn't have casting calls like that. We had to get a bunch of ex-prostitutes to be in those.

The girl with the long wig who looked like a mermaid? Not only did I pick her, I dated her. The girl I thought had the best ass of all had a banana skirt on. She's only in the video for a couple of seconds because she was shy. She was like, "Most people tease me for my butt." I said, "Well, they won't after this song, baby."

Once the video went to number one, MTV got complaints and decided to show it only during the evening. They said it offended a lot of people. I thought my career was over. The record company was like, "This is great!"

ANN CARLI: We were thrilled when Will Smith got a show on NBC, *The Fresh Prince of Bel-Air.* But I wasn't surprised. You could see it had to go that way. Rap was becoming undeniable. The rise of hip-hop and its infiltration into the mainstream has a little to do with why we elected an African-American president.

Chapter 40

"EGO-FUCKING-MANIACS"

MICHAEL BAY, CHER, AND
ALL 9:08 OF "NOVEMBER RAIN"

A T FIRST, VIDEO DIRECTORS HAD ENTERED AN UNSURE, unestablished, underfunded industry. A few years later, when Russell Mulcahy and Steve Barron began making feature films, it altered the industry—now, young directors saw music videos as an elevator to Hollywood, a faster and more certain route than starting with a career in costume design (Joel Schumacher), acting (Peter Bogdanovich), stand-up comedy (Woody Allen), or directing softcore porn (Francis Ford Coppola).

While he was a film student, Michael Bay "knew exactly what I was going to do," he's said. "I was going to do videos—that's when videos were fun." Two weeks after graduating in 1988, he had a $165,000 budget to return Donny Osmond to stardom. Instead, the video made a star of Bay, who became the biggest action director of all time. The loud-and-large fireball mentality he brought to *Bad Boys*, *The Rock*, *Armageddon*, and *Transformers* was evident even on MTV, where he ushered in a new era of excess. "This guy had a *plane crash* in a *music video*," Will Smith—whom Bay turned from a video star into a film star, in *Bad Boys*—once said. "I was like, *Damn*." Bay's trilogy of videos for Meat Loaf included, in addition to the plane crash, a girl getting hosed down while washing a red convertible and wearing a sheer dress, a girl in a bathtub, the same girl in bed with another girl, a motorcycle, another motorcycle, a helicopter, a graveyard, a medieval mansion, Jack Daniel's, gangbangers, an exploding jukebox, an exploding TV set, and Angelina Jolie. Axl Rose probably saw this as one-upsmanship.

Bay has never believed in understatement—as a fifteen-year-old intern on

Raiders of the Lost Ark, just two years out of Hebrew school, he met Steven Spielberg and announced that he thought the film "was going to suck." Bay refers to himself as "a frank guy," and success has not made him falsely modest. After starring two *Transformers* films, Megan Fox described him as behaving "like Hitler," which is unfair—Michael Bay would never do anything as small as invade Poland.

MICK KLEBER: Capitol had just signed Donny Osmond, and we put out his first "adult" album, *Soldier of Love*. Although Donny was one of the most unlikely MTV artists imaginable, they agreed to support a "Sacred Emotion" video if it worked for their audience. My objective was to erase the perception of Donny as a cheesy pretty boy. A talented young woman named Paula Walker started to make a great video featuring a troupe of exotic models in haute couture lingerie.

Donny's manager came in from Utah with a colleague who was introduced as a production adviser. The adviser said, "I know sexy, and this isn't it." I said, "You're an expert on sexy?" He said, "I'm a Mormon with six kids. We have more sex with beautiful women than anybody." Things got tense enough that I had to cancel the shoot. Now I had half the original budget to work with. I thought that it was going to take a miracle to bring back Donny Osmond.

And then I thought, *That's what this video has to be about. It has to be about a miracle.* So I came up with this idea of making it rain in the desert. We'd do a version of the barn-raising scene in *Witness*, but make it sexy, with hot guys and girls; they'd build a stage and then it would rain. After about a week of being turned down by different directors, I looked through my pile of demo reels, and liked one from this kid at the Pasadena Art Center. So I brought him in, gave him the treatment I'd written, and asked if he could do it for $120,000. He said, "We'll make it work." They went off and shot for three days in the Arizona desert.

The next Friday, Donny was on *The Today Show* to sing "Sacred Emotion," and they played a little of the video, which wasn't finished yet. When I got to work, my message book was filled with people wanting to know who directed the Donny Osmond video. And by the end of the day, Michael Bay was signed to Propaganda.

ANNE-MARIE MACKAY: The work was beautiful. We signed him immediately to Propaganda.

JONI SIGHVATSSON: Michael Bay was polarizing. Anne-Marie said, "I found this guy who did a great video for Donny Osmond." And we're like, "Anne-Marie, are you insane?" We thought we were much too cool for Donny Osmond. The video wasn't to everyone's taste—it was sleek and commercial—but I was amazed by the technical proficiency. I knew Bay was going to be a big.

ADAM HOROVITZ: When the Beastie Boys moved to LA and signed to Capitol Records, they had a huge party for us on the roof. We thought, *This is great. The label loves us.* The next day, the label president gets fired.

The new president is this motherfucker named Hale Milgrim. He's in charge when Capitol puts out *Paul's Boutique*, and nothing is happening with our record. We go to see Milgrim, the dude's got a mini-ponytail and a brand-new tie-dyed Grateful Dead shirt. Classic look. He said, "I know you worked hard on this record, but I'm pushing the new Donny Osmond record right now, so you guys have to wait till next time." We're like, "Wait—Donny Osmond? From the Osmonds?" And he was dead serious. I remember that Donny Osmond video. It's Donny Osmond out in the desert, and he's trying to do Michael Jackson dance moves. That shit sucked.

JOHN BEUG: Michael Bay did a couple of videos for me. I don't think I was particularly encouraging to his career, shall we say. He did a Chicago video, and I told him I wasn't blown away by his talent, which he reminded me of at the *Pearl Harbor* premiere ten years later.

TARSEM SINGH: Michael Bay was in film school with me. We had an assignment to do a video to anybody's song; most people used Tom Waits, something like that. But Michael Bay cut his reel to Berlin's "You Take My Breath Away." It moved his soul! It was *shit*, but it moved his soul! When people say he sold out, I say *bullshit*, because he's true to himself. When you see a Michael Bay film, you might say it's the biggest piece of shit, or the most brilliant and successful film, but you see *him*.

ALAN NIVEN: Michael Bay: That's the only fucker I ever fired off a video shoot. Mick Kleber introduced Michael to do a Great White video, "Call It Rock n' Roll." And the collection of women Michael turned up with at the shoot was totally over the top. He spent more of the day chasing hemlines with his lens than he did shooting my band. I called Capitol and said, "I'm about to fire your goddamn director." Capitol drove out to the shoot in a panic, because they wanted to keep their relationship with Michael. And Kleber and I finished the video. So when I watch *Pearl Harbor,* I do quietly smile.

GREG GOLD: Whenever Michael Bay was casting a video, you'd pull up to Propaganda and see beautiful girls lined up outside the building. They were usually, uh, endowed. He never grew out of that.

LIONEL RICHIE: Michael Bay directed "Do It to Me One More Time." That video had *two* amazing—no, *three* amazing—girls. It's the only shoot I've ever been on where the entire crew showed up *early.*

DOMINIC SENA: Michael Bay was the first guy beyond the original founders who was invited to join Propaganda. David Fincher and Michael were not each other's biggest fans. David was not fond of Michael's work. They were oil and water. They never spoke to each other. They were highly competitive and preferred not to associate. Which remains true to this day.

HOWARD WOFFINDEN: I got on well with Michael. But he was as excitable then as he is now. He could get volatile with people for no good reason. He was charismatic, though, and well connected. His dad was rich, and he seemed to know every person in LA.

Michael was a sponge, which drove everybody at Propaganda crazy. He would grab all the directors' show reels and spend his night watching everybody's videos. A couple of weeks later, those same scenes would come up in his videos. I used to think of him as a re-imager—he would find images in people's reels and breathe new life into them. Michael would add a sexy, voluptuous girl and you'd think, *Oh my god, she's getting hosed down—and it's windy as well!*

RICHARD MARX: Every once in a while, my kids go, "Wait a minute. You did a video with Michael Bay?"

KIP WINGER: After the "Hungry" video, I was like, "I want the next video to be like a Coke commercial." We hired Michael Bay to shoot "Can't Get Enuff." He was like the young David Fincher, and at the time, Fincher was *the* guy. Michael Bay walked in to watch our rehearsal, and the first thing out of his mouth was "This is going to be rough." He really didn't care about the band—it was the Michael Bay show. Visually, it's by far our best-looking video.

DENNIS DeYOUNG: "Show Me the Way," my favorite Styx video, was directed by Michael Bay. He's a serious dude; he has a very low humor threshold. Given his track record since, you would never believe that he directed that video. All I can say is, if you want to be enormously successful in the film business, come to me first and do a video.

VANILLA ICE: Michael Bay directed "I Love You." Ugh, I hate that song. Charles Koppelman, the president of my record company, said, "We need you to do a slow song." And I was like, "I really don't want to do that, man." And he's like, "Here's a couple million bucks, now do us a slow song." I said, "When do I go in the studio?"

JULIANA ROBERTS: I loved Michael. He was totally hyper. And he kind of worshipped David Fincher. We'd always crack up, because Michael would follow David around the Propaganda offices.

JONI SIGHVATSSON: Fincher and Bay became adversaries. It wasn't spoken, but it created a great deal of tension. Fincher was sophisticated. He was inspired by great photographers such as Robert Frank and Horst P. Horst. Bay was a technical genius like Fincher, but he had the mind of a teenager. His sensibility was juvenile.

JEFF AYEROFF: Michael Bay was known as "the little Fincher." That's how he was pitched to me. They said, "He's not as artistic, but he's got drive, he's gonna chew through everything." He did the Divinyls' "I Touch Myself" for me at Virgin. He was an ego-fucking-maniac.

JERRY BRUCKHEIMER: We used a lot of MTV directors to make our films, Michael Bay being the premier one. When we were looking for a director for *Bad Boys*, we saw his commercials and his videos. Besides being a phenomenal shooter, we loved Michael's sense of lighting and his sense of humor. Whatever he did had a wink and a smile. He'd done an excellent Donny Osmond video, and that was another thing that helped sell him to us.

CHYNNA PHILLIPS: We made "You Won't See Me Cry" with Michael Bay. He's a great director, but he went for the sexy lingerie look, which was a mistake. Management felt we needed to be more sexy, instead of wearing jeans all the time. We were already extremely successful, so why were we changing our image?

MEAT LOAF: I asked David Fincher to direct "Anything for Love." I gave him the whole *Beauty and the Beast* premise, and Fincher said, "Ah, I love it." And he gave me a budget of $2.3 million. I said, "I-I . . ." I stuttered. And he goes, "Let me try to rework the budget." So he came back a few days later and gave me a budget of $1.7 million. I said, "David, we don't have that kind of money." And Fincher said, "Well then, get Michael Bay." That's the last time Michael Bay was the cheaper option.

JONI SIGHVATSSON: Fincher was very expensive. He and the label were at an impasse over the Meat Loaf video, so I said, "Why don't we just give this to Michael Bay?" Fincher gave it to Bay, we ended up spending $750,000, and it was a seminal video. Michael directed, and it was David's concept. That was the first and last time Fincher and Bay collaborated.

BRIAN GRANT: Once the four of us at MGM got quite successful, we grew into a massive company. We made five feature films—*Sid and Nancy* was the first. Then the stock market crashed. We were highly leveraged, and when the banks panicked and pulled the money, the whole company collapsed. Within a week. By then, the baton had been passed, to Propaganda in particular. They were the next generation.

ANNE-MARIE MACKAY: There was a tremendous meeting of the minds between Madonna and David Fincher. She's very well read, and she came to the table with a lot of references and ideas. It was Madonna who came up with the *Metropolis* motif for "Express Yourself," then the set designer, Vance Lorenzini, ran with that and built the incredible sets.

RANDY SKINNER: "Express Yourself" was a four-day shoot. If my memory serves me, it cost $1.7 million.

PAULA ABDUL: I was saving money from my choreography to make demos. Janet Jackson was the one who kept saying, "You can do this." And I'd say, "Eh, I'd better stick to my day job." But she encouraged me. The bottom line—and I've always known this—is that I may not be the best dancer and I'm not the best singer, but I do know how to be a brilliant performer.

DANIEL KLEINMAN: Paula choreographed a few videos I'd done, and she wanted me to direct her first video, "Knocked Out." We were quite good mates—we'd gone on a few dinner dates—but frankly, I didn't like the song. Paula wanted the video to focus on the choreography, so I tried to film the dancing in an interesting way, which I don't think I did. Quite rightly, Jeff Ayeroff hired David Fincher to do her next video.

PAULA ABDUL: I loved making videos. Loved, loved, loved it. MTV and music videos were a huge reason I got signed, and why I became so popular. My videos were everything. Even when I was collecting demos, I was putting together the videos in my head.

JEFF AYEROFF: When I left Warners to become co-president of Virgin Records, I hired David Fincher to do Paula's videos. The first one, "The Way That You Love Me," was only okay. For the next one, I said, "Make it black-and-white. Highly graphic, stylized, and make her look fucking great. Have Arsenio Hall do a cameo in it. Figure out something." That's where "Straight Up" came from. It became the biggest video of the year.

PAULA ABDUL: Jeff had already signed me to Virgin Records, so the deal was that I'd choreograph a video for David Fincher, and David would direct "Straight Up" right after that. At first I was so bummed that David wanted to do "Straight Up" in black-and-white Super 8. I was like, *This is my big chance! I do color videos!* I think the main reason he shot in black-and-white is that it doesn't cost as much as color, and he wanted to bank the difference. But of course, it ended up being a brilliant move. "Straight Up" was career-defining, it was style-defining—everything about it helped define me as an artist. And obviously, David turned out to be a genius.

JONI SIGHVATSSON: We all thought Paula Abdul sucked. Ayeroff had been good to Fincher, and David's a very loyal person.

PETER BARON: I played David Fincher the Aerosmith song "Janie's Got a Gun," which no one outside the offices had heard yet. I said, "David, I want you to do this video." I pressed play again and he listened for a couple of minutes and said, "Okay, this is what we're going to do. The first shot's going to have yellow police tape, rippling in the wind . . ." He already had a visual of how to start the video.

JOHN TAYLOR: To me, David Fincher was not a video pioneer. By this point, video had gone corporate. I would guess that the budget for "Janie's Got a Gun" was the total of our first eight videos.

PETER BARON: I walked into David Geffen's office and said, "I need $400,000 for 'Janie's Got a Gun.'" He said, "You have a director?" I said, "I've got David Fincher." He said, "Go make the video."

JULIANA ROBERTS: "Janie's Got a Gun" was the first video I worked on that seemed like a movie.

GARY GERSH: Around '89, we really got on a roll at Geffen, from every angle in our company. Aerosmith, Guns N' Roses, Cher: We didn't spare any expense when we were trying to get it done.

JOHN KALODNER: Marty Callner directed Aerosmith's "Love in an Elevator" and Cher's "If I Could Turn Back Time." He was incredibly expensive. When Marty wanted a $10,000 light, and there was only one in all of Hollywood, he got it.

MARTY CALLNER: On "Love in an Elevator," I worked Aerosmith for thirty-five straight hours, and then they had to wait around for three days while we set up the final shot. They were already pissed at me. We set up an outdoor elevator in Santa Monica, and there was a long line of chicks waiting to get in the elevator with Steven Tyler. You know, love in an elevator! The producer had obtained a permit, but instead of writing that we'd finish at 1 A.M., he mistakenly wrote 10 P.M. So at ten, as I'm ready to do the final shot, they shut us down and said, "If you roll a foot of film, we're putting you in jail." The band didn't talk to me for months.

JOHN KALODNER: Cher was difficult to work with. So lazy and thoughtless. One of the biggest stars ever, and not a pleasure. When I approached her in 1987 to do a record, she said, "I don't want to be a singer again." I said, "I'll pick the songs, I'll pick the producers, all you have to do is sing." I did everything for those records except sing them, and she never so much as gave me a thank-you. That was Cher. But "If I Could Turn Back Time"—the song and especially Marty Callner's video—was incredible. It gave her career a whole new life.

CHER, artist: John Kalodner really did believe in me when no one else did. David Geffen introduced us, and John told me he thought I should be making records, which I hadn't done for many years. He was a fabulous record executive and gave me a lot of confidence. But about his comments: What is he, a fuckin' ventriloquist?

MARTY CALLNER: We were on the USS *Missouri*, making "If I Could Turn Back Time." Cher asked me, "What should I wear?" I told her, "The last time I looked, you were Cher, so wear something outrageous." Unbeknownst to me, she'd called her longtime costume designer Bob Mackie and had him design something special. Now we're shooting the video, and my crew tells me, "The lights are ready, let's do rehearsal." Ever the dutiful director, I go to her Winnebago to escort her to the ship, and I open the door, and I'm in shock. She's standing there in that fishnet body thong. I froze. I didn't know what to say. And as I looked over my right shoulder as she was walking by me, I saw tattoos on her ass. And I said, "How clever. Tattoo underwear."

CHER: It was my design. Bob Mackie said, "Don't tell anyone I designed *that* for you." We shot for two or three days. I arrived in the night mist, in a coach and a big cape. I rode in a speedboat and had to climb a ladder in high heels, up the side of the ship, but they didn't use that scene. The Japanese surrendered to the United States on that ship. All the sailors called me "ma'am."

MARTY CALLNER: So we're rehearsing, and she's straddling the guns, and all the commanding officers are whooping it up. We're getting as phallic as you can possibly get. Our liaison from the USS *Missouri* was a guy named Steve Honda. The take ends, he says, "Marty, can I talk to you a second?" He says, "She can't wear that. If she wears that, I'll end up in the Aleutian Islands." He was really adamant about it. So finally I said, "Look I'll make you a deal. You go tell her she can't wear it." And he did not have the nuts to tell her.

JOHN CANNELLI: I had a very good relationship with Cher. She used to pick me up at the office and we'd have ice cream at Serendipity. My dad passed away during the time I was dealing with her, and she talked to my mom on the phone and consoled her. On one of her tours, she actually sent a limousine for my mom to bring her to a concert.

MARTY CALLNER: Initially, Abbey Konowitch and John Cannelli were over the moon about the video. When MTV aired it, they got tons of flack from the navy. Then they decided they would only play the video after 9 P.M. I took the position that the video with Cher on the battleship was good for the navy's recruiting. They couldn't really argue the point.

ABBEY KONOWITCH: "If I Could Turn Back Time" was hugely controversial. Tom Freston and I decided to play the video only after 9 P.M. Tom said, "We need to have a public statement as to why we're not playing this until after nine." I said, "Why don't we say, 'Too much butt for the morning' or 'No butts about it.'" He goes, "You're onto something. We can't take ourselves too seriously. We're just a music network." We were under the gun, and I said the Yiddish word *tush*. And Tom, who was the furthest thing from a Jewish guy, says, "That's it! That's our position." So when I went on Larry King to discuss it, I said, "She's a big star, but it was just too much tush for nine o'clock in the morning."

CHER: It worked out well, because the controversy—which I didn't plan—made more people want to see the video.

JOHN KALODNER: Nobody was ever allowed to make a video on a United States naval ship after "Turn Back Time."

MARTY CALLNER: People always ask me, why'd you make the Cher video on a ship? I was looking for an interesting location. It was the same reason Bon Jovi went to the top of a mountain for "Blaze of Glory." Because it was there.

WAYNE ISHAM: People always want to know how much Bon Jovi's "Blaze of Glory" cost. I'll be honest, I don't know. We came up with the idea of creating the last drive-in on earth, on top of a butte in Utah. So we helicoptered in our own drive-in screen, all the old cars and trucks you see, everything. Just getting all that shit up there was expensive. We even brought blenders with us, for margaritas. There's a shot of Jon sitting and playing his guitar on the edge of a cliff. Doc McGhee was freaking out, going, "You're gonna kill my artist."

DOC McGHEE: There was a thunderstorm on top of this butte, and Wayne tells Johnny to hang over a rock while he's playing guitar. If he falls fifteen hundred feet and dies, then I lose my commission and have to walk home! So what do you think I'm going to say? Johnny's hair was standing on end because of the electricity. He looked like Buckwheat.

WAYNE ISHAM: If you look closely, underneath the ledge right next to Jon is a bottle of Cuervo. We spent the night on the cliffs of Moab in sleeping bags, woke up at sunrise, rode motorcycles, shot the video, made margaritas. That's shit that you did. That was the life.

CURT MARVIS: The Rolling Stones wanted to do a video to promote their Steel Wheels tour, and they brought on Peter Mensch and Cliff Burnstein as consultants. That's how our relationship with the Stones started. Wayne Isham and I were in DC one week, getting ready for a video, and we got pretty wasted. We staggered back to our hotel at one-thirty in the morning and Peter said, "Keith wants to talk to you." We walked into the hotel bar, which was closed to everyone but us.

Keith starts, "You fucking bastards!" He found out we were charging $300,000 for this video, and he's convinced that it's way too much money. He said, "I'm gonna slit your throat, sonny!" and he took out his knife and brought it across his throat. Peter Mensch said, "Does anybody need a drink?" Keith said, "I want two Long Island iced teas." Mensch goes, "*Two?* Why do you want *two?*" Keith said, "Get me two fucking Long Island iced teas!"

So Mensch brings over the drinks, and Keith keeps yelling at us. He's screaming, waving his arms around, and while he's swinging his arms he hits one of the Long Island iced teas and knocks it to the floor. The glass shatters. He looks at Mensch and goes, "Now you know why I ordered *two!*"

TONY DiSANTO: When Guns N' Roses started getting some fame, we shot interviews with them at the Chelsea Hotel, and their energy was so I-don't-give-a-fuck, so punk rock. When *Use Your Illusion* came out, the next set of interviews was with Kurt Loder in Axl's beautiful LA backyard. His hair was blow-dried, his teeth were all perfect, and he looked like an angel. I was like, "Wow, they've sure changed."

ANDY MORAHAN: Two of Axl's favorite artists were Elton John and George Michael. Which was bizarre. As a matter of fact, he hated most other rock bands. If you spoke to him about Van Halen or Nirvana, he'd be spitting feathers, but when it came time to talk about Elton John, he'd go all misty-eyed. One of his favorite videos was George Michael's "Father Figure," and he wanted to make some big, epic narrative-driven videos.

DOUG GOLDSTEIN: After Axl fired Alan Niven, I walked into Eddie Rosenblatt's office and said, "We're gonna make an expensive video." And he said, "Doug, we're out of the video business with you. You pay for your own videos. We'll front the money, but we'll take it back, and then you guys own the rights to your videos."

ALAN NIVEN: The videos that were done under my watch totaled something like $500,000, of which half went into "Paradise City." I was told it cost $1.25 million to shoot "November Rain," which to me is a preposterous waste of money.

STEVEN ADLER: I think that video would have been better if I was a part of it. But I'd been kicked out of the band for partying—and the biggest irony is, I was partying *with* the guys in the band.

DOUG GOLDSTEIN: The videos caused tension in the band. Axl would just not show up for a day of shooting, so it doubled the cost. He did that on every video. Everybody else in the band was upset about it, and Slash was the only one who spoke up.

DAVE GROHL: When a musician starts to use the phrase "mini-movie" to describe a video, it's time to quit. Some videos I enjoyed just because they were train wrecks, like "November Rain." I looked forward to seeing that on TV because I didn't need those nine minutes of my life anymore.

DANIEL PEARL: Axl was as unreliable a person as you could possibly imagine, but at the same time he was a good benefactor. I did three big videos with Andy Morahan for Guns N' Roses—"Don't Cry," "November Rain," and "Estranged"— and each one cost over a million dollars, God bless 'em.

DOUG GOLDSTEIN: Oh fuck. To be honest, I blank on the *Use Your Illusion* videos, because they all seem like the same video to me.

ANDY MORAHAN: Axl had written a trilogy of videos based around a short story by his friend Del James. We made "Don't Cry" the first video. Axl was undergoing regressive therapy, he'd gone through bouts of severe depression and wanting to blow his brains out, and his personal madness became part of the video's story line. Izzy Stradlin had left the band, and the cracks were starting to appear—the trilogy was Axl's way of saying, "I'm gonna take control here." Before we started those videos, *Use Your Illusion* was up to about 8 or 9 million in sales. After those videos, it went up to 22 million.

If I wanted to do a daylight scene, I'd have to keep the band up all night and shoot it first thing in the morning. They were like vampires. I had a day set aside for the graveyard scene. I had half of the LA County cemetery closed down, and a cortege and two hundred extras and four rain machines, and Axl didn't show up until it was dark. That's why the graveyard scene is at night.

PETER BARON: Andy Morahan shot part of "Don't Cry" on the top of the Transamerica Center in downtown LA. We had two helicopters. It was mayhem. We got in a lot of trouble from the city because we completely stalled traffic on a Friday night.

ANDY MORAHAN: Stephanie Seymour and Axl were lovey-dovey on the first video. Stephanie had no shame in cuddling up to Axl in front of me and saying, "Hey Axl, why don't you work with some really big Hollywood directors?" *Thanks, Steph. Love you, too.*

PETER BARON: When the "Don't Cry" shoot finally ended, I got on the freight elevator by myself to go down to my car. I press the button, and just as the doors start to close, who walks in but Axl and Stephanie Seymour. And they proceed to make out. I'm not going to say he was dry humping her, but he was dry humping her. He just did not care that there was someone else in the elevator. He was a rock star, and he was having a rock star moment.

DOUG GOLDSTEIN: Their relationship was tumultuous. Axl loved that girl to death. I'd say Stephanie was the unstable one in that relationship. The first time I met her, she opened the door naked. She goes, "No, you can come in." *Sorry, gotta go.*

ANDY MORAHAN: We couldn't figure out what we were going to do with Slash in "November Rain." I said to him, "Wouldn't it be cool if you walked out of the church into a completely different environment?" And he said, "Yeah, let's go to New Mexico and do that." So we did. Weirdly enough, Anton Corbijn was staying in the same hotel as us in New Mexico. I'd known Anton for a while, and I invited him to come to the shoot. After about a half hour he said to me, "Andy, this is incredible. You've got five cameras, cranes, helicopter, this big crew. Is this the whole video?" I said, "No, it's about twenty-seven seconds of it."

I've had calls from Sofia Coppola's people over the years asking to buy the original storyboards from "November Rain."

All three songs—"Don't Cry," "November Rain," and "Estranged"—are overblown power ballads. And all three videos are crazy. It was like *Spinal Tap* with money. I still don't know to this day why, in "November Rain," you see only half of Stephanie Seymour's face in the coffin.

DOUG GOLDSTEIN: Axl jumping off the oil tanker in "Estranged," that's got to be the most extravagant thing I've ever seen.

BILL BENNETT, record executive: I got a notice at work one day that Sunset Boulevard was going to be closed all afternoon for a video, and thought, *Who the fuck would close down Sunset?* Guns N' Roses, that's who, for "Estranged." Their videos were late, bloated, and expensive. The band was so big, they did whatever they wanted.

ANDY MORAHAN: By the time we got to "Estranged," Axl had split up with Stephanie Seymour, and he said, "I never want a girl in a video again. I'd rather go out with a dolphin." Which is why I put dolphins all over the video. I've been asked by students about the metaphorical imagery in those videos, and I'm like, "Fuck if I know."

Chapter 41

———

"I WANT TO HAVE A NICKNAME"

HOW MTV HELPED MICHAEL JACKSON ELECT HIMSELF "THE KING OF POP"

"ERE'S A UNIQUE ONE," MTV'S MATT FARBER wrote in a November 1991 memo to staff. "We need to refer to Michael Jackson as 'The King of Pop' on-air." This was not MTV's idea—it was Jackson's. That week, he was debuting an eleven-minute video, "Black or White" (his first with John Landis since "Thriller"), and any network that wanted the extravaganza had to agree to call him by the nickname he'd chosen. MTV was willing to do whatever was required to keep him happy. "I know this is a bizarre request," Farber wrote apologetically, as he outlined a system for pleasing Jackson: Each VJ had to refer to him on-air as "The King of Pop" at least twice per week. Farber added one more instruction: "Please be sure to note which segments you do this in case we need to send dubs to the King of Pop himself." Jackson had made MTV huge, and now he was monitoring the channel, to make sure they expressed their gratitude toward him.

JONI SIGHVATSSON: Propaganda had a contract to produce all of Michael Jackson's videos for his *Dangerous* album. In retrospect, the spiraling budgets weren't healthy, and some of the work wasn't great. I met Michael at Sound Recorder Studios in Hollywood. It was a Thursday. The meeting was supposed to start at 6 P.M., but Michael—and Bubbles, his chimp—didn't arrive until eight. We started the meeting, and at eight-thirty Michael suddenly says, "Oh, we have to stop. *The Simpsons* is coming on." We stopped the meeting and watched *The Simpsons*.

JOHN LANDIS: Propaganda had a deal to make the videos for *Dangerous*. I got a call from Propaganda, asking if I would do "Black or White." I said, "Listen, Michael owes me a lot of money from "Thriller," so I don't think so." Michael called, and he kept coming over to my house, pleading, "John, come on, come on." So finally I said, "All right. But I want to be paid weekly." I got a lot of money to direct that, because the label and Propaganda were having terrible trouble with Michael—he wasn't cooperating and he kept wanting to spend more and more money. I thought I'd be working on it for a month. It ended up being three months. By the time of "Black or White," Michael was not entirely on this earth. My job on "Black or White" became clear: Try to make a video where Michael did not look too crazy.

Michael kept wanting to add more and more scenes. He'd tell the production crew to get a Louma Crane and a Chapman Crane and a Steadicam, all this equipment. I would say, "Wait, what's going on?" And they'd say, "Well, Michael wanted . . ." So I go to Michael and say, "Michael, why do you want all this?" "Well, maybe we'll get an idea." I said, "You're spending several hundred thousand dollars, in case we get inspired?" I don't know the exact total, but that video must have cost millions. There was one day when we had a lot of dancers on the set, and Michael didn't show up. We're all wondering, "Where the fuck is he?" Turned out he had gone to Toys "R" Us with Macaulay Culkin and they'd spent something like $50,000. It's *hard* to spend $50,000 at Toys "R" Us.

I thought for "Black or White" it would be neat to see human faces morphing into one another. I went to a friend, John Whitney, Jr. His dad, John Whitney, Sr., was a fine artist who was basically the father of what we call CGI—computer generated imagery—and John Jr. owned the company that did graphics for the first computer-generated movie, *The Last Starfighter*. John sent me to a company called PDI, and PDI did it. It was very expensive—it cost $100,000 and took a month. I shot the live action pieces and then PDI morphed them. At the time, it was totally mind-blowing, because it was so seamless. Now, of course, you can buy the software at Best Buy and do it on your laptop.

Ronald and Nancy Reagan came by to watch Michael make "Black or White." We were on a stage in Hollywood, and Michael says, "John, would you like to have lunch with President and Mrs. Reagan today?" I said, "Absolutely not," and went out for lunch to make sure we didn't see them.

Then there was the famous scene where Michael morphs from a panther. He's dancing on top of a car, and all of a sudden he grabs his crotch and starts rubbing himself. I yelled, "Cut!" I said, "Michael, what are you doing?" He said, "I'm expressing myself." I said, "Michael, that's weird, don't do that." He said, "Madonna does it. Prince does it." I said, "You're not Madonna or Prince. You're Mickey Mouse." So we're shooting again, and he actually unzips his fly and puts his hand in there. I went, "Cut!" I said, "Mike, I am really not comfortable with you touching your nuts and stroking your cock. I just don't think it's acceptable." And Michael turns to our choreographer, Vince Patterson, and says, "Well, what do you think, Vince?" And Vince says, "I didn't really like it either." Michael says, "Well, let's call Sandy." At that time, Michael was managed by Sandy Gallin, who also represented Dolly Parton and Cher. Sandy was a screaming queen. A very flamboyant homosexual. Sandy Gallin comes to the set, looks at the playback, and he goes, "Do it, Michael! Do it! Do it!"

Maybe this was part of Michael's genius, because when "Black or White" aired, it created huge controversy. It premiered simultaneously in sixty-some countries. It had one of the largest viewing audiences in history. I know it had more audience than the moon landing.

TOMMY MOTTOLA: Michael Jackson spent $6 or $7 million sometimes, but 90 percent of that was his own money. When I came in as president of CBS Records, I never was in favor of huge-budget videos. And many times we got criticized by artists about that. But when you're drawing up a marketing plan, and it's seven figures just for one video, it's hard to justify that cost.

LARRY STESSEL: By that point, I'd become head of worldwide marketing and was no longer involved with Michael on a day-to-day basis. But when they showed me "Black or White," I said, "Are you crazy? A black guy beating the shit out of cars, in the ghetto? You can't send that to MTV." But Michael's new team were all yes-men. Dave Glew and Polly Anthony, who were running Epic, said, "It's great." Sure enough, MTV showed it once and the backlash was so strong, they had to recut the video.

JOHN LANDIS: When Michael came back from one of his Saudi Arabian adventures, I went to see him and he'd had further surgery, and he had, like, no nose. He looked like the Phantom of the Opera. I was horrified. He wanted me to do another video for him, but I honestly couldn't figure out how to film his face.

TARSEM SINGH: Michael Jackson was obsessed with the video I did for Deep Forest. I was told, "Michael wants you to hear his new song. Please come to LA and the song will be played for you." I said, "I have no interest in it." They sent me a piece of paper; just sign this, it says you won't give the song to anybody, and we'll send it to you. I wouldn't sign it. Then a guy flew over to London and played me the song. Guess what? I loved the song. And I said, "Okay, I'll meet him."

When I saw him and had a look at his face, I realized there's no way this man should be filmed. And I said, "I have an idea: You'll sing behind a tree. I'll see your body language, but I'll never see you. You dance behind a tree, and I'll film the tree." He said, "Can I come out occasionally?" And I said, "No." I didn't know what to do with him.

DOUG HERZOG: Judy, Abbey, and I were in a conference room with Michael's manager Sandy Gallin, discussing Michael's participation in our tenth anniversary special on ABC. Sandy says, "Well, you know, you have to give Michael an award. He loves awards." We said, "Of course." Sandy said, "And it's gotta be BIG . . . really BIG . . . HUGE!" We were like, "Uh, okay. Artist of the Decade? Artist of the Century? Artist of the Universe? You name it." Sandy said, "No . . . I mean PHYSICALLY BIG!"

JUDY McGRATH: Sandy told Doug that Michael wanted a Moonman. We thought, "Oh that's easy." Turned out Michael wanted a *life-size* Moonman. A Moonman that was *his* size. So we gave him a six-foot Moonman.

JOEL GALLEN: I produced MTV's tenth anniversary special for ABC. We had all the biggest stars participating from different locations: Madonna, George Michael, Aerosmith, R.E.M., and celebrities doing the introductions: Mel Gibson, Tom Cruise, Cher. Madonna didn't want to perform, she wanted to do a monologue. Typical Madonna. And Michael Jackson closed the show. He did two songs at the Barker Hangar in Santa Monica: "Black or White," with Slash, and "Will You Be There." After that, we had twenty-four hours to edit Michael's performance. That was it. And Michael came into the edit room and sat with me for all twenty-four hours. There was a moment where he wanted a certain edit, and I said, "Michael, if we do it that way, your mic will be in your right hand in the first shot and then in your left hand the next." And he said, "But the children will think it's magic."

LARRY STESSEL: Michael called me one day and said, "I want to have a nickname, like 'The Boss' or 'The King.'" I said, "Well, Bruce Springsteen is 'The Boss,' and Elvis Presley is 'The King.' You can't be the King because you'll never live it down. The press will rip you apart." But Michael would not let this go.

He hired his own personal publicist, Bob Jones. And one day, Bob issued a press release announcing that Michael Jackson was the King of Pop. Michael went rogue on us. And sure enough, he got slammed. Everyone laughed.

STEVE ISAACS: The VJs got a memo that instructed us to refer to Michael Jackson as the King of Pop. There was a quota—we had to do it at least twice a week for two weeks. But what I love is, that memo came out in a *Rolling Stone* article soon after. And who used to be a writer at *Rolling Stone*? Kurt Loder. From what I understand, he blew the whistle on that memo and gave the story to *Rolling Stone*.

ADAM CURRY: We were doing a Michael Jackson Weekend. We taped it on Thursday, and that night I got a call that we had to rerecord all the segments, because we didn't refer to Michael as the King of Pop.

KEVIN SEAL: I was genuinely appalled when we were directed to always refer to Michael Jackson on-air as the King of Pop. It didn't seem effective. If you tell everybody they have to love this guy, why would they love him?

Chapter 42

"RHYTHM NATION"

SUPERSTARS AND ONE-HIT WONDERS STAGE
A DANCE-OFF IN YOUR LIVING ROOM

MORE AND MORE, MTV GREW TO LOOK LIKE *CLUB MTV.* Metal, rap, and alternative rock had individual shows, tucked away late at night. For the other twenty-two hours of the day, MTV played the hits, especially videos that incorporated old-Hollywood conventions, like dancing and glamour. MC Hammer replaced Run-DMC. Vanilla Ice replaced Beastie Boys. Dance routines gave video directors another way to display body parts. Academics had previously taken interest in the medium, and now that interest bloomed—with MTV in an exhibitionist stage, scholars heatedly debated video's relationship to materialism and female objectification, leading to articles like "Sex as a Weapon: Feminist Rock Music Videos" and "Temporary Insanity: Fun, Games, and Transformational Ritual in American Music Video." As a prelude to the debut of *Total Request Live* in the late '90s, the Top 40 was aimed right at the hearts of young girls.

DOMINIC SENA: When I started working with Janet Jackson, she was in Michael's shadow and was looking to break out. She was still living at her parents' house, and Michael's stuff was everywhere: glass cases filled with memorabilia, gold records, all that. We talked for a while, and she took me out to this small house in the backyard that had been built for Michael. Inside was a candy store, a garage-size structure that was filled with aisles of candy. She said, "Help yourself."

JANET JACKSON: I knew who I wanted to direct "Rhythm Nation," that was simple: Dominic Sena. After working with him on "Let's Wait Awhile," I absolutely fell in love with him. He would get so excited and so expressive with his hands—

I can see him right now—and he'd put his hair behind his ear with his finger. Dominic understood story, and he could put onscreen, from front to back, the whole picture you had in your head. The foggy, smoky street and the dark, black-and-white tone, that was all intentional. When you've done a lot of videos, it can be difficult to keep it fresh and new. You have to try something you've never done, in fear of looking like something you've already created.

DOMINIC SENA: I'd done a couple of videos for Janet—"Let's Wait Awhile" and "The Pleasure Principle"—before *Rhythm Nation*. We'd gotten along really well and they got a lot of airplay, and then Janet and her boyfriend Rene Elizondo wanted to do a short movie. We incorporated three or four songs into a thirty-minute film. It was a big deal at the time; they spent something like $1.7 million on this film to promote *Rhythm Nation*.

We shot "Rhythm Nation" at this old electrical plant in Pasadena. I had found a wonderful setting in the bowels of the basement, with all these pipes and steam. So we moved the cameras down there, and the crew was getting ready when somebody said, "Listen, the dancers don't want to dance down here." I said, "Jesus Christ, what do you mean? We can't afford to lose three or four hours of shooting." He said, "There's asbestos everywhere." I went downstairs and the whole crew was wearing white gas masks. The signs were so corroded and dusty that at first nobody had bothered to clean them off. But they said, WARNING: ASBESTOS.

JANET JACKSON: A lot of times, I would see a commercial and wonder, *Who directed that?* I saw a commercial Peter Smillie had done, and it had a whimsical feel. I loved the tones and the cinematography, how it was edited. Peter had never done a video before, and I think he was a little nervous. He did "Escapade," which has a mischievous feel to it. A lot of that had to do with it taking place at night. The hours were very long, but you're not thinking about that when you're a kid.

"Alright" pays homage to a lot of the great stars from the old musical era, the days of bright yellow zoot suits. I wanted Gene Kelly to be in the video, and he told me, "Janet, I just don't dance anymore. I'm too old." But we had Cyd Charisse, the Nicholas Brothers, and Cab Calloway. Julien Temple, who directed, loved color, and "Alright" is very vibrant. He loved to make the camera move and travel. We were transporting you to a completely different place and time.

DOMINIC SENA: After I'd done the *Rhythm Nation* videos, I got a call from Pia Zadora's people. Pia was this very sweet C-list actress who married an extremely wealthy older man, Meshulam Riklis. She was pursuing a music career, and they asked me to shoot a video for a song called "Heartbeat of Love." I thought, *Thanks, but no thanks.* Then they said, "She'll pay any price." So I figured I could make a down payment on a house, *and* try out film techniques I'd been wanting to learn. I wrote the biggest, most expensive video I could dream up, and the concept included every possible thing I wanted to do: I used a snorkel camera in one scene. It was an $800,000 video, and I don't think it ever got a single play on MTV or VH1. The husband was a nice guy, but he got visibly upset when he turned up at the shoot and saw hunky shirtless male dancers groping her. We had to back off some of the more sexy stuff until he left.

JANET JACKSON: I was so used to being a tomboy, covered from head to toe, and I told Herb Ritts I wanted to do something different for the last video from *Rhythm Nation*, "Love Will Never Do." I said, "I want to even wear a dress for this one." And he said, "Just wear some jeans and a little top. And maybe a blond wig." I was comfortable with the jeans, but with the top half, I never wore something so tiny in my life. And I didn't have on a bra.

CHRIS ISAAK: Herb Ritts called and said, "We can try to go for a big name for the 'Wicked Game' video, or if you don't mind I would like to use this girl, Helena Christensen." I'll put it this way: I was not unaware that she was a good-lookin' woman. She was cordial, but we were making a video. People say, "Oh, you guys were really making love on the beach." It's a nice fantasy. A lot of the reason we held on to each other is because she was freezing. Look at her skin—she's covered in goose bumps. They kept trying to make us look wet, and they were throwing buckets of cold ocean water on us, so we'd glisten. Her hair was covering her nipples, and that was all that was covering them. They put double-stick tape on her nipples, then put her hair over her nipples, and of course it would come loose. The only way to cover her for the video was for me to hold her against me. At least, that's the story I told the judge.

I like the fact that I don't get the girl. She's not kissing me, she's kind of ignoring me through the whole video and that matches the song, which is, you know, "I'm in love with you, but you're playing with me." When I saw the video, I said, "MTV's not going to play it. I don't think it's sexy enough." I remember that comment because it was so stupid.

CINDY CRAWFORD: British *Vogue* had done a cover with five girls on it: me, Christy Turlington, Linda Evangelista, Tatjana Patitz, and Naomi Campbell. George Michael got fixated on that idea for his "Freedom '90" video; it had to be those same five. We shot it with David Fincher, over a weekend in London, and somehow they corralled us all.

Jake Nava, who directs a lot of music videos, recently told me he was working with Beyoncé and they tried to replicate the shot of me in the bathtub. He was like, "How did you *do* that?" Well, there was no water in the tub. I was sitting on an apple box, to lift me up, and I had glycerine all over me, to look wet. Was it comfortable? Models don't ask themselves that question. If you're not passing out, it's comfortable.

ADAM LEVINE: My first masturbatory fantasies were to videos on MTV. I was obsessed with music at an early age, and I was also getting sexed up at a young age, because every image on MTV at that point was highly sexual. God, Billy Idol's "Cradle of Love" video killed me. There's one scene where the woman is crawling on the floor—it's just epic. I jerked off to that video so many times!

ANNE-MARIE MACKAY: "Cradle of Love" was interesting, because Billy had broken his leg in a motorcycle accident, and that's why the concept of him appearing as paintings on the wall came into being. He couldn't perform, so David Fincher came up with a way of basically posterizing him.

BILLY IDOL: I'd been in this horrible motorcycle accident that crushed my right leg, from the knee down. How were we going to do a video when I wasn't mobile? David Fincher had an idea for a really long time, that a young girl would come to a nerd's house and seduce him to a record. It was fantastic, because I could narrate the video from these pictures on the wall. And then Fincher threw in the girl doing sexual somersaults on the bed. A load of guys love that video.

BETSY LYNN GEORGE, actress: I wasn't a flashy, big-boob Hollywood girl, and I don't even know if David Fincher liked me. The casting director said I wasn't his first pick, and I'd need to put on a push-up bra. I was skinny and didn't have much of anything.

There's a scene where I crawl across the floor, which I didn't know I had to do. The first couple of times I did it, I could see David getting frustrated. He said, "Crawl like you want it," or something like that. I cried after I did the scene, because I felt so embarrassed.

David was very specific in the bedroom scene—he wanted me to go completely wild, as if I was dancing alone in my bedroom. The choreographer said, "Do some acrobatics on the bed." I was a competitive gymnast for many years, and I'm very flexible.

BILLY IDOL: I went out to dinner with the actress from "Cradle of Love." She came out in sandals. That just put me off completely. Especially because I was in leather trousers.

BETSY LYNN GEORGE: We went to a little Italian restaurant, and he didn't like my shoes. Then we went up to his house and sat by the pool. When I said it was time for me to go home, Billy was very cordial: "Okay, we'll take you home." His assistant said, "You're not staying? Why aren't you staying?" It was like *every* woman stayed and spent the night.

After the video was released, Propaganda got a letter from a mothers' group that wanted to see a copy of my driver's license, because they thought I might be under 18.

JOHN DIAZ: In 1982, MTV banned Billy's "Hot in the City" video, mainly because we'd put Perri Lister up on a crucifix. But they put "Like a Prayer" in heavy rotation, with a burning cross. It was simply because Madonna was their golden girl.

ANN CARLI: I was in the MTV office the day they got the Madonna video for "Like a Prayer." Abbey Konowitch played it for me and goes, "I don't know what we're going to do with this."

JUDY McGRATH: To me, playing "Like a Prayer" was braver than playing something that's sexually provocative. That was a transformative video. It pushed buttons on race, religion, sex, burning crosses, making out with Jesus. I loved it.

MARY LAMBERT: Madonna enjoyed controversy, and so did I. I grew up in Arkansas, at a time when there was a lot of racial tension and violence, and it was really offensive to me. One of the reasons I used a burning cross in "Like a Prayer" was to force people to deal with that image I grew up with.

LIZ ROSENBERG: I don't know that "enjoyed" would be the right word, but Madonna seemed to be amused and entertained whenever a big fuss was unfurling in the media. She was never defensive about anything she was accused of, never felt like she had to explain. I'd never seen an artist besides Johnny Rotten who was able to let people throw sticks and stones and not back down.

FREDDY DeMANN: The "Like a Prayer"/Pepsi episode was quite dramatic. I arranged for Madonna to do a commercial for Pepsi featuring "Like a Prayer." She was to receive $5 million, and Pepsi was going to premiere the commercial and the song during *The Cosby Show*, which was the number one show on TV. Meanwhile, Madonna had cut the "Like a Prayer" music video with Mary Lambert, which was much darker than the Pepsi commercial. She kissed the feet of a black saint; I knew that would offend the Pepsi people, and when they got wind of the video, they said, "Send us the video!" I didn't want to send them the video. And I didn't. The commercial ran, then MTV premiered "Like a Prayer" the next day. And of course Pepsi immediately pulled the commercial and never aired it again. The controversy got phenomenal coverage. I loved every minute of it.

LEE MASTERS: Freddy DeMann showed me "Like a Prayer," and I said, "Freddy, Pepsi is gonna go *nuts*." He said, "Wh-what you do you mean?" He was all innocent. Of course that's exactly what happened. Which I believe Freddy knew all along. I think Freddy was so smart that he had this figured out from the get-go. He didn't care about the money from Pepsi. He did it for the publicity.

FREDDY DeMANN: Madonna loved racy. When MTV saw "Justify My Love," they said, "We can't play that." My comment was, "Great, we'll sell it on our own." We did, and we did quite well on it. The publicity generated by them *not* playing it was great for business.

TONY WARD: When Madonna and I started dating, we watched a lot of old Italian movies—Fellini, Rossellini, the Pasolini movie that's got the shit eating. I don't know if she would agree, but I would say the idea for "Justify My Love" came from me. She was editing *Truth or Dare*, and we talked about sexual scenarios, being voyeuristic. Seeing two girls make out, that made her excited.

JEAN-BAPTISTE MONDINO: We don't see ass and tits in "Justify My Love"—maybe a little bit, but this was not the point. The idea was simply that a woman is to be loved emotionally and sexually, at the same time. Most of the time, we think sex is something that is for the man. If a woman admits that she likes sex, we think she's not a respectable person, which is completely stupid.

When the day of the shoot arrived, I freaked out. I said, "Fuck, what am I going to do?" Because usually, you have a storyboard. All I knew was that at the start of the video, Madonna had a suitcase, and at the end, after some sexual experiences, she leaves the hotel completely happy. The kisses were real. We weren't faking anything. I rented a hotel for two days and nights, and we shot nonstop. We didn't use any lights, only the lights that were in the hotel.

In a video, I like to reveal something within a person—I'm like a shrink. With Madonna, there's no bullshit. So I learned things, while making videos. Not learning where to put the camera and how to become famous—this is a joke. But with Madonna, I learned to be honest, be clear, and not to lie—which is a big deal for men, because we are liars and cowards.

ABBEY KONOWITCH: When I saw "Justify My Love," I assumed Madonna was sending it to us for effect, and she had another version of it for television. And for the next twenty-four hours or so, Tom Freston and I tried to figure out what to do. She was our biggest star and we couldn't play her new video. Not in our wildest dreams. I called Freddy DeMann and asked him what he wanted us to do. He said, "I want you to play it." He never wavered from that position.

LIZ ROSENBERG: Madonna said to me, "They'd never not run a Madonna video." But she was wrong. Then we decided to sell the video in stores, and it was a huge success, and Madonna was called a "marketing genius."

JEAN-BAPTISTE MONDINO: Madonna made even more money from MTV's stupid decision, and it made the video more famous, so it was good.

RANDY SKINNER: All hell broke loose with "Justify My Love." When they were finished shooting, I went to the telecine in Paris to pull twenty seconds or so of the video to send back to the States, because MTV wanted to start running promos. They got the footage, ran the promos, and then when they got the finished video, the shit hit the fan. Everyone at the label was angry at MTV for not airing the video, but certainly no one was surprised.

ABBEY KONOWITCH: There was a moment when Madonna threatened to pull out of the MTV tenth anniversary special on ABC. She knew Michael Jackson was planning a huge performance, and in a head-to-head competition with him, the best she could do was a draw. A draw wasn't good enough for Madonna. But I knew she'd do the show. Her absence would have been more notable than her presence. Which was the line I used with Freddy DeMann, and he told me to go fuck myself. She ended up delivering a brilliant three-minute monologue about the first ten years of MTV.

DEBBIE GIBSON: The first time I met Madonna was at a fashion show, and she was going through one of her holier-than-thou moments where she had to act like a diva and be mean to people in public or her image would have been ruined. She totally ignored me. The second time I met her was backstage at a Vanilla Ice concert, when she was rumored to be dating him. This time she was relaxed and sweet and chatty. I guess the lesson is that you can't act very cool at a Vanilla Ice concert.

VANILLA ICE: The "Ice Ice Baby" video was made on a rooftop on Martin Luther King Boulevard in downtown Dallas. The building was abandoned, so we climbed the fire escape. I'd rehearsed the dance moves for two weeks, and I brought two changes of clothes. We didn't have time to go to a gas station, so in the scene where I was rolling in the 5.0, I ran out of gas. I was being pushed by three of my buddies, out of frame. It wasn't MTV who picked up the video first, it was The Box. So of course we kept calling The Box and requesting "Ice Ice Baby." The video cost $5,000 and probably made $3 billion. Not a bad return.

MTV had a lot to do with my success, but they made billions and billions of dollars on my videos. I figured there should be a mutual respect for that. But to them, we're just products on the shelf. When everything in my life crashed and I was having hard times—I had a weekend that lasted a few years—I came on their show *25 Lame* [a 1999 special where "Ice Ice Baby" was named the ninth lamest video of all time]. And they tried to humiliate me. I destroyed the whole set. It was real, it wasn't staged. It got stupid crazy ratings. I probably made them another couple million dollars.

MC HAMMER: I loved "Ice Ice Baby," like everybody else. It showed that rap wasn't limited to African-Americans. It was a direct reflection of the power of hip-hop, that a kid like him had grown up consuming enough hip-hop that he could perform it in a manner that was more than acceptable. He did a few of my dance moves in his video, and God bless him.

VANILLA ICE: The Club MTV tour with Hammer and En Vogue was a wild time. When my song went to number one, Hammer was pretty pissed off about it. He moved my dressing room in the huge arenas to the bathroom.

MC HAMMER: The video for "Too Legit to Quit" was a thirty-day project.

RUPERT WAINWRIGHT: Yes, but it felt like sixty. The big thing was that we were doing two videos: "Too Legit" and "Addams Groove." And with "Addams Groove," we had to rebuild the sets from the movie, but they weren't big enough, so we had to make them bigger. Then Anjelica Houston wanted to be in it, and she was going on holiday, so we had to build half the set and shoot her two weeks early. You couldn't shoot two days in a row, because every day was an eighteen- or twenty-hour day. I mean, every single scene was bigger than the next. It was huge. And then, get this, Charles Addams's widow, who lived somewhere in Switzerland, had total creative control. "Mrs. Addams didn't approve it. Come up with something different. Oh, and you're shooting tomorrow." And remember, some of these videos came out in movie theaters, so you're not shooting them for a thirty-two-inch CRT, you're shooting them for an eighty-foot screen. "Too Legit" and "Addams Groove," together, cost somewhere in between $4 and $5 million. But, you know, it was *huge* at the time.

MICK KLEBER: "Too Legit to Quit" was based on a book I was reading, Joseph Campbell's *Hero with a Thousand Faces*, about the structure of the monomyth that supposedly was the basis for the *Star Wars* trilogy, and now virtually every movie in Hollywood. So we structured "Too Legit" on the typical hero's journey, which in this case is Hammer being called by the mentor, James Brown, to retrieve "the glove," which is obviously a reference to Michael Jackson. Then he and his dancers are transported in a flying globe to a concert hall. For one of the big auditorium shots, we actually had a crane on top of a crane. And sometime during that segment Hammer descends in an elevator into a fiery abyss, where he's joined by more dancers. Eventually, we go back to the auditorium, where different celebrities flash the "Too Legit" hand signal on a big screen behind him, culminating, at the end, with Michael Jackson's supposed gloved hand making the "Too Legit" signal. The sense of competition between Hammer and Michael at that moment was fierce.

RUPERT WAINWRIGHT: Hammer wanted the opening scene to be him going into Hades and meeting James Brown. One small hitch: James Brown was in jail. When is he getting out? The day before our shoot. Okay, I don't have much pull with the Atlanta Corrections Department, but I'll do what I can to make sure he gets there on time. So Hammer goes, "Rupes, he's the godfather of soul. I owe this man everything. Just send a private jet to pick him up." So we send a private jet and James Brown comes with his wife, the one who sadly passed away under the knife doing like eight operations all at once.

So then, James goes, "So, Rupes, I'm heading back on Friday, right? You still got the jet?" I'm like, "No, we're sending you commercial, James." There's a pause. Hammer comes up to me afterwards and goes, "Get the jet back. Fly James back to Atlanta, but route him through Vegas and have the jet on standby for him all weekend" Only one? What happens if he doesn't like the color of it? I'd constantly tell him, "The budget's gonna be expensive, Hammer." And he'd say, "Rupes, Rupes, Rupes, don't worry about the money." It was always, "Do it bigger, do it better."

MC HAMMER: It cost me over $1 million.

MICK KLEBER: That album, I heard through the grapevine at Capitol, generated $44 million. I know we spent in the vicinity of $1.2 million of that on the "Too Legit to Quit" video. We felt that we were in head-to-head competition with Michael Jackson, who was doing "Black or White" at the time. We would get reports from the set of the Michael Jackson video: "He didn't show up today. Now the budget's up to $7 million." And we were going, "Can that really be true?

MC HAMMER: Michael Jackson was staying one floor beneath me at the Universal Sheraton while I was filming. Every day when I came home, I would yell to him through the floor: "I'm back, Mike! I'm telling you, you're gonna love this video!"

I put in a call to Michael, because part of the theme of the video was, I was going after the glove. It was tongue-in-cheek. When Michael called me back, it was 7 A.M. I said, "My wife is here, I'm trying to sleep," and I slammed the phone in his face. Not for one minute did I think it was Michael Jackson.

So the phone rings again and I knew it was really him. I said, "Michael, you're the greatest dancer ever." And he said, "Oh no, Hammer, you're the best." We compliment each other back and forth. So I said, "Michael, listen, I want you to look at my new video, I'm almost finished with the editing. If you don't approve the whole theme, I'll take it out." He goes, "No, it's okay. I like it." I said, "You like it? You haven't seen it." He said, "I've seen it. I like it, MC." And I started laughing. That's the power of Michael Jackson: He had spies going in, putting my video on tape, and bringing it to him.

MICK KLEBER: We did a lot of different versions of that video. There was an edited version, a sixteen-minute version that featured Jim Belushi as an anchorman, and an hour-long documentary video. It had a life force of its own.

MC HAMMER: It had Milli Vanilli, Mark Wahlberg, Queen Latifah, Chevy Chase, Danny Glover, a who's who of the music industry and actors. It had fifteen athletes who are today in the Hall of Fame.

MICK KLEBER: We also did a video called "Addams Groove" for the *Addams Family* movie that used a computer-generated, 3D mapping of Hammer's head. I don't know that any music video had ever used that technology before. We cut off his head and the head would bounce around. A few months later, I went to his house and I saw the the gold-plated lavatories, and I thought, "I don't know, I'm getting a bad feeling about this."

MARK PELLINGTON: I got out of MTV in '90 as it started to become a global monster. I got the sense that the days of old were declining, and it was more focused on the business. It wasn't just art and freedom and attitude and spirit; now sales and audiences were coming into play.

ALAN NIVEN: I heard rumors of people buying BMWs off video budgets and hiding it in the numbers. There was a day where a lot of people harvested it for all they were worth.

NICK RHODES: By 1990 or so, they stopped even inviting us to the VMAs. I was in LA and thought I would go, and they weren't even interested in giving us tickets.

MARK GHUNEIM: When I went to work at Columbia, New Kids on the Block was one of the first acts I promoted. MTV was not in love with this band. They didn't care for that type of music. My pitch wasn't, here's great music and you've got to put it on. It was, here's music that your audience needs to see, and I don't care if you like it or not. You want ratings, play New Kids.

TAMRA DAVIS: New Kids on the Block were the biggest band in America, and they no longer would talk with their label. There was no communication. The record company gave me a plane ticket and a backstage pass and said, "Go find them, talk to them, and see if you can make a video with them."

I started hanging out with them, listening to what they wanted to do. They were having a crazy time, sleeping with lots of different girls every night. I was saying, "You guys better have condoms." They were totally unsupervised and had everything they wanted, as much as they wanted. Even the record company girls were trying to sleep with them.

ALEK KESHISHIAN, director: When the Bobby Brown track "Don't Be Cruel" came around, a lot of directors passed on it. That was my first video. I met Bobby, and when he finally piped in, he said, "In this video, I want to have a maid and a Mercedes." Isn't that brilliant? So the opening shot of "Don't Be Cruel" is a Mercedes. The closest I got to the maid was putting the girl in a black outfit.

LIZ HELLER: None of us had any idea of the electricity of Bobby until Alek started filming. That was Bobby's first solo outing and everybody loved the track, but I don't think anybody had any idea that Bobby was gonna turn it on like that until it happened.

ALEK KESHISHIAN: Then they came back to me to do "My Prerogative," and I said I would direct it only if Bobby did exactly what I asked him to do. Believe it or not, I thought, *Why can't we position him as kind of a black George Michael?* Urban, but stylish and chic.

I wanted him to wear a headpiece microphone, and Bobby goes, "I can't wear that. That's gonna ruin my hair, and my hair is my image." I went, "Bobby, you don't *have* an image. That's why you're wearing this headpiece mic. That's gonna be part of your image." "My Prerogative" was his breakthrough on MTV.

BOBBY BROWN: I didn't expect it—I prayed for it—but once it happened, it was heaven on wheels. The director, Alek, was a cool dude. We had a lot of fucking fun.

LIZ HELLER: I had known Bobby since he was thirteen, and he was very difficult. When we were making "Every Little Step," I needed to make sure he'd get on a plane and fly in to LA for the video. So I sent a guy who worked for me, named Abe. I had to go through this whole drill with Abe about how he was going to have to knock on the door and physically get Bobby out of bed, onto an airplane, and over to the video shoot. I don't even know if Bobby knew for sure that he was going to be doing a music video. Abe started calling me every twenty seconds, because he couldn't get Bobby out of bed. But finally Abe got him up and got him on the plane. Bobby came right to the video shoot from the airport. He had zero rehearsal. But it's such a great performance, especially if you realize the condition he was in. He just turned it on, did his takes, and left.

BOBBY BROWN: For "Every Little Step," they asked me to actually write out a script for the video. I was on tour. I said, "Script? Just give me a white background, spell out 'Every Little Step' in big letters, and let us dance." That was the most popular video I ever did.

ALEK KESHISHIAN: Bobby had such a raw talent, and once he trusted me, he let me style him and image him. By the time of "Every Little Step," he didn't even know what the concept was. He just walked out of the limo and I told him, "Here, put these clothes on." I'd designed a black suit with "Bobby" written down the sleeve. He was like, "Wow, look at these letters."

There was a moment when "Every Little Step" was gonna be more elaborate. We met at the Sunset Marquis in LA, and I guess some gang had threatened Bobby's life. Me, Liz Heller, Bobby, and Bobby's brother were talking, and all of a sudden the bodyguard goes, "Everybody down!" And we're on the ground at the fucking hotel, still *talking* about the video concept.

My videos were an integral part of creating Bobby's brand, and when all was said and done, I made *maybe* $80,000 for, like, seven videos. That was before taxes. So I walked away. In 1992, when he had another album, Bobby's people were coming back, like, "We have a $500,000 budget." "We have $600,000."

"We'll pick you up in a limo." By that point, I'd heard the stories of what he was like, and I just wasn't interested.

LIONEL MARTIN: I loved Bobby Brown from the beginning. He was cocky and spoke his piece. Bobby was like Flavor Flav. He'd show up late, and he had an entourage. He was a major star, and he was just about to marry Whitney Houston. The things he did were kind of crazy. It was a big part of his performances at the time to take his shirt off, even though he had a bit of a belly. In the "Humpin' Around" video I did, he was in an elevator with a beautiful girl, one of the Fly Girls from *In Living Color*. His hands were all over the place. I mean, I turned red. But he didn't care. Girls were coming up to us during casting, like, "We'll do it for free, we just want to be in the video." He had a lot of juice.

ANDY MORAHAN: When I worked with Bobby and Whitney, they'd just had a baby and they were sweet and happy. They weren't crazy drug addicts. Although at the end of the shoot, Whitney went home with the baby and Bobby came out drinking with us in Miami, and we had to pull him out of a potential fight.

LIONEL MARTIN: Somebody called me from Arista's video department: "Lionel, we're thinking about doing a Whitney Houston video, and we're looking at you, Ernest Dickerson, and Spike Lee." I was insulted. And I said, "You should go with Ernest, he's really good." *Click.* I hung up the phone. I had this swagger, because I'd done a lot of hip-hop videos. They called me back five minutes later. I said, "No, seriously, I'm too busy right now." To do an R&B video for Whitney Houston wasn't something I was excited about.

They flew me to Ohio to meet her, so I guess the cockiness paid off. We sat down and were kind of staring each other down. She said, "I've heard some things about you." I said, "Well, I've heard some things about you, too." She said, "I've heard you're kind of arrogant." I said, "I heard you were a bitch to work with." That broke the ice right there, she started laughing and talking. And she hired me.

JULIEN TEMPLE: Whitney Houston was very much her own person. She was much less subordinate to the record company than I'd thought she'd be. We shot part of "I'm Your Baby Tonight" at a park on the Hudson River, on New York's west side. When I got there the record company had put up all these black drapes along the middle of the park where we were shooting—*huge*, five-hundred-meter runners. I said, "What the hell are you doing that for?" And they said, "We didn't want Miss Houston to see the homeless people in the park." When she got there, she went mad. She said, "What the fuck's going on? Take those down. What do you think I am?" It was fantastic.

Chapter 43

"YOUR MANAGER'S AN ASSHOLE"

FISTFIGHTS AND PYRO FARTS: WAR BREAKS OUT AT THE MOSCOW PEACE FESTIVAL

ADAM CURRY: Doc McGhee had gotten busted for importing a huge amount of marijuana. His get-out-of-jail-free card was creating an anti-drug, anti-alcohol concert in Moscow. We left from Newark Airport and everyone was hammered. Ozzy had to take a piss and someone was in the lavatory, so he pissed his pants right there. He's like, "Sharon!"

DOC McGHEE: My conviction had nothing to do with the Moscow concert, okay? I mean, no judge says, "Oh, for being involved in a conspiracy to smuggle seventy thousand pounds of pot into the U.S., you have to put on a concert in Moscow." They don't say stuff like that. We always wanted to go to Moscow and do the first rock show in the Soviet Union. I wanted to do their Woodstock. Remember, I had gone through rehabs with Mötley and family members, so I said, "Let's do this for kids that are being fried in the brain by electroshock therapy." Because that's the way they treated kids who abused drugs and alcohol. So how are they going to say *no* to us, if the proceeds from the show go to the Make A Difference Foundation, which I started, and we bring doctors to teach them how to treat addiction? It didn't count for anything in court. It didn't help me—except that it helped me personally, because it was the first rock show ever on Russian television, and it was televised in fifty-two countries.

We couldn't get permits. Russian officials would say, "Sure, this is a great idea," but nobody would stick their neck out and sanction it. We never had a permit to do anything. I brought sixty-four tractor-trailers into Russia with no permits. That show was absolutely insane. I almost had a nervous breakdown.

TOMMY LEE: This was the one time when all four of us in Mötley Crüe were sober. And everyone else on the airplane was drinking, doing blow, everything. Geezer Butler from Black Sabbath commandeered the liquor cart and was rolling it up and down the aisle. Ozzy had passed out in his seat. We were in agony because everyone was partying except us.

SEBASTIAN BACH: Zakk Wylde smuggled in Jack Daniel's, and we were drinking it in the back. Geezer Butler was yelling, "Why the fuck am I playing in Russia? I should be at home with my kids." Then he picked up the food cart and ran down the middle of the plane.

JOHN CANNELLI: I was on the private jet that transported all the artists from Newark Airport. Richie Sambora was dating Cher, who said to me, "Take good care of my honey!" There was really bad tension between Bon Jovi and Mötley Crüe. Mötley thought Bon Jovi were pussies.

ADAM CURRY: Before the broadcast went up to the satellite, it had to go through the Russian censors. They had a gray Volkswagen bus—that was the KGB. At that moment, I knew the Cold War was bullshit, because these guys had no technology.

DOC McGHEE: In that era, you could do the craziest shit, all around the world. I owned it. I was the fucking ringleader. Wayne Isham filmed himself pissing in front of Lenin's tomb in Red Square, in the middle of the night, singing "God Bless America" with the Russian flag flying in the background.

ADAM CURRY: A couple of us went to the hooker boat—a boat that had hookers. But everyone was like, "Let's leave. These are not our kind of hookers."

JONATHAN DAYTON: Wayne Isham was directing the live shoot and he hired us to come with him to Moscow. We ended up working for three days straight. At one point, I thought Val had died. She passed out and Russian paramedics had to come.

VALERIE FARIS: We had gone seventy-two hours without sleeping, and I was exhausted. A Russian paramedic stuck his finger down my throat to gag me, and I woke up.

There was a group of kids in Moscow that did tattoos with ballpoint pens and electric shavers, like a prison tattoo. We arranged for the guys in Skid Row to get tattoos, and the doctor who was with the tour advised against it. He thought they might catch hepatitis. The Russian kids were laughing that a heavy metal band was scared to get tattoos.

SEBASTIAN BACH: We were on at 1 P.M. So by one-thirty, I was getting fucked up. I could barely stand, and Doc's brother Scott took my bottle from me. I was walking around, looking for booze, while Doc was doing a press conference against alcohol and drugs. I burst in screaming, "Somebody get me a bottle of vodka." While Doc is talking about not drinking!

Doc's brother Scott McGhee ran at me—he's an ex–football player, for the Chicago Bears—and I ran to my dressing room and shut the door. He kicked the door down and put his knee into my throat, going, "You motherfucker. I love you so much, man. You can't do that." He's crying, my tour manager—also an ex–football player—is crying. We're all crying, the dressing room is destroyed, I'm fucking shit-faced. Those were some good times.

TOMMY LEE: We were told there would be no pyro—none of the bands were allowed to use it. And Mötley was synonymous with pyro. Then Bon Jovi started their set and they had these big explosions. I ran around the arena to the backstage area and saw Doc. He said, "What?" I ran at him and hit him in the chest. He went flying through the air. I said, "Tomorrow, when you wake up, you can get a job managing the Chipmunks, because you do not manage Mötley Crüe anymore." And that was it.

SEBASTIAN BACH: I was right there. Tommy said to me, "Your manager's a fucking asshole." Then he grabbed my bottle of vodka and chugged it—I mean, like, gulp, gulp, gulp, gulp, gulp—ran over to Doc, and punched him in the head. Doc was walking around with tears in his eyes. It was a bad fucking scene. Mötley wouldn't fly back in the same plane with Doc.

DOC McGHEE: Mötley felt like I fucked them, which I didn't. There was a malfunction—one tiny piece of pyro went off on one side of Lenin Stadium. It was a popcorn fart. I was backstage, and I didn't even hear it. When Tommy came at me, I was shocked. I had no idea what he was talking about.

We were all kinda burned out. Nikki almost died of an overdose a year and a half before that. Vince had killed a kid in a car crash with the drummer from

Hanoi Rocks, and crippled two other kids. I mean, the catshit was piling up. And when the catshit gets bigger than the cat, you've got to get rid of the cat.

ADAM CURRY: On the way back, everyone was ripped from this ten-day journey. Jon Bon Jovi had his personal doctor along for the ride, and he started handing out yellow pills. It was Halcion. A few years later, Halcion was taken off the market in some countries because people were committing suicide. We certainly slept, but I was fucked up for a week.

Chapter 44

"KERMIT UNPLUGGED"

AN ACOUSTIC MUSIC SHOW MORPHS
INTO A WORLDWIDE MEGABRAND

OST OF THE PEOPLE WHO DESPISED MTV CITED the channel's preference for pageantry over authenticity, which had been the measure of all musical acts until the end of the '70s. Authenticity meant Bob Dylan, aiming his songs against violence, injustice, the government, and conformity. In the video universe, it didn't matter if you wrote your own songs or performed with the assistance of dancers and prerecorded vocals—Paula Abdul and Bruce Springsteen might equally make a great video. MTV grew more confident in its beliefs as time passed, until pageantry became almost the entirety of the channel: lip-syncing Germans, rappers who danced better than they rapped, rock bands whose hair was better than their music, and millionaires whose new songs doubled as beer or soda commercials. MTV needed some balance, and it came from two producers who didn't work at the channel and were disgusted that "hot chicks and cute boys" now ruled the music business.

JIM BURNS, TV producer: Bob Small and I went to a Bruce Springsteen show at Madison Square Garden, and Bruce kept getting called out to do encores. The last encore, he came out alone, sat down on a stool, and sang and played an acoustic guitar. As we were leaving, I said to Bob, "You know, I think that could be a show."

I've known Bob since 1970, when I was a freshman in college and we worked on the same political campaign for two weeks. My mother got me a job on Wall

Street, then she got me a job at the Metropolitan Museum. But I'd always wanted to be in show business.

BOB SMALL, TV producer: I'd been a roadie in college: Bowie, during the East Coast leg of the "Diamond Dogs" tour, Jefferson Starship, Peter Frampton, Elvis Costello's first American appearance. I did a couple of Brecht plays, and after I realized, *This is where the girls hang out*, I became a theater major. You see *Threepenny Opera* and then you see Bowie, and you see a connection. I was driving a cab, working in off-Broadway theaters, and hanging lights with Mark Brickman.

JIM BURNS: We sublet space from Fred/Alan, the advertising agency for MTV Networks. We were their in-house production company, and we did specials for HBO and Lifetime. And we wanted to start pitching shows.

BOB SMALL: We pitched an acoustic music show. They said, "Well, folk music doesn't work on MTV." We tried to explain, it's not folk music. I'm an old hippie. Music shouldn't be reduced to how cute you are, or how clever the filmmaker is. I directed music videos, and the labels would say, "Could you stretch the video and make them look thinner?" You didn't see fat guys with beards on MTV, you saw hot chicks and cute boys. There are other things besides pop music. I've got a big mouth, so I kept pursuing it.

JIM BURNS: Our one ally at MTV was Judy McGrath. She had us pitch the show to two or three different people, and nobody liked it. They kept turning us down. We also pitched it to PBS, who didn't like the show. Then Judy got some added responsibilities, took over the running of the studios, and she said, "I have a little bit of money. Can you shoot a pilot in the VH1 studios?"

JUDY McGRATH: When they came in with the idea, they said everybody told them MTV would never do the show. The minute I heard it, I knew it would be fantastic for us.

BOB SMALL: *Yo! MTV Raps* had just started. It was the height of metal. Nobody took out an acoustic guitar. It just didn't happen. Nobody believed in *Unplugged*. We had four hours to set up the pilot, and four hours to shoot it. The budget was like $18,000. I couldn't get money to hire a director. They said, "You direct it." I was carrying drapes and hanging them on the set. We couldn't get people there. If you look at the first few shows, the makeup person and the PAs are sitting in the audience. I remember handing out cards in the street, "Come see Sinead O'Connor."

JIM BURNS: It's a simple idea, which is why a lot of people take credit for it.

JOEL GALLEN: *Unplugged* was my baby. It sort of started at the '89 VMAs, with Jon Bon Jovi and Richie Sambora sitting down with acoustic guitars, doing "Livin' on a Prayer" and "Wanted Dead or Alive." That was the jumping-off point. *Unplugged* came from an outside production company. I was the one who said, "In order for this to be very MTV, we have to do what Jon and Richie did. We have to find big rock bands who are normally loud and electric, and strip it all away and have them play acoustic. *That* would be cool."

ABBEY KONOWITCH: I needed Bon Jovi to be on the VMAs in 1989. Doc McGhee said, "There's no way they can do it. The band isn't even together on that date. A couple of the guys are in Europe." I said, "I really need them." Doc said, "I can't make it happen." So I said, "If Johnny and Richie sat in the middle of the stage without the band and did 'Wanted Dead or Alive' acoustic, it would be as good as having Bon Jovi on the show." So they played "Wanted Dead or Alive" in the middle of the stage at the MTV Awards, acoustic, and it was the showstopper.

ALEX COLETTI: Jon Bon Jovi thinks he created *Unplugged*, but Bob and Jim had a development deal in place for months. A thousand people claim they created *Unplugged*.

BOB SMALL: Please do not credit Bon Jovi for creating *Unplugged*. Jon Bon Jovi thinks he was the inspiration for it. He wouldn't even *do* the fucking show until 2007.

JIM BURNS: The VMAs happened in the first week of September 1989, and Joel Gallen—who was executive producer on *Unplugged* as well as as the VMAs— suggested to Jon Bon Jovi and Richie Sambora that they do an acoustic set at the VMAs. It was a success, people liked it, and that did help sell *Unplugged* to the network. But Jon did not create the show. The credit says, "Created by Jim Burns and Bob Small."

BOB SMALL: Joel Gallen was upset that Jim and I got the "Created by" credit. He went after us with a vengeance. I have faxes from him saying, "You can't say this to the press." He successfully took center stage. By the time the show was getting nominated for Emmys, you would think it was all him. Taking our producer credit away eliminated us from being on the Emmy list. I have said that to him many times, to his face.

JIM BURNS: Bob and I created the show. We sold the show to MTV. Joel did a great job as executive producer, I can't fault him on the work he did. But he has claimed credit for creating it. It's really a character flaw. That's my grievance with Joel. There was always tension between us.

ALEX COLETTI: The fifth episode was billed as Joe Walsh and Friends, and Joe showed up with only one friend—Ricky, his bass player. We thought it meant his famous friends, but apparently that got lost in translation. Bob Small found Dr. John in the bathroom at National Studios—he was appearing on Carol Leifer's talk show. We rolled in a piano, and Dr. John and Walsh did the Eagles song "Desperado."

JOEL GALLEN: Joe Walsh was our breakthrough show. He played "Desperado," and Don Henley, who wrote the song, wouldn't give us permission to air it. Abbey Konowitch reached out to him, and Henley sent back a three-page fax about why he didn't want Joe Walsh performing the song. We said to Don, "Why don't you come on and perform 'Desperado' the way it should be?"

JIM BURNS: Before that, the show was two groups doing a couple of songs each, then doing a song together. Jules Shear was the host. But when Henley came on, he didn't want to play with anybody else. And Jules was very awkward with Henley. That's really when it changed.

BOB SMALL: Don Henley kept an audience waiting outside in the sun in LA for four hours while they tuned a piano to his liking.

JOEL GALLEN: Once Henley did *Unplugged*, more people took notice. We got a call from Capitol Records saying Paul McCartney wanted to do it. I said, "Let's have this be the first one-hour *Unplugged*." Until that point, we only did half-hour *Unplugged*s.

We went to London in January 1991, when the first Gulf War was under way. We flew over about four days before the taping and drove to McCartney's farmhouse, north of London. He had a barn he'd turned into his rehearsal space. Paul said, "Okay, Joel, let me run the set for you." He and his band did twenty-two songs, and something like nineteen of them were Beatles songs. "And I Love Her," "We Can Work It Out," "Blackbird." And on the Beatles songs, he's reading the lyrics off pieces of paper. I said, "Paul, when we do the show, you're not gonna need a music stand, are you?" He explained that he hadn't performed many of these songs since he'd recorded them, because the Beatles stopped touring so early. There's a charming moment in the show where he botched the lyrics to "We Can Work It Out." He actually stopped it and had to start again.

BOB SMALL: During the Aerosmith taping, there was a girl between Steven Tyler and Joe Perry whose panties you could see on camera. Apparently, when McCartney did the show, he said, "Make sure that doesn't happen to me." We had Crosby, Stills & Nash, and Steve Stills's throat closed up the day of the show. David Crosby said to me, "Listen, I don't care if you stitch his mouth together, if you put a hot girl in the front row, he'll sing." So we did that.

ROBERT SMITH: The only time I've been nervous about performing was *MTV Unplugged*. It was so stripped down and bare, and the audience was so close. There was no escape. It was one of the best things we ever did, actually.

JIM BURNS: The most difficult *Unplugged* was Neil Young. We shot him at the Ed Sullivan Theater, the same night we shot Aerosmith. Neil was onstage, he was singing, and suddenly, for whatever reason, he got agitated and ran outside. He ran down Broadway, and Alex Coletti ran after him. Neil never came back to finish the show.

BOB SMALL: Neil came running out of the Ed Sullivan Theater and jumped over a police barrier. I said, "I think we've got a problem."

JIM BURNS: Elton John kept people waiting for hours. We had a piano tuner come in, but at rehearsal, Elton said, "It's out of tune." So the piano tuner started from the beginning again. After an hour, Elton said, "No, it's still out of tune." Another three hours, Elton came out, played the piano, and said, "No, there's still a little problem." Finally, he said, "When I was starting out, I played in bars that didn't have half these keys. Let's just do it."

The biggest star behavior I saw was Mariah Carey. She had a hair person, of course; a makeup person, of course; a costume person, of course; and a woman who made tea for her.

BOB SMALL: When Mariah Carey came in with her two lighting designers, the show went from credibility to prima donnas.

JIM BURNS: The only image I can remember from the *Yo! Unplugged* show is LL Cool J's deodorant. He had a wife-beater on, and when he lifted his arms, all you saw was his caked-on white deodorant. But he did a great job.

BOB SMALL: Is that the kind of thing you stop a show for? This is the greatest show ever done, are you gonna stop filming because the audience can see his deodorant? And we're still talking about it to this day, so there you go.

RICK KRIM: I remember fighting Abbey to do Pearl Jam *Unplugged*. It was unprecedented to do an *Unplugged* on a new band. I don't remember how, but I finally convinced him, and we taped Pearl Jam at 1 A.M. on the same day we taped Mariah Carey, to save money. I still get chills thinking about that show. It was one of the few times in my life that I saw a show and thought, *This band is about to become huge.* The moment where they did "Porch," and Eddie stood up on his stool and started writing "PRO CHOICE!!!" on his arm, that was a seminal moment in their life. Mine, too.

JIM BURNS: Bruce Springsteen was rehearsing with his band in LA, and we heard he wasn't happy with how the band sounded. So he did an electric show, which was disappointing, I have to tell you. He was the inspiration to do *Unplugged*, and he couldn't bring himself to do a couple of songs acoustically?

BOB SMALL: When it became a big success, Jim and I were pushed further and further out of it. The network didn't want us being promoted as the creators of the show. They would say, "We're not big on credits here." So I pounded the table and said, "You've given me so little, you can't give me credit? You're throwing me a few dollars and you're not allowing me to take bows for it?" The little bit of money I got, I usually used hiring lawyers to fight for a bit of recognition. I said to them, "Why don't you give us a VMA? Isn't there an award for having an impact on music?"

JIM BURNS: Bob and I get a piece of the money on *MTV Unplugged* records, DVDs, CDs, downloads. I bought a Mercedes, which I named "Rod Stewart," because I got a big check for the *Rod Stewart Unplugged* record. He essentially paid for that car.

BOB SMALL: *Unplugged* was not only popular, not only saved MTV's ass in the music industry, it brought in a lot of revenue. There are over five hundred *MTV Unplugged*s around the world, 390 of which I just found out about in the last year. There's an *MTV Unplugged* perfume in India. Lately, they've given us our royalties for shows that were done without telling us. But I'm not as wealthy as you would imagine.

JIM BURNS: Bob and I split up our professional partnership in '92. I got tired of going in every day and apologizing to people who were working for us. Bob had a hot temper. He'd fly off the handle and scream at people. He was very angry that I left, so I had to deal with that for a couple of years.

BOB SMALL: There's a lot of stuff out there called *Unplugged*, including a *Kermit Unplugged*.

JIM BURNS: "Unplugged" became part of the lexicon. I think it's in the dictionary.

BOB SMALL: The acoustic guitar became acceptable again. I saw U2 during the Zoo TV tour, and they did an acoustic set in the round. That had to be from *Unplugged*. I mean, some people think of *Unplugged* as the greatest influence on music in the last twenty years. I think it's probably the greatest music show, next to *American Bandstand*.

JIM BURNS: One person we could never get, because he was dead at the time, was John Lennon. I think that would have been the ultimate.

Chapter 45

"SILLY, SUPERFICIAL, AND WONDERFUL"

CINDY CRAWFORD AND JON STEWART BRING BEAUTY AND LAUGHS TO MTV

MUSIC WAS STILL THE BASE OF THE NETWORK, TO use Lee Masters's phrase, but the base was getting smaller. Fashion—a significant component of MTV since the days when small-town kids began dressing like the Stray Cats or Madonna—came to the forefront with *House of Style*, hosted by Cindy Crawford, a goddess made human by her earthiness and stiff delivery. "MTV helped people relate to me as more than just an image," says Crawford, who became an integral part of the channel, via VMA broadcasts and even comedy interstitials. Ben Stiller had his own MTV show, where he impersonated Bono and Bruce Springsteen, before moving on to network TV and Hollywood. And for *You Wrote It, You Watch It*, an early experiment in crowd-sourcing, MTV hired Jon Stewart, a self-described "bitter little hairy man" who a year earlier hosted *Short Attention Span Theater* on Comedy Central. *You Wrote It*—which has become synonymous with the phrase "short-lived"—also propelled the comedy careers of Michael Ian Black, Michael Showalter, David Wain, and Thomas Lennon. When it fell apart, Stewart became the host of MTV's long-gestating talk show, which would be "far more casual" than Conan O'Brien's or David Letterman's shows, he told a reporter. "I'll be wearing a cocktail dress." Stewart drew more viewers than music-video programming did, and soon, MTV was airing it three times a day. As the channel got bigger, the videos got smaller.

CINDY CRAWFORD: *House of Style* was like a comedy club where you try out your material. It didn't have to be perfect. If you could think it up, you were given a chance to try it.

ALISA MARIE BELLETTINI: I started at MTV in September of 1988, as a segment producer in the news department. They said, "Go interview the Beastie Boys." It was so much fun—they poured beer on my head. One day, Doug Herzog said, "We're gonna start covering fashion, and you're gonna do it." I was always stylish. And the two other writers in the news department, one was a Rastafarian and the other was reading Hitler books all the time.

Kurt Loder was our main news anchor, and fashion stories had to come out of Kurt's mouth. He was not comfortable doing it. The look on his face, going from a Guns N' Roses story to a fashion story—he looked like he was about to die. We got a memo from Tom Freston which said, "What the fuck? Why do we have Kurt Loder talking about fashion?" That night, I wrote up a paragraph saying we should do a show about style. Within twenty-four hours, Doug Herzog said, "You've got $25,000 for your budget and you have to find a host." My first host suggestion for *House of Style* was Johnny Rotten.

CINDY CRAWFORD: I don't think Alisa ever told me that. "We couldn't get Johnny Rotten, but we got you."

ALISA MARIE BELLETTINI: Herzog said, "Please go back to the drawing board." He told me to look at fashion magazines, which I never read. But I saw there were these girls called "supermodels." I saw photos of Cindy Crawford and thought she was a great idea because she was considered a sex symbol and I'd read an interview where she said she was already tired of modeling.

CINDY CRAWFORD: Alisa was looking for someone who had credibility in the fashion world but who guys could also relate to, because MTV had a very male audience. And I'd just posed for *Playboy*. Alisa wanted me for *House of Style*, even though I had zero experience doing anything like that.

DOUG HERZOG: I'd become smitten with Cindy Crawford. She was on the cover of all my wife's magazines. So we asked, and not only did she say yes, but she agreed to host the show for free. That's how badly she wanted to be on TV.

ALISA MARIE BELLETTINI: Her manager said *no*. Her modeling agency said *no*. I asked them to have her call me. When she did, I said, "Would you like to do a show about fashion? I don't have any money to pay you." She immediately said *yes*. The whole first year, she worked for free.

CINDY CRAWFORD: My agents thought it was a waste of my time. I was making so much money modeling, per day, why take away from that? Other than Elsa Klensch on CNN, there was no fashion on TV. Look at how much TV has changed since then. Now, of course, an agent would say, "Yes, you should do it. And you should do a blog."

ALISA MARIE BELLETTINI: The first show aired in May 1989. When the ratings came in, Herzog high-fived me and said, "You've got a show."

CINDY CRAWFORD: I was like a cardboard cutout in that first show. It's cool that Alisa didn't can me.

ALISA MARIE BELLETTINI: It wasn't an easy show to do at first. People like Annie Lennox felt that if they talked about fashion, their music wouldn't be taken seriously. So we covered a lot of hip-hop, because they were cool about style. We weren't covering high-end designers, we were covering the cool ones: Anna Sui, Mark Jacobs, Todd Oldham. I wanted the audience to be girls in the Midwest who we could teach about style.

JOHN VARVATOS, fashion designer: *House of Style* definitely had an effect on pop culture. To certain people, especially in the Midwest, it was their bible—it was their guidepost to fashion. There really wasn't anything like it.

CINDY CRAWFORD: *House of Style* seemed like it was on weekly, because they air the shit out of stuff on MTV. It seemed like each show was on a hundred times a week.

ALISA MARIE BELLETTINI: We weren't showing big butts and breasts—the show was respectful to women.

CINDY CRAWFORD: We talked a lot about demystifying beauty. We showed Naomi Campbell putting zit cream on at night. We also said, "Look, fashion is great, but we're holding our stomachs in at photo shoots." One reviewer said *House of Style* was "silly, superficial, and wonderful." I loved that quote. We couldn't ask for a better review of the show, because that's what fashion is all about.

NICK RHODES: Going on *House of Style* was one of the funniest things we ever did on MTV. Cindy Crawford took us to Sears and we had to spend $200 on clothes.

CINDY CRAWFORD: Simon and Nick were wearing dresses at one point, that's all I remember.

SIMON LE BON: I ended up in drag, wearing a zip-and-dash dress. And Nick made a suit out of ties, I believe. It's hilarious.

BETH McCARTHY: When MTV started making its own programming, there was that Judy Garland/Mickey Rooney feeling: "My mom has some costumes, my dad has a barn, c'mon, let's put on a show!"

MICHAEL IAN BLACK: MTV knew how to build their brand as a cool destination for youth, a cool place to hang out. But they didn't know how to develop original shows. They needed cheap, youthful programming, and a large amount of it. The way to do that is to hire inexperienced people who will work for almost nothing—like the State, a sketch-comedy troupe I helped start at NYU in 1988. Fairly quickly, we ended up on MTV, which then launched the careers of several marginally successful comedians who you may or may not know today.

LAUREN CORRAO: We did the original *Ben Stiller Show* in 1990. It was sort of a show-within-a-show: three or four music videos, and sketches in between. Fox saw it, and offered a sketch show to Ben. Their *Ben Stiller Show* won an Emmy. Losing Ben to Fox was an eye-opening moment. We realized people were poaching our talent. Ken Ober had gone off to do *Parenthood*, Colin Quinn had a development deal at Fox. Joe Davola also moved to Fox, and he was tapping all our talent. We would discover people and put them on the air, and then they'd get agents and move on.

In 1992, we had a show hosted by Jon Stewart called *You Wrote It, You Watch It*. Viewers sent in funny stories, and they'd be reenacted by members of the State. *You Wrote It, You Watch It* was the precursor to both *The Jon Stewart Show* and *The State* sketch show on MTV the next year.

MICHAEL IAN BLACK: *You Wrote It, You Watch It* was Jon Stewart's first regular television job. It was not a success, largely because it was terrible. I mean, even when you say the idea, it sounds terrible. It was canceled, and we got our own show, *The State*. It was also clear that Jon Stewart had a future, and MTV gave him a talk show not that much later. It was exactly what you'd think an MTV talk show at that time would be. His coffee table was a knock-hockey table, and that seemed to embody what the show was. He had a semi-retarded sidekick named Howard, who was a cabdriver and sometime comedian. It was all the things you like about Jon Stewart—he was smart, charming, and funny, and also awkward. He was figuring out how to make a talk show.

BETH McCARTHY: MTV had a problem holding on to talent. They'd discover Ben Stiller and Jon Stewart, but couldn't do talent-holding deals, because the budgets were so small, and talent would eventually leave. But then MTV would go in the other direction, like with poor Mike Judge, who created *Beavis and Butt-head*. MTV robbed that guy. He got nothing.

ABBY TERKUHLE, MTV executive: I was the animation guy at MTV—and *Liquid Television* was a testing ground for weird, animated characters. It was sort of like, "Where's our *Ren and Stimpy*?" When I saw Mike Judge's short film *Frog Baseball*—which was Beavis and Butt-head playing baseball with a frog—I got excited and flew Mike to New York. He was a musician in Texas, and created *Frog Baseball* while babysitting his kids.

I told him we wanted to make twenty-six short films of *Beavis and Butt-head*. He asked if he should change the drawing. I said, "It's perfect, it looks like a fourteen-year-old drew it." Then he was worried, and he said, "Will I have to quit my band?" And I said, "Well, maybe." We went on the air, and it was an instant hit. It carried on our tradition of irreverence, and also suggested that if you watched MTV all day, you might end up like Beavis or Butt-head.

I went to see an Anthrax concert with Mike in New York, and this guy comes up to him and introduces himself—he was in some metal band. Mike and I both started backing up, afraid, and he said, "I love your show. You trashed my video, but wait until you see the next one—it sucks even *more*."

Chapter 46

"TIRED OF CHEAP SEX SONGS"

R.E.M., U2, AND VAN HALEN (!) ELEVATE THE ART FORM IN THE NINETIES

WHEN CDs WERE INTRODUCED IN 1983, FEWER than a million were sold. Four years later, annual sales were at 102 million, surpassing the number of LPs sold. After another four years, CDs were outselling cassettes. This funneled a lot of money into the record business and created a bubble that lasted well into the '90s—not only were CDs priced higher than the other formats, many people were now buying CD versions of music they already owned on album or cassette. Labels had more money, and they spent more money.

Video budgets had been growing steadily, and now the money was put to good use. U2 and R.E.M. crossed over into the mainstream, and brought artsy, cinematic sensibilities to big-bucks productions. Bono said U2 was "reacting against the perfect cinematography and the beautiful art direction—it's all too beautiful, too much like an ad." He added, "These days we are being fed a very airbrushed, advertising-man's way of seeing the world." For years, R.E.M. had made anti-video videos: singer Michael Stipe called one clip a "response to videos which objectify and berate women." Now Stipe starred in a deluxe video, shot in a style that could be called Gothic Technicolor, directed by an eccentric Indian immigrant who more or less retired from videos after winning six VMAs.

The spirit of invention even spread all the way to Van Halen, who made a video without any hot chicks in it.

TARSEM SINGH: Record labels were pursuing me to make videos while I was at the Art Center College of Design in Pasadena, California. My work in school was fucking awesome! Most people did music videos so they could go on to do commercials. But I did music videos because I *loved* them. I was like a prostitute in love with his profession; I would've fucked them for free, but they were paying me!

I did some videos while I was in school—En Vogue, Suzanne Vega—but after I graduated, I only did two. The first was R.E.M.'s "Losing My Religion."

I'd grown up in Iran and India, so with my vocabulary of English being limited, I didn't think "religion" had another meaning. So I took Michael Stipe's poetry and fucked it up, and did a literal interpretation of it.

I took a rough story from Gabriel García Márquez's "A Very Old Man with Enormous Wings," about an angel who falls down into this plane, and becomes an inspiration for some and a circus show for others. And I said, "I want to do Caravaggio-style paintings of one world, another world of Russian propaganda posters, and a third of heaven, from where the angel falls," which is very much like how Indians treat their gods and goddesses—which in the West, I think you'd call "very gay."

PATTI GALLUZZI: Tom Freston started saying, "I hate being so much about hair bands. I hate hair bands. We need to play less hair bands." And I thought, *Oh my God, yes, thank you.* Because we were so Winger, Slaughter heavy.

MICHAEL STIPE: "Losing My Religion" was the first video I'd ever lip-synced in, so it was an important moment for me. The thing that brought me to that was seeing Sinead O'Connor's "Nothing Compares 2 U," which is unbelievably raw and powerful. In what appeared to be a single shot, she stared down a camera and meant it and actually cried tears. I saw that and thought, *You know what? This isn't fake.*

PATTI GALLUZZI: R.E.M. are my favorite band of all time, and when "Losing My Religion" came in, and it was spectacular, I put it into ultra-heavy rotation. Yes, we had Queensryche in heavy rotation at the same time. But it was like, *Now this is my channel. I'm doing what I want. I don't care that R.E.M.'s not that popular.*

TARSEM SINGH: I shot with them for eight hours, we did expensive things, and it was dreadful. I was getting so nervous, I kept throwing up in the toilet, and of course the AD thought I was on drugs. I threw up like mad, and when I got out of the toilet, I gathered everybody and said, "Let's just have the rest of the band stand in the back and Michael dance in front of this window." When it was done, I said, "I hope they like it. They could call it gay, they could call it pretentious."

I didn't do another video for two and a half years, when I put in four months and $40,000 of my own money to make Deep Forest's "Sweet Lullaby." What else is money for if you aren't gonna blow it?

MICHAEL STIPE: Tarsem had this idea to put me in classical Bollywood poses, on my knees, twisted to one side, with one arm raised and staring into the camera. And it was not working, and it was not working, and it was not working. He went off and vomited. He said, "I threw up in the bathroom. This isn't working. What do we do?" We talked for a bit, and I said, "Let me be a performer. Let me do what I do."

I did a herky-jerky dance based on Sinead O'Connor's "Last Day of Our Acquaintance" video, plus a little David Byrne. You can see Peter Buck in the background, looking super-dour.

ANTON CORBIJN: Many years after "Pride," when I'd been told not to get near U2 with a video camera, I was approached by Bono to make a video for "One." It was a weird situation again. I put all these ideas into it: Berlin, which had been two cities, had just become one; the Father, the Son, and the Holy Ghost are one; man and woman are one. The band dressed as women, to illustrate that. It was very easy to get them in drag. Which of them looked cutest in a dress? Well, it wasn't Bono.

PAUL McGUINNESS: We found some pushback from programmers who didn't like the idea of men in drag. We decided to make another video so they would have a choice. That's probably my favorite U2 video, Anton's "One."

ANTON CORBIJN: But they wouldn't give it to MTV. They said the video wouldn't work for them. They took a beautiful David Wojnarowicz photo of bisons and quickly made that into a video for the time being, while they commissioned somebody else to do a video, Phil Joanou, and he shot Bono and some models in a bar. To me, it had nothing to do with the song. After the song had gone out of the charts, they revisited my video and gave it to MTV, after the event. A few years later, Bono said it was his favorite U2 video. At the time, I was disillusioned. I took it personally, after putting so much into it. I thought I'd made an amazing video.

MEIERT AVIS: Anton Corbijn's a bit northern European for my taste. I know Anton, but his prevailing emotion is *Let's commit suicide.*

MARK PELLINGTON: I'd made a seven-minute video by Disposable Heroes of Hiphoprisy, called "Television: The Drug of a Nation." U2 got turned on to that idea: "Let's attack the media and be self-aware and kind of meta." They hired me to create videos for their Zoo TV tour.

Bono gave me a David Wojnarowicz photo of a buffalo and said, "Make a piece based on that." I got some stock footage of buffaloes, blew it up, slowed it down, blew it up more, and blurred it. I think the thing took forty-five minutes. "Okay, slow it down. Slow it down more."

U2 were like family to me. Not having the band in the video was, at that time, pretty radical. Mine was so slow that people were complaining it wasn't a video. Then they made the third video for "One," which I call "the Heineken video," with Bono in the bar.

PAUL McGUINNESS: Mark's video featured buffalos throwing themselves over a cliff. It was a fine piece of work. But it was somewhat short on what we need in a video, which is imagery of the band.

KEVIN GODLEY: Like Sting, the camera loves Bono. He's prepared to try anything—I've had him falling out of cars, writhing around on the ground, wearing a silly hat. He is a musical actor.

PAUL McGUINNESS: Bono's a performer, and over the years he's seen enough film of himself that he didn't like to put some effort into understanding the process. He knows about lenses, he knows about timing, he knows how to connect with the camera. He shares with Bruce Springsteen and Mick Jagger that intuitive ability to connect. All the singers I know—Mick, Bono, Sting—are extraordinary mimics. The singer gene seems to be the same as the mimicry gene. I had lunch with Mick Jagger and Bono, and they were talking about Bob Dylan, who they both know well, and they started to perform competing versions of Bob. I was the only audience for this, and they were both brilliant.

SAMMY HAGAR, Van Halen: I was tired of writing cheap sex songs. Eddie and I wanted to get serious and talk about world issues. "Right Now" was the best lyric I'd ever written for Van Halen. The treatment for the video was bullshit:

"Right now, Sammy's looking in the mirror and licking the milk off his mustache," or something. I told the director, "Fuck you, man. People ain't even going to be listening to what I'm singing because they're going to be reading these subtitles." I thought, *How dare they?* People probably don't know this: I refused to do the video.

MICHAEL ANTHONY: Because of the lyric of the song, we wanted something that was a little more meaningful than the usual party stuff. I was really proud of that video.

JOHN BEUG: The video I'm probably proudest of is Van Halen's "Right Now." A commercial director and copywriter named Mark Fenske came up with the concept. The band didn't understand what we were doing. Sammy Hagar didn't want the video to come out. He said, "How dare you put type on top of my lyrics." He finally relented and "Right Now" won Video of the Year at the 1992 VMAs.

SAMMY HAGAR: Mo Ostin, the chairman of Warner Bros. Records, called me personally when he heard I hated it. He goes, "Sammy, this is going to be the biggest video you've ever had." I go, "You're crazy. This stinks." I didn't want to talk about it, so I took my girlfriend—who's now my wife—and we flew off to Kiawah, South Carolina. No one knew where I was.

MARK FENSKE, director: I'd written and produced a few TV commercials that used type on the screen. The record company was scrambling to get a video done. I doubt they'd have given me a shot except for that. When I met the band in a hotel room the night before the shoot, Sammy said, "I can't argue with this guy, look at him." I'm six-four and 250 pounds. If he was unhappy, I didn't see it. But I was busy and nervous enough to not have noticed a lot of things. It was my first music video. And I'd brought my mother into town, to be the actress in one of the shots.

We didn't have much money or time. Except for Van Halen, every person you see in the video worked on the crew or, in my mother's case, was related to me. For the idea of a girl setting fire to a guy's photo, I had a photo of me at twenty-four that I didn't mind burning.

SAMMY HAGAR: I had pneumonia and a 104-degree temperature. When you see me in the video folding my arms, refusing to lip-sync, it's because I was pissed off. The director's going, "Oh, that's great!" When I slammed the door into the dressing room at the end of the video, that was for real. I was pissed off.

I don't think "Right Now" is a great video at all. It was groundbreaking and interesting, but the look and the feel didn't do much for me. I don't think it's enough about the band.

MARK FENSKE: When "Right Now" won Video of the Year, I didn't know whether or not I should go up to the podium, so I didn't. Music videos are that kind of gig. It's someone else's music, and all you're doing is adding a visual or a context for the song, so it's probably best to not overvalue your contribution.

I brought my mom as my date to the VMAs. While I was staring at the girls from En Vogue, Flea from the Red Hot Chili Peppers walked past us. My mom leaned over to me and said, "That man is only wearing underpants."

Chapter 47

"A MONKEY COULD DO IT"

PAULY SHORE AND THE THIRD GENERATION OF VJs

THE THIRD WAVE OF VJs WERE YOUNGER THAN THEIR predecessors and had more success in their post-MTV careers. Karyn Bryant joined the network right after graduating from an Ivy League college, then worked for TBS, CNN, TNT, ESPN, and MMA. Dan Cortese, a hunky ex–college quarterback, was promoted from production assistant to host of *MTV Sports*, which led to roles on *Melrose Place* and *Seinfeld*. Lisa Kennedy Montgomery, known as Kennedy, was hired when she was nineteen and debuted in September 1992. She says she began receiving hate mail "like the second week I was on the air," likely because of her brash wisecracking, but possibly because she declared herself to be both a virgin and a young Republican. "Dear Kennedy, you disgust me greatly . . ." began a letter she posted on her office door. Nonetheless, she lasted six years at MTV.

Steve Isaacs was an LA singer/songwriter, and after a brief but influential stint at MTV, he played in a band with Dave Navarro and Stephen Perkins of Jane's Addiction, then became a Web site designer and creative director for digital media. Karen Duffy, a quick-witted model and nursing-home recreational therapist, snuck in digs at Bryan Adams's complexion, and even the viewing audience ("MTV—we play the classics because you fear the unfamiliar"). She was named to *People* magazine's 50 Most Beautiful People list, had a film career that lasted from *Reality Bites* to *Fantastic Mr. Fox*, and wrote a best-selling book about living with sarcoidosis, a potentially fatal autoimmune disorder.

And then there was Pauly Shore, an intensely and deliberately annoying LA comic who had more interest in girls' breasts ("melons") than in videos—and who in 1992, with *Encino Man*, became the first VJ to star in a hit movie. It's MTV's version of a rags-to-riches tale.

DOUG HERZOG: Nobody at MTV wanted anything to do with Pauly Shore. We were doing a show called *The Half-Hour Comedy Hour*, and having some success with it, so we decided to do a full comedy concert. We booked five comedians we liked, doing fifteen minutes apiece, and let Pauly be the warm-up act.

PAULY SHORE: They said, "We want you to host it, but your shit's not going to air." So I went out and killed. It was my time. My shot at Spring Break was a year or two too early.

DOUG HERZOG: He was the best act of the night. Everybody who worked on the show said, "We'd better take the Pauly thing seriously." Next thing we knew, we were in business with the Weez.

PAULY SHORE: I did thirty-second vignettes called *Totally MTV*, shot on film. I was doing a gig at a comedy club in West Palm Beach, Florida, sharing a condo with a comedian named Jonathan Katz, the bald guy. All of a sudden, *Totally MTV* came on, and I screamed: "Oh my god, I'm gonna get laid! I'm on TV!" The next day, Jonathan switched condos.

The buzz started at MTV: Who was this guy with his own vocabulary? *Weasel* and *buddy* and *grindage*. When I'd say, "Hey, check out my buff wood that you created," MTV didn't know it meant, "Hey girls, look at my dick that you just got hard." It was a subliminal language to the kids.

They offered me a three-month trial run for my own show, *Totally Pauly*, in June 1990. MTV was so East Coast: Ken Ober, Kevin Seal, Adam—what's his name, with the hair? Adam Curry. I represented freedom, wildness, California dreaming. I was twenty-one, I acted retarded, and I looked retarded. I had long hair, I was wearing tie-dye shirts, jean shorts, and scarves from my mom's closet, talking to the sluts on Sunset Blvd.

KAREN DUFFY, MTV VJ: I had a post-grad degree as a recreational therapist, working with severely and profoundly disabled people. I loved my job at the Village Nursing Home on Twelfth and Hudson, working with an Alzheimer's population who had a two-second attention span. And that translated beautifully to the MTV audience.

I kept getting big commercial gigs without any experience. I was the Calvin Klein girl, I did commercials for Cover Girl, Skippy Peanut Butter, Vidal Sassoon, Revlon. I was twenty-nine and still working at the nursing home. Being a VJ looked like fun. So I made a cheeseball videotape and sent it to MTV the Thursday before Memorial Day. By Tuesday, they asked me to audition.

I was with Click Models and they told me, "Don't take this job." My modeling agent said I'd be taking a pay cut. Everybody said it'd be the worst thing I could do for my career.

I didn't know a lot about music, and that made me work harder. I went to the Museum of Broadcasting and watched old Frank Sinatra variety shows. I noticed that Frank always dolled up, and seemed to not take himself seriously. Even at the height of grunge, I was always in stockings and high heels and a dress. I was hosting the evening shift and kind of wanted it to feel like that.

MTV was the greatest job of my life, because it was money undiluted by labor. It was pure fun. Being a VJ? A monkey could do it.

STEVE ISAACS: When I got to MTV, the two big acts were Guns N' Roses and fucking Vanilla Ice. I was twenty-one, and at that point, MTV still played music. The first round of VJs had to think on their feet and know about music. Starting with round two—Adam Curry, Julie Brown—MTV didn't give a crap about that. It was just *Get some kids, put them on the air, see how it works out.* I was a musician, doing an open-mic night in LA, and I hope they hired me because I had a bit more music knowledge. I was part of what everybody referred to as phase three: me, Karen Duffy, and later, Kennedy.

KENNEDY: I got negative mail as soon as I got on the air. It was a little shocking— angry letters from girls in Macon, Georgia, threatening to hurt me if I kept flirting with Steve Isaacs. There was also a postcard from someone who accused me of being a fat liberal Jew, and I remember saying, "I'm not liberal!" Why was I voted Most Annoying VJ after only a few months? I still don't know. I think a lot of women on TV at the time were not as acerbic and outspoken.

TONY DiSANTO: Steve Isaacs was the guy who turned me on to Rage Against the Machine. The first time I heard Pearl Jam was from Steve Isaacs. He was part of that new generation.

STEVE ISAACS: I got in trouble with Michael Jackson one time. He went on Oprah, and she asked why his skin had become white. "Why are you white now, Michael Jackson?" He said he had vitiligo, and that was why he was getting brighter. I mentioned it on the air and said he was on his way to becoming fluorescent. It's not even a funny line. But let's be honest, the guy became white.

Apparently, he was watching. I got called into one of the boss's offices and they said, "Michael's pissed off, and to make up for it, we have to do a Michael Jackson weekend."

I was shocked at how much new artists would bend over backwards to get on the channel. And then there was a tipping point where artists like Michael Jackson, Madonna, and Guns N' Roses could tell MTV to do anything. It was strange to see artists hold that kind of power over MTV.

KENNEDY: More than one artist complained about me, or refused to let me interview them. I had a pretty good head on my shoulders, so when someone said they liked me, I assumed they wanted something from me, like Duff's phone number.

KAREN DUFFY: MTV really kept us on our toes. People were getting sacked left and right. I was on a six-week contract, and MTV would renew it for another six weeks. The network fed you with an eyedropper full of love. My friend Steve Isaacs was making $22,000 a year. He'd negotiated his own contract.

I was covering the Grammys at Radio City Music Hall, and afterwards there was a party at the Rainbow Room, where Howard Stern was doing a live broadcast, and he started talking about me. The next day my agents called and said, "What the hell happened? MTV just offered you a big contract." That was a turning point. I owe it all to Howard Stern.

DAVE HOLMES: Karen Duffy is beautiful and spunky, and she knows everybody. Literally, everywhere you go, she knows everybody. She's like the mayor.

KAREN DUFFY: I used the privilege of MTV to go to a lot of *Saturday Night Live* shows. I was dating Chris Farley and I was *crazy* about him. One time we were going to the Museum of Natural History to watch a shark movie. I was starstruck that I was on a date with him. It's snowing like crazy, we were cutting through Central Park, and Chris kept falling. He kicked my feet from underneath me, and I did a face plant in the snow. We get up, we laugh. We get to the museum and everyone's looking at me. I'm thinking it's because I'm on a date with Chris. Then I looked in the mirror in the bathroom and all my makeup had run down my face, like Alice Cooper. I'm like, "Dude, why didn't you tell me?" And he's like, "I wanted you to look ugly so nobody else would go out with you."

He jilted me for the most beautiful girl in the world, Laura Bagley. But every night I went out with Chris, he had women throw themselves at him. I don't know any man that could scoop the poozle like Chris Farley.

KENNEDY: I was really disappointed by the way a few women at MTV responded to me. Karyn Bryant already had a reputation as being difficult, and she provided a great roadmap of what not to do. She was gone within a few months, so maybe she had reasons to be insecure. But being super-bitchy to someone who's never been on TV? That was lame, and there's no excuse for it.

PAULY SHORE: I'd been on MTV for about a month, and Sam Kinison asked me to open for him in Virginia Beach. I got to the venue and there were screaming teenage girls. About a year after I started at MTV, Jeffrey Katzenberg at Disney offered me a three-movie deal.

TONY DiSANTO: I was Pauly's intern. When he sees me, he still says, "Get me a cappuccino, Fat Boy." That was his term of endearment for me. I once brought a script to his hotel room at Spring Break in Daytona. I knocked and nobody answered, so I opened the door and it was like a video—Pauly sitting in bed with twenty bikini-clad, big-haired '80s girls. He said, "So, give me my script."

We became great friends, and I ended up producing his show. Pauly was the first VJ who had nothing to do with music. He wasn't a former radio DJ or a music expert. He was a comedian and a personality. His material wasn't even all that great. It was more about his delivery and attitude. The music became secondary when he was on. When he did VJ segments, he didn't even say the name of the next video. I think Pauly was the network's first attempt at developing a youth culture–driven personality, as opposed to a music-driven one.

JOEY ALLEN: Pauly Shore came out on the road with Warrant, in our tour bus. He was with Savannah, the porn star, when we played Vegas. He was smarter than a lot of people understood at the time. He had no shortage of pussy, trust me.

PAULY SHORE: There was a lot of girls. There was Debbie Laufer, who was a *Penthouse* Pet in 1988. I was dating a *Playboy* Playmate, Cady Cantrell. There was a model named Jill Fink, who married Patrick Dempsey. And then obviously Savannah.

There were groupies, all the time. That was kind of my thing. I used to have a road manager, Nick Light—his brother is Rob Light, one of the head guys at CAA—and he made it clear to them: If they came on the bus, they had to hook up with me. If they said, "Oh, I just want to meet him," he wouldn't let them on the bus. In the back of my bus, which I called "The Wood Den," I had a basket of buttons that said GRINDAGE, and another basket that had condoms. I'd have sex with them with a condom, and they'd leave with a button. So it was win-win.

Chapter 48

"A PEP RALLY GONE WRONG"

"SMELLS LIKE TEEN SPIRIT," GRUNGE, AND THE HAIR METAL APOCALYPSE

MTV HAD BECOME SICKENINGLY DECADENT, AND Nirvana came along as a corrective to the show-business follies of Paula Abdul and Pauly Shore, an enema to the idiocy of corporate rock—that's the conventional plot synopsis of grunge. Here's how one Nirvana biographer summarized the popularity of *Nevermind*, the band's 1991 album, which (oh, the symbolism!) knocked Michael Jackson out of number one on the U.S. album chart and has sold more than 30 million copies: "People were choosing substance over image." Juxtapositions and morality tales are convenient, but the truth is more complicated—Nirvana was as deliberate about their image as any other band of the MTV era, and far smarter about it, too.

Punk rock is usually said to be about refusal, saying *no* to mainstream culture and values. But Nirvana was not uncooperative with the mainstream. Rather than deciding to not make videos—as their contemporaries Pearl Jam quickly did, after MTV would not air the original version of "Jeremy"—Nirvana made great videos, meticulously overseen by Kurt Cobain. No matter how much they might have despised MTV, they made themselves part of it: videos, *Headbangers Ball*, the VMAs, *Unplugged*, interviews, a lengthy seven-song live set at MTV's studios in January 1992, a day off before taping *Saturday Night Live*.

Sure, Nirvana's roaring music and disorienting videos made other bands look conventional, and "Smells Like Teen Spirt" had as much effect as any video since "Thriller." But MTV was too big and stable to be changed by any one band. A new roster of rock bands came on the air—Nirvana, Pearl Jam, and Alice in

Chains, and soon Smashing Pumpkins, Stone Temple Pilots, and dozens more—but even as Nirvana's "Come as You Are" gained in heavy rotation, MTV was also playing pre-grunge holdovers, including Def Leppard, Genesis, Vince Neil, Mr. Big, Slaughter, and Richard Marx. Nirvana didn't kill video stars—they joined them.

AMY FINNERTY: I met Kurt Cobain and Krist Novoselic at a World Party concert at the old Roseland in New York. I said to Kurt, "Aren't you in that band Nirvana?" He was like, "Wow. You know who we are?" I said, "I work at MTV." At which point he and Krist couldn't make fun of me fast enough.

Everyone in the MTV programming department was at a listening party for the new Guns N' Roses album, and Mark Kates at Geffen slipped me an advance copy of *Nevermind*. From then on, I was determined to get this band all over MTV.

SAMUEL BAYER: I'd spent every dime I had to put together a spec reel. I knew Robin Sloane at Geffen Records, and I took her to lunch—I couldn't even afford to order anything—and told her I was desperate for a job. I think she took pity on me.

ROBIN SLOANE: Kurt Cobain was the only artist I've ever known who had brilliant, fully realized ideas he could express in one sentence. With "Smells Like Teen Spirit," Kurt said, "My idea for the video is a pep rally gone wrong." Kurt got some ideas for directors from watching MTV and taking notice of directors' names. He liked Matt Mahurin, and I knew Matt's assistant, Sam Bayer, and had seen his reel. He hadn't made a video yet, but he'd been doing a lot of shooting on his own. Kurt looked at Sam's reel and loved it, so I hired Sam. But there were a lot of problems between Sam and Kurt.

COURTNEY LOVE, artist: Kurt hated Sam Bayer. For "Teen Spirit," Kurt wanted fat cheerleaders, he wanted black kids, he wanted to tell the world how fucked up high school was. But Sam put hot girls in the video. The crazy thing is, it still worked.

SAMUEL BAYER: Kurt wanted to make something that felt like a cross between the movies *Over the Edge* and *Rock 'n' Roll High School*. I had in mind something darker and more gothic.

DAVE GROHL: The idea was, the kids take over and burn down the school gymnasium, just as Matt Dillon did in *Over the Edge*, with the rec center. Kurt was a *huge* fan of that movie.

We walked into that whole thing really cautiously, because we didn't want to misrepresent the band. There were certain things we found to be really funny about music videos—tits and ass and pyrotechnics, shit like that—and when we showed up at the video shoot, we were like, *Wait a minute, those cheerleaders look like strippers. There's fire over there? Hold on.* A lot of people we worked with didn't understand the underground scene or punk rock.

SAMUEL BAYER: I scouted LA strip clubs for the cheerleaders. Kurt didn't like them; he thought they were too pretty. I couldn't understand why he wanted to put unattractive women in the video. I think Kurt looked at me—the way I talked, the way I acted, everything—and saw himself selling out to the corporate way of doing a music video. So anything I did was construed as corporate. But to me, these were nasty girls. They had rug burns on their knees. In my eyes, the whole video was dirty. It's all yellows and browns. It was the opposite of everything I saw on MTV at the time; every video was blue and backlit with big xenon lights. It was MC Hammer dancing, and Guns N' Roses swimming with dolphins. It was ridiculous. I was a painter. I was trying to rip on Caravaggio and Goya. I just wanted to make the greatest music video you ever saw for $25,000.

ROBIN SLOANE: The problems at the shoot weren't Sam's fault. All the kids in the bleachers were drunk, and they seriously wrecked the set. It was out of control. To Sam's credit, he kept shooting.

DAVE GROHL: We did a couple of takes and the audience just started destroying the stage, tearing shit apart. People were out of control and the director's on a bullhorn screaming, "Stop! Cut!" And that's when it started to make sense to me: This is like a Nirvana show.

SAMUEL BAYER: The day of the video shoot was pure pain. Kurt was miserable. We didn't get along. He hated being there. I think at one point my nerves were fried, the set was chaotic, the band didn't like stuff, and I yelled, "Shut up!" at the kids we'd recruited. That was a turning point. I became the enemy. And then Kurt refused to lip-sync. Danny Goldberg, or some other big cheese on the set, had to beg Kurt to sing the song a couple times. And maybe it was his venom coming through, but I've been on two hundred music-video sets since, and that was the best performance I've ever seen.

ROBIN SLOANE: Sam didn't know how to edit. Most directors hire editors, but Matt Mahurin is a control freak, and Sam learned from Matt. Sam's edit had a lot of footage of the janitor and not nearly enough of the band. He fixated on the janitor. He'd have him on screen for thirty seconds in a row. He said, "The janitor shot is so great." But of course the most interesting thing in this video is Kurt. Fuck the janitor.

I said to Sam, "You've got to edit this the way Kurt wants." Sam was like, "Fuck you, I'm the director." And I'm like, "Fuck you, I'm the record company. I'm taking it away now." Which is what we did. We hired an outside editor to finish it. It was a very ugly scene.

SAMUEL BAYER: I was a young filmmaker, and when you're young you get too close to your subject matter and things become too precious. There were some characters in the video, a principal and a teacher, that Kurt was adamant had to come out. He was right, but I couldn't see it. Kurt flew down to LA, and it was the last time I saw him. It was a very contentious meeting. And Robin Sloane, who was great to me, made the decision to bring in an outside editor to finish cutting the video. The editor was Angus Wall, who became David Fincher's editor—he won the Academy Award for *The Social Network*. "Smells Like Teen Spirit" was one of his first jobs.

GARY GERSH: Not everybody at Geffen was excited by Nirvana. A lot of executives were shaking their heads, going, *This is all well and good, but we're having a lot of success with Cher and Whitesnake.* The first pressing of the album was thirty thousand copies, and I made a bet with someone in the sales group, for a relatively large amount of money, that we'd sell thirty thousand within the first month. More than one person took the bet. We sold thirty thousand the day it came out. Within the next seven days, I think we shipped half a million records.

AMY FINNERTY: Initially, Abbey Konowitch said, "Look, the visuals are great, and they have a catchy name, but beyond that, I don't really know what this is gonna do." And I basically testified for Nirvana. I said, "I'm your target audience. I understand why we're playing Bobby Brown and Paula Abdul and Whitesnake. But this is what we should be playing. And if there isn't a place for this, I don't know what I'm doing here. Give this video significant rotation for a month, and I promise you'll see some return. If you don't, you can reconsider my position."

COURTNEY LOVE: The first time Kurt and I slept together was at a Days Inn in Chicago, 'cause, you know, that's how Nirvana rolled. I'd seen "Smells Like Teen Spirit" quite a few times by that point, but we were having our first postcoital moment, and we're watching MTV and the video came on. I pulled away from him when the video came on, because it was his video, his moment, he was the king of the fucking world, and he put his arm around me and held my hand and pulled me closer to him. Which was symbolic, like, "I'm letting you into my life." That really endeared him to me.

The next time I saw the video with him was at the Omni Northstar Hotel in Minneapolis. I'd flown there to fuck Billy Corgan, who still had lots of hair. I hadn't had sex in a while and I needed to have some. I didn't even know Nirvana were playing that night. Kurt and I wound up at the Northstar Hotel and our daughter Frances was basically made that night. "Smells Like Teen Spirit" was on MTV every five fucking minutes.

SAMUEL BAYER: I was at a girlfriend's house one afternoon, laying on the bed watching TV, and I saw it. That video immediately gave me a career. Everyone wanted to do a Nirvana-type video: Ozzy Osbourne, Johnny Lydon, the Ramones. They all wanted that look. That first year, the videos I did were all just imitations of Nirvana.

KEVIN KERSLAKE: "Teen Spirit" crossed the Rubicon. Nirvana became the mold for success, the way Poison had been four years before. There are many ironies within the history of MTV, and that is one of them: The revolutionary fights the dictator, and ultimately becomes the dictator. It's just swapping chairs.

AMY FINNERTY: The first time I saw Kurt after the video took off was backstage at *Saturday Night Live*. We were in the greenroom and he said in that scratchy voice, "Hey, Amy. I heard you played our video. Thank you so much. I thought you were the VP of Post-it notes over there, I didn't know you had any power." He really didn't know that I was in the programming department. He had no idea what my position was.

DAVE GROHL: It all came down to Amy Finnerty. She championed the band. And she became a part of my family—coming down to Virginia and staying with my family and vacationing with us in North Carolina.

"WEIRD AL" YANKOVIC: My manager was having a very tough time getting Nirvana's management to return his phone calls, and I very much wanted to do my "Smells Like Teen Spirit" parody. So I called Victoria Jackson, who I'd just done a movie with—she was on *Saturday Night Live* and Nirvana was performing there. And I said, "If you get Kurt Cobain alone in a room, please put him on the phone with me." And she did.

So I talked to Kurt and he said, "Is it going to be a song about food?" I said, "Actually, it's going to be about how nobody can understand your lyrics." And he's like, "That's great. Go ahead." That was the last video of mine MTV put in heavy rotation.

AMY FINNERTY: When MTV News reported on the *Vanity Fair* article about Courtney's drug use while pregnant, she and Kurt would complain to me about Kurt Loder. They didn't want to talk to him again. And then—I'm not sure why—Kurt decided he wanted to make up with Loder. I told the news department and they were thrilled, and we jumped on a plane to Minneapolis. Kurt and Kurt did the interview, and then Loder and Krist Novoselic decided to go to Krist's room and have a couple of drinks.

After a while, I went to check on them, and the door was ajar. I walked in, and no one was there, but the room was completely destroyed. I mean, broken glass tables, broken televisions, a full wet bar with every glass broken. It was totaled. I went down to Loder's room and same thing: The room was completely wrecked. And there sat Loder and Novoselic, each smoking a cigarette and drinking a brandy. I was like, "What happened?" And they just smiled and smoked. Loder denied any participation, but I have a hard time believing Krist would ruin his room and then ruin Kurt's room, too. Nirvana's tour manager and I had to settle up with the hotel. They did upwards of $30,000 in damage.

PETER BARON: I took Kurt and Krist to do *Headbangers Ball*. Kurt wore a big yellow ball gown. He was completely fucked up. He was sleeping the entire time we were waiting to go on.

RIKI RACHTMAN: I was so excited to meet Kurt Cobain, and he was passed out in the greenroom. And when he came on the show, he was high as a kite. He wasn't even really talking. That clip is all over YouTube.

STEVE ISAACS: I had no problem with being called "the grunge VJ." I was wearing combat boots, I had flannel shirts, I was obsessed with Nirvana and Pearl Jam. It felt like my generation had its moment, and MTV was depicting it. Nirvana broke about two months after I got to MTV. *Boom*, "Smells Like Teen Spirit," and everything was different.

GARY GERSH: There was a Nirvana show in LA, early on, at the Palace, and backstage there was, like, the royalty of hard rock and hair metal bands. They were there to see what was up.

KIP WINGER: I was talking to Rick Krim on the phone and he said, "You haven't heard of Nirvana?" So I watched "Smells Like Teen Spirit" and I thought, *All right, we're finished*. We all knew it. It was obvious. There was no "Won't you play our video?" MTV wiped the slate.

JOHN KALODNER: When I saw "Smells Like Teen Spirit," my immediate thought was *My bands are in real trouble*. I took Kip Winger to lunch, and he was so dejected because Beavis and Butt-head were making fun of him. Mike Judd or whatever that fuck's name is. Fuck him. I mean how, how dare they? Hard rock bands made that network.

JANI LANE: My manager and I flew to New York to say, "Please play our new video, 'Bitter Pill.' Just give it a shot." And Rick Krim said, "I can't do it." It was a real blow. I went home thinking, *My career's over*.

RIKI RACHTMAN: People think grunge killed metal, and that's not true. The musical climate is always changing. Nobody said that A Flock of Seagulls killed Adam & the Ants. Everybody was toning down. All of a sudden, you weren't seeing pyro at shows.

JOEY ALLEN: Warrant had five number one videos at MTV. But I saw the writing on the wall from the Seattle bands—Pearl Jam's *Ten* was killer. We were at a Grammy party in LA. I had a few drinks in me and I bumped into Rick Krim. I'd played golf with him a few times, we were friends. I pulled out every credit card in my wallet, all the cash I had, and said, "Please play my video!"

MEIERT AVIS: After "Smells Like Teen Spirit," I could not get arrested. I'd done a couple of Warrant videos, and if you'd ever done a hair band, the Seattle bands would not touch you. Suddenly everything had to be like Sam Bayer. It was like a wave that cleaned a whole bunch of crappy directors out of the system.

BRET MICHAELS: I don't blame grunge for anything. Poison was imploding anyway. I thought "Smells Like Teen Spirit" was phenomenal. And let's be straight honest: Grunge collapsed quickly. It exploded and then collapsed.

JANI LANE: All of a sudden, we were scapegoats. I remember an interview, on MTV I believe, where Joe Elliott said, "Warrant ruined the '80s."

ANDY MORAHAN: I wanted to cry when I saw "Teen Spirit." I thought it was perfect. In a way, Guns N' Roses, myself, we became the dinosaurs, the kind of artists punk rockers hated. We'd become overblown and indulgent and kind of stupid, and then Nirvana happened and suddenly everything was grunge and cheap, and thank god for it, you know?

KEVIN KERSLAKE: The Michael Bays of the world, their aesthetic was so foreign to me. I wanted nothing to do with it, and it fueled a lot of defiance in the indie world, musically and visually. There was enough gloss to go around, so our approach was anti-gloss. Nirvana talked under their breath to me about "Teen Spirit," and they just wanted to move on and do something different.

DAVE GROHL: By the time we did "Come as You Are," we felt like we had the license to do whatever we wanted to do. So as things went on, the videos got a little darker. In "In Bloom," we were making fun of the hysteria around the band by using footage from old *Ed Sullivan* shows, of girls screaming in black-and-white for their favorite teenybopper. Plus, we just wanted to meet Doug Llewelyn from *People's Court*.

KEVIN KERSLAKE: There was one thing Kurt wanted in "Come as You Are," and that was not to be in the video. I had to develop a tool in which he was seen but wasn't seen, whether it was dark lighting or using a sheet of water in front of the camera that distorts his face.

The videos got darker because their psyches got darker. Any band that goes through that transition, it's so explosive and intoxicating and dark as fuck. Kurt wanted substance, and fame at that level doesn't offer much substance.

The idea on "In Bloom" was to satirize the spectacle of fan adoration, where you have expectations of pop stars who are squeaky clean. The band wore dresses, which was a spontaneous thought that Kurt came up with. We shot with old cameras, and did something you're really not supposed to do, which is change the lens in the middle of a shot to make jarring shifts. Then the cherry on top was when the band ripped the set to shreds, which is almost identical to the end of "Teen Spirit," actually.

DAVE GROHL: At that point, it was all about making people uncomfortable, really. The content and the visuals got heavier. Before Kurt had any idea for "Heart-Shaped Box" or any director in mind, he said, "You know what I want to do for the next video? I want to spend a *million* dollars." And everybody said, "Okay!"

COURTNEY LOVE: Kurt controlled every aspect of his videos. He wrote the treatment for every Nirvana video, except for "Lithium," because he was too fucked up, so he let Kevin Kerslake do it. I stupidly recommended Kevin. I didn't realize the level of my reach and influence with Kurt. And Kevin Kerslake ended up suing Kurt on the day of his funeral.

ROBIN SLOANE: Kevin Kerslake made a few Nirvana videos: "Lithium," "In Bloom," "Come as You Are." His videos were just okay, but he and Kurt were friendly. Kurt and Kevin had a couple of phone conversations about "Heart-Shaped Box," and Kevin wasn't going where Kurt wanted. Kurt said he wanted to work with someone else, so I suggested Anton Corbijn. And then Kevin sued the band for stealing his ideas. They were never his ideas. Even after Kurt's death, this suit was going on. Kevin went nuts.

DAVE GROHL: Kurt wrote a treatment for "Heart-Shaped Box" and gave it to Kevin Kerslake. He started working on the treatment but couldn't get it together in time, so we moved on and did it with Anton Corbijn, and Kerslake came out and said, "Nope, that was my idea." Which I think is fucking bullshit.

KEVIN KERSLAKE: Legally, I can't talk about the lawsuit. It had to do with copyright infringement. There was a resolution to the case—a financial settlement—and I signed a non-disclosure agreement. There are only two people who know the truth, one of whom is sadly not with us any longer, and we are both at peace with it, even if certain people on the margins of the litigation still use it as an excuse to exorcise their personal demons.

ROBIN SLOANE: Kurt had an idea of doing something that looked like the poppies in *The Wizard of Oz*, so I suggested that we shoot the video in Technicolor. Kurt loved that idea. There is no more Technicolor, actually—there's only one facility, in China—but Anton and his producers found a way to make it look like Technicolor. The video had a weird, beautiful look to it, and it was all over MTV. Videos don't get much better than that.

ANTON CORBIJN: Courtney knew my Echo & the Bunnymen videos, and Nirvana asked me to do the video for "Heart-Shaped Box." Kurt was fantastic. He wrote most of the ideas for the video. He sent me a fax, very detailed, of how he saw it: the field, the poppies, the crucifix, the fetuses hanging on a tree, the girl with the Ku Klux Klan–type outfit. I've never even seen a director be that detailed about a video.

It was very long finishing that video, because we shot in color, then transferred to black-and-white and hand-tinted every frame. Kurt wanted to shoot in Technicolor, and Technicolor had been sold to China, so he wanted to shoot it in China. My producer didn't like that idea very much. So we used colorization, a technique Ted Turner used for old black-and-white films, which created really vibrant colors.

Because it's so colorful, it got past the MTV censorship board. They didn't ask for a single change. "Heart-Shaped Box" got an award for Best Video and I was not invited onstage. I made the video! MTV gave the awards to the bands. Crazy.

STEVE ISAACS: There was an asinine rivalry between Nirvana and Pearl Jam. I loved them both. But Kurt said in *Rolling Stone* that Pearl Jam's music was "false," and he accused them of jumping on a bandwagon. The story was everywhere: *Nirvana hates Pearl Jam.* I wrote a letter to *Rolling Stone* saying Pearl Jam was a great band and calling Kurt pretentious. That pissed Kurt off. I was supposed to interview Nirvana in Madrid a few months later, but they faxed over a letter that said, "Anybody can interview us except Steve Isaacs."

RICK KRIM: Steve Backer, who did video promotion at Epic, said, "You've gotta see this band Pearl Jam," and I went to the famous show at Roseland in '91 where they opened for Smashing Pumpkins and the Red Hot Chili Peppers. Saw the show, was blown away, and shortly thereafter we got the "Alive" video.

STEVE BACKER: As Krim's watching, he turned to me and said, "I get it." That meant he'd be there when we needed him. He'd be their advocate. Rick came to Boston with me to take Pearl Jam to a Knicks/Celtics game. He became incredibly close with the band.

MARC REITER, record executive: I was the product manager for Pearl Jam at Epic Records. They shot their first video, "Alive," at the Off Ramp in Seattle, and insisted on using a friend of theirs, Josh Taft, to direct. *Headbangers Ball* was the only show that would play it. In fact, *Headbangers Ball* did the first-ever interview with Pearl Jam. And the band had a hard time with that. They just didn't think of themselves as aligned with that kind of music.

"Even Flow" was the next single. We shot a concept video at Griffith Park Zoo with a director named Rocky Schenck that never saw the light of day. He had done an Alice in Chains video everyone liked, but when we saw the first edit on this, we pushed the abort button right away. So we ate the $40,000 and went back to Josh Taft and shot another live video.

RICK KRIM: "Alive" and "Even Flow" were great performance clips, but "Jeremy" was going to be their first concept video. We were incredibly excited. Steve Backer came in and showed it to me. It's an amazing video. It's even more powerful in the version we didn't air. I still have the original, in my office closet.

MARC REITER: The band gave me a list of five directors and said, "This is who we will consider working with." And if I have a claim to fame, this is it: I sent them six reels. The sixth was Mark Pellington.

MARK PELLINGTON: Eddie Vedder told me he loved the Disposable Heroes of Hiphoprisy video I did, and the Public Enemy video. He told me the story of Jeremy, the real story of the kid. He didn't say what they were looking for, other than the band didn't really need to be performing in it. Which was good, because I don't love shooting drummers.

When we cast the role of Jeremy, all these kids were being angst-ridden, but it didn't feel authentic. This one kid, Trevor Wilson, was listless and dull and had one droopy eye. He looked really uncomfortable. I found out later he was sick as a dog, but he had this certain thing about him, so we cast him.

I'll never forget dollying around Eddie and oh my god, the hair was rising on the back of my neck at the end. It felt like he was rising from the dead. You don't really direct that, you just unleash it.

JOHN CANNELLI: Part of my responsibilities at the network was working with standards and practices, and giving the labels and artists ideas of how to make the videos more acceptable. I had to be the bad guy. I got on the phone with Michelle Anthony at Epic and Eddie Vedder and explained the changes we felt were necessary for the "Jeremy" video.

MARC REITER: In the initial video, the kid who plays Jeremy takes the gun, puts it in his mouth, and pulls the trigger. The band wanted it in. Pellington wanted it in. For five days, I went back and forth with Pellington and Krim.

STEVE BACKER: MTV came back to us and said, "We love it, but there's no way we're playing it with that ending." And I didn't blame them. The kid blows his brains out.

MARC REITER: In the final version, you see Jeremy walk into the classroom and extend his arm toward his head, but you don't see his hand, and you don't see a gun. For one split second, you see him close his eyes. And then you see his classmates, frozen, covered in blood. Some people thought, incorrectly, that Jeremy shot the kids in the front row, or shot the teacher.

MARK PELLINGTON: Eddie wasn't anti-video. He became that way after "Jeremy." It was edited and censored; it was misinterpreted by people who thought Jeremy shot his classmates, and Eddie was really pissed off by that. They were artists, man.

JUDY McGRATH: When Pearl Jam decided, after "Jeremy," not to make any more videos, Eddie Vedder said to me, "Look it's not personal, we're just not gonna make these things anymore." I adored Pearl Jam and totally respected what he was doing. But we could not have played "Jeremy" without editing it. Anything involving kids and suicide was extremely touchy.

MARC REITER: Pre-"Jeremy," the album had sold between 500,000 and 1 million copies. And it had taken ten months to get there. After "Jeremy," it was a blockbuster. It went to 2 million copies in a flash. And then 4 million, and 5 million. That's when it became a blur.

ABBEY KONOWITCH: Grunge was a watershed moment, because it proved a huge musical movement could exist outside of us, not just because of us. For me, it began to signal the end of MTV's musical impact.

JOEL GALLEN: 1992 was my favorite VMAs. We held the show at the Universal Amphitheater from '89 to '91, and the energy in the house was always a little low. I convinced MTV to move to a bigger arena and to put real fans in the front. We got Pauley Pavilion on the campus of UCLA to let us do it at the gymnasium, and I gave fans all the good seats, and gave the VIPs the seats on the side. A lot of people were angry about that, including Tom Freston.

JUDY McGRATH: I'll never forget the '92 VMAs. We had Pearl Jam, Bobby Brown, Guns N' Roses, Eric Clapton, and Nirvana. I could have died right then and there. A half hour before showtime, Nirvana weren't there. Kurt called, said he was driving and he was lost. He was in the car with Courtney and Frances, looking for the Pauley Pavilion and trying to get directions.

JOEL GALLEN: We asked Nirvana to open the show with "Smells Like Teen Spirit," the biggest song of the year. And Nirvana said they didn't want to play "Teen Spirit"—they wanted to play "Rape Me," a song nobody had ever heard. I said, "You can't play 'Rape Me.'"

JUDY McGRATH: Nobody had heard the song yet, and it's the opening of the show . . . *and it's called "Rape Me."* But they were Nirvana; we should have let them do whatever they wanted. Every time we've gone against an artist, I've regretted it. Every single time. Whether it was Neil Young's "This Note's for You" or Nirvana at the VMAs.

RICK KRIM: The 1992 VMAs were the greatest VMAs ever. We had Pearl Jam, Nirvana, Guns N' Roses with Elton John, Tom Petty, Black Crowes, U2 via satellite on the Zoo TV tour, Eric Clapton, Howard Stern as "Fartman." And of course, Nirvana wanted to play "Rape Me." I remember Judy telling Nirvana's manager Danny Goldberg, "You can't put a song called 'Rape Me' on the Video Music Awards."

AMY FINNERTY: Kurt wanted to give MTV a new song that hadn't been released yet. In his mind, he was giving us something special. There were some uncomfortable conversations back and forth about whether or not they were going to play the show. While this was taking place, Kurt was in rehab. Courtney and I drove to the rehab clinic together, walked in, and she *ran* up to Kurt, like before I got through the door, and said, "Amy's here to try to convince you to play 'Smells Like Teen Spirit.' Don't do it, don't do it!" I said, "I'm not going to try to talk you into anything. I just want to know what your feeling is about this."

COURTNEY LOVE: Kurt was very ill, very frail, around the time of the 1992 VMAs. He was in rehab and he was propped up on some kind of high-end methadone. He was real fucked up, that's for sure. He hadn't seen Frances in a long time, and we'd been through a lot because of the *Vanity Fair* article. Anyway, Kurt did not want to play "Smells Like Teen Spirit" on the VMAs because he was a full-on contrarian.

GARY GERSH: There was a posse of us advocating for them to play "Rape Me." What was MTV gonna do? Ban Nirvana? That would only have made the record bigger.

DAVE GROHL: It seemed hypocritical to us that MTV was tackling all these really important issues and trying to change the world, and we can't say the word *rape*.

JOEL GALLEN: To play it safe, we decided not to open with Nirvana. The Black Crowes opened. Nirvana promised to do "Lithium." We introduced them, and they went into the first four bars of "Rape Me." Right before panic really set in, they switched to "Lithium." That was a great moment.

DAVE GROHL: Kurt played those few bars of "Rape Me" just to give everybody a brief heart attack. I didn't know he was gonna do it. I don't think Krist did either. Believe me, I was used to worse than that.

AMY FINNERTY: I was standing next to Judy McGrath when they started "Rape Me." She grabbed my hand and we looked at each other, and she locked eyes with our stage manager and said, "No, leave it, leave it, leave it." As soon as they launched into "Lithium," the two of us just cracked up. We were so relieved.

SIR MIX-A-LOT: I was standing right near the stage when Nirvana was playing and Krist Novoselic threw his guitar way up in the air and it came down, hit him right in the face and knocked him out.

AMY FINNERTY: During the show, Eddie Vedder and Kurt made up by slow-dancing to Eric Clapton's "Tears in Heaven."

COURTNEY LOVE: We're sitting backstage at the VMAs. Everybody in the world is in this big tent, and there's a Guns N' Roses camp and there's a Nirvana camp. Literally, our roadies and their roadies are getting in fights. We stayed in our trailer most of the time because Kurt was sick, but we got bored, probably because there weren't any drugs to do, except coke, and we wouldn't have noticed that. So Kurt and I wander out to the main trailer with Frances, and Axl Rose comes over and he looks nervous. Everyone was watching us. I said something to him, I can't remember what, and he said to Kurt, "Get your bitch to shut up or I'll take you to the pavement." Kurt was holding Frances, and in a moment of pure brilliance he said to me, "Shut up, bitch," in the most deadpan possible voice. The whole room laughed at Axl. It was like your worst Freudian nightmare of a whole room laughing at you. I knew it would be a story I'd be telling many years later. Then Stephanie Seymour thought she'd be clever, and said to me, "Aren't you a model?" And I said, "No, aren't you a nuclear physicist?" At that moment, the world was definitely on our side.

DOUG GOLDSTEIN: I'd love to straighten out the story about Axl and Kurt Cobain. Axl loved Kurt's music, but Kurt used to say not very nice things about Axl. And Axl could never understand why.

So we're walking along, it's me and Stephanie and Axl, and all of a sudden I hear this voice: "It's Asshole Rose. It's Asshole Rose." It was Courtney. Axl said, "Fuck off," and kept walking. She said, "*Asshole.* What are you doing, *Asshole?*" So finally, Axl was pissed off and he walked over to Kurt and said, "Look, if you can't shut that bitch's trap, maybe I should shut yours." The instigator in this situation was Courtney.

AMY FINNERTY: Courtney was obviously trying to rile Axl. He said to Kurt, "You better get a handle on your woman." So Kurt screamed at Courtney, "Woman! You better listen to me!" At which point we all cracked up. But when Axl walked away, Kurt quietly said, "Honestly, that was really scary."

DAVE GROHL: That was a really weird night. It felt like I was back in high school, and that's one of the reasons I'd dropped out in the first place.

AMY FINNERTY: After the show I went back to Nirvana's trailer. As I got there, I saw Duff McKagan and a couple of the guys from the Guns N' Roses camp rocking the trailer back and forth, trying to tip it over. They were trying to get back at Kurt for his comments. I started screaming at them, "The baby's in there, the baby's in there!" They stopped, but it was ugly for a second.

MARK PELLINGTON: I was sitting behind Kurt Cobain at the VMAs. When they announced my name, he put up his hand and I shook it. And I remember Sharon Stone having had a lot of wine. She handed me my award and said, "Here you go, dude." I ended up at David Fincher's house. He was sitting in the bathroom, really depressed. I was like, "Dude, you're a genius, what are you unhappy about?"

SAMMY HAGAR: Eddie Van Halen and I were in the men's room with Flea and Anthony from the Red Hot Chili Peppers. They were saying, "What the fuck? You guys got our award. We wanted Video of the Year for 'Under the Bridge.'" And "Under the Bridge" should have been Video of the Year. That fucking thing was killing.

RICK KRIM: Pearl Jam wanted to play the Dead Boys' "Sonic Reducer" instead of "Jeremy." They gave in and played "Jeremy" on the VMAs, then made up for it the next night. It was the party for Cameron Crowe's movie *Singles*, which featured Pearl Jam and Soundgarden on the soundtrack. MTV threw the premiere party in downtown LA, and we booked Pearl Jam to perform. Fame was still difficult for Eddie to deal with, and he'd had to compromise the night before. In his mind, he'd sold out and played the hit. So he had a bunch of cocktails before the show. I saw him backstage, wearing an army helmet and kicking field goals with beer bottles. The show was a mess. He was wasted onstage. He kept yelling at security to let more people in, and the fire marshal kept coming onstage to shut things down. We had to carry Eddie off the stage and throw him in a car, because the show nearly turned into a riot.

STEVE BACKER: Eddie dragged me into a closet and started ripping for a half hour about how hard this was for him. He wanted to thank me for everything I'd done for them at MTV, but it was also kind of a good-bye. After that, Pearl Jam put everybody on notice that they weren't doing videos anymore. Pearl Jam were awesome guys, but they weren't, like, *fun* guys.

PETER MENSCH: Those VMAs were about as apocalyptic an event in the music business as I've ever been to. We managed Def Leppard. They went out there and played "Let's Get Rocked," the first single on an album that sounded way too slick for the times, and they got killed. It became clear to me that night that there was a whole new movement that I had completely missed. There was something transcendent going on, and we were not part of it. It really caused Cliff and me to think hard about our future as managers. We would go out to lunch every day and go, "What are we going to do?" It was clear that our bands from the '80s, except for Metallica, were basically done.

DOC McGHEE: See, MTV was a culture for about ten years, before they forgot what lifestyle was. MTV would be on in your house twenty-four hours a day. The culture they started was Bon Jovi, Mötley Crüe, Scorpions, Skid Row. And Kurt Cobain killed that culture like a light switch. I didn't sign any band in the '90s, except for KISS, because I couldn't get Rage Against the Machine or Pearl Jam, and the rest of the stuff stunk. Record companies signed every band that looked slightly like the Ramones. It wasn't about showmanship. It was no fun. And I'm a fun guy.

Maybe it was time to be a little more socially conscious. There'd been so much decadence for ten or fifteen years. And I feel bad for anybody that has mental problems and commits suicide. That's as sad as you can get. But if Kurt Cobain had done it four years earlier, that would have probably made me another $40 million. And I mean that in the nicest way.

Chapter 49

"YOU'RE NO BETTER THAN A RABBIT!"

FEARLESS TWENTYSOMETHINGS SHAPE A PRESIDENTIAL ELECTION

THE 26TH AMENDMENT TO THE CONSTITUTION GAVE eighteen-year-olds the right to vote, which they politely declined. Almost half of eighteen- to twenty-one-year-olds cast a vote for president after the amendment passed in 1971; by 1988, the percentage had eroded to less than a third.

Judy McGrath, one of the original MTV employees, had accrued a lot of influence at the network. She was an early advocate for *Yo! MTV Raps* and *Unplugged*, even though many staffers were opposed to the shows, and when both became hits, Tom Freston rewarded her foresight with a promotion to head of programming in 1990. She immersed the network in social issues, launching "Choose or Lose" as a way to encourage viewers to register to vote.

Next, MTV decided to cover the presidential race, assigning it to Tabitha Soren, who'd been out of college for two years when she took a job network reporters wait twenty years to fill. But Soren was "about as hard-driving and ambitious as they come," Judith Miller wrote in the *New York Times*. Though Soren had less experience than her colleagues on the campaign trail, she had no less confidence.

When Bill Clinton contested George H. W. Bush's reelection, young people voted in record numbers, and overwhelmingly supported the Democrat. After he was elected, Clinton appeared at MTV's Inaugural Ball in Washington DC and certified the network's influence by announcing, "I think everybody here knows that MTV had a lot to do with the Clinton-Gore victory."

A video network had changed presidential politics. This was not public service—as Soren points out, MTV gained new advertisers and political influence by virtue of their role. Presidential coverage, one insider said, "helped redefine MTV" as more than a video network.

ABBEY KONOWITCH: 1990 through 1992 was the second golden era of MTV. We knew who we were. There was an exciting balance of videos, music programming, and pop-culture programming. Our news department was influential. MTV had a great relationship with Madison Avenue and a great relationship with the record industry. We became so powerful that we got credit for every change in music.

JUDY McGRATH: I believed social issues, politics, and culture were all part of music. And so we brought in the "Choose or Lose" campaign. I had a lot of debates with people over that. I thought we could have a voice in politics. And others believed that was a big mistake, that we were an entertainment network, and we weren't equipped, nobody would watch, and we'd be be laughed out of town. I thought the adults in Washington needed to pay attention to our viewers, and they needed to do so on the viewers' terms. And clearly, Bill Clinton understood the value of Arsenio Hall and MTV. There's a hilarious interview with Kurt Loder and Ross Perot. Kurt sat down with Ross, and Ross turned it into a public service announcement to the MTV audience. He said something like "Now, if you're out there and you're doing drugs and you're having sex, you're no better than a rabbit. You're a rabbit!"

LINDA CORRADINA: "Choose or Lose" is the thing I'm most proud of doing at MTV News. I loved getting young people to understand the electoral process. We sugarcoated it, so it didn't feel like we were teaching anything, but we were. And we kept MTV on the air! When cable operators were complaining about Spring Break coverage, MTV would get grief and they'd want to drop us, so we'd point to MTV News. We were the smart department that did something good.

TOM FRESTON: During the 1992 presidential election, we decided to enter the political realm. We thought we could activate young voters in a nonpartisan way, because voting among the eighteen- to twenty-four-year-old demographic has always been the lowest. And Doug and Judy and Dave Sirulnick thought we could get the presidential candidates involved. I knew this PR guy, Ken Lerer, through Pittman. He worked with Robinson Lake Lerer and had helped us through various controversies. They were very active in Washington, very politically connected. We couldn't get arrested in Washington, and Kenny became our point person.

TABITHA SOREN: I worked at *World News Tonight with Peter Jennings* after my college classes, then I'd change out of my suit, into jeans, and go to MTV. They needed someone to write the news for *Headbangers Ball.* MTV was my part-time job throughout college, and I also worked at CNN and WNBC-TV. When I graduated in '89, I got a job as a reporter at the ABC station in Burlington, Vermont, covering the state house. After a year, they promoted me to anchor. It was kind of impressive, but it was a rinky-dink station, third in the ratings. Vermont bored me to tears, so I quit and came back to New York.

Kurt Loder had scheduled a two- or three- or four-week vacation in Barbados, and he was not going to cancel that, no matter what. They didn't have a substitute to do the news. Dave Sirulnick had me read the teleprompter at the studio, and I didn't make any mistakes. I was a really good fill-in.

The news department started to get much bigger and more professional, less like a playpen. Kurt's a total curmudgeon. He smoked in the building, even though he wasn't supposed to. When you walked into his office, you felt like you were in an ashtray. He had little patience for the stupid machinery around bands. It was great to have him setting parameters for the rest of us. Now, would he show up at the airport with his photo ID? Not always. Would he remember his credit card, so he could rent a car? Not so much.

Kurt was going to get all the veterans. I was never going to interview Mick Jagger or Bruce Springsteen, no one who had a son my age, because I would have made them look old. Kurt couldn't sit down with the Black Crowes and see them as anything but ripoffs of the Rolling Stones, whereas I thought, *The more bands that sound like the Rolling Stones, the better.* So it was useful for MTV to have somebody who wouldn't be pissy to a band that sounded slightly derivative.

ALISON STEWART: I moved from the production department to MTV News by showing them some writing samples. The news department was changing. It wasn't just going to be a PR machine for artists, which was always the difficulty:

You wanted to ask a confrontational question, but the artist's video was in heavy rotation.

TABITHA SOREN: Even though I was twenty-four, it seemed logical to me that I could cover a presidential race. I come from a middle-class background; my dad's in the military. I went to college to get a job, not to get an education. As a freshman, I was already trying to find a place to work. In New York, I'd covered Ed Koch's mayoral campaign. When I was in Vermont, I'd covered a gubernatorial race, as well as Bernie Sanders running for the House of Representatives. I had mayoral, gubernatorial, and congressional races under my belt. Dave Sirulnick was interested in having serious news, so I suggested we cover the presidential campaign. He said, "I'd have to have people who are really passionate about doing it." And I said, "That would be me."

ALISON STEWART: I was sitting in the newsroom and Dave Sirulnick walked through and said, "Alison, you like politics, right? We're going to cover the presidential election. I'd like you to produce it. Can you go to New Hampshire next week with Tabitha Soren?" Within a week, we were in a New Hampshire classroom with Bill Clinton. We were overwhelmed. CBS takes up two hotel rooms just for their editing equipment. Here we are, a tall, aggressive redheaded woman and her short, black, frizzy-haired producer, with a computer and some folders. I was twenty-five. Other reporters made fun of us. "*MTV News*? Isn't that an oxymoron?" I can't tell you how many times I heard that. These were the same people who, a year later, were asking me for tickets to the Rock n' Roll Inaugural Ball.

DAVE SIRULNICK: During the course of the campaign, we probably interviewed then-governor Clinton six or seven times. Some reporter asked President Bush, "Would you ever go on MTV?" And his answer was, "That teenybopper network? Why would I do that?" All year, we asked to do an interview with the president. Then, forty-eight hours before the election, we get a call from the White House: President Bush will do an interview with you.

TABITHA SOREN: I was given ten minutes in the back of a train with George Bush, who was snarky and dismissive. I had prepared; he hadn't. I asked a question about his tax returns, and they stopped the interview.

ALISON STEWART: The Clinton campaign got it right away. Bob Kerrey got it. Jerry Brown changed his clothes before we interviewed him, from a suit into a flannel shirt. Tom Harkin was like, "Hey you kids, get off my lawn."

We didn't need to talk about social security or tax cuts. We focused on jobs, student loans, gays in the military. It was a big risk. We would have been a laughingstock if we hadn't done a good job.

ETHAN ZINDLER, Bill Clinton campaign staff: My title in the Clinton campaign was assistant press secretary for youth media outreach. I wrote George Stephanopoulos a long memo in June, outlining a strategy for targeting youth media, including MTV, college papers, college radio, etc. MTV's coverage was huge. In retrospect, it seems rather antiquated, given how far we've come with the Internet and Facebook, but back then, putting a politician on anything other than mainstream network television news was considered way unconventional.

DOUG HERZOG: I was dumbstruck at how fast our election coverage took off, and how seriously we were taken. We hired a woman who worked for CNN to host part of it, and it turned out to be a disaster, because she sucked and was completely wrong for us. I was convinced we couldn't throw a bunch of kids at the president, and it turned out that was exactly what we did, and exactly what we should have been doing.

TABITHA SOREN: The network threw a lot of weight behind our coverage. The key was, it opened up a lot of new advertisers for them—maybe cars, maybe AT&T. It became lucrative for them. Also, it allowed Viacom to throw more weight around in Congress, at a time when there was lots of cable legislation.

TOM FRESTON: I went with Ken Lerer and Judy Miller to the '92 Republican Convention. The same Judy Miller who worked at the *New York Times* during the run-up to the the Iraq War. She decided she wanted to do a *New York Times Magazine* piece on MTV's political impact.

TABITHA SOREN: As soon as they saw I wasn't showing up in a halter top, as soon as I started talking, it was pretty clear I was there to ask politicians about their platforms. The reporters scratched their heads at us, but once the *New York Times* followed me around and wrote about us, it legitimized us.

DAVE MUSTAINE: My goal as an MTV correspondent at the '92 Democratic Convention was to show that there are people in metal who are intelligent and articulate. So I went up to Oliver Stone at the convention, and he seemed like he was out of his mind on drugs. I also talked to two politicians with the same last name: Bob Kerrey, the war vet that lost his leg? Nice guy. But John Kerry is a total asshole. He and Phil Jackson, the Chicago Bulls coach, were two of the rudest guys I've ever talked to. Phil Jackson looked into the camera and said, "Fuck MTV."

TABITHA SOREN: They gave me a mix of assignments. I flew to Colorado to interview Tom Petty, and he wouldn't talk to me. His manager said, "Tom is sick." I thought, *This is rude. I am not going home without an interview. Fuck that.* I was relentless, and finally the manager called MTV. They apologized to him for me doing my job. I got a call from the news department: "You're pissing everybody off." Well, did you send me here to get an interview with Tom Petty or not? Christ, if Bill Clinton can talk to me, so can Tom Fucking Petty.

ALISON STEWART: Tabitha had a lot thrown at her at a young age, and I don't know if she handled it as well as she could have. I'll say that diplomatically. Professionally, we were terrific, but personally, we clashed quite a bit. She got a lot of attention, and you know what happens to young people who get a lot of attention. She could be hard on people behind the scenes who were trying to help her, and I wasn't ever sure why. There's no reason to be short with a cameraman. There's no reason to yell at an intern.

ADAM CURRY: Her nickname was Crabitha. That's what we called her. She was cranky and nasty and gnarly.

LINDA CORRADINA: Tabitha could be moody and crabby, for sure. We'd send her out on pieces and she'd come back with the goods—breaking down "What is a caucus?" and "What is a primary?" She was doing a job way beyond her experience, and doing it well, but it took a toll, I'm sure.

TABITHA SOREN: After the primaries, there was a lull in the news. I was at odds with the MTV publicity department, because I was being interviewed all the time. I was on *Letterman, The Tonight Show, The Today Show, Good Morning*

America, any CNN show. No one was ever patronizing towards me; I think I was more in danger of patronizing them. Sorry, that sounds kind of jerky.

ALISON STEWART: I think our coverage changed the election. MTV helped Bill Clinton get himself elected. A lot of people were saying, "MTV is biased for Clinton." But he was the one candidate made most available to us.

JUDY McGRATH: I loved the early '90s era of MTV. It was among the lowest-rated eras of MTV, and among the most influential.

Chapter 50

"GETTING OUT OF
THE MUSIC BUSINESS"

THIS IS THE TRUE STORY . . . OF WHAT HAPPENED
WHEN *THE REAL WORLD* . . . TOOK OVER MTV . . .
AND MADE MUSIC VIDEOS . . . OBSOLETE

MTV HAD BEEN PLOTTING THEIR OWN VERSION OF a soap opera for years, and it finally arrived in May 1992. Except it wasn't a soap opera, because MTV couldn't afford scripts, costumes, actors, and sets. Instead, the original idea had mutated into *The Real World*, a show that invented the modern reality-TV show and brought landslide ratings to the network. Everyday people were the new rock stars.

AMY FINNERTY: I saw flyers up around the halls of MTV for the casting of the first *Real World*, and I thought, *Who the hell would sign up for something like that?*

TOM FRESTON: People asked me, "How did you come up with *The Real World*? That is genius." It was just because we didn't have any money.

VAN TOFFLER: Joe Davola, Doug Herzog, and I looked at statistics about how much our audience watched soap operas during the day. So we said, "Let's do a soap opera."

DOUG HERZOG: We decided to do a teen soap opera, with a rock n' roll attitude. Fred Silverman, of all people, the former president of NBC, recommended a woman named Mary-Ellis Bunim, who came from the world of soap operas.

JONATHAN MURRAY, TV producer: Mary-Ellis had produced daytime soaps like *As the World Turns*, and she was working with MTV on *St. Marks Place*, a scripted show about young people on the Lower East Side. When we put together a budget, MTV was like, "Oh my god, we can't spend this much money. We get our music videos for free, and now we're going to spend $300,000 for a half hour of television?"

LAUREN CORRAO: It would have cost around $500,000 a week. In comparison, *Remote Control* was about $15,000 an episode.

JONATHAN MURRAY: But Mary-Ellis and I saw this as our big break, and we couldn't let it go. So we pitched a new idea: six young, diverse people living together. We'd put them in a loft, follow their lives with cameras and create half-hour episodes. There'd be conflict and growth, and that would give us our story arc. We pitched it at breakfast and it was bought by lunch.

LAUREN CORRAO: I'll never forget, Mary-Ellis said, "What if you could do a soap opera with no actors and no writers?"

JUDY McGRATH: Someone at Nickelodeon said, "You can't put an unscripted soap opera on television!" Which immediately made me competitive and certain that we could.

JONATHAN MURRAY: We delivered two twenty-two-minute pilot shows. MTV tested it, and it tested through the roof. And then we waited. And waited. They had six months to make a decision about giving us the go-ahead for season one, and they took all six months. I think they knew they were crossing a bridge that could change the channel forever. God, for the first ten years of *The Real World*, MTV never promoted the fact that the show was getting huge ratings, because they didn't want it known that music videos *weren't* getting huge ratings.

KEVIN POWELL, cast member, The Real World: I was a freelance journalist, and I'd started writing about music. I was interviewing an R&B group called Joe Public at a diner in midtown Manhattan. They were four black guys who wore their hair the way we all did back then, in little twisties or high-tops. You know, beginning dreadlocks. A woman named Tracie Fiss came to our table and said, "I really like the way you guys look. We're doing a documentary-type show for MTV, would any of you be interested?" I can't say I watched a lot of MTV, but I took her card. I'd been a student leader at Rutgers University and was politically active, so I thought, *If I try out for the show and get on*—which was far-fetched—*maybe it will lead to some college speaking appearances.*

ERIC NIES, cast member, *The Real World*: I was cast for *The Real World* through my modeling agency. I had no idea what I was getting into. I was twenty years old. I was going to clubs, having a good time. It was an opportunity to work with MTV, which could be a stepping stone for my career. And I was getting a free place to stay.

KEVIN POWELL: Jon and Mary-Ellis had an incredible vision. Outside of *An American Family* on PBS in the '70s, there wasn't anything like it. I was really into their idea of combining documentary filmmaking with a soap opera. I thought it a fascinating social experiment.

When Julie and I had our famous "race" argument on the sidewalk, we were so passionate about our positions that we were oblivious not only to the cameras, but to the crowd of people that had gathered. She was a Southerner, I was a Yankee, and we had completely different perspectives on the world. People have told me that was the first time they'd ever seen race talked about in that way on national television. People have written dissertations on our argument.

ERIC NIES: I'd posed naked for a Bruce Weber book, and the producers decided to throw the book on the coffee table in our apartment for everybody to see. They felt they had to create conflict. But for me, it was all good. It grabbed me more attention and helped my career. Obviously, that's what the show is all about.

LAUREN CORRAO: Of that cast from the first season, Heather B. was a rap artist, Andre was in a rock band, Becky was a folk singer, Julie was a dancer. It fit into MTV's pop culture universe. There was enough music on that first season to calm some of the fears about doing a non-music show.

KEVIN POWELL: In September of '92, we were flown to LA for the VMAs. You're talking Red Hot Chili Peppers, Nirvana, Howard Stern—and then the cast of *The Real World*. And I swear, bro, the fans screamed for us as if we were the Beatles. That's when I really knew the show was a game-changer.

NICK RHODES: That's really when MTV ended. That's when it became entirely crap.

SIMON LE BON: When you saw *The Real World*, you knew it was gone.

JONATHAN MURRAY: When *The Real World* debuted in 1992, MTV was still mostly music videos. In fact, the show sometimes began at three minutes before the hour, or three minutes after the hour, depending on when a music video ended. When the first episode aired, we came out of a 0.3 rating for the videos, and *The Real World* popped to a 0.9. We tripled our lead-in.

ERIC NIES: We each made $1,400 for appearing on *The Real World*. It was *completely* unfair. That show made millions and millions of dollars for MTV. I made $1,400.

STEVE ISAACS: I remember MTV saying there was no way to hold a steady rating when they played videos. If they played rock, rap fans would turn the channel, and vice versa. There was a schism in music.

KEN R. CLARK: There was a time when I'd walk down a street in New York City wearing an MTV staff jacket, and people would yell, "Wow, man, MTV is so cool." By the time we were airing *Real World*, people would yell "MTV sucks!" And a lot of us were starting to think it did.

DOUG HERZOG: To show you what an idiot I am, when *The Real World* took off, I thought, *Well, this can only work once.* My thinking was, those kids who did the first season, they had zero expectations coming in. But since they'd become stars, the next group of kids were going to expect to become stars, too, and they'd be over the top and obnoxious and the audience wouldn't want to see that. Wrong! That's exactly what the audience wanted to see.

LAUREN CORRAO: After the first season aired, kids wanted to be on the show as a means to an end. But that first group was not about that. We couldn't even get anyone to kiss on camera that season. And now look what happens on the show.

DAVE HOLMES: Have you seen the first season of *The Real World* lately? It seems like a fucking Ken Burns documentary from today's perspective. The scenes and conversations go on forever. It's like, you can't believe how much shorter our attention spans have gotten since then.

JUDY McGRATH: Academics were quick to latch on to *The Real World*. All of a sudden, I was getting invitations from universities, and people were writing that it was either the death of everything or the beginning of everything.

KEVIN POWELL: Our season of *The Real World* opened a new chapter in television history. For our show to be part of American pop culture, that's incredible.

Still, it's a mixed bag. On the one hand, I'm proud when people say to me, "Your conversation about race had an impact on my life," or "Norman coming out and being an openly gay male on TV had an impact on me." That's important. But when people ask, "How can I get on reality TV?" I mean, come on, man. I'm in my forties. I've run for Congress twice. I could care less about that stuff.

NICK RHODES: I saw a newspaper headline once that stuck with me: TOYS "R" US WANT TO GET OUT OF THE TOY BUSINESS. That's what happened to MTV. They wanted to get out of the music business.

LAUREN CORRAO: I still feel a little guilty about being the one responsible for the non-music shows.

JOHN LACK: *The Real World* was the end of music as we know it on MTV.

DOUG HERZOG: We didn't know what to do with the kids from the first season. We felt responsible for them. We gave Eric Nies a job hosting *The Grind*. We hired Julie Oliver in HR, but she started looking up all the executives' salaries and telling Bunim-Murray, so we fired her. Heather B worked on *Yo!* for a while. I bought a very bad painting from Norm.

Chapter 51

"LET'S GET CRAZY TONIGHT"

TEARS, TEQUILA, AND BROKEN GLASS:
MTV VIPs CELEBRATE THE FIRST DECADE

TOM FRESTON: I threw a ten-year anniversary party at the Tribeca Grill in 1991, and invited John Lack and Bob Pittman and all the executives. People who had passed through, and crashed and burned, and hated each other, they all came together this night. We were upstairs in a private room, drinking tequila shots.

FRED SEIBERT: I was looking at all these old, rich people in suits, thinking, *Really? This is what I miss?*

JOHN LACK: Many of us hadn't been together for five, six years. For a lot of people, MTV was their Camelot. It was the greatest time of their lives.

TOM FRESTON: I toasted John Lack as the father of MTV and gave him a bottle of champagne. He was so emotional, being publicly recognized once again, in front of those people, that he *was* indeed the guy who had the idea.

JOHN LACK: After I left MTV, history got a little altered. Bob Pittman began to think that he created the thing, and he went around telling everybody that it was his idea. So when Tom introduced me, I think he wanted to set the record straight in front of everyone. And he did.

FRED SEIBERT: Tom was fucking awesome about giving John his due. For the first time among his peers, it was publicly acknowledged that John maybe hadn't gotten the credit he deserved. And Bob raised his glass, too. It was good to get it out there like that, in front of everybody.

ROBERT MORTON: When people were filing in, Pittman said to me, "Let's get crazy tonight." Sure. No problem. So after I made my toast, I took my glass and threw it against a wall, thinking, *All right, this is crazy enough.* At which point sixty people started throwing glasses at the wall.

BOB PITTMAN: One of the MTV traditions was that we would shoot tequila and break the shot glasses. At my going-away party at the Cadillac Bar and Grill, paramedics had to come and stitch up people's feet. The tenth anniversary party was at the Tribeca Grill, which is not the kind of restaurant where you throw glasses. But we all did, of course. Freston blamed it on me, which was okay, because he was still working there and I wasn't.

TOM FRESTON: It was crazy. Soon, everyone was standing up and throwing their glasses. It was like a Greek wedding. Management ran in and said, "Get the fuck out of here." We ended up getting thrown out of the Tribeca Grill that night. It made Page Six.

ROBERT MORTON: I was producing *Late Night with David Letterman.* When I went back to the Tribeca Grill with friends, the owner, Drew Nieporent, didn't talk to me for years. *I* was the one Pittman blamed. He said *I* incited the breaking glass. That pussy hung me out to dry, but *he* incited the goddamn thing. I tease him about it every time I see him.

BRIAN DIAMOND: Tom Freston had a great line that night. He stood up with John Lack on one said and Bob Pittman on the other side, and said, "MTV: It's a club you can't get into, and you can't get out of."

Chapter 52

"FAT CITY"

THE BUBBLE BURSTS ON
MUSIC VIDEOS' GOLDEN ERA

NITIALLY, MTV WAS SOMETHING YOU COULD FIND ONLY by watching MTV. As its influence spread, its uniqueness dissipated.

After MTV proved the value of a teen market, Rupert Murdoch and Barry Diller launched the Fox network, which by 1993 had seven nights of prime-time programming, and launched beloved shows: *Married . . . with Children, 21 Jump Street, The Arsenio Hall Show, The Simpsons, Beverly Hills 90210, Melrose Place*, and *The X-Files*. Robert Morton, an early MTV employee who left because he thought the network would fail, was executive producing *Late Night with David Letterman*, which brought anti-authoritarian absurdity to mainstream NBC. Specialization became rampant across cable—MTV's comedy programming had to compete with an entire comedy network, Comedy Central, and its news department vied with E! Entertainment Television for celebrity interviews.

Simultaneously, as MTV attitude became pervasive, videos began to feel commonplace. The idea of MTV—as something new and sheltered, hidden from adults or older siblings—had passed away; once the initial audience matured, the following wave of schoolkids didn't feel the same private delight. They had Nintendo and Sega, which revitalized home gaming; Mosaic soon made the Internet accessible. Active technology was supplanting passive technology. Offering MTV to a kid in 1993 was like offering a board game to a kid in 1981.

Also, videos had begun to lose their spark. Most of the people who created the video industry agree that by '92, the Golden Age was winding down. Videos were now carefully controlled by record labels, minimizing the chance of imaginative work. Large budgets substituted for fresh ideas. The arrival of digital editing, in the form of Avid, made it easy for directors to flit breathlessly between images. "Directors started putting as many cuts as they could into five seconds, but none of the cuts meant anything," says David Mallet. "Music videos were the first genre to encompass nonlinear editing. That's when they started to go *bang bang bang bang bang*. It got hugely abused."

Novice directors increasingly saw videos as a way to showcase their own talents, rather than the band; music video had become an internship for Hollywood employment. In December 1992, MTV began listing directors' names in chyron credits. Videos had been ads for a song, or a band, or a way of living and dressing. Now that their names were credited at the beginning and end of each video, directors were also making ads for an additional product: themselves.

The Golden Age—an era of creativity, invention, freedom, outrage, dancing zombies, bold hairstyles, profane VMA speeches, laughable costumes, cheesy special FX, midgets—came to a close. Rap videos, in particular, became more predictable and codified than hair metal videos ever were. Given the relative success of *The Real World* compared to MTV's ratings for video, the audience seemed to agree with comedian Denis Leary (*Newsday* called him "the most happening act on MTV right now"), whose lustful rants about Cindy Crawford in 1992 depicted her as the pinnacle of the network's content. "No MTV news, unless it's news about Cindy. No music, unless it's songs about Cindy," Leary woofed.

Of all MTV's long-form programming, *The Real World* had the most tenuous connection to music. Its success speeded video's dismissal from MTV, and was bad news for record labels: MTV had thought to make themselves independent of the labels, but the labels never thought to make themselves independent of MTV. When MTV reduced the number of videos played per week, labels that once wanted nothing to do with the network felt betrayed by their unrequited devotion to MTV.

From humble beginnings twelve years earlier as the Cable Channel Least Likely to Succeed, MTV had spread its influence across TV, radio, advertising, film, art, and fashion. In a final display of potency, it proved influential in the election of Bill Clinton (who, given his attitude and sexual exploits, might be called "the first MTV president"). Once you've helped determine a presidential election, what's left? Another Winger video?

ABBEY KONOWITCH: *The Real World* turned television upside down. It was good for MTV, but it wasn't good for music. The scary thing, the most important thing to look at in this era, is the amount of power MTV had. We were perceived as the panacea for the record business. We were the crutch. If MTV played your video, you had a shot. If MTV didn't, you didn't. That was a flaw in the business. When MTV didn't play videos, the record industry suffered.

MIKE ROSS: When they started to phase out videos, we ran up against some walls that irritated me. In 1993, they had one slot to add a rap video—it was either our Pharcyde video, "Passin' Me By," or "Slam" by Onyx. Only *one* could get added. And they added "Slam." It was a huge blow for us, and cost us a million, maybe two million, in record sales.

RICK RUBIN: The labels became dependent on MTV, absolutely. Their entire marketing campaign was to make an expensive video, as though the fact that it was expensive solved the problem of there not being a great idea. So these expensive, mediocre things were being made, to get play on MTV, and then MTV started to go away. It caused a great deal of confusion. It's like, MTV changed everything when it came, and it changed everything when it left.

KEVIN GODLEY: People got bored with music videos. Because—guess what?— they were boring. They were safe, they were the same, they were the results of marketing experiments as opposed to creative experiments. They were more to do with selling the artist than the song. They were more to do with sales than with art. It's always Art vs. Commerce, but in the beginning, art won out because commerce didn't understand it.

MICHAEL NESMITH: There was a golden age of music video—an innocence and a flowering—and then a rolloff in the late '80s or early '90s.

TIM NEWMAN: In the beginning, it was laissez-faire and ad hoc. Each label had a head of video production, but in many cases they didn't do anything, didn't show up to the set. It was pure freedom and fun. In the late '80s, there were more people in the business who frankly didn't know what they were doing. As time went on, managers more and more thought they were experts.

JEFF STEIN: The scariest phrase I ever heard doing music videos was the record company executive saying, "I have an idea for the video." And the second scariest phrase was the band's manager saying, "I have an idea for the video."

ANTON CORBIJN: When budgets increase, more people get paranoid about money being misspent and they want to have a say in the video. And you know, art is not created by committee. If that happens, it's a problem.

TOM BAILEY: The music business was held hostage by videos. Media barons and lawyers took over the record companies, because it was about the way you spent money, to focus your bombardments of the audience. So whilst I have MTV to thank for opening America to the Thompson Twins, it also killed us off, in a way. Video was a fantastic servant, but not a very good master.

ADAM DUBIN: In music videos, there are three distinct forces—the unholy triumvirate, I call it. The artist and their management each have an idea of what the video should be. The record company has another vision, but they also have the money. You needed two of the three camps aligned for your concept, but the other camp usually fought back. And sometimes management and the record company would line up together and force a concept down the artist's throat: "Either you do this, or there will be no video."

If you shoot the video and get into the edit room, all three forces battle it out. It becomes a place for old scores to be settled. Or band members squabble among themselves over screen time.

JEFF STEIN: As MTV became a phenomenon, and record companies and managers became more involved and put their fingerprints all over videos, it became big business. It became overcommercialized and homogenized. And eventually in 1992, it became euthanized.

ABBEY KONOWITCH: The balance at MTV was moving away from music and that's when I left, in '92. The things we did, whether it was Guns N' Roses or a hundred others, we couldn't do it anymore. There weren't enough video hours, and more important, there wasn't the commitment that music was important to the channel.

KEVIN SEAL: Around 1991, it fizzled out for me. Somebody asked if I really wanted to do this job, and I made a noncommital shrug. They eased me out. The idea that somebody new should be on all the time sounded reasonable. For example, I was amazed Kurt Loder could be on year after year, because he was not any more into it than I was. As long as they were still paying, he could go out and drink after work. One night we went to a dive bar near Penn Station and ordered every zany cocktail we'd never had. "Brandy Alexander? That sounds like a stripper's name!"

KENNEDY: I had the pleasure of sitting down with all five original VJs at the Hotel Nikko in LA the night before the 1993 VMAs. J.J. Jackson was a sweet teddy bear. Alan seemed a little confounded by the direction of the network. Even back then, people were complaining there wasn't enough music on MTV.

ADAM CURRY: I quit on the air in the summer of 1993. I was doing the *Top 20 Countdown*, Beck was number one with "Loser," and I said, "Beck is number one. That's it, I really think the Internet is the place to be, I had a great seven years, I'll see you on the Internet." I walked out and never went back.

TRACEY JORDAN: What I call the pimp-rap videos had started. Rappers were throwing gang signs up, there was gunplay, and women were more like body parts and props.

RICK RUBIN: The budgets got bigger over time, but the concepts never got better.

SIMON LE BON: The simple ideas, which are always cheap, got used up. If you haven't got a great idea, one thing you can do to make it look good is throw money at it. That became the ethic.

SCOTT IAN, Anthrax: Here's what was fucked up: In 1993, Anthrax was about to shoot a video, when Mark Pellington came up with a treatment for a different song. But he wasn't available until the fall. So we waited, which was a huge mistake. During our summer tour, we had no single out. It was a stupid decision. Our record company talked to us into waiting because Mark was *the* hot guy at the time. Videos ruled the business.

JOHN SAYLES: I know somebody who worked on a Taylor Dayne video, and it was reshot three times because they didn't like the way her hair looked.

ANN WILSON: As it went along, videos really stopped trying to interact with the music. The video had a story of its own, and the music was a subtext. It became about how the stylists wanted to make you look. It got less fun for us because of that.

AL TELLER: Every artist and manager felt it was their right to make a top-notch video. Meanwhile, MTV tightened up their playlists and started to air fewer and fewer videos. Plus, they started branching off into non-music programming. So you had two conflicting curves: a rapidly climbing curve of expenses for a video, and a rapidly declining curve of the number of videos being exposed. It became impossible.

MICK KLEBER: Most of the early videos were made for $20,000 or less. Duran Duran's "Hungry Like the Wolf" and "Save a Prayer" in Sri Lanka were a package deal at $35,000. By the end of my run in 1993, Capitol had produced music videos with budgets eclipsing $1 million, and annual video expenditures for the label were nearly $15 million.

EDDIE ROSENBLATT: Videos were singularly the biggest cost in a marketing budget. Once you spent $100,000 or $300,000 or $500,000, if MTV didn't play the video, it was a waste of money. And even though you had different arrangements with artists relative to recoupment, if they didn't sell any albums, there was nothing to recoup.

MARTHA DAVIS: Record companies were so fat that they did what everything does in the law of physics: they blew up. And they started making stupid choices. Part of it was drug-induced. Because there was so much money, the price of making a video was going up like crazy.

I remember the year when the record industry grossed more than the film industry, or something crazy. It was like fat city. Secretaries were going to lunch in limos. We fall for the bubble thing, every time. We fall for it.

NICK RHODES: The record labels were such thieves—the budgets we were spending on videos, they were spending on wine at lunch.

JOHN BEUG: I'd started working in the music business in '72 for a guy named Lou Adler. We made a couple of movies: *The Rocky Horror Picture Show* and Cheech and Chong's *Up in Smoke*. Then I went to work for movie studios. Having worked in motion pictures, it annoyed the crap out of me that the money being spent on videos often didn't wind up on screen. They were wasting it. Directors wanted a steady camera *and* a stage crane, even though they only used one or the other. I used to marvel that we made *Up in Smoke* for $1 million, and here we were spending $1 million on a music video.

ANN WILSON: A whole day would be spent auditioning the effect on a snare drum. Talk about wasteful activity.

NANCY WILSON: It was a huge, spectacular, corporate explosion. And it was exciting to be part of it, at first. But videos, like the production of music in that time, became bombastic and costly. How many dancers were employed? How many makeup artists and stylists? *How* big did the hair get? *How* much did it cost?

Chapter 53

"YOU HAVE NO IDEA HOW I MISS IT"

FANS, STARS, STAFF, AND DETRACTORS
REFLECT ON THE VIDEO AGE

SAMMY HAGAR: I was fucking shocked. *These bastards don't play videos any-more. How dare they call themselves MTV?*

MICHAEL NESMITH: MTV switched to reality programming and became more of a social network, which may have been prescient.

DAVE HOLMES: MTV doesn't really want to acknowledge their age. I hosted a twentieth anniversary special with the original five VJs and the ratings were not good. At all. The kids don't really want to watch people who are old. So the twenty-fifth anniversary passed without a peep.

BOB PITTMAN: If I had stayed at MTV, I'm not sure I'd have *ever* switched it to mostly shows. I understand that if the advertiser says, "I'll give you more money for it," you do it. But I'm one of those old-fashioned guys that goes, "If I have something the consumer likes, my job is to convince the advertiser to advertise in *this*, not to change my programming to what the advertiser wants."

JUDY McGRATH: The people who were there when MTV started were disappointed when we stopped being the home of music videos. I'm *still* sad about it. But things had to evolve.

NICK RHODES: At some point the *M* in MTV changed from *Music* to *Money*.

MEIERT AVIS: The rampant abuse of music-video directors in the past thirty years has been appalling. We have no ownership over our work. We have no protection from having it re-edited or repackaged. Directors are paid a flat fee, which is pathetic to begin with. And now MTV is a giant corporation, thanks to music videos. You're not even allowed to talk about this shit. It's career-busting if you try.

JAC BENSON: I understand the economics of television. But you fell in love with a channel that promoted itself as giving you that thing you wanted and couldn't find anywhere else, that represented you, and then that channel changed. It's sad and disappointing.

DAVE HOLMES: Sitting in front of a TV certainly looks passive. But watching MTV made me want to grow up and be a creative person. It made me want to write, it made me want to get onstage. MTV was instrumental in me not being a banker, and not being a banker has made all the difference in my life.

JOHN TAYLOR: Once a year or so, I meet somebody that tells me that they were living in Iowa or Ohio, fifteen years old, when MTV came on. And it changed the direction of their life. Whereas they thought they were gonna be a lawyer, they ended up moving to New York and becoming an art director. There must be thousands of people working in the arts—graphic design, Madison Avenue, film, photography—because of the influence of MTV. And all the hairdressers, of course.

HUEY LEWIS: For a long time, the '80s were dismissed. But the '80s gave us twenty-four-hour-a-day music television, and the drum machine. Both changed music forever.

ALAN NIVEN: You know the old expression "You can't shine shit"? Video did. It shined shit.

ANDY SUMMERS: My real thought about music videos is that you shouldn't have music videos. But one didn't really express these thoughts too much at the time, being huge beneficiaries of the medium.

BOY GEORGE: Videos were like postcards, going to every corner of the world. People living in small towns in the middle of nowhere were able to have access to what artists were doing. That's the positive aspect of MTV. The negative of that is that it turned music into a product, like a can of beans, and that's why we're in the situation we're in now. Everything is cross-collateralized: movies and pop, fashion and pop, advertising and pop. Back in the '70s, pop music was its own untouchable empire. You would never have seen David Bowie advertising anything. Pop stars were kind of nebulous and saintly. Whereas nowadays, anyone can be like a pop star, and video played a part in that.

MARTY CALLNER: MTV was great for music and great for the country. The Beatles changed everything, and nothing else changed again until MTV. Everybody watched it to get their style, to know what was hip and cool. It was a lifestyle channel.

ANNE-MARIE MACKAY: Music videos were a new form of storytelling, with their own visual literacy. Young people understood them. They could say, "These are the new myths." They were tribal about it. Music videos changed the way people absorbed information. They changed entertainment forever. When MTV changed its format and started airing reality shows, I hated it with a passion and I still hate it. They made the music-video industry, and they killed the music-video industry.

DAVE HOLMES: It's just kind of a network now, you know? They outsource all their shows to external production companies, instead of using their own sets and producers.

BILLY GIBBONS: It's not unusual for people to ask me, "When will MTV go back to playing music?" And I say, "You'll have to go to Europe."

ABBEY KONOWITCH: MTV and radio were gurus for what was cool, what mattered in pop culture. Today it's all tiny little factions. MTV was the last national radio station. There is no mass media anymore.

STEVE BARRON: The '80s was a great decade for treading new ground. Punk had come in and chucked everything in the air, so there was this clear path. We had the freedom to decide how to combine new music with a new visual medium. It was kismet, a time that will never happen again. Some of what we created was really sweet and some was really tacky and terrible, but it was what it was.

ANN WILSON: Whatever happened in the '80s, I can barely remember. But it was good.

STEVEN ADLER: Rock n' roll ended after the '80s. I see bands on TV nowadays, and I could swear it's the same guy I just bought a Whopper from at Burger King. Nobody has a look, nobody really cares.

TIM NEWMAN: I don't direct commercials anymore and have no interest in doing them. But I'd do another video at the drop of a hat. I am available, yes.

ADAM CURRY: I don't get invited to the reunion shows. People at MTV hate me. I'd love to go back.

NICK RHODES: The one mistake we made with MTV, without a doubt: We didn't buy shares.

MEIERT AVIS: Most of the videos on MTV were really bad. Duran Duran, or silly hair band: It was all phony people doing phony shit in phony situations.

JOHN TAYLOR: Call me prideful, but I think the *Duran Duran Greatest* DVD is the best video compilation there is.

DAVE HOLMES: I don't think kids twenty-five years from now will be talking about a specific episode of *My Super Sweet 16* the way we remember things about Duran Duran videos. I'm sure *The Hills* got good ratings, but it weakens the brand.

STEVE ISAACS: I mean, Heidi Montag and her fucking double-G breasts, and her psychopathic ex-husband—that I know this much about those people, I can only blame on MTV.

KAREN DUFFY: The name of my production company is Dewey, Cheatem, and Howe. This company called me back recently to make sure my credit card was real. And they said, "You've got the same name as the girl from MTV. Is that you?' And I said, "Yeah." And they go, "Wow, you're Duff? You must be, like, sixty."

JULIE BROWN: When my daughter and I go out together, people come up and mention my work, which makes both of us very proud. If that's all I got out of MTV, then money has nothing to do with it. Then again, that's because I'm rich. If I was broke, living in my car, I'd be like, "Up yours!"

CINDY CRAWFORD: I get a lot of people tweeting, "I loved *House of Style*."

PAULY SHORE: The Web site Funny or Die reminds me of how MTV was when I first started: no money, but as much freedom as you want.

ADAM CURRY: I believe I'm the only VJ who has been successful in business after leaving MTV. That is a badge I am often given, and I wear it with pride. I cofounded an Internet company, Think News Ideas, Inc., that sold in 1999 for $450 million, just before the Internet bubble burst. I cofounded another broadcasting company, MEVIO, and we raised almost $50 million from premier venture capital firms.

ALAN HUNTER: When people see the VJs, they have a sense-memory flashback. We were in their lives every day, and we got seared into their brains. We're like a neuron that got triggered, never to be turned off. Some days, it seems like it was yesterday.

SUSANNA HOFFS: The fact that the '80s are now a beloved era is shocking. I never in my life thought I'd meet a person who'd tell me, "The '80s are my favorite era for music." My knee-jerk response, when I started hearing this, was to say, "Are you crazy? It was terrible. The '60s, *that's* the golden age." But I realize, there is something wonderful about the lightheartedness of the decade.

JEAN-BAPTISTE MONDINO: I thank God it's over now. I'm happy that MTV doesn't play videos. As soon as they stopped, music came back. People are making music for the pleasure of it, not to make money, because money's not there any longer. There are good videos on the Internet, done by kids with no money, that are poetic and beautiful. Videos now are better than videos were in the '80s, because they are not made as packaging.

DAVE GROHL: Ten or eleven years ago, Foo Fighters played a gig at a little bar in the Valley, to warm up for a festival tour. Afterwards we had a party and I was talking to this one chick who was a porn star. She was gorgeous. And she said, "I've met you before." I thought, *Uh-oh, what have I done?*

And she said, "I was one of the cheerleaders in the 'Teen Spirit' video." I'm like, *Oh my god, now she's a porn star?* Talk about the arc of MTV.

TARSEM SINGH: My generation of directors—me, Fincher, Spike Jonze, Mark Romanek—we ruined your visual world. We grew up on a completely visual culture, and we brought our candy video eyeballs to cinema. It'll always be looked down on, shat on, and they accuse us of being bad for the film world. There's a saying: Politicians, prostitutes, and ugly buildings all get respectable if they last long enough. The same is true for film movements. Shitty or not, in about twenty years, it will seem valid.

LEE RITENOUR: MTV spawned *American Idol* and YouTube. The entertainment world is visual today because of MTV.

BOB PITTMAN: Before MTV, concerts mainly consisted of artists standing on-stage, looking at each other. I went to a David Bowie concert in the '70s that was considered state of the art because they had a cherry picker that lifted him up when he did "Major Tom." But after Michael Jackson and Madonna, shows became *performances*, with spectacular choreography and light shows. MTV changed live concerts.

SCOTT IAN: I couldn't be happier that it's gone. Videos were bigger than radio—that's why so many bands sucked live, because you could just make a video and never have to tour. It enabled bands to become lazy. Now, if you want to sell records, you have to be a good live band and go on tour for eighteen months, like you did before videos.

SEBASTIAN BACH: It's an era that needs to be remembered, if only as a caution-ary tale about the music industry and how killer it was, how fucking profitable and successful and fun. It wasn't *American Idol*, it was Americans who were fuckin' idols. We didn't do a karaoke routine to an Aretha Franklin song.

FRED SCHNEIDER: We want to put B52's videos out on DVD, but who's going to buy the DVD if you can get it for free on YouTube?

CLIFF BURNSTEIN: Videos are now short-lived phenomena on YouTube. I read a study that 78 percent of YouTube views come within the first ten days of a video. That shows it's totally fan-driven. You're appealing to the people who already liked you. And what good is that?

PAUL McGUINNESS: MTV and Viacom's utter failure to transfer their huge, worldwide audience from cable television onto the Internet will go down in his-tory as a disaster.

KARI WUHRER: This *Jersey Shore* crap? What the fuck is that?

ADAM HOROVITZ: I fucking love *Jersey Shore.* "You're excluded from cutlet night!" That's one of my favorite lines ever.

ALAN NIVEN: *Jersey Shore,* what does that perpetuate except for the most negative aspects of human behavior? It makes the old, cliché-ridden hard rock videos look tame by comparison.

DAVE KENDALL: MTV was demonized by intellectuals who thought we were debasing pop culture, and by right-wing Christians who saw it as polluting America's youth. I hear the same debate now, about reality programming. It's arrogant and holier-than-thou. People like reality TV. Who am I to judge that?

JOHN SYKES: If you look at MTV recently, they were belly-up, until Snooki saved the network.

MIKE DUGAN: It's not my cup of tea, but God bless them. They're getting 8.0 ratings on that show. If we got a 3.0, we were dancing in the aisles.

JOHN TAYLOR: I don't suppose *Punk'd* ever changed anybody's life. I can't imagine anybody watching that and going, "Hey, now I know what I'm gonna do with my life!"

SINEAD O'CONNOR: MTV has quite a lot to answer for. When video came around, the business transformed, and it became important how you looked. It became more visual and more materialistic. I mean, I hold MTV entirely responsible for the bling culture. It started when they made that show *Cribs.* Now you have a whole generation of young people who've been brought up to believe that fame and material wealth is what it's all about. You don't have young people saying, "I really want to be a singer," they say, "I really want to be famous." Then you've created a culture of people who feel they're nothing unless they live in a huge house and have seven cars.

NIGEL DICK: I often find myself defending MTV these days. MTV wanted to keep people watching for half an hour at a time. They couldn't do that by playing a Guns N' Roses video, then a Dire Straits video, then an Eddie Money video. Coke and Nike and Ford weren't going to buy ads unless they knew a viewer was going to sit through the whole program. That's how television works. You place an Apple ad in the middle of *Two and a Half Men* and you've got a guaranteed audience. End of story.

TONY DiSANTO: Every new generation has made MTV its own. It was no longer their parents' MTV, or their older brother's—it was *their* MTV, and therefore it had to be a very different MTV than what it was before. The audience that misses the old MTV? It's time for them to move on. It's still a network for and about youth culture, whether you're talking *Jersey Shore* or a new Lady Gaga video. MTV was always about being loud and irreverent. It's a different network than when it started, but I think its soul is the same.

LADY GAGA: I do miss when MTV played more music videos. However, it's important to be modern and change with the times. As MTV changes, so does the Internet, and we all change with it. It's now up to the artist to re-revolutionize what it means to put film to music.

MICHAEL IAN BLACK: There's a sense of mourning for MTV among my generation, which I don't share. There are so many other outlets now to find music. The Internet is better suited for that job; within twenty minutes, you can find twenty bands you've never heard of, and see videos from bands you'd likely never hear of, even if MTV still existed in its old form. For a few years, MTV was a great place, if you were into white music. But it was also a business. And the business evolved.

LOU STELLATO: Is Kurt Loder still at MTV? Is he a pile of dust?

ED LOVER: Where is hip-hop on MTV? Bring it back. MTV needs to find two cool guys that love hip-hop as much as Dre and I, and bring back *Yo! MTV Raps*.

FAB 5 FREDDY: People come up to me and say, "Fab, we wish there was *Yo! MTV Raps*." I tell them, "So you *really* would want to see me standing there interviewing Soulja Boy?" Then it hits them. I go, "Dude it's not me, it was the music."

"WEIRD AL" YANKOVIC: I haven't really followed the programming since it became the all-reality, all-Snooki channel. But I very much miss the old MTV.

FLEA: When they were great, music videos on MTV were like a short film festival for housewives in Nebraska. A couple of years ago, I was talking to the film director Milos Forman. He said, "I loved MTV. All those short little films . . . how great." And it dawned on me how right he was. And now that it's gone, I really miss it.

STEVIE NICKS: I just want to say, *I* want my MTV. And I'm so sad that MTV doesn't play videos all the time. It breaks my heart. I do, I want it back.

RIKI RACHTMAN: You have no idea how I miss it. If they wanted me to host a rock show again, I'd probably do it for free.

GREG HAYMES: If you Google "worst music videos of the '80s," I think Blotto are in the Top 10 results. As long as they remember us, that's all we care about.

TREVOR HORN: A couple of years ago, I met a very prominent politician. And he said, condescendingly, "Oh, you're that 'Video Killed the Radio Star' chap." And I thought, *Yes. And they'll remember me long after they've forgotten you, mate.*

Acknowledgments

Carrie Thornton thinks "Let's Dance" is the greatest video ever made and still has a videocassette copy of *The Cure Unplugged*. She was an avid champion of the book at Dutton, and a superb editor in the old-fashioned and seemingly defunct sense of the word. Her assistant, Stephanie Hitchcock, educated us on technological advancements we'd somehow missed in the past twenty years and reminded us helpfully of our production schedule and gently of our failures to be on time. PJ Mark at Janklow & Nesbit took us to lunch, let us choose the restaurant, represented our interests with maternal fervor, and never once asked nervously, "Are you guys making progress with this book, or what?"

Thank you to the one-hit wonders, Hall of Famers, MTV alumni, lifelong bizzers, cue-card-reading VJs, madcap directors, long-suffering producers, and briefly famous extras who shared their memories and insights with us. Thanks to John Lack, for starting MTV. A tip of the hat to Joni Abbott, Ted Demme, J.J. Jackson, and Ken Ober, MTV fixtures who were recalled lovingly by all who knew them.

A list that acknowledged everyone whose assistance we appreciate would be a separate book in itself. These are some of the people who were especially generous in helping us: Bill Adler, Jennifer Ballantyne, Lisa Barbaris, Angela Barkan, Michelle Bega, Brian Bumbery, Sharon Cho, Ed Christman, Tom Cording, Dennis Dennehy, Sarah Weinstein Dennison, Gayle Fine, Paul Freundlich, Billy F. Gibbons, Carrie Gordon, Randy Haecker, Ambrosia Healy, Robert Hilburn, Darren Hill, C.C. Hirsch, Anne Kreamer, Jolyn Matsumuro, Michelle McDevitt, Claire Mercuri, Jim Merlis, Fachtna O'Ceallaigh, Mitch Schneider, Gina Schulman, and Jill Siegel. Warm thanks to MTV's Jeannie Kedas, who replied without fail to each and every one of our beseeching e-mails.

A very special thank-you to the MTV and music executives who provided not only their recollections, but personal photographs, as well as many invaluable introductions: Jeff Ayeroff, Peter Baron, Ken R. Clark, Adam Curry, Amy Finnerty, Tom Freston, Les Garland, Doug Herzog, Abbey Konowitch, Rick Krim, Judy McGrath, Bob Pittman, Fred Seibert, and John Sykes.

We ruthlessly exploited our uncomplaining interns: Rituleen Dhingra, Janay Meertens-Deans, Meghan O'Connor, Adam Olivo, Eric Sandler, and Rachel Yecco; Aaron Gonsher and Joe Jasko especially distinguished themselves with uncompensated toil. We hope they have long editorial careers and assign us lucrative work in our sunset years.

Dorian Lynskey sent encouragement and insight from England. Elizabeth Goodman and Rob Kemp helped us organize an overgrowth of research.

Judythe Cohen was stellar with the tedious task of transcribing our audio files. Trinitie Kedrowski of Kedrowski Transcriptions was as quick as she was accurate, and Luke McCormick and Cory Merrill added timely assistance as well.

There were several books we found useful in our research: *Inside MTV*, by R. Serge Denisoff; *MTV: The Making of a Revolution*, by Tom McGrath; *MTV Uncensored*, an authorized history created by MTV; *The Rolling Stone Book of Rock Video*, by Michael Shore; *Dancing in the Distraction Factory: Music Television and Popular Culture*, by Andrew Goodwin; *Money for Nothing: A History of the Music Video from the Beatles to the White Stripes*, by Saul Austerlitz; and *Sound and Vision: The Music Video Reader*, edited by Simon Frith, Andrew Goodwin, and Lawrence Grossberg.

Our ideals for writing an oral history came from reading two great ones: *Live from New York: An Uncensored History of Saturday Night Live, as Told By Its Stars, Writers, and Guests* by Tom Shales and James Andrew Miller, and *Please Kill Me: The Uncensored Oral History of Punk*, by Legs McNeil and Gillian McCain.

We also made prodigious use of the Web site MVDB.com, a remarkably comprehensive and accurate database of music-video information compiled by the saintly Alex S. Garcia.

A note on sourcing: All quotes in the book come from interviews conducted by Craig Marks and Rob Tannenbaum. The main introduction and some chapter introductions incorporate a few quotes from other sources—we've denoted those quotes by placing them in the past tense ("Keith Richards said") rather than the present tense ("Janet Jackson says").

The writing of this book was made easier by some products we love: Apple Computers, Diet Coke, DropBox, Facebook, Gmail, LinkedIn, Scrivener, Skype, Valium, Wellbutrin, YouSendIt, and YouTube. We don't know how Charles Dickens survived without them.

From Craig Marks: Thanks to my employers and coworkers at *Billboard* magazine and Popdust, who pretended not to notice while I YouTubed early-'80s new wave videos at my desk. Thanks to my friends and fellow music journalists, whose ideas about and knowledge of videos I blithely ransacked and whose support for this book was incalculably fortifying. And I'm indebted to René Steinke, who selflessly put my needs, and our son's, ahead of her own over and over and over again. I can only hope that this book is one one-hundredth as good as her next one is sure to be.

From Rob Tannenbaum: Thanks to Gabriela Shelley, for encouragement, for making me laugh, for leaving me alone, and for timing the birth of our child to follow book publication by three months; to my parents, Mort and Sydelle, who would have kvelled; to my aunt and uncle, Sylvia and Julian Ander, for, respectively, cooking brisket whenever I ask and finding a good red wine to accompany it; to my brother, Rick, and his family, for love, support, advice, and assistance; and to Steve Randall and Jimmy Jellinek, for not pointing out that watching videos had become way more important to me than some of my other contractual responsibilities.

The authors can be reached by e-mail at IWantMyMTVBook@gmail.com. Where appropriate, corrections will be made in subsequent editions of this book. Please find us on Facebook (www.facebook.com/IWantMyMTV), Twitter (@ IWant MyMTVbook), and YouTube (www.youtube.com/user/IWantMyMTVbook). God save the Buggles.

Cast of Characters

PAULA ABDUL is a choreographer and singer who won four Video Music Awards in 1989 for the David Fincher–directed "Straight Up." She is currently a judge on Fox's *The X Factor*.

BRYAN ADAMS had many hit singles in the 1980s, including "Cuts Like a Knife," "Run to You," "Heaven," and "Summer of '69."

BILL ADLER worked as the director of publicity for Def Jam Recordings and Rush Artist Management from 1984 to 1990.

STEVEN ADLER was the drummer for Guns N' Roses from 1985 to 1990.

BRUCE ALLEN has managed Bryan Adams for many years and also represented Loverboy in the 1980s.

JOEY ALLEN is the lead guitarist of Warrant.

PETE ANGELUS conceived and directed the Van Halen videos "Hot for Teacher" and "Jump," managed David Lee Roth from 1985 to 1990, and conceived/directed Roth's "California Girls" and "Just a Gigolo" videos. He has managed the Black Crowes since 1990.

ADAM ANT gained popularity as the leader of the new wave group Adam & the Ants and later as a solo artist and actor.

MICHAEL ANTHONY played bass in Van Halen, of which he was a founding and long-time member. He now plays in Chickenfoot with Sammy Hagar.

MIKE ARMSTRONG was a writer on *Remote Control*.

DANIÈLE ARNAUD is a French-born model who starred in ZZ Top's three most famous videos. She represents painters and photographers in the San Diego area.

MEIERT AVIS is an Irish music-video and commercial director who's worked with U2 and Bruce Springsteen.

JEFF AYEROFF was the creative director of Warner Bros. Records and the co-chairman of Virgin Records America. Now semiretired in Kauai, Hawaii, he's the copresident of Shangri-La Music.

B-REAL is a founding member of the California rap group Cypress Hill, who debuted in 1991.

SEBASTIAN BACH was the front man for the hard rock band Skid Row from 1987 to 1996.

STEVE BACKER was a promotion executive for Epic Records. He is currently a managing partner at One Haven Music Publishing.

TOM BAILEY led the new wave band Thompson Twins from 1977 until 1993. He has several current bands and also writes film scores.

CAROLYN BAKER was MTV's original head of talent and acquisitions. She is the CEO of Carolyn B. Baker & Associates, a philanthropy consulting firm.

JOHNNY BARBIS is a former record executive. He manages Elton John.

DON BARNES is the lead singer and a founding member of the Southern rock band .38 Special.

PETER BARON was a video production executive for Arista Records and Geffen Records.

SIOBHAN BARRON was a cofounder of Limelight Productions with her brother, Steve.

STEVE BARRON is an Irish film director. His videos rank among the artform's best loved: Michael Jackson's "Billie Jean," a-ha's "Take on Me," and Dire Straits' "Money for Nothing," among others. He was a cofounder of Limelight Productions.

TONI BASIL is a singer, choreographer, director, and actor. She has been nominated for a Grammy, in the Long Form Video category, and an Emmy, and is best known for her worldwide number one hit "Mickey" from 1982.

SAMUEL BAYER is a music-video and film director. His first video was Nirvana's "Smells Like Teen Spirit."

ALISA MARIE BELLETTINI was the creator and executive producer of *House of Style*.

PAT BENATAR has won four Grammy Awards and sold more than 22 million records in a career that has produced nineteen Top 40 singles.

DAVID BENJAMIN is the former head of business affairs for CBS Records. He is currently a senior vice president at the Universal Music Group.

JAC BENSON was a producer for *Yo! MTV Raps*.

GEORGIA "JO" BERGMAN is an executive at Warner Bros. Records, where she's worked since 1972. She was Warner Bros.' first director of video and television.

MARSHALL BERLE managed the LA rock band Ratt and later cofounded Laugh .Com, a comedy record label.

JOHN BEUG was a senior vice president of video production for Warner Bros. Records.

BIG DADDY KANE is a Brooklyn-born rapper whose 1988 debut album was *Long Live the Kane*.

MICHAEL IAN BLACK is a member of the State, the first comedy troupe with their own MTV series. He has starred in the TV shows *Ed*, *Viva Variety*, *Stella*, and *Michael & Michael Have Issues*, and the film *Wet Hot American Summer*.

NINA BLACKWOOD was one of the five original MTV VJs. She hosts a daily show on Sirius XM Radio's '80s on 8 station.

REBECCA BLAKE is a photographer and director. She directed three videos for Prince, including "Kiss."

SUSAN BLOND was vice president of media relations for Epic Records, where she worked with Michael Jackson.

JULIA BOLINO was a model who appeared in the video for Robert Palmer's "Addicted to Love." She currently owns a makeup service in London.

BOY GEORGE is the lead singer of Culture Club.

DALE BOZZIO became famous as the lead singer of the 1980s pop/new wave band Missing Persons.

GEORGE BRADT worked at MTV from 1983 to 1988 as research analyst, supervisor of music scheduling, and associate producer, and later cofounded Kinetic Records.

MARCY BRAFMAN was Fred Seibert's first hire at MTV, in March 1981. She is now a visual artist and set-design consultant.

RONALD "BUZZ" BRINDLE joined MTV in 1981 as director of programming. Before and after his time there, he worked extensively in the radio industry.

BETH BRODAY is a music-video and television producer.

BOBBIE BROWN was Miss Louisiana Teen USA in 1987, a *Star Search* champion, and star of Warrant's "Cherry Pie" video.

BOBBY BROWN is an R&B singer and a former member of New Edition.

JULIE BROWN was a dancer on a British TV show before moving to New York at age twenty-six to work as an MTV VJ.

JERRY BRUCKHEIMER has produced more than forty feature films, including *Top Gun*, *Beverly Hills Cop*, *Flashdance*, and three *Pirates of the Caribbean* films.

JIM BURNS is a television producer who created *Unplugged* with Bob Small.

CLIFF BURNSTEIN is the cofounder of Q Prime Management, whose clients include Def Leppard, Metallica, and the Red Hot Chili Peppers.

JONATHAN CAIN is the keyboardist for the band Journey.

MARTY CALLNER is a television and music-video director. He has filmed videos for Twisted Sister, Heart, Whitesnake, Aerosmith, and Cher, among many acts.

JOHN CANNELLI was a senior vice president of talent and artist relations for MTV.

ANN CARLI was senior vice president of artist development at Jive Records.

GERRY CASALE is a video director and also a singer and founding member of Devo.

STEVE CASEY was a founding programming executive for MTV. He is currently a radio consultant.

CHER is a recording artist and actress. She has won an Academy Award, a Grammy Award, and an Emmy Award.

CHILLI rose to fame as a member of the R&B singing group TLC. She later starred in the VH1 reality show *What Chilli Wants*.

CHUCK D is a rapper and author. He helped create politically conscious hip-hop in the 1980s as the leader of Public Enemy.

KEN R. CLARK was a production assistant to MTV's original five VJs, and later manager of on-air talent. He is currently a real-estate broker in Portland, Oregon.

TIM CLAWSON was the head of production for Propaganda Films from 1988 to 1999. He is now an executive vice president at the Weinstein Company.

LISA COLEMAN played keyboards for Prince's backing band, the Revolution, and was one half of the musical duo Wendy and Lisa, with Wendy Melvoin. She and Melvoin won an Emmy in 2010 for their theme to the TV show *Nurse Jackie*.

ALEX COLETTI was an executive producer and director for MTV and is now an independent producer.

PHIL COLLEN is the guitarist for Def Leppard.

PHIL COLLINS is a best-selling solo recording artist and drummer. He was inducted into the Rock and Roll Hall of Fame in 2010 as a member of the band Genesis.

MILES COPELAND was the founder of I.R.S. Records and the manager of the band the Police.

STEWART COPELAND is best known as the drummer for the Police.

ANTON CORBIJN is a Dutch photographer, stage designer, and director of feature films and music videos.

LINDA CORRADINA worked at CNN and ABC News before joining MTV and running the news department.

LAUREN CORRAO was a production executive at MTV. She is currently the president of Ellen Degeneres's production company, A Very Good Production.

CINDY CRAWFORD is a model and an entrepreneur, as well as the first host of MTV's *House of Style*.

LOL CREME was a member of the 1970s rock group 10cc and later worked as a music-video director, usually in partnership with Kevin Godley.

KEVIN CRONIN is the lead singer for REO Speedwagon and wrote their number one hits "Keep On Loving You" and "Can't Fight This Feeling."

ROBERTA CRUGER was a director of talent relations at MTV. She currently works as a freelance journalist.

ADAM CURRY was an MTV VJ from 1987 to 1993. He founded and sold an interactive advertising firm, cofounded the Mevio video site, and now cohosts the No Agenda podcast and hosts the Big App Show.

DJ JAZZY JEFF and rapper turned actor Will Smith comprised the hip-hop group DJ Jazzy Jeff & the Fresh Prince.

DMC is a member of the hip-hop group Run-DMC.

CLIVE DAVIS is the chief creative officer of Sony Music Entertainment Worldwide. He was the founder of Arista Records and its president from 1975 through 2000.

MARTHA DAVIS was the lead singer of the Motels, an LA rock band, from 1978 to 1987, when she began a solo career.

TAMRA DAVIS has directed music videos as well as feature films, including *CB4*, *Billy Madison*, *Half-Baked*, and *Crossroads*.

JOE DAVOLA cocreated MTV's *Remote Control*. Later, he was executive producer of the TV shows *Smallville*, *One Tree Hill*, and *What I Like About You*.

JONATHAN DAYTON and Valerie Faris codirected MTV's *The Cutting Edge*, many music videos, and the 2006 film *Little Miss Sunshine*, which won two Academy Awards.

PAUL DEAN has been the guitarist in Loverboy since 1978.

FREDDY DeMANN is a music executive who has managed the careers of Michael Jackson and Madonna.

WARREN DeMARTINI was the lead guitarist in Ratt, and cowrote their biggest hit, "Round and Round."

HOWIE DEUTCH has directed feature films including *Pretty in Pink*, *Some Kind of Wonderful*, and *The Replacements*, plus music videos.

DENNIS DeYOUNG is a founding member and former lead singer of the band Styx.

BRIAN DIAMOND joined MTV as an associate producer in 1981, moved to London in 1986 to launch MTV Europe, and is now a senior vice president at Spike TV.

JIM DIAMOND sang and played guitar in Ph.D, who had the fifth video played on MTV.

JOHN DIAZ is a music-video, television, and concert producer.

NIGEL DICK is a music-video and film director whose credits include Guns N' Roses' "Welcome to the Jungle" and Britney Spears's ". . . Baby One More Time." He was a cofounder of Propaganda Films.

BRUCE DICKINSON was a product manager at Columbia Records in the early '80s and has worked in many different departments for a number of record labels.

TONY DISANTO is a television producer who got his start as an intern at MTV in 1987. Later, as MTV's president of programming, he was responsible for the hit reality programs *The Hills* and *Jersey Shore*.

THOMAS DOLBY is a musician and producer best known for his 1982 hit "She Blinded Me with Science."

KEVIN DOLE has directed *Pee-wee's Playhouse*, music videos, and hundreds of TV ads. His first film, *Kiss the Frog*, is scheduled to begin production in 2012.

PETER DOUGHERTY joined MTV as a freelance production assistant, cocreated *Yo! MTV Raps*, and worked as creative director of MTV Europe.

ADAM DUBIN directed the Metallica documentary *A Year and a Half in the Life of Metallica* and codirected two Beastie Boys videos.

KAREN DUFFY joined MTV as a VJ in 1991. She has modeled for Revlon and wrote a book, *Model Patient: My Life as an Incurable Wiseass*, about her struggle with sarcoidosis.

MICHAEL DUGAN has written for *Remote Control*, *Beavis and Butt-head*, *The Jon Stewart Show*, *The Tom Green Show*, and many other TV comedies.

JONATHAN ELIAS wrote the MTV "Moon Landing" theme and produced Duran Duran's 1988 album *Big Thing*.

JOE ELLIOTT is the singer for Def Leppard. The Sheffield, England–based band has sold more than 35 million albums in the U.S.

LEN EPAND was a video production executive for PolyGram Records.

EVERLAST wrote and rapped on House of Pain's 1992 hit "Jump Around" and made three albums with the group.

FAB 5 FREDDY is a graffiti artist, filmmaker, hip-hop pioneer, and the original host of *Yo! MTV Raps*.

SIOBHAN FAHEY is a founding member of the 1980s British trio Bananarama and later started the band Shakespear's Sister.

VALERIE FARIS and Jonathan Dayton codirected MTV's *The Cutting Edge*, many music videos, and the 2006 film *Little Miss Sunshine*, which won two Academy Awards.

TIM FARRISS plays guitar with INXS, whose sixth album, *Kick*, was a worldwide blockbuster, selling six million copies in the U.S. and earning five Video Music Awards, including Best Video.

MARK FENSKE wrote and directed commercials and music videos, including Van Halen's "Right Now," and is a professor at Virginia Commonwealth University.

SIMON FIELDS is a music-video, TV, and movie producer. He was a cofounder of Limelight Productions and is currently a partner at JLE/Nuyorican Productions.

AMY FINNERTY was a music programming executive at MTV from 1989 to 2000.

PAUL FLATTERY was an English music-video producer who worked for Jon Rose-man before cofounding his own production firm with Bruce Gowers and Simon Fields.

FLEA is the cofounder and bassist for Red Hot Chili Peppers.

WISH FOLEY was a regular on the 1970s TV series *Family* and later played Alice in Tom Petty's "Don't Come Around Here No More" video.

TOM FRESTON was the CEO of MTV Networks from 1987 to 2006. Hired in March 1980, he was MTV's first head of marketing. He runs Firefly3, a media investment and consulting company whose clients include Oprah Winfrey, Vice Media, and Tolo TV in Afghanistan. He is the chairman of the ONE campaign, an antipoverty advocacy group.

MARTIN FRY and his group ABC had five Top 40 hits in the U.S. between 1981 and 1990.

JOEL GALLEN is an Emmy-winning television producer who produced MTV's Video Music Awards and *Unplugged*.

PATTI GALLUZZI joined MTV in 1988 and rose to senior vice president of music and talent.

LES GARLAND, a former radio programmer and record executive, was the executive vice president of programming for MTV from 1982 to 1987. He currently owns a media consultancy firm, AfterPlay Entertainment.

BOB GELDOF fronted the Boomtown Rats, starred in *The Wall*, and was the impetus behind "Do They Know It's Christmas?" and Live Aid.

BETSY LYNN GEORGE was Devon, the tempting teen in Billy Idol's "Cradle of Love." She was also seen in Deep Purple's "King of Dreams," TV shows including *Wild Palms*, and movies including *Point Break*. She lives in Pennsylvania and teaches yoga.

GERARDO is a Latin rapper/singer who had a Top 10 hit in 1991 with "Rico Suave."

GARY GERSH is a music-industry executive who signed Nirvana to Geffen Records. He later comanaged Nirvana, and currently manages John Legend and Soundgarden.

MARK GHUNEIM did video promotion for Beggars Banquet/4AD and for Columbia Records. He's the founder and CEO of the marketing agency Wiredset.

BILLY GIBBONS sings and plays guitar in ZZ Top.

DEBBIE GIBSON is a singer whose 1987 debut album, *Out of the Blue*, released when she was seventeen, produced four Top 5 singles.

MAK GILCHRIST is a British model who appeared in Robert Palmer's "Addicted to Love" video.

BOB GIRALDI has directed short films, award-winning TV ads, and videos, including Michael Jackson's "Beat It," Pat Benatar's "Love Is a Battlefield," and Lionel Richie's "Hello."

NEIL "SPYDER" GIRALDO is Pat Benatar's guitarist, producer, and husband.

COREY GLOVER has been the lead singer in Living Colour since 1986.

KEVIN GODLEY was a member of the 1970s rock group 10cc and later worked as a music-video director, usually in partnership with Lol Creme.

GREG GOLD is a producer and director. He was a cofounder of Propaganda Films.

JULIAN GOLDBERG was an executive producer at MTV from 1981 to 1987.

DOUG GOLDSTEIN was the tour manager for Guns N' Roses from 1986 through 1989, then managed the band from 1989 to 2003.

MARK GOODMAN was one of the five original MTV VJs. He currently hosts a variety of shows on Sirius XM Radio.

BRUCE GOWERS is a music-video and television director whose clip for Queen's "Bohemian Rhapsody," in 1975, is often considered the most influential pre-MTV music video.

CAMILLE GRAMMER was a dancer on *Club MTV*. She later posed for *Playboy*, married (and divorced) actor Kelsey Grammer, and starred on the *Real Housewives of Beverly Hills*.

BRIAN GRANT is a music-video and television director and producer. He was the cofounder of MGMM Productions, with Scott Millaney, Russell Mulcahy, and David Mallet.

CEE LO GREEN has been a solo artist, a member of Gnarls Barkley, a member of Goodie Mob, and a coach on NBC's *The Voice*.

PAULA GREIF is a music-video and commercial director.

MEG GRIFFIN has been a radio DJ since 1975 and was briefly an MTV VJ. She currently hosts several shows on Sirius XM.

DAVE GROHL was the drummer for Nirvana and started his own band, Foo Fighters, in 1994.

ALLEN GRUBMAN is an entertainment industry lawyer.

SAMMY HAGAR recorded eight solo albums before joining Van Halen in 1986.

ARSENIO HALL is an actor, comedian, and former host of *The Arsenio Hall Show*, which ran from 1989 to 1994. He hosted the Video Music Awards from 1988 to 1991.

DARYL HALL is a cofounder of the duo Hall & Oates, which has sold more than 60 million albums. He created and hosts the Web series *Live from Daryl's House*.

HERBIE HANCOCK is a jazz pianist and composer. The video for his hip-hop song "Rockit," directed by Godley and Creme, won five Moonmen at the inaugural Video Music Awards in 1984.

JERRY HARRISON played guitar and keyboards in Talking Heads.

DEBBIE HARRY is the lead singer of Blondie, who released the first-ever album-length music video, *Eat to the Beat*, in 1979.

COLIN HAY is an Australian recording artist. He's best known as the singer for the 1980s band Men at Work.

GREG HAYMES is lead singer of Blotto, under the name Sergeant Blotto. Their "I Wanna Be a Lifeguard" video was an early MTV staple.

CAROLYNE HELDMAN was an MTV VJ from 1986 to 1988. She is currently the program director of Aspen Public Radio.

LIZ HELLER was a video promotion executive for MCA Records.

DOUG HERZOG is the president of MTV Networks Entertainment Group. He joined MTV in 1984 as director of news.

SUSANNA HOFFS is a singer/guitarist for the band the Bangles.

DAVE HOLMES is a comic and writer who joined MTV after placing second in the 1998 "Wanna Be a VJ" contest.

PETER HOOK played bass for Joy Division and New Order.

TREVOR HORN is a record producer, a cofounder of the ZTT record label, and bassist/singer for the Buggles, the first band ever shown on MTV.

ADAM HOROVITZ, also known as Ad-Rock, is a member of the hip-hop group the Beastie Boys.

ALAN HUNTER was one of the original five VJs on MTV, starting in 1981.

TOM HUNTER joined MTV in 1987 as the vice president of music programming. He went on to become the president of MTV Latin America.

TIMOTHY HUTTON won an Academy Award at the age of twenty for his role in *Ordinary People*. He has starred in many films, plays, and TV shows, and his career as a director includes music videos for the Cars and Don Henley.

SCOTT IAN is the guitarist and main lyricist in Anthrax and is married to Meat Loaf's daughter.

BILLY IDOL has had many hits, including "Dancing with Myself," "Rebel Yell," and "White Wedding."

STEVE ISAACS was a VJ on MTV from 1991 to 1993. He is the creative director at BLT & Associates.

CHRIS ISAAK released his first album in 1985, had his own TV shows on Showtime and Biography, and appeared in the films *Married to the Mob* and *The Silence of the Lambs*, among others.

WAYNE ISAAK worked at A&M Records from 1982 to 1994 and held the title executive vice president at east coast ops & publicity.

WAYNE ISHAM is a director whose run of hit videos began in 1985 with Mötley Crüe's "Home Sweet Home" and includes Bon Jovi's "Living on a Prayer," Metallica's "Enter Sandman," and the Backstreet Boys' "I Want It That Way."

JANET JACKSON has sold more than 100 million records worldwide. Her hits include "Escapade," "Miss You Much," "Nasty," and "When I Think of You."

JOE JACKSON is an English singer-songwriter whose MTV hits include "Steppin' Out."

KURT JEFFERIS of Phoenixville, Pennsylvania, won MTV's "Lost Weekend with Van Halen" contest in 1984.

BILLY JOEL is a singer, songwriter, and pianist. He ranks as the sixth best-selling recording artist of all time, with more than 79 million albums sold in the U.S.

STEVEN R. JOHNSON is a music-video and television director. His video for Peter Gabriel's "Sledgehammer" won nine Video Music Awards in 1987, a record that still stands. Johnson directed the first season of the children's TV show *Pee-wee's Playhouse*.

HOWARD JONES had many '80s hits, including "Things Can Only Get Better," "No One Is to Blame," and "What Is Love?"

MICK JONES sang and played guitar in the Clash and later formed the band Big Audio Dynamite.

TRACEY JORDAN was vice president of music programming and talent development at MTV from 1992 to 1994. She has worked at Motown and Arista Records and works as a consultant with Aretha Franklin and ABKCO Records.

ROB KAHANE managed George Michael from 1986 to 1992.

SAM KAISER was vice president of programming for MTV from 1986 to 1988. He owns a music consultancy firm, MVP Entertainment.

JOHN KALODNER was an A&R executive for Atlantic Records and Geffen Records. He signed Foreigner and Phil Collins to Atlantic, and Whitesnake, Cher, and Aerosmith to Geffen.

SCOTT KALVERT is a director and producer of music videos and movies.

DAVE KENDALL is a British-born journalist who hosted *120 Minutes* for many years.

JEANA TOMASINA KEOUGH was the November 1980 *Playboy* playmate. She is featured in three ZZ Top videos, was a *Real Housewives of Orange County* cast member, and is a real-estate broker in California.

KEVIN KERSLAKE has directed videos for Nirvana, Green Day, R.E.M., the Red Hot Chili Peppers, and others, as well as TV shows, short films, commercials, and documentaries about surfing, EDM culture, and the Ramones.

ALEK KESHISHIAN directed the 1991 Madonna documentary, *Truth or Dare*. He made four videos for Bobby Brown, including "My Prerogrative" and "Every Little Step."

TAWNY KITAEN is an actress who starred alongside Tom Hanks in *Bachelor Party*, then rose to fame with a string of gyrating appearances in hit videos for the band Whitesnake. She was married to the group's singer, David Coverdale, from 1989 to 1991.

MICK KLEBER ran the video department at Capitol Records between 1980 and 1993.

JANET KLEINBAUM is the senior vice president of video and DVD production for Jive Records.

DANIEL KLEINMAN is a British music-video and commercial director.

ABBEY KONOWITCH was MTV's senior VP of music and talent from 1988 to 1992. He has worked as a record executive at Arista Records, Maverick Records, and Hollywood Records.

KOOL MOE DEE was the first rapper to perform at the Grammys. His hits include "How Ya Like Me Now" and "Wild Wild West."

LENNY KRAVITZ is a Grammy Award–winning singer, songwriter, and guitarist. His debut 1989 video, "Let Love Rule," was directed by his then-wife, *Cosby Show* star Lisa Bonet.

RICK KRIM joined MTV in 1982, tasked with filing Les Garland's expense reports. He eventually worked his way up to vice president of music and talent. He is currently the executive vice president of music and talent programming at VH1.

JOHN LACK was the executive vice president of the Warner Amex Satellite Entertainment Company, or WASEC. It was Lack who came up with the idea for MTV. He served as an executive vice president at ESPN and is currently the chief partner at FireMedia Partners, a digital media company.

LADY GAGA is a singer and songwriter whose second album, *Born This Way*, debuted at number one on the *Billboard* album charts with first week sales of 1.1 million copies.

MARY LAMBERT directed the Madonna videos "Borderline," "Material Girl," "Like a Virgin," and "Like a Prayer." She is currently a film director.

JON LANDAU manages Bruce Springsteen.

JOHN LANDIS is a film director whose credits include *National Lampoon's Animal House* and *Trading Places*. His video for Michael Jackson's "Thriller" was the first music video inducted into the National Film Registry.

JANI LANE was Warrant's singer during their heyday, when they had five number one videos on MTV.

CYNDI LAUPER won Best Female Video at the first VMAs for "Girls Just Want to Have Fun" and has sold more than thirty million albums in her unusual career.

SIMON LE BON is a former child actor and the front man in Duran Duran.

TOMMY LEE plays drums in Mötley Crüe. He married Heather Locklear in 1986 and after their divorce dated Bobbie Brown.

HARVEY LEEDS was the national director of video promotion for Epic Records. He currently runs Headquarters Media, a management and consulting company.

STEVE LEEDS was head of on-air talent for MTV from 1987 to 1990. He is currently the vice president of talent and industry affairs at Sirius XM Radio.

ANNIE LENNOX is a Grammy Award–winning singer who performed with Dave Stewart in the 1980s duo Eurythmics.

DON LETTS directed videos for the Clash and Musical Youth and has made several films, including *Punk: Attitude* and *The Punk Rock Movie*.

ADAM LEVINE is Maroon 5's singer and a costar of NBC's *The Voice*.

HUEY LEWIS is the leader of Huey Lewis and the News. They performed "I Want a New Drug" at the first MTV Video Music Awards in 1984.

PAM LEWIS was national media director at Warner Amex Satellite from 1980 to 1984. She later comanaged Garth Brooks, from the start of his career to the peak of his superstardom, as well as Trisha Yearwood.

GARY LIEBERTHAL is a TV executive and the former chairman and CEO of Columbia Pictures Television.

LIMAHL was seen on MTV with Kajagoogoo ("Too Shy") and as a solo artist. His "Love in Your Eyes" video was directed by Russell Mulcahy.

PERRI LISTER is an English dancer and choreographer. She has appeared in music videos for Def Leppard, Duran Duran, and former boyfriend Billy Idol.

GEORGE LOIS is a legendary advertising executive who may or may not have created the phrase "I Want My MTV."

ROBERT LOMBARD is a Hollywood producer who worked with Van Halen and Fleetwood Mac and cast many soft-core porn films.

COURTNEY LOVE is the leader of the band Hole. She is the widow of the late Nirvana singer-songwriter Kurt Cobain.

ED LOVER cohosted the weekday *Yo! MTV Raps* with Dr. Dre and blogs at cmonson online.com.

STEVE LUKATHER is the lead guitarist for the band Toto.

MONICA LYNCH worked as a go-go dancer before rising to the presidency of the rap label Tommy Boy Records.

ANNE-MARIE MACKAY was the head of music video at Propaganda Films. She is now executive director/chief creative officer at the media production company Wondros.

MATT MAHURIN is an illustrator, photographer, and director who has worked with U2, Metallica, Peter Gabriel, and R.E.M.

DAVID MALLET is a British director who has worked extensively with David Bowie, as well as Queen, Def Leppard, Billy Idol, Scorpions, and INXS.

AIMEE MANN and her band 'Til Tuesday won Best New Artist at the 1985 Video Music Awards. She has been a solo artist since 1993.

MICHAEL MANN was executive producer of the TV series *Miami Vice*. He directed the films *Heat*, *The Insider*, and *Collateral*.

KIM MARLOWE manages Fab Morvan, formerly of Milli Vanilli.

LIONEL MARTIN cohosted *Video Music Box*, one of the first TV shows to feature rap videos, and as a director worked with Public Enemy, Bobby Brown, and Whitney Houston, among others.

CURT MARVIS was a partner with Wayne Isham in the music-video production company The Company. He is currently the president of digital media at Lionsgate Entertainment.

RICHARD MARX released seven consecutive Top 5 singles between 1987 and 1990.

LEE MASTERS, born Jarl Mohn, was the general manager of MTV from 1986 to 1989. He founded E! Entertainment Television in 1990 and is currently an investor in a number of broadcast, cable programming, and Internet companies.

MC HAMMER recorded the hits "U Can't Touch This," "Pray," and "Too Legit to Quit." *Please Hammer, Don't Hurt 'Em* was the first rap album to sell 10 million copies.

RON McCARRELL was vice president of marketing at Epic, Portrait, and CBS Associated Labels, then worked at Capitol and Windham Hill. He later launched record labels for the House of Blues and for the World Wrestling Federation.

BETH McCARTHY was a director at MTV whose credits include *Nirvana Unplugged*. She directed *Saturday Night Live* from 1995 to 2006 and frequently directs the comedy series *30 Rock*.

DOC McGHEE managed Bon Jovi, Mötley Crüe, Scorpions, and Skid Row at the height of each band's career.

JUDY McGRATH began as a copywriter at MTV in November 1981. She was appointed chairman/CEO of MTV Networks in 2004 and stepped down from the post in May 2011.

PAUL McGUINNESS has managed U2 since 1978.

MEAT LOAF is a singer and actor. His 1977 album *Bat Out of Hell* has sold an estimated 43 million copies worldwide.

RIC MENELLO directed LL Cool J's "Going Back to Cali" and codirected (and had cameos in) Beastie Boys' "Fight for Your Right" and "No Sleep Till Brooklyn."

PETER MENSCH is the cofounder of Q Prime Management.

BOB MERLIS was senior vice president of worldwide corporate communications at Warner Bros. Records, where he worked for twenty-nine years.

MARK METCALF is an actor best known for his role as Doug Neidermeyer in *National Lampoon's Animal House*, a part he reprised in two Twisted Sister videos, "We're Not Gonna Take It" and "I Wanna Rock."

GEORGE MICHAEL has sold more than 100 million records worldwide, and received a Video Vanguard Award from MTV in 1989.

BRET MICHAELS is the singer for the hard rock band Poison. He starred in three seasons of the VH1 reality show *Rock of Love*.

JEAN-BAPTISTE MONDINO is a French-born fashion photographer and video director who has worked with Madonna, Don Henley, David Bowie, Prince, Sting, Björk, and Bryan Ferry.

TOM MOHLER comanaged Billy Squier and later managed Poison.

ANDY MORAHAN is a British music-video and commercial director. He directed George Michael's "Faith" and Guns N' Roses' "November Rain," among many clips.

ROBERT MORTON served as creative director of MTV prior to the network's launch. He was the longtime executive producer of David Letterman's late-night talk show.

FAB MORVAN was born in Paris and lived in Munich when he met Rob Pilatus. The two performed as Milli Vanilli, one of the biggest pop acts of the late '80s.

MARK MOTHERSBAUGH is a cofounder of Devo, who were early adopters of music video. He has scored many TV shows and movies.

TOMMY MOTTOLA managed Hall & Oates, became president of CBS Records in 1988 and chairman and CEO of Sony Music five years later.

RUSSELL MULCAHY is an Australian film and TV director. His exotic trilogy of videos for Duran Duran—"Hungry Like the Wolf," "Rio," and "Save a Prayer"—propelled the band to worldwide stardom. He has directed several episodes of MTV's original series *Teen Wolf*.

SOPHIE MULLER directed many videos for Eurythmics and also worked with Sinead O'Connor.

JONATHAN MURRAY is a television producer and cocreator, along with the late Mary-Ellis Bunim, of MTV's *The Real World*. Among the reality programs that Bunim/Murray Productions cocreated or executive produced are *Road Rules*, *Making the Band*, Fox's *The Simple Life*, and all the Kardashian series on E!

DAVE MUSTAINE is the founder of the heavy metal band Megadeth.

JOAN MYERS was an assistant to MTV vice president of programming Les Garland. She is currently the owner of the public relations and marketing firm Myers Media.

DAVE NAVARRO plays guitar in Jane's Addiction, whose "Been Caught Stealing" was a highlight of MTV's 1990 playlists.

MICHAEL NESMITH became a music and TV star in the 1960s with the Monkees and made his first music video, "Rio," in 1977. He created the *Pop Clips* TV show, which fueled the origins of MTV.

ALLEN NEWMAN is a TV director and producer who has worked for ABC, NBC, PBS, BBC, HBO, and NHK. He began his career at MTV and worked there from 1981 to 1987.

DEBBIE NEWMAN was Columbia Records' first video production executive. She is currently a music industry consultant.

TIM NEWMAN won the award for best direction for ZZ Top's "Sharp Dressed Man" at the first VMAs in 1984 and also directed Lou Reed and Huey Lewis & the News.

OLIVIA NEWTON-JOHN played Sandy in the 1978 film *Grease* and landed on MTV with her video for "Physical," a song that was banned on some radio stations.

STEVIE NICKS has had many hit records, as a solo artist and with Fleetwood Mac, starting in 1977.

ERIC NIES gained fame as a cast member on the first season of *The Real World*. He later hosted MTV's dance show *The Grind*.

ALAN NIVEN is a New Zealand–born songwriter and producer who managed Guns N' Roses between 1986 and 1991 and Great White from 1982 to 1995.

TERRI NUNN fronted the LA band Berlin.

CONAN O'BRIEN hosted *The Tonight Show* for seven months and now stars in the TBS talk show *Conan*.

SINEAD O'CONNOR is an Irish singer and songwriter. She won a Best Video Award at the 1990 VMAs for "Nothing Compares 2 U," the first time a woman won that category.

SHARON ORECK is the author of *Video Slut*, a memoir of her adventures in the 1980s as a music-video producer and executive.

STEPHEN PEARCY sings with the LA hard rock band Ratt, whose "Back for More" video was the MTV debut of Tawny Kitaen.

DANIEL PEARL is a director of photography who has worked on feature films (1974's *The Texas Chainsaw Massacre*), commercials, and music videos, including the Police's "Every Breath You Take," U2's "With or Without You," and Guns N' Roses' "November Rain."

MARK PELLINGTON started at MTV as an intern, worked in the on-air promotions department, and after leaving the network directed Pearl Jam's "Jeremy," which won four VMAs. He has directed and produced feature films, short films, documentaries, and TV shows.

RAQUEL PENA is a Spanish–West Indian model featured in Bryan Adams's "Cuts Like a Knife" and Michael Jackson's "Billie Jean."

PEPA cofounded the rap group Salt-N-Pepa, who appeared on the first episode of *House of Style*. She met rapper Treach at MTV's 1991 Spring Break and later married him.

VICKI PETERSON is a guitarist/singer with the band the Bangles.

TOM PETTY is a singer, songwriter, and guitarist who, along with his band the Heartbreakers, was inducted into the Rock and Roll Hall of Fame in 2002.

CHYNNA PHILLIPS is one-third of the vocal group Wilson Phillips.

RANDY PHILLIPS is the CEO of the live entertainment company AEG Live. He has managed acts including Rod Stewart, Lionel Richie, and Guns N' Roses.

BOB PITTMAN is one of the founders of MTV. He led the network from its inception until his departure in 1987. Pittman was the first CEO of MTV Networks. He has served as president of America Online and as COO of AOL Time Warner. He is cofounder of the Pilot Group, a private investment firm, and is currently chairman of media and entertainment platforms for Clear Channel Communications.

DALE PON is an advertising executive and one of the creators of the "I Want My MTV" ad campaign.

KEVIN POWELL got into a wicked fight with Julie during season one of *The Real World*. He is now a political activist and author.

COLIN QUINN was the cigarette-voiced sidekick on three seasons of MTV's *Remote Control*. He later joined *Saturday Night Live*, where he hosted Weekend Update, and hosted *Tough Crowd with Colin Quinn* on Comedy Central.

MARTHA QUINN was the last of the five original VJs hired by MTV. She hosts a daily show on Sirius XM Radio's '80s on 8 station.

CHIP RACHLIN joined MTV in 1982 as director of acquistions. He is now the president of Rachlin Entertainment.

RIKI RACHTMAN owned the Cat Club, an LA metal venue, and began hosting *Headbangers Ball* in 1990 after being recommended to MTV by his friend Axl Rose.

VERNON REID is the guitarist and primary songwriter in Living Colour, whose "Cult of Personality" won three awards at the 1989 VMAs.

MARC REITER is a manager at Q Prime. He was a product manager at Epic Records, where he worked with Pearl Jam.

MIKE RENO is the singer in Loverboy, whose hits include "Turn Me Loose" and "Working for the Weekend."

NICK RHODES is the keyboard player in Duran Duran and was an early advocate of men wearing mascara.

LIONEL RICHIE is a top-selling singer, songwriter, and musician. His 1983 album *Can't Slow Down*, featuring the singles "All Night Long" and "Hello," won the Grammy for Album of the Year.

LEE RITENOUR is a Grammy-winning jazz guitarist. Two of his videos were shown on the first day of MTV, but rarely thereafter.

JULIANA ROBERTS is a music-video, film, and TV producer. She was a producer for Propaganda Films' hard rock division, The Foundry.

DAVID ROBINSON plays drums in the Cars, who won Video of the Year at the first VMAs. He owns an art gallery and is a jewelry maker.

JAMES D. ROBINSON III was the CEO of American Express Co. from 1977 until his retirement in 1993.

JON ROSEMAN was the founder of Jon Roseman Productions. Among the videos he produced are Queen's "Bohemian Rhapsody" and Eurythmics' "Sweet Dreams (Are Made of This)."

LIZ ROSENBERG has been Madonna's press agent since 1982 and was a senior vice president at Warner Bros. Records, where she worked for thirty-nine years.

EDDIE ROSENBLATT was the CEO of Geffen Records.

CAROL ROSENSTEIN is a music-video and television producer.

MICHAEL ROSS cofounded the LA hip-hop label Delicious Vinyl in 1987 and released records by Tone-Lōc and Young MC.

JORDAN ROST was hired as vice president of research at WASEC, making him the company's first department head, and later became vice president of sales. He then spent sixteen years at the Warner Music Group, as senior vice president of marketing and new technology, and is now a consultant.

RICK RUBIN cofounded Def Jam Records as a college student and has produced music by LL Cool J, Beastie Boys, Run-DMC, Johnny Cash, and Red Hot Chili Peppers.

TODD RUNDGREN has been writing, singing, and producing hit songs since the late 1960s. He tried to launch a music-video network before MTV.

DONNA RUPERT placed second in the Miss Canada 1981 pageant, modeled for the Wilhelmina agency, and played the teacher in Van Halen's "Hot for Teacher."

SALT cofounded the rap group Salt-N-Pepa, who appeared on the first episode of *House of Style.*

RICHIE SAMBORA is the longtime lead guitarist of Bon Jovi.

DEBBIE SAMUELSON was a music-video promotion and production executive for Columbia Records.

JOHN SAYLES directed three Bruce Springsteen videos and has made sixteen feature films, including *The Return of the Secaucus 7, Eight Men Out,* and *Lone Star.*

SCARFACE is a hip-hop artist and a former member of the pioneering gangsta-rap group the Geto Boys.

RUDOLF SCHENKER is a guitarist and founding member of Scorpions, Germany's best-selling heavy metal band.

RICHARD SCHENKMAN is a writer/director/producer who joined the program services department of MTV in February 1981.

FRED SCHNEIDER and the B-52's won two VMAs in 1990 for "Love Shack."

JACK SCHNEIDER had a long career as chief of the CBS Broadcast Group before becoming the original president and CEO of WASEC. Schneider left the company in 1984 and later served as the managing director of the investment firm Allen & Co.

STEVE SCHNUR began his career as an intern for Les Garland in the programming department of MTV. He is currently worldwide executive of music and marketing for videogame developer Electronic Arts.

MIKE SCORE worked as a hairdresser before singing and playing the synthesizer in the British foursome A Flock of Seagulls.

KEVIN SEAL was a college student when MTV hired him as a VJ in 1987. He left the network in 1991 and is now a stay-at-home dad and handyman who does voice-over work for radio ads.

DENNIS SEATON sang with the young Jamaican group Musical Youth. Their hit "Pass the Dutchie" was the first reggae song on MTV.

FRED SEIBERT was Bob Pittman's first hire at The Movie Channel, in May 1980, and was MTV's head of program services at its launch. He oversaw the design of the MTV logo and the creation of the "I Want My MTV" ad campaign. He is the founder of Frederator Studios, which makes cartoons for TV, movies, and the Internet.

DOMINIC SENA is a music-video and film director. He was a cofounder of Propaganda Films.

ANDY SETOS began at WASEC as vice president, engineering, and was promoted to senior vice president at Viacom. He is now president, engineering, at the Fox Group's television and film operations.

BRIAN SETZER and the Stray Cats were one of the first bands to become stars from MTV airplay.

SHOCK G is the mastermind of rap group Digital Underground, whose 1990 debut was *Sex Packets*.

HANK SHOCKLEE is a music producer and former Def Jam executive who was integral to the creation of Public Enemy's sound and videos.

PAULY SHORE joined MTV in 1989 and was soon hosting his own show, *Totally Pauly*. His first starring film role was in *Encino Man*, a surprise hit that grossed more than $40 million.

JONI SIGHVATSSON is a movie producer and a cofounder of Propaganda Films.

SUSAN SILVERMAN was a video production executive for Warner Bros. Records.

TARSEM SINGH grew up in India and moved to the U.S. at the age of twenty-four. He has directed commercials, R.E.M.'s "Losing My Religion" video, and the feature films *The Cell* and *The Fall*.

SIR MIX-A-LOT is a Seattle-based rapper best known for his 1992 number one hit "Baby Got Back." He likes big butts.

DAVE SIRULNICK is currently the executive vice president of news and production for MTV, overseeing the news and docs department, as well as studio-based programming and event productions. Sirulnick joined MTV in 1987 as a news producer.

NIKKI SIXX plays bass and writes songs for Mötley Crüe and published a best-selling memoir, *The Heroin Diaries*.

RANDY SKINNER was a video production executive at Warner Bros. Records.

ROBIN SLOANE was a video production executive at Elektra Records and creative director at Geffen Records.

BOB SMALL created *Unplugged* with Jim Burns and has produced shows for Comedy Central, HBO, and Nickelodeon.

CURT SMITH founded Tears for Fears in 1981 with Roland Orzabal and is the featured singer on "Mad World" and "Everybody Wants to Rule the World."

ROBERT SMITH has been the Cure's front man since 1979.

PATTY SMYTH is a singer and musician who was the front woman for the band Scandal.

DEE SNIDER is the lead singer of the band Twisted Sister. He hosted the first heavy metal show on MTV, *Heavy Metal Mania*.

TABITHA SOREN was formerly a reporter for MTV News and is now a professional photographer.

GALE SPARROW was the director of talent and artist relations at MTV from 1981 to 1985. She co-owns an estate liquidation company that serves the greater Philadelphia area.

RICK SPRINGFIELD is an Australian singer and actor known for the 1981 number one single "Jessie's Girl."

BILLY SQUIER had multiple hits from his first two records: "The Stroke," "In the Dark," "My Kind of Lover," and "Everybody Wants You." His third record included "Rock Me Tonite," widely considered the worst music video of all time.

JEFF STEIN directed a film about the Who, *The Kids Are Alright*, and many memorable videos, including Tom Petty's "Don't Come Around Here No More," the Cars' "You Might Think," and Warrant's "Cherry Pie."

SUE STEINBERG was MTV's first executive producer, responsible for the casting of the five original VJs. Now retired, she enjoyed a long career as a television producer.

LOU STELLATO was a producer at MTV. He is currently creative director at the advertising firm the Warehouse Agency.

LARRY STESSEL was a marketing executive at Epic Records from 1975 to 1991. He is now a managing partner at the Revolver Marketing Group.

ALISON STEWART began her broadcast career at MTV News, then reported for *CBS Sunday Morning* and *48 Hours*, anchored ABC's *World News Now*, and contributed to *NBC Nightly News* and *The Today Show*. Most recently, she has hosted and reported for NPR and PBS.

DAVE STEWART is a musician, songwriter, and producer who performed as one half of the 1980s duo Eurythmics.

ARNOLD STIEFEL has managed Rod Stewart for many years and also managed Billy Squier.

MICHAEL STIPE is the singer in R.E.M. He started a film company in 1987 and was a producer of *Being John Malkovich* and an executive producer of *Velvet Goldmine*.

DONNA SUMMER worked in musical theater before recording a string of dance, R&B, pop, and rock hits.

ANDY SUMMERS is a guitarist best known as a member of the band the Police.

JAZZ SUMMERS managed Wham!, along with Simon Napier-Bell, and launched the career of George Michael.

JOHN SYKES is a founding executive of MTV. He was the network's director of promotion at launch and became vice president of programming before his departure in 1986. He later served as president of VH1 from 1994 to 2002 and as CEO of Infinity Radio. Sykes is currently president, national ventures, for Clear Channel Communications.

GEOFF TATE sings with the progressive rock band Queensrÿche, who won a Viewer's Choice VMA for "Silent Lucidity" in 1991.

JOHN TAYLOR plays bass in Duran Duran, which he cofounded.

AL TELLER was president of Columbia and CBS Records from 1981 to 1988. He later became chairman/CEO of the MCA Music Entertainment Group.

JULIEN TEMPLE directed the 1980 Sex Pistols "mockumentary" *The Great Rock 'n' Roll Swindle* and the 2000 Sex Pistols documentary *The Filth and the Fury*. He has made videos for Culture Club, the Rolling Stones, Neil Young, Tom Petty, and Whitney Houston, among many acts. He is currently a documentary and feature film director.

ABBY TERKUHLE was creative director of MTV and the founder and president of MTV Animation. He executive produced MTV's animation showcase *Liquid Television*, which spawned the hit series *Beavis and Butt-head*. Terkuhle is currently the president of Aboriginal Entertainment, a production company.

VAN TOFFLER is president of MTV Networks Music/Films/Logo Group. He began working at MTV in 1987 in the business affairs department.

TREACH is a member of the hip-hop group Naughty by Nature. He was married to Pepa, whom he met at an MTV Spring Break.

RALPH TRESVANT was a founding member of the R&B group New Edition.

LARS ULRICH is the drummer and cofounder of Metallica.

USHER is a singer, dancer, songwriter, and actor who released his first album in 1994.

KATHY VALENTINE plays bass in the Go-Go's and cowrote the singles "Vacation" and "Head over Heels."

VANILLA ICE is a rapper whose smash 1990 single "Ice Ice Baby" was "retired" nine years later on the MTV show *25 Lame*. He currently hosts a home-improvement TV series on the DIY Network.

JOHN VARVATOS is a fashion designer who grew up in Detroit and has played guitar onstage with Cheap Trick, ZZ Top, and Guns N' Roses.

MICHELLE VONFELD was the head of the standards and practices department at MTV.

RUPERT WAINWRIGHT directed videos for MC Hammer and N.W.A, and the films *Stigmata* and *The Fog*.

TONY WARD is a model and actor who starred in a number of music videos, most memorably Madonna's "Justify My Love."

CHARLIE WARNER was a radio and TV executive for many years. He hired Bob Pittman as a program director and gave John Lack his first job at CBS, and now teaches at NYU's Stern School of Business.

RON WEISNER is the former comanager of Michael Jackson.

PAUL WESTERBERG made albums with his band the Replacements from 1981 to 1990.

JANE WIEDLIN plays guitar in the Go-Go's and cowrote their hit "Our Lips Are Sealed."

ANN WILSON is the main singer in Heart, which she leads with her older sister Nancy. The group has sold more than 35 million albums worldwide.

NANCY WILSON plays guitar in Heart, which she leads with her younger sister Ann. They were one of the few 1970s bands to have hits on MTV.

KIP WINGER led the 1980s band Winger. He now composes classical music under the name C. F. Kip Winger.

HOWARD WOFFINDEN is a commercial producer who worked at Propaganda Films from 1986 to 1996.

KARI WUHRER was a model and an actress before she was hired for the cast of *Remote Control* while still in college. Since then she has been in many films and TV shows, including *Sliders* and *General Hospital*.

"WEIRD AL" YANKOVIC got lots of MTV play for his song parodies "Eat It" and "Smells Like Nirvana" and hosted many episodes of *Al-TV* on the channel.

WALTER YETNIKOFF was the head of CBS Records from 1975 to 1990. He is the author of the music-industry memoir *Howling at the Moon: Confessions of a Music Mogul in an Age of Excess*.

YOUNG MC cowrote Tone-Lōc's "Wild Thing" while enrolled at USC before releasing his own 1989 crossover hit, "Bust a Move."

JIM YUKICH may have directed more music videos than anyone in this book (192, according to MVDB.com). His collaborations with Phil Collins and Genesis are legion; thirty-seven videos in all, including the award-winning "Land of Confusion." He is currently a TV director and producer.

PETER ZAREMBA hosted MTV's monthly alternative-music show *The Cutting Edge* from 1984 to 1987. He is the lead singer of NYC's long-running garage-rock band the Fleshtones.

ETHAN ZINDLER was youth outreach coordinator, at the age of twenty-three, for Bill Clinton's 1992 presidential campaign. He has since worked for MTV and the White House, and now heads policy research for a clean-energy market-research firm.

Index

ABC (group), 96, 116, 168
Abdul, Paula, 208–9, 285, 296, 323, 339, 396, 401, 469–70, 526, 529, 577
Abrams, Lee, 331
AC/DC, 19
Aykroyd, Dan, 256
Adam & the Ants, 27, 125
Adams, Bryan, 92, 96, 107, 188, 234, 271, 520, 577
Adams, Cey, 279
Addams, Charles, 491
Adler, Bill, 170, 275, 419, 435, 461, 577
Adler, Lou, 562
Adler, Steven, 437–38, 441–44, 475, 567, 577
Ad-Rock. *See* Horovitz, Adam
Aerosmith, 19, 276–78, 344–45, 470–71, 506
A-ha (DJ), 16
a-ha (group), 234–36, 238–39
Aiello, Danny, 189
Ailes, Roger, 44
Alaia, Azzedine, 307
Allen, Bruce, 106, 161, 230, 307, 577
Allen, Joey, 307, 347–40, 446, 524, 532, 577
Alonso, Maria Conchita, 133
Anderson, Jon, 322
Anderson, Laurie, 166
Angelus, Pete, 87, 153–55, 217–20, 225–26, 252, 321, 334, 577
Anger, Kenneth, 30, 36
Ant, Adam, 19, 81, 90, 125, 165, 238, 577
Anthony, Michael, 86–87, 155, 217–19, 222, 518, 537, 541, 577
Anthony, Polly, 480
Antonioni, Michelangelo, 283
Armatrading, Joan, 166, 175
Armstrong, Mike, 387–88, 392–94, 398, 577
Armstrong, Neil, 54
Arnaud, Daniele, 146–47, 577

Asher, Dick, 47
Astaire, Fred, 186–87, 459
Astley, Rick, 398
Aucoin, Bill, 203–4
Avis, Meiert, 115–16, 287–88, 358–61, 517, 533, 564–67, 577
Ayeroff, Jeff, 46, 89, 119–20, 128, 130, 147–48, 168–69, 174, 190–95, 214, 234–42, 292–97, 309, 338, 345, 358, 468, 470, 577
Azoff, Irving, 110, 327
Azoff, Shelli, 327

B-52s, 92
Babineau, Marko, 414
Bach, Sebastian, 28, 151, 160, 324, 351–52, 499–500, 569, 578
Backer, Steve, 137, 405, 413, 416, 442, 535–37, 542, 578
Bagley, Laura, 524
Bailey, Bunty, 235
Bailey, Tom, 114–15, 248, 290–91, 560, 578
Bak, Sunny, 279
Baker, Anita, 303
Baker, Carolyn, 50, 65, 143, 167–68, 177, 578
Baker, Rick, 182
Ballhaus, Michael, 212
Bananarama, 271
Bangles, 103, 305
Banks, Tony, 300
Barbis, Johnny, 95, 578
Barnes, Don, 67, 308, 578
Baron, Peter, 262, 304, 443, 470–71, 476, 531, 578
Barron, Siobhan, 35, 89, 127, 179, 238, 578
Barron, Steve, 34–34, 88, 99, 107, 119–20, 127, 161, 174–75, 179–80, 190–91, 234–38, 294, 297, 464, 566, 578
Base, Rob, 425

Basil, Toni, 104–5, 187, 578
Bators, Stiv, 62
Bauer, Axel, 236
Bay, Michael, 17, 464–69, 533
Bayer, Samuel, 86, 358–59, 527–30, 578
Beach, Reb, 346–47
Beard, Frank, 25
Beastie Boys, 196, 273, 278–83, 406, 434, 436, 466, 483, 510
Beatles, 21, 31–32, 35, 43, 111, 123, 359, 566
Beatty, Warren, 35, 186
Beck, 561
Bellettini, Alisa Marie, 330, 510–11, 578
Belushi, Jim, 493
Belushi, John, 272
Belzer, Richard, 56
Benatar, Pat, 27, 65–67, 81–82, 90, 95, 159, 200, 578
Benitez, Jellybean, 192
Benjamin, David, 173, 177, 578
Bennett, Bill, 477
Benson, Jac, 427–35, 565, 578
Bergman, Georgia "Jo," 31, 145, 340, 578
Berle, Marshall, 154–57, 336, 578
Berle, Milton, 156–57
Berlin, 96, 466
Bernhard, Sandra, 327
Bernstein, Adam, 453, 463
Berrow, Michael, 70, 307
Berrow, Paul, 122
Bertinelli, Valerie, 153, 222
Beug, John, 235, 466, 518, 562–63, 578
Bicknell, Ed, 238
Bigelow, Kathryn, 357
Biondi, Frank, 383
Bissett, Josie, 348
Biz Markie, 462
Black Crowes, 538–39, 545
Black, Michael Ian, 27–28, 389–90, 509, 512–13, 571, 579
Blackwell, Chris, 35
Blackwood, Nina, 56–57, 61–62, 245, 256, 368–70, 405, 579
Blake, Rebecca, 301, 308–9, 579
Blond, Susan, 176–77, 179, 579
Blondie, 32, 39, 422
Bloom, Howard, 55
Blotto, 68–69, 572
Blotzer, Bobby, 157
Bolino, Julia, 305–7, 579
Bonaduce, Danny, 388
Bone, Mike, 125
Bonet, Lisa, 362
Bon Jovi, 17, 161–64, 332–36, 445, 448, 473–74, 499, 501, 504, 542

Bono, 103, 234, 355, 359–60, 514, 516–17
Boogaloo Sam, 104
Boomtown Rats, 32, 245
Bowie, David, 27, 33–34, 39, 81–82, 117–18, 152, 168, 225, 268, 566, 569
Bow Wow Wow, 27
Boy George, 123, 126–30, 150, 220, 246, 271, 565–66, 579
Bozzio, Dale, 103, 134–35, 579
Bradt, George, 168, 275, 299, 317, 321, 373, 415, 445, 579
Brafman, Marcy, 53, 138, 140, 199, 267, 405, 579
Branca, John, 184
Brando, Miko, 227
Braun, David, 46–47
B-Real, 28, 425–26, 428, 578
Brickman, Mark, 503
Brindle, Ronald "Buzz," 58, 77, 125, 133–34, 166, 179, 303, 579
Briscoe, Jimmy, 87
Britny Fox, 393–94
Broday, Beth, 35, 159, 228–30, 269–70, 289–94, 579
Brown, Bobbie, 348–50, 579
Brown, Bobby, 169, 185, 323–24, 461, 494–96, 529, 538, 579
Brown, James, 168, 187, 321, 491–92
Brown, Jerry, 547
Brown, Julie, 16, 367–76, 397–402, 406–8, 522, 567, 579
Bruck, Connie, 260
Bruckheimer, Jerry, 22, 31, 468, 579
Bryant, Karyn, 520, 524
Buck, Peter, 363, 516
Buckholtz, Tom, 91
Buggles, 64–65
Bullet Boys, 365
Bunim, Mary-Ellis, 550–52, 554
Burns, Jim, 502–8, 579
Burnstein, Cliff, 74, 116, 187, 292, 341–42, 447–49, 474, 569, 579
Burroughs, William, 202
Bus Boys, 166
Bush, George H. W., 543, 546–47
Busload of Faith, 364
Butler, Geezer, 499
Byrne, David, 92, 104–5, 285, 296–97, 516

Cabasa, Lisa Ann, 452–53
Cain, Jonathan, 91–92, 579
Callner, Marty, 109, 157–60, 227–28, 301–2, 305, 316, 331–32, 335–40, 344–45, 471–73, 566, 579
Calloway, Cab, 20, 484

Cameo, 276, 397
Cammell, Donald, 234
Campbell, Joseph, 147, 491
Campbell, Naomi, 486, 511
Cannelli, John, 338, 345, 350, 373, 405, 415–16, 436–43, 472–73, 499, 537, 579
Cantrell, Cady, 525
Capps, Roger, 90
Carey, Mariah, 374, 507
Carli, Ann, 96, 156, 169, 275–76, 303, 418–19, 422, 456–57, 463, 487, 579
Carnes, Kim, 109
Carradine, Keith, 189
Carrasco, Joe King, 69
Cars, 96, 102, 104, 205–7, 229–30, 314
Casale, Bob, 36
Casale, Jerry, 30, 36, 68, 102, 144, 230, 233–34, 271, 579
Casey, Steve, 43, 50, 52, 64–66, 332, 579
Casper and Cooley, 187
Catherall, Joanne, 119
Chapman, Tracy, 361–62, 436
Charisse, Cyd, 484
Chase, Chevy, 493
Cheap Trick, 45
Cher, 259, 322–23, 440, 471–73, 499, 580
Chicago, 237
Chilli. See Thomas, Rozonda
Chilton, Alex, 354
Christensen, Helena, 485
Chuck D, 28, 95, 276, 281, 426–27, 457–48, 580
Cinemax, 262
Clapton, Eric, 248, 325, 538, 540
Clark, Dick, 326
Clark, Ken R., 58–63, 134, 337, 356, 369–80, 397, 431, 553, 580
Clash, 31, 106, 170
Classix Nouveau, 68
Clawson, Tim, 309, 580
Clay, Andrew Dice, 325–26
Cliff, Jimmy, 354
Clinton, Bill, 543–49, 559
Cobain, Kurt, 116, 526–35, 538–42
Cocks, Jay, 22
Cohen, Lyor, 428–29, 431
Coldplay, 366
Coleman, Lisa, 169, 215–16, 309, 580
Coleman, Signy, 308
Coleridge, Tanya, 311
Coletti, Alex, 310, 372–73, 379–80, 398–99, 405–7, 412, 422, 434, 504–6, 580
Collen, Phil, 151, 250, 580
Collins, Phil, 93–94, 229, 299–300, 580
Combonation, 237
Commodores, 274

Conner, Bruce, 30, 105
Copeland, Miles, 48, 92–93, 133, 199, 580
Copeland, Stewart, 35, 102, 128–30, 230, 580
Coppola, Sofia, 477
Corbijn, Anton, 234, 287, 365–66, 477, 516–17, 534–35, 560, 580
Corgan, Billy, 530
Cornyn, Stan, 50
Corradina, Linda, 369, 414–15, 544, 548, 580
Corrao, Lauren, 369, 393, 512, 551–54, 580
Cortese, Dan, 520
Costello, Elvis, 120, 503
Coverdale, David, 153, 337–40
Cox, Courteney, 211
Crawford, Cindy, 16, 193, 327–30, 385, 486, 509–12, 558, 567, 580
Creme, Lol, 33–34, 70–71, 88, 108, 127–29, 170–71, 233, 259, 270, 289–91, 580
Cribiore, Alberto, 264
Critchley, Eric, 175
Cronin, Kevin, 55, 57, 67, 92, 232–33, 580
Crosby, David, 248, 506
Crosby, Robbin, 153, 157
Cross, Christopher, 293
Crowe, Cameron, 541
Cruger, Roberta, 132, 137, 179, 253, 321, 580
Cuesta, Michael, 164
Culkin, Macaulay, 479
Culture Club, 114, 123, 126–27, 150, 225
Cure, 32
Curry, Adam, 59, 367, 370–72, 375–77, 380, 384, 404, 413, 431, 444–46, 482, 498–501, 521–22, 548, 561, 567–68, 580
Curtis, Bill, 81
Cutting Crew, 288
Cutting Edge, The, 353–55, 382
Cypress Hill, 28

Dajani, Nadia, 279
Dall, Bobby, 344
Danforth, John, 313
Danger Danger, 416
Daniels, Charlie, 45
Danzig, Glenn, 346
Dargis, Manohla, 30
Davies, Kathy, 306
Davis, Clive, 198, 304, 400, 412, 581
Davis, Maria, 293
Davis, Martha, 94–95, 103, 293, 562, 581
Davis, Tamra, 288, 364, 451–55, 494, 581
Davola, Joe, 132, 137, 249, 276, 321, 387–94, 404, 406, 512, 550, 581
Dayne, Taylor, 397, 561
Dayton, Jonathan, 354, 358, 499, 581
Dead Milkmen, 399

Dean, Paul, 160, 581
Decouflé, Philippe, 357
Def Leppard, 74, 90, 149, 151–53, 250, 330,
    334, 341–42, 542
De La Soul, 423
DeMann, Freddy, 174–80, 187–90, 193–96,
    254, 258–59, 488–90, 581
DeMartini, Warren, 156–57, 581
Demme, Jonathan, 358
Demme, Ted, 397–98, 418–21, 424, 429–30,
    433–35
Dempsey, Don, 176, 182
Dempsey, Patrick, 525
De Niro, Robert, 304, 349
De Palma, Brian, 210–11
Depeche Mode, 144, 365–66
Depp, Johnny, 434
Deutch, Howie, 205, 581
DeVille, CC, 329, 351
Devo, 30, 35–36, 68, 102, 116, 144
DeYoung, Dennis, 68, 111, 468, 581
Diamond, Brian, 321, 556, 581
Diamond, Jim, 67, 581
Diaz, John, 88, 91, 204–7, 271, 286, 310, 456,
    487, 581
Dick, Nigel, 31, 230–31, 245–46, 294, 337, 341,
    345, 437–43, 570, 581
Dickerson, Ernest, 212, 496
Dickinson, Bruce, 101, 176, 581
Dickinson, Janice, 191
Dike, Matt, 451–42
DiLeo, Frank, 174, 413
Diller, Barry, 141, 385, 557
Dillon, Matt, 528
Dio, Ronnie, 336–37
Di Palma, Carlo, 360–61
Dire Straits, 237–39, 317, 436
DiSanto, Tony, 435, 445, 474, 522, 524, 570–71,
    581
Disney, Lillian, 186
Divinyls, 468
Dixie Dregs, 347
Dixon, Jerry, 347
Dixon, Willie, 354
DJ Hurricane, 281
DJ Jazzy Jeff, 419–22, 429, 455–57, 580
DJ Red Alert, 274
DMC, 273–78, 423, 580
Doebler, Margaret, 139
Dokken, Don, 333, 337
Dolby, Thomas, 60, 125–26, 581
Dole, Kevin, 232–33, 581
Donovan, Terence, 301, 306
Doors, 21
Dors, Diana, 125

Dougherty, Peter, 53, 276, 281, 420–22, 427,
    429, 434, 581
Drake, Bill, 48
Dr. Dre, 423–25, 430–32, 455
Dr. John, 505
Dubin, Adam, 92, 94, 219–20, 279–83, 335,
    449–50, 560, 581
Duffy, Karen, 520–24, 567, 581–82
Dugan, Michael, 387–95, 570, 582
Duran Duran, 27, 32, 48, 54, 70–74, 104, 106,
    113–16, 123, 144, 149–50, 165, 188, 202,
    225, 248–49, 252, 255, 290, 322, 562, 567
Durst, Stephen, 159
Dylan, Bob, 21, 113, 517

Eagles, 272
Eazy-E, 455
Eber, José, 368
Eberhardt, Allie, 310
Edwards, Blake, 279
Eisenstein, Sergei, 31
Electric Boogaloos, 104
Elias, Jonathan, 54, 582
Elizondo, Rene, 484
Elkes, Terry, 265–67, 383–84
Ellington, Duke, 20
Elliott, Joe, 90, 123, 151–53, 242, 341–42, 533,
    582
Enrico, Roger, 226
En Vogue, 491, 515
Epand, Lee, 47–48, 164, 335, 582
Epstein, Howie, 314
Eric B & Rakim, 423–24
Ertegun, Ahmet, 157
Eurythmics, 113–14, 118–19
Evangelista, Linda, 486
Everett, Kenny, 33–34
Everlast, 275, 428, 434, 462–63, 582
Everly, Erin, 440, 442
Exene, 380

Fab 5 Freddy, 281, 283, 420–24, 427–32, 435,
    462, 571, 582
Fabian, Ava, 294
Fahey, Siobhan, 271, 582
Farber, Matt, 478
Fargnoli, Steve, 214–15, 309
Farian, Frank, 396, 400, 402
Faris, Valerie, 162, 230, 353–54, 358, 499–500,
    582
Farley, Chris, 523–24
Farriss, Tim, 90, 582
Feldman, Corey, 410
Fellini, Federico, 283
Fenske, Mark, 518–19, 582

Ferry, Bryan, 247
Fields, Simon, 35, 93, 98–99, 107, 175, 190–91, 194–95, 215–16, 286, 299, 582
Fincher, David, 17, 282, 285–86, 292–96, 358, 467–71, 486–87, 529, 541, 568
Fink, Jill, 525
Finnerty, Amy, 435, 527–31, 539–41, 550, 582
Fiorvante, Don, 303
Fiss, Tracie, 551
Fixx, 116
Flattery, Paul, 88–89, 94, 98, 107, 109, 176, 179–80, 198, 207, 241, 270, 294, 299–300, 582
Flavor Fav, 426–27
Flea, 365, 406–7, 453, 519, 541, 571, 582
Fleetwood Mac, 25, 99–100, 109, 269
Fleetwood, Mick, 100
Fleischer, Charles, 41
Flics, Seymour, 304
Flock of Seagulls, 116–17, 370
Fluck, Peter, 300
Flynt, Larry, 450
Foley, Wish, 314–15, 322, 582
Folsey, George, 182–83
Foo Fighters, 216, 568
Forman, Milos, 571
Forstmann, Nick and Ted, 263–65
Fox, Megan, 465
Fox, Michael J., 62, 434
Fox, Samantha, 303, 336
Frank, Robert, 358, 468
Frankie Goes to Hollywood, 114
Franklin, Aretha, 49
Frantz, Chris, 192
Fraser, Wendy, 148
Freston, Tom, 49, 51–54, 65, 68, 73–79, 83, 125, 137, 141–42, 167, 186, 196, 223, 263–68, 325–26, 367, 378, 382–88, 395, 417, 439, 473, 489, 510, 515, 538, 543–47, 550, 555–56, 582
Frey, Glenn, 321
Friedman, Dana, 328
Friend, Lonn, 450
Frost, Deborah, 331
Fry, Martin, 96, 114, 116, 130, 582
Fuentes, Daisy, 377

Gabriel, Peter, 297–99, 302
Gaff, Billy, 98
Gahan, Dave, 366
Gallen, Joel, 323–25, 328, 481, 504–6, 538–39, 582
Gallin, Sandy, 480–81
Galluzzi, Patti, 318–19, 414, 432–33, 515, 583
Gap Band, 93, 274

Garland, Les, 17, 48–50, 75–76, 80–82, 97, 125, 127, 131–40, 151, 158, 166–67, 171, 176–78, 184, 186, 189–90, 201, 211, 226, 237–38, 247, 257–59, 262, 267–68, 272, 316, 320–21, 343, 386, 583
Garvey, Marcus, 422
Geffen, David, 141, 198, 265, 267, 338, 344–45, 417, 436–41, 471–72, 476
Geldof, Bob, 245–47, 321, 583
Genesis, 299–300
George, Betsy Lynn, 486–87, 583
Gerardo, 409, 583
Gersh, Gary, 74, 102, 117, 439, 471, 529, 532, 539, 583
Gerstner, Lou, 50
Geto Boys, 423, 425
Ghuneim, Mark, 355, 416, 494, 583
Gibbons, Billy, 25, 144–48, 566, 583
Gibson, Brian, 111–12
Gibson, Debbie, 193, 202, 322, 399, 490, 583
Gibson, Mel, 103, 425
Gilchrist, Mak, 305–7, 583
Gilmer, Bruce, 398
Giraldi, Bob, 180–82, 190, 200, 226–27, 251, 269–70, 287, 583
Giraldo, Neil "Spyder," 67, 160, 583
Giraldo, Patricia, 67
Glew, Dave, 416, 480
Glover, Corey, 413, 583
Glover, Danny, 493
Godley, Kevin, 33–34, 70–72, 87, 127–29, 170–71, 229–30, 259, 290–91, 363, 517, 559, 583
Go-Go's, 29, 101, 225
Gold, Andrew, 68
Gold, Greg, 228–29, 293–96, 467, 583
Goldberg, Danny, 528, 539
Goldberg, Julian, 62, 583
Goldblatt, Steven, 112
Goldsmith, Harvey, 247
Goldstein, Doug, 438–44, 475–77, 540, 583
Golin, Steve, 294
Goodman, Mark, 57–63, 68, 134–37, 154, 168, 196, 245, 278, 310, 355, 367, 370–71, 409, 583
Goodwin, Andrew, 166
Gore, Al, 313, 316
Gore, Tipper, 313–16
Gorman, Ken, 266–67, 383
Gortner, Marjoe, 405
Gottfried, Gilbert, 405
Goude, Jean-Paul, 282
Gowers, Bruce, 31–32, 37, 68, 86, 88, 98, 583
Grammer, Camille, 308, 397–99, 407–8, 583
Grammer, Kelsey, 397, 399

Grant, Brian, 32, 34, 97, 107–10, 116, 202, 289, 305, 469, 583
Grant, Eddy, 166
Grasshoff, Alex and Marilyn, 453–54
Gravatte, Marianne, 308
Great White, 161, 331, 337, 341, 345–46, 437, 466
Green, Cee Lo, 185, 425–26, 584
Greif, Paula, 288–90, 584
Grein, Paul, 173
Grey, Glenn, 272
Griffin, Meg, 57–58, 584
Grohl, Dave, 25, 216, 270, 355, 475, 528, 531–34, 539, 541, 568, 584
Grombacher, Myron, 90
Grubman, Allen, 45–46, 242–43, 384, 584
Guns N' Roses, 17, 285, 324, 347, 436–46, 471, 474–77, 522–23, 533, 538–41

Hagar, Sammy, 517–19, 541, 564, 584
Haircut 100, 27
Hall, Arsenio, 322–29, 402, 451, 544, 584
Hall, Daryl, 90, 110, 207, 229, 247, 271, 584
Hall & Oates, 27, 48, 90, 276
Ham, Bill, 145, 257
Ham, Greg, 101
Hancock, Herbie, 170–71, 259, 320, 584
Handler, Chelsea, 103
Harket, Morten, 235
Harkin, Tom, 547
Harrison, Jerry, 104–5, 296–97, 584
Harry, Debbie, 32, 584
Harvey, Gene, 304
Hay, Colin, 101, 584
Haymes, Greg, 68–69, 572, 584
Headbangers Ball, 382, 432, 438–39, 444–47, 526, 531, 536, 545
Heart, 29, 232, 301–2
Heather B., 552, 554
Heavy D, 429, 432–33
Heldman, Carolyne, 370–71, 376–77, 380, 584
Heller, Liz, 88, 198, 316, 494–95, 584
Hendrix, Jimi, 210
Henley, Don, 236–37, 326–27, 505
Herbert, Herbie, 91
Herbert, Jim, 93
Herman, Pee-wee, 328
Herrin, Kym, 148
Herzog, Doug, 249, 326, 328, 369, 382, 385–89, 392–95, 405–9, 445, 481, 510, 521, 547, 550, 553, 584
Hetfield, James, 448–50
Heyward, Julia, 104
Hilburn, Robert, 64
Hill, Anita, 414

Hill, Benny, 116
Hilton, David, 201
Hilton, Kathy, 229
Hilton, Paris, 229
Hoffs, Susanna, 305, 568, 584
Holmes, Dave, 28, 66–69, 94, 115, 123, 149, 186, 379, 394, 523, 553, 564–67, 584
Honda, Steve, 472
Hook, Peter, 357–58, 364, 584
Hooters, 292
Hopper, Dennis, 330
Horn, Trevor, 65, 246, 278, 572, 584
Horovitz, Adam (Ad-Rock), 196, 278–82, 406, 453–54, 466, 569, 584
Horowitz, David, 82, 261–63, 316
Horst, Horst P., 468
House of Style, 385, 509–12, 567
Houston, Angelica, 491
Houston, Whitney, 304–5, 334, 496–97
Hubley, John, 79
Hughes Brothers, 430
Human League, 114, 119, 174
Hunter, Alan, 33, 60–63, 245–48, 256, 355, 368–71, 381, 405, 409, 561, 568, 584
Hunter, Rachel, 347
Hunter, Tom, 262, 268, 340, 347, 376, 382–87, 397, 415–16, 420–21, 438–40, 444–45, 584
Hüsker Dü, 354
Hutton, Timothy, 207, 585

Ian, Scott, 561, 569, 585
Ice Cube, 427, 432, 455
Ice-T, 423, 428
Idol, Billy, 81, 124–25, 138, 160, 197, 203–5, 208, 220, 328, 374, 486–87, 585
Ienner, Donnie, 198, 304, 348
Isaacs, Steve, 150, 482, 520–23, 532, 535, 553, 567, 585
Isaak, Chris, 27, 102, 317, 485, 585
Isaak, Wayne, 129, 585
Isham, Wayne, 34, 129, 149, 162–63, 176, 194, 288, 333–35, 342–46, 351, 447–49, 473–74, 499, 585

Jackson, Jackie, 185, 208
Jackson, Janet, 18, 26, 188, 289, 327, 397, 469, 483–85, 585
Jackson, J.J., 58–60, 168, 245, 310, 355, 369–70, 561
Jackson, Joe, 54, 120, 166, 189, 289, 585
Jackson, Michael, 16, 18, 20, 104, 106, 169, 172–89, 198, 207–9, 226–27, 239, 252, 259, 273, 275, 285, 317, 413, 418, 427, 461, 478–83, 490–93, 523, 526, 562, 569
Jackson, Phil, 548

Jackson, Randy, 185
Jackson, Tito, 185
Jackson, Victoria, 531
Jacksons, 207–9, 316
Jacobs, Mark, 511
Jacquet, Illinois, 128
Jagger, Mick, 31, 79–81, 87, 94, 99, 440, 517
Jam, 34
James, Del, 475
James, Rick, 167, 174, 186, 228, 273–74
Jam Master Jay, 276–78
Jane's Addiction, 25, 328, 365, 520
Jefferis, Kurt, 221–24, 585
Jeung, Kathy, 310–11
JJ Fad, 420
Joanou, Phil, 516
Jobs, Steve, 38
Joel, Billy, 94, 97, 105, 108–9, 402, 585
Joe Public, 551
John, Elton, 19, 95, 97, 108, 198, 474, 506, 538
Johnson, Brian, 150
Johnson, Stephen R., 191, 237, 296–99, 585
Jolie, Angelina, 464
Jones, Bob, 482
Jones, Grace, 282
Jones, Howard, 115, 130, 233, 248, 291, 585
Jones, Jo, 128
Jones, Mick, 31, 106, 585
Jones, Quincy, 174, 178–79, 184, 257
Jones, Rickie Lee, 192
Jonze, Spike, 568
Jordan, Tracey, 323–24, 561, 585
Journey, 88, 91, 113, 139, 178
Judge, Mike, 513, 532

Kagan, Peter, 290
Kahane, Rob, 309–12, 318, 562, 585
Kaiser, Sam, 317, 332, 335, 338–39, 345–46, 412, 436, 585
Kajagoogoo, 114
Kalodner, John, 62, 101, 338, 340, 345, 471, 473, 532, 585
Kalvert, Scott, 315, 418–19, 424, 456, 586
Kane, Big Daddy, 425, 428–29, 462, 578
Kane, Bob, 152
Kates, Mark, 527
Katz, Jonathan, 521
Katzenberg, Jeffrey, 524
Kaufman, Howard, 338
Kelly, Gene, 186, 484
Kelly, Patty, 306
Kendall, Dave, 318, 353–56, 570, 586
Kendall, Mark, 337
Kennedy. See Montgomery, Lisa
Kenny G, 262, 436

Kensch, Elsa, 511
Keough, Jeana Tomasina, 146, 148, 586
Kerrey, Bob, 547–48
Kerry, John, 548
Kerslake, Kevin, 357, 530, 533–35, 586
Keshishian, Alek, 494–96, 586
Kiedis, Anthony, 330
Kimmel, Adam, 283–84
King, Carole, 425
King, Don, 430, 456–57
King, Kerry, 282
Kinison, Sam, 322, 345, 405, 524
Kirshner, Don, 21
Kiss, 337, 542
Kitaen, Tawny, 16, 149, 153, 338–41, 586
Kleber, Mick, 74, 88, 90, 94, 96, 232, 236, 250–55, 270, 293, 302, 317, 335, 337, 341, 344, 459, 465–67, 491–93, 562, 586
Kleinbaum, Janet, 408, 414, 419, 586
Kleinman, Daniel, 191, 196, 286, 336–37, 469–70, 586
Klinsky, Steve, 263
Kluger, Barry, 326
Knopfler, Mark, 237–38
Konowitch, Abbey, 138, 172, 198, 326–27, 347, 350, 399–400, 411–17, 421, 432, 448, 473, 487–90, 504–7, 529–30, 538, 544, 559–60, 566, 586
Kool G Rap, 462
Kool Moe Dee, 273, 276, 308, 419–20, 586
Koppelman, Charles, 468
Kragen, Ken, 247
Krasnow, Bob, 150
Kravitz, Lenny, 26–27, 362, 409, 586
Kresti, Chris, 390
Krim, Rick, 68, 133, 339, 343–44, 347, 352, 355, 384, 416, 436, 507, 532, 535–41, 586
KRS-One, 422
Kuchar Brothers, 30, 36
Kurfirst, Gary, 92

Lack, John, 16, 39–55, 60, 65, 73, 76–78, 82–83, 131, 140–43, 261, 554–56, 586
Lack, Sandy, 143
Lady Gaga, 27, 339, 570–71, 586
Lage, Milt, 399
Lambert, Mary, 189, 192–96, 214–15, 289, 487–88, 586
Landau, Jon, 97, 199, 209–13, 246–47, 360, 384, 586
Landis, John, 182–87, 239, 323, 478–81, 587
Lane, Jani, 152, 348–40, 446, 532–33, 587
Laufer, Debbie, 525
Lauper, Cyndi, 82, 103, 200, 220, 225
Law, Roger, 300

Laybourne, Gerry, 383
Leaders of the New School, 423
Lean, David, 30
Lear, Norman, 41
Leary, Denis, 388–89, 393, 434, 558
Le Bon, Simon, 17, 48, 54, 71–72, 102–3, 120–24, 202, 246, 290, 307, 512, 552, 561, 587
Led Zeppelin, 49, 376, 437
Lee, Spike, 212, 457–48, 496
Lee, Tommy, 153, 157, 162–63, 334–35, 342–43, 348, 412–13, 499–500, 587
Leeds, Harvey, 127, 133, 138, 182, 185, 198, 587
Leeds, Steve, 143, 367, 374–80, 399–401, 421, 587
Leer, Cindy, 453
Leifer, Carol, 56, 505
Lenahan, Jim, 37, 324
Lennon, Thomas, 509
Lennox, Annie, 118–19, 126, 511, 587
Lenzer, Don, 222
Lerer, Ken, 545, 547
Letterman, David, 275, 386, 389, 557
Letts, Don, 93, 106–7, 156–57, 169–70, 424, 587
Levey, Jay, 182
Levine, Adam, 350, 486, 587
Levine, Arnold, 97
Levy, Charlie, 206
Levy, Steven, 165
Lewis, Drew, 141–42
Lewis, Huey, 95, 127, 134, 220, 225, 259, 291, 307, 565, 587
Lewis, Jerry Lee, 275
Lewis, Pam, 59, 65, 587
Lieberthal, Gary, 41–42, 587
Light, Nick, 409, 525
Limahl, 114–15, 119, 232, 587
Lindsay-Hogg, Michael, 31
Lister, Perri, 33, 124–25, 153, 202–5, 208, 487, 587
Little, Brian, 263
Little Jimmy, 461
Live Aid, 245–49, 321
Living Colour, 104, 413
LL Cool J, 282–83, 308, 411, 423, 425, 507
Locklear, Heather, 343–44
Loder, Kurt, 248, 369–72, 376, 474, 482, 510, 531, 544–45, 561
Lois, George, 78–80, 83, 587
Lombard, Robert, 86–87, 154–55, 271, 587
Longo, Robert, 357
Lopez, Jennifer, 423
Lorenzini, Vance, 469
Love, Courtney, 527, 530–31, 534–41, 587

Lover, Ed, 186, 423–34, 571, 587
Loverboy, 106, 160–61, 292, 296
Lucas, George, 285, 293
Lukather, Steve, 37, 62, 94, 112, 242, 270, 587
Lundvall, Bruce, 47
Lydon, John, 356, 530
Lynyrd Skynyrd, 113
Lynch, Monica, 423, 587
Lynch, Stan, 314
Lynch, Tom, 274, 588

Mac, Bernie, 434
Mackay, Anne-Marie, 292–96, 308, 465, 469, 486, 566, 588
Mackie, Bob, 472
Madness, 116
Madonna, 17, 18, 134, 187–200, 225, 247, 257–59, 285–86, 310, 317–20, 327, 354, 357, 362, 370, 436, 469, 481, 487–90, 523, 569
Magness, Bob, 77
Magnoli, Albert, 216
Mahurin, Matt, 287, 358–63, 527, 529, 588
Malcolm X, 422
Mallet, David, 30–34, 37, 98, 117, 124–25, 149–52, 160, 204, 232, 251, 286, 294, 302, 304, 558, 588
Malone, John, 77–78, 83, 261–62
Mandel, Howie, 41
Manhattan Design, 52
Manitoba's Wild Kingdom, 308
Mann, Aimee, 229, 286, 588
Mann, Michael, 22, 31, 588
Marley, Ziggy, 428
Marlowe, Kim, 400–402, 588
Maroon 5, 350
Mars, Mick, 151
Marshall, Dana, 442
Martin, Chris, 366
Martin, Dean, 35
Martin, Lionel, 274, 276, 279, 426–27, 462, 496, 588
Martindale, Wink, 318
Martinez, Eddie, 274
Marvis, Curt, 163, 333, 342–44, 447, 474, 588
Marx, Richard, 28, 103, 129, 294–95, 335, 467, 588
Masters, Lee, 21, 44, 187, 262, 326, 332, 374, 386–87, 411–12, 418, 420–21, 432, 438–39, 488, 509, 588
Mattiussi, Jeanne, 89, 137, 292, 296, 303
Maybury, John, 363–64
Mays, Brian, 32
Mazza, Jim, 253
McCarrell, Ron, 178, 588

McCarthy, Beth, 134, 278, 370–76, 389, 392, 397–400, 404, 512–13, 588

McCarthy, Jenny, 431

McCartney, Paul, 41, 182, 248, 505–6

McDaniels, Ralph, 274, 420

McFarland, Spanky, 186

McGee, Jerry, 53

McGhee, Doc, 160–64, 288, 333–36, 343, 351, 473–74, 498–501, 504, 542, 588

McGhee, Scott, 500

McGrath, Judy, 53, 75, 77, 115, 137, 140, 167, 248, 323, 332, 345, 350, 355, 376–78, 382–87, 420, 432–33, 481, 487, 503, 537–40, 543–44, 551, 553, 564, 588

McGroarty, Bob, 49, 77–78, 82–83

McGuinness, Paul, 115–16, 213–14, 234, 241, 360, 516–17, 569, 588

MC Hammer, 187, 326–27, 412, 423, 425, 458–61, 483, 490–93, 588

McKay, Jim, 357

McNally, Keith, 60

McVie, Christine, 99, 269

McVie, John, 99

Meat Loaf, 32–33, 39, 94, 464, 469, 588

Megadeth, 26, 369

Mekas, Jonas, 105

Melendez, Melissa, 283

Mellencamp, John Cougar, 98–99, 198–99

Melman, Larry "Bud," 275

Melvoin, Wendy, 309

Men at Work, 101–2, 166, 173

Menello, Ric, 278–84, 346, 461–62, 588

Mensch, Peter, 152, 448–49, 474, 542, 589

Mercury, Freddie, 232, 330

Merlis, Bob, 325, 589

Messer, Kate, 353

Messman, Jack, 261

Metallica, 26, 436, 447–50

Metcalf, Mark, 157–59, 227–28, 589

Meyer, Russ, 30

Michael, George, 18, 188, 200–202, 246, 285, 310–12, 474, 486, 589

Michaels, Bret, 27, 329, 344, 351, 533, 589

Midler, Bette, 256

Milano, Alyssa, 381

Milgrim, Hale, 466

Mili, Gjon, 128

Miller, Ali Espley, 115

Miller, Dennis, 115

Miller, Judith, 543, 547

Miller, Steve, 94

Milligan, Spike, 125

Milli Vanilli, 396–403, 493

Minnelli, Liza, 296

Minutemen, 353–54

Missing Persons, 135

Mister Mister, 408

Mitchell, Tony, 204–5

Mohler, Tom, 227, 251–54, 589

Mondino, Jean-Baptiste, 236–37, 288, 296, 301, 488–89, 568, 589

Money, Eddie, 292–93

Monk, Noel, 155

Monkees, 21, 35–36, 385

Montag, Heidi, 567

Montgomery, Lisa "Kennedy," 123, 379, 520–24, 561

Moon, Keith, 203

Morahan, Andy, 114, 200, 287, 294, 310–11, 474–77, 496, 533, 589

Morris, Doug, 48–50

Morrissey, 354

Morton, Robert, 44, 49, 56–58, 139, 556–57, 589

Morvan, Fab, 396–403, 589

Moss, Jon, 127, 271

Motels, 94–95, 293

Mothersbaugh, Mark, 35–36, 240, 589

Mötley Crüe, 18, 149–51, 157, 159, 161–64, 324, 332–33, 342–43, 412–13, 499–501, 542

Mottola, Tommy, 48, 83, 140, 198, 242, 304, 374, 480, 589

Mulcahy, Russell, 34, 65, 97–100, 108–11, 121–22, 202–3, 235, 294, 305, 322, 464, 589

Muller, Sophie, 287, 341, 589

Munro, Caroline, 125

Murdoch, Rupert, 557

Murphy, Eddie, 17, 134, 167, 206, 320–23, 434

Murray, Jonathan, 550–54, 589

Musical Youth, 169–70

Mustaine, Dave, 26, 369, 446, 548, 589

MTV News, 369, 380, 531, 544–49

M-Walk, 452

Myers, Joan, 80, 103, 133, 138, 589

Napier-Bell, Simon, 200–201

Natividad, Kitten, 416

Naughty by Nature, 179

Nava, Jake, 486

Navarro, Dave, 25, 61, 328–29, 365, 520, 589

Neil, Vince, 324

Nelson, Matthew, 349

Nelson, Rick, 21

Nelson, Tyka, 302

Nesmith, Michael, 35–36, 39–42, 51, 143, 559, 564, 590

Nevil, Robbie, 398

New Edition, 169

New Kids on the Block, 396, 494
Newman, Alfred, 145
Newman, Allen, 133–34, 138–40, 267, 409, 590
Newman, Debbie, 47, 88–92, 137, 171, 590
Newman, Lionel, 145
Newman, Randy, 145
Newman, Tim, 88, 129, 144–48, 198, 243, 259, 287, 559–60, 567, 590
New Order, 357–58
Newton-John, Olivia, 103–4, 107–8, 590
Nicholas Brothers, 186, 484
Nicholson, Jack, 247
Nicks, Stevie, 25, 29, 99–100, 103, 110, 269, 571, 590
Nieporent, Drew, 556
Nies, Eric, 552–54, 590
Nine Inch Nails, 351
Nirvana, 25, 216, 526–35, 538–41
Niven, Alan, 161, 324, 333, 337, 341, 437–43, 466–67, 475, 493, 565, 569, 590
No Face, 431
Novoselic, Krist, 527, 531, 539–40
Numan, Gary, 116
Nunn, Terri, 96, 103, 590
N.W.A., 427, 454–55, 461
Nykvist, Sven, 116

Oakey, Phil, 119
Oates, John, 229
Ober, Ken, 388–92, 394, 512, 521
O'Brien, Conan, 26, 61, 235, 590
Ocasek, Ric, 102, 104, 229–30
Ochs, Meegan Lee, 195
O'Connor, Sinead, 200, 302, 327, 362–64, 515–16, 570, 590
O'Hanlon, Ned, 290
Ohlmeyer, Don, 256–57
Oldham, Todd, 327, 511
Olinsky, Frank, 52–53
Oliver, Julie, 552, 554
Onassis, Jackie Kennedy, 186
Onyx, 559
Orbison, Roy, 86
Oreck, Sharon, 93, 110, 191–92, 195, 214–17, 270, 289–90, 346, 358, 590
Ortega, Kenny, 108, 112, 251–54
Orzabal, Roland, 231
Osbourne, Ozzy, 346, 498–99, 530
Osmond, Donny, 464–66, 468
Osmonds, 176
Ostin, Mo, 148, 238, 518
Outfield, 292
Ovitz, Mike, 268, 412
Owens, Buck, 21

Paay, Patricia, 375–76
Page, Jimmy, 247
Paik, Nam June, 42
Palmer, Robert, 301, 305–7, 451
Pankhurst, Julie, 306
Parents Music Resource Center (PMRC), 165, 313–14, 316, 318, 331
Park, Nick, 298
Parker, Bill, 228
Patitz, Tajan, 486
Patterson, Michael, 235
Patterson, Vince, 181, 480
Paynter, Bob, 182
Pearcy, Stephen, 156–57, 308, 336, 590
Pearl, Daniel, 37, 109, 129, 175, 209–10, 475, 590
Pearl Jam, 507, 522, 526, 532, 535–38, 541–42
Pellington, Mark, 134, 384, 493, 517, 536–37, 541, 590
Pena, Raquel, 107, 175, 590
Penn, Sean, 195–96
Pepa, 408–9, 590
Perenchio, Jerry, 41
Perkins, Stephen, 520
Perot, Ross, 544
Perry, Joe, 345, 506
Perry, Steve, 91–92
Peters, Michael, 181, 200
Peterson, Vicki, 103, 590
Petty, Tom, 37, 95, 106, 138, 145, 242, 272, 307, 313–18, 324, 348, 538, 548, 591
Pharcyde, 559
Phillips, Chynna, 28, 468, 591
Phillips, Julianne, 308
Phillips, Randy, 75–76, 82, 135–36, 257, 591
Pierson, Arthur, 194
Pilatus, Rob, 396–97, 400–402
Pink Floyd, 19, 113
Piscopo, Joe, 247
Pittman, Bob, 15–16, 20–21, 39–51, 54–60, 64–68, 73–84, 116, 131–32, 138–43, 166–68, 173–79, 183–87, 197, 238, 242–43, 256–68, 321, 331, 367–68, 383–86, 420, 440, 545, 555–56, 564, 569, 591
Plant, Robert, 59, 376–77
Podbielniak, Nancy, 79
Poison, 27, 317, 344, 348, 533
Police, 17, 35, 37, 82, 127–30, 187, 256
Pon, Dale, 44, 78–80, 82–84, 591
Pop, Iggy, 354
Pope, Bill, 448
Pope, Tim, 201, 229
Porcaro, Steve, 62
Porizkova, Paulina, 207

Portman, Natalie, 434
Powell, Kevin, 551–53, 591
Powell, Rickey, 280
Powell, Tony, 245–46
Presley, Elvis, 21, 111, 125, 482
Pressburger, Emeric, 117
Pretenders, 95
Prince, 27, 93, 146, 166, 197–98, 214–17, 302, 308–10, 436
Prokofiev, Sergei, 31
Propaganda, 294–95, 341, 465–69, 478–79, 487
Public Enemy, 28, 273, 281, 422–23, 426–27, 457–58
Pyke, Dr. Magnus, 126

Quay Brothers, 297–98
Queen, 21, 31, 232, 248
Queen Latifah, 428, 432, 493
Queenrÿche, 413
Quiet Riot, 318
Quinn, Colin, 308, 388–94, 397–98, 512, 591
Quinn, Martha, 16, 58–62, 83, 245–48, 283–84, 355, 368–71, 591

Rachlin, Chip, 247, 257–58, 385, 591
Rachtman, Riki, 150, 442, 445–47, 532, 571, 591
Radecki, Dr. Thomas, 165–66
Rage Against the Machine, 522, 542
Raitt, Bonnie, 94
Ramones, 453, 530, 542
Ransohoff, Marty, 141
Ratt, 153, 156–59, 336
Rauschenberg, Robert, 36
Reagan, Nancy, 479
Real World, The, 18, 550–54, 558–59
Reagan, Ronald, 212, 479
Reardon, John, 326
Reddy, Helen, 21
Red Hot Chili Peppers, 330, 353–54, 365, 406–7, 453, 519
Redstone, Sumner, 382–85
Reed, Lou, 363–64
Regehr, Bob, 190
Reid, John, 108, 198
Reid, Vernon, 104, 274, 591
Reiter, Marc, 536–38, 591
R.E.M., 93, 353–55, 363, 514–16
Remote Control, 16, 385–95, 411, 551
Reno, Mike, 88, 91, 160–61, 591
REO Speedwagon, 45, 47, 55, 65, 68, 113, 233
Replacements, 354, 356
Reshovsky, Marc, 414
Revolt, 420
Reyes, Simone, 282

Rhodes, Nick, 54, 71, 83, 103, 113, 118–23, 171, 202, 258, 493, 511–12, 552, 554, 562, 564, 567, 591
Rice, Ron, 406
Richards, Keith, 21, 31, 37, 99, 137, 440, 474
Richie, Lionel, 188, 227, 273, 467, 591
Richman, Jonathan, 354
Ridgeley, Andrew, 201
Riklis, Meshulam, 485
Ritenour, Lee, 67, 569, 591
Ritts, Herb, 301, 485
Roberts, Elliott, 102
Roberts, Juliana, 448, 468, 471, 591
Robinson, Carol, 370
Robinson, Chris, 330
Robinson, Dar, 449
Robinson, David, 96, 230, 248, 591
Robinson, James D., III, 39, 40–51, 263, 592
Robinson, Smokey, 228
Robinson, Troy, 449
Rock, Bob, 449
Rock, Chris, 411
Rockett, Rikki, 344
Rodgers, Nile, 248
Roganti, Bob, 268, 383
Rolling Stone, 107, 165, 194, 199, 225, 350, 369, 385, 443, 482
Rolling Stones, 21, 31, 37, 49, 79–81, 87, 94, 99, 138, 282, 334, 440, 474
Rollins, Henry, 354
Romanek, Mark, 296, 568
Rose, Axl, 324, 437–46, 464, 474–77, 540
Roseman, Jon, 39, 98, 118, 126, 200, 592
Rosenberg, Liz, 258, 488–89, 592
Rosenblatt, Eddie, 339, 439, 475, 562, 592
Rosenstein, Carol, 98, 592
Ross, Diana, 186, 304
Ross, Mike, 451–53, 559, 592
Ross, Steve, 39, 45, 50–51, 83, 142, 178, 257, 261–65
Rost, Jordan, 43, 76, 137, 143, 166–67, 261, 592
Roth, David Lee, 20, 86, 154–56, 218–22, 282, 308, 317, 321–22
Rotten, Johnny, 356, 380, 488, 510
Roxette, 398
Roxy Music, 114
Rubin, Rick, 241, 273–84, 346, 463, 559, 561, 592
Rundgren, Todd, 39, 42–43, 60, 106, 592
Run-D.M.C., 273–78, 344, 420–23, 452, 483
Rupert, Donna, 218–19, 592
Russell, Jack, 337

Salley, John, 374
Salt, 434, 592
Salt-n-Pepa, 408, 434

Sambora, Richie, 334, 336, 349, 499, 504, 592
Samuelson, Debbie, 88–89, 161, 292, 592
Sandler, Adam, 16, 378, 392–94, 405
Sassa, Scott, 274
Satellites, Georgia, 416
Saturday Night Live, 44, 45, 386
Savannah, 524–25
Sayles, John, 211–13, 561, 592
Scandal, 27, 111
Scarface, 425, 592
Scarlett-Davies, John, 166
Scheer, Amanda, 434
Schenck, Rocky, 536
Schenker, Rudolf, 28, 91, 160, 250, 345, 592
Schenkman, Richard, 52–53, 68, 138, 221–23, 592
Schilling, Peter, 125
Schmidt, Michael, 351
Schneider, Fred, 92, 259, 569, 592
Schneider, Jack, 39–41, 44, 47, 50–53, 61, 77–78, 81–82, 142–43, 261, 592
Schnur, Steve, 62, 133–35, 151, 337, 342–43, 448–49, 592–93
Scopitones, 20–21
Score, Mike, 117, 593
Scorpions, 28, 159–61, 542
Scott, Mike, 361
Scott, Tony, 311
Seal, Kevin, 355, 378–80, 408, 444, 482, 521, 561, 593
Seaton, Dennis, 170, 593
Sednaoui, Stéphane, 301, 365
Seger, Bob, 94
Seibert, Fred, 43–44, 52–54, 65, 78–79, 82–84, 138–41, 555, 593
Seinfeld, Jerry, 323
Sellers, Peter, 125
Sena, Dominic, 228, 269, 293–96, 303, 467, 483–85, 593
Setos, Andy, 44, 53, 66, 68, 143, 593
Setzer, Brian, 102, 307, 593
Sex Pistols, 32, 380
Seymour, Stephanie, 476–77, 540
Shabba-Doo, 104
Shakur, Tupac, 430, 432
Shalamar, 274
Shamberg, Michael, 357
Shante, Roxanne, 273, 276
Shaw, Tommy, 112
Shear, Jules, 505
Shear, Rhonda, 392
Sheila E., 214–15
Sheinberg, Sidney, 39, 46–47, 267
Sherwood, Bob, 101–2, 176
Shock G, 454, 593

Shocklee, Hank, 426, 457–58, 593
Shore, Pauly, 409–10, 520–26, 568, 593
Showalter, Michael, 509
Showtime, 183, 264
Siberry, Jane, 233–34
Sighvatsson, Joni, 294, 466–70, 478, 593
Silverman, Fred, 550
Silverman, Susan, 89, 190, 322, 593
Simmons, Gene, 415–16
Simmons, Russell, 273–78, 419–20, 433, 456–57, 461
Simon & Garfunkel, 31
Simpson, O.J., 153
Singh, Tarsem, 330, 466, 481, 514–16, 568–69, 593
Sir Mix-A-Lot, 116, 427–28, 463, 540, 593
Sirulnick, David, 371–72, 544–46, 593
Siskel, Gene, 166
Sixx, Nikki, 150–53, 157, 160, 163, 334, 343, 500–501, 593
Skid Row, 28, 161, 351, 542
Skinner, Randy, 89, 97, 216–19, 237, 292–93, 363, 469, 489, 594
Slash, 436, 443–44, 475–77, 481
Slater, Andy, 236
Slater, Christian, 410
Slick, Grace, 134
Slick Rick, 461–62
Sloane, Robin, 34, 125, 150–51, 162, 174, 205–6, 292, 342–43, 447–48, 527–29, 534–35, 594
Small, Bob, 502–8, 594
Smear, Pat, 216
Smell the Glove, 160
Smillie, Peter, 484
Smith, Chad, 406–7
Smith, Curt, 120, 139, 231, 247, 286, 594
Smith, Keely, 307
Smith, Larry, 274
Smith, Robert, 32, 95, 271, 356, 506, 594
Smith, Tony, 300
Smith, Will, 419, 422, 463–64
Smokin' in the Boys Room, 159, 162
Smyth, Patty, 27, 95, 111, 292, 594
Snider, Dee, 149, 158–59, 227–28, 241, 316, 331–32, 594
Snyder, Tom, 44
Somerville, Jimmy, 415
Sonic Youth, 357
Soren, Tabitha, 280, 327, 371, 385, 437, 543–49, 594
Spandau Ballet, 168
Sparks, David, 280
Sparrow, Gale, 46, 48, 69, 82, 102, 125, 132, 137, 161, 171, 176, 190, 198, 247, 276, 594